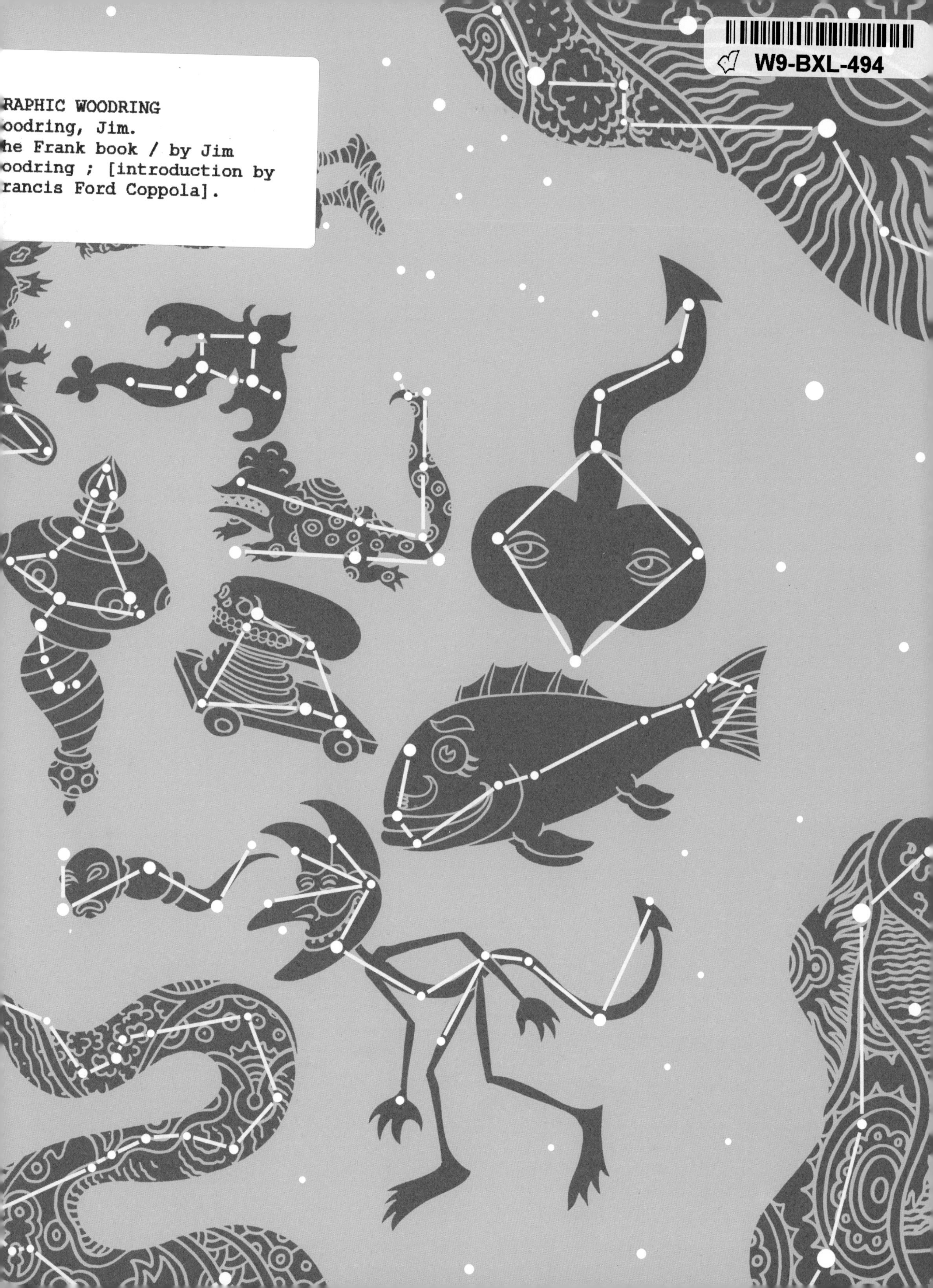

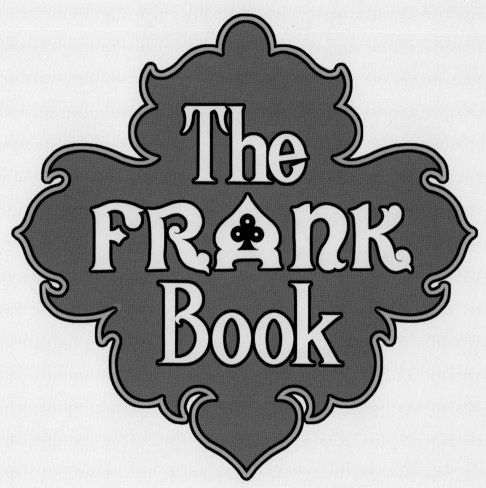

by Jim Woodring

FANTAGRAPHICS BOOKS

THANKS

रामकृष्ण

Ted Blackman
Francis Coppola
John Dorman
Michael Dowers
Kevin Eastman
Gary Groth
Mrs. Lahr
Mark Landman
Mark Martin
Eric Reynolds
Howard Rheingold
Kim Thompson

Fantagraphics Books, 7563 Lake City Way NE, Seattle, WA 98115. • Edited and designed by Jim Woodring. Production by Paul Baresh and Dale Yarger. Production manager: Kim Thompson. Associate publisher: Eric Reynolds..Published by Gary Groth and Kim Thompson. • All contents copyright © 2003, 2011 Jim Woodring. This edition copyright © 2003, 2011 Fantagraphics Books. The stories in this volume originally appeared in *BUZZ, Dramatis Personae, FRANK, Heavy Metal, Hyena, JIM, Measles, The Millennium Whole Earth Catalog, Pictopia, PULSE!, Snake Eyes, The Stranger*, and *Tantalizing Stories* between 1991 and 2001. All rights reserved. Permission to quote or reproduce material for reviews or notices must by obtained from the author or publisher. • Third Fantagraphics Books edition: July, 2011. • ISBN: 978-1-60699-513-6 (previous edition: 978-1-56097-534-2). • Visit the Fantagraphics Books website at www.fantagraphics.com; visit Jim Woodring's website at www.jimwoodring.com • Printed in China.

Contents

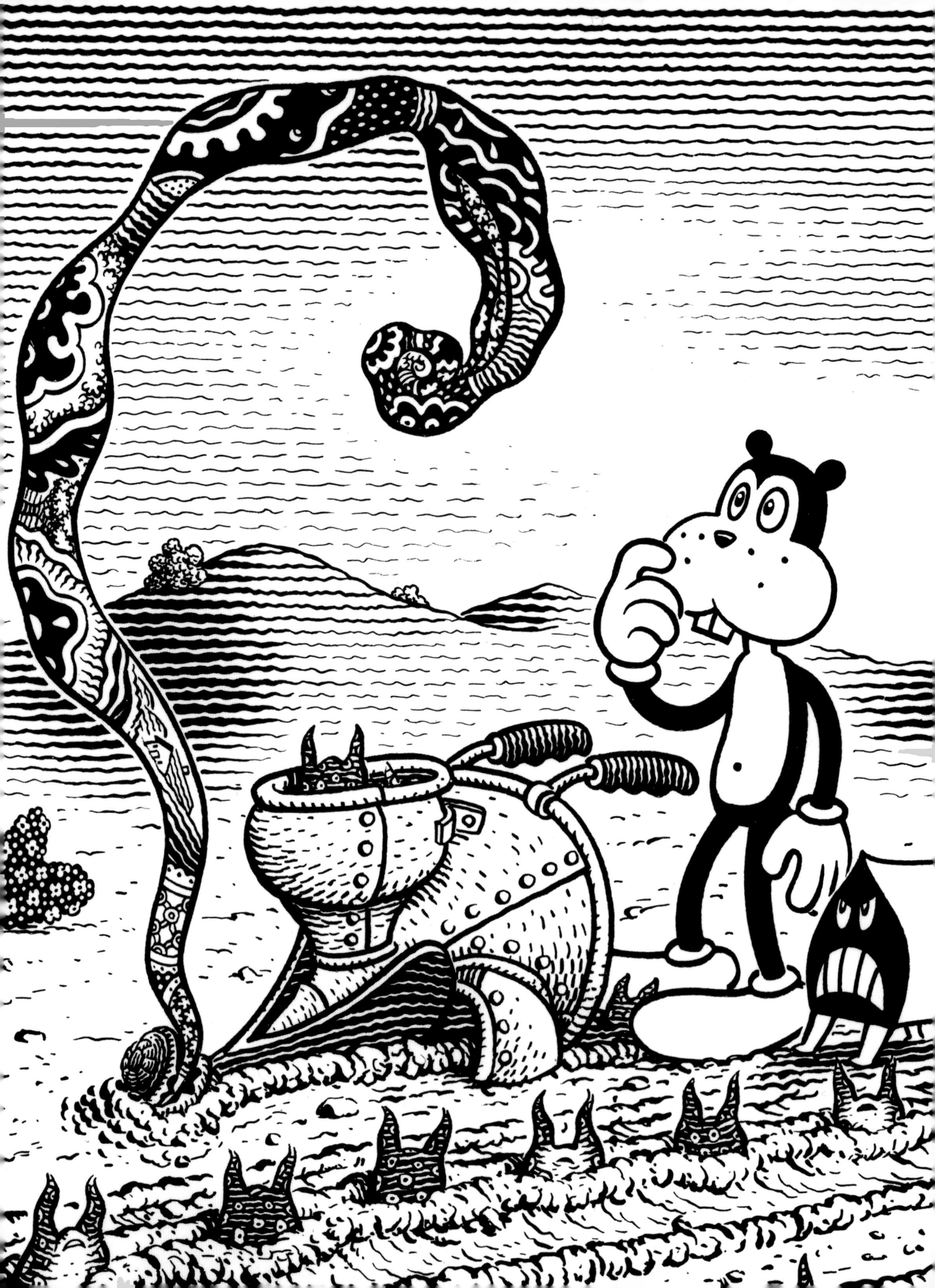

Introduction

by Francis Ford Coppola

FRANK is such a strange creation that I hardly know how to describe it. Wordless, timeless, placeless, full of unprecedented characters and experiences, it exists on its own bizarre terms. It offers vivid tableaus of tenderness and bloodshed, cruelty and and sacrifice, love and betrayal, terror and bliss; and it offers them wrapped like candies from another planet.

The artist has always used his or her inner "stuff", the very substance of the soul, mixing it with the subject's own essence and deriving droplets of imagery from this alchemy. Jim Woodring has taken the time and trouble to master the cartoonist's craft in order to express his vision of the universe in a way that any person in any culture can absorb. It is difficult to imagine these tales being told as well in any other medium. As for exactly what it is they are saying, that is something readers will have to discover on their own. The events that unfold in these stories are nearly impossible to explain; yet on some level we understand them.

The ancient myths and folk tales of all cultures which have been preserved for so many centuries have meaning for us today because the fantastic elements in them are rooted in immutable reality. The Frank stories belong to this class of literature. As with the enduring heroic allegories, the ultimate significance of Frank's bewildering adventures often seems maliciously oblique; and yet we feel a subtle sense of resolution, letting us know that in Woodring's world the equation has been thoroughly worked out and presented, and that the results are worth understanding.

THE FRANK BOOK is one man's puzzling gift to a puzzling world. It brings a hidden world to light and lets us examine it minutely. You may proceed with caution or not, as you like.

For
The Terrible Madame W,
with eternal love.

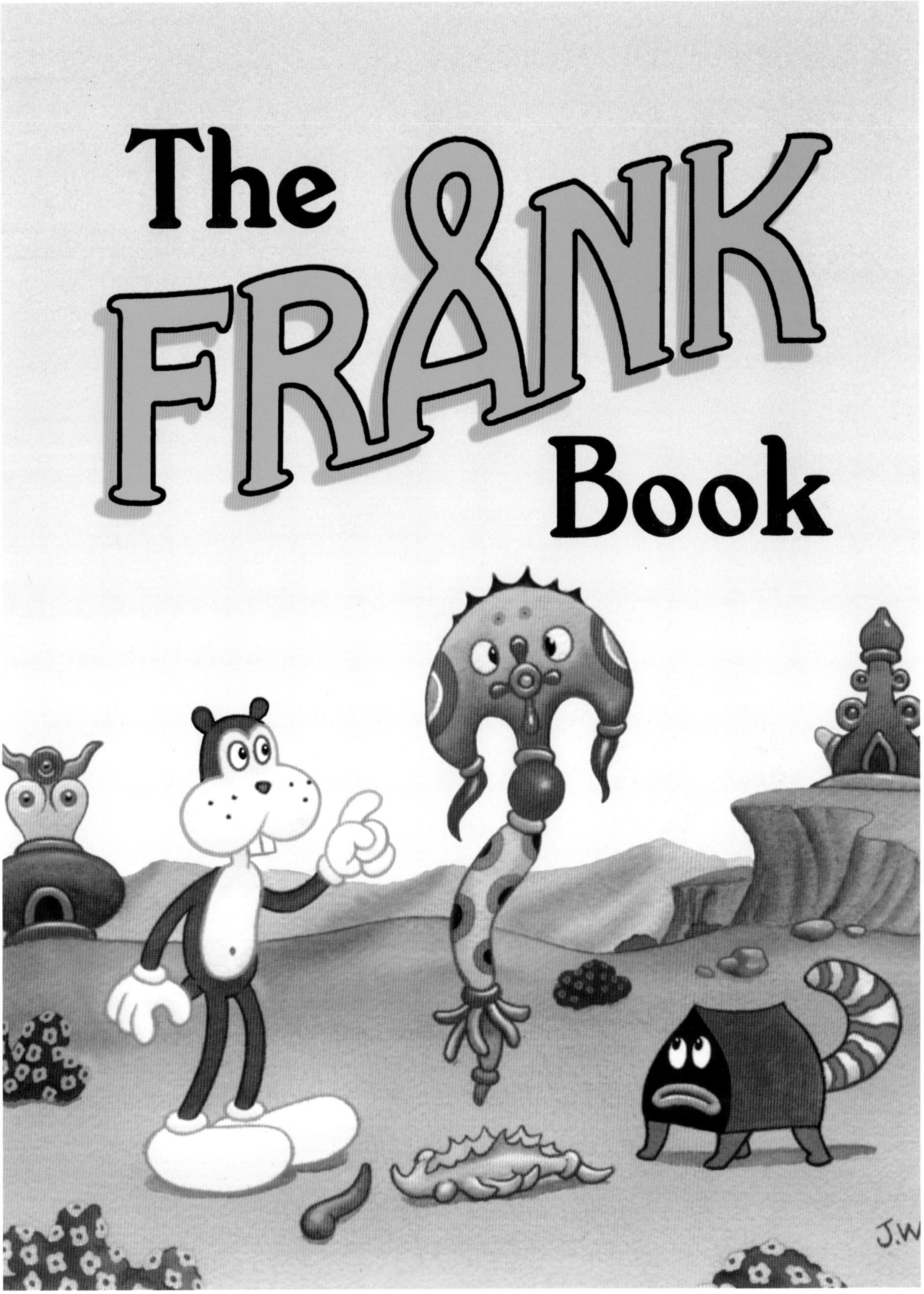
The
FRANK
Book

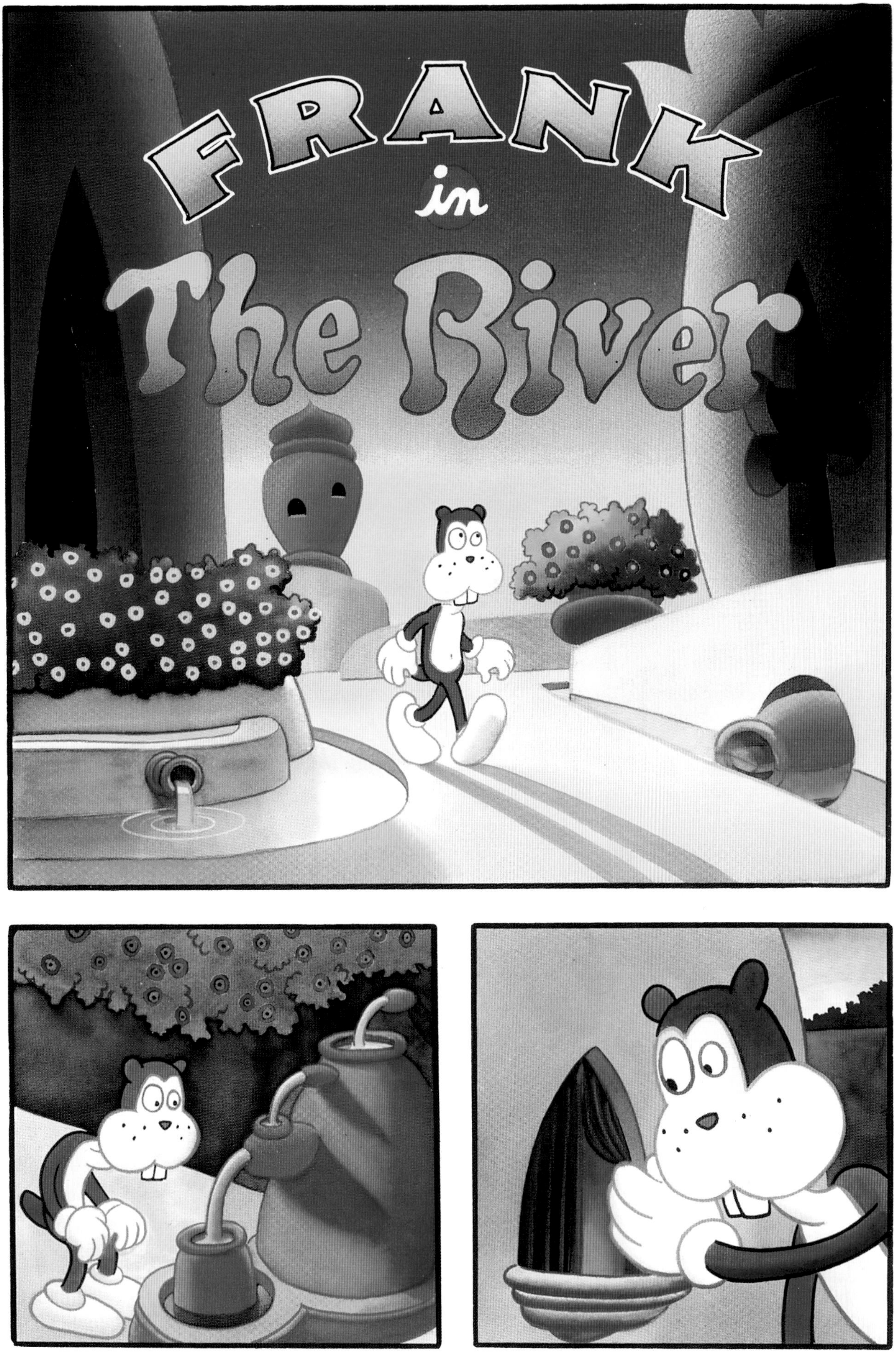
FRANK
in
The River

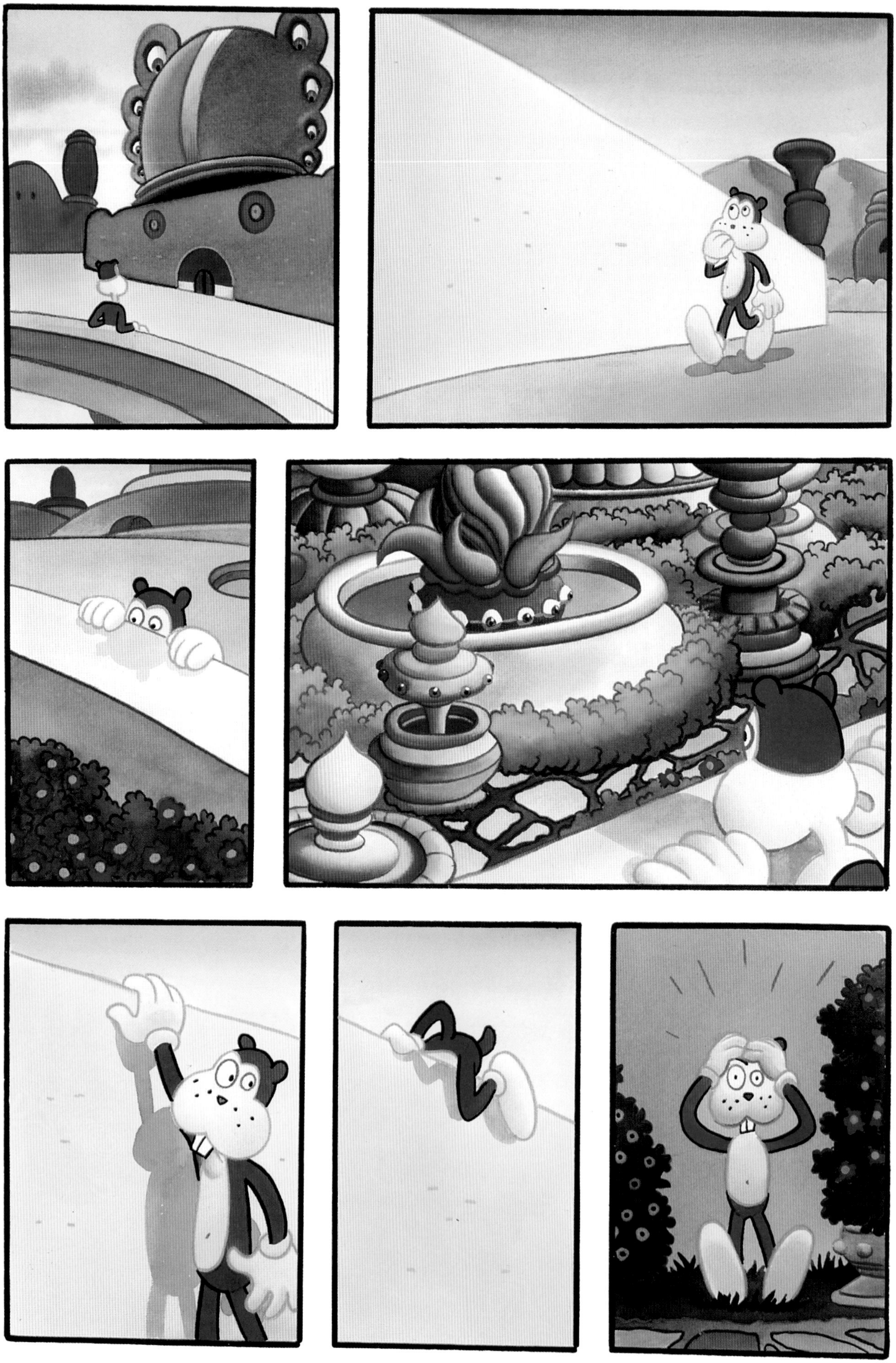

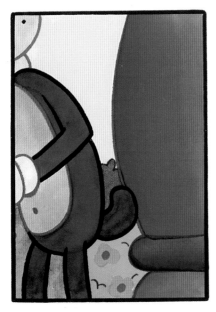

11

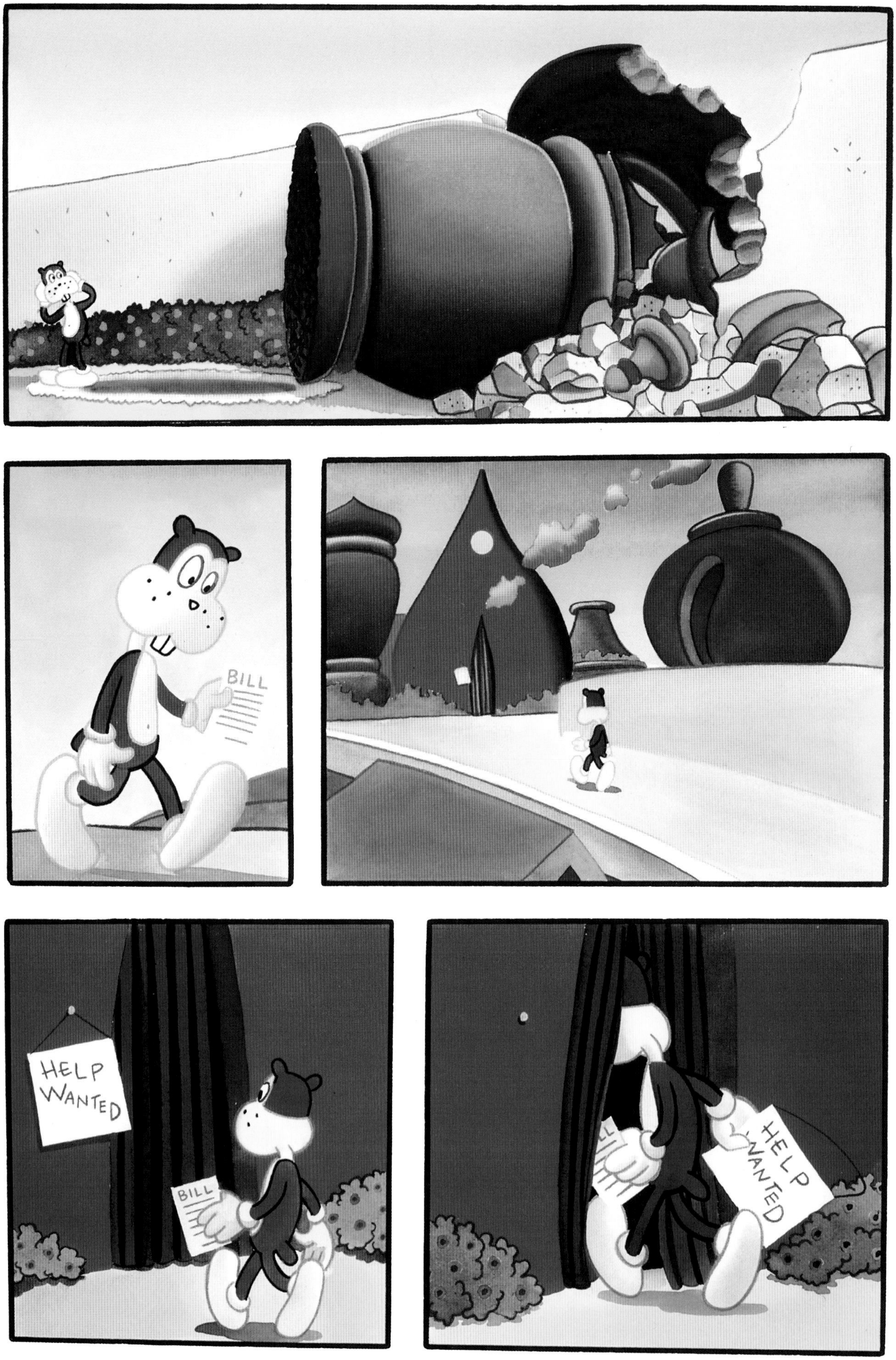
BILL
HELP WANTED
BILL
HELP WANTED

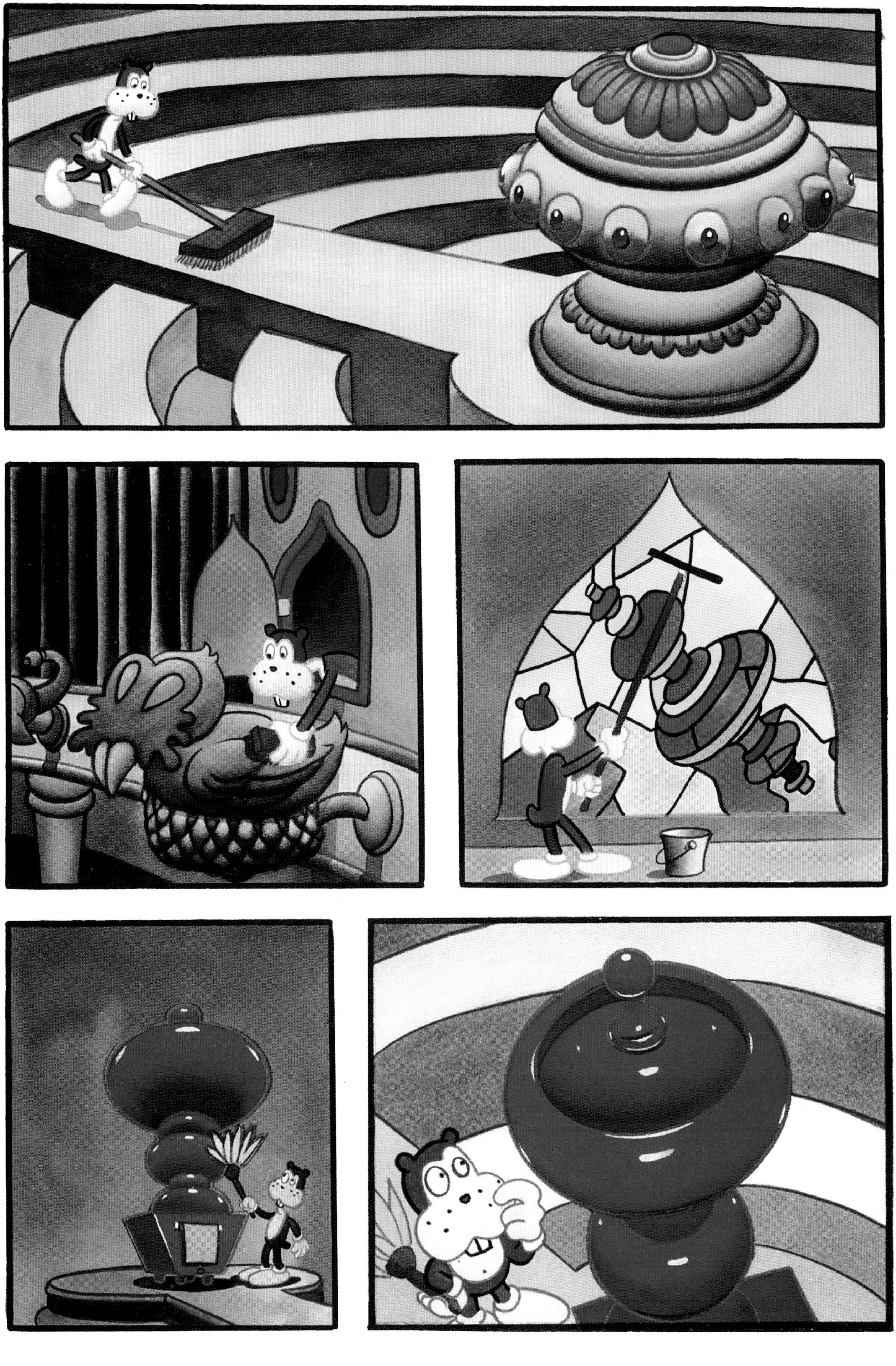

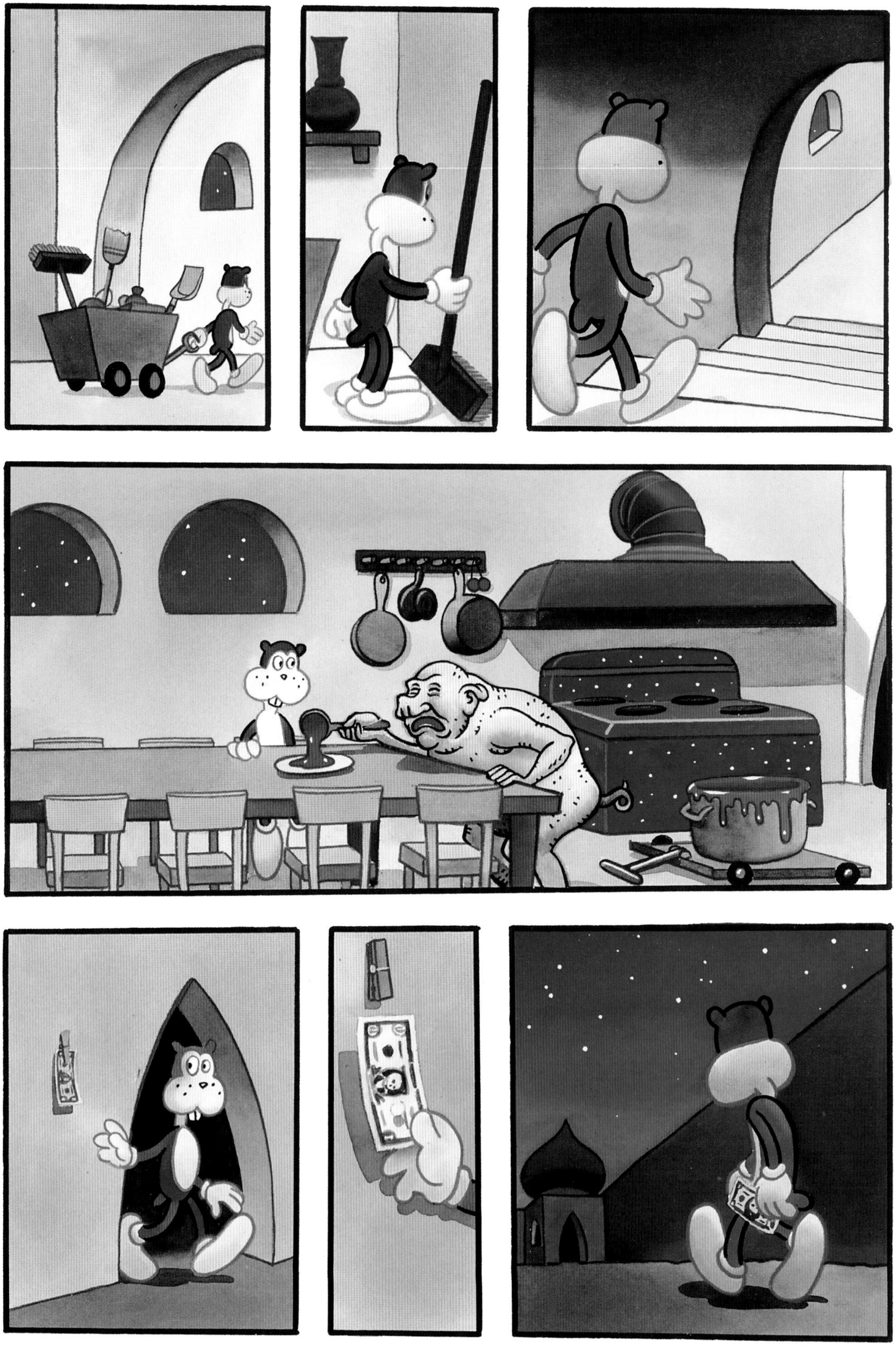

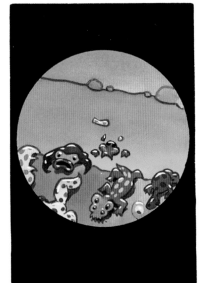

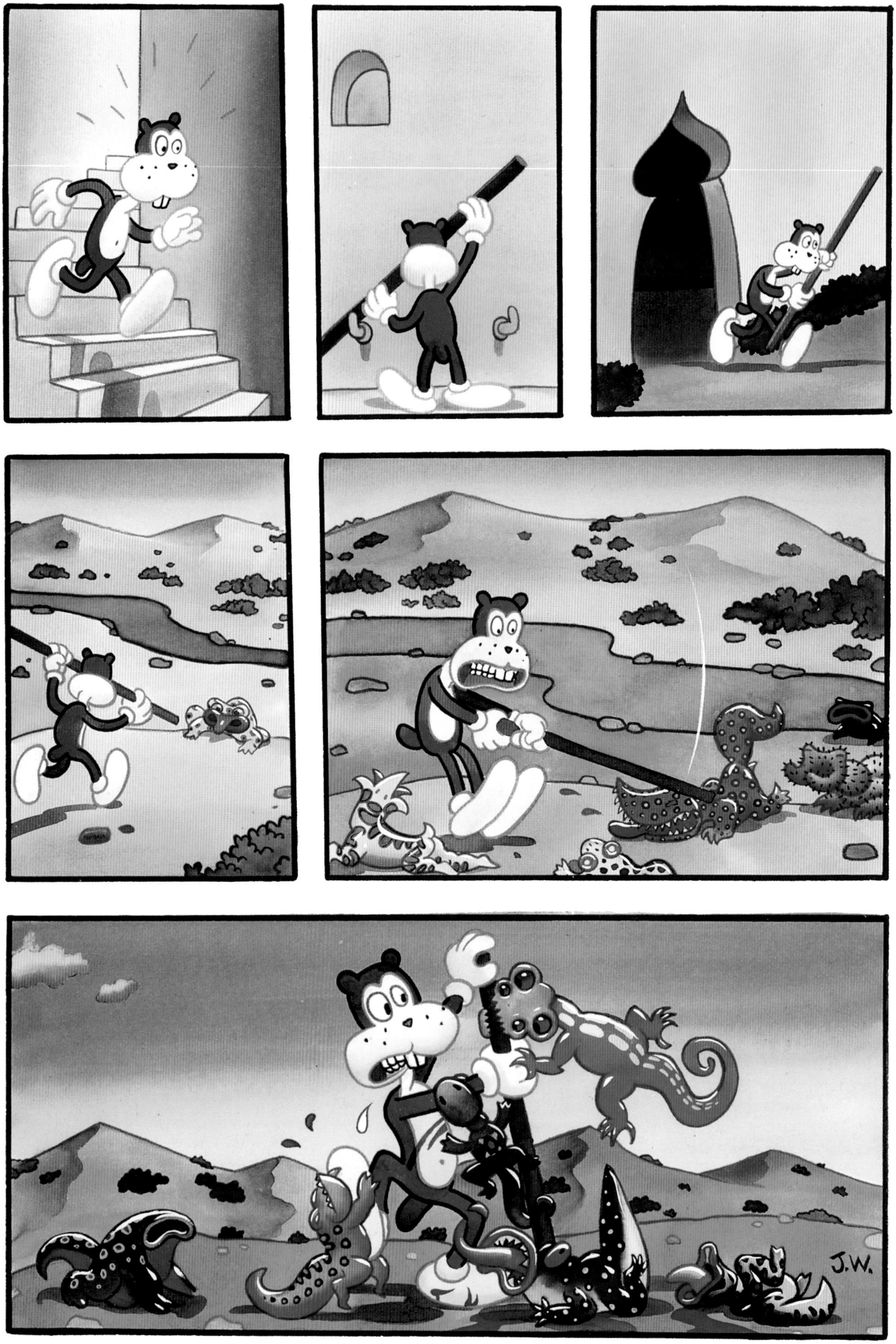
J.W.

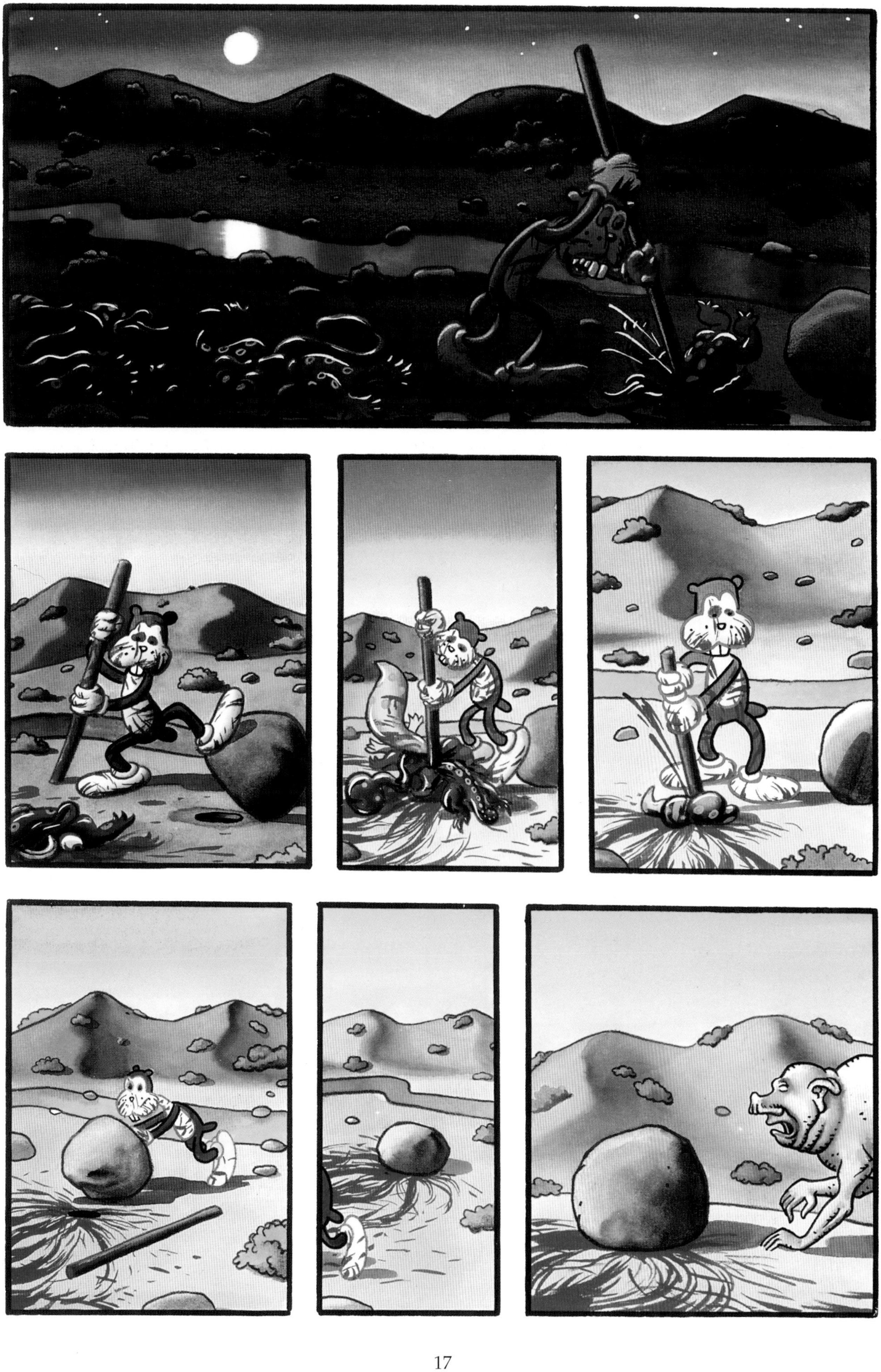

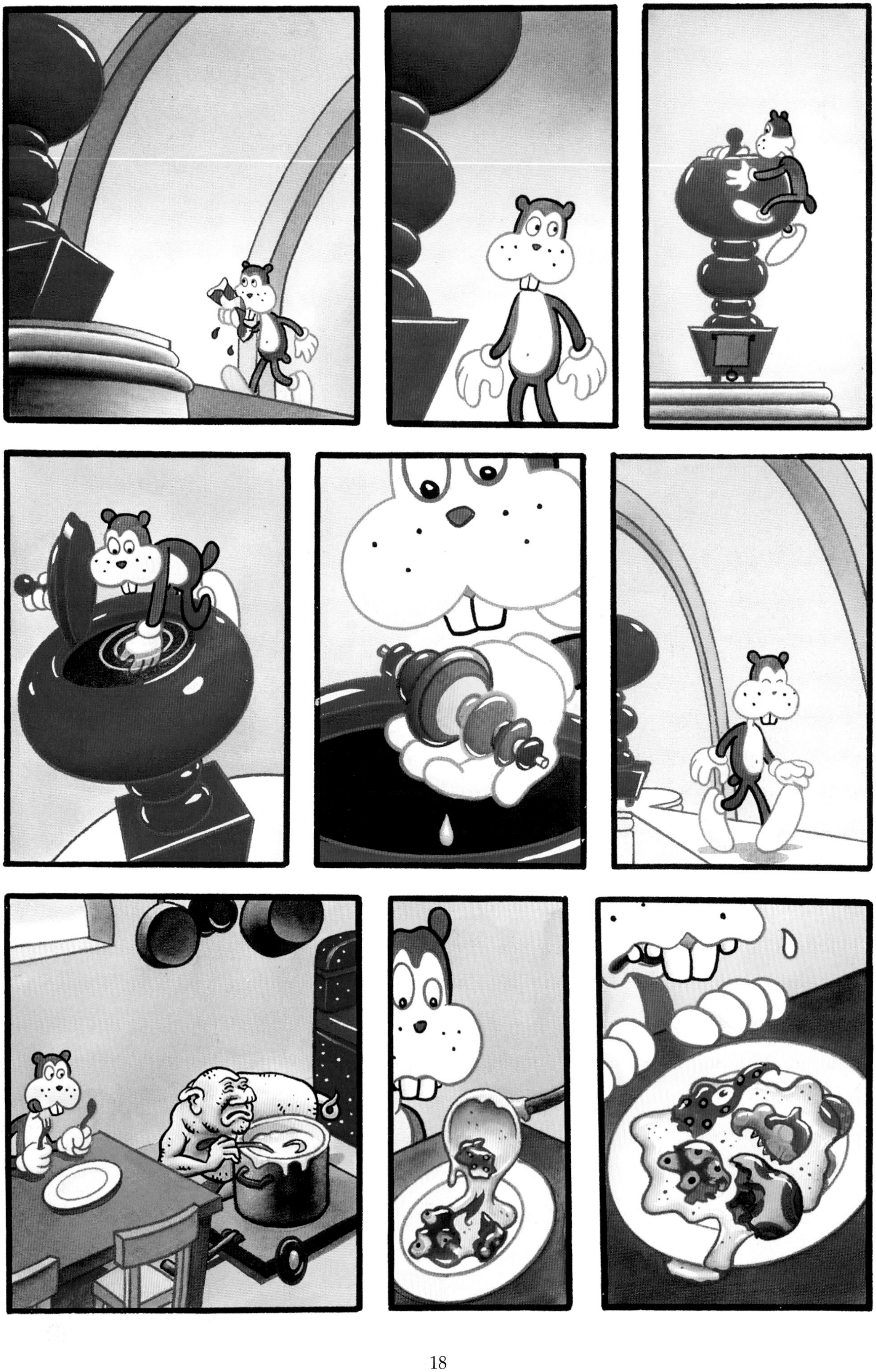

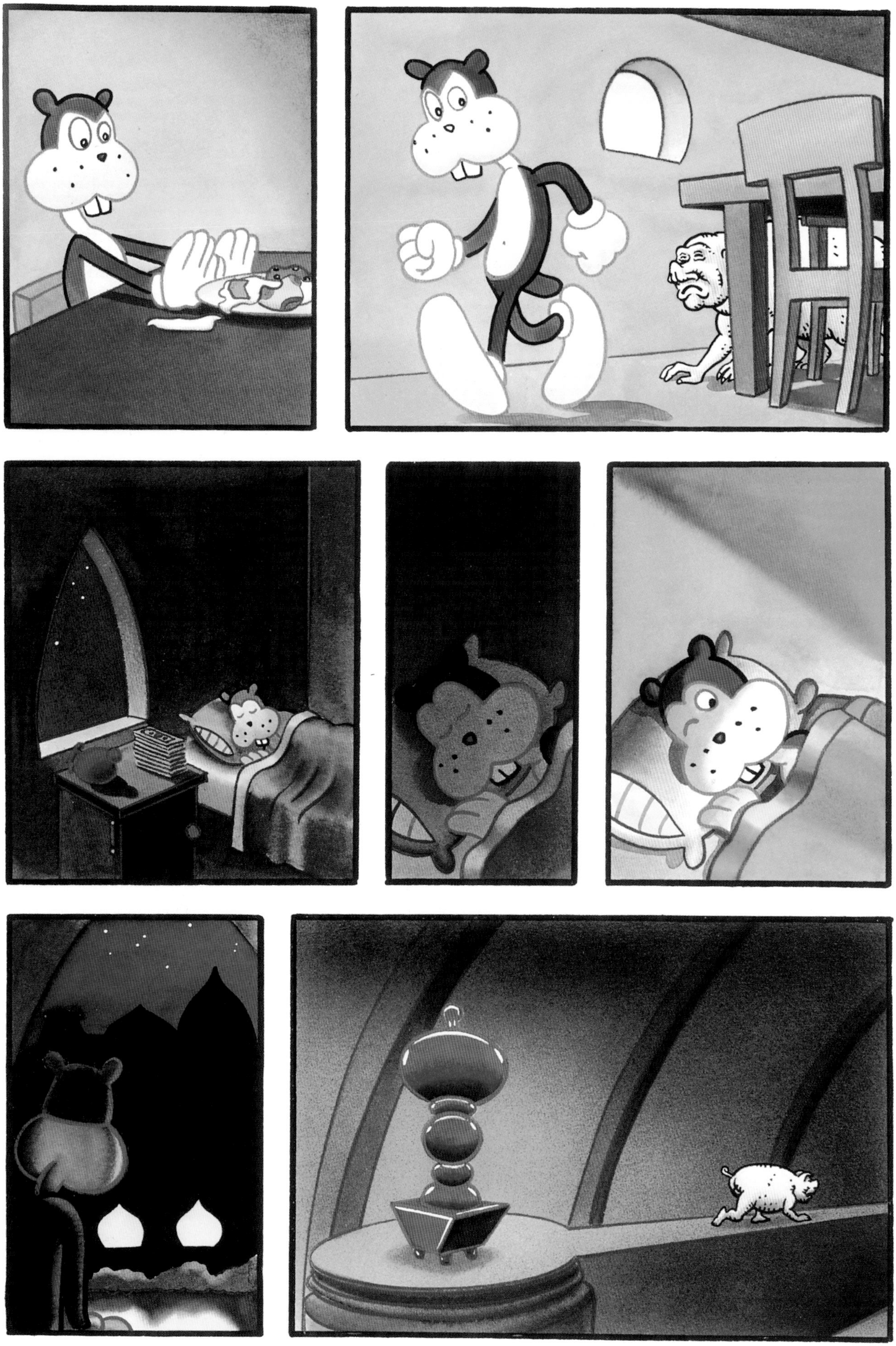

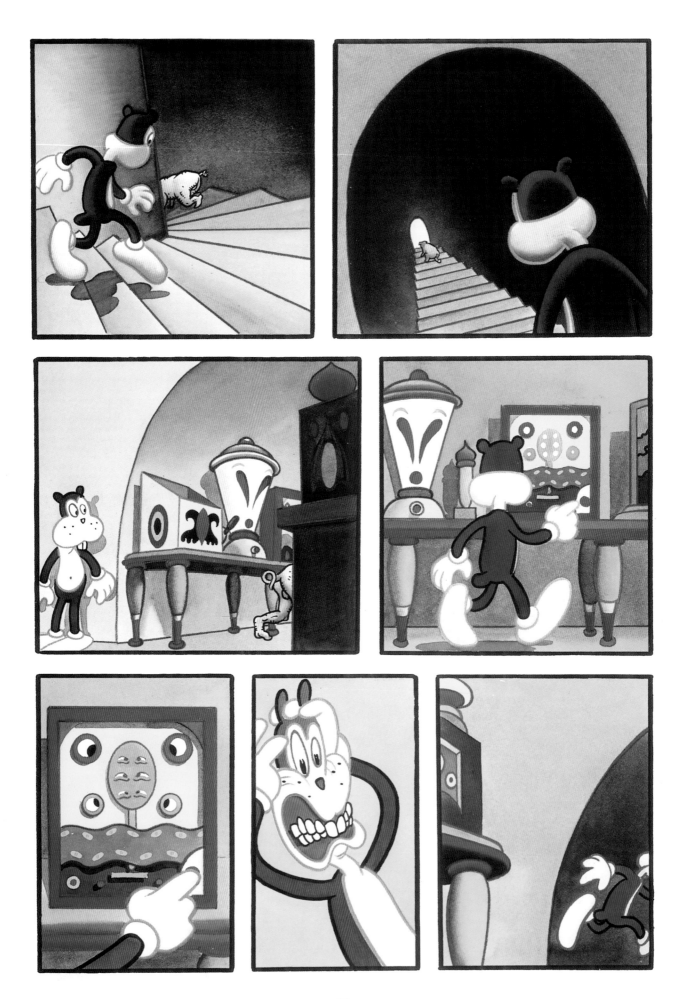

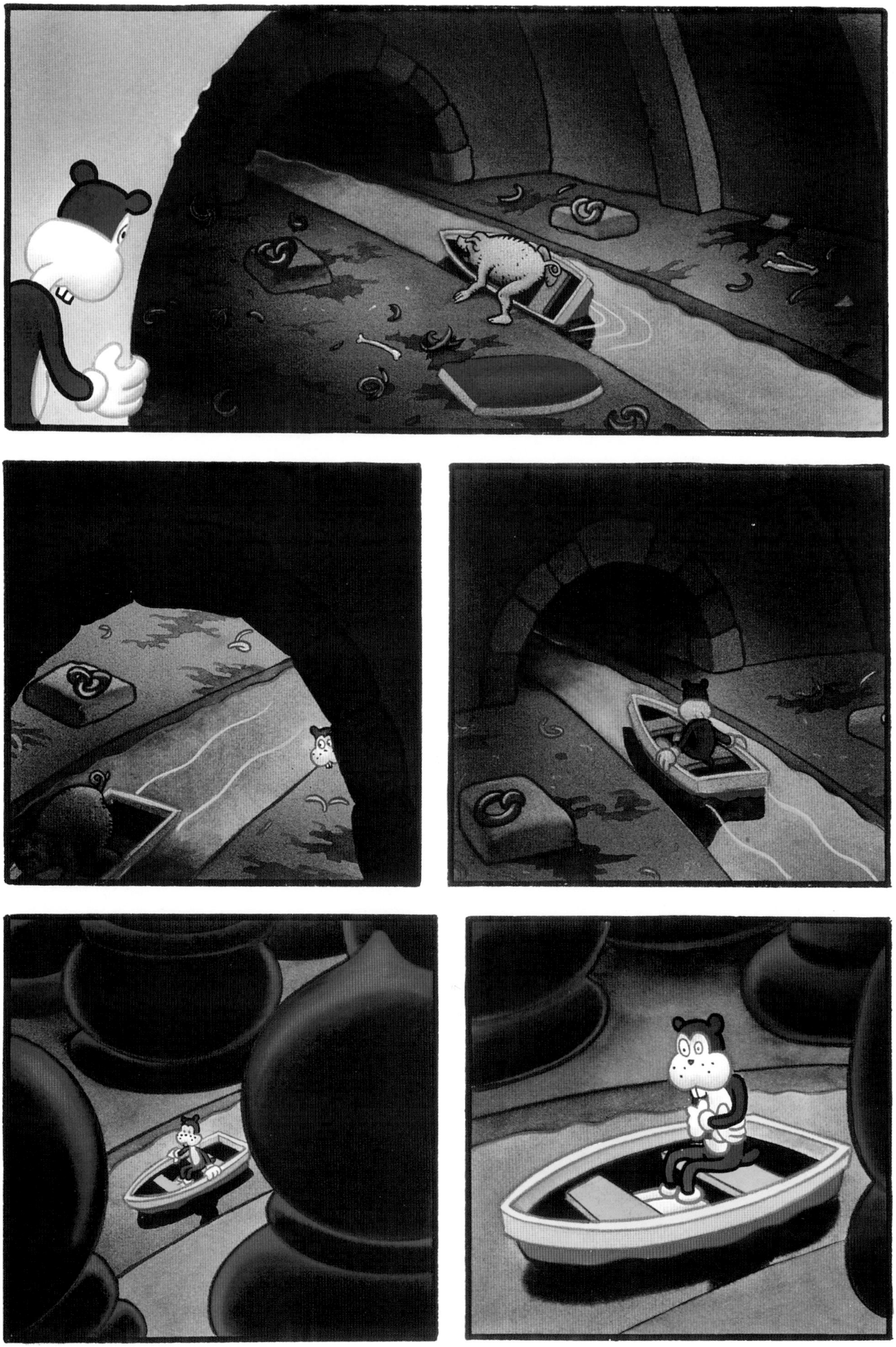

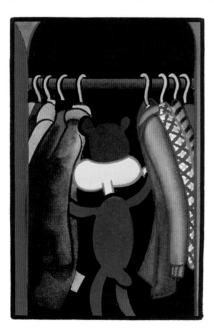

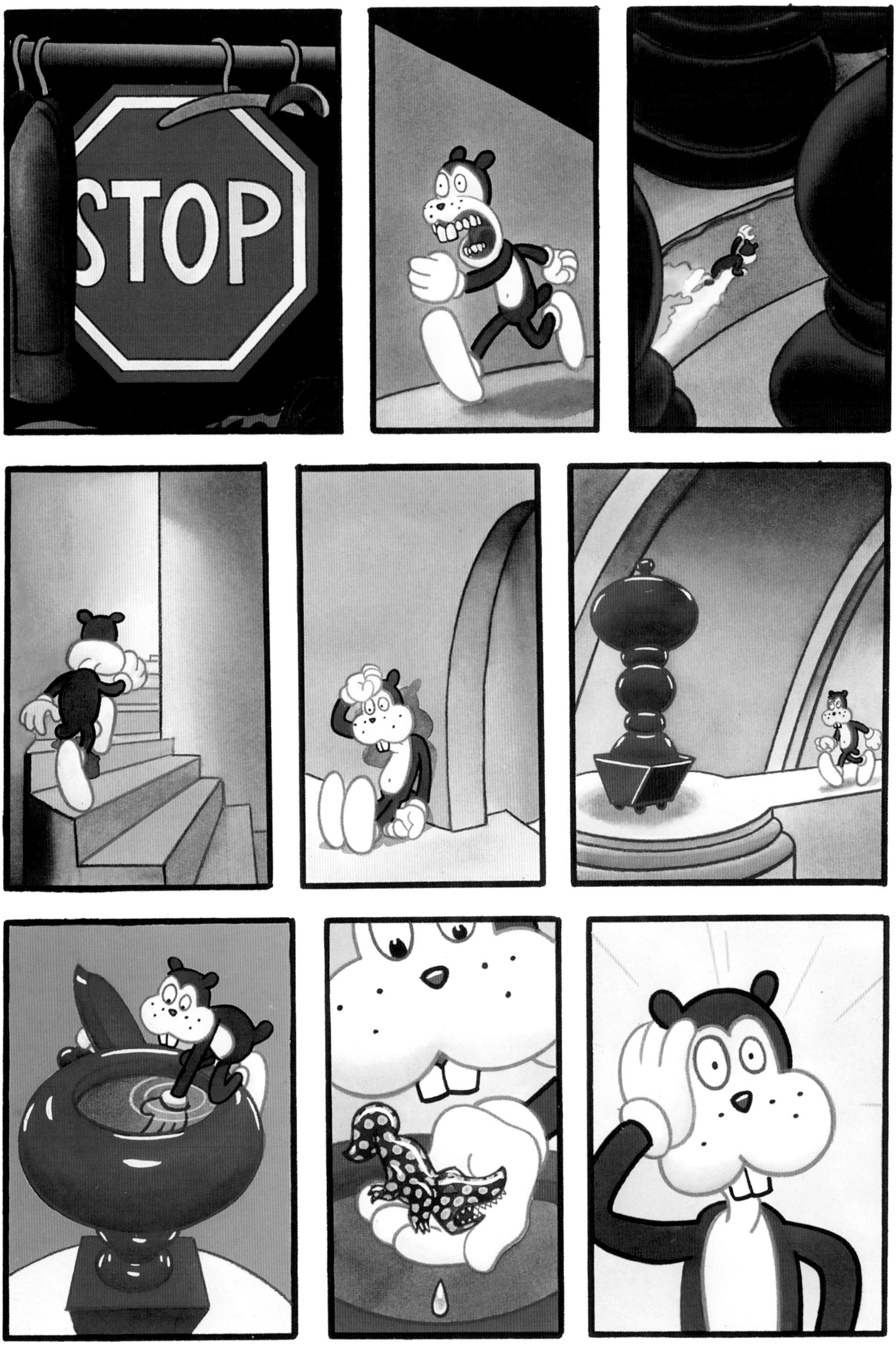
STOP

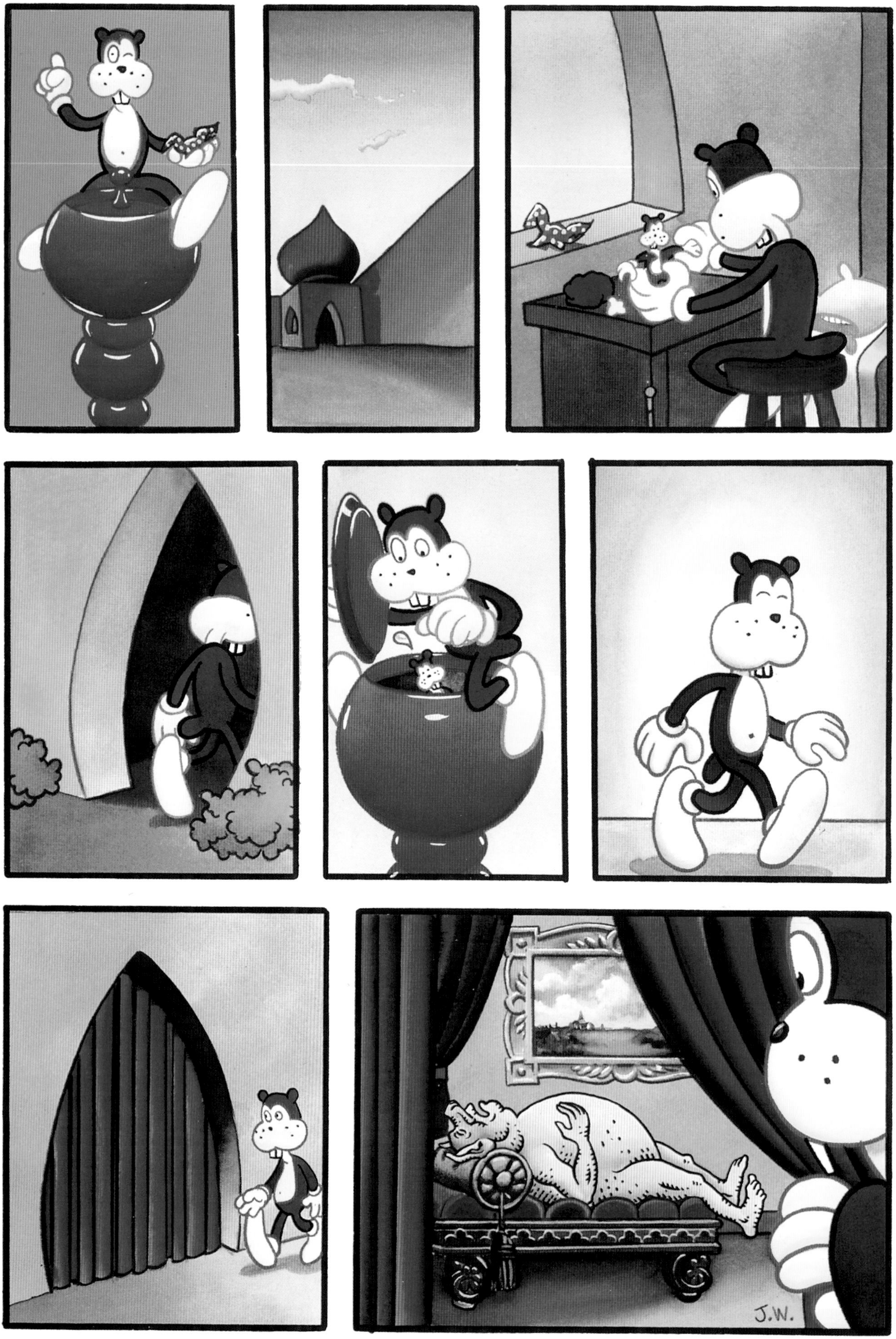
J.W.

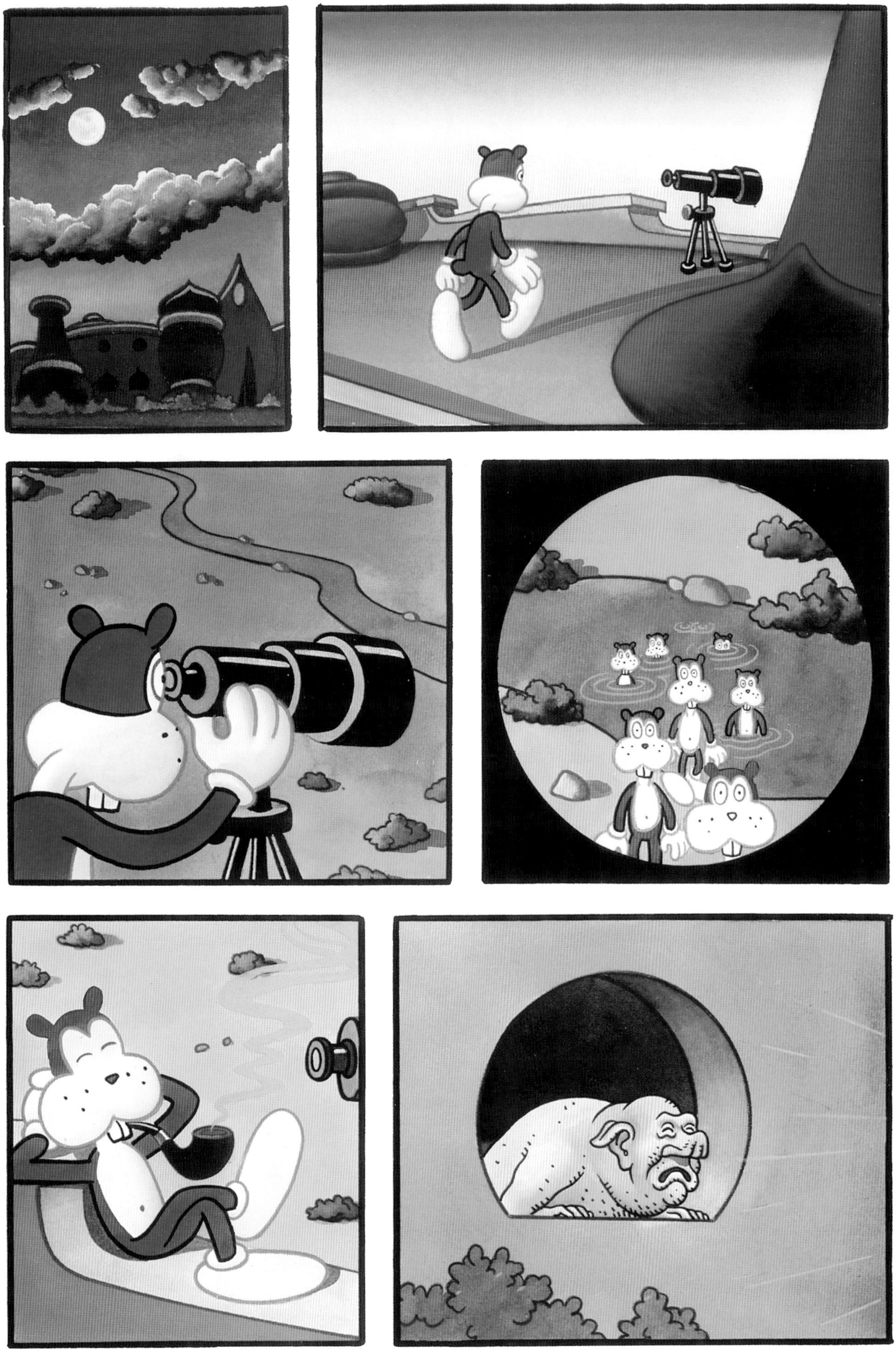

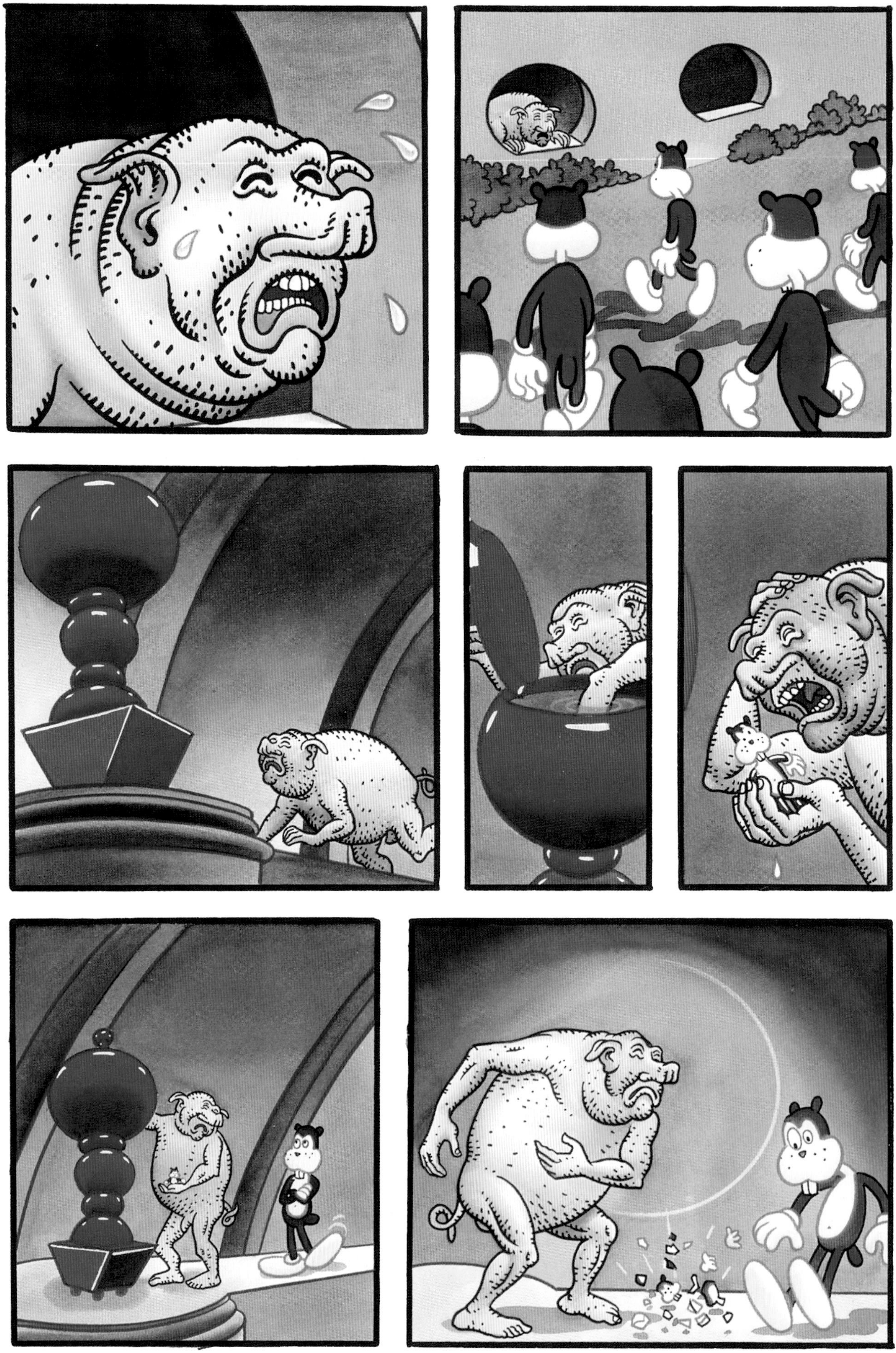

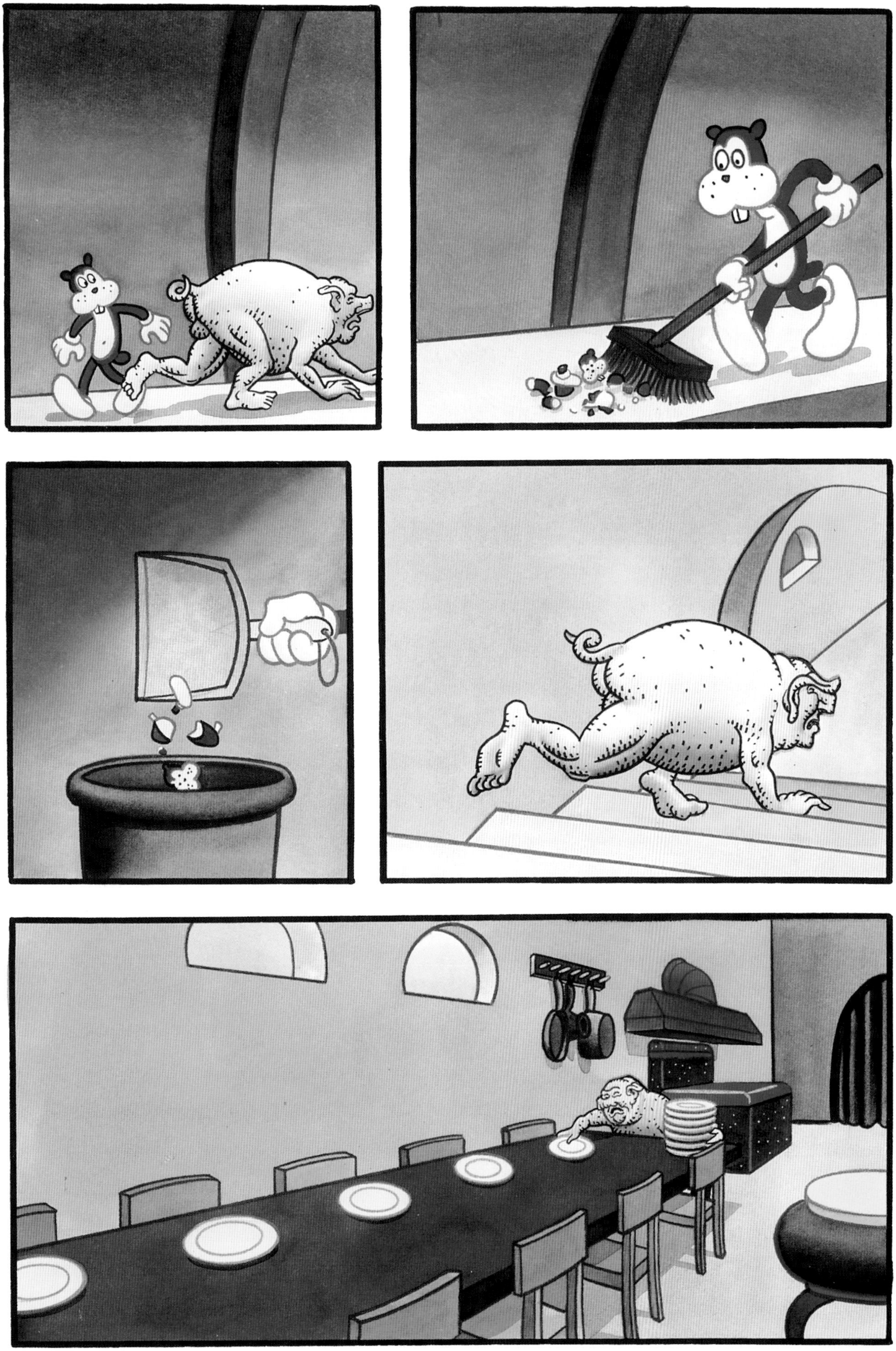

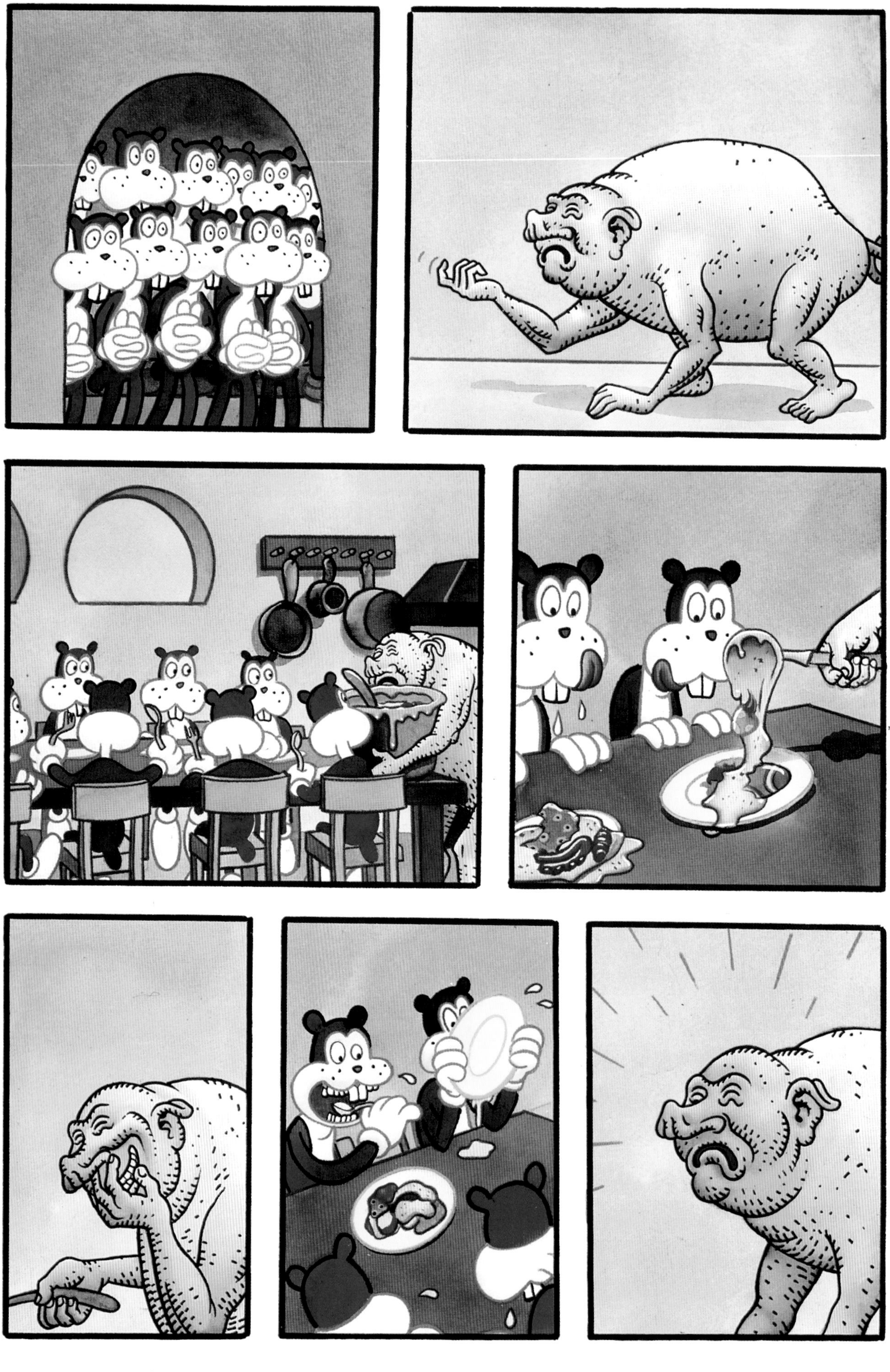

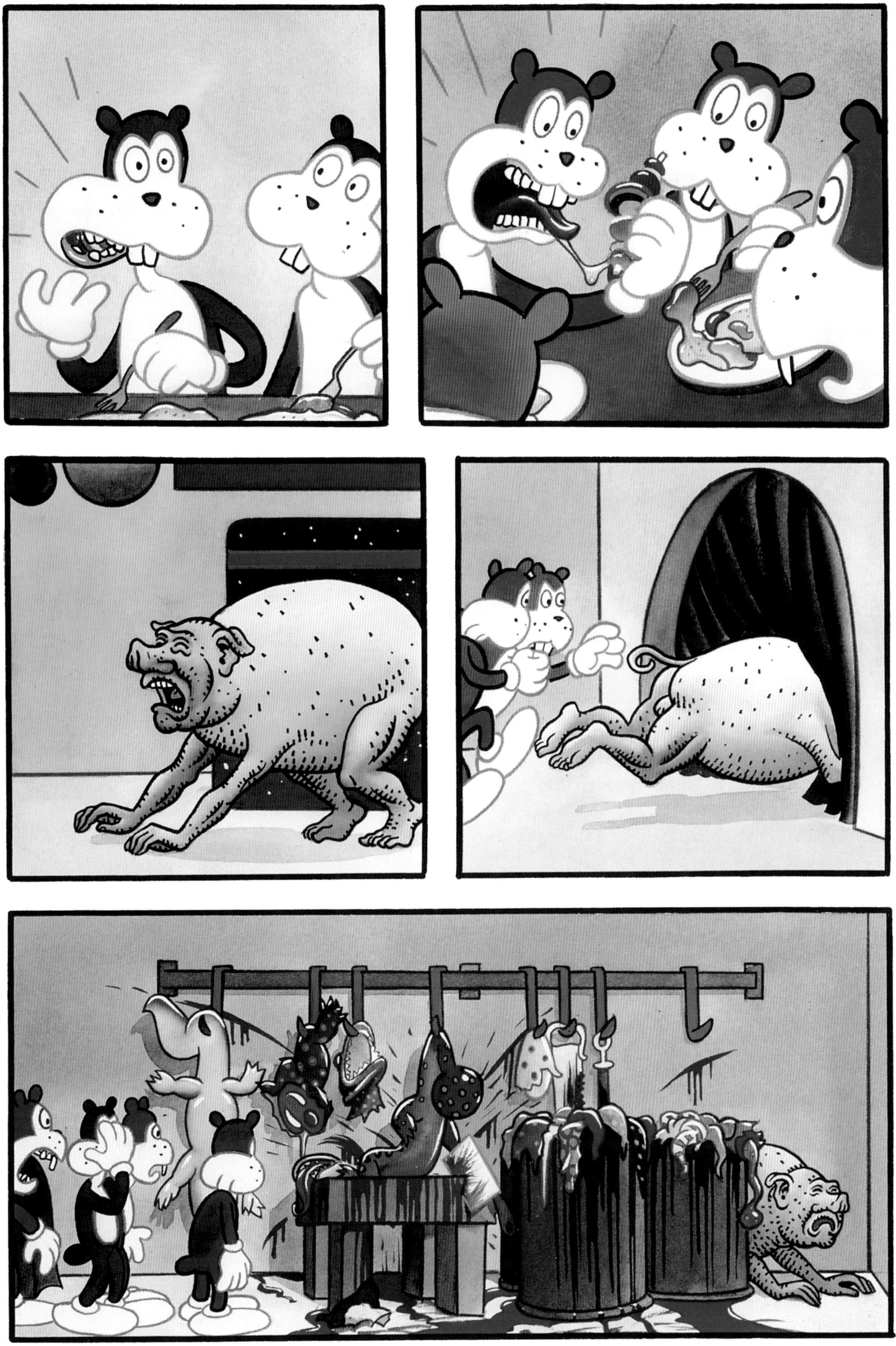

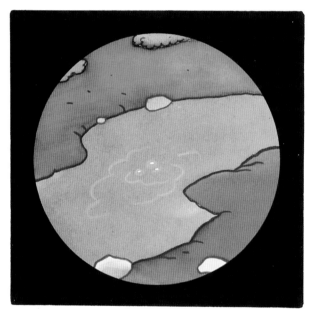

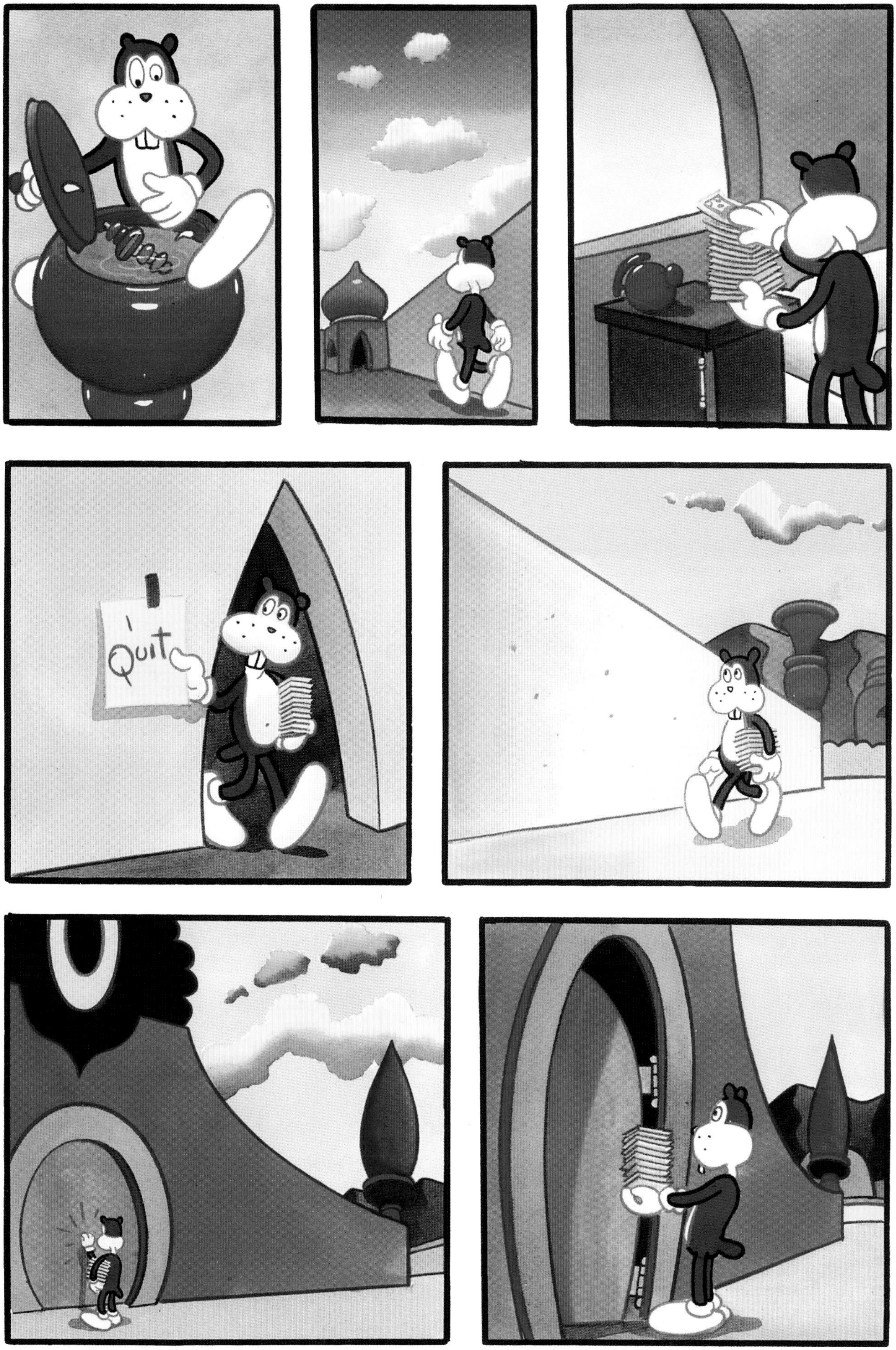
I
Quit

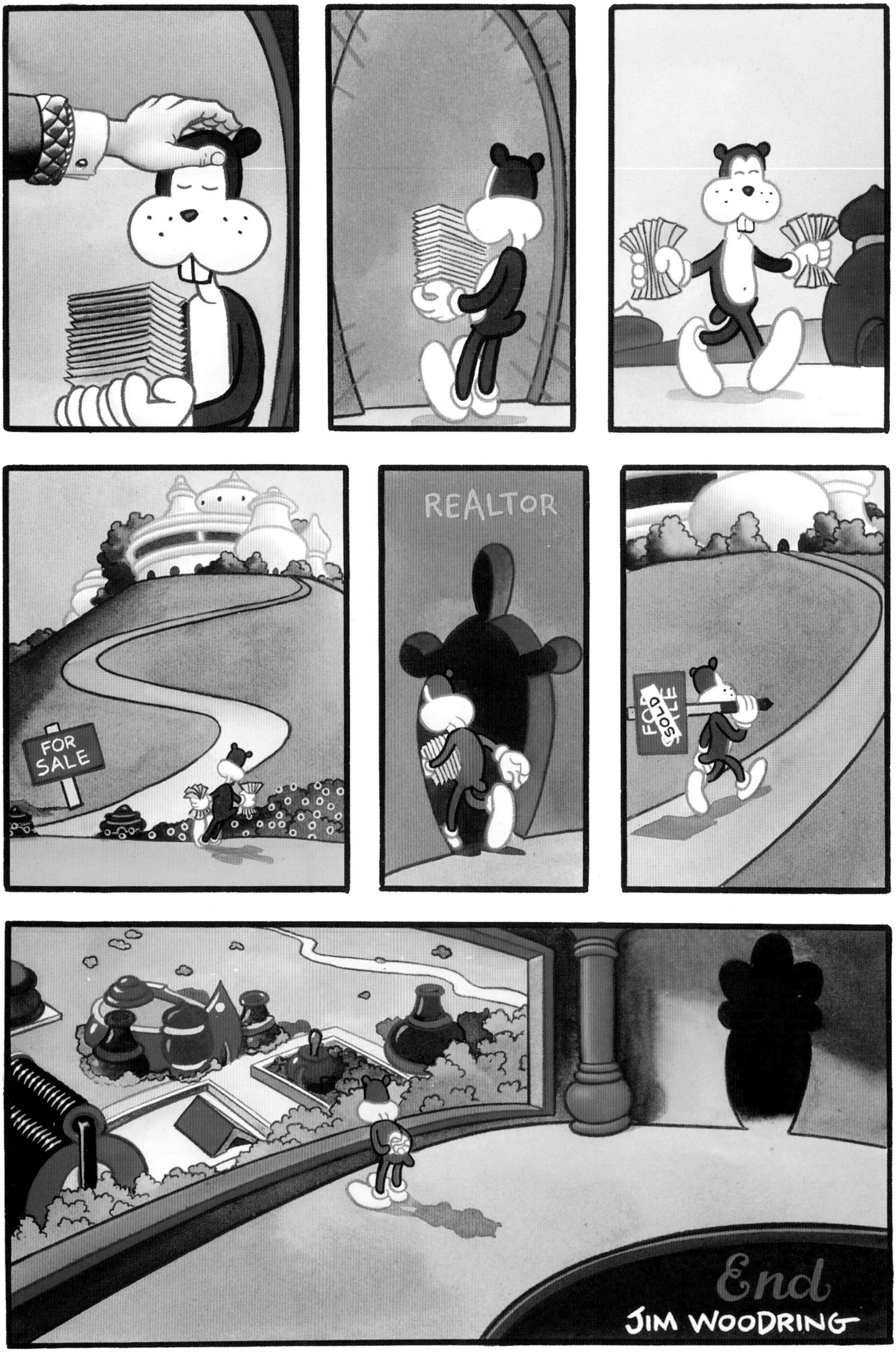
FOR SALE
REALTOR
FOR SALE
SOLD
End
JIM WOODRING

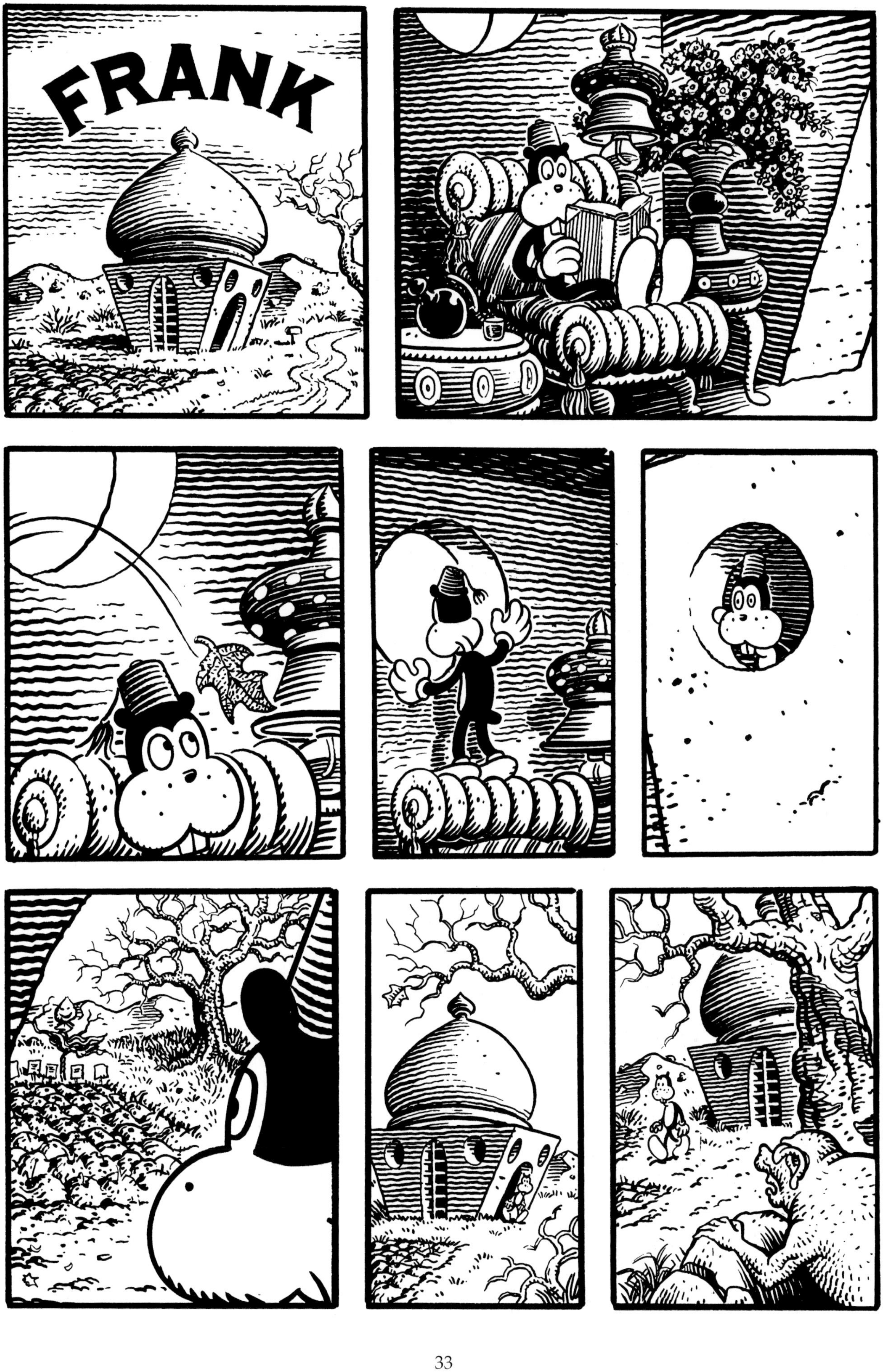
FRANK

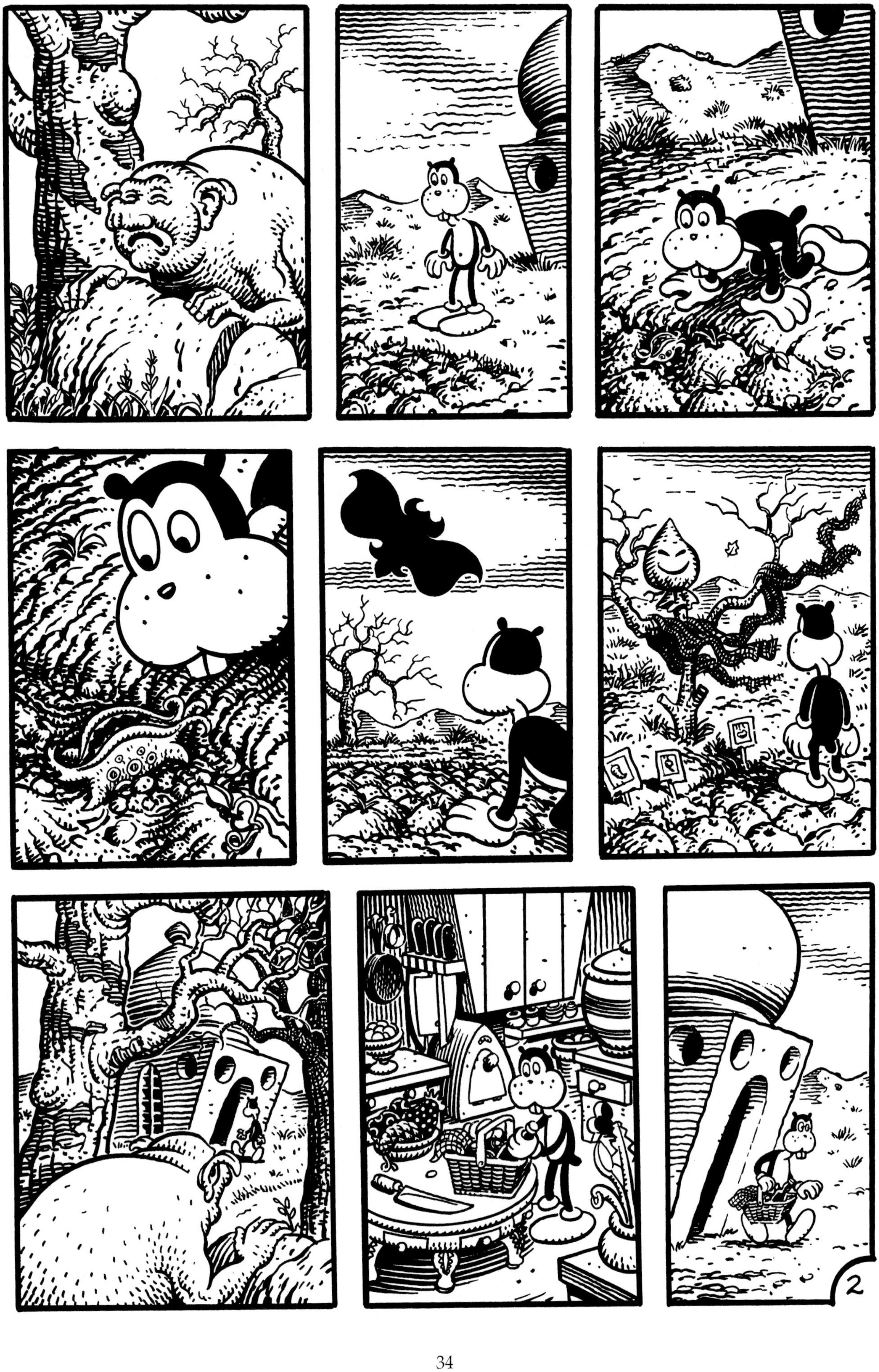
2

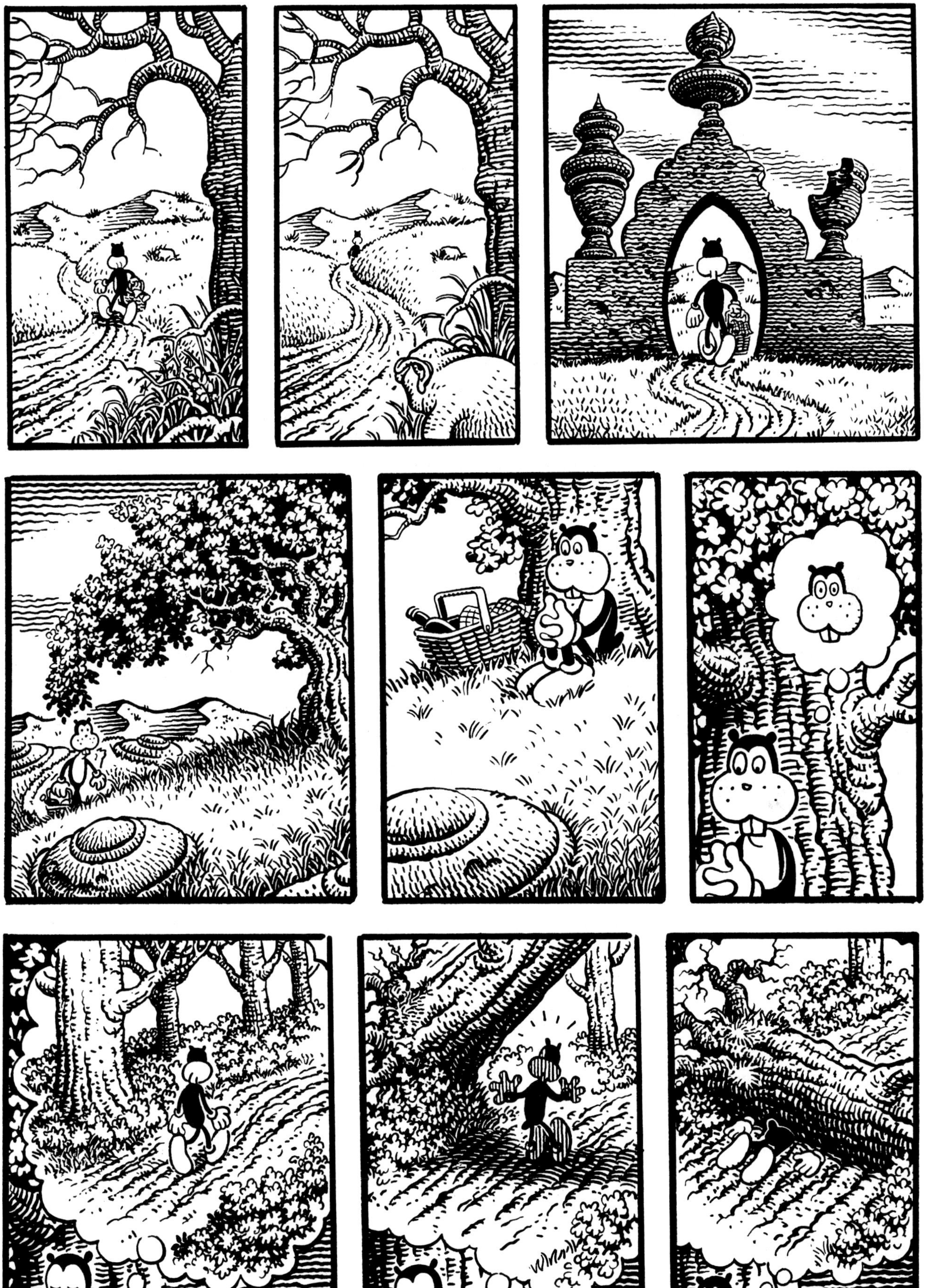
3

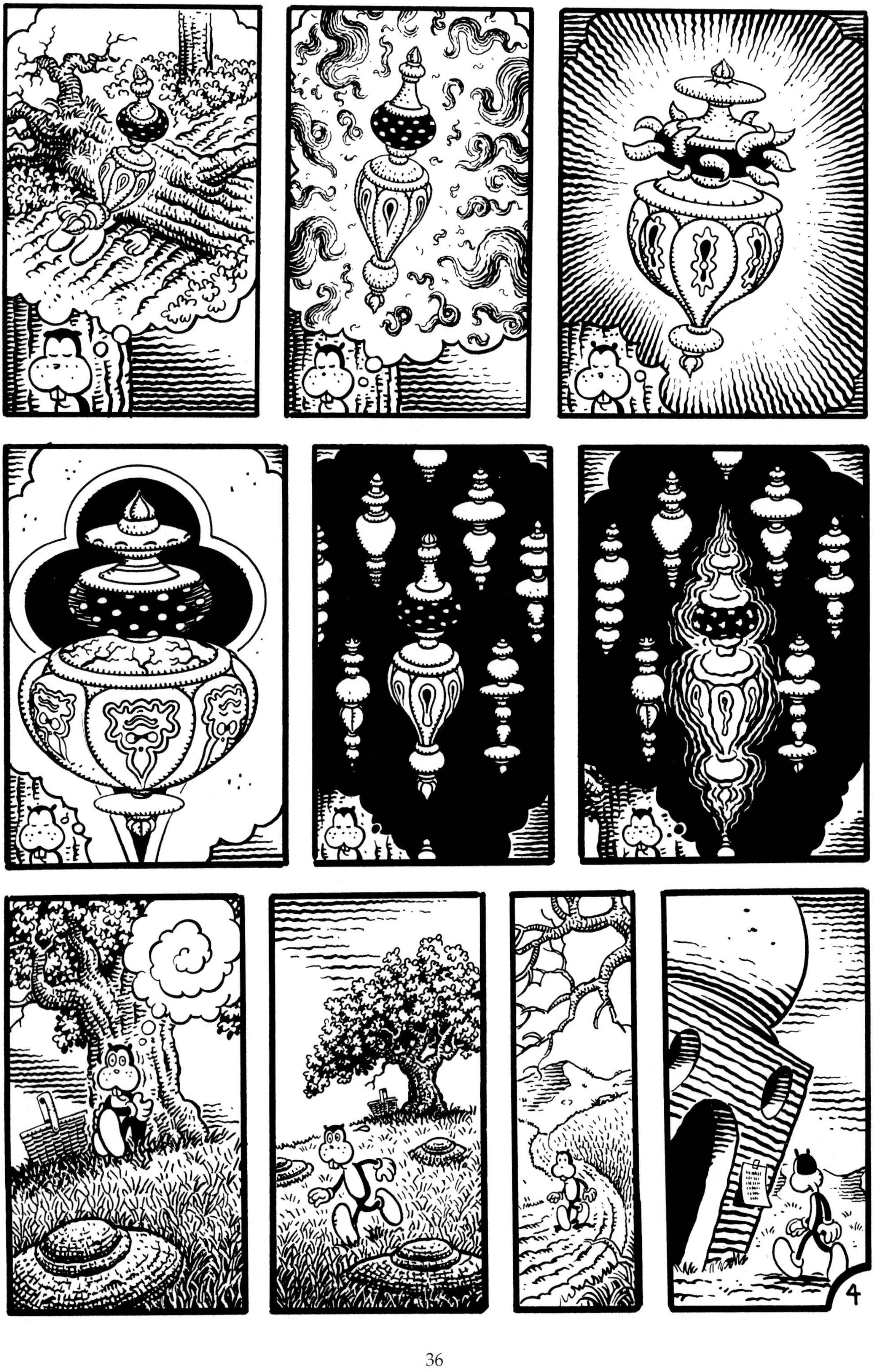
4

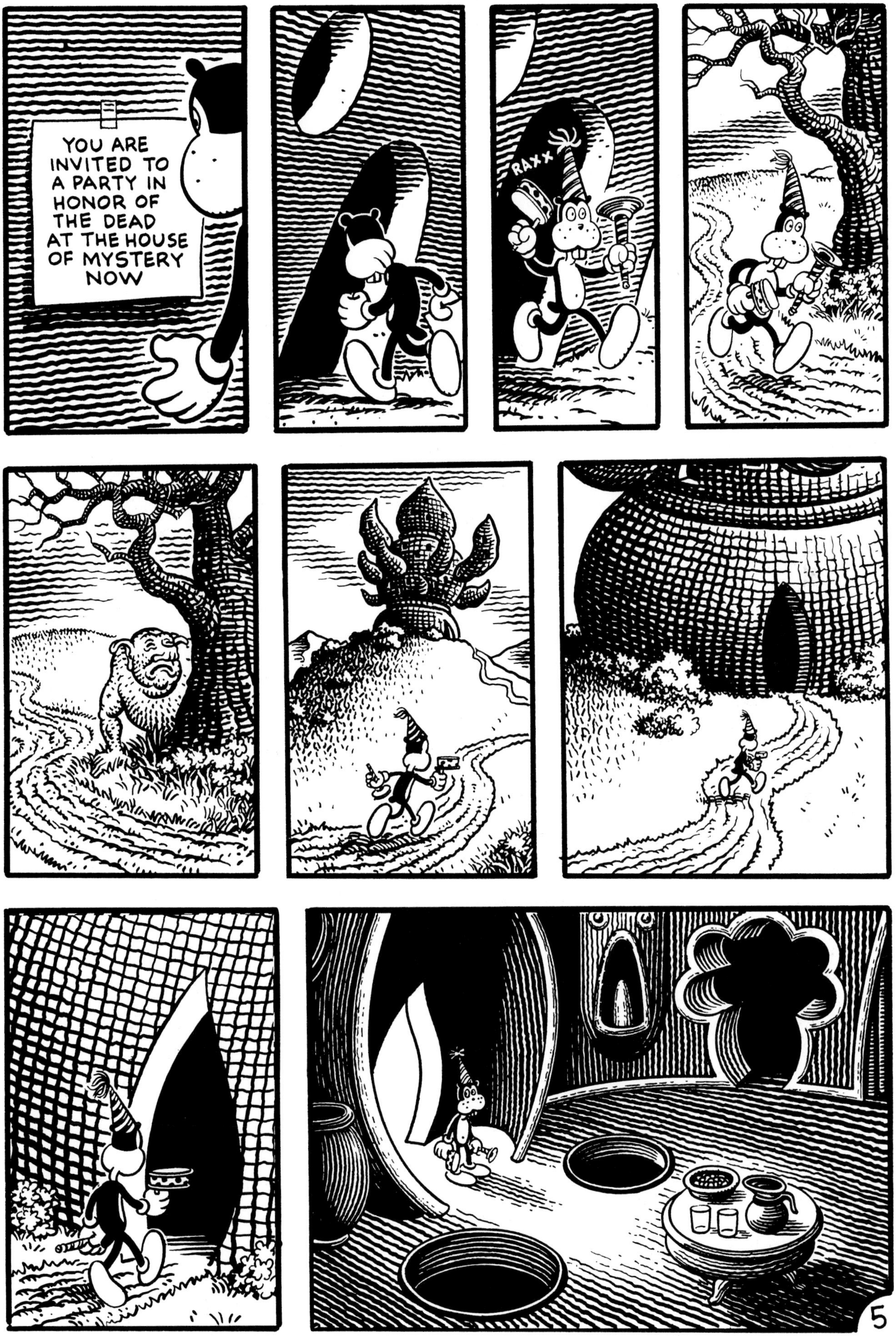
YOU ARE INVITED TO A PARTY IN HONOR OF THE DEAD AT THE HOUSE OF MYSTERY NOW
RAXX
5

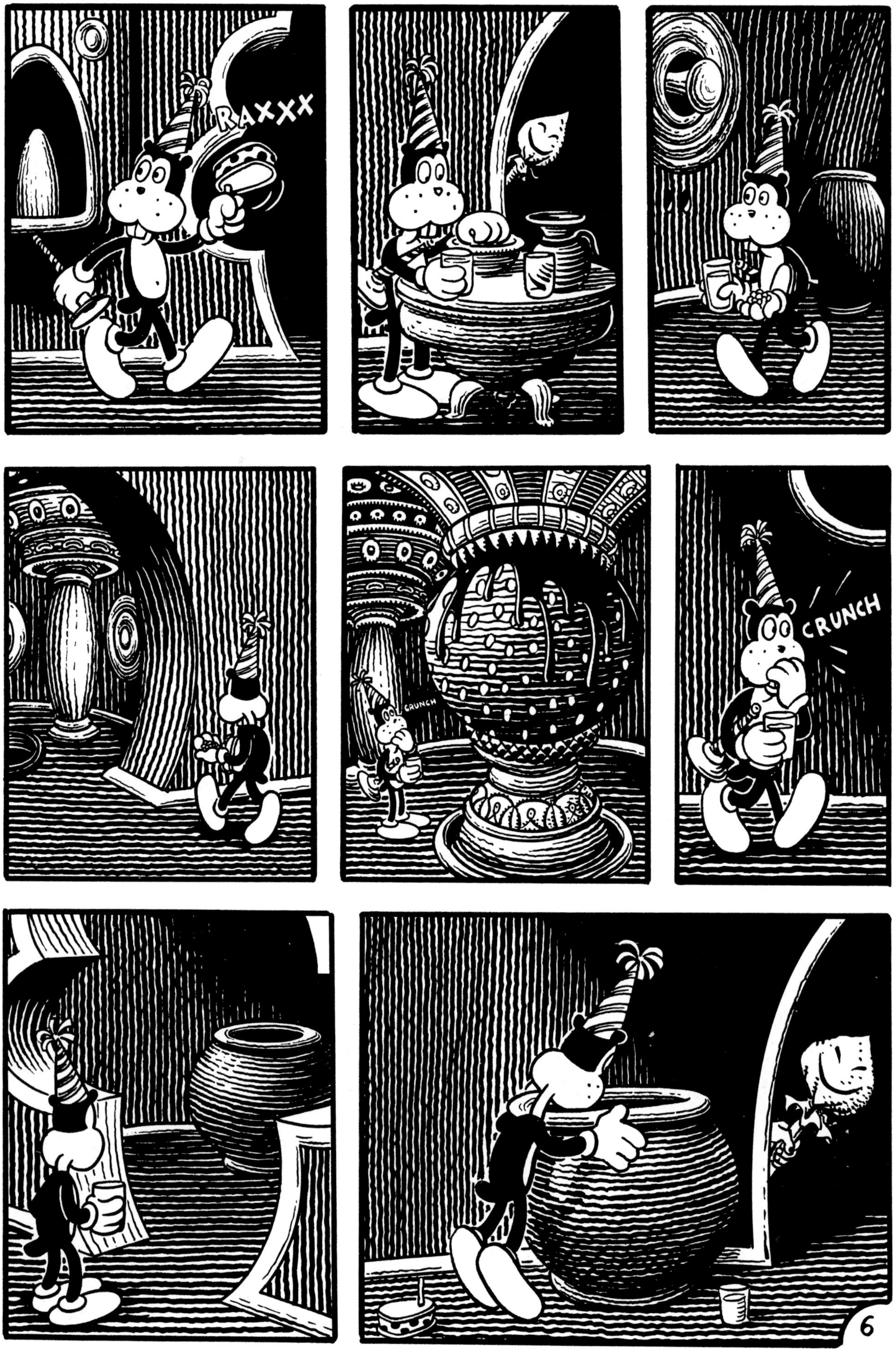
RAXXX
CRUNCH
CRUNCH
6

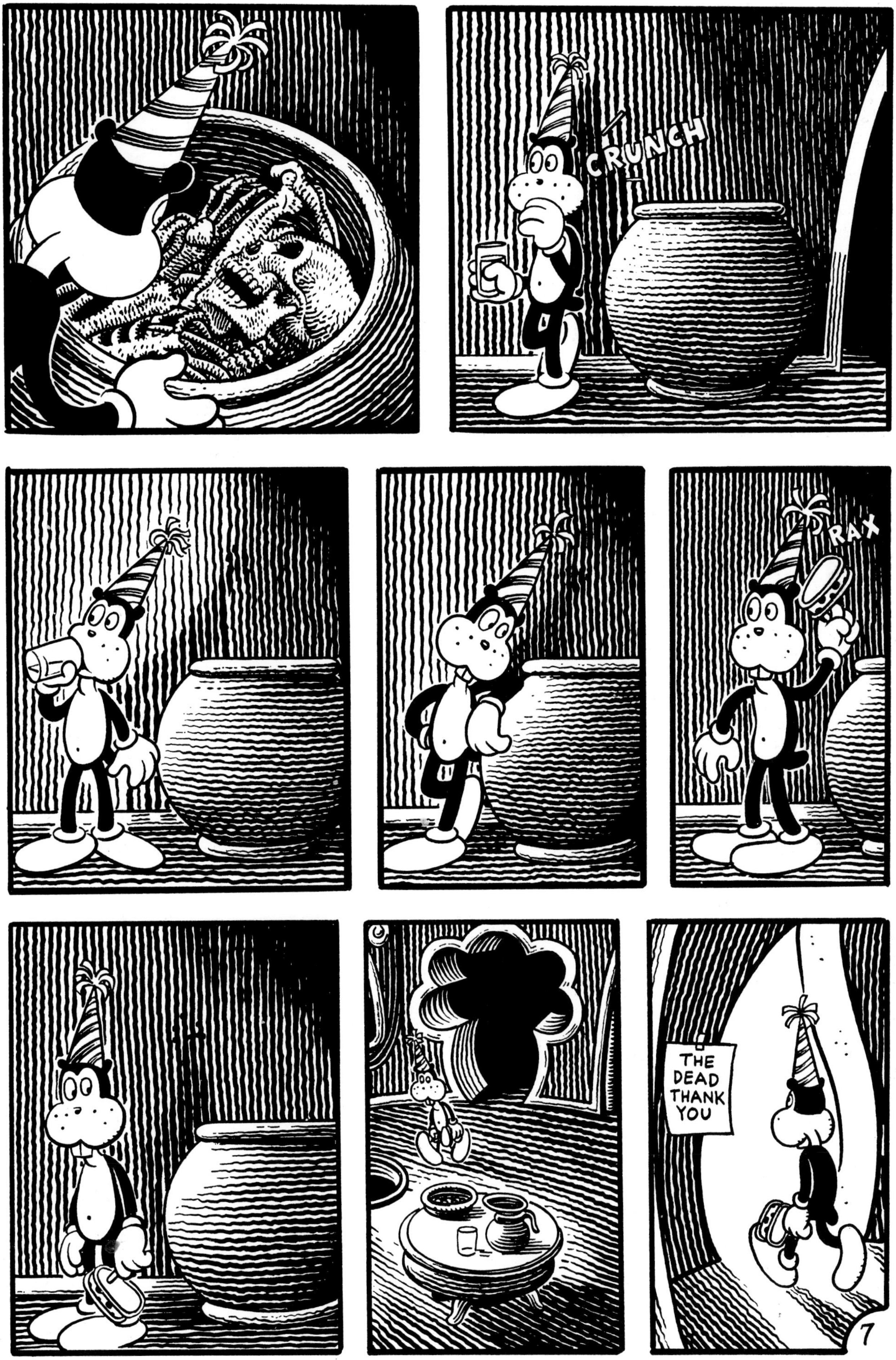
CRUNCH
RAX
THE DEAD THANK YOU
7

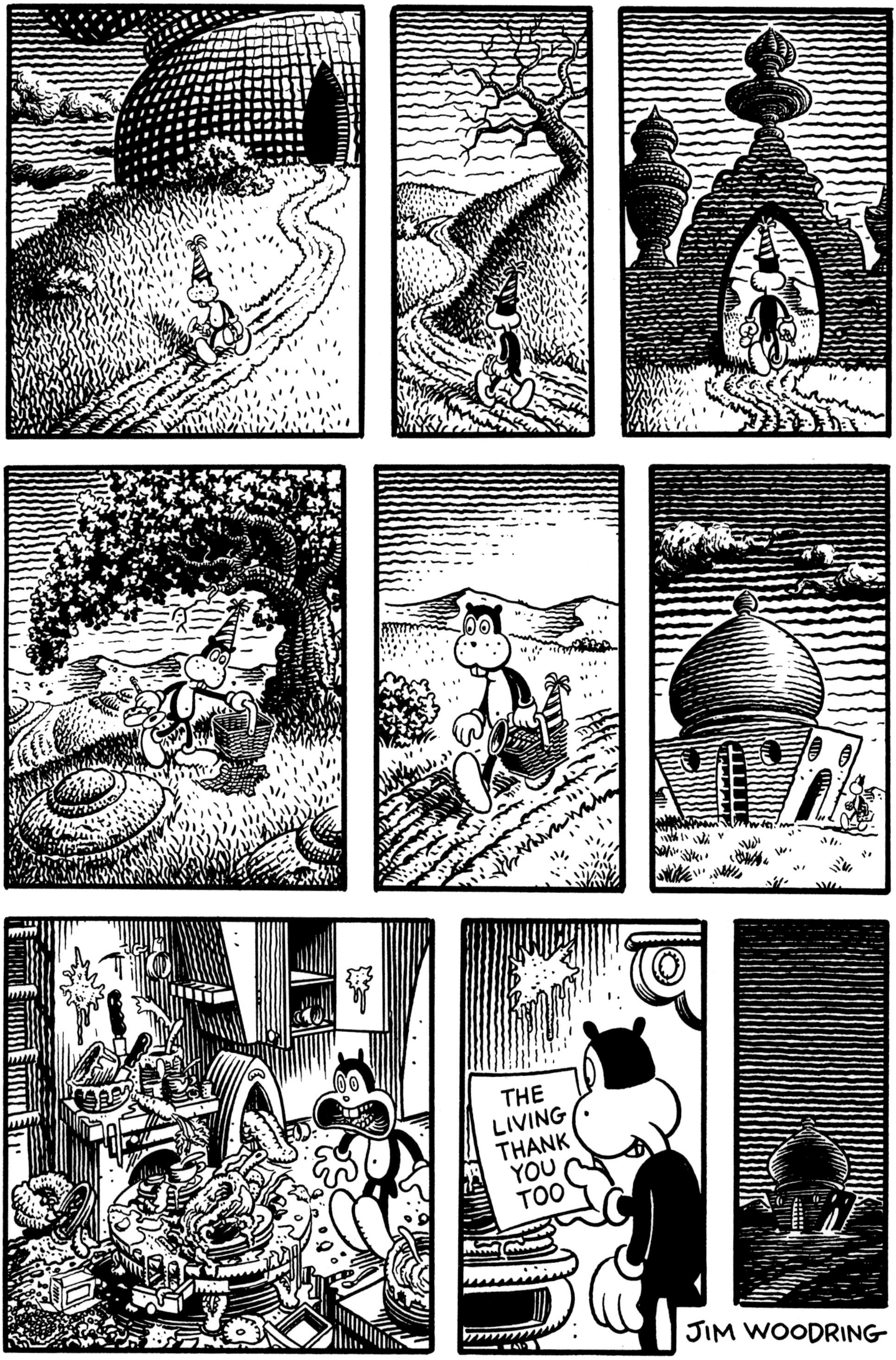
THE LIVING THANK YOU TOO
JIM WOODRING

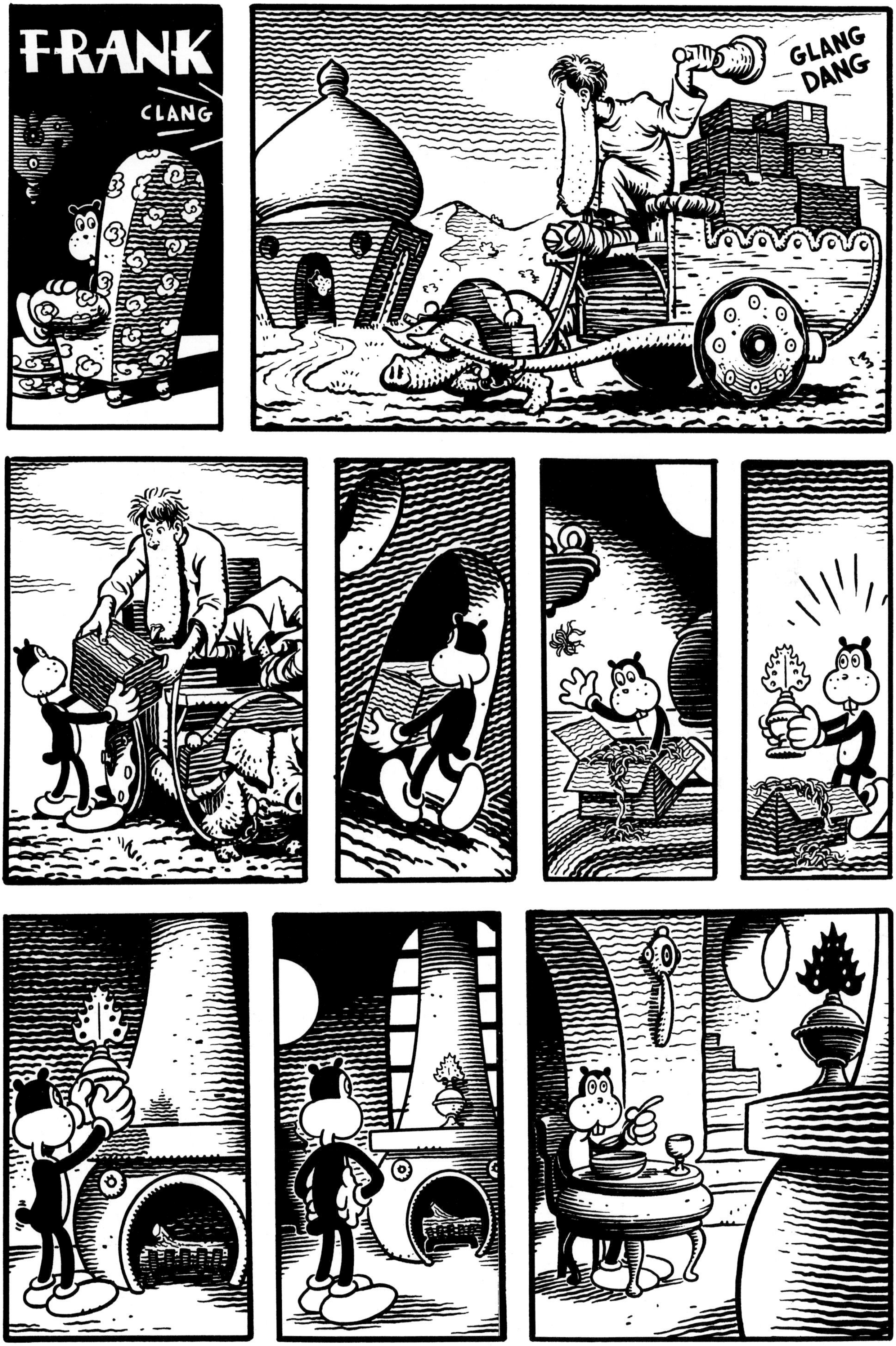
FRANK
CLANG
GLANG
DANG

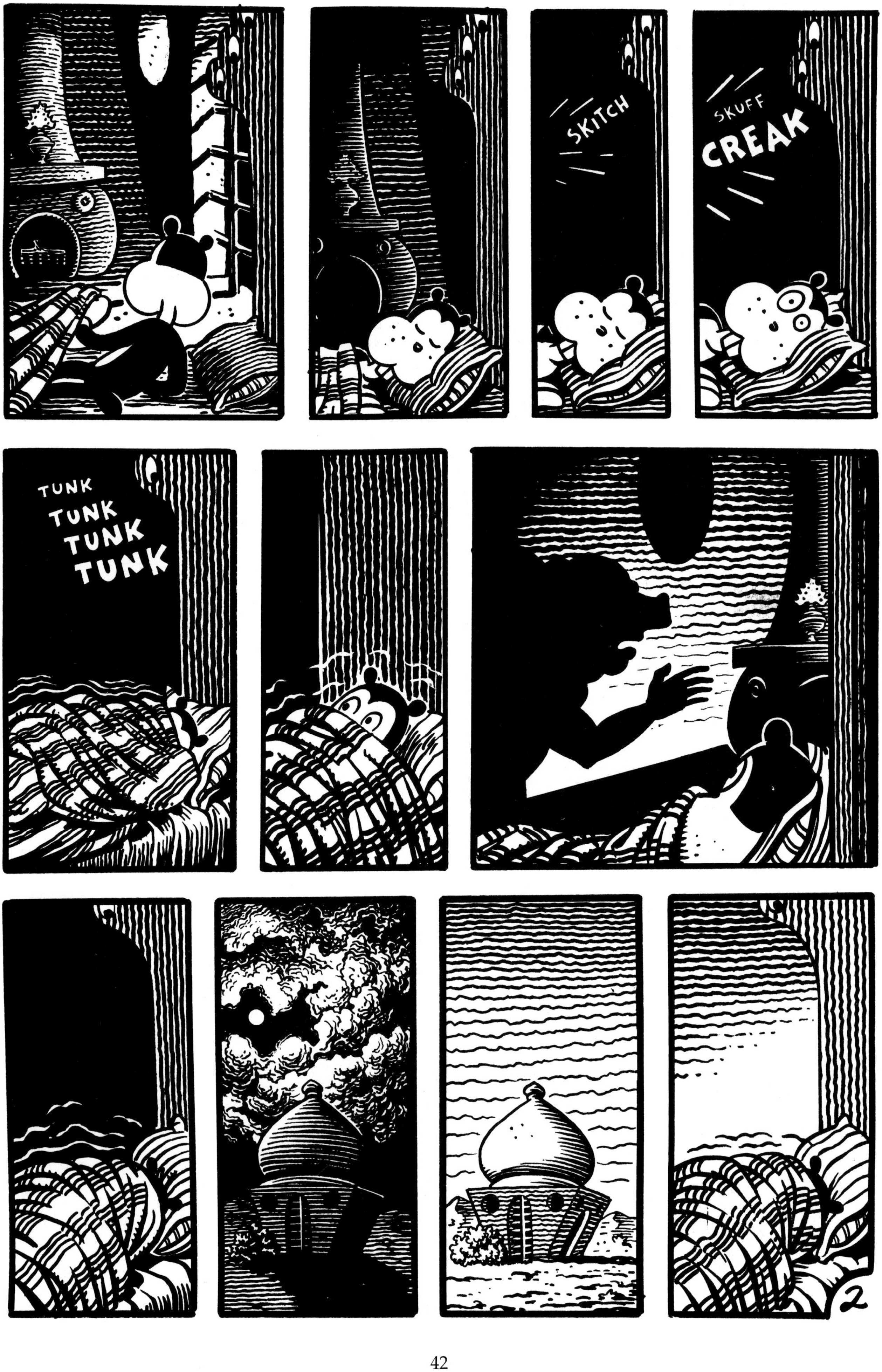
SKITCH
SKUFF
CREAK
TUNK
TUNK
TUNK
TUNK
2

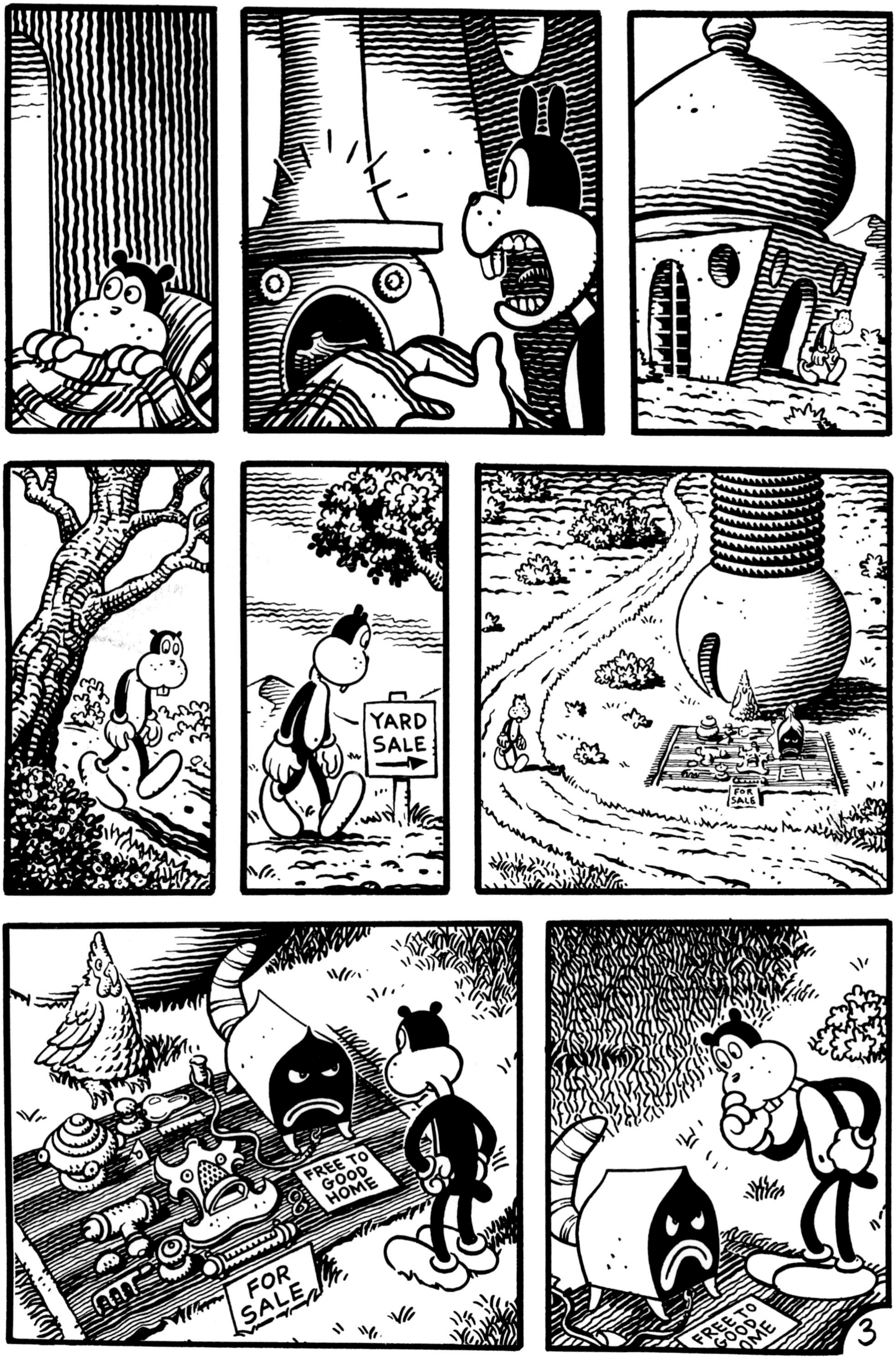
YARD
SALE
FOR
SALE
FREE TO
GOOD
HOME
FOR
SALE
FREE TO
GOOD
HOME
3

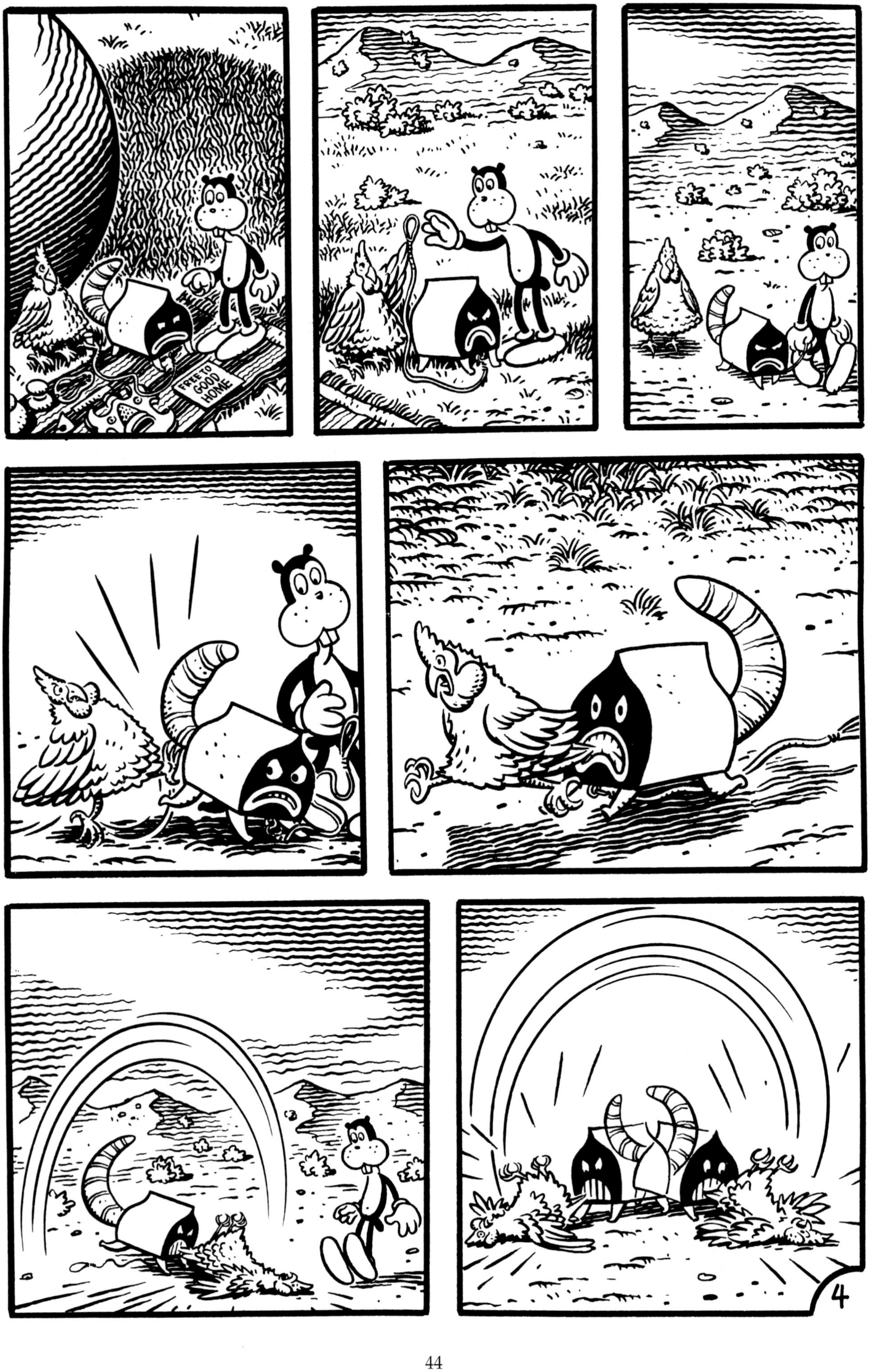
FREE TO GOOD HOME
4

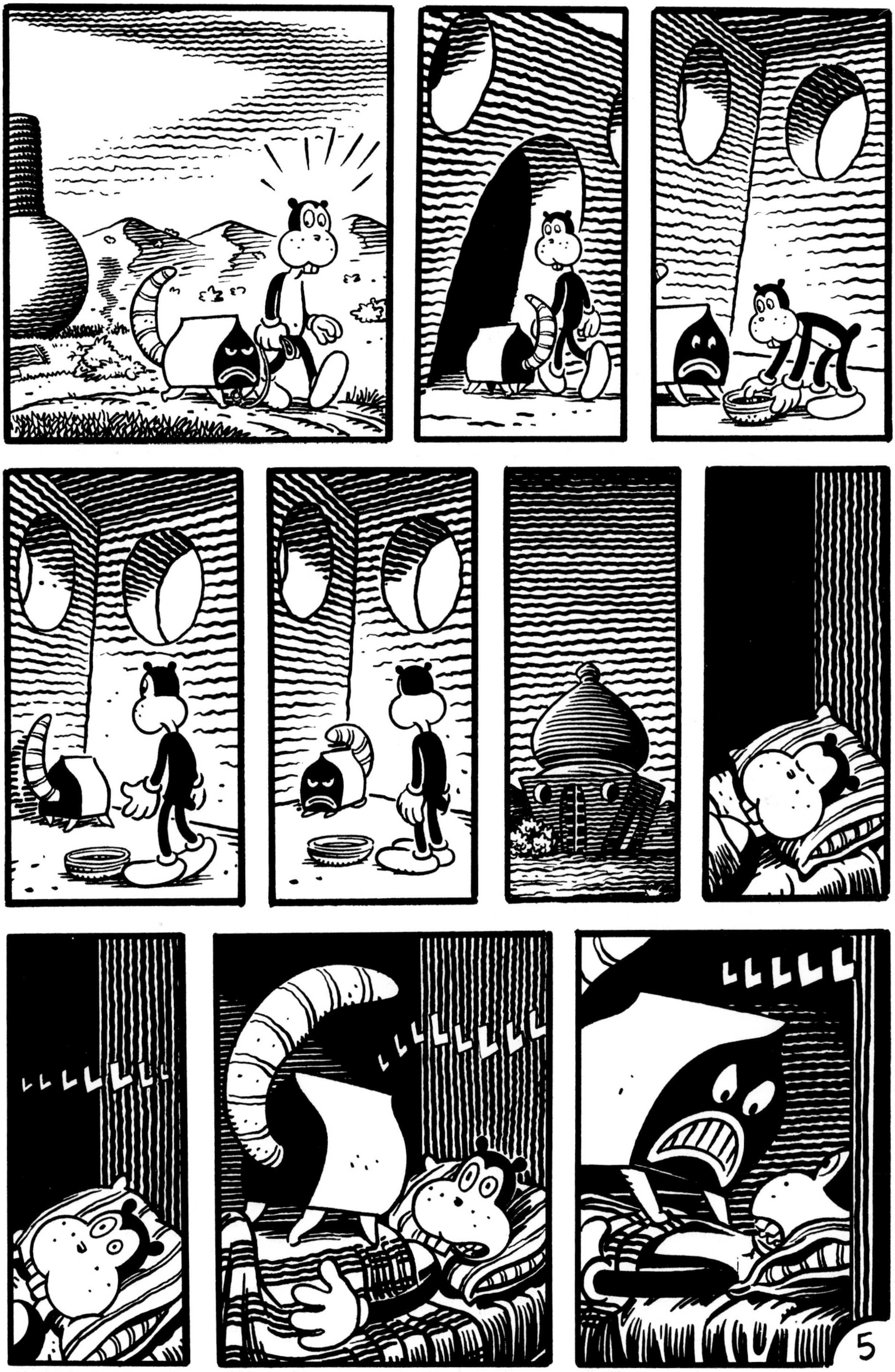
5

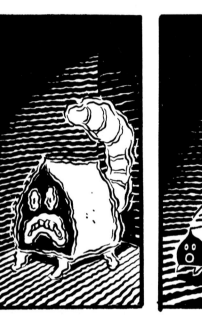

6

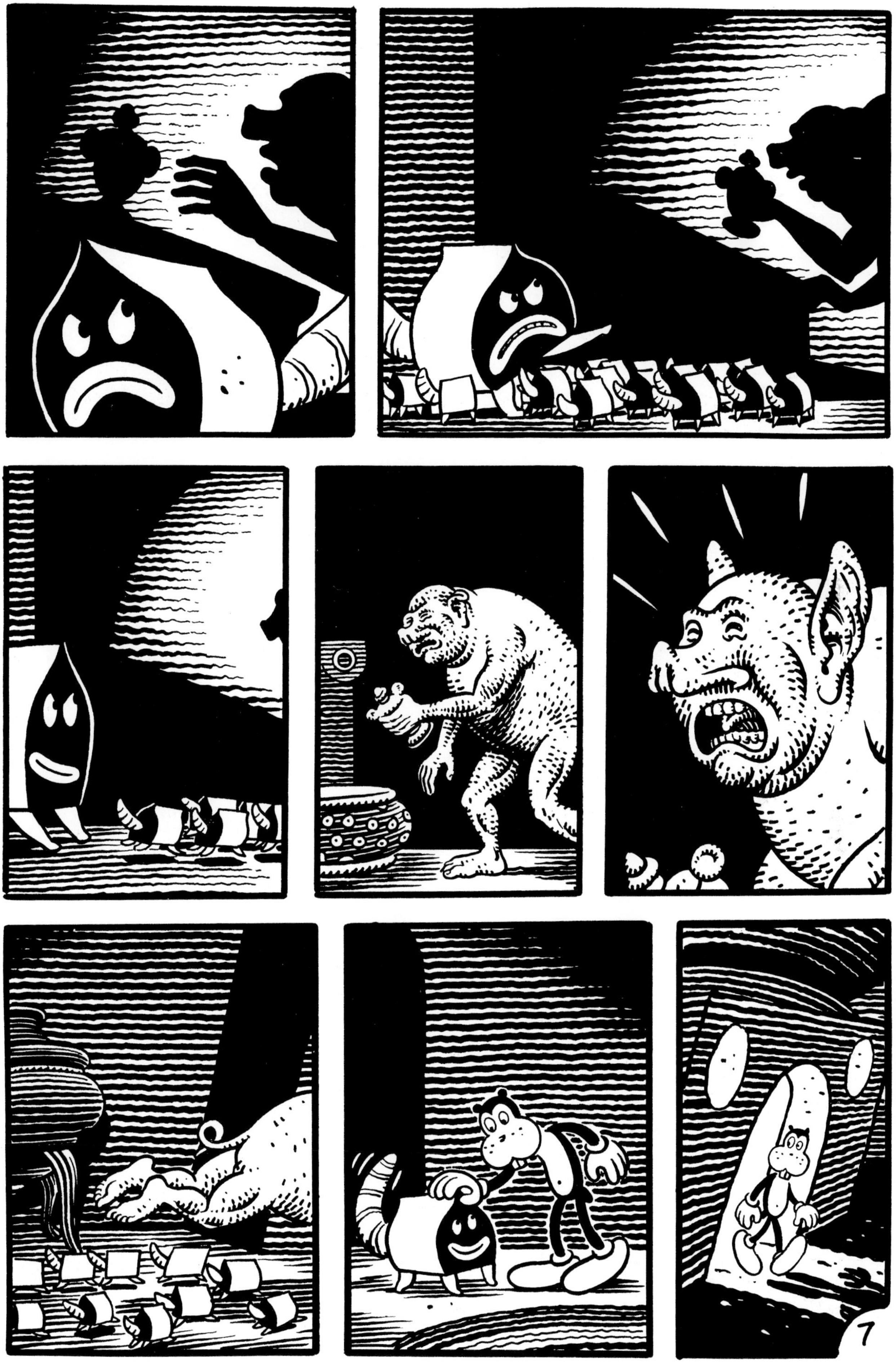
7

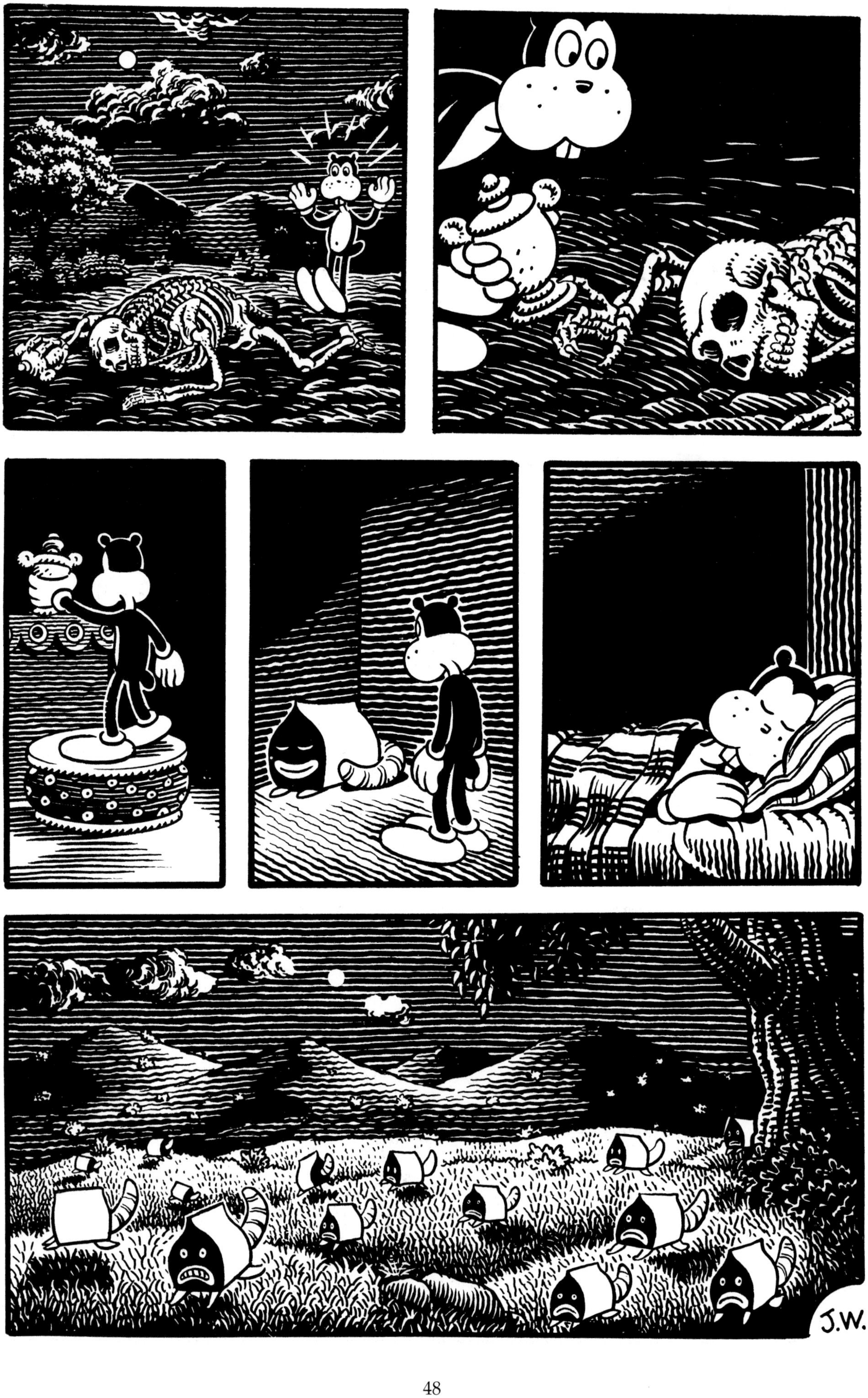
J.W.

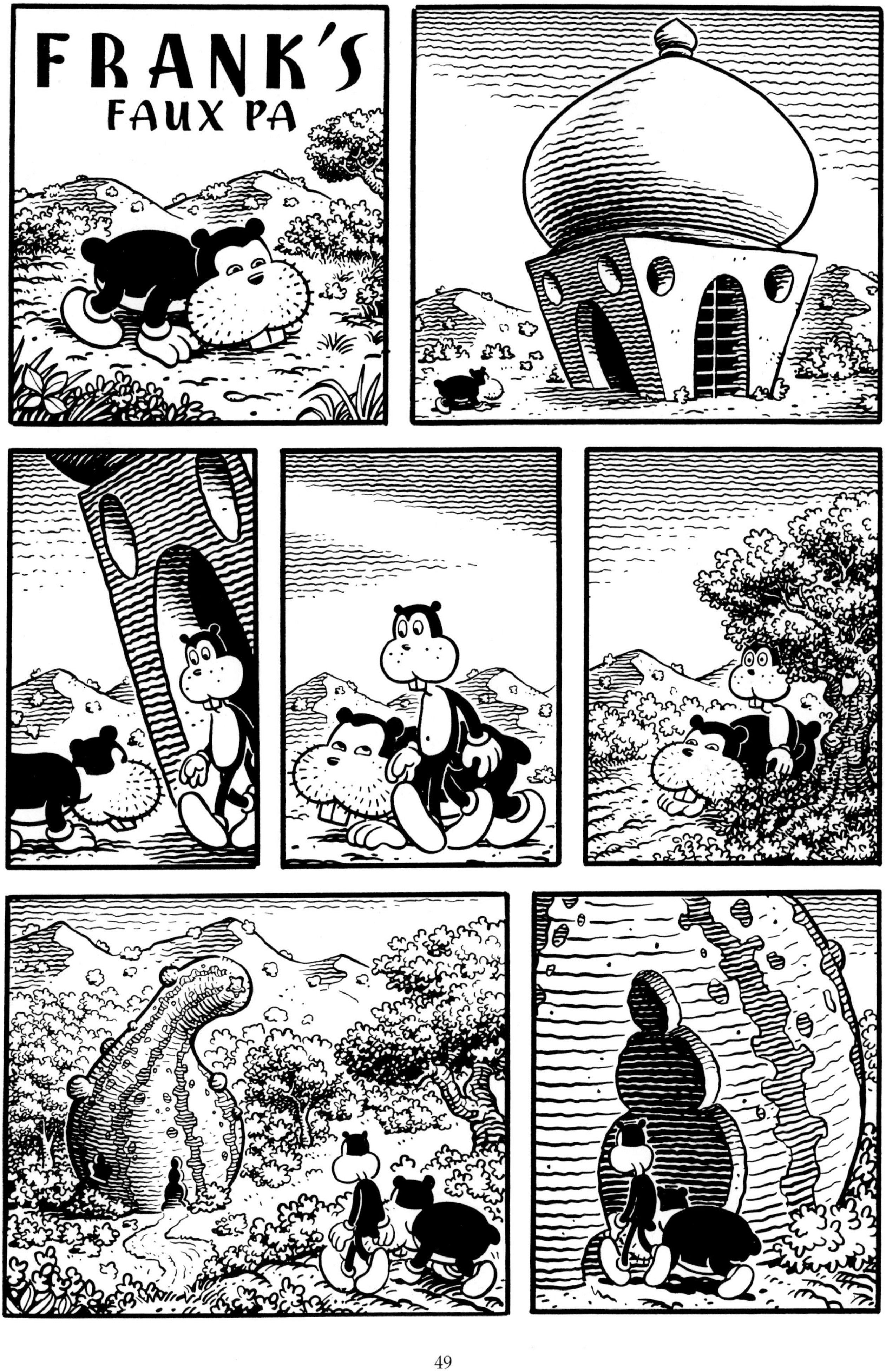
FRANK'S
FAUX PA

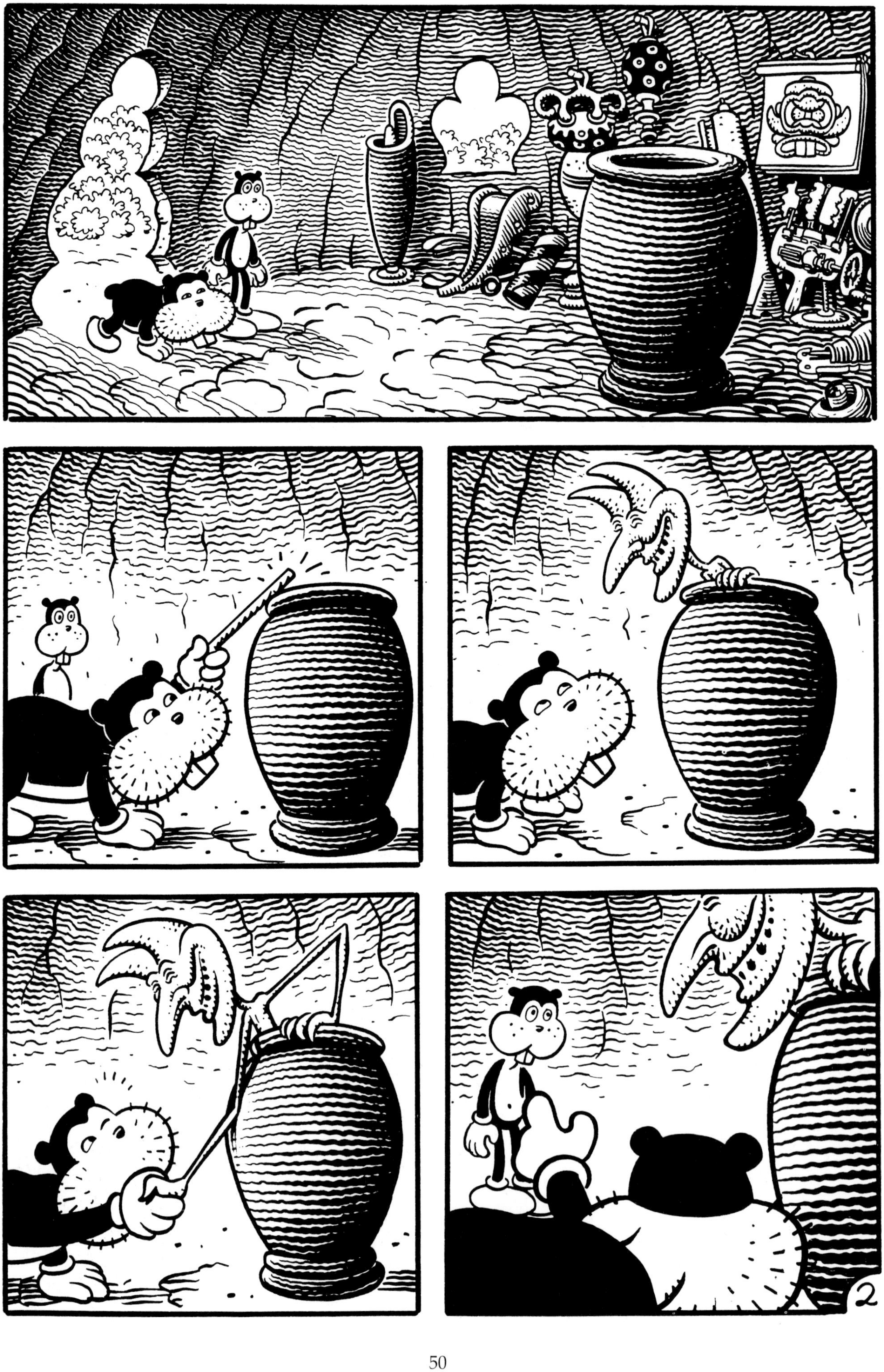

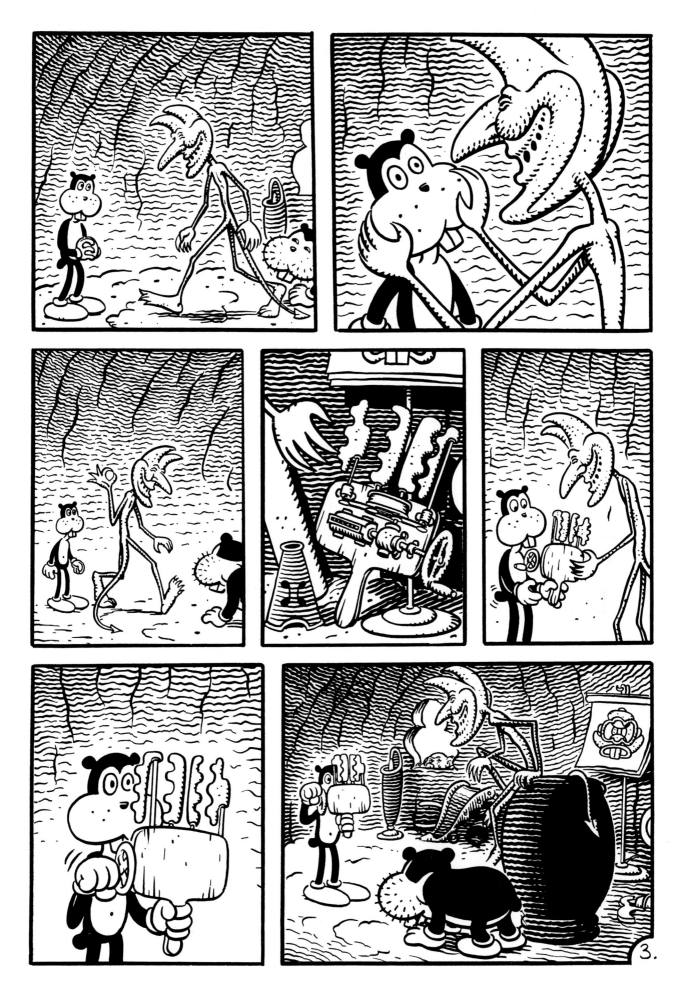

"AND YOU CALL YOURSELF A GENTLEMAN"
5.

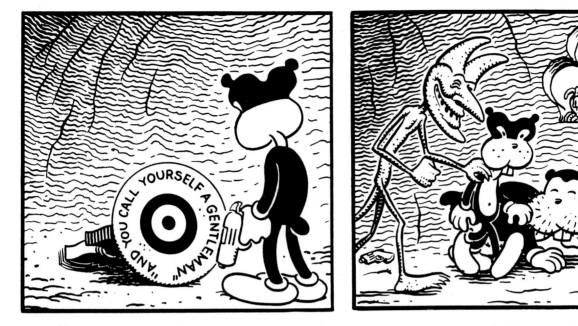

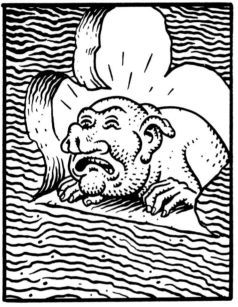

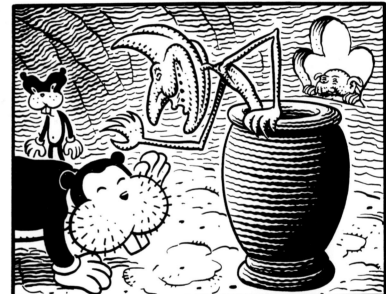

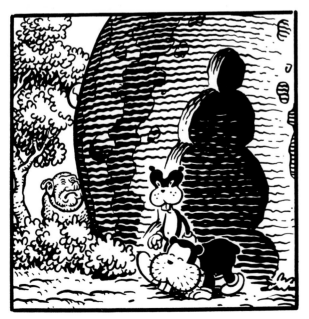

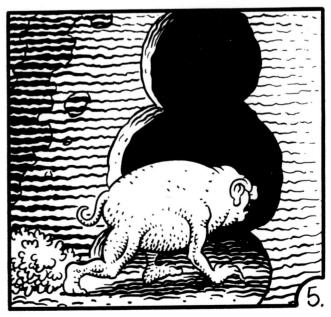

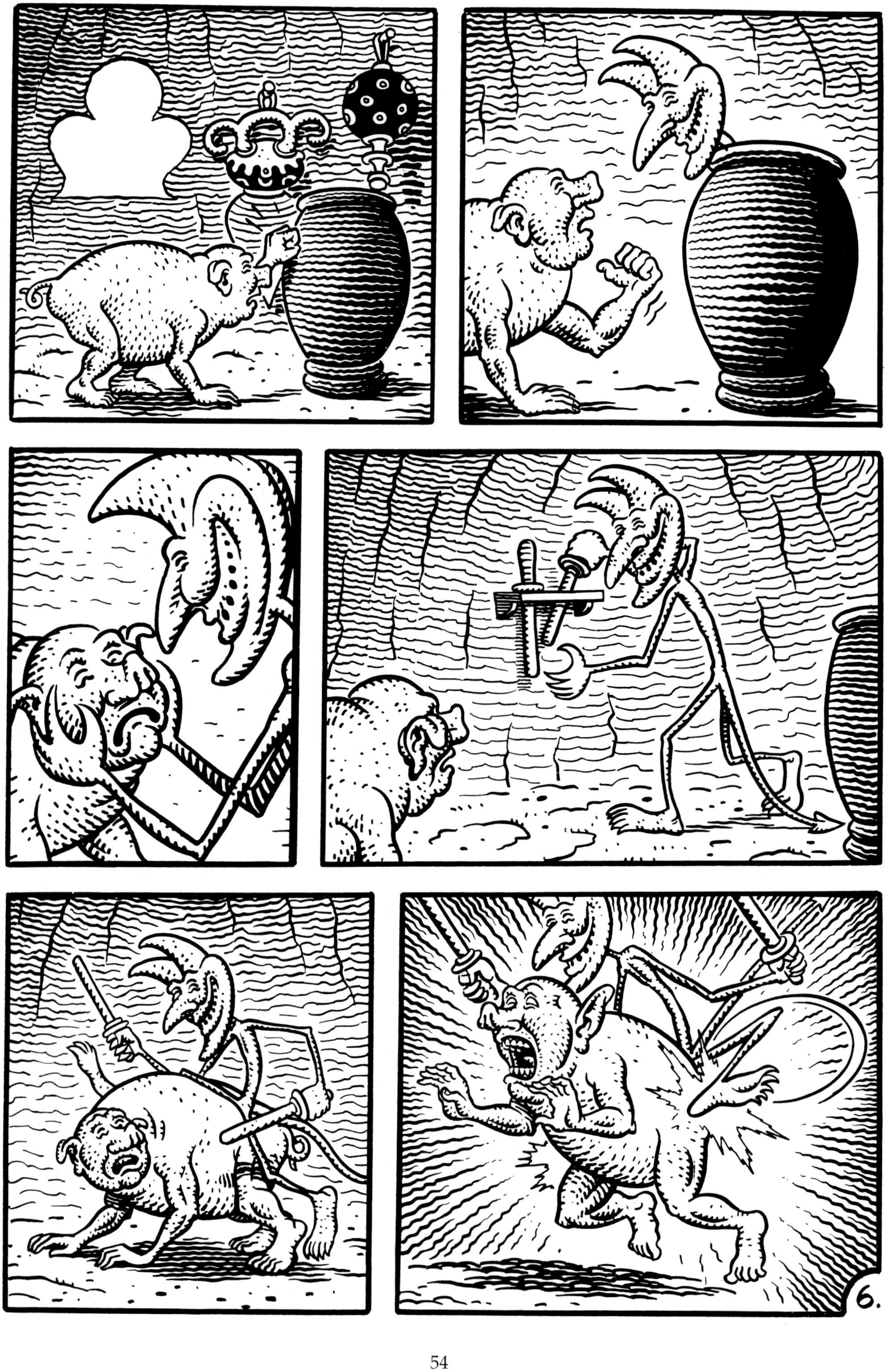
6.

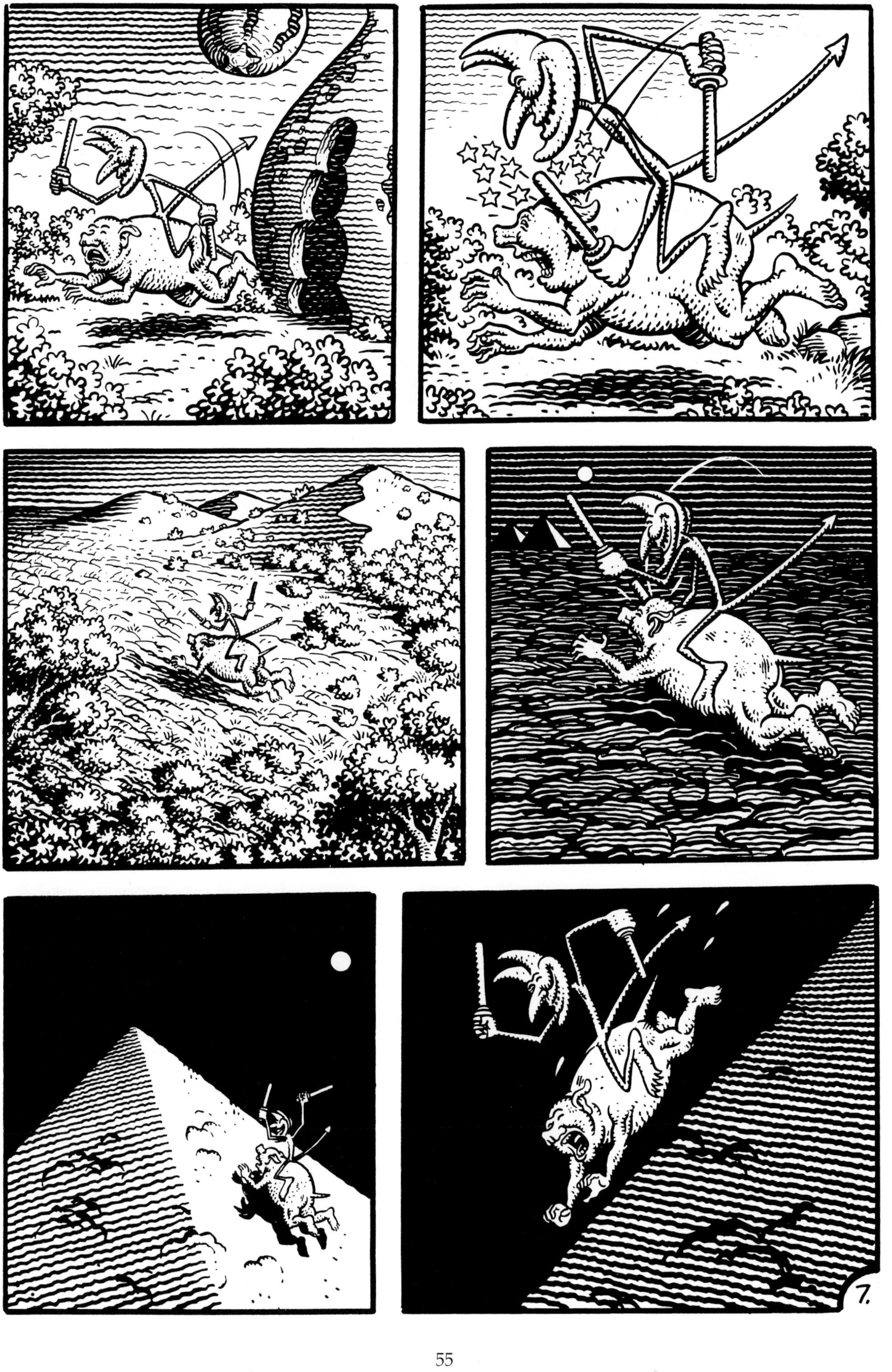
7.

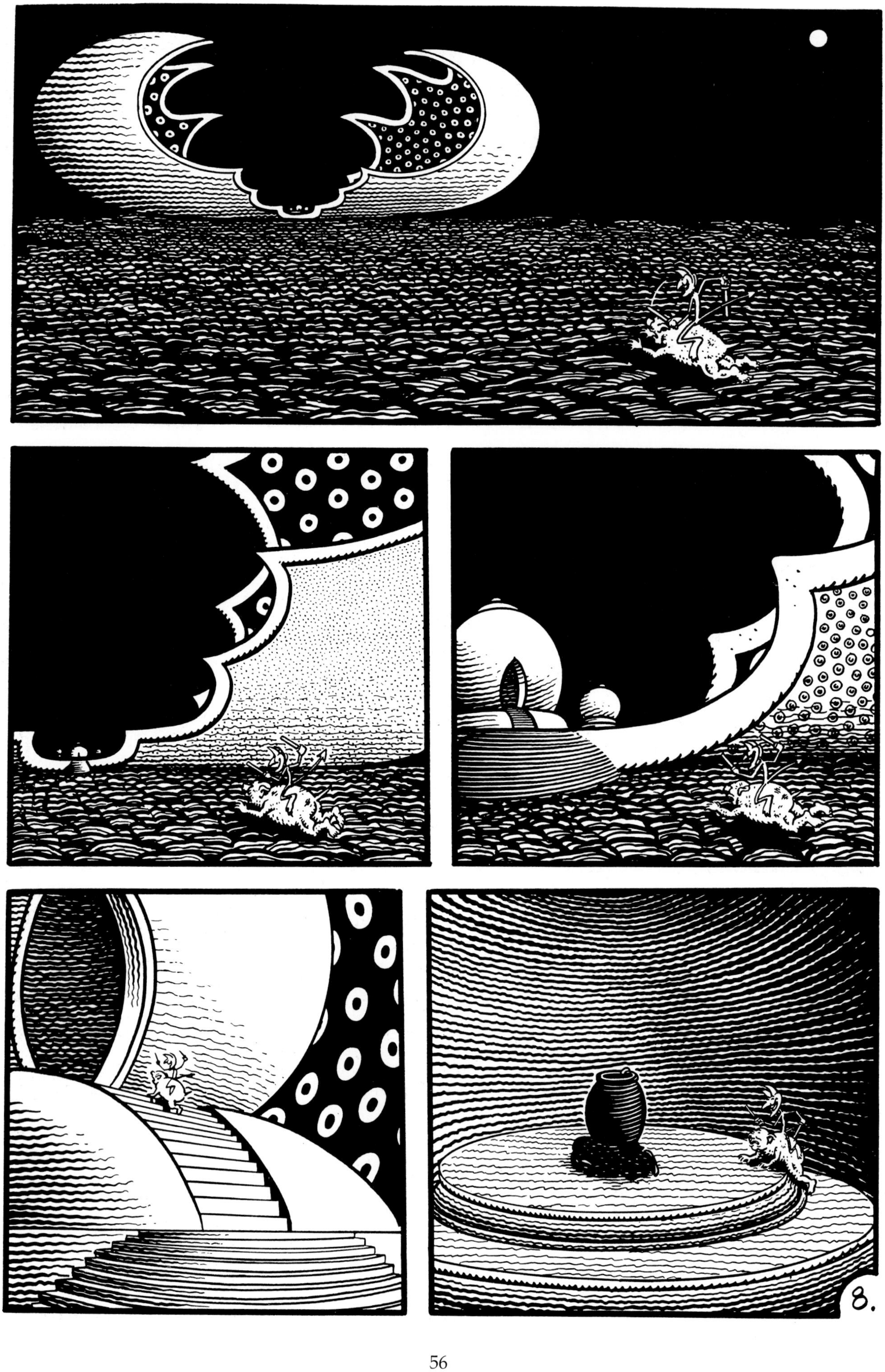
8.

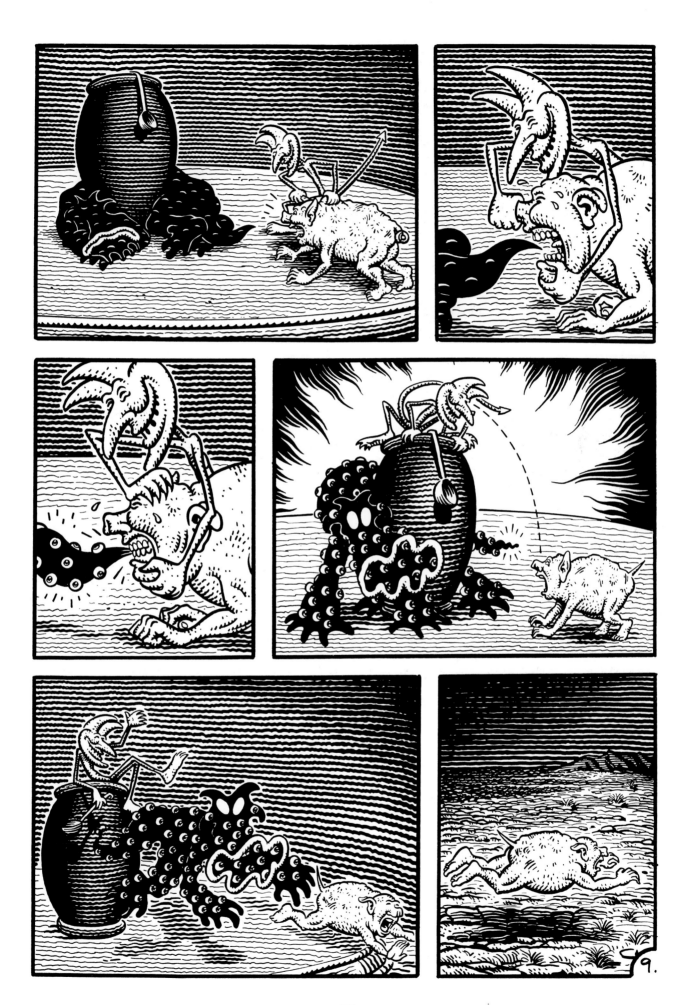

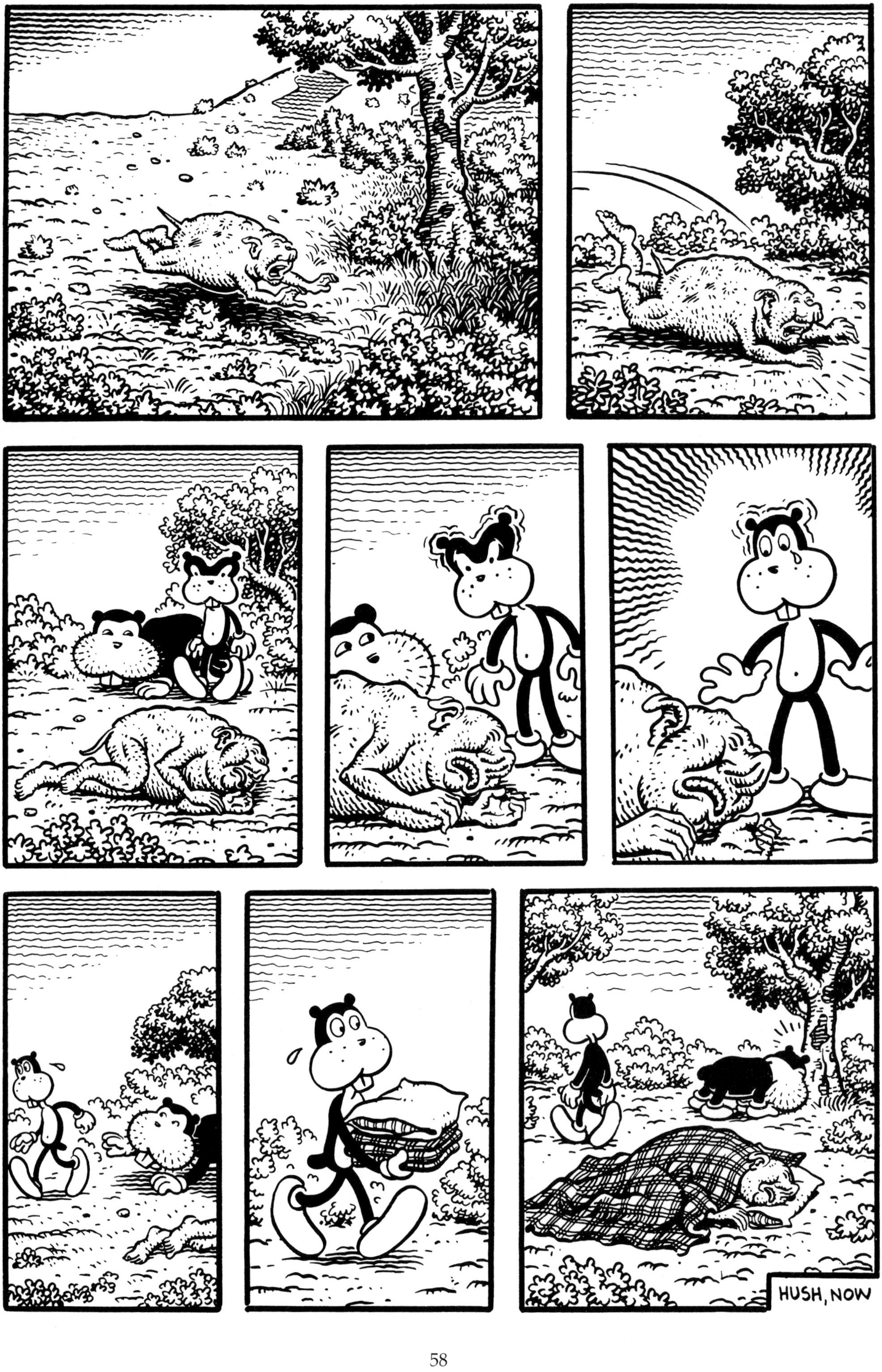
HUSH, NOW

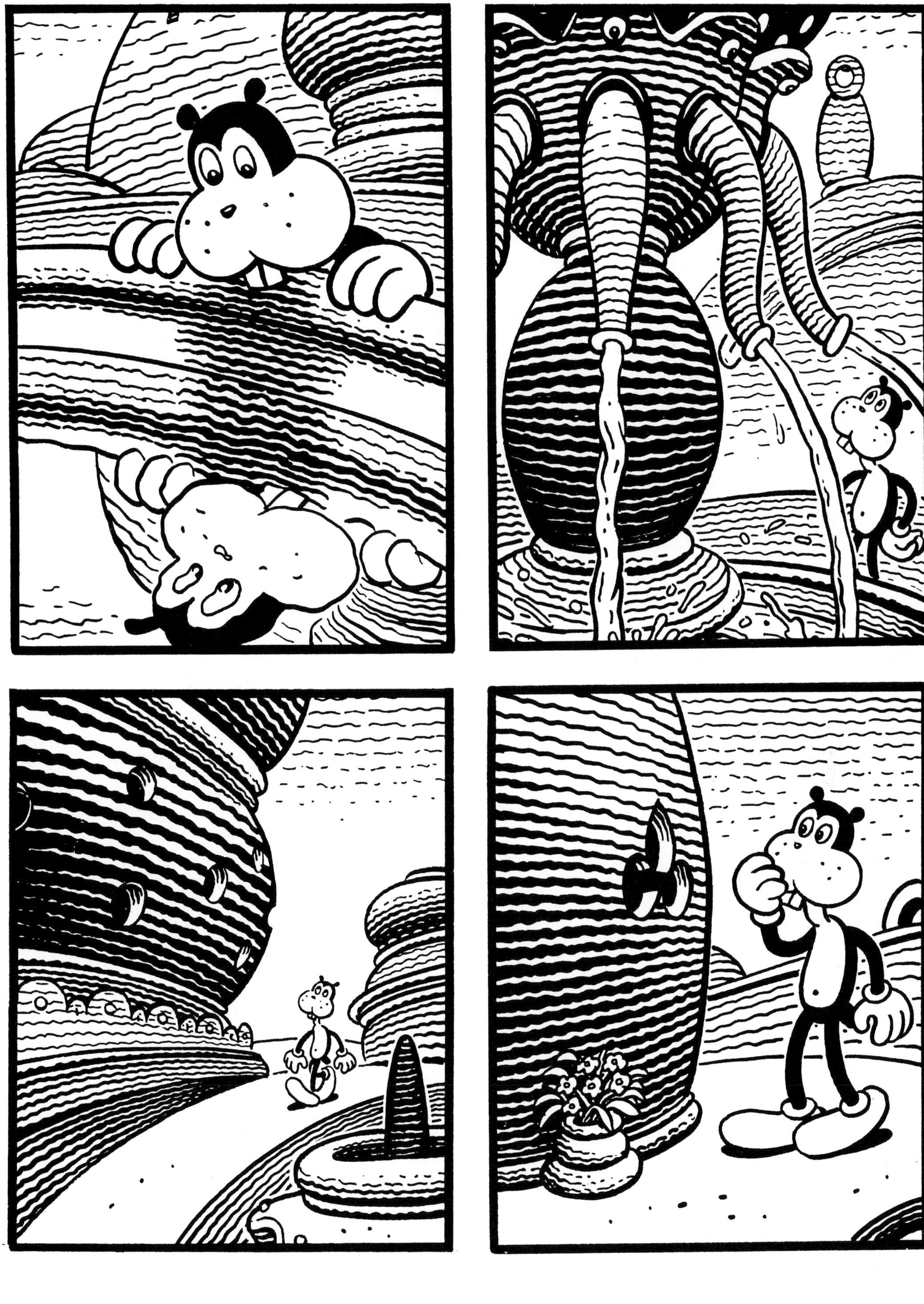

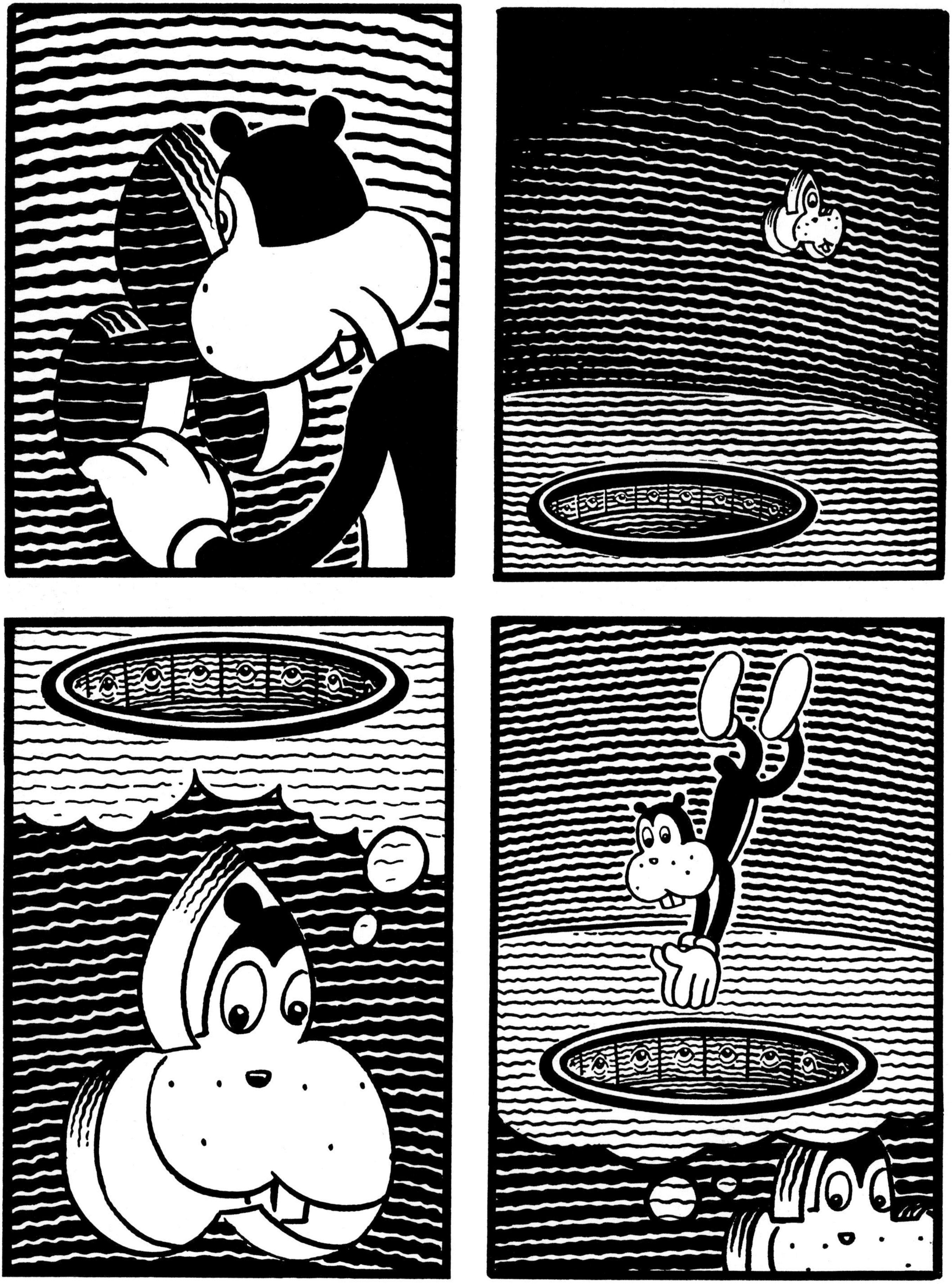

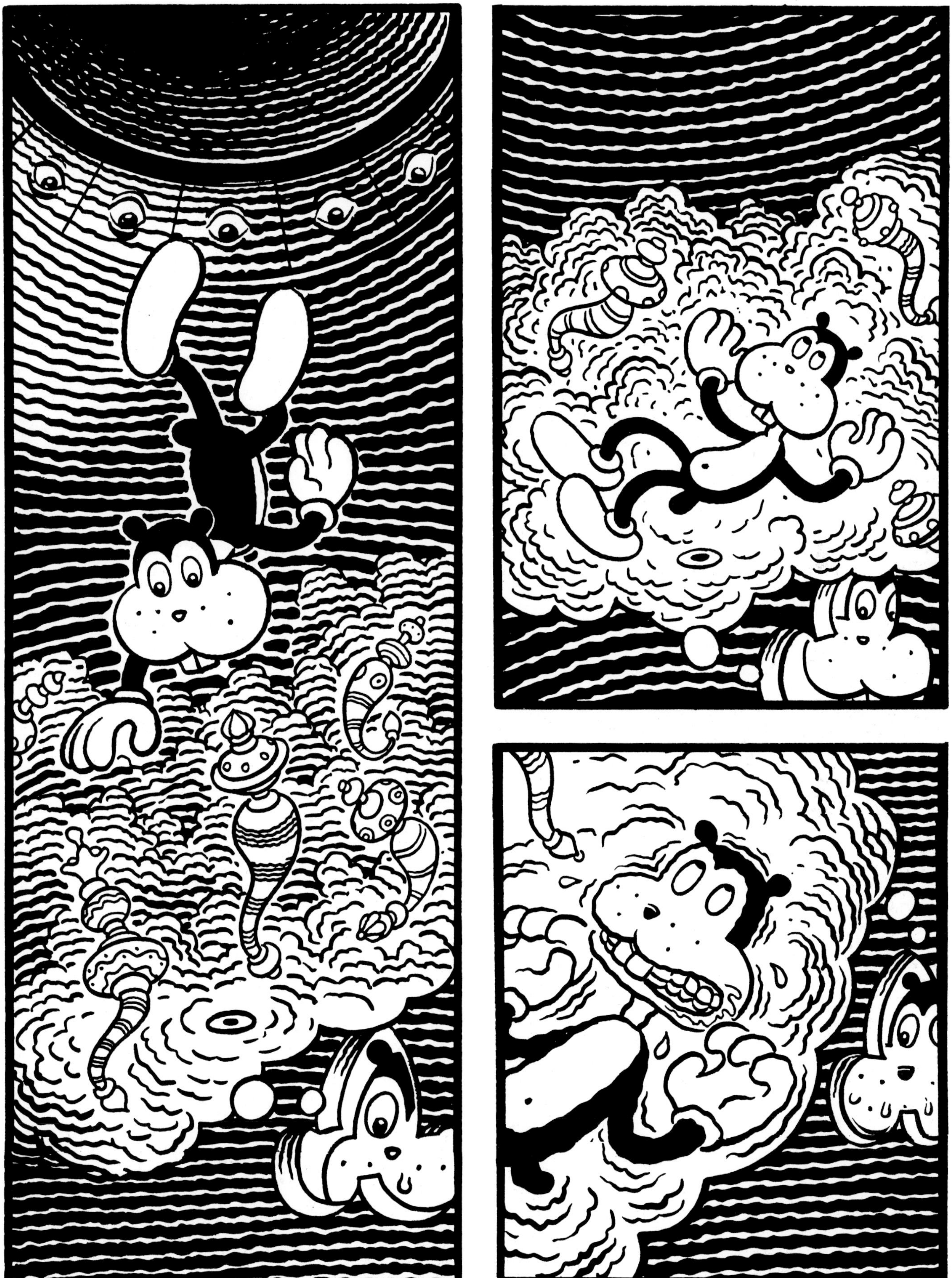

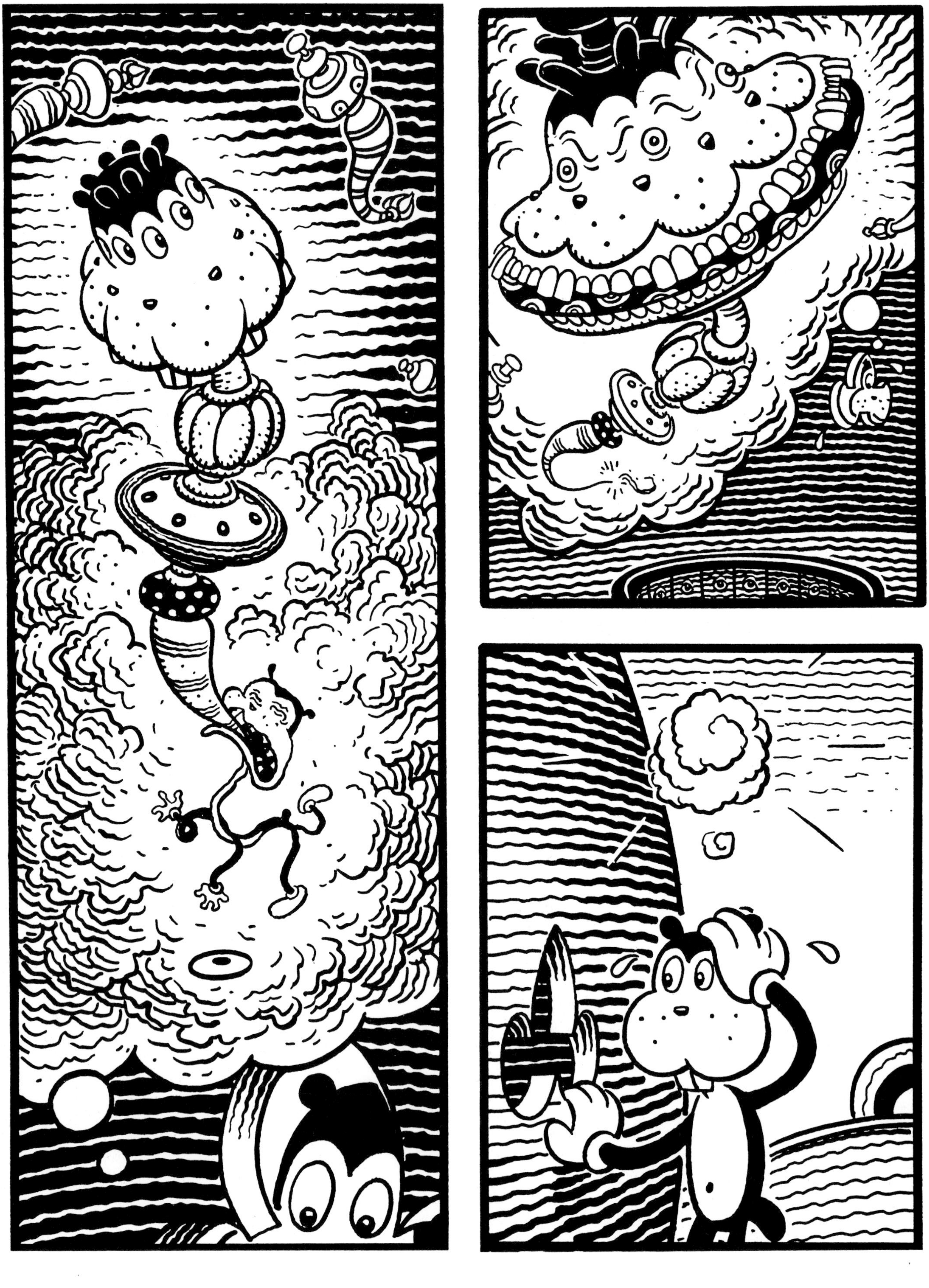

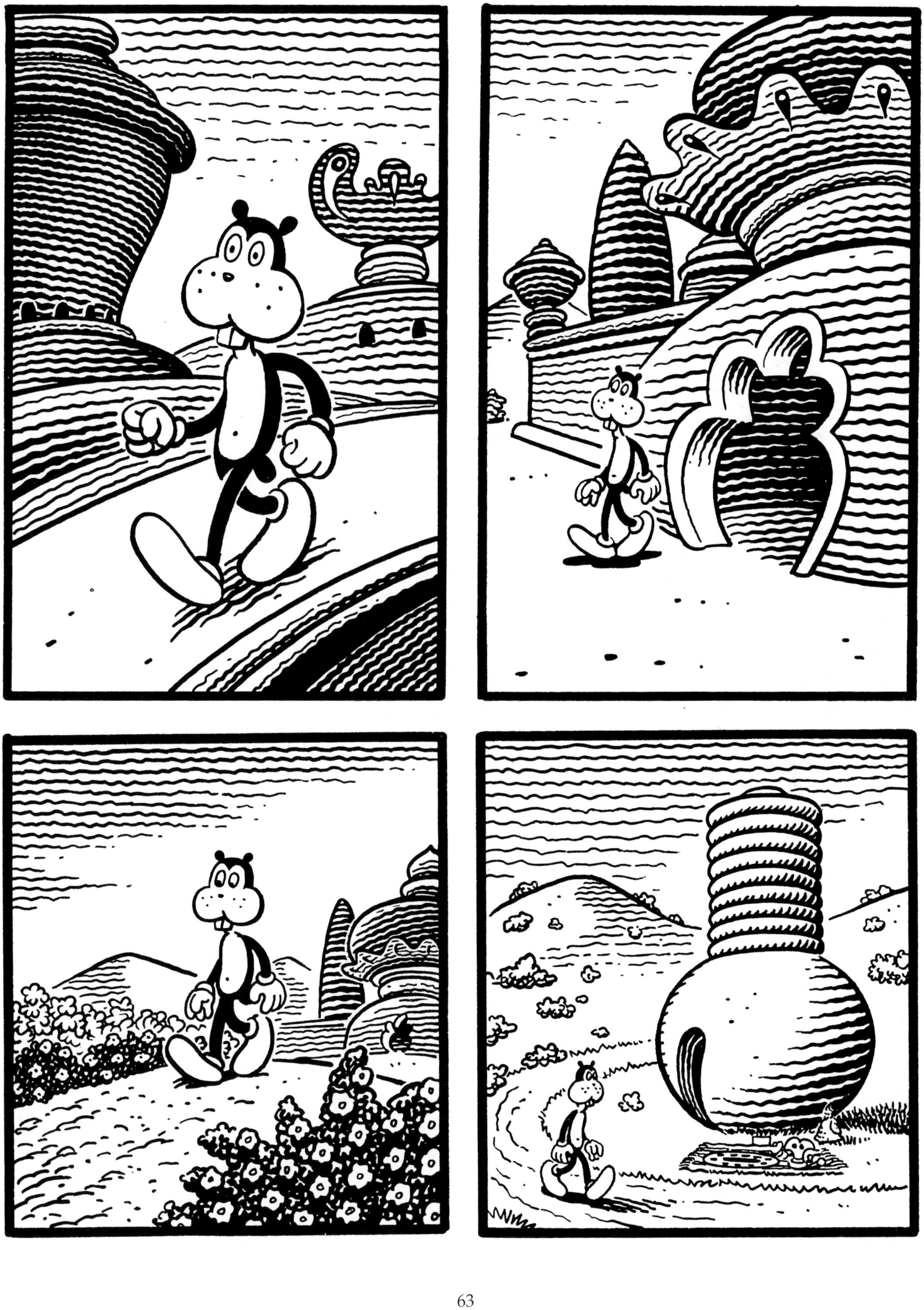

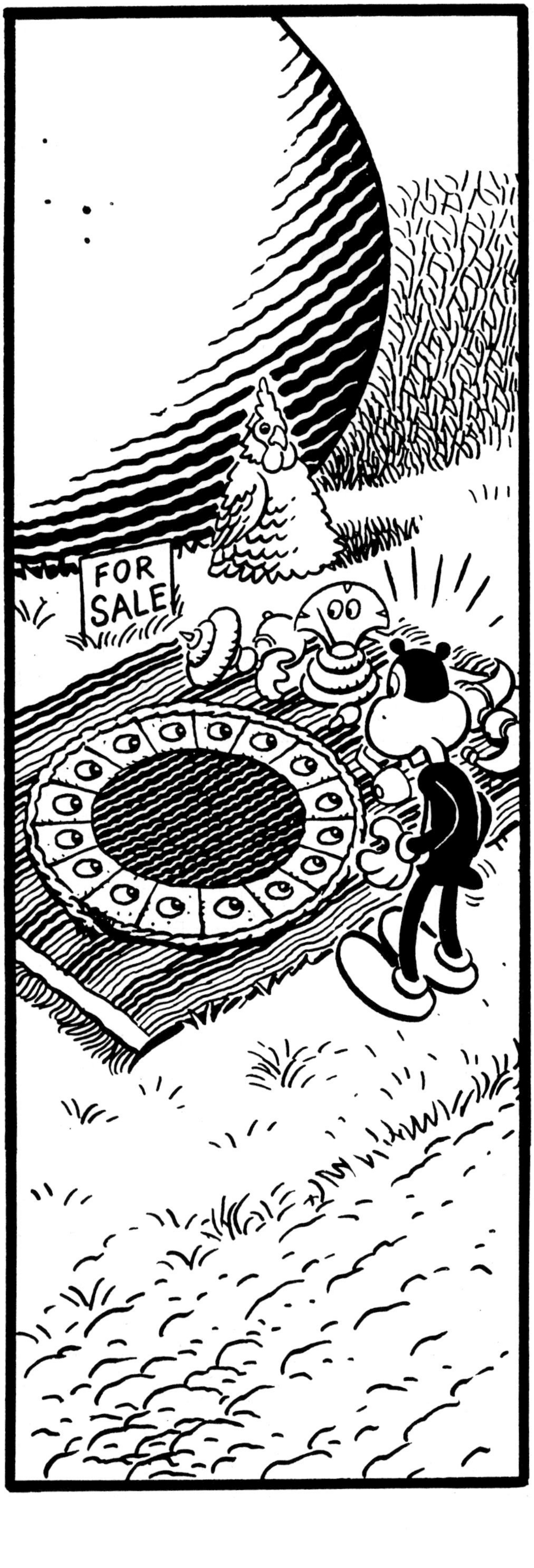
FOR SALE

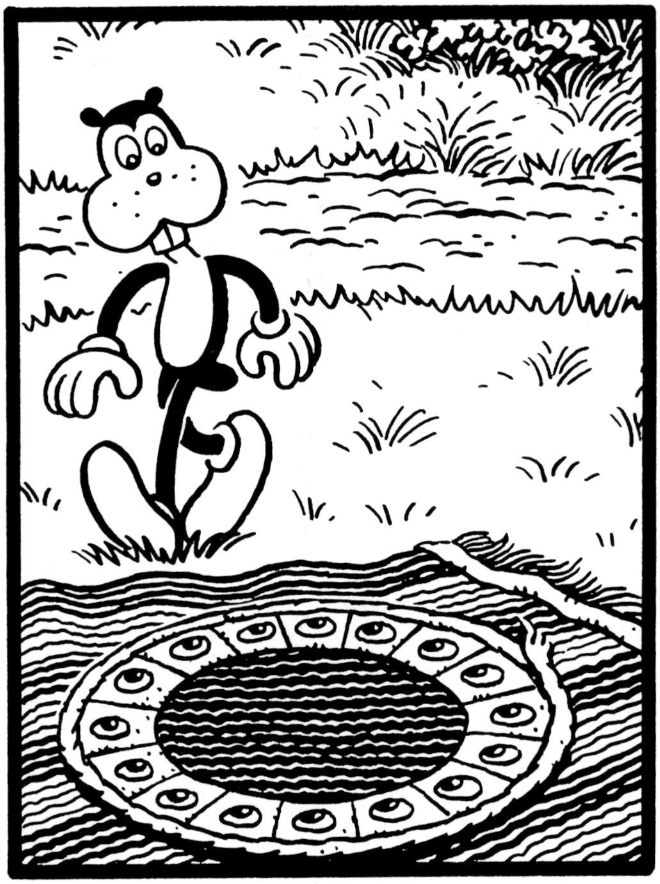

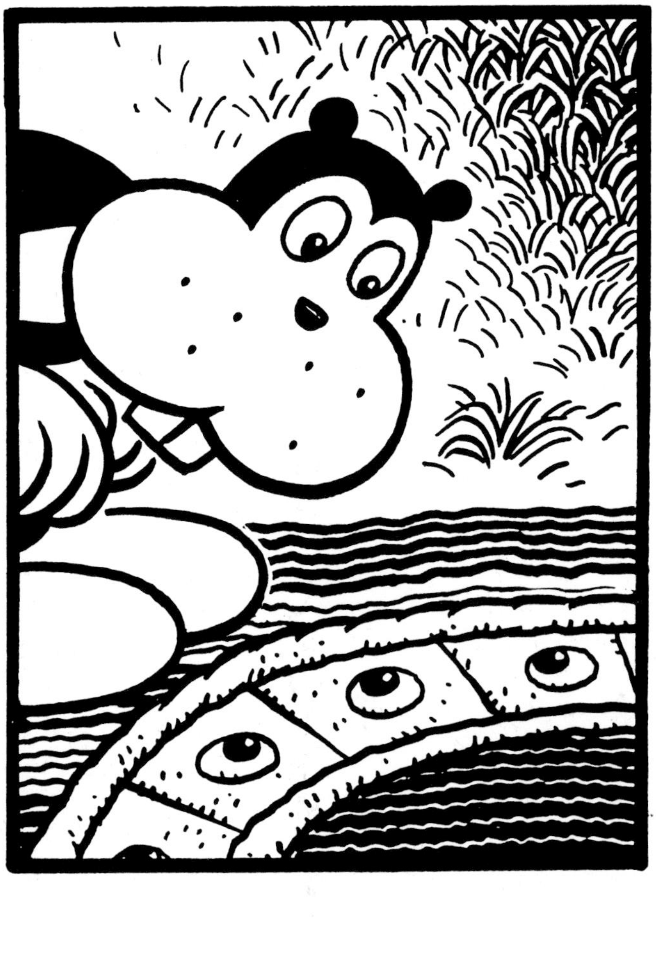

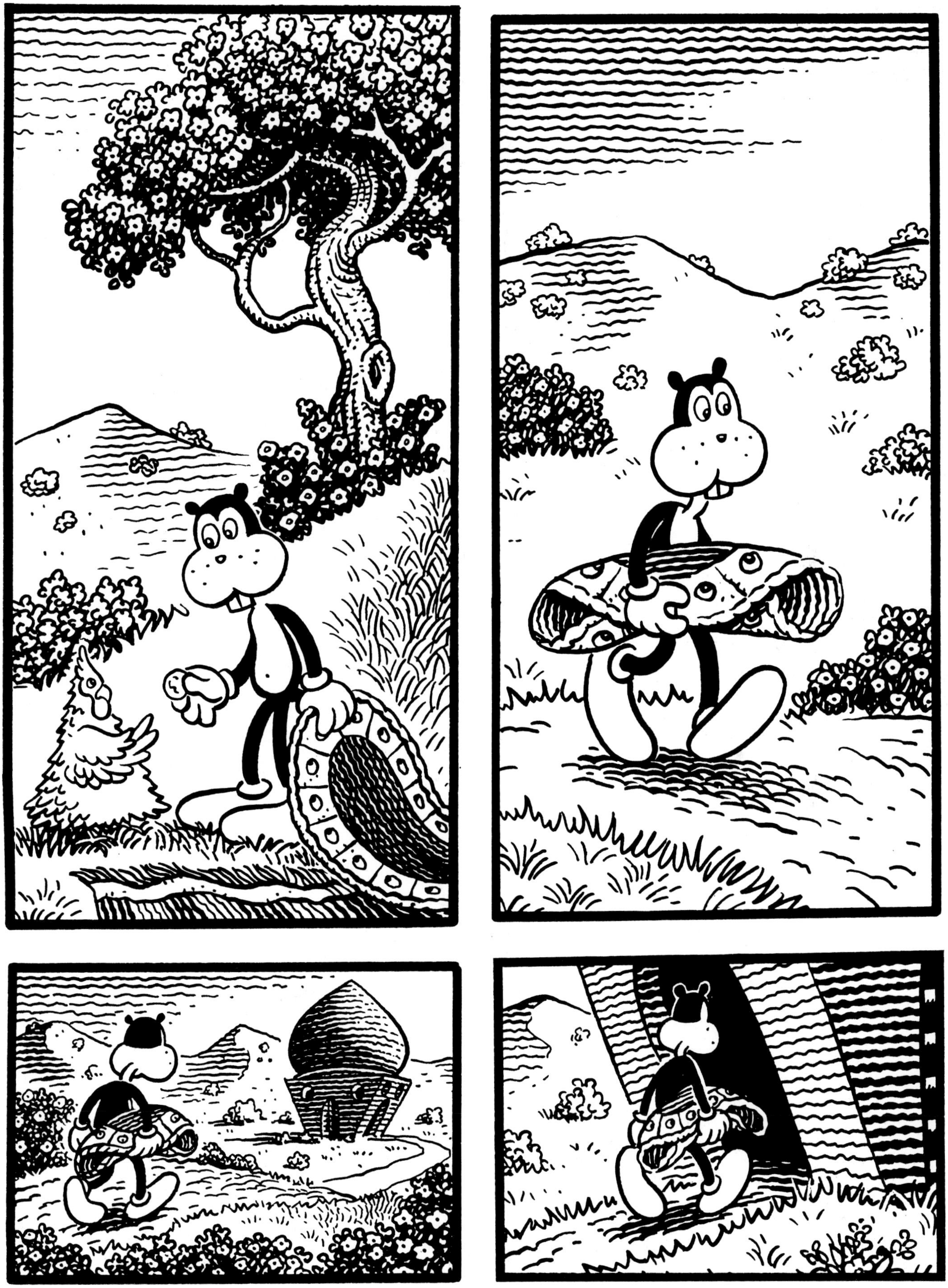

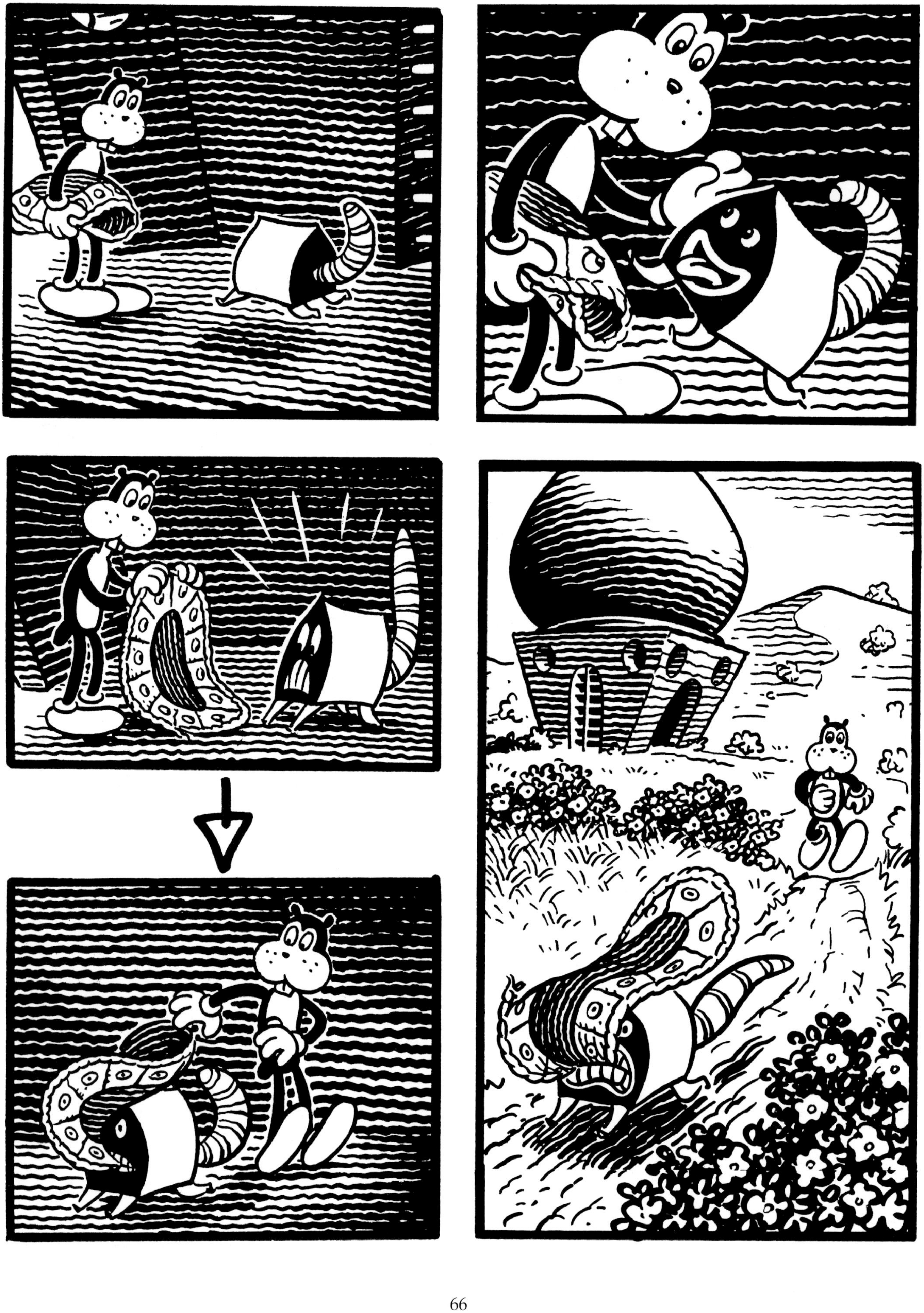

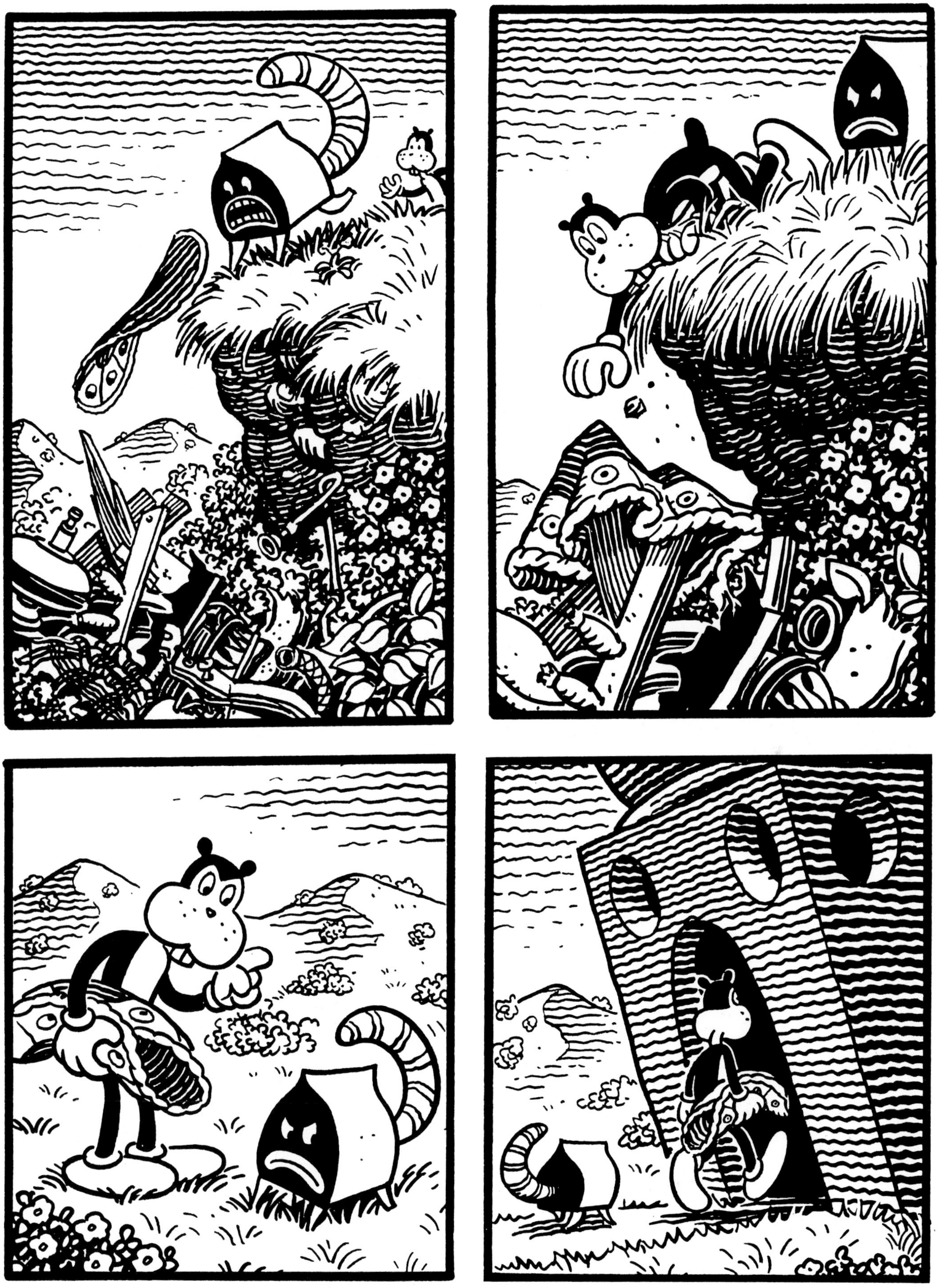

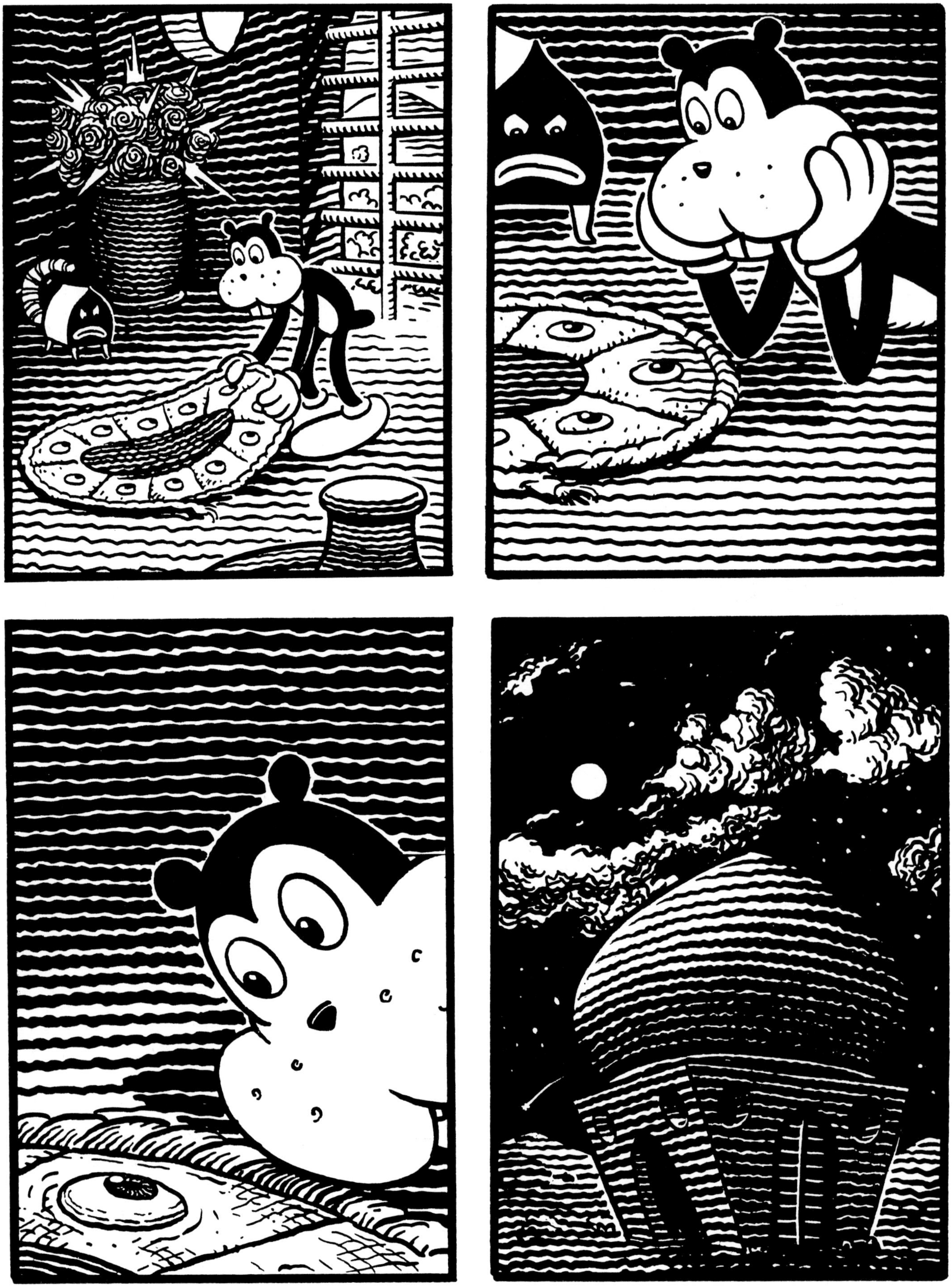

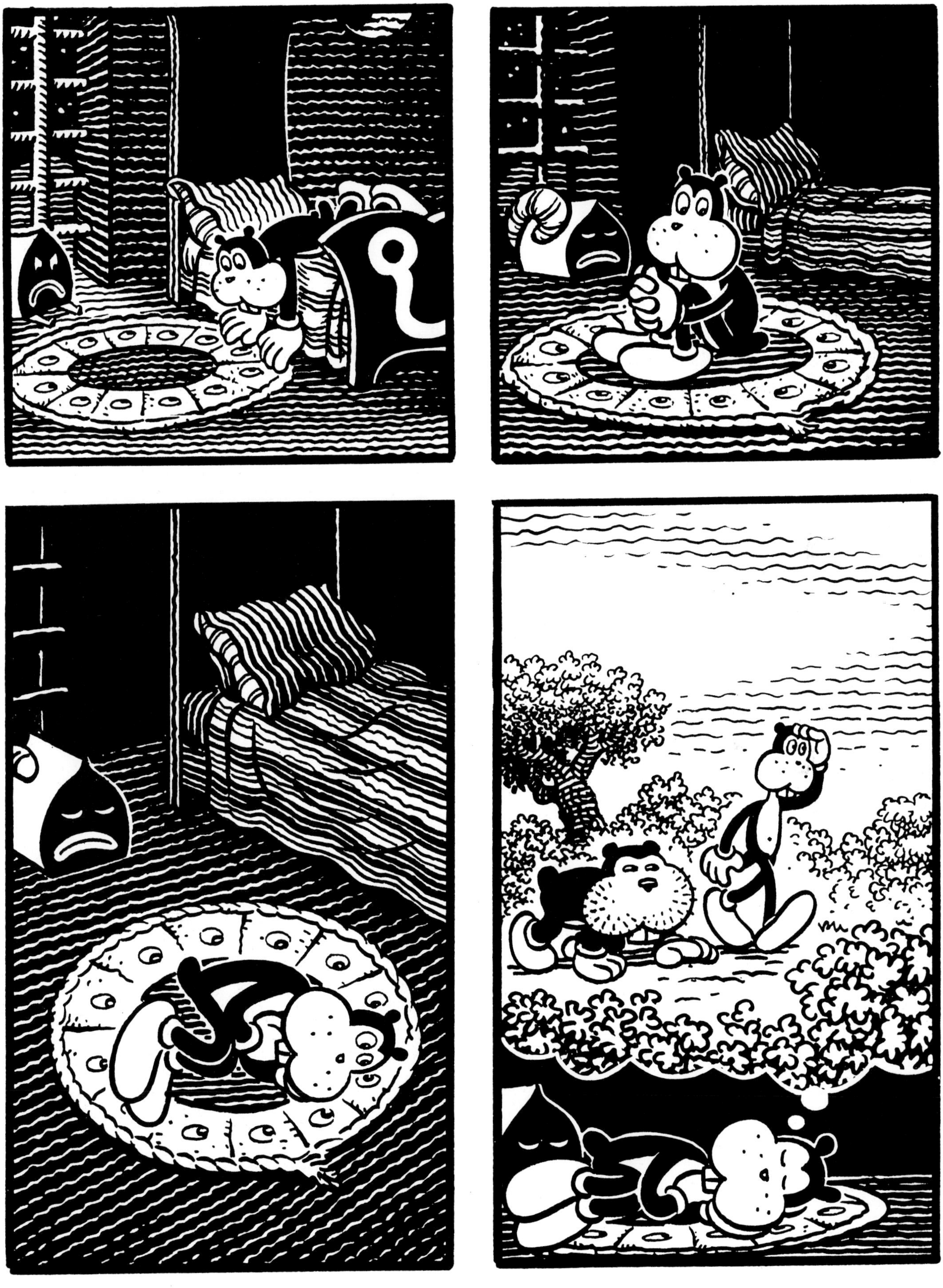

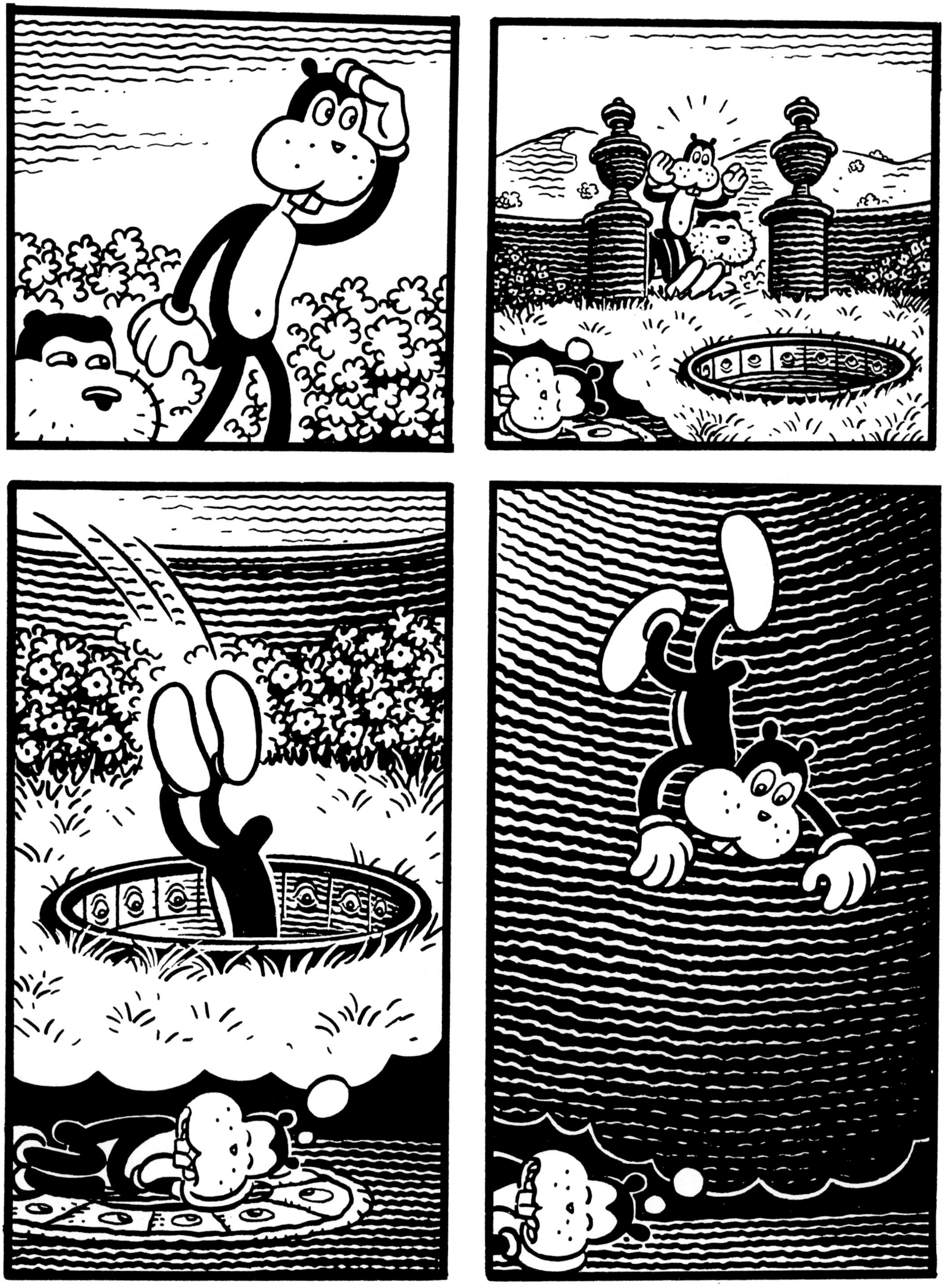

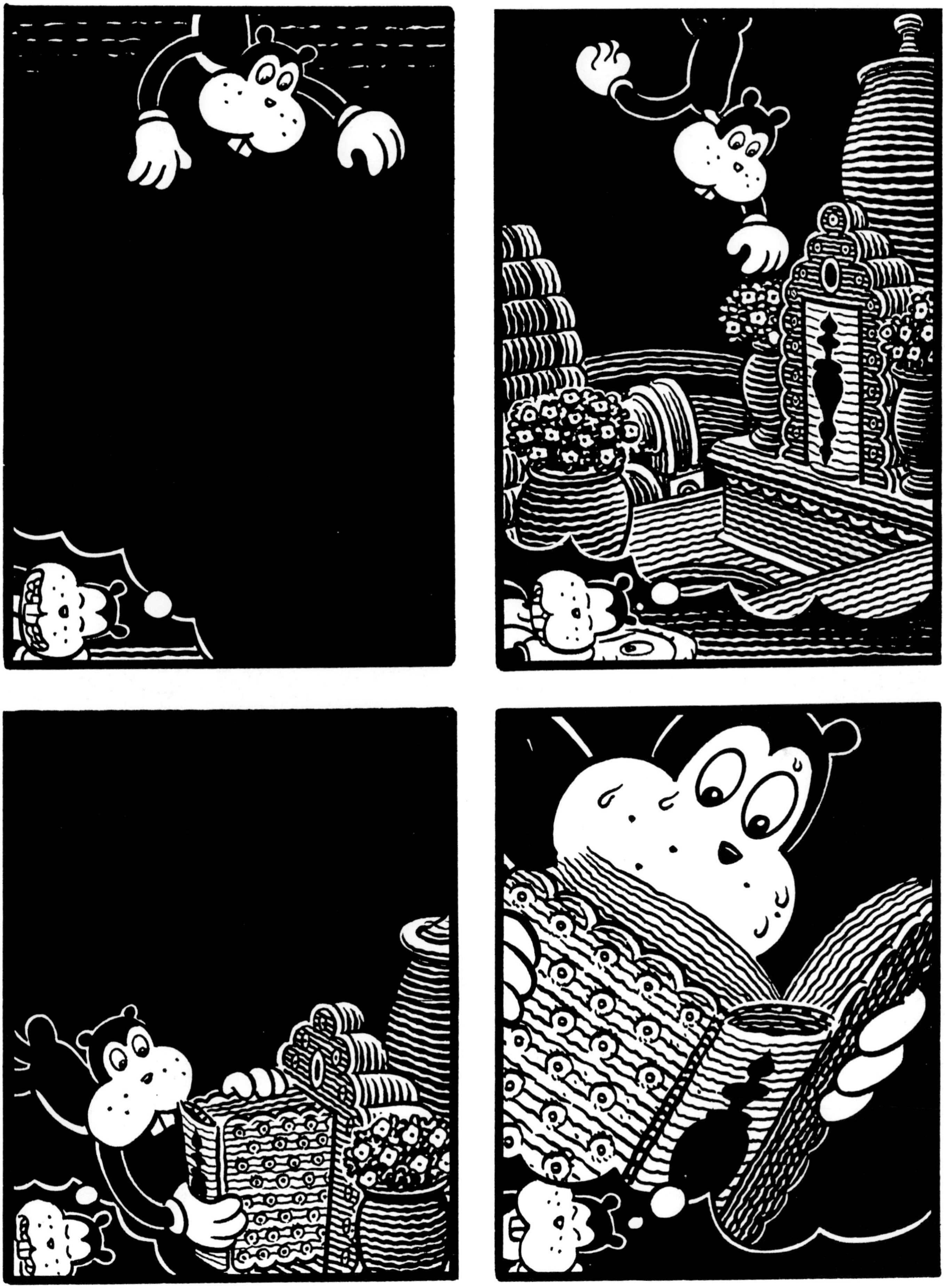

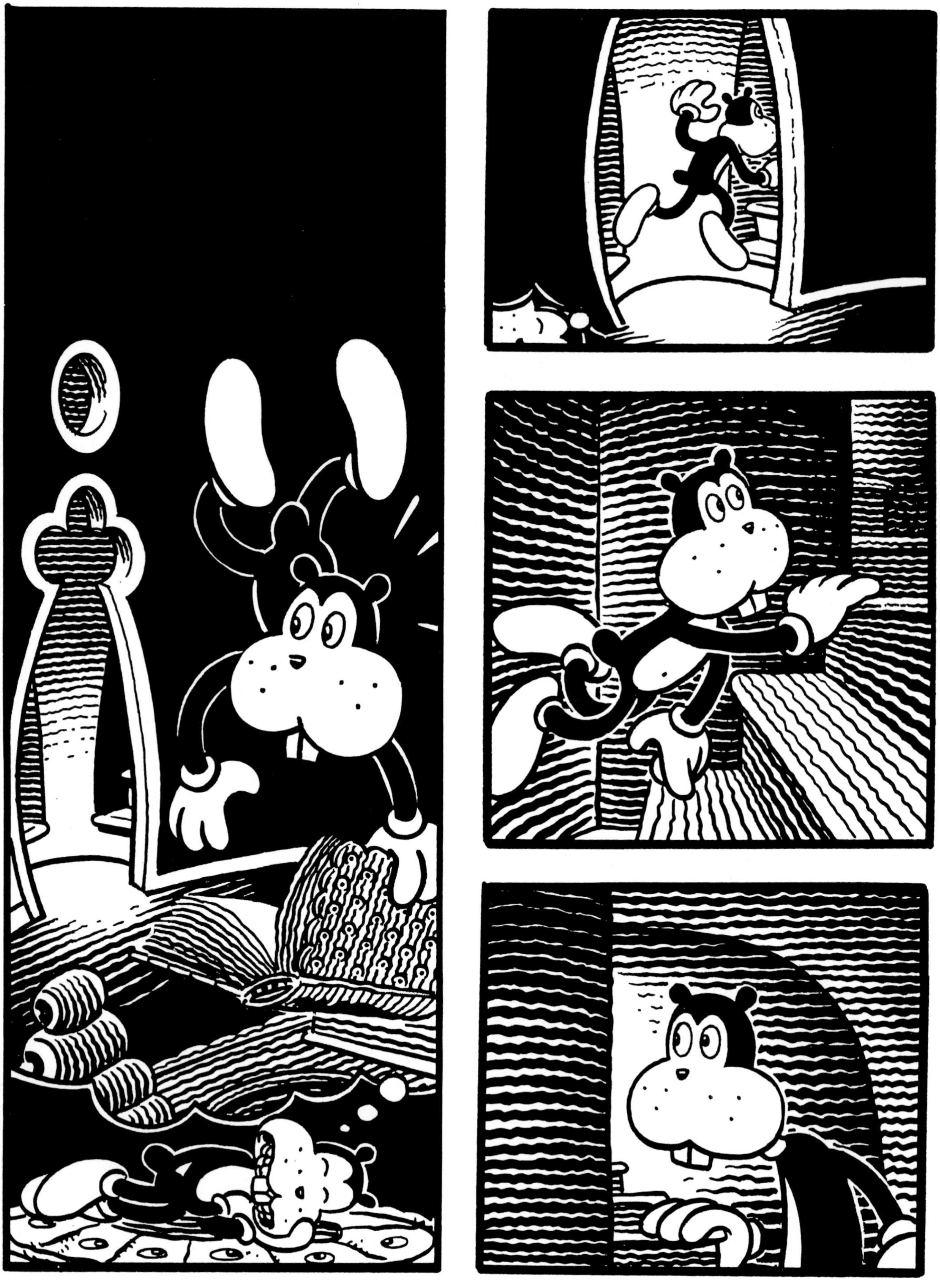

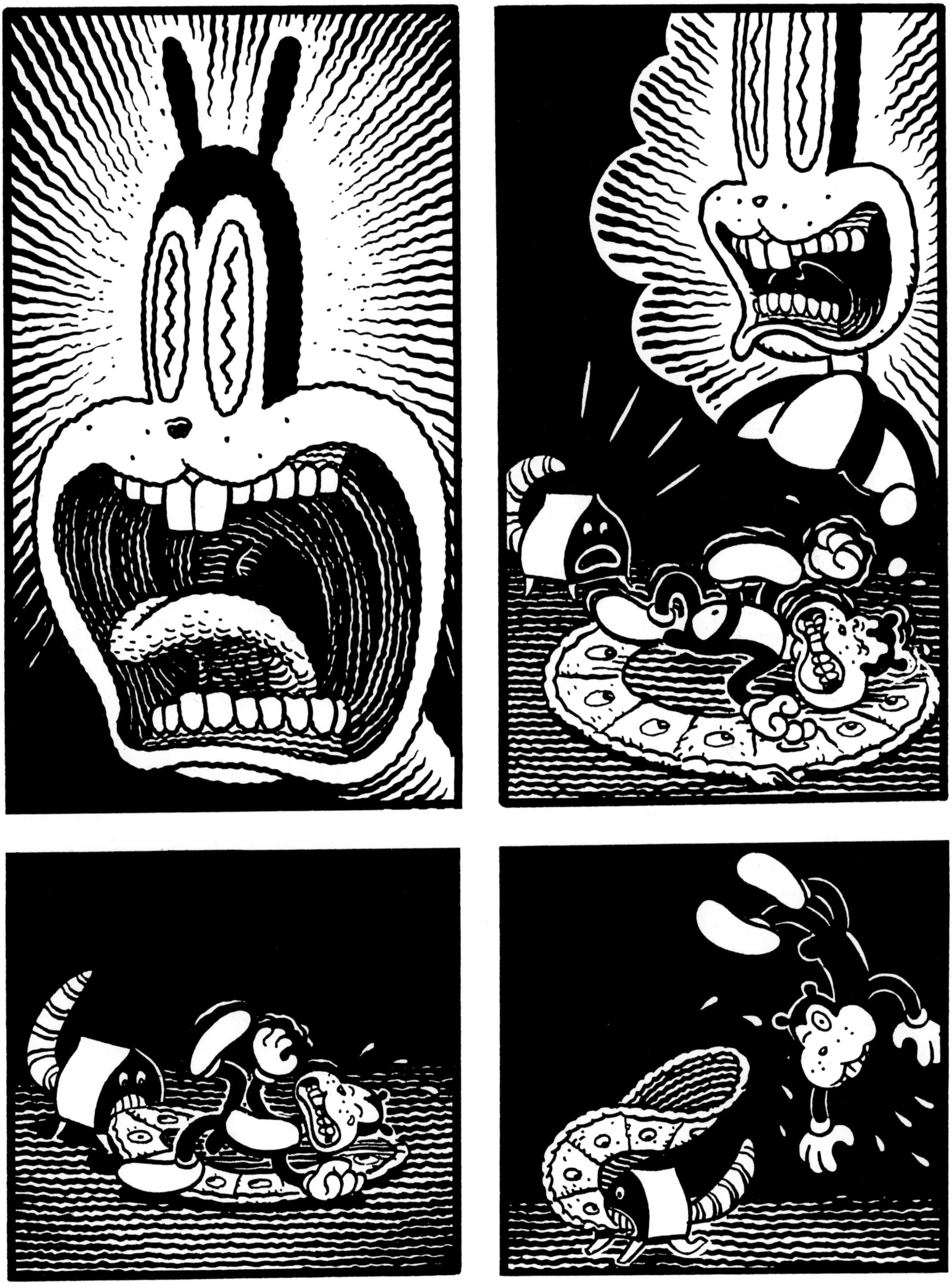

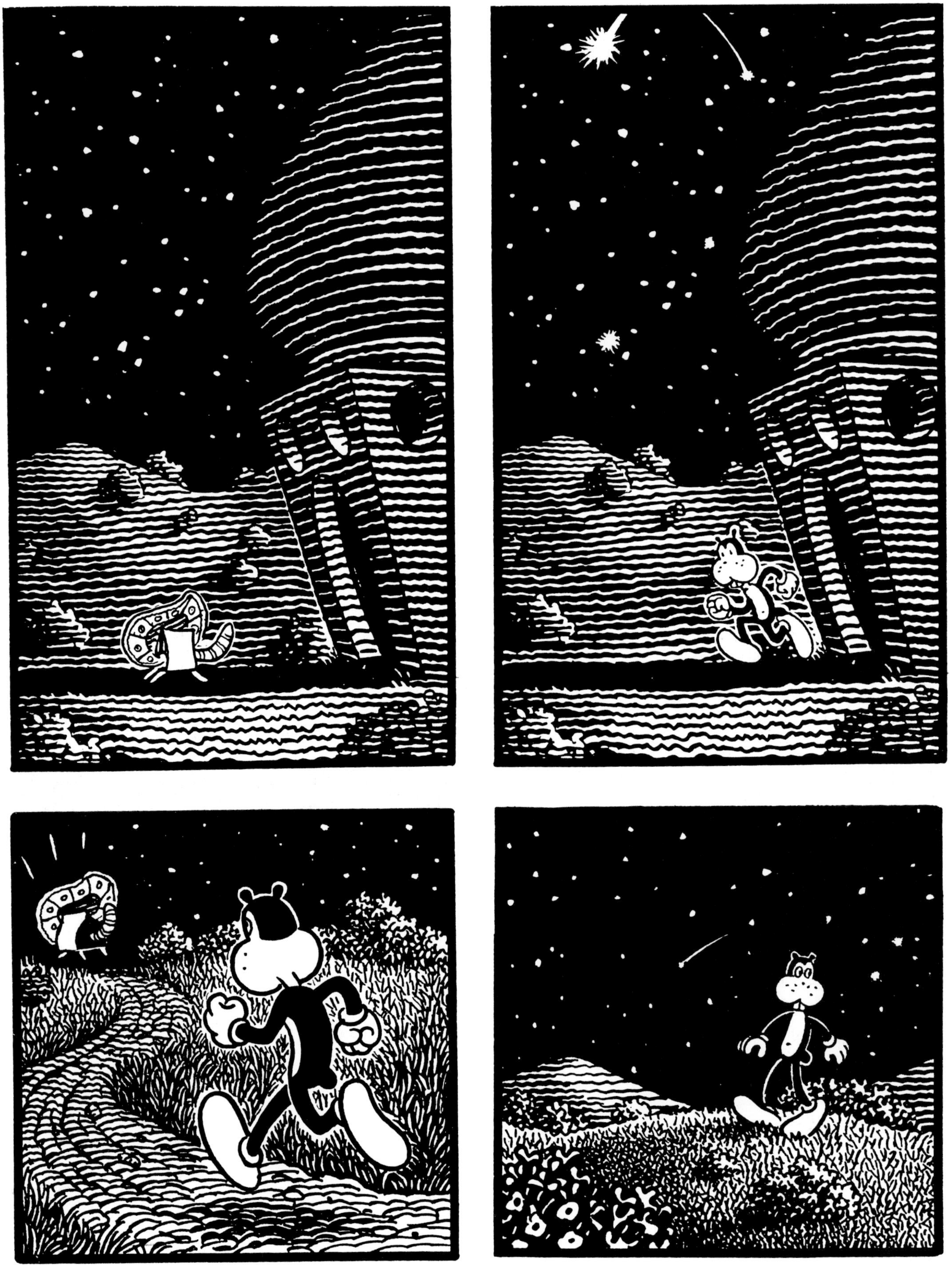

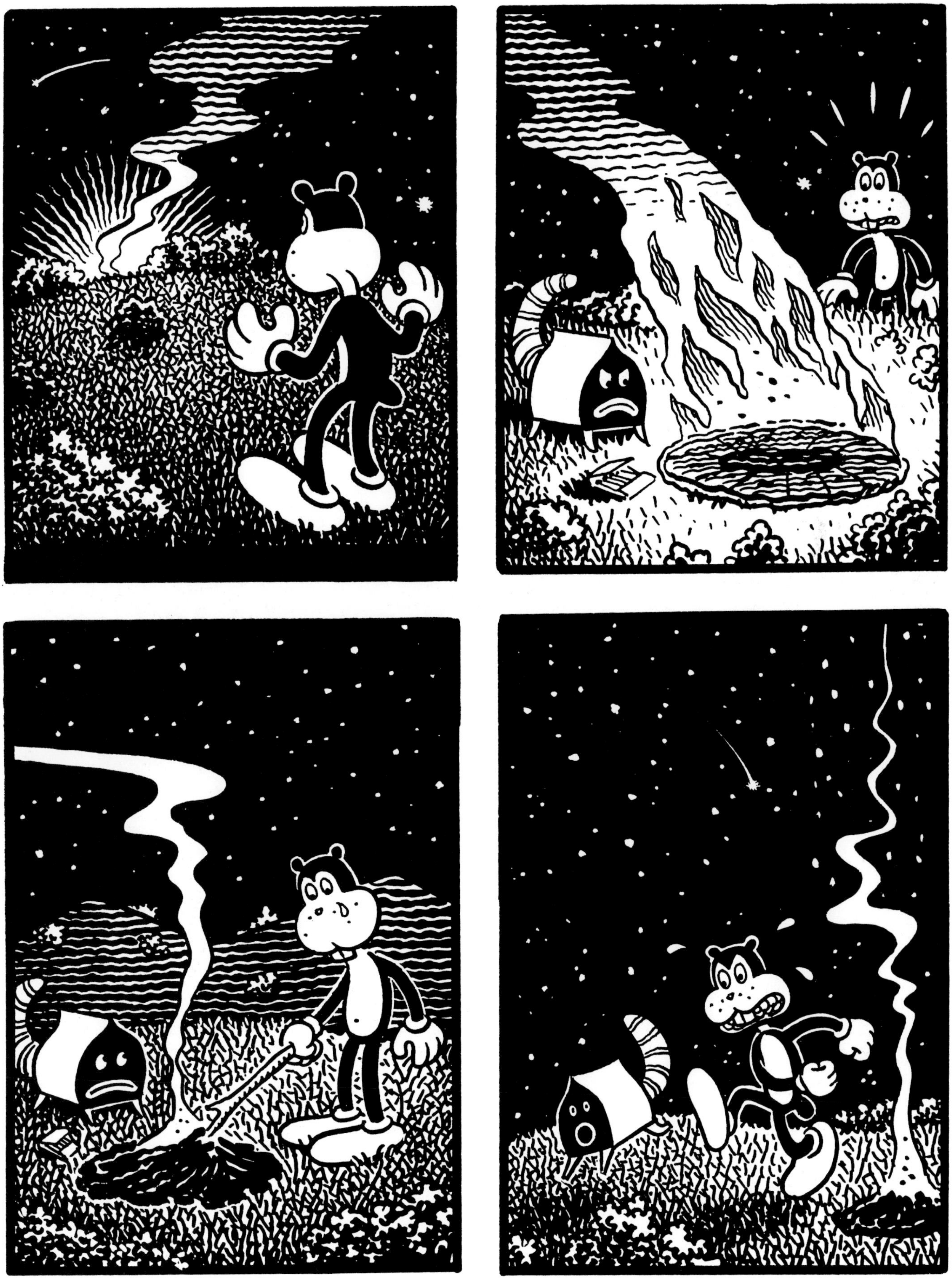

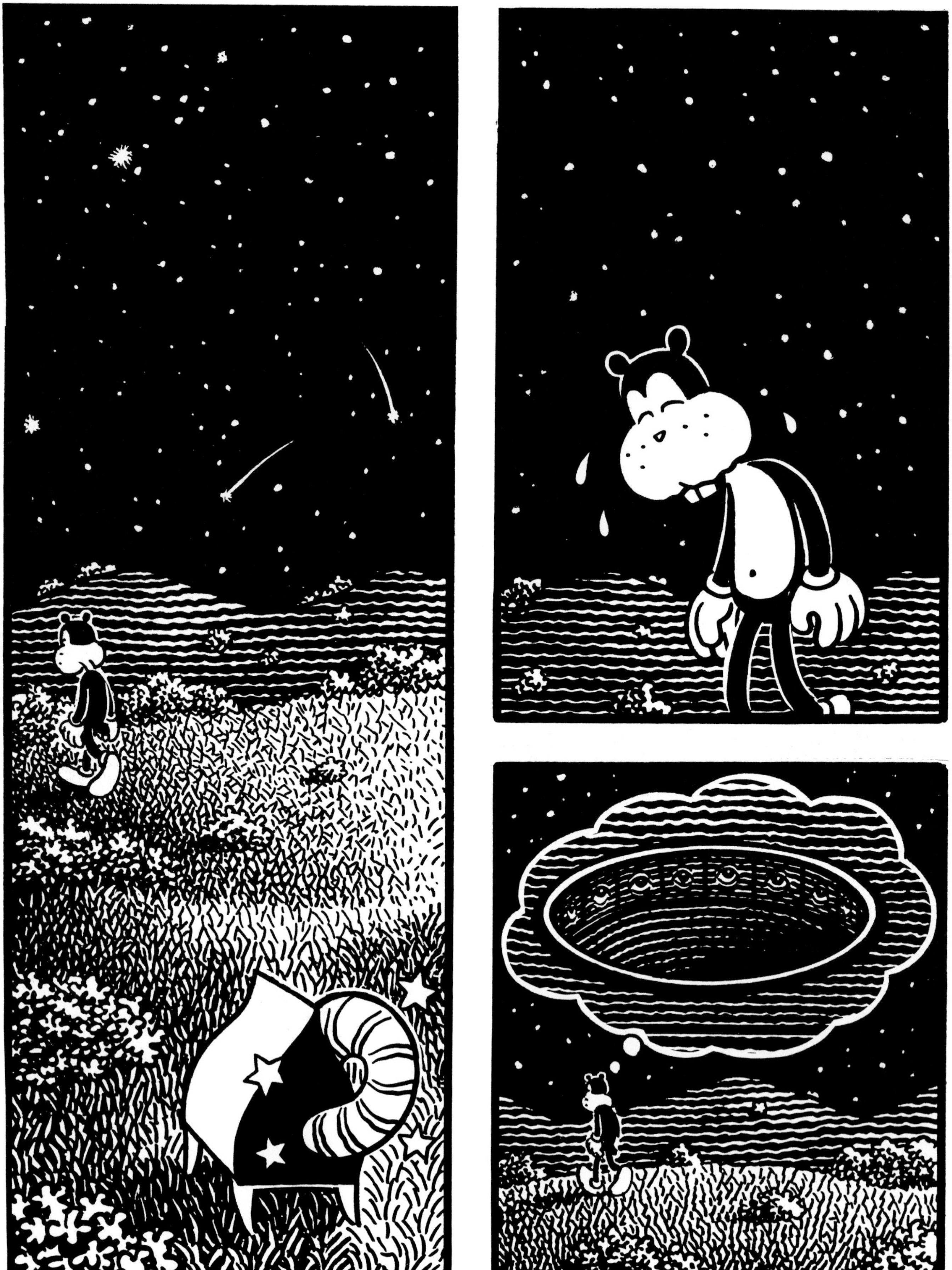

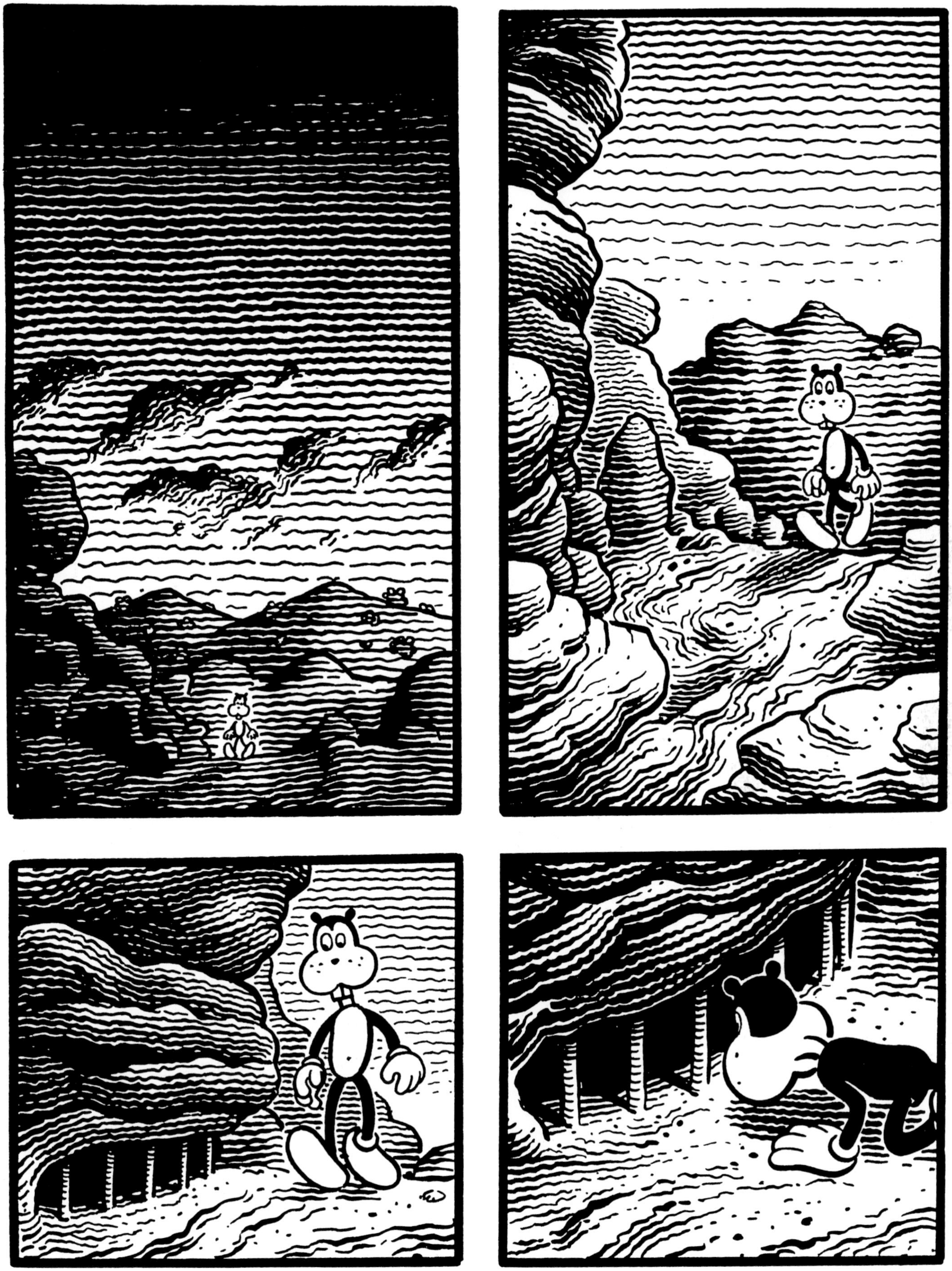

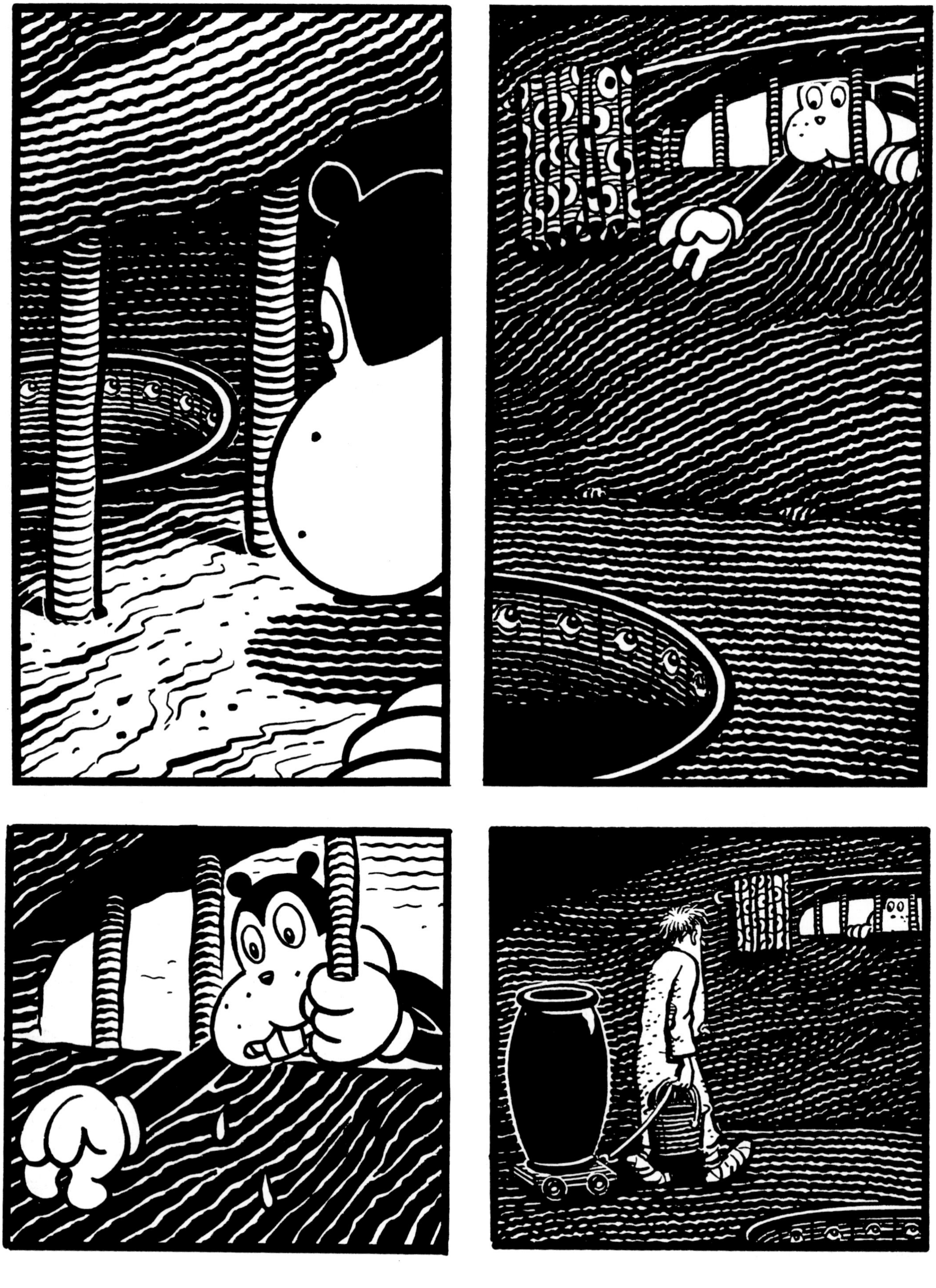

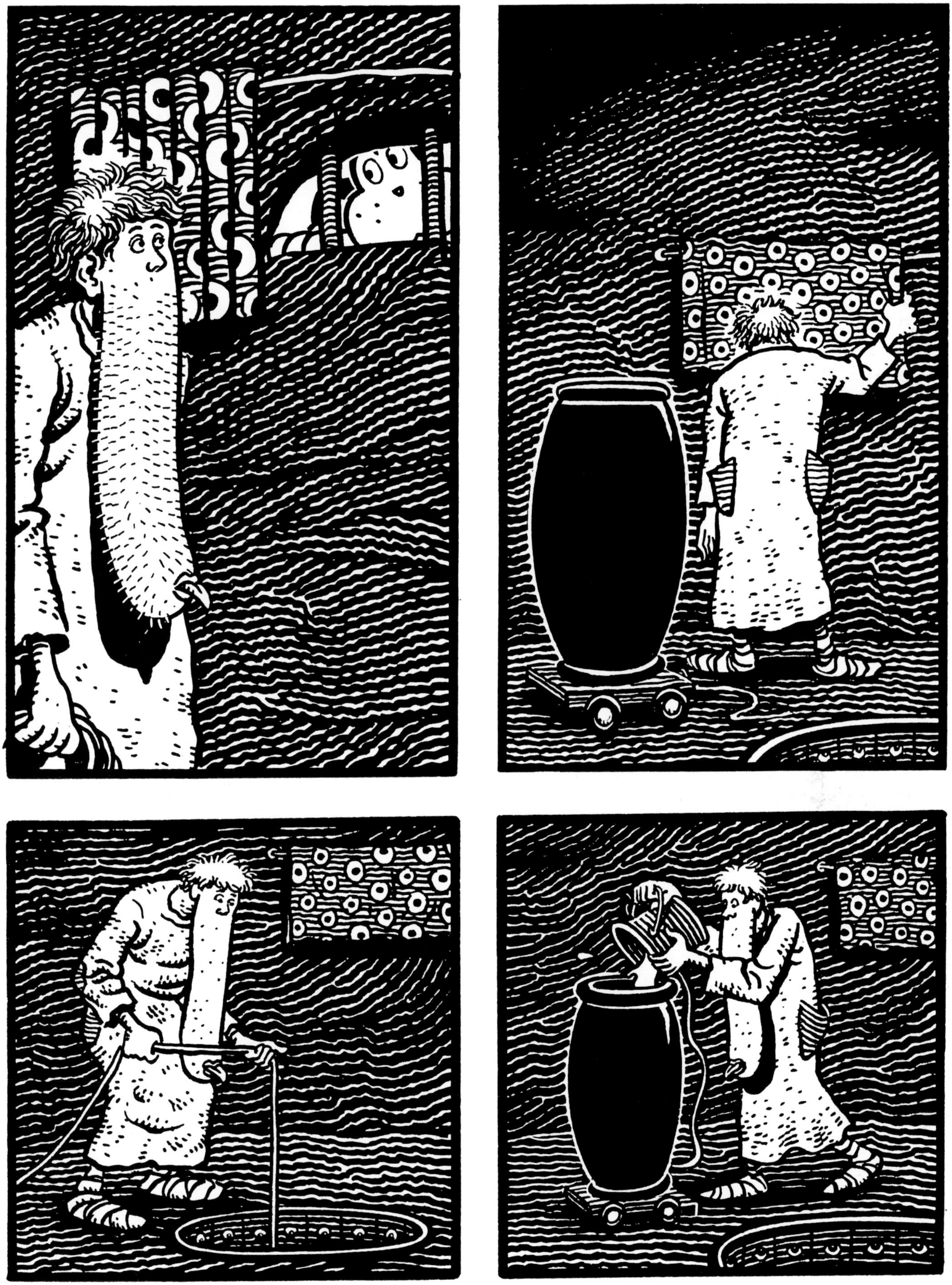

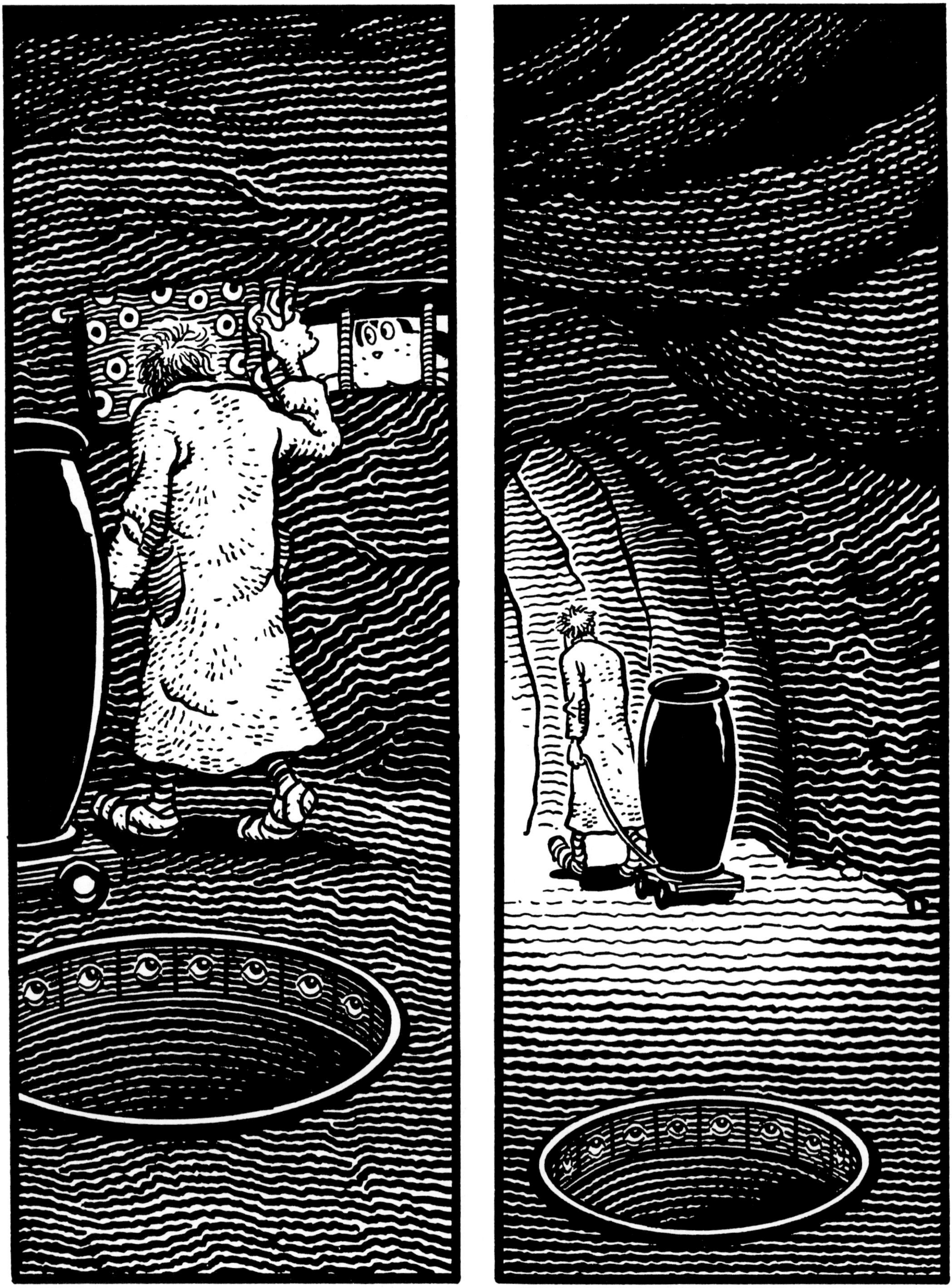

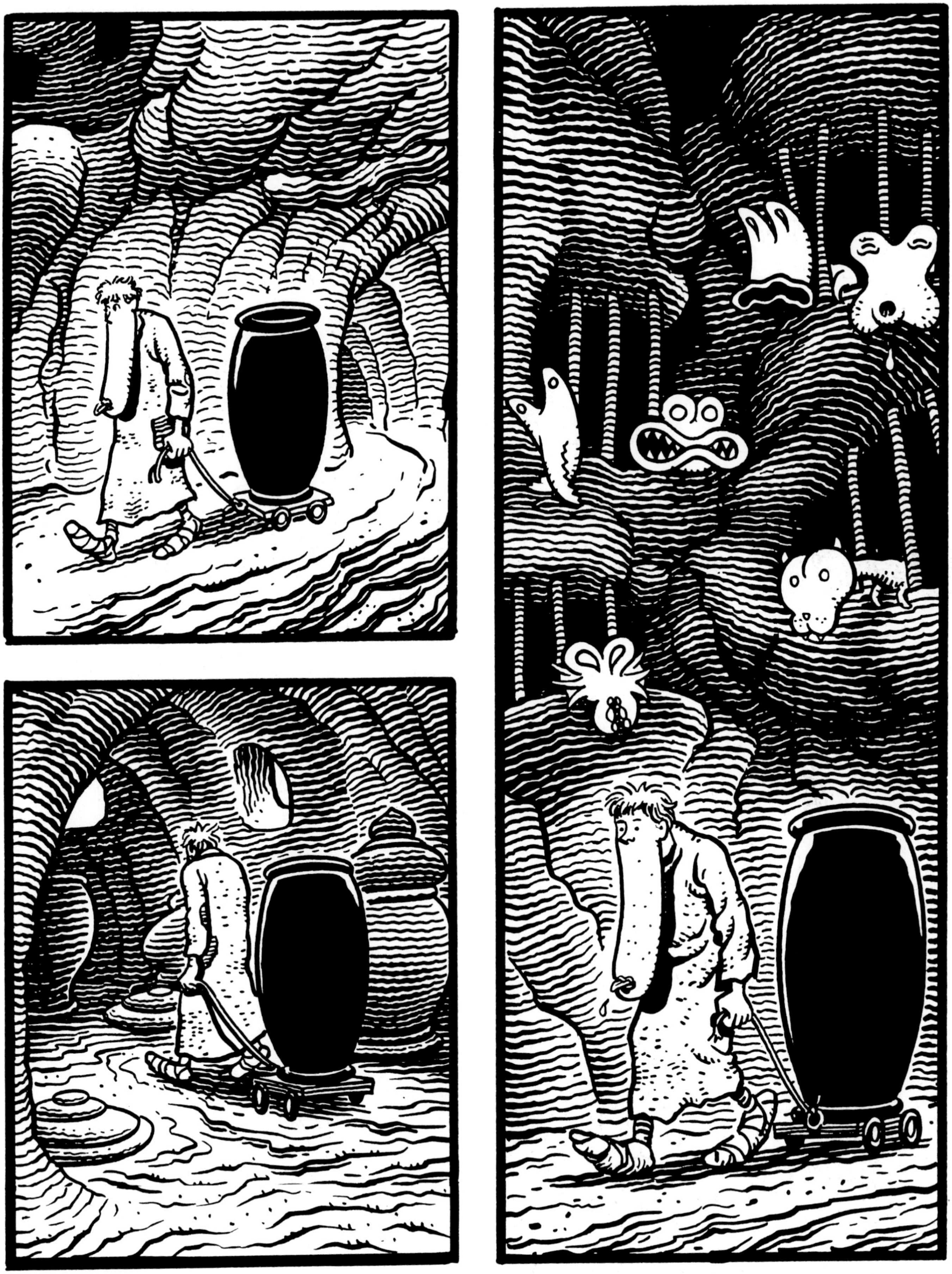

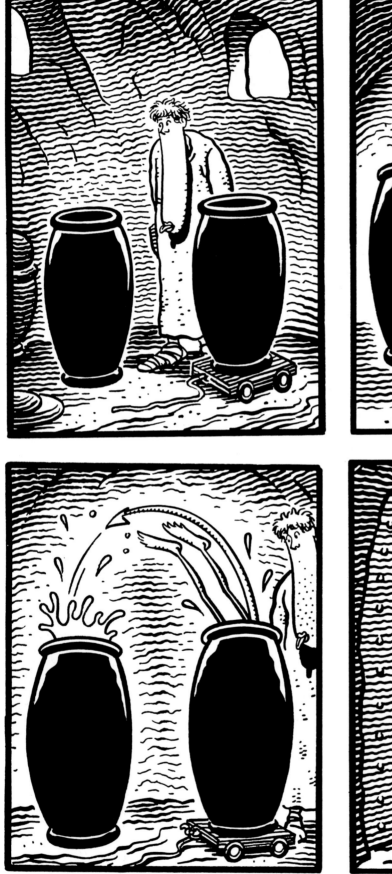

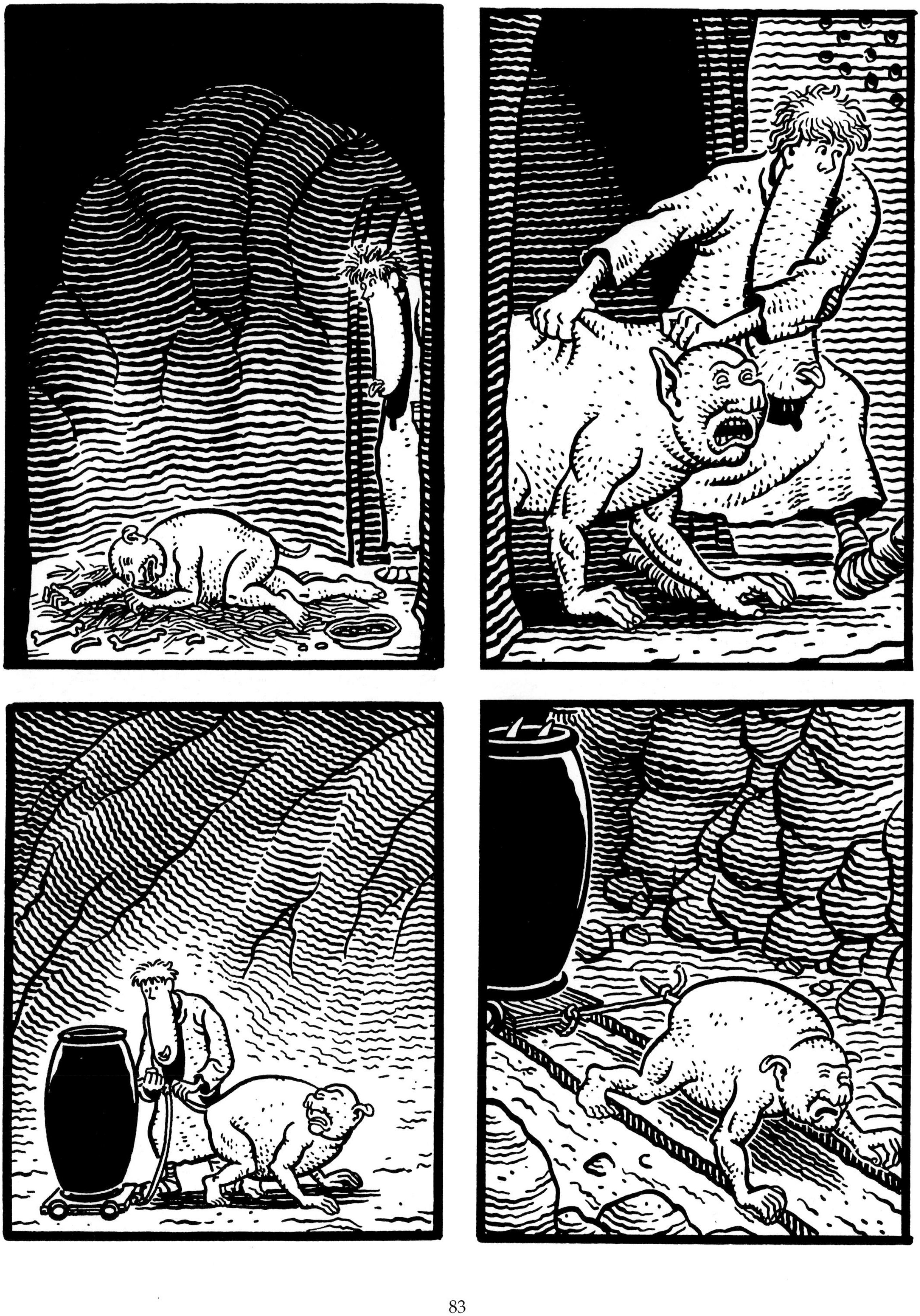

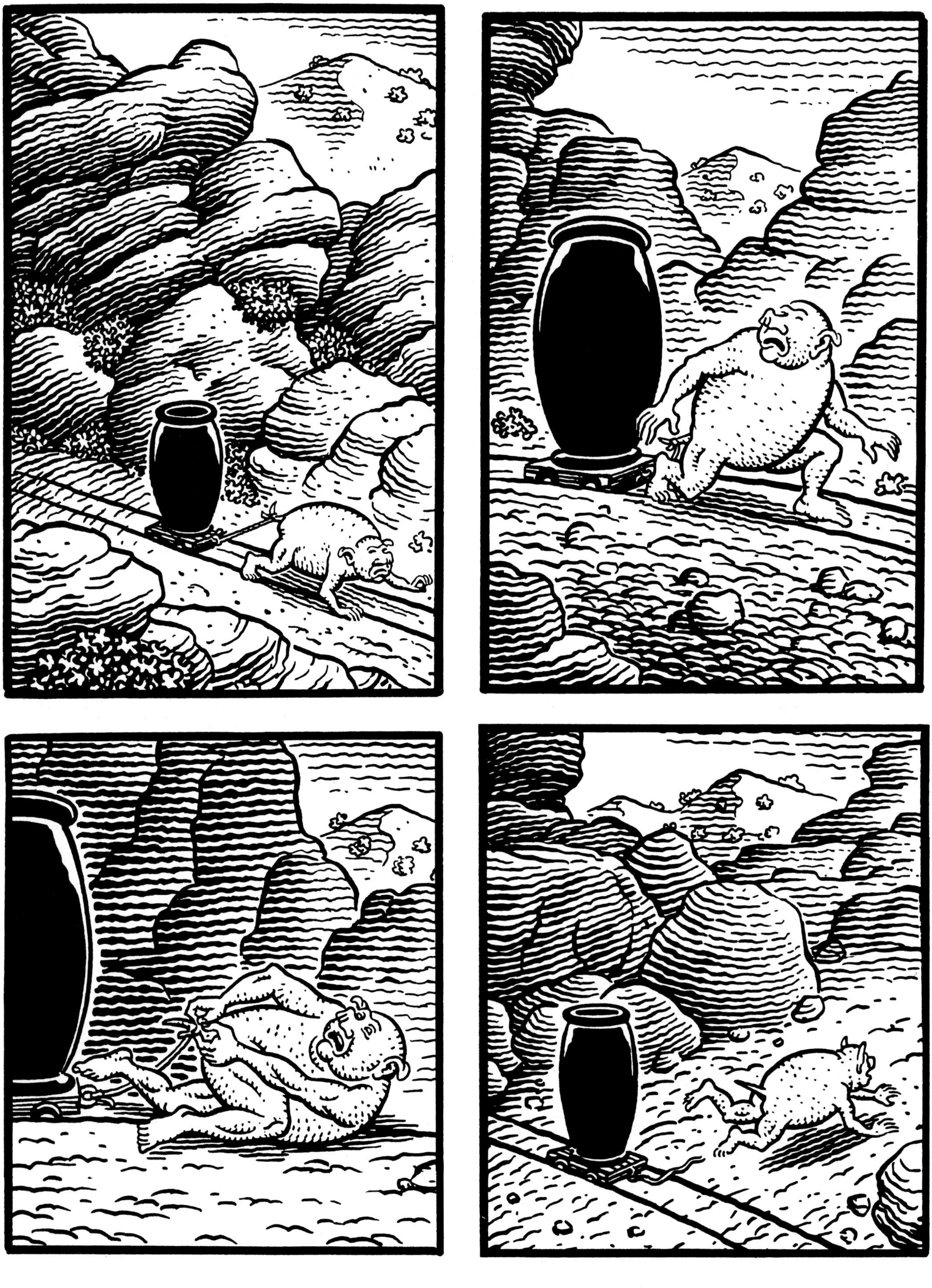

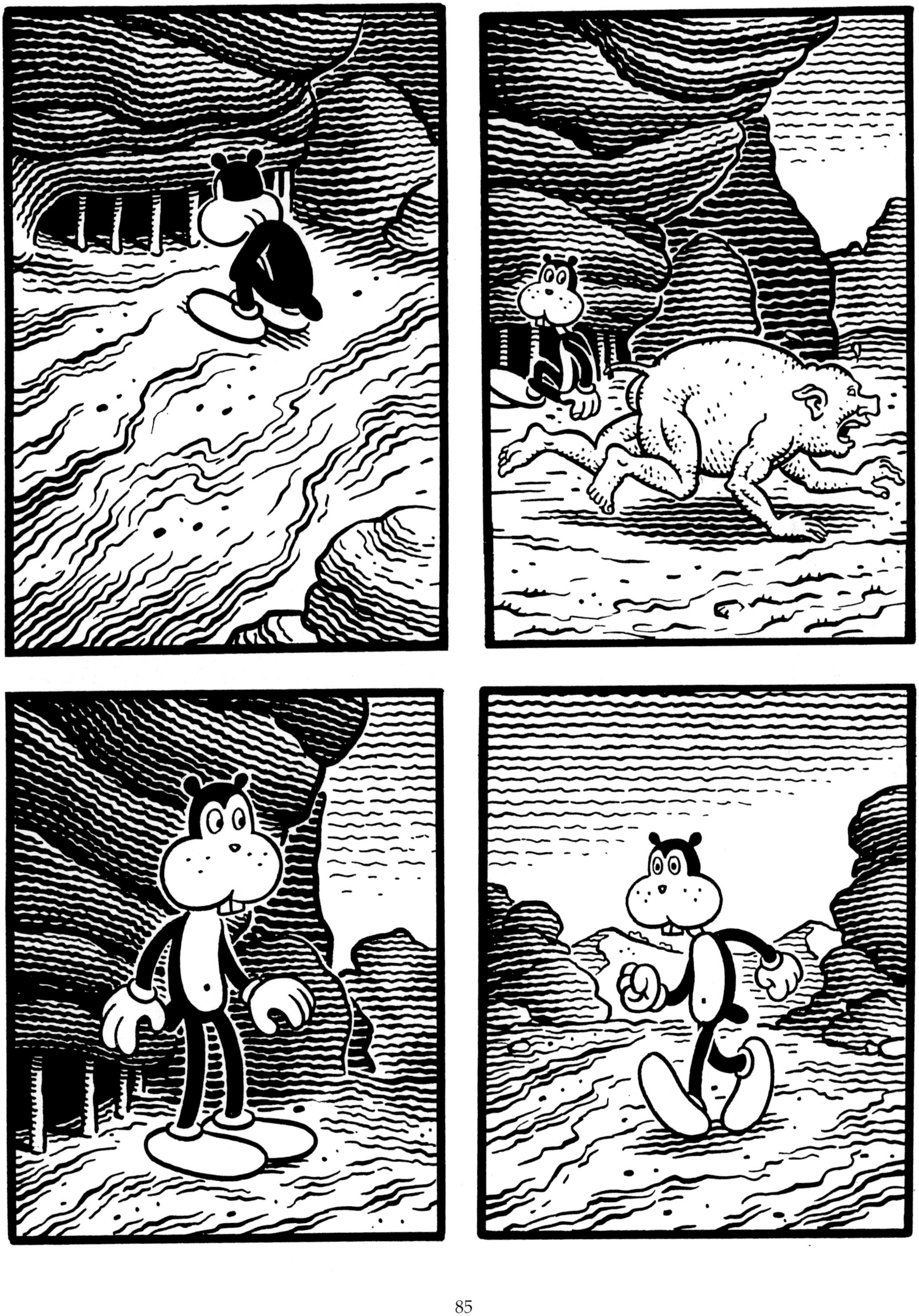

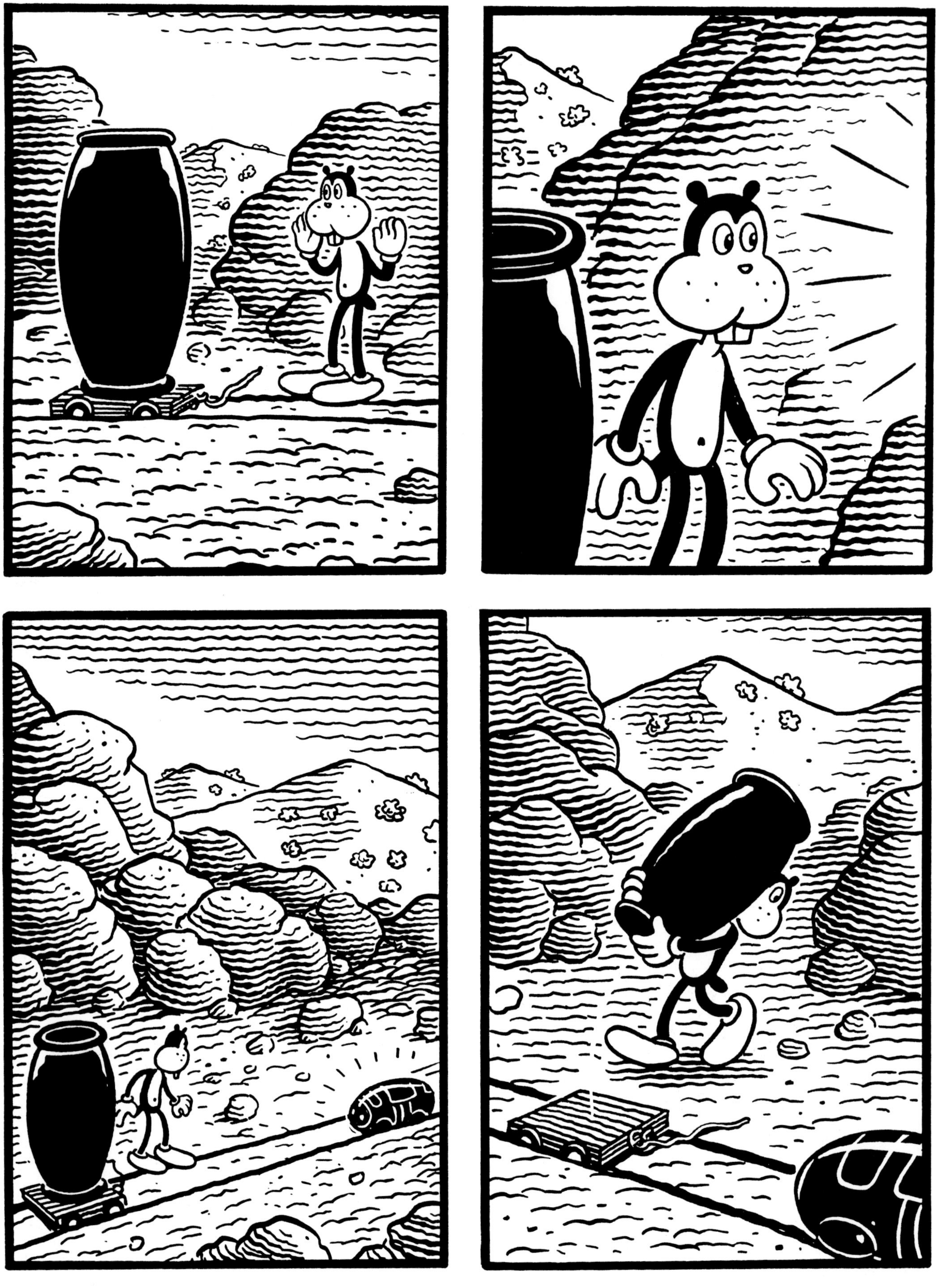

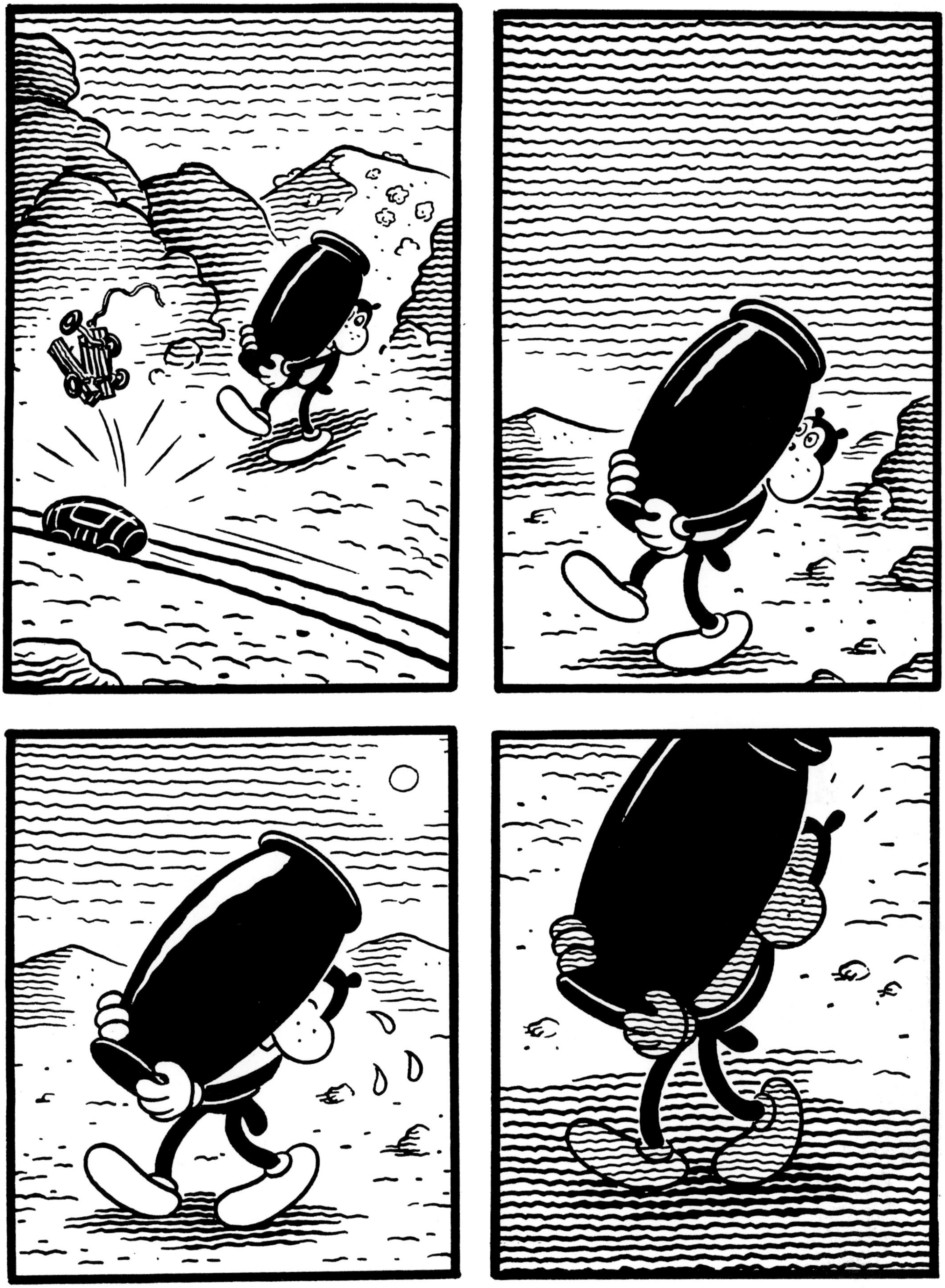

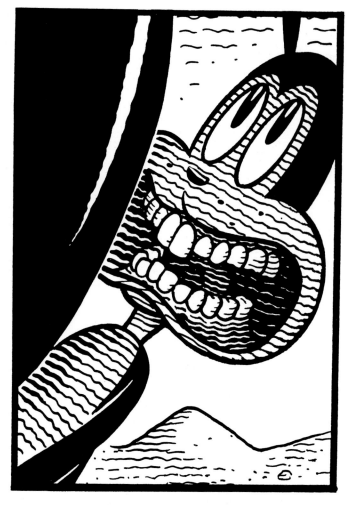

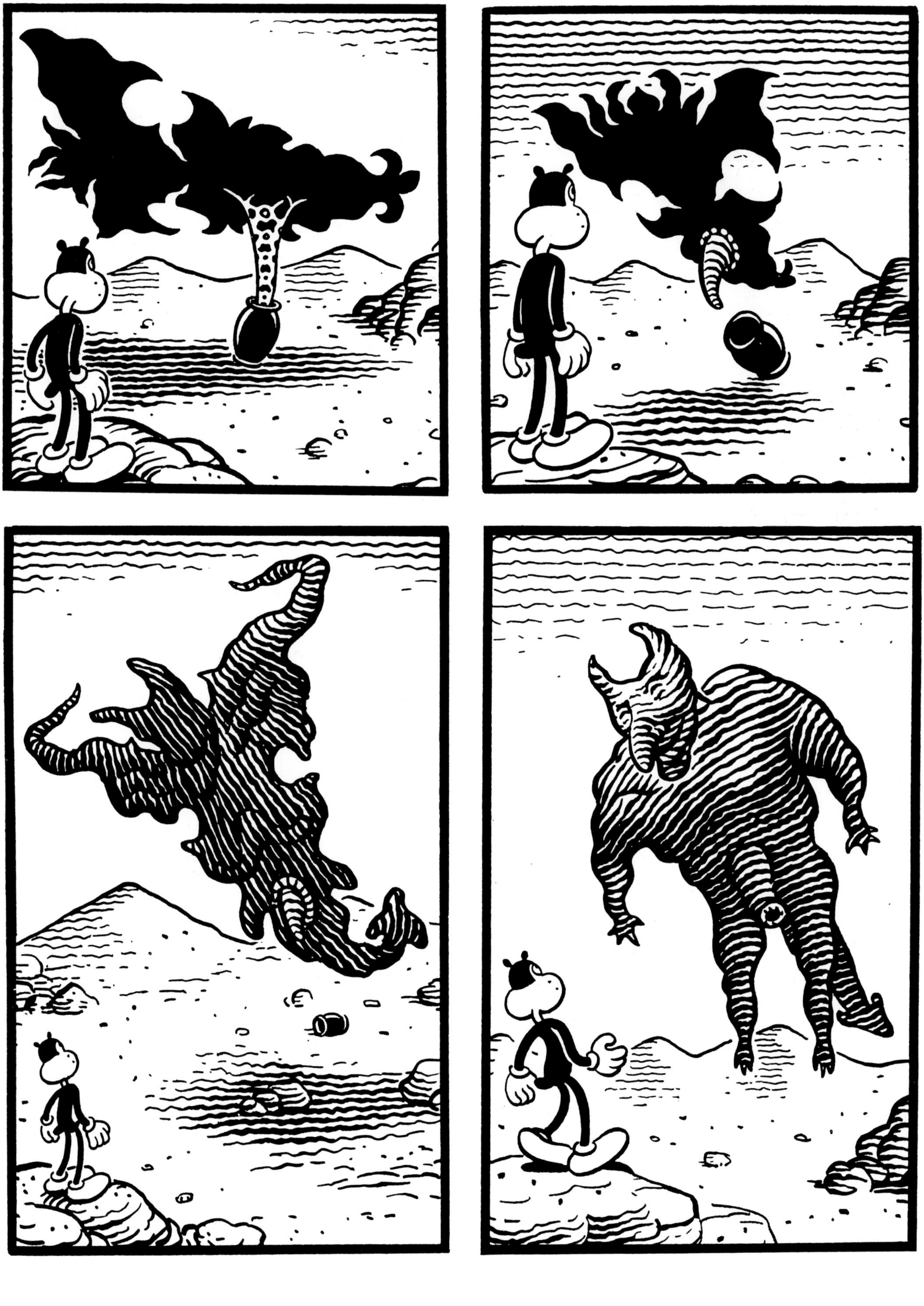

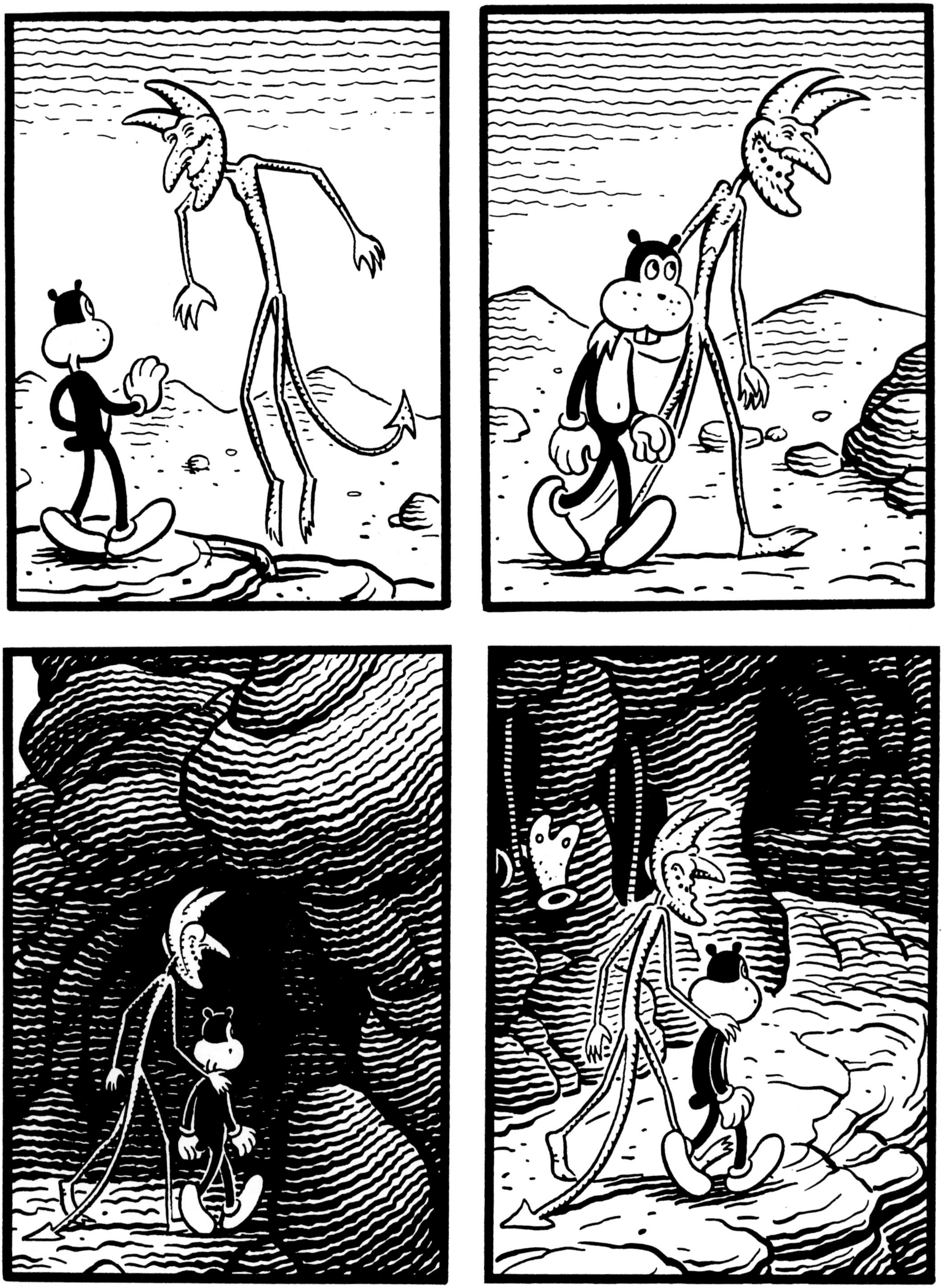

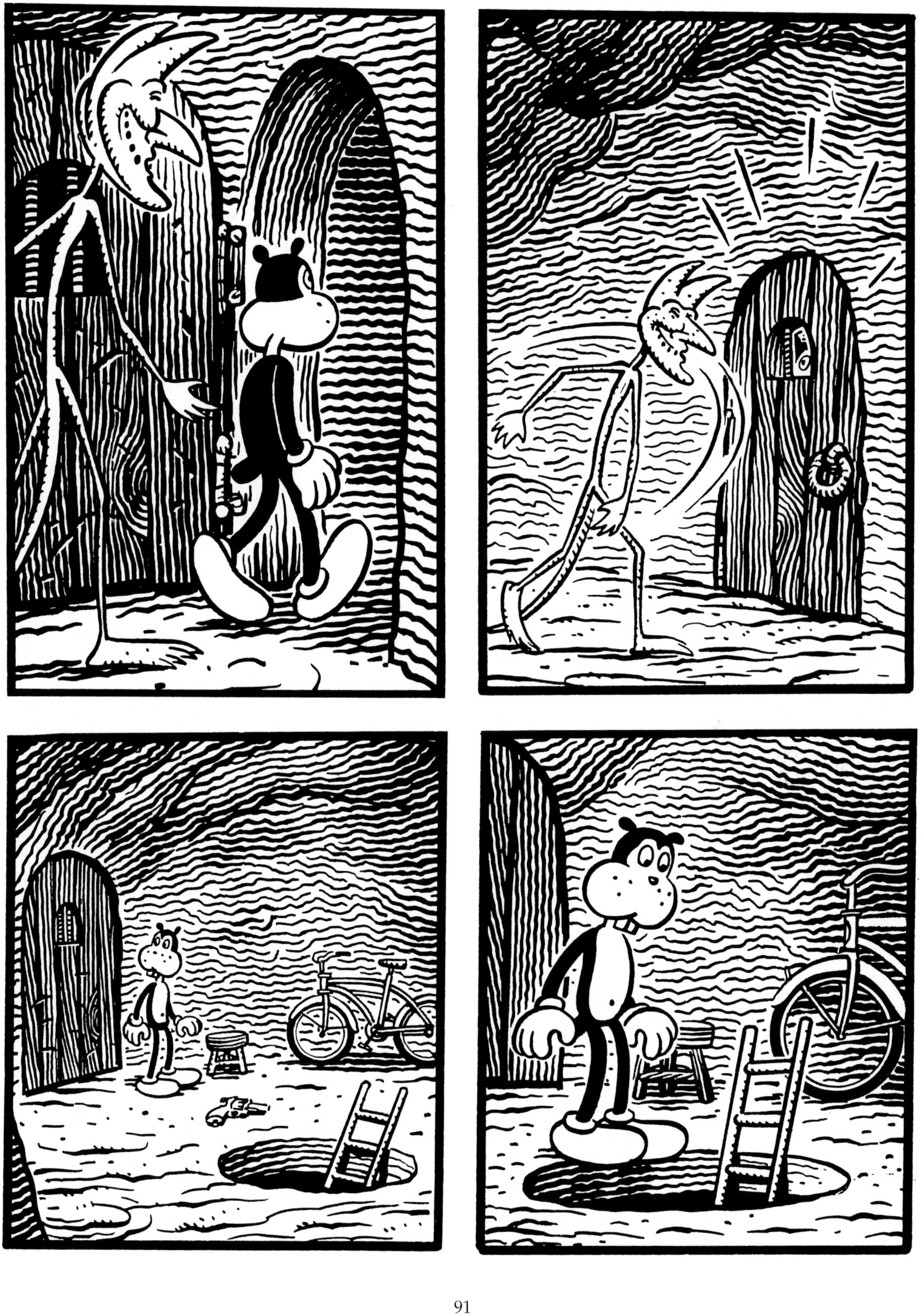

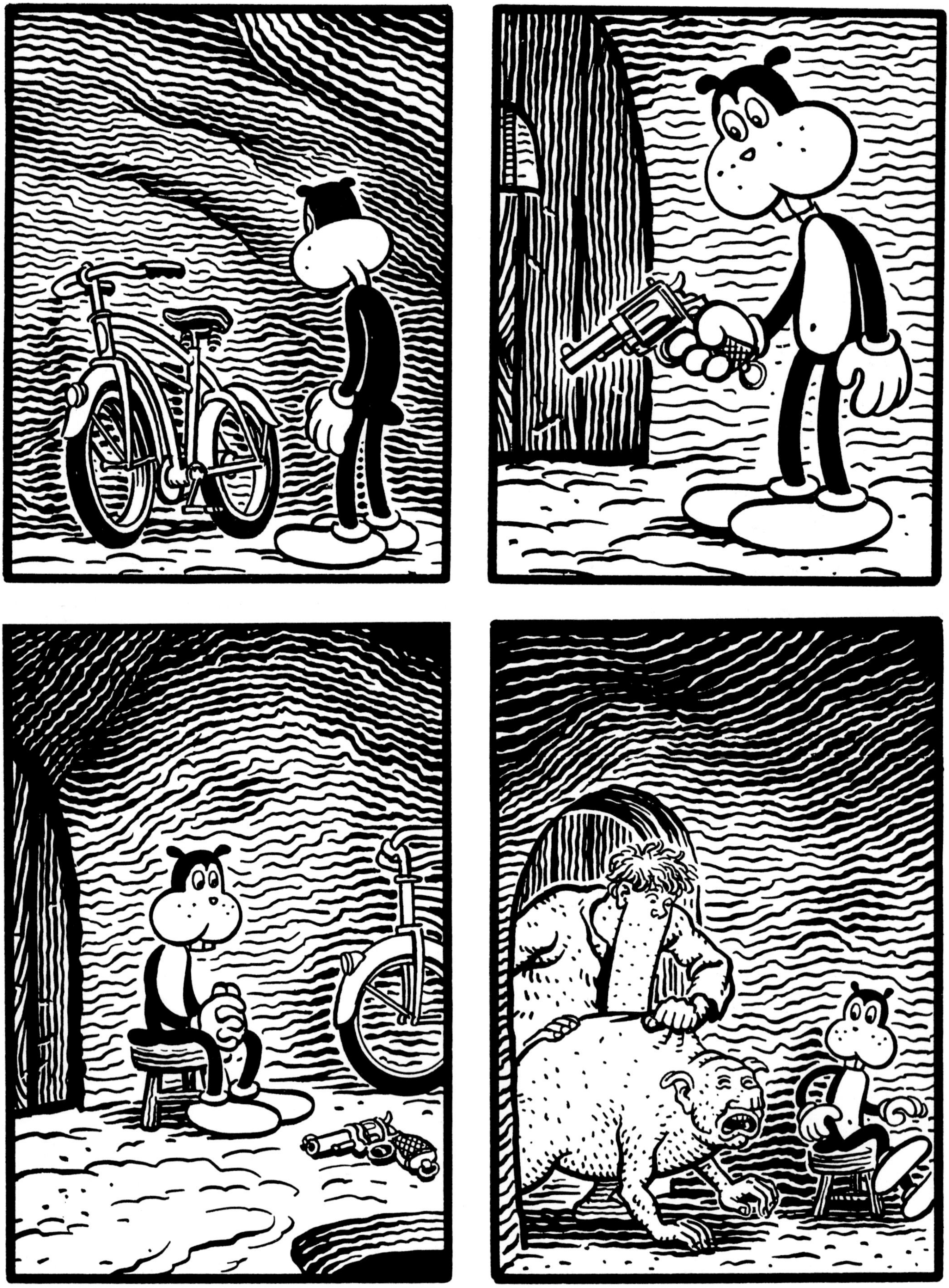

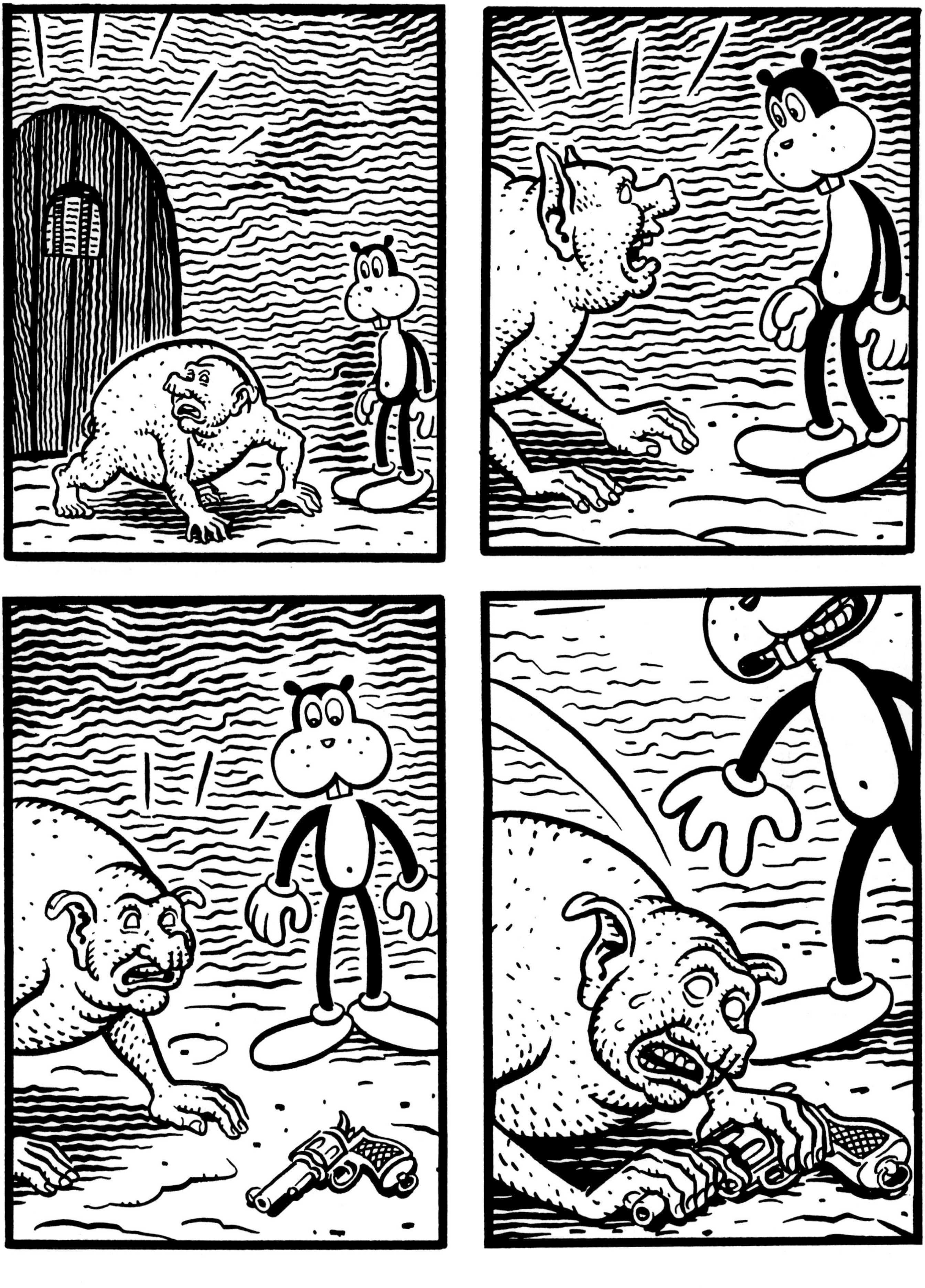

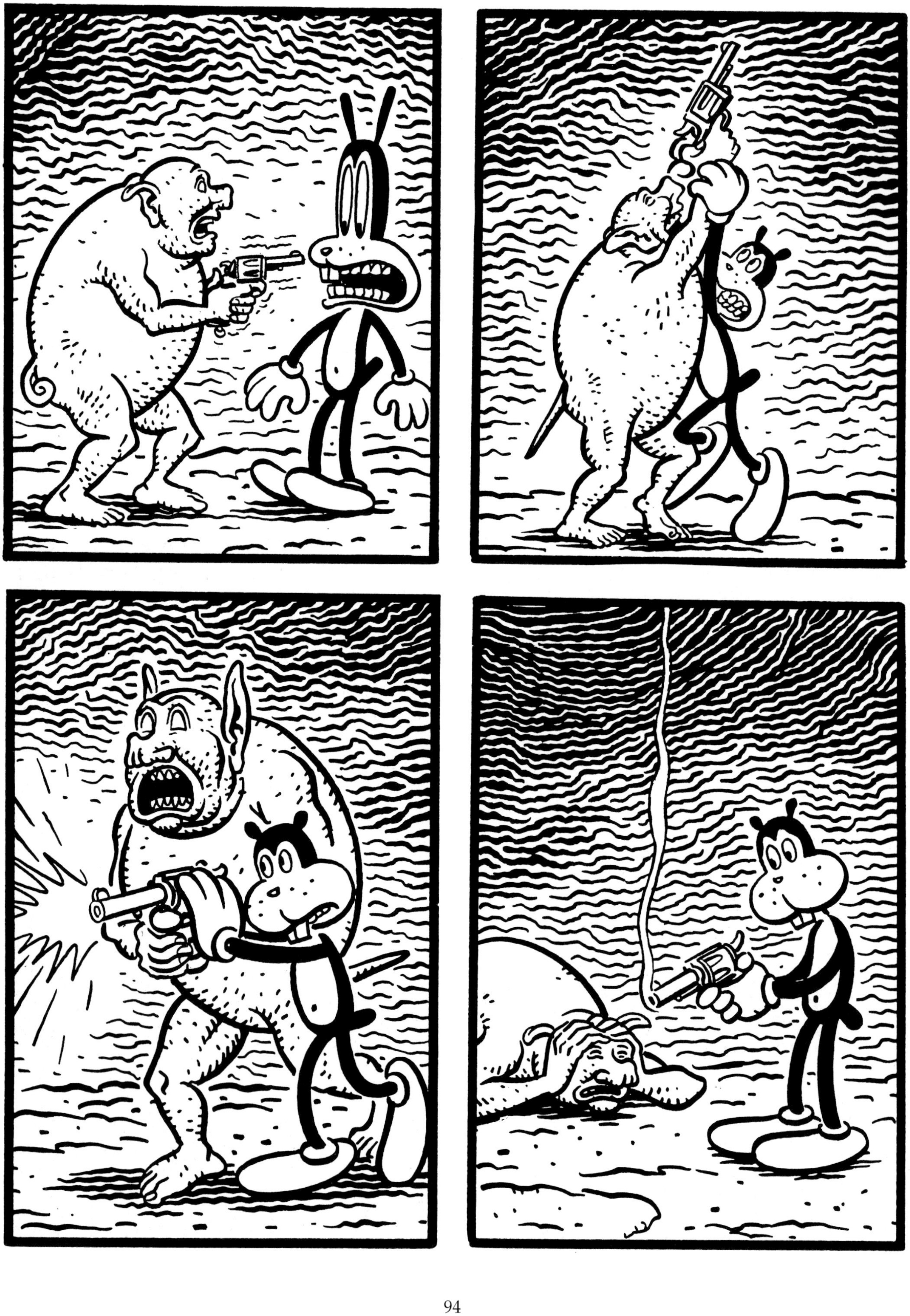

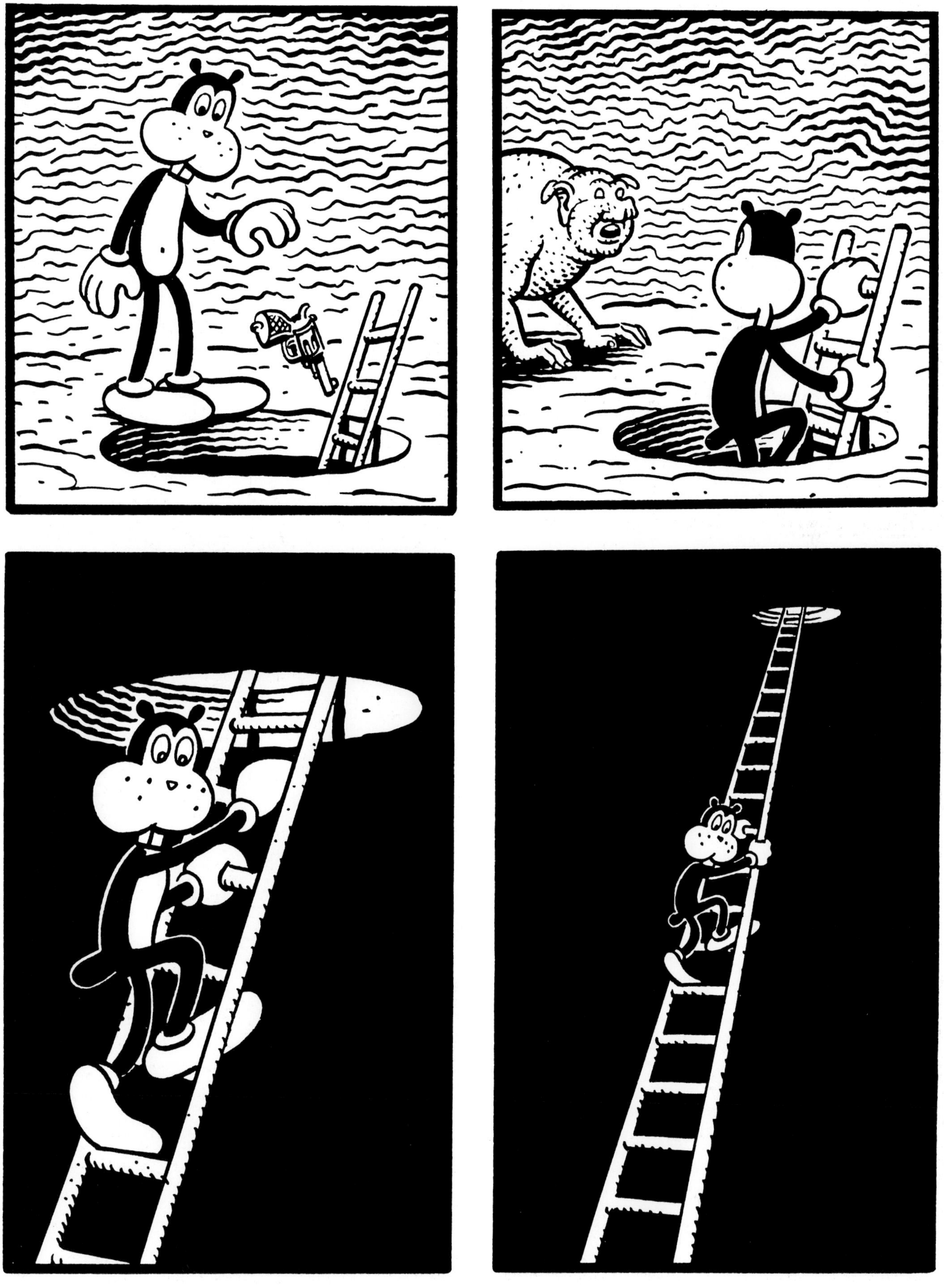

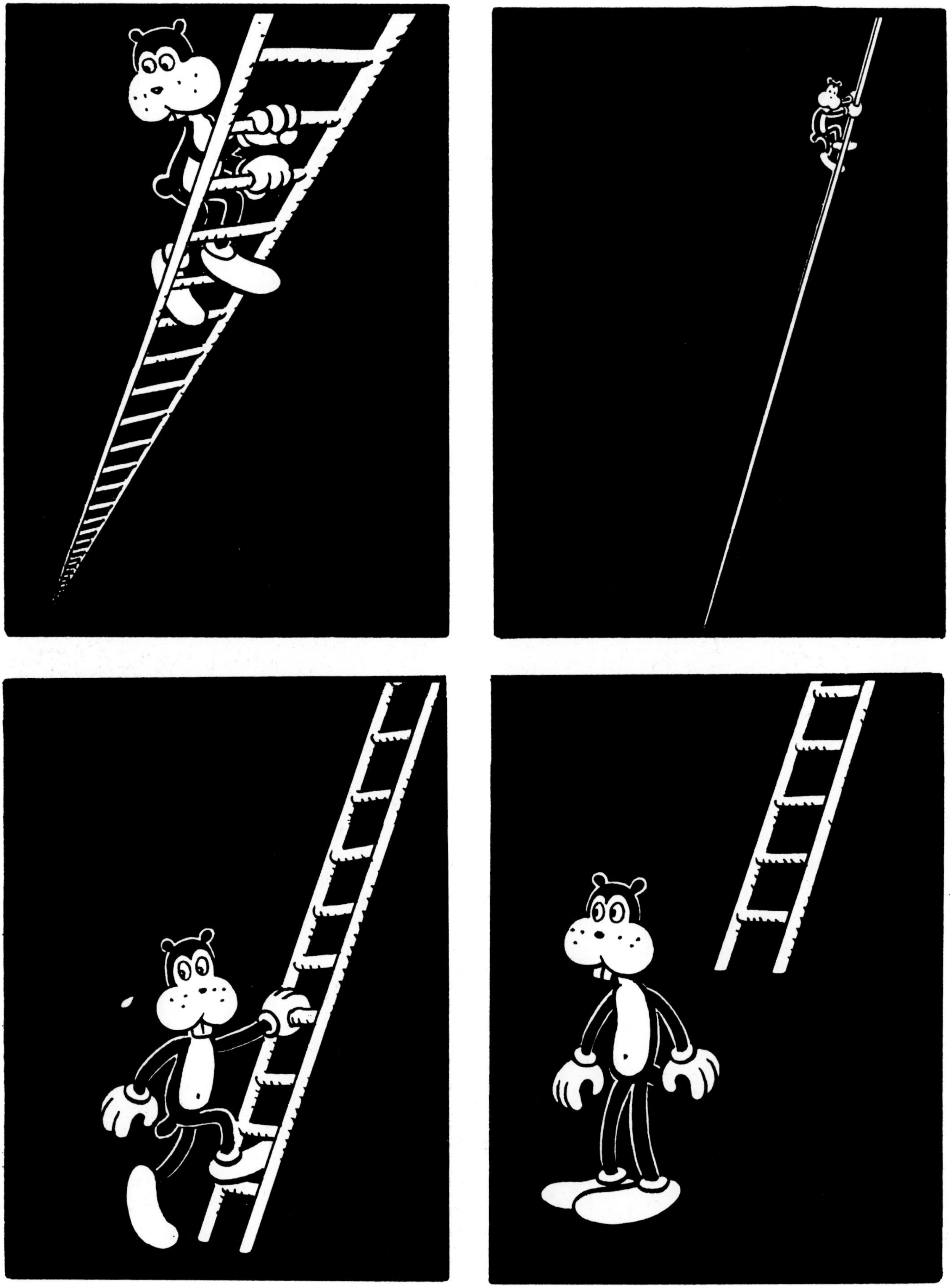

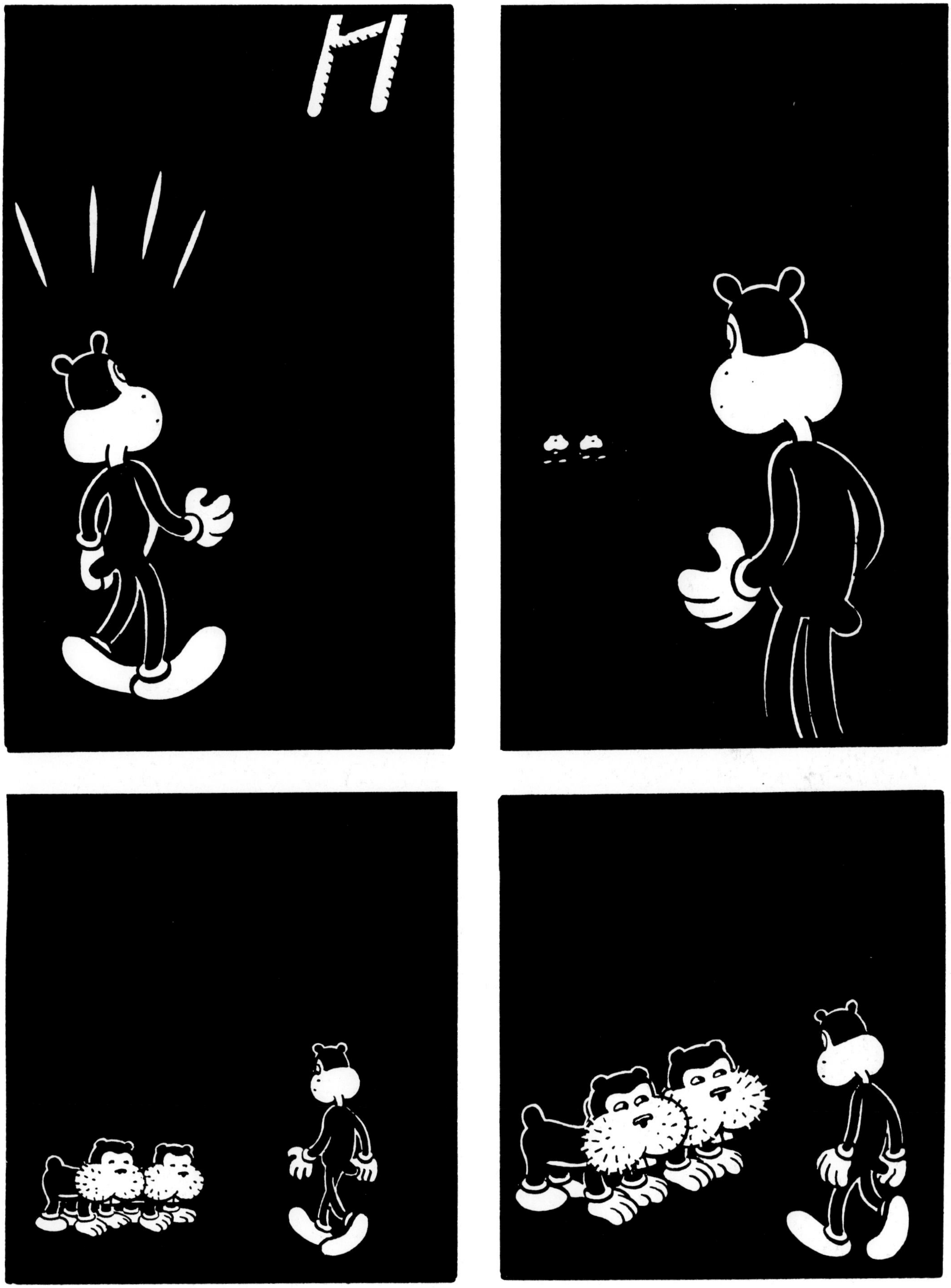

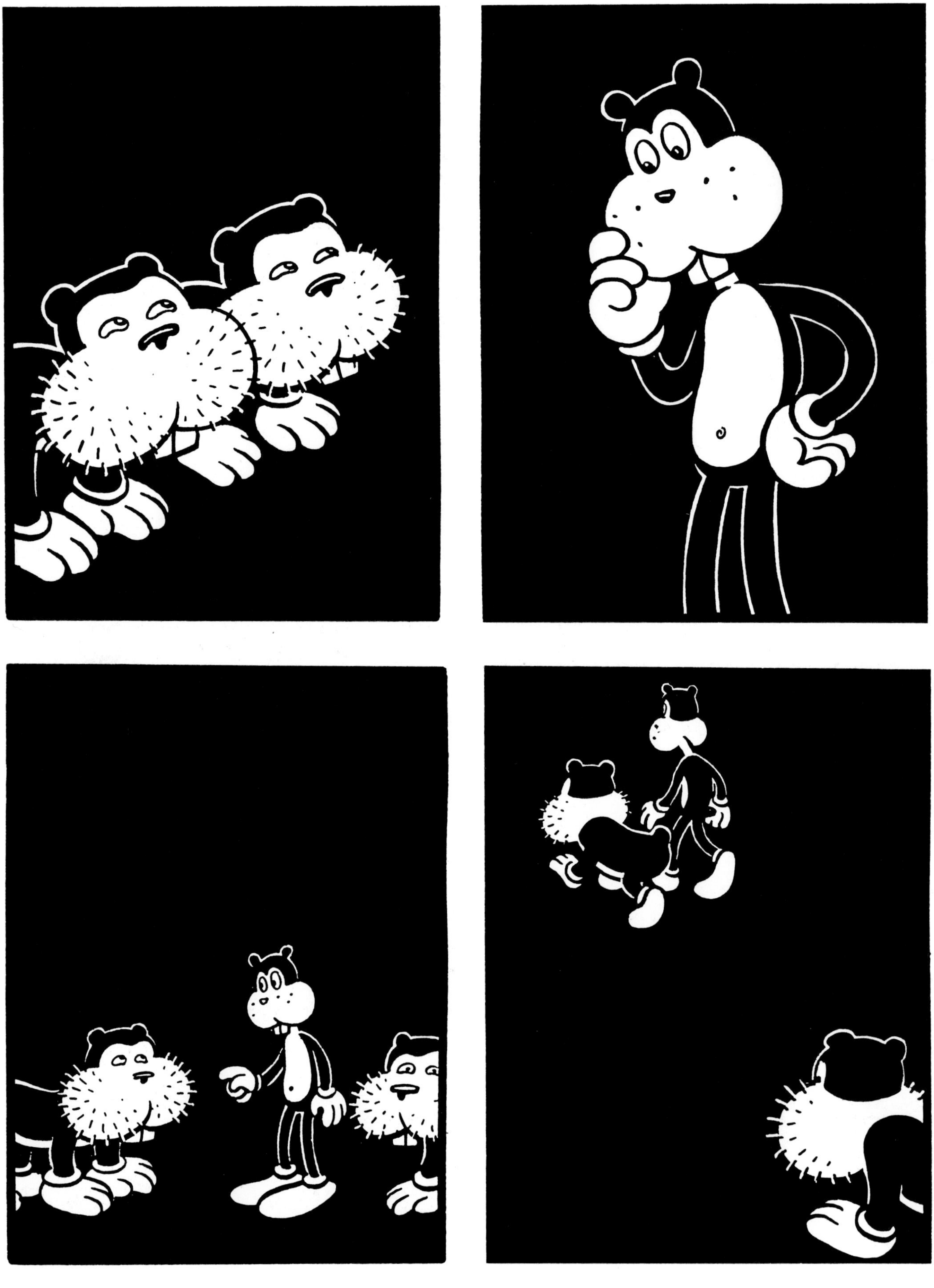

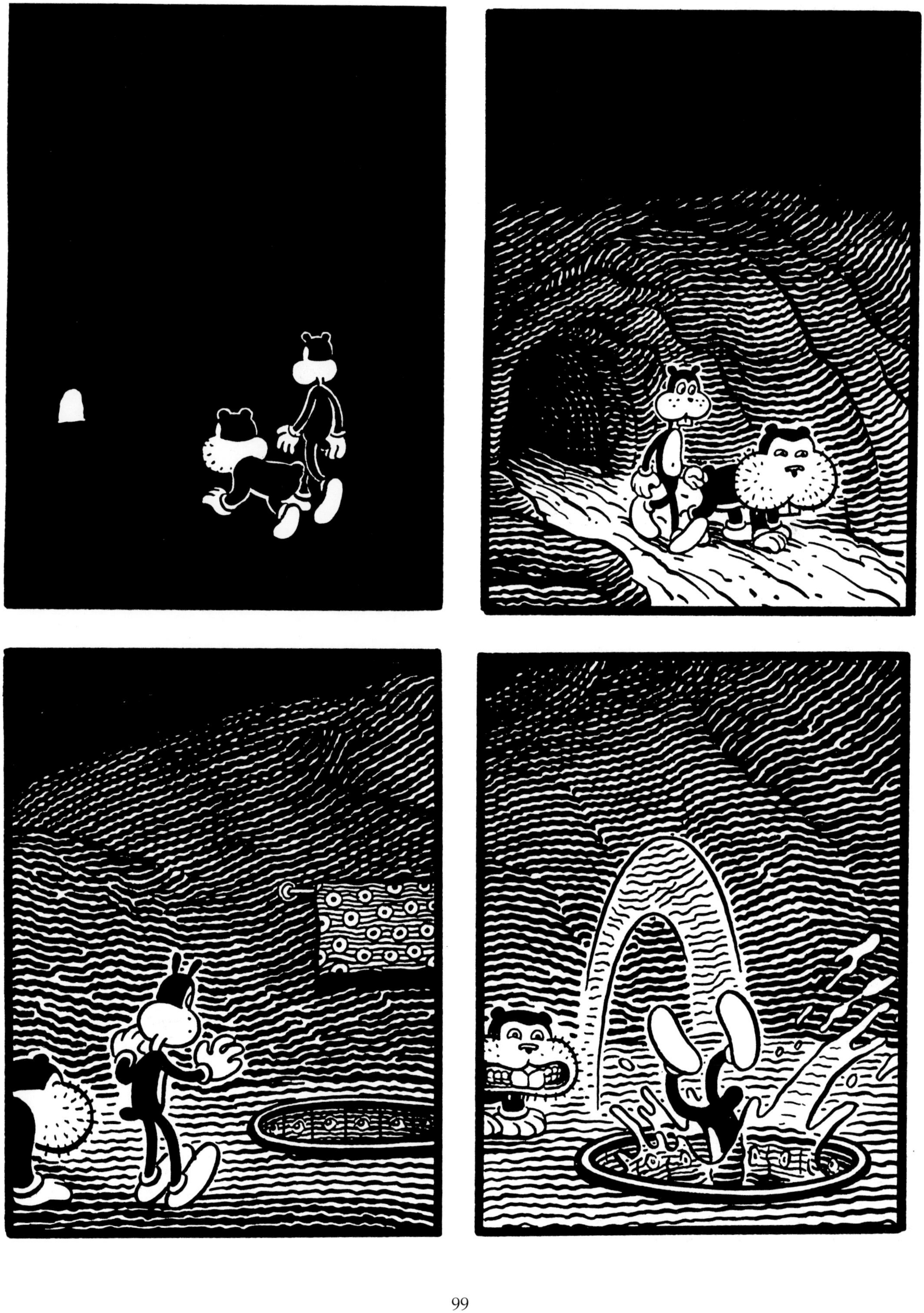

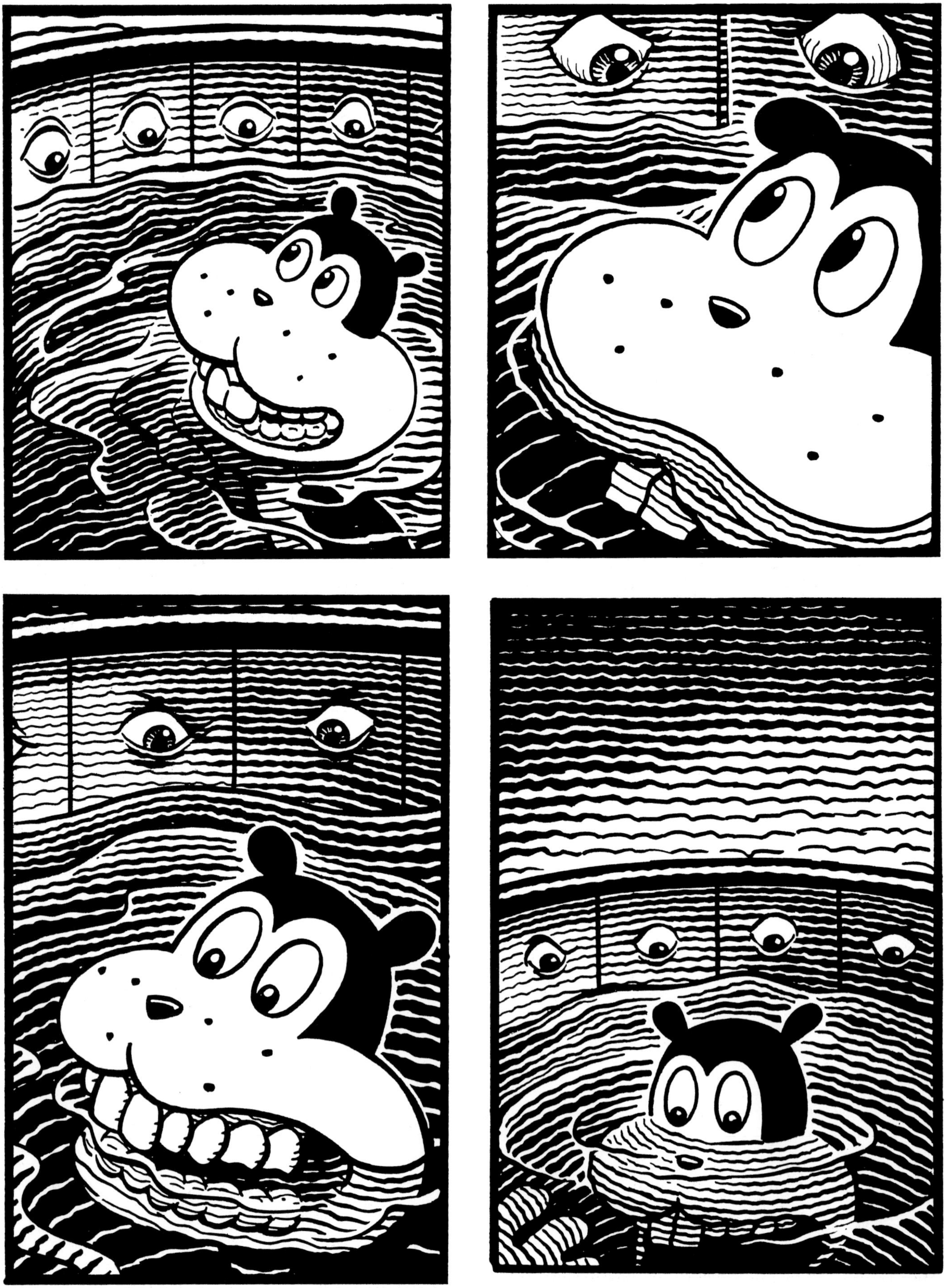

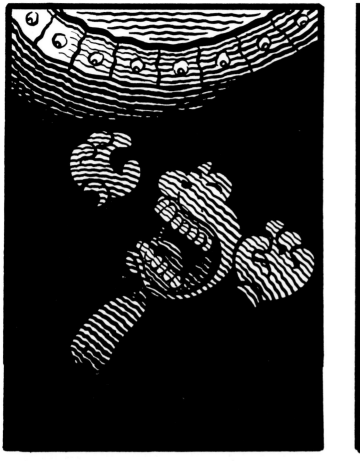

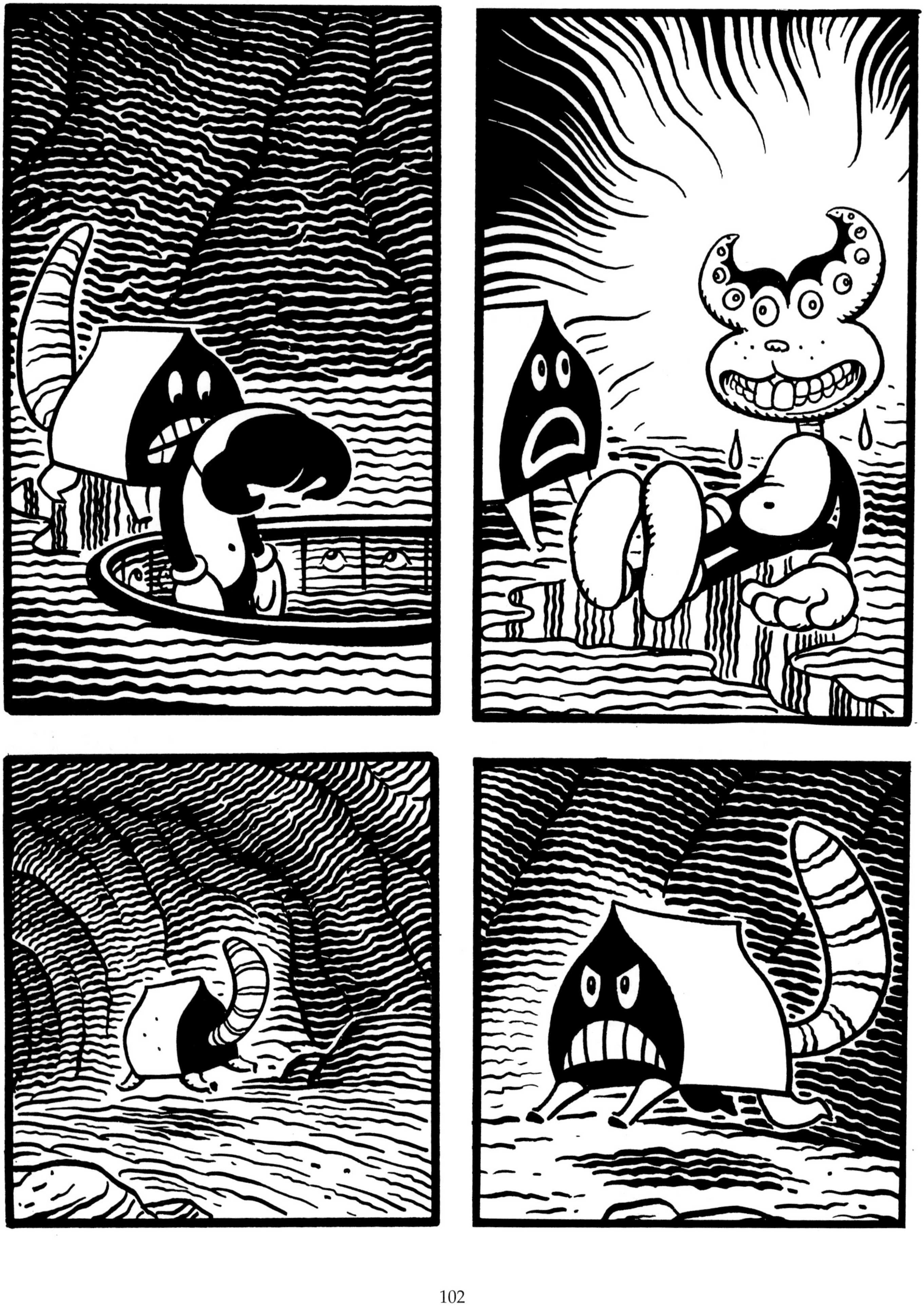

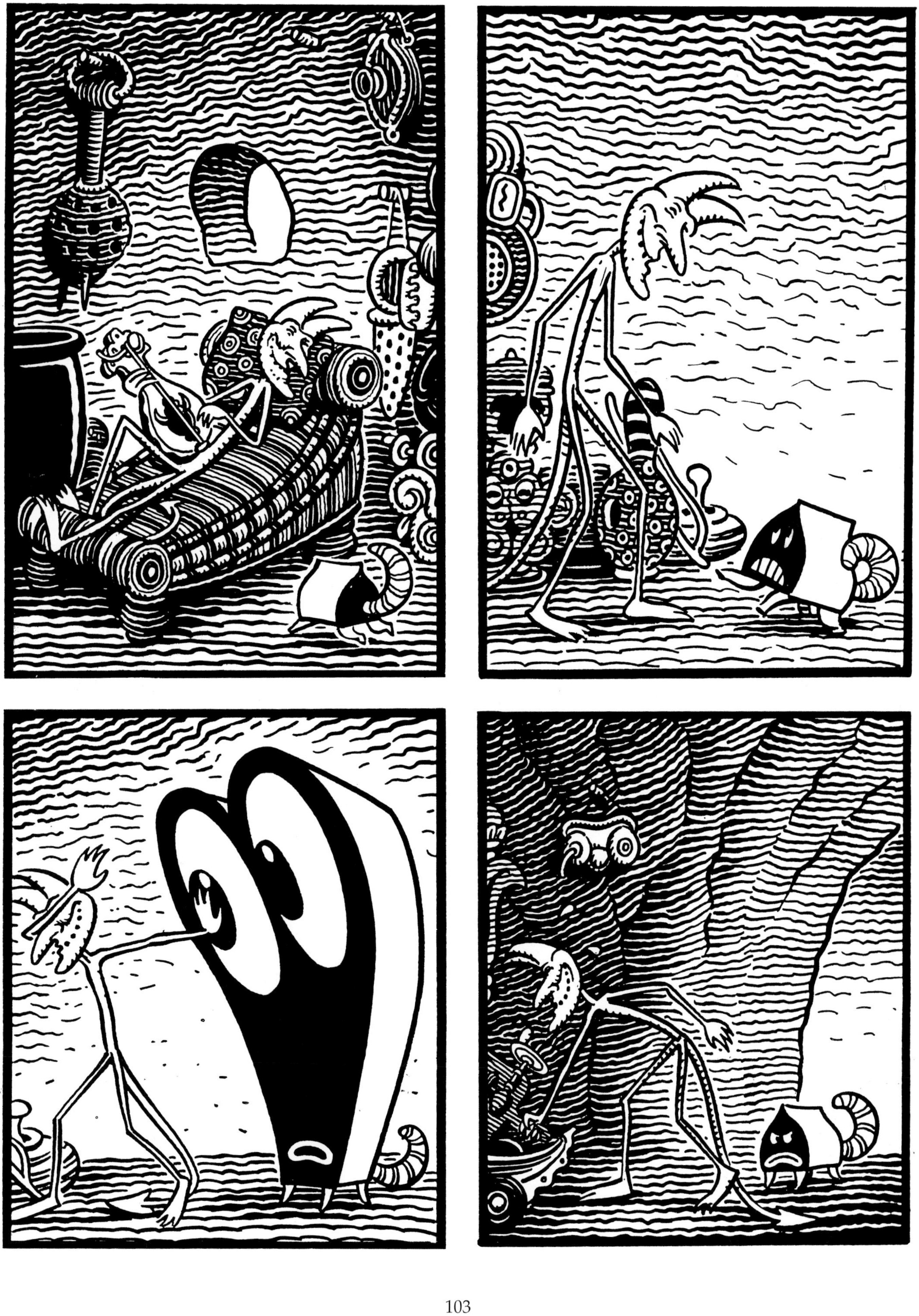

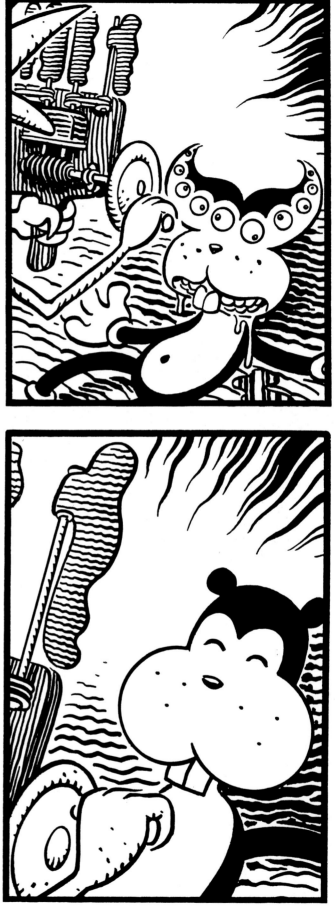

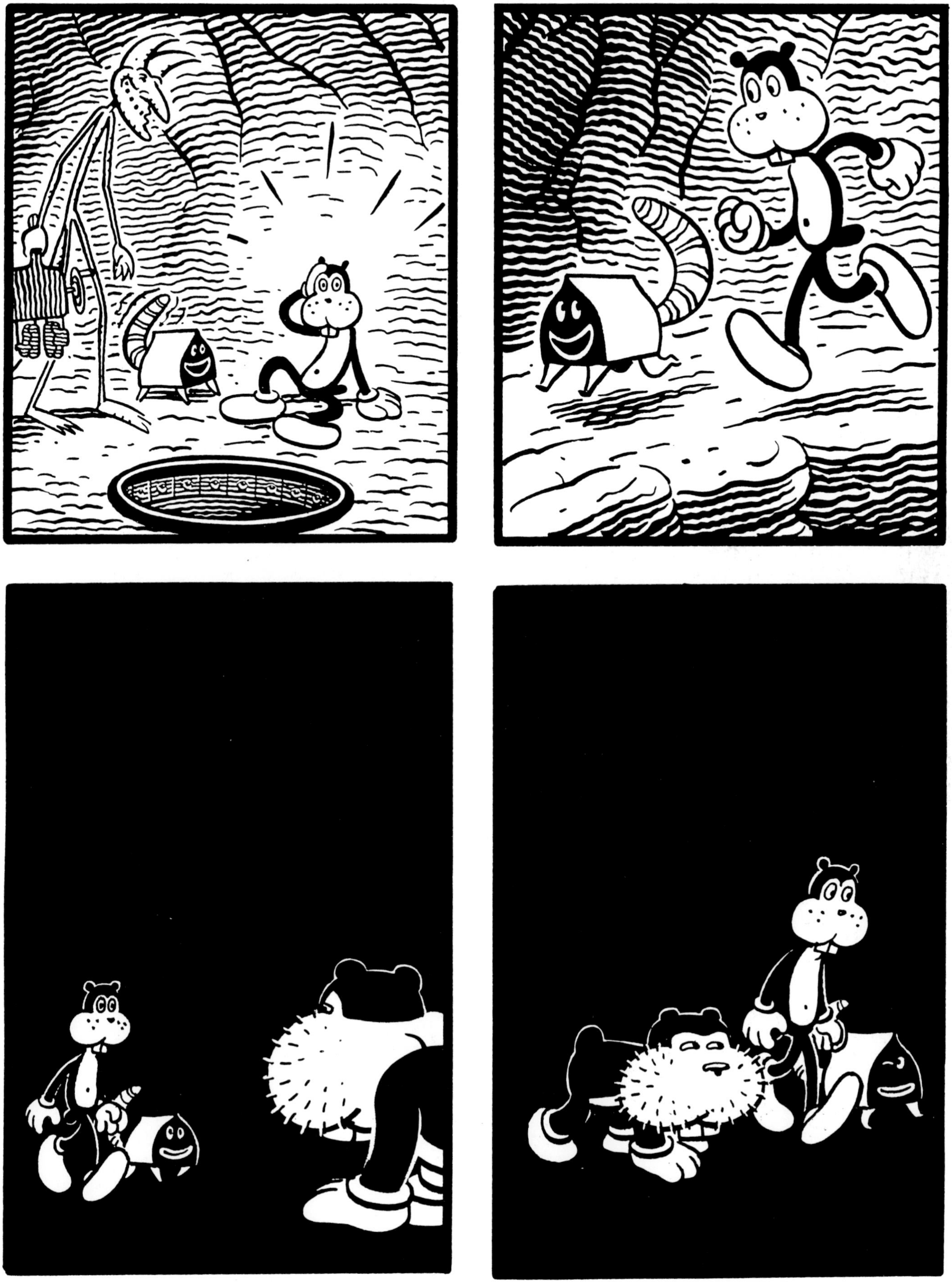

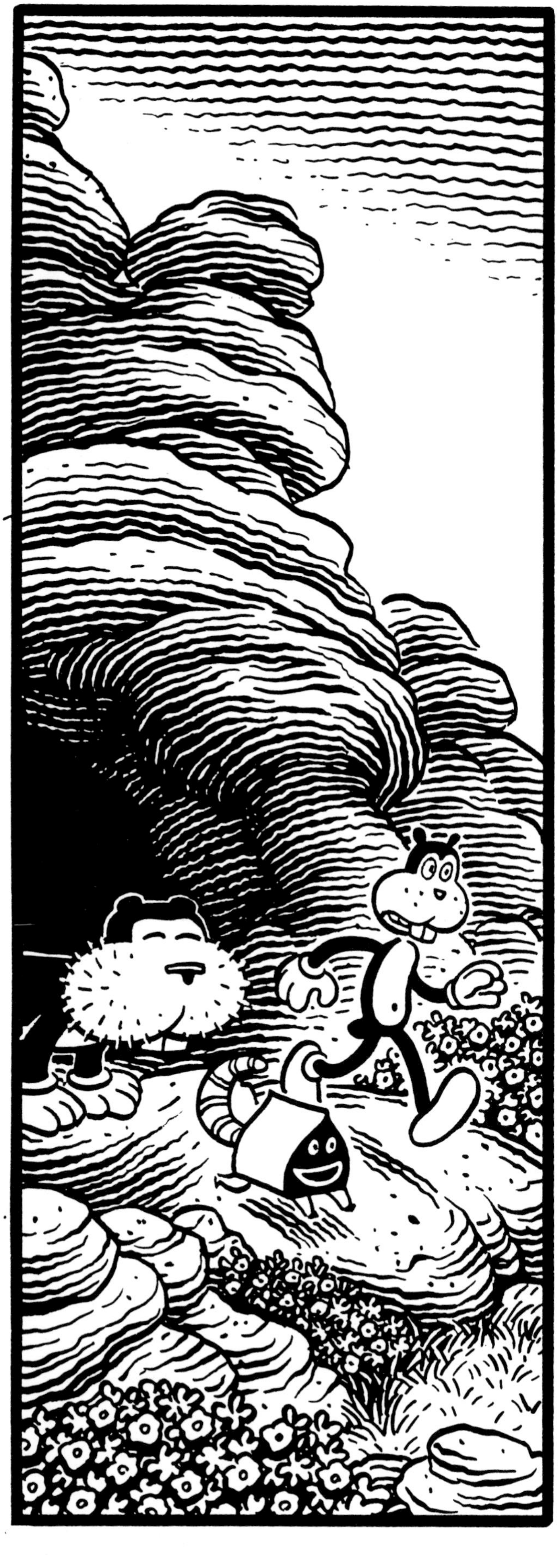

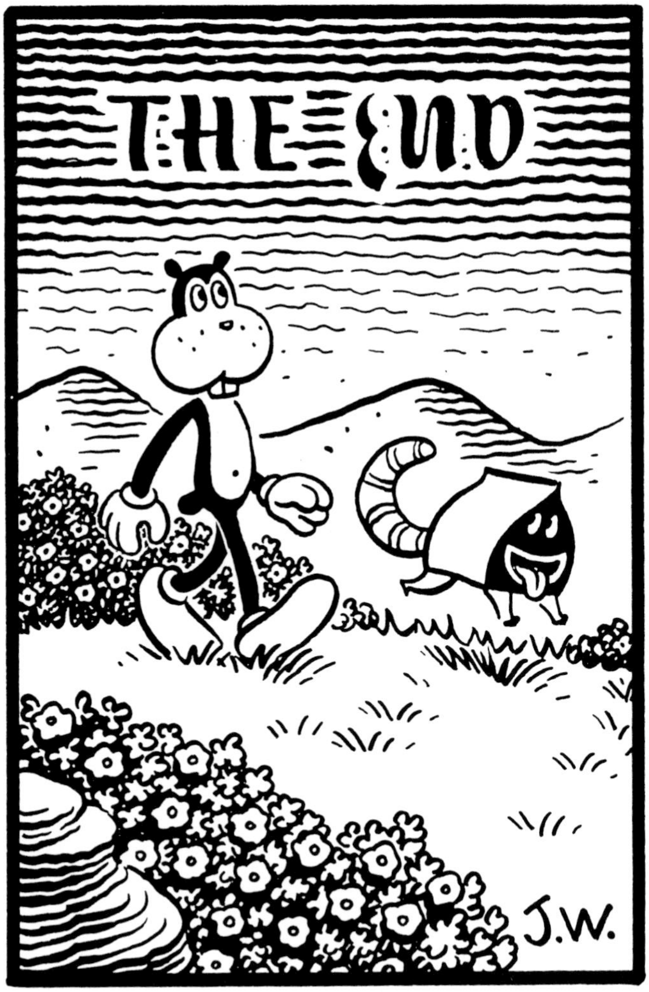
THE END
J.W.

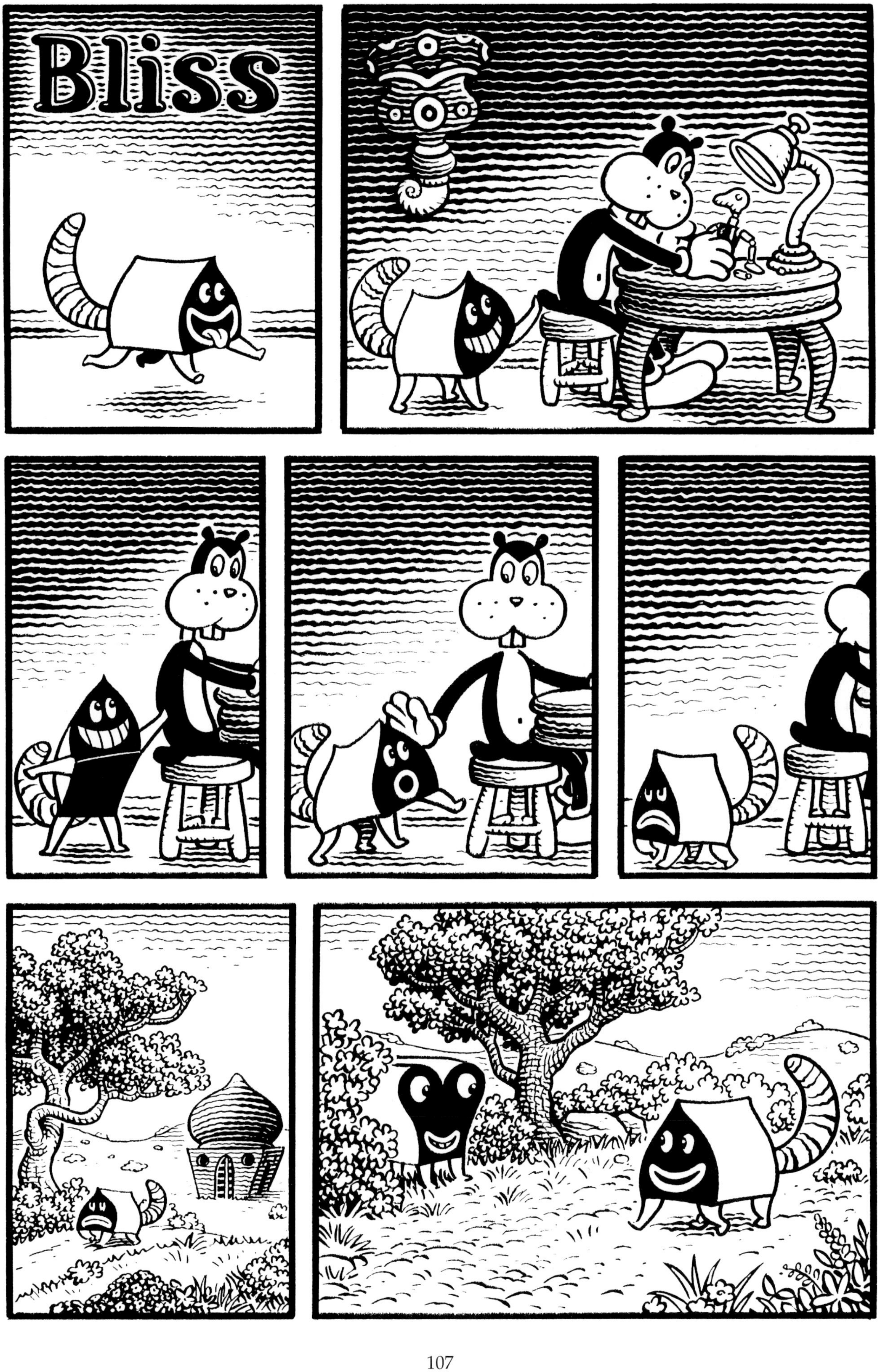
Bliss

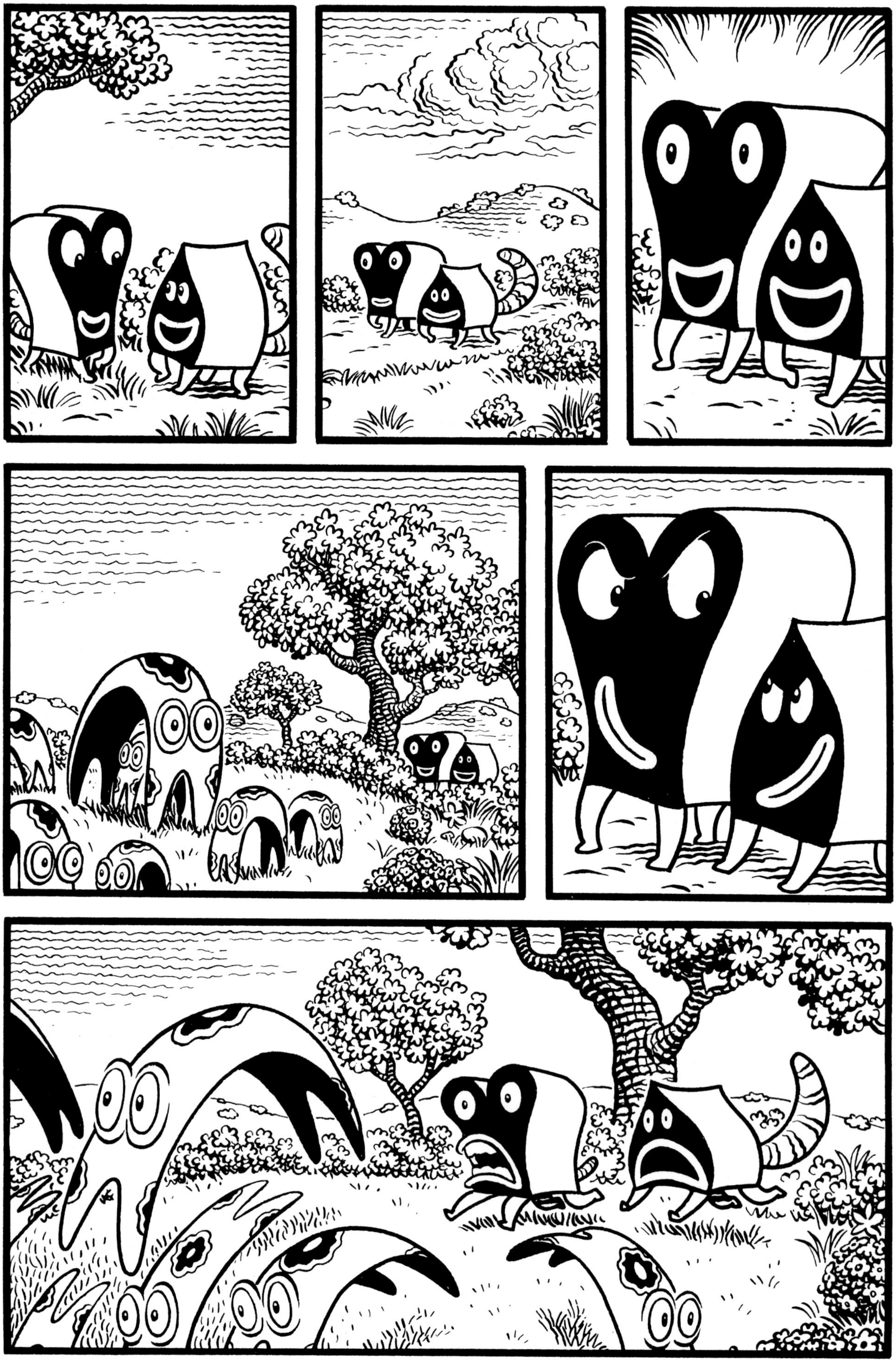

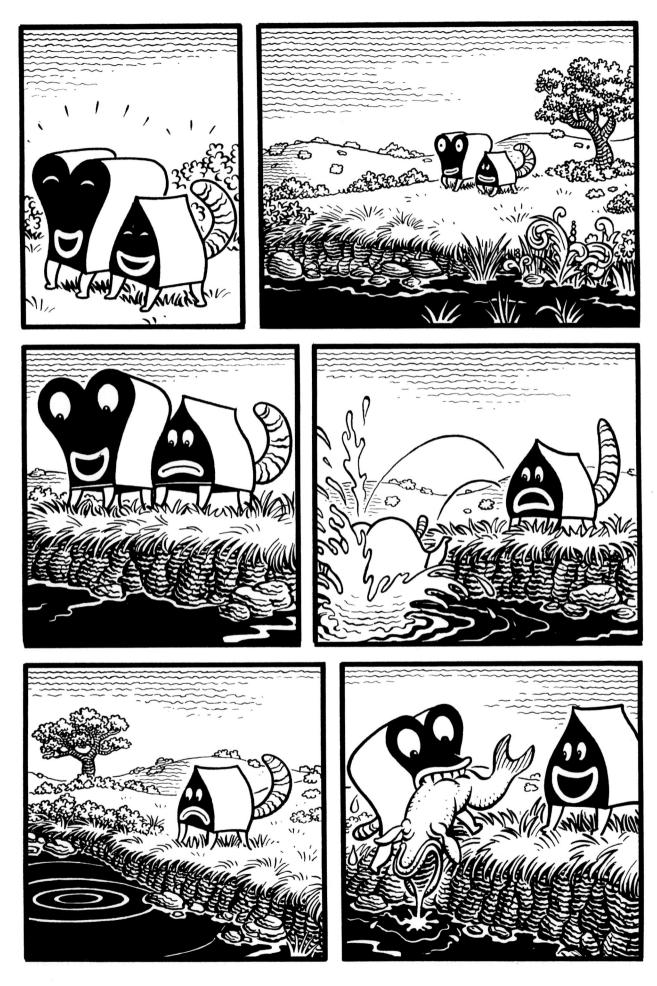

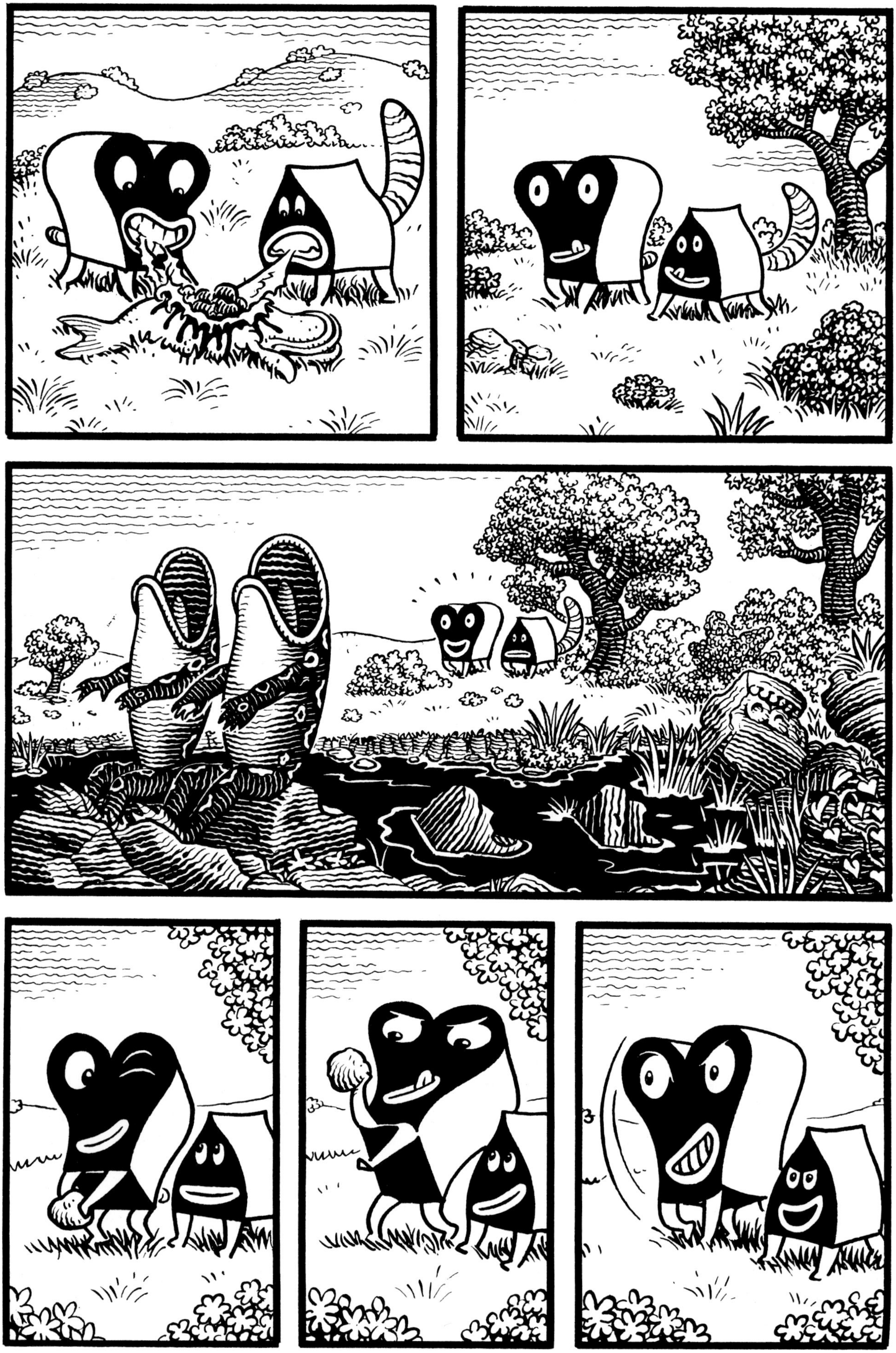

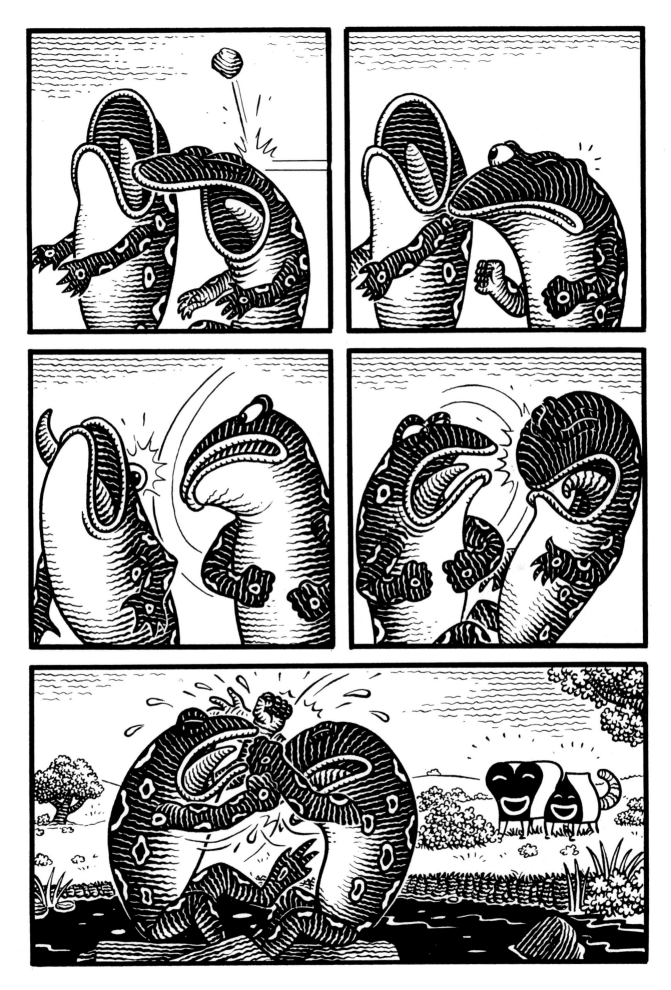

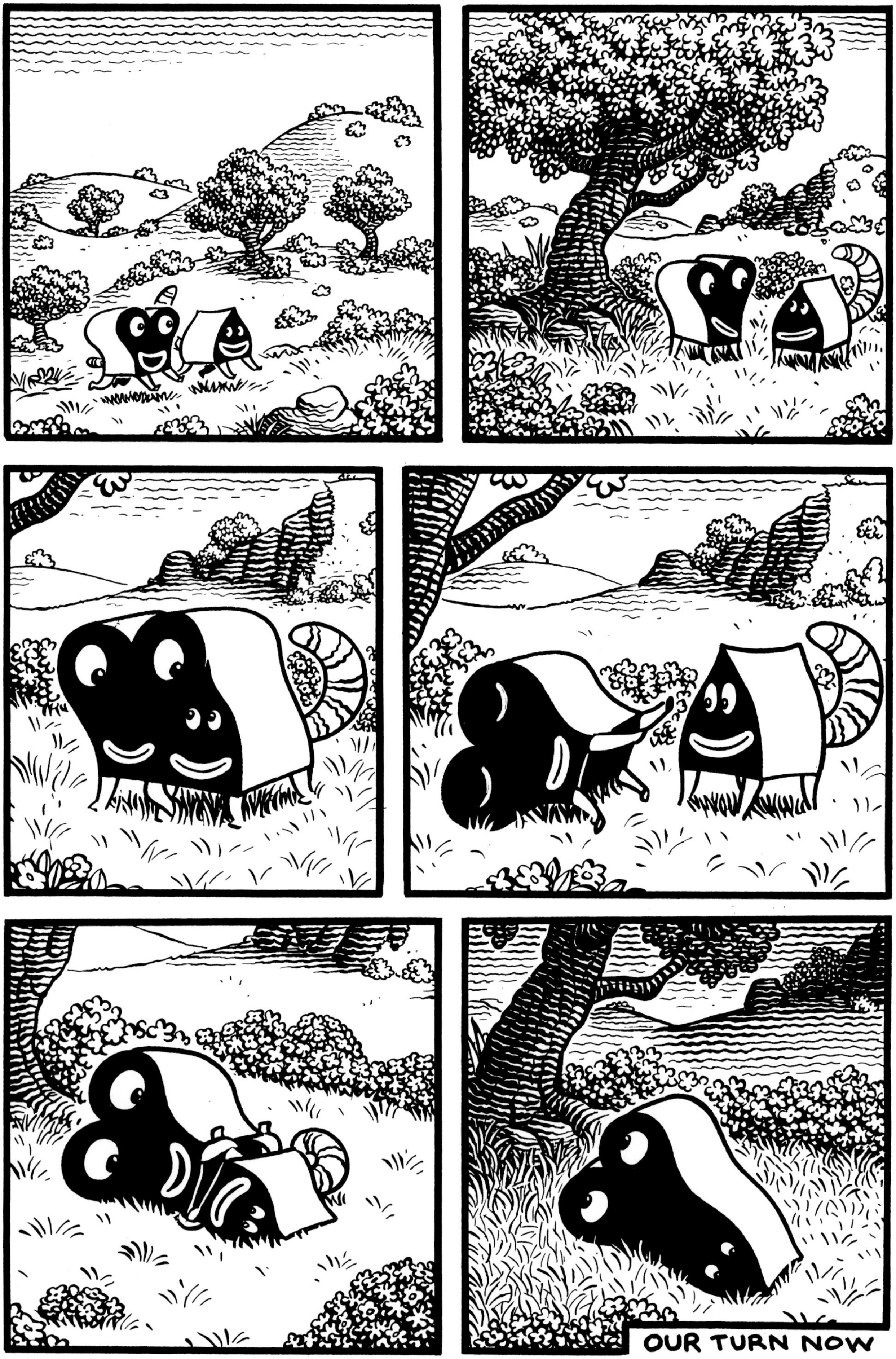
OUR TURN NOW

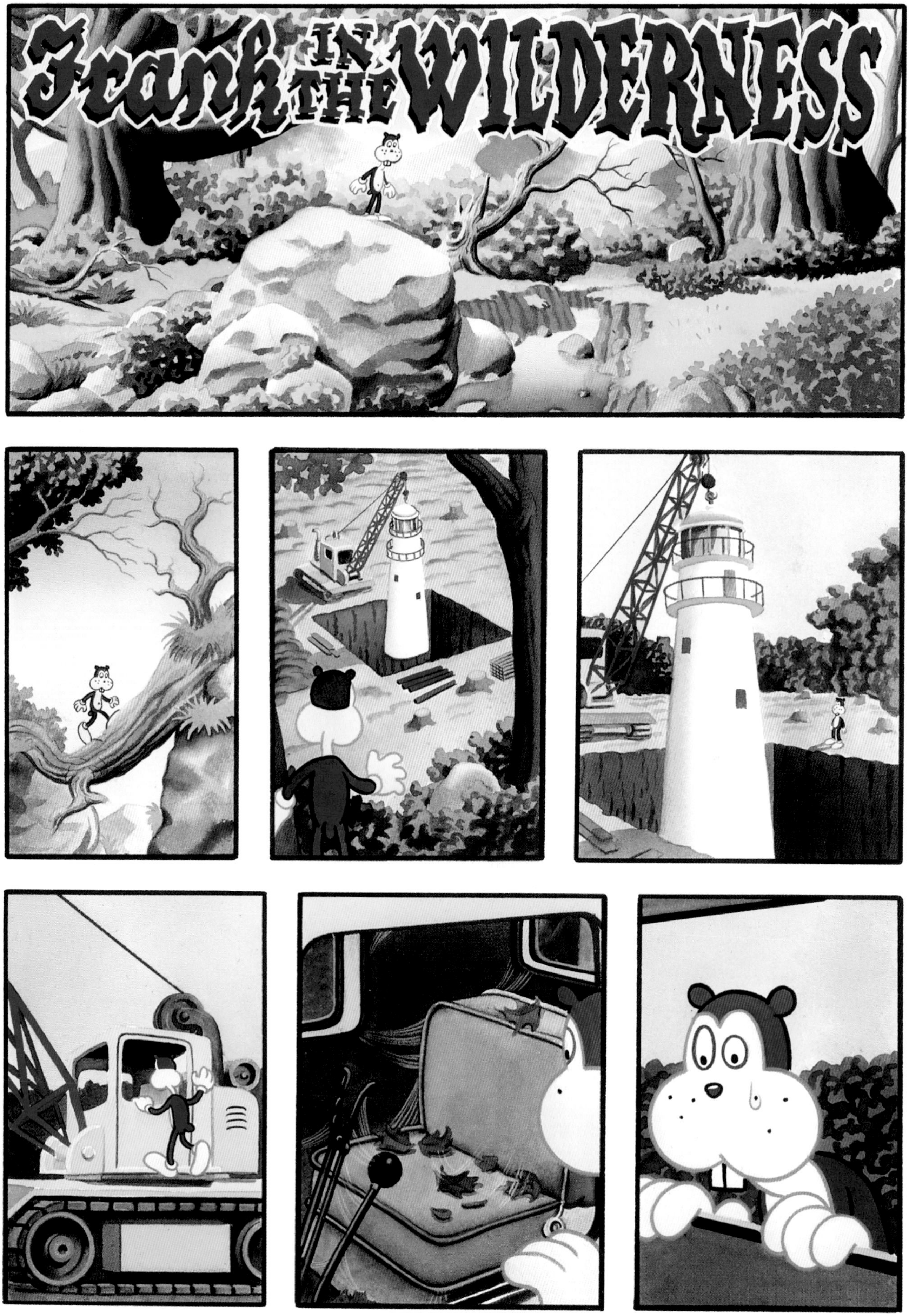
Frank IN THE WILDERNESS

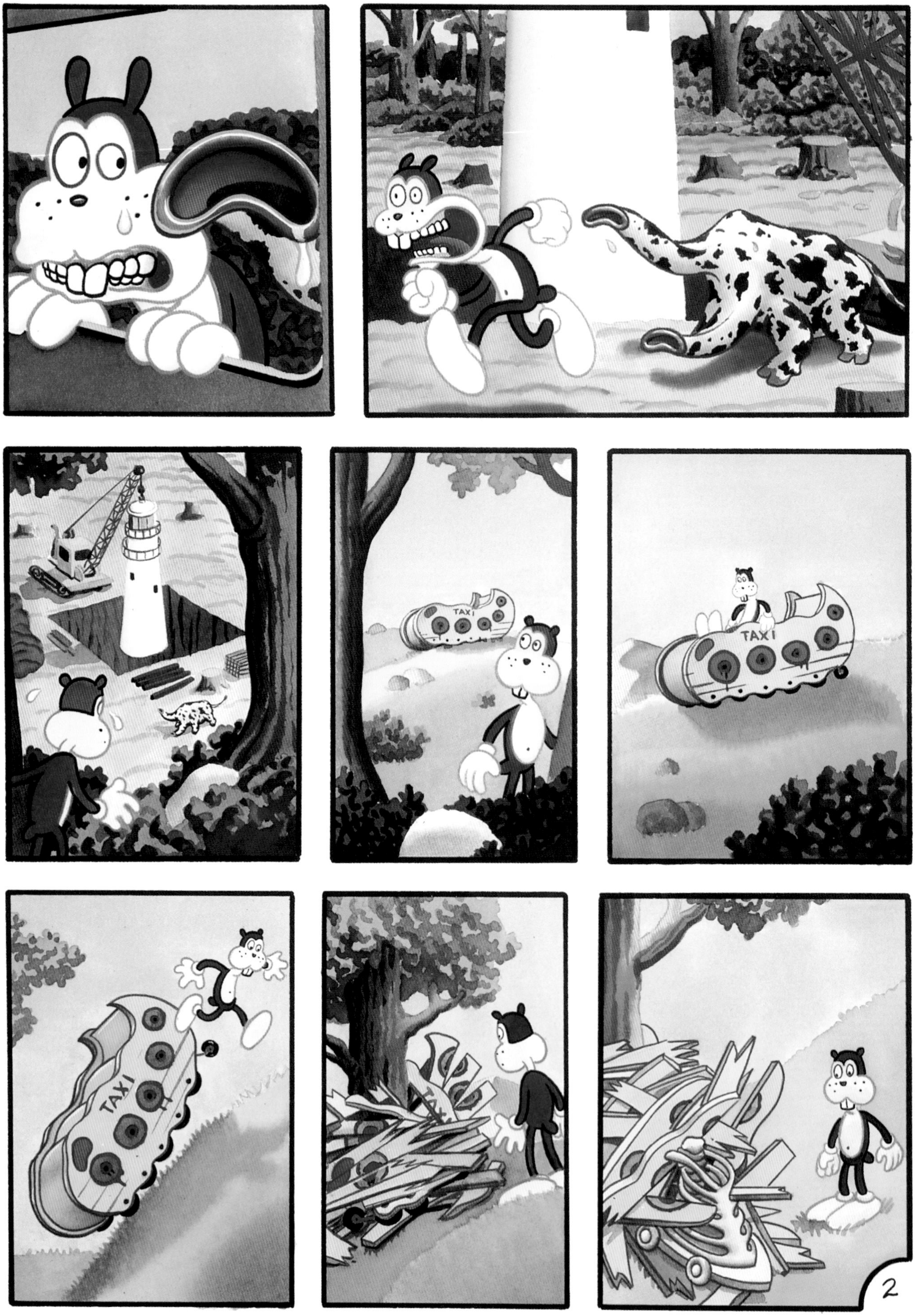
TAXI
TAXI
TAXI
2

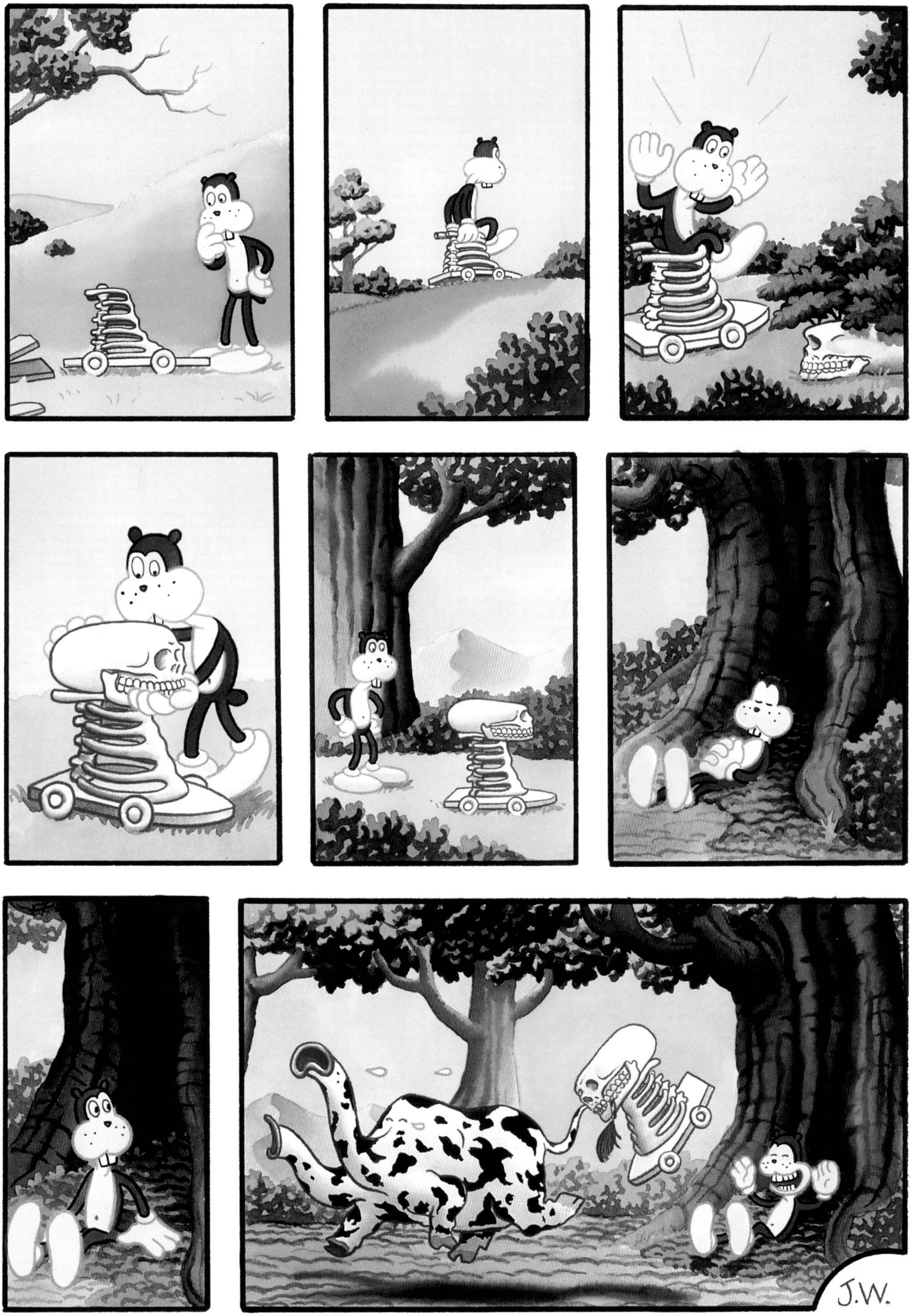
J.W.

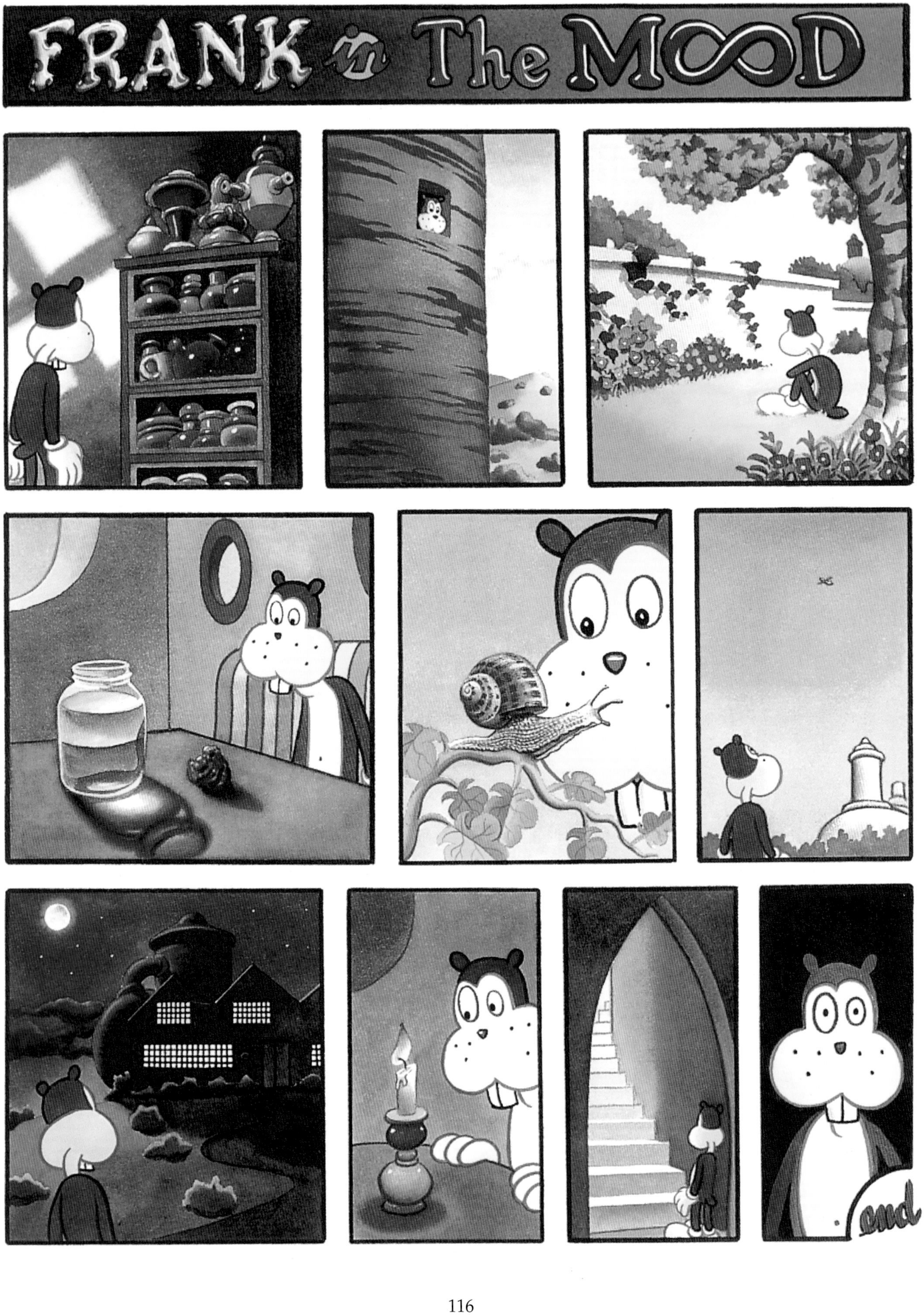
FRANK in The MOOD
end

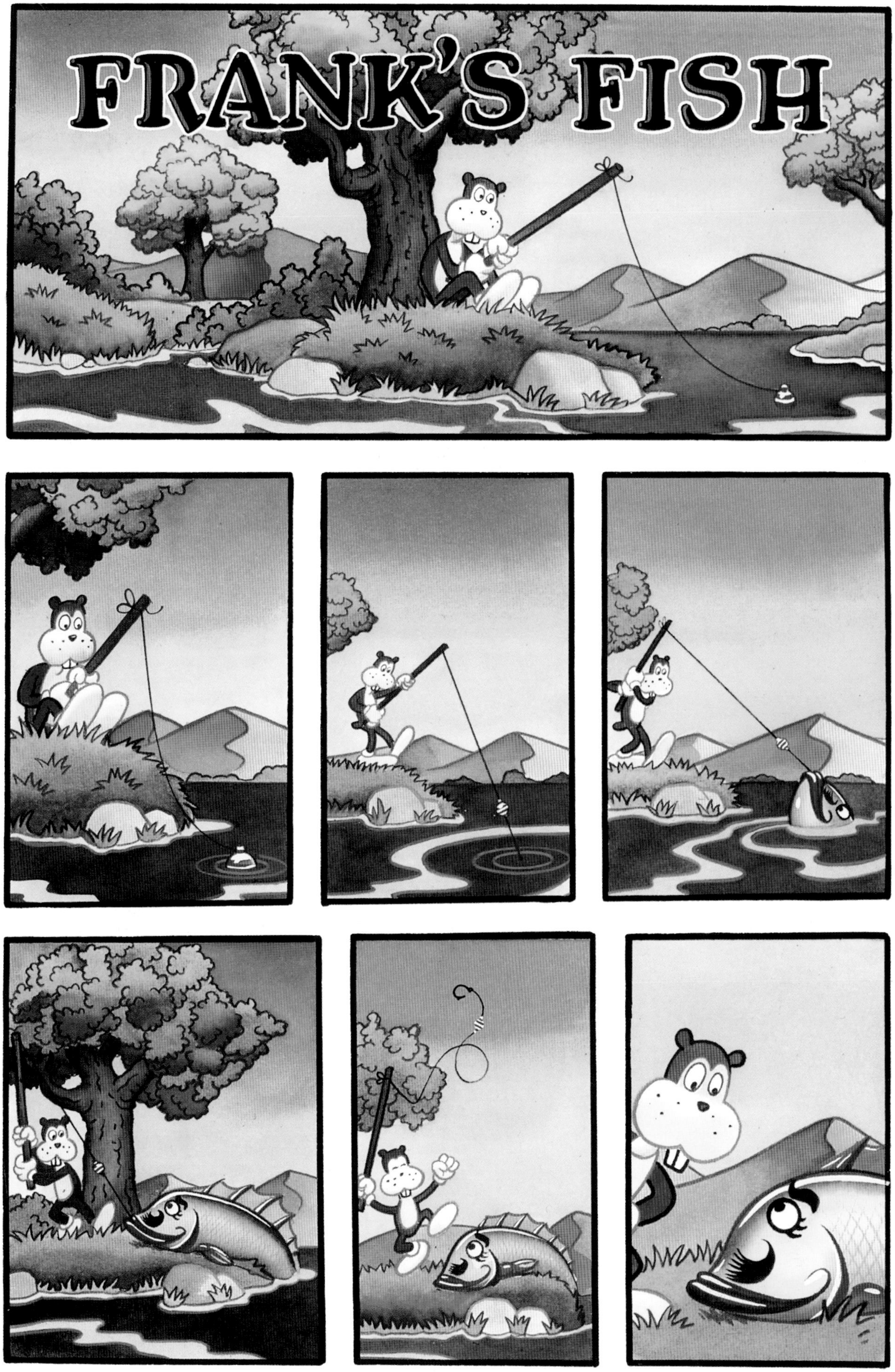
FRANK'S FISH

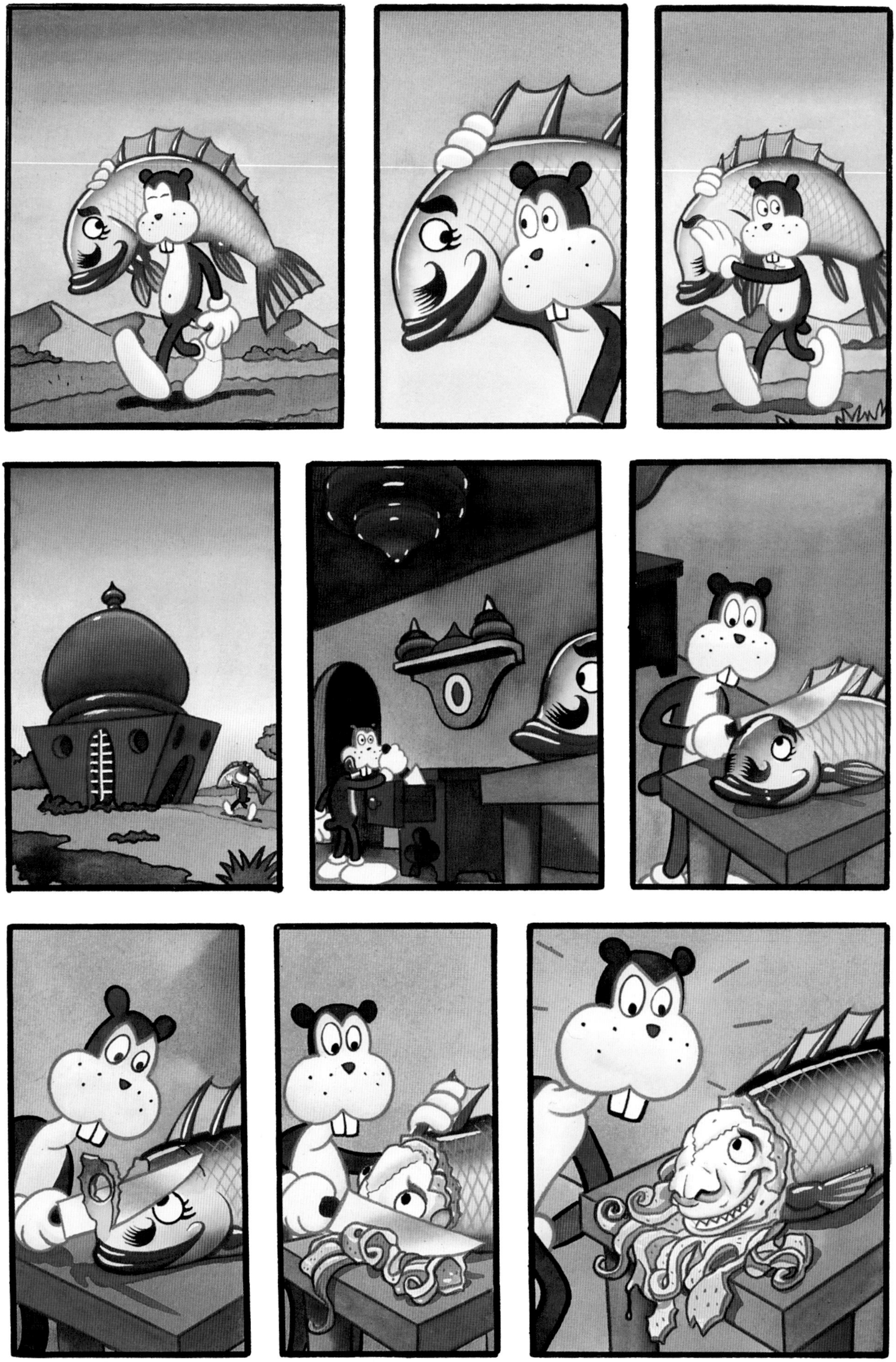

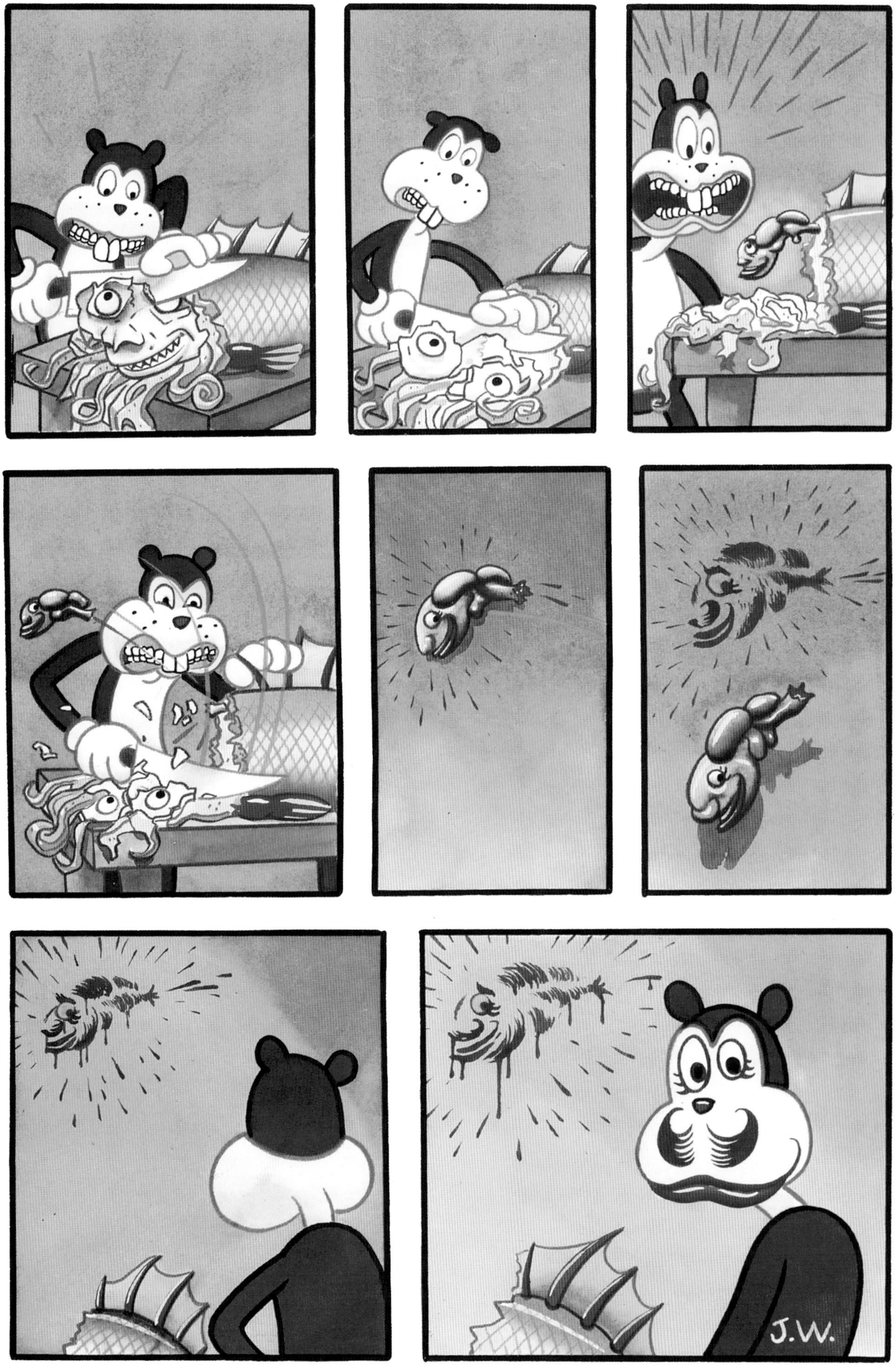
J.W.

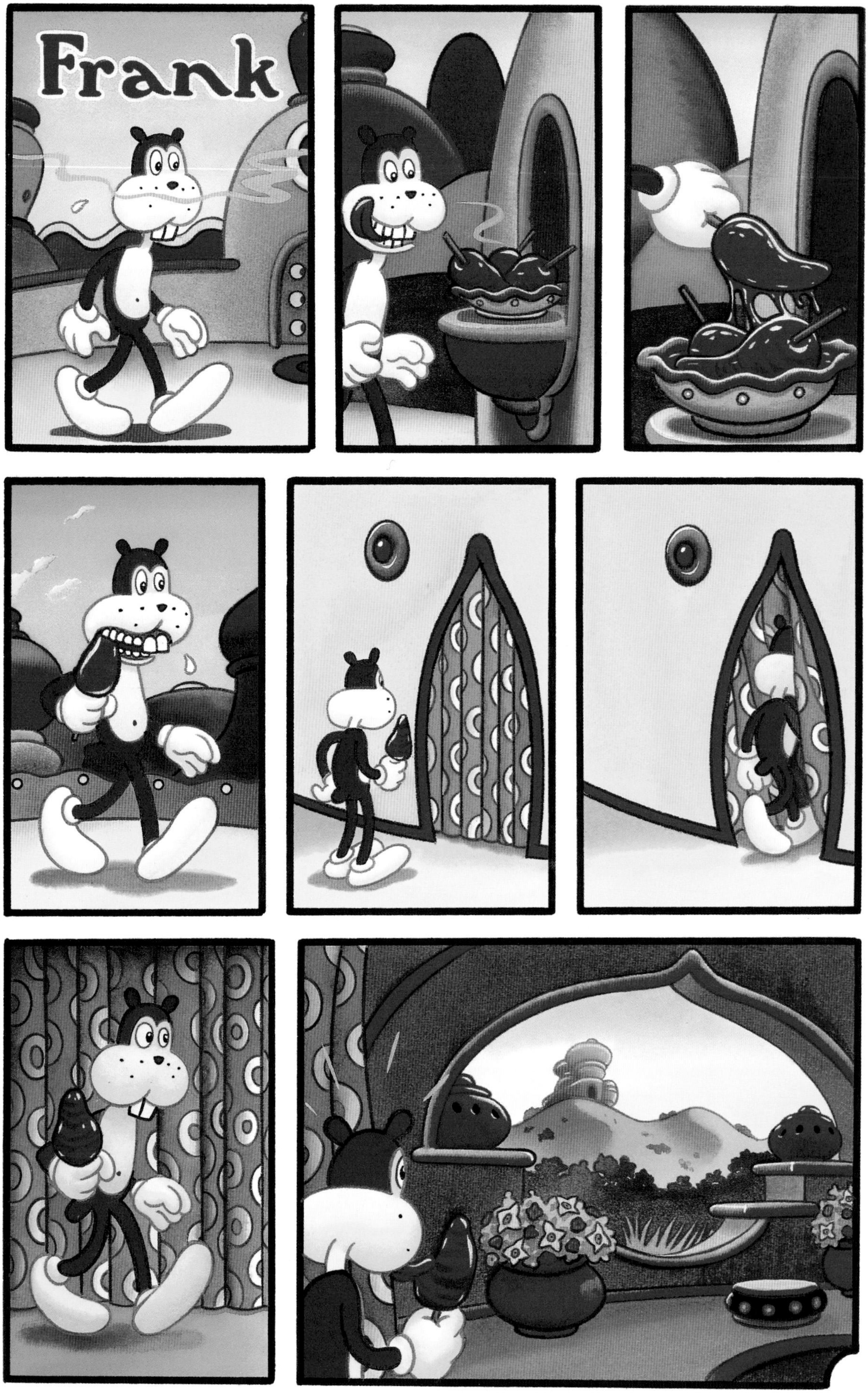
Frank

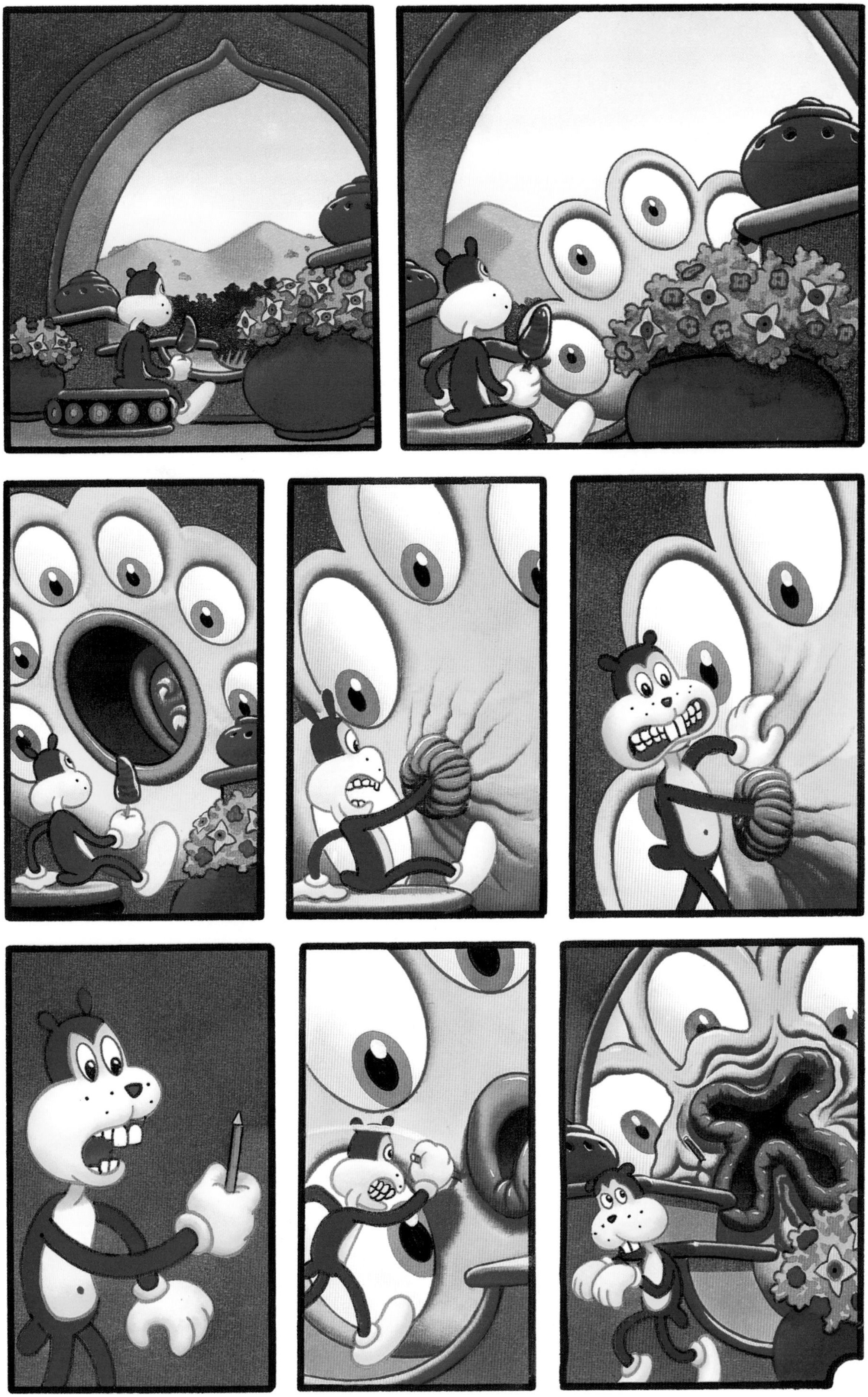

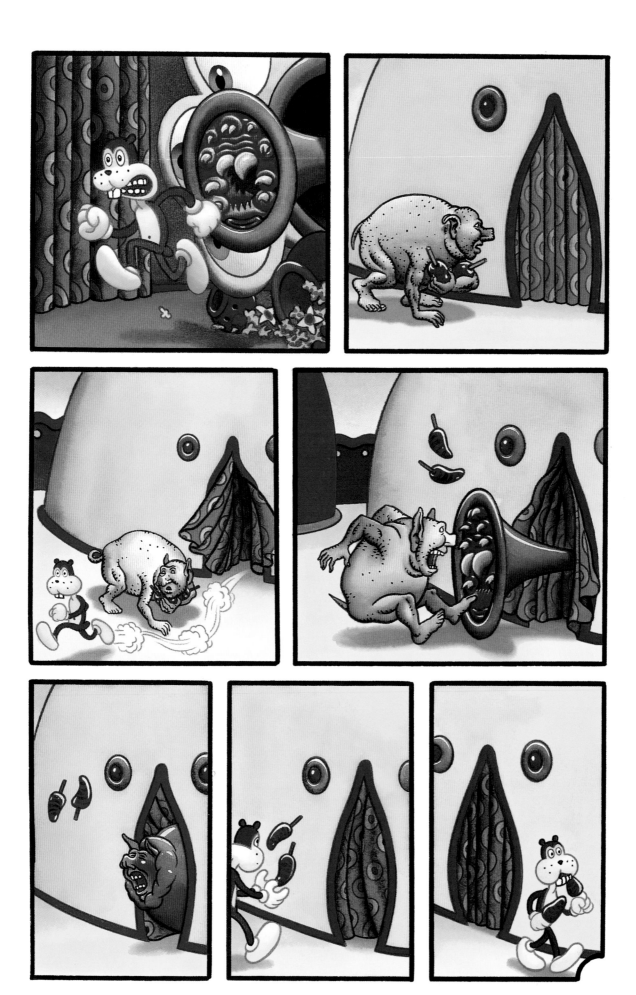

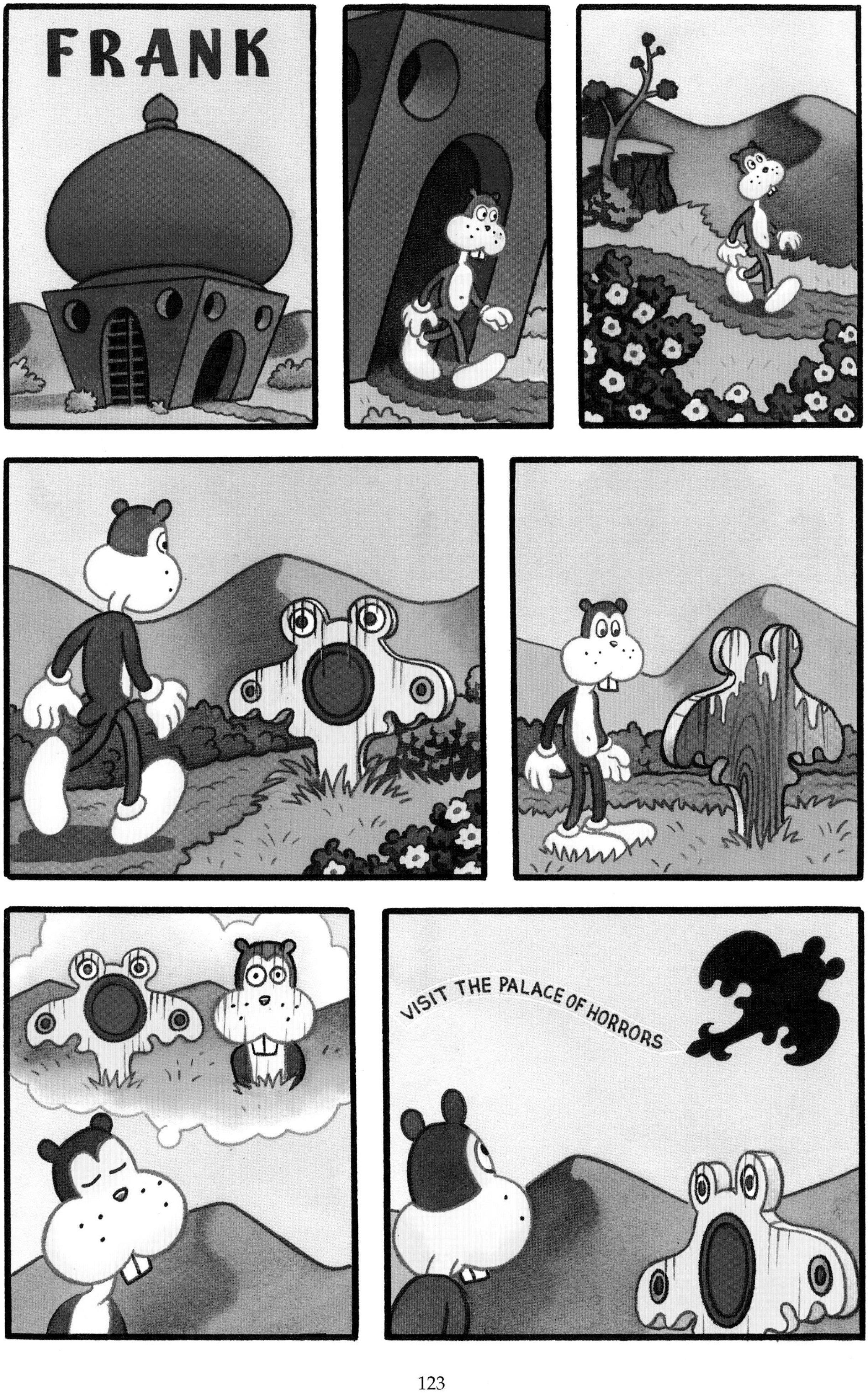
FRANK
VISIT THE PALACE OF HORRORS

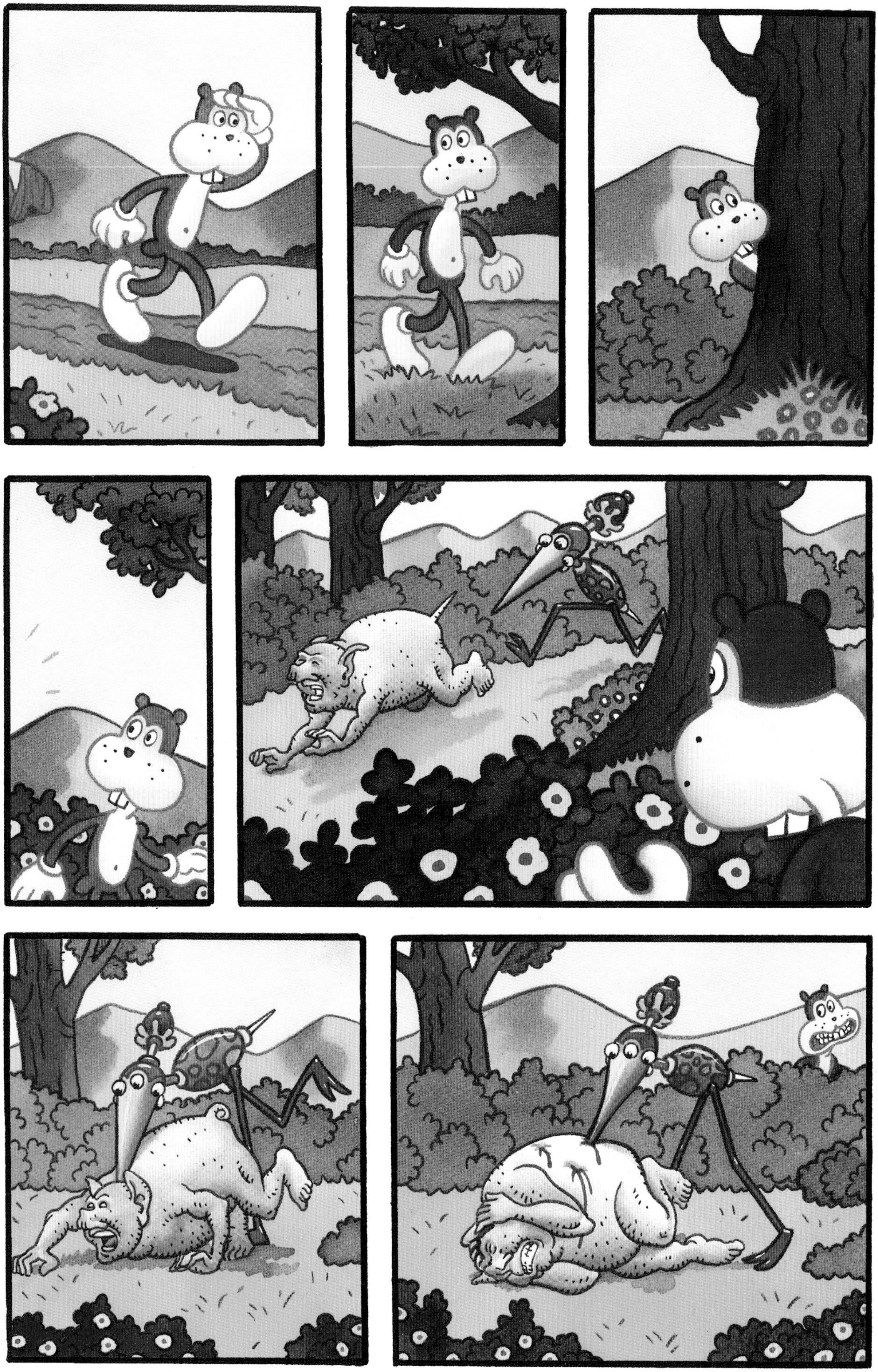

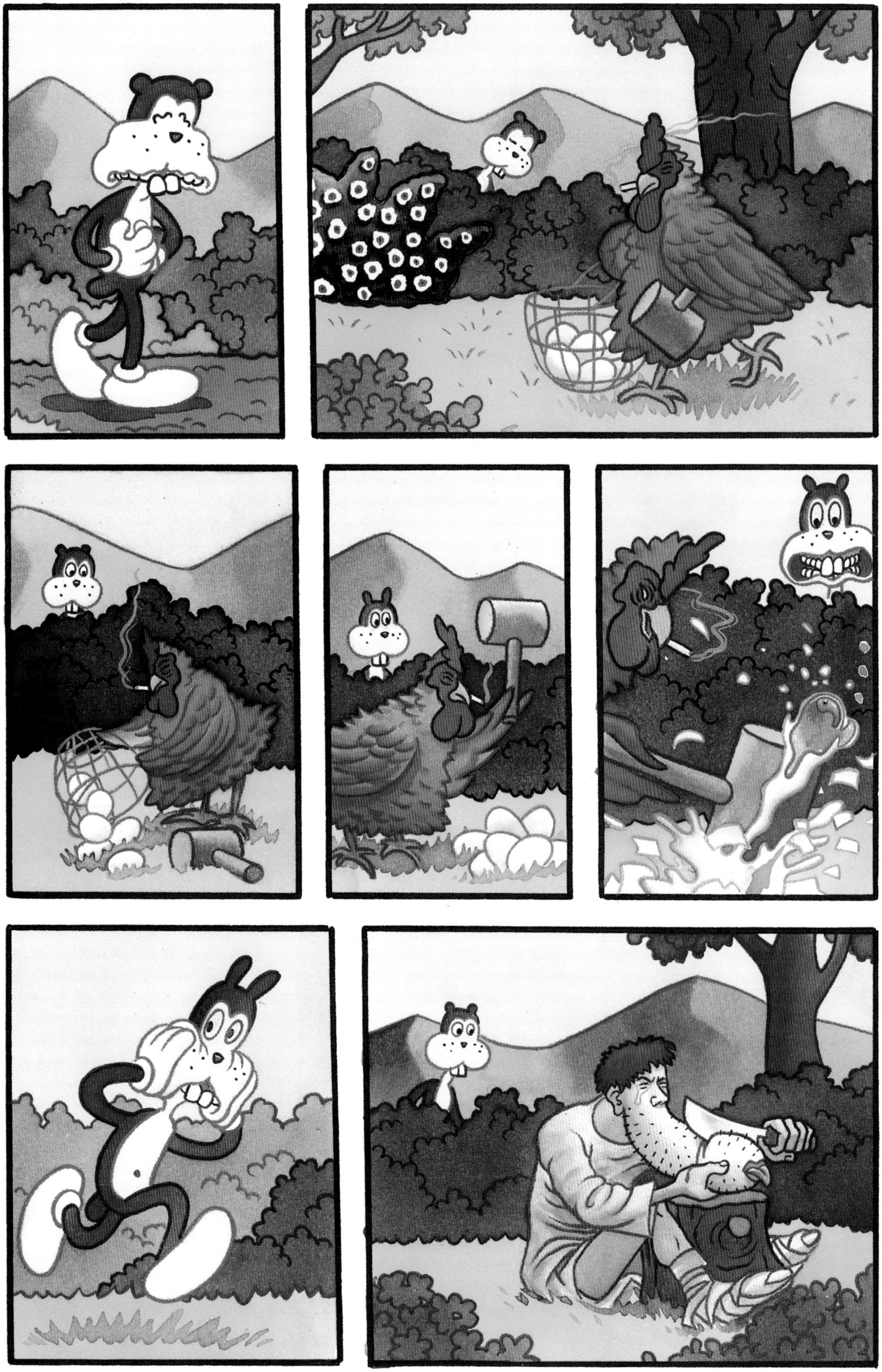

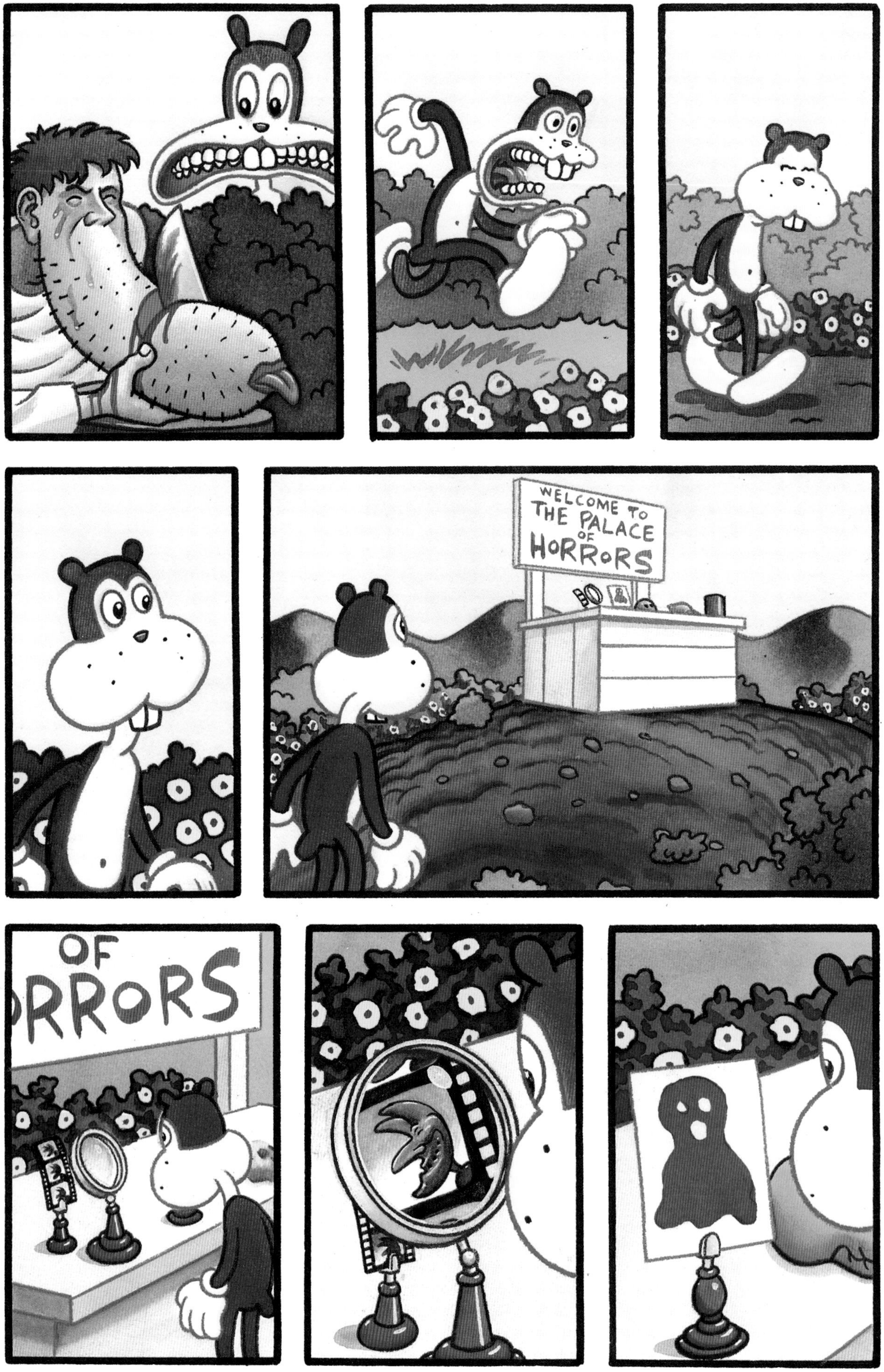
WELCOME TO
THE PALACE
OF
HORRORS
OF
RRORS

DONATIONS
ACE
RS
DONATIONS
WELCOM
THE PA
OF
HORRO

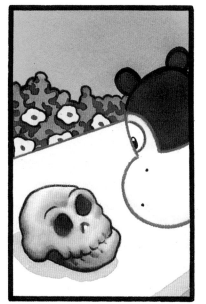

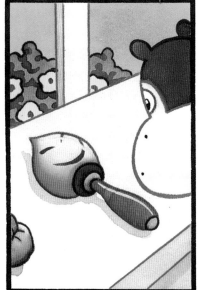

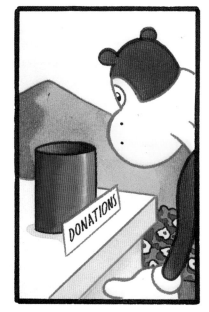

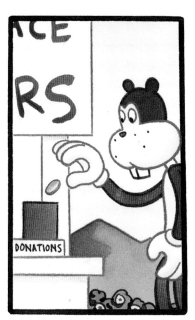

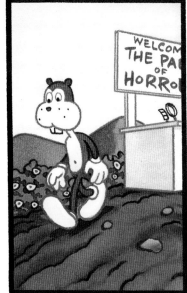

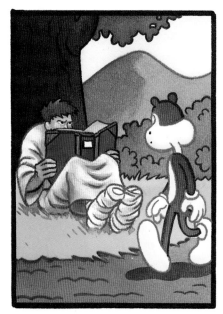

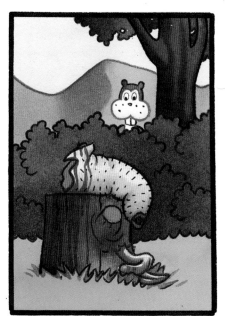

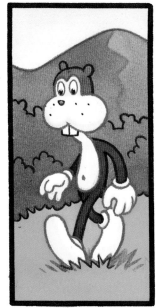

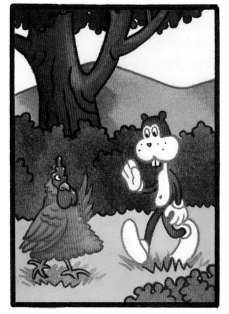

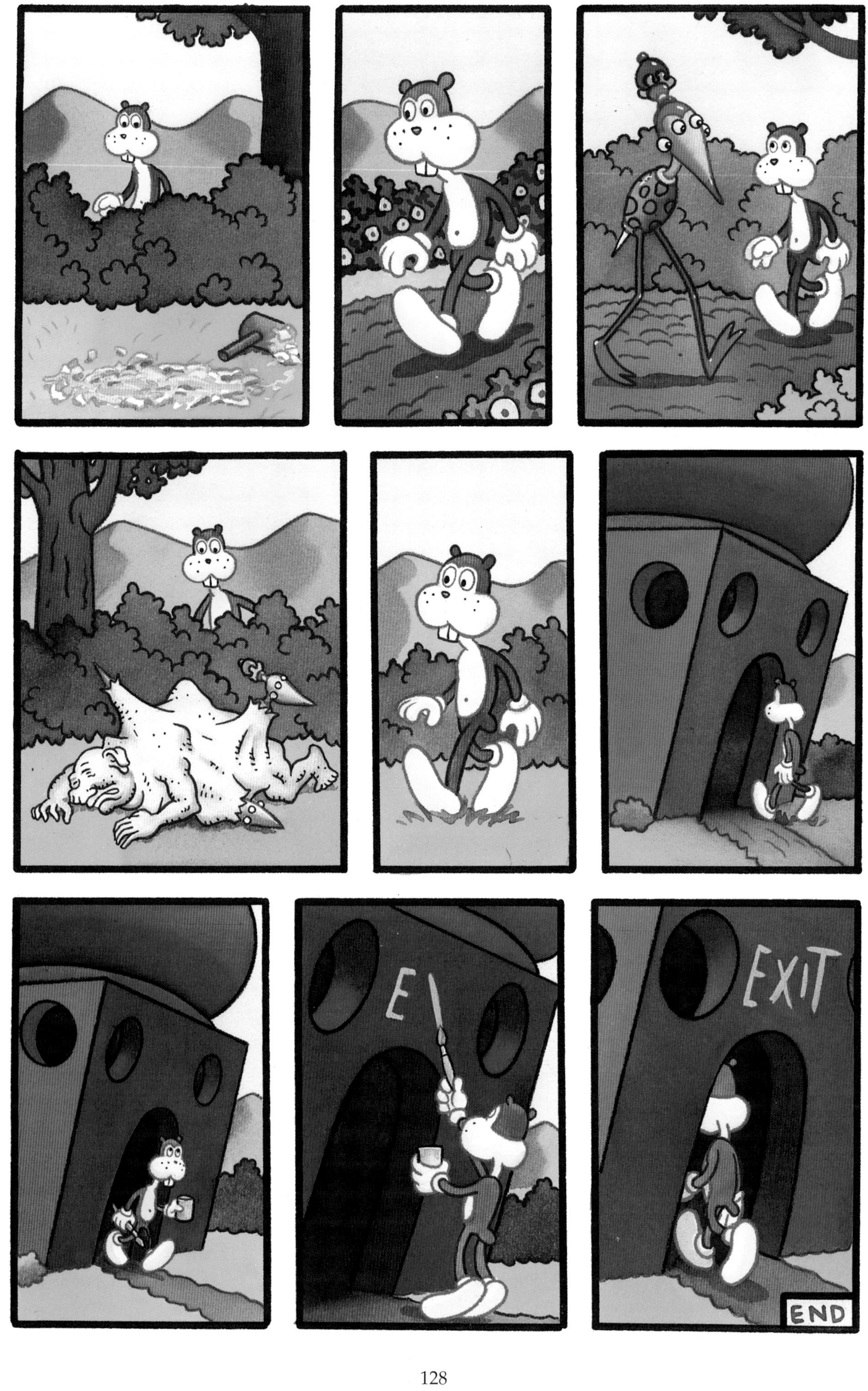
E
EXIT
END

FRANK AND THE TRUTH ABOUT PLENITUDE

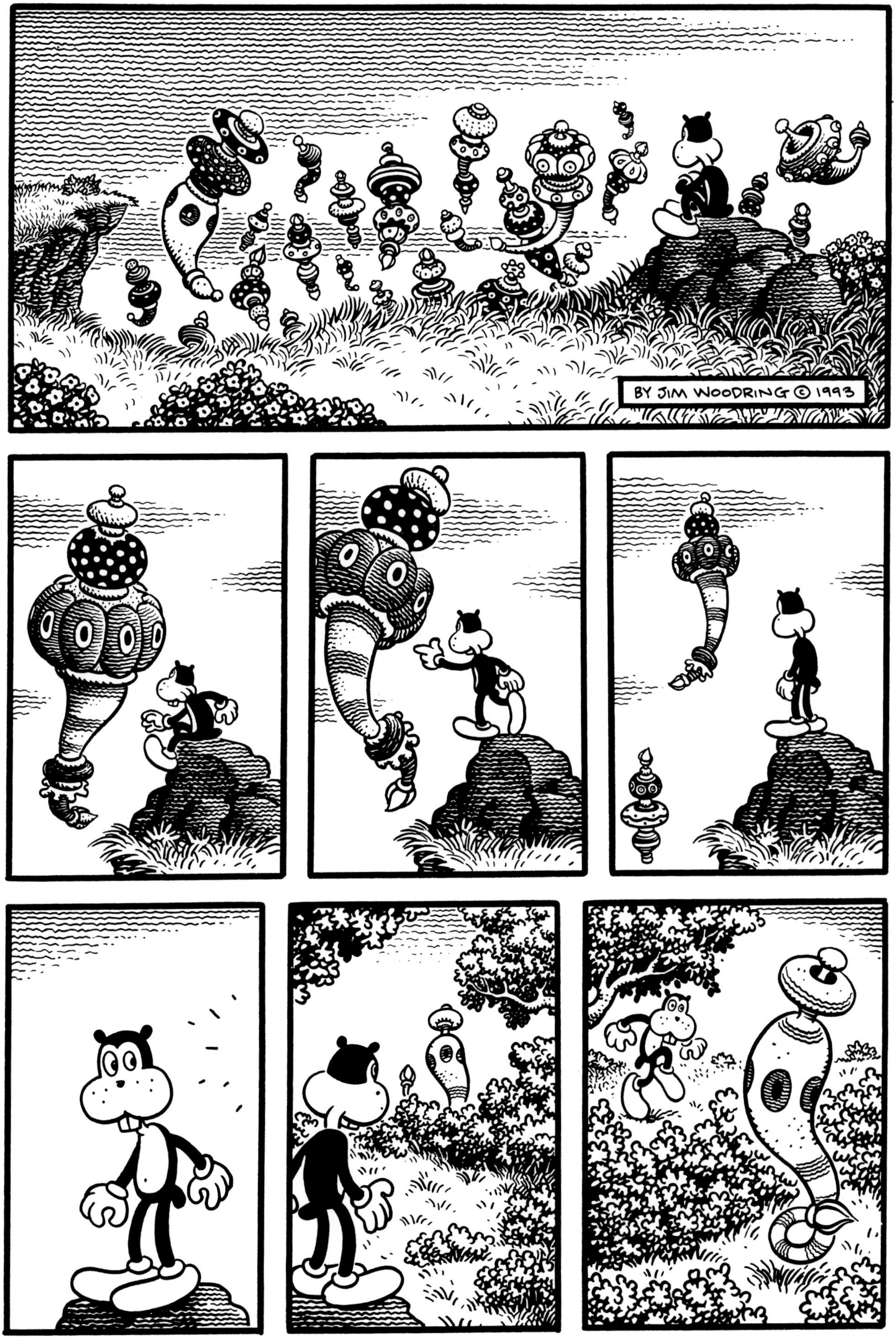
BY JIM WOODRING © 1993

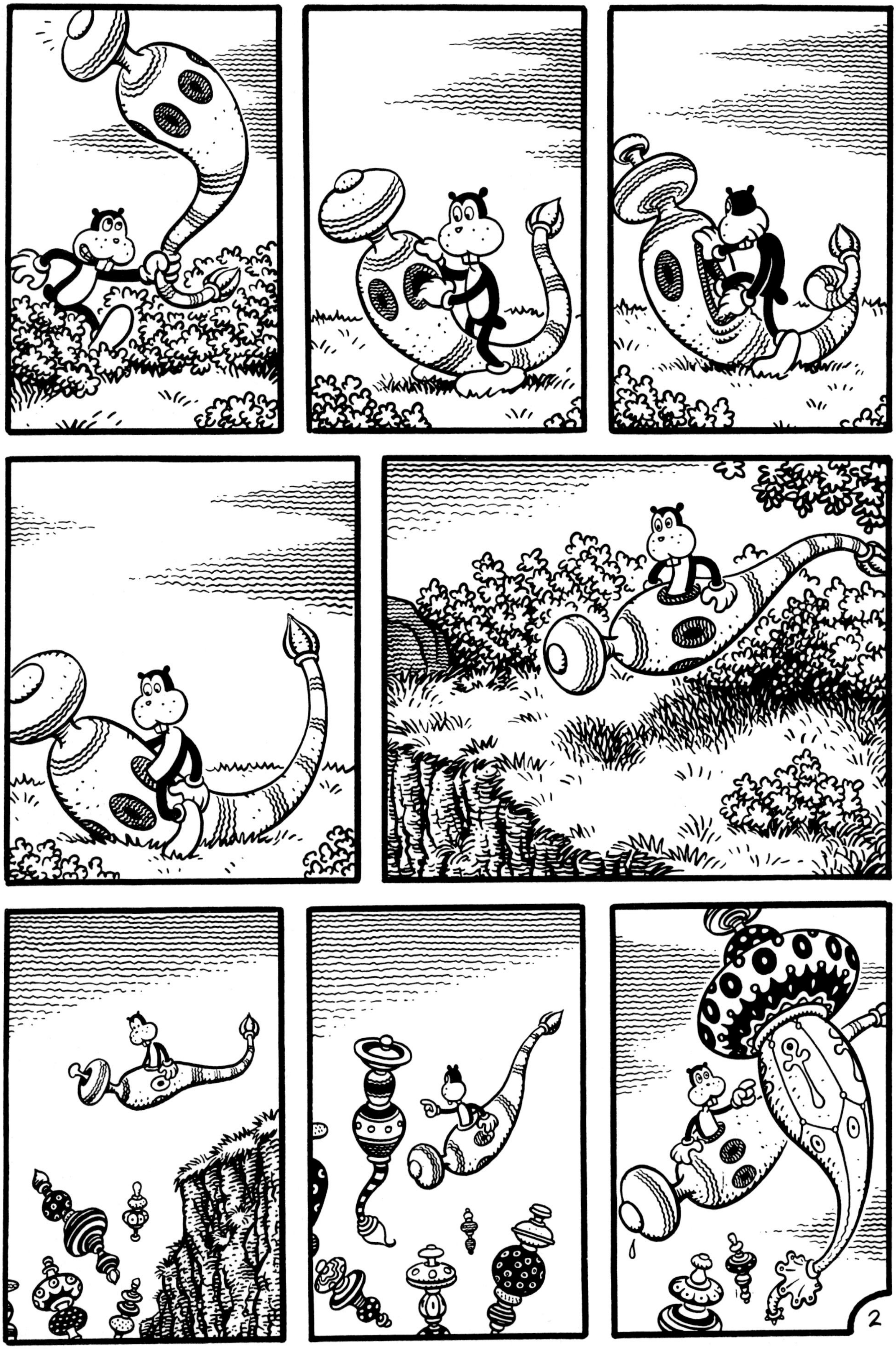
2

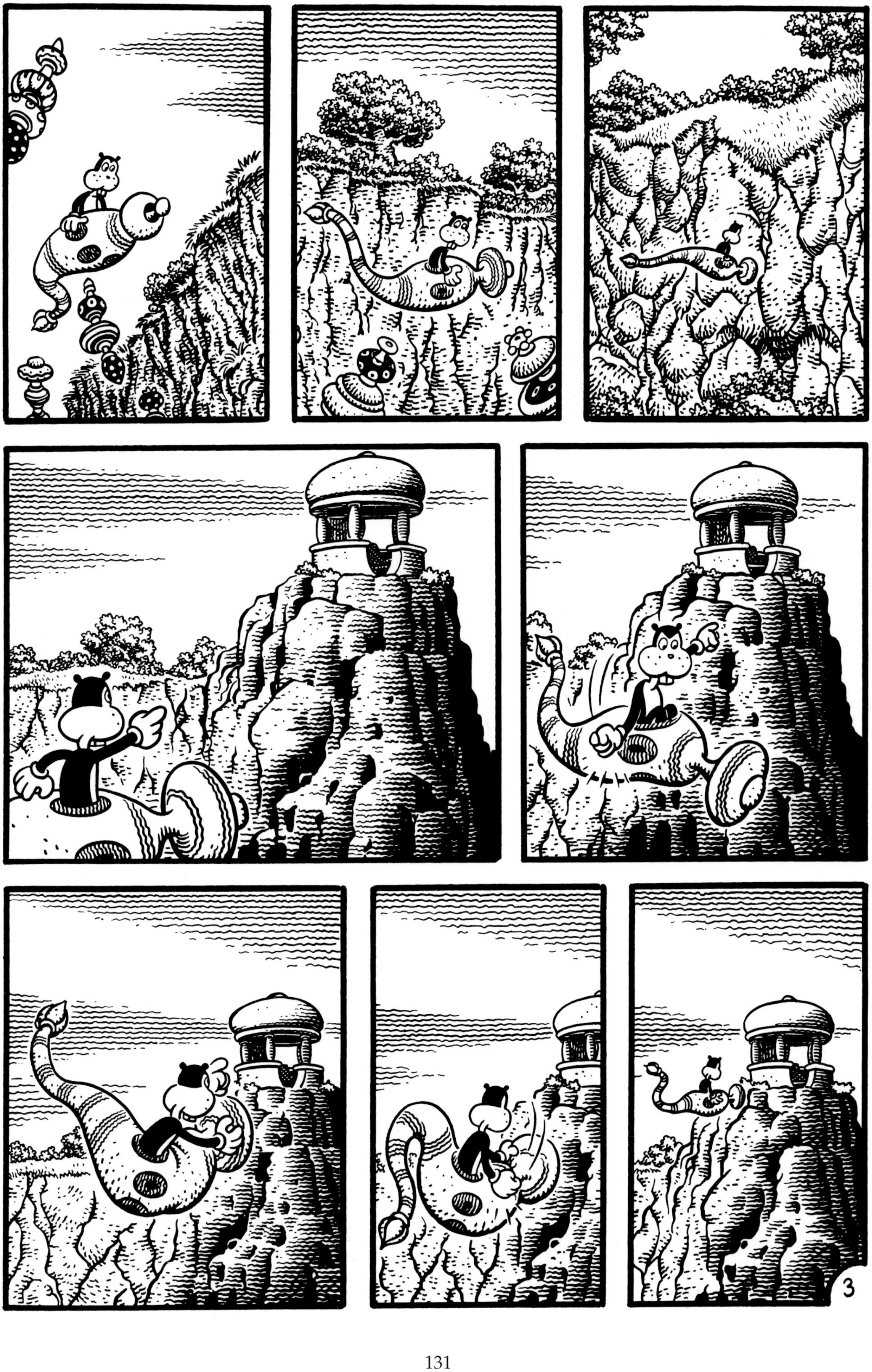
3

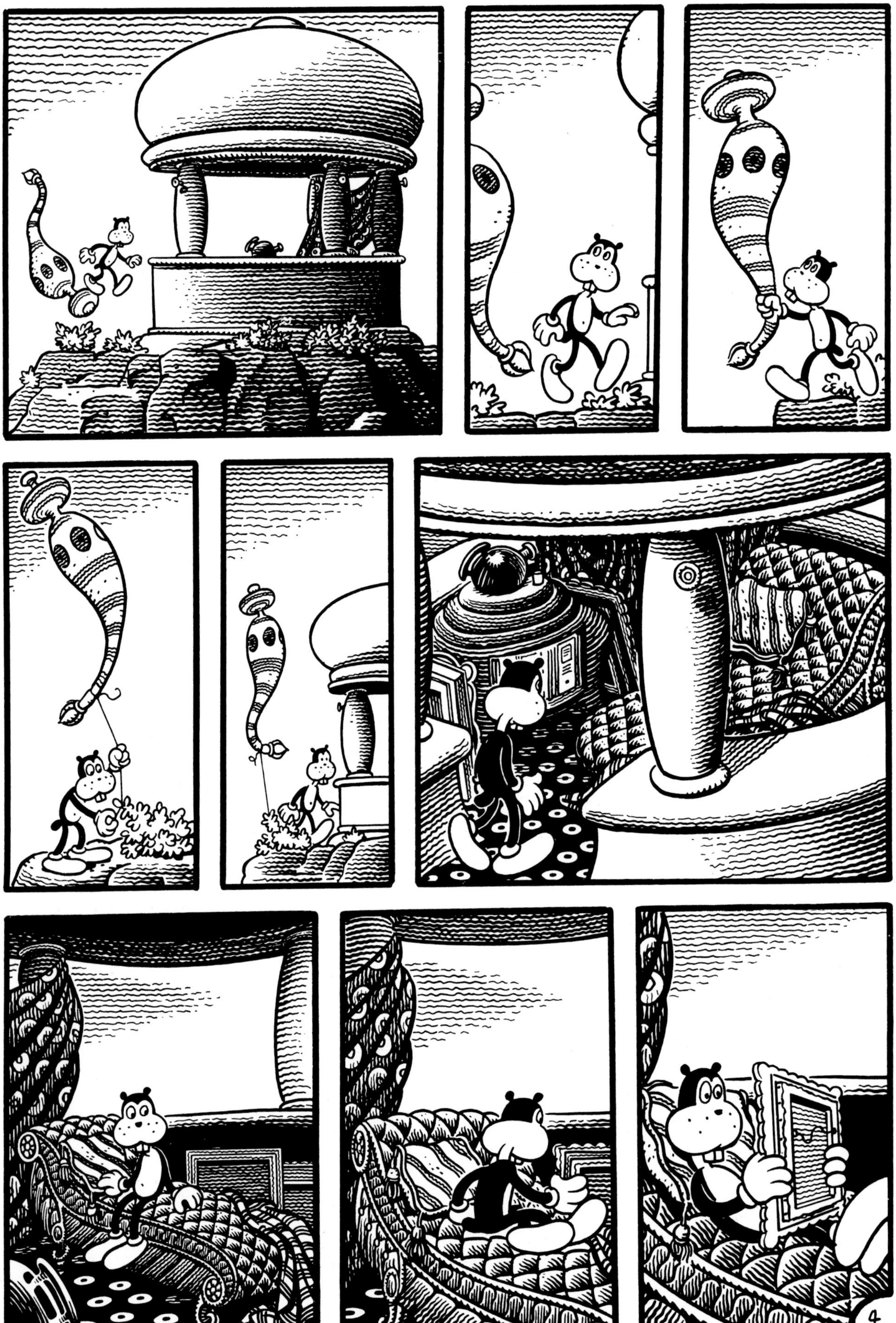
4

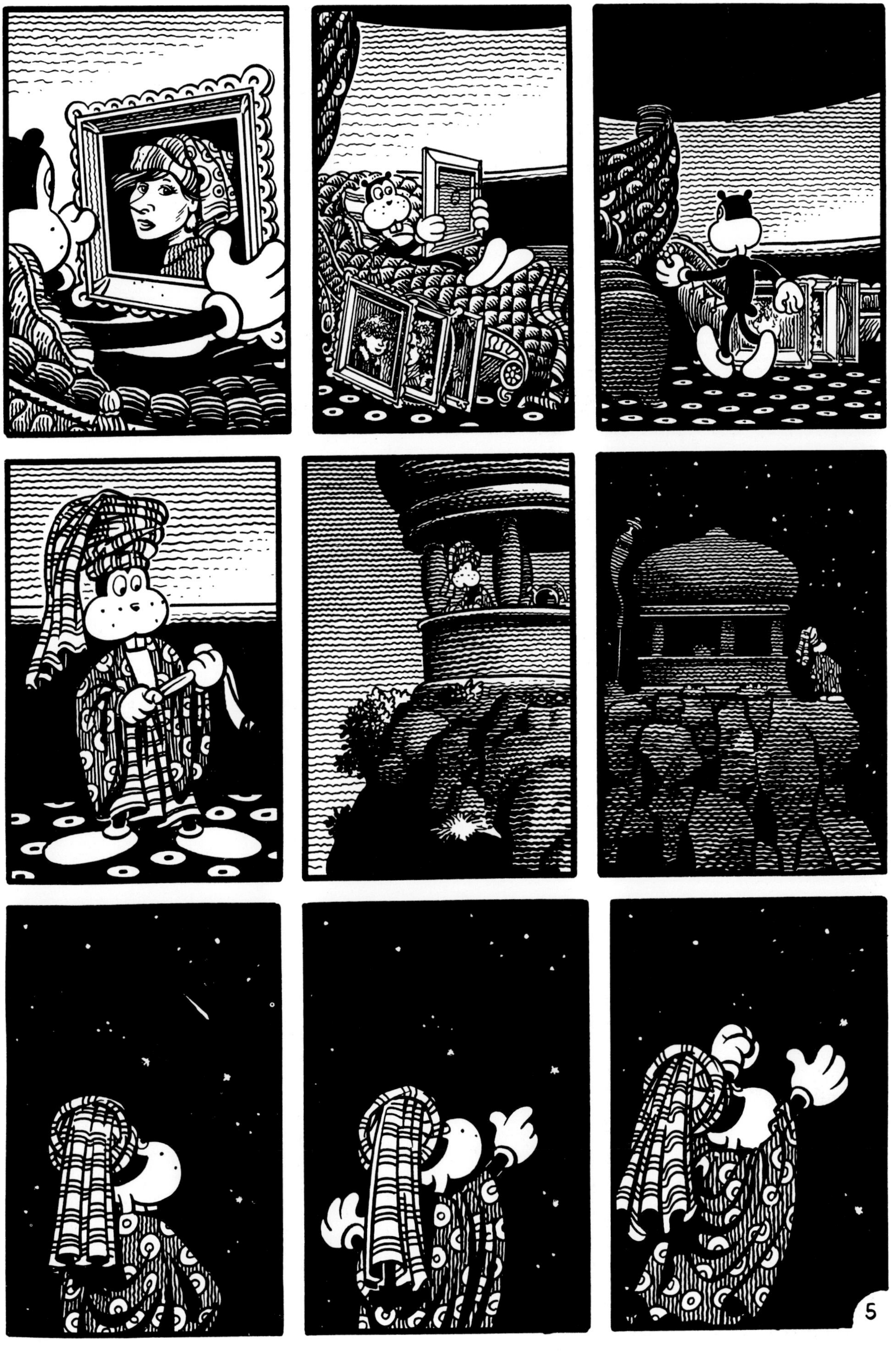
5

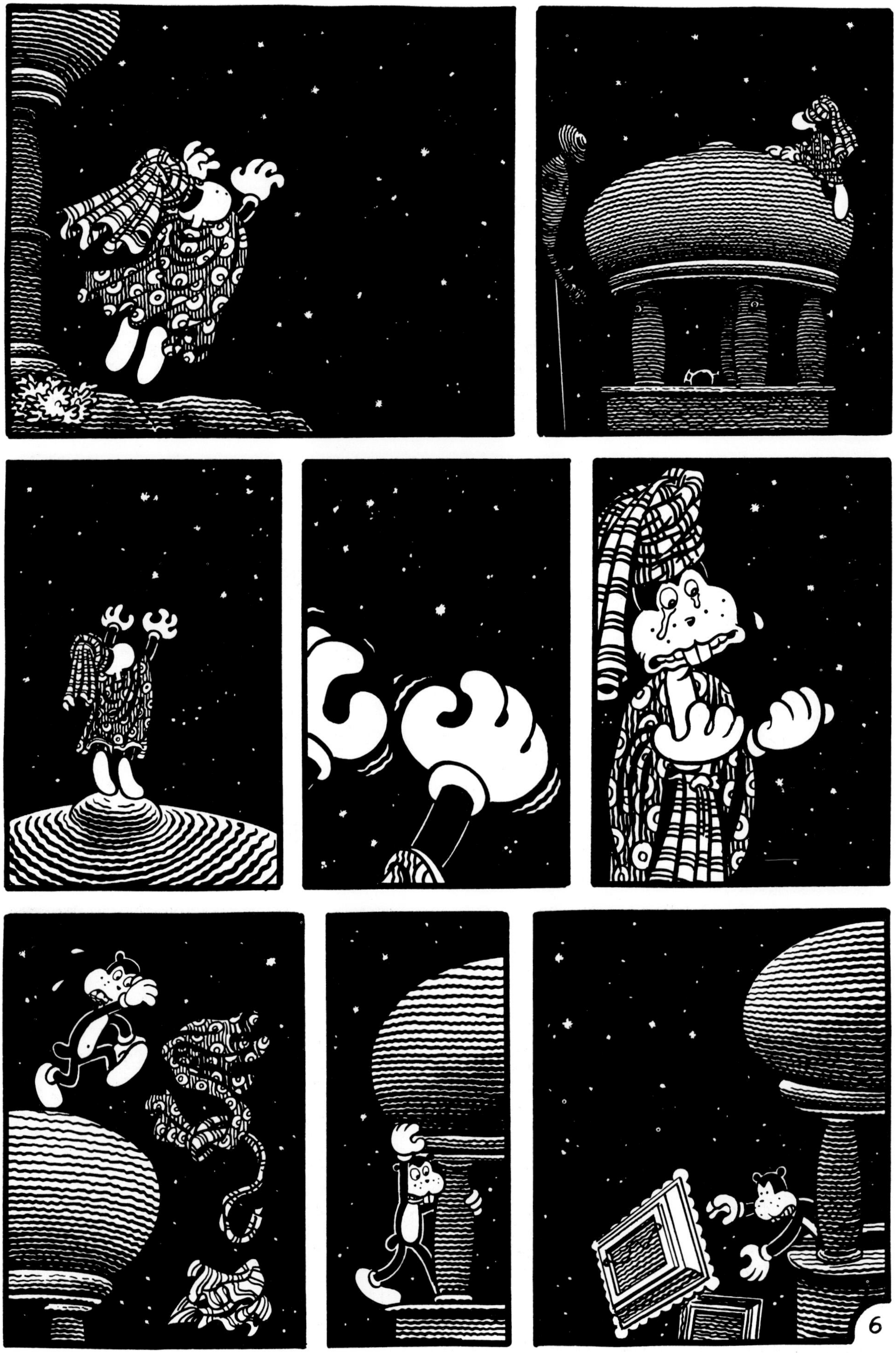
6

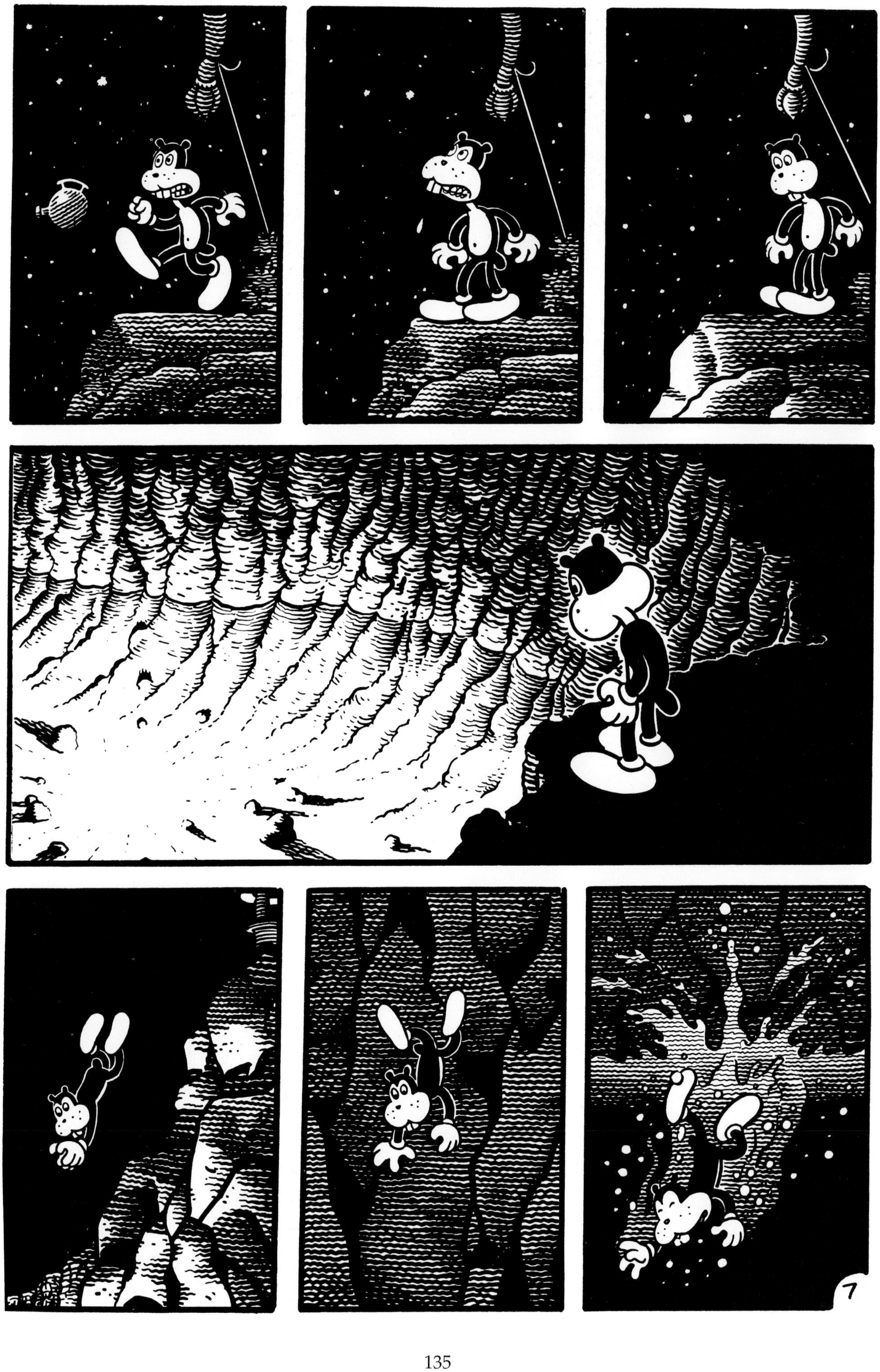

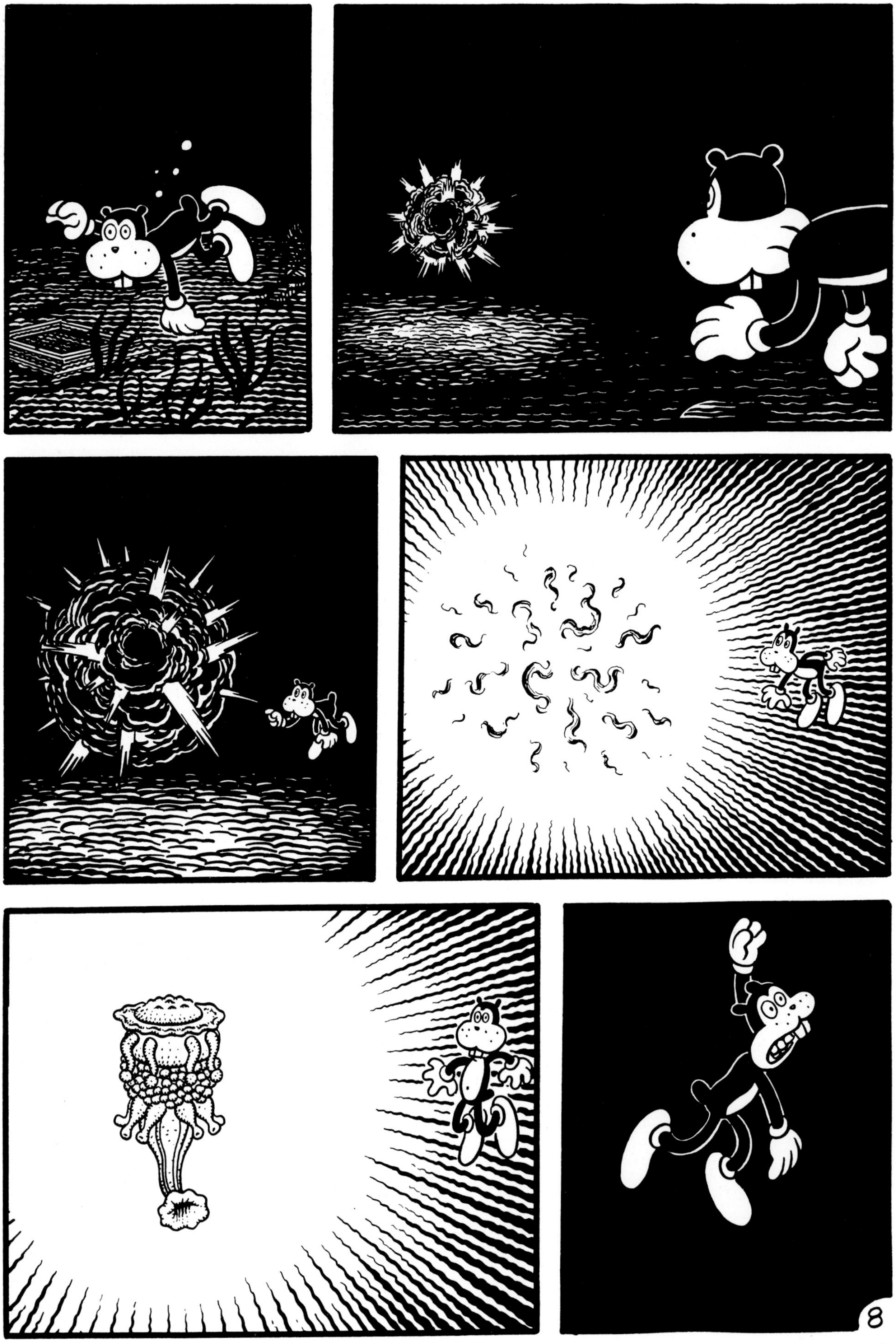
8

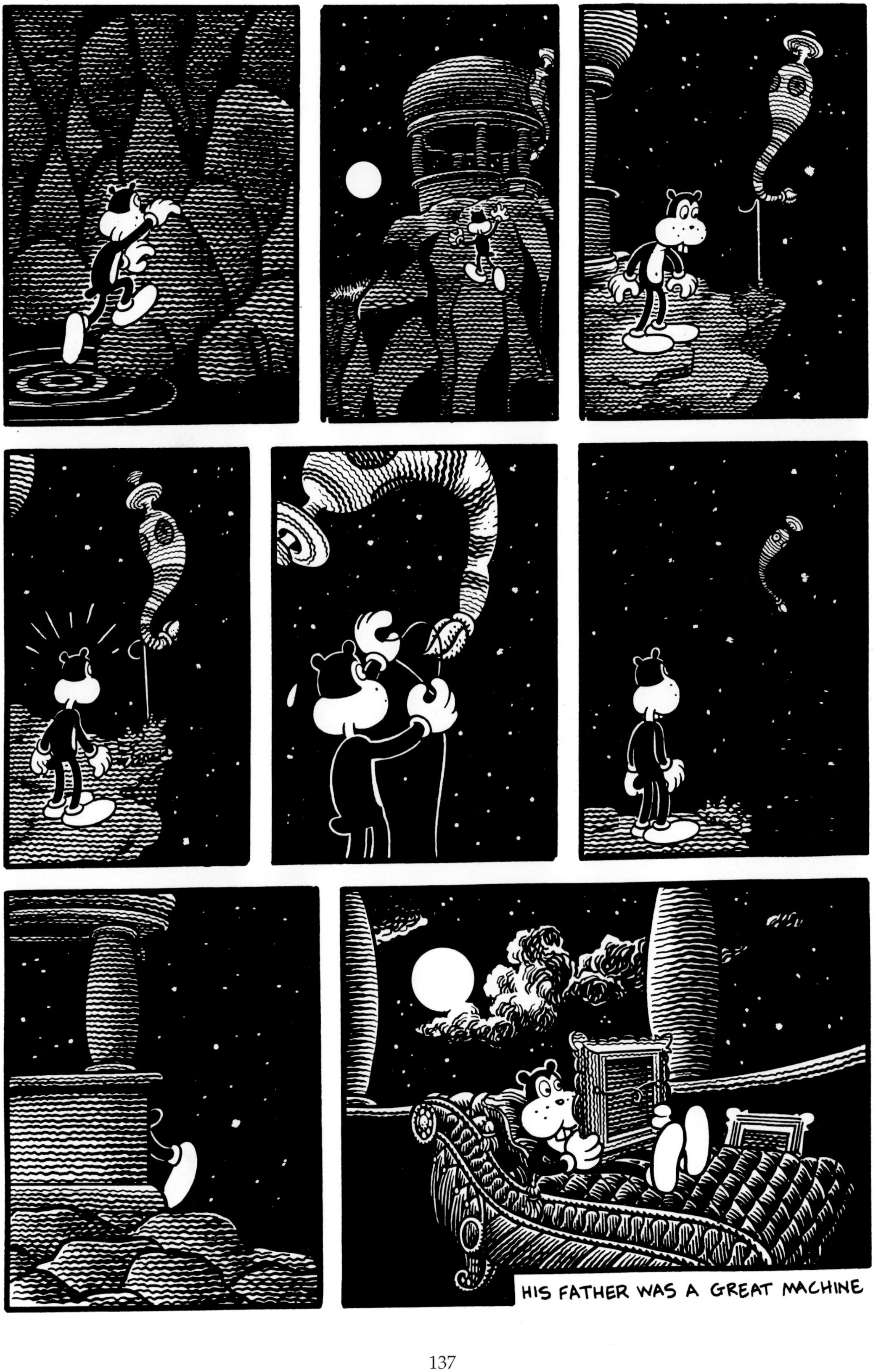
HIS FATHER WAS A GREAT MACHINE

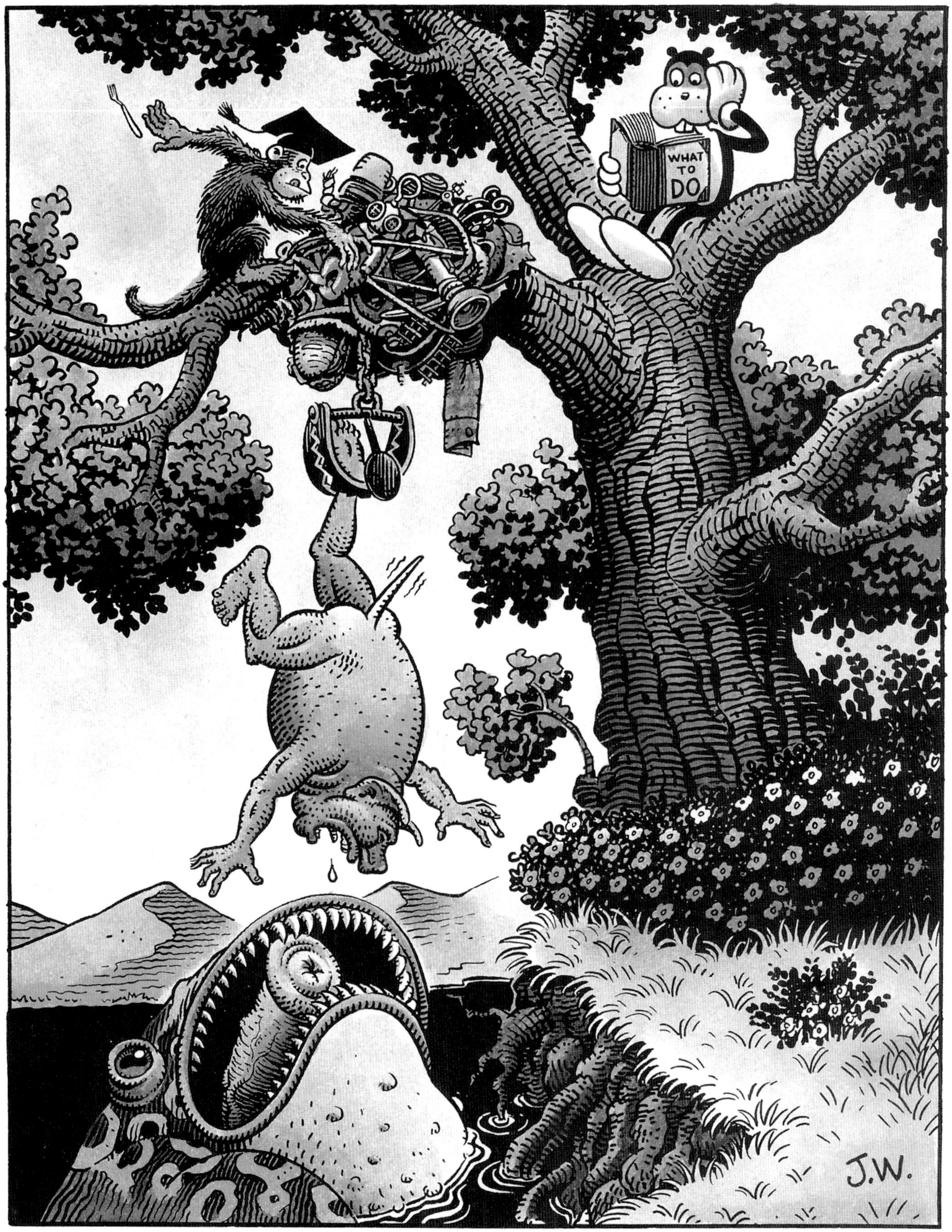
WHAT
TO
DO
J.W.

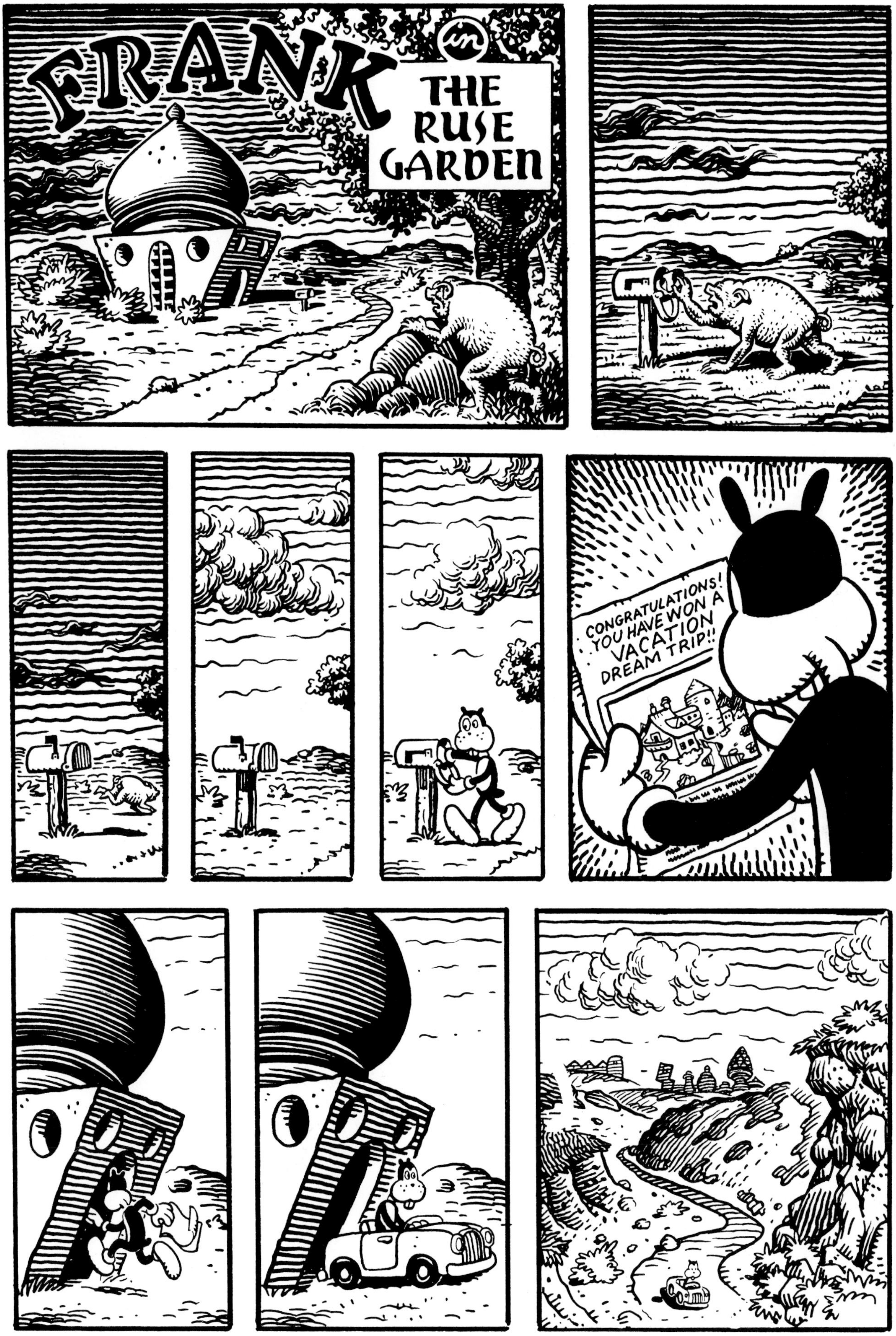
FRANK in THE RUSE GARDEN
CONGRATULATIONS! YOU HAVE WON A VACATION DREAM TRIP!!

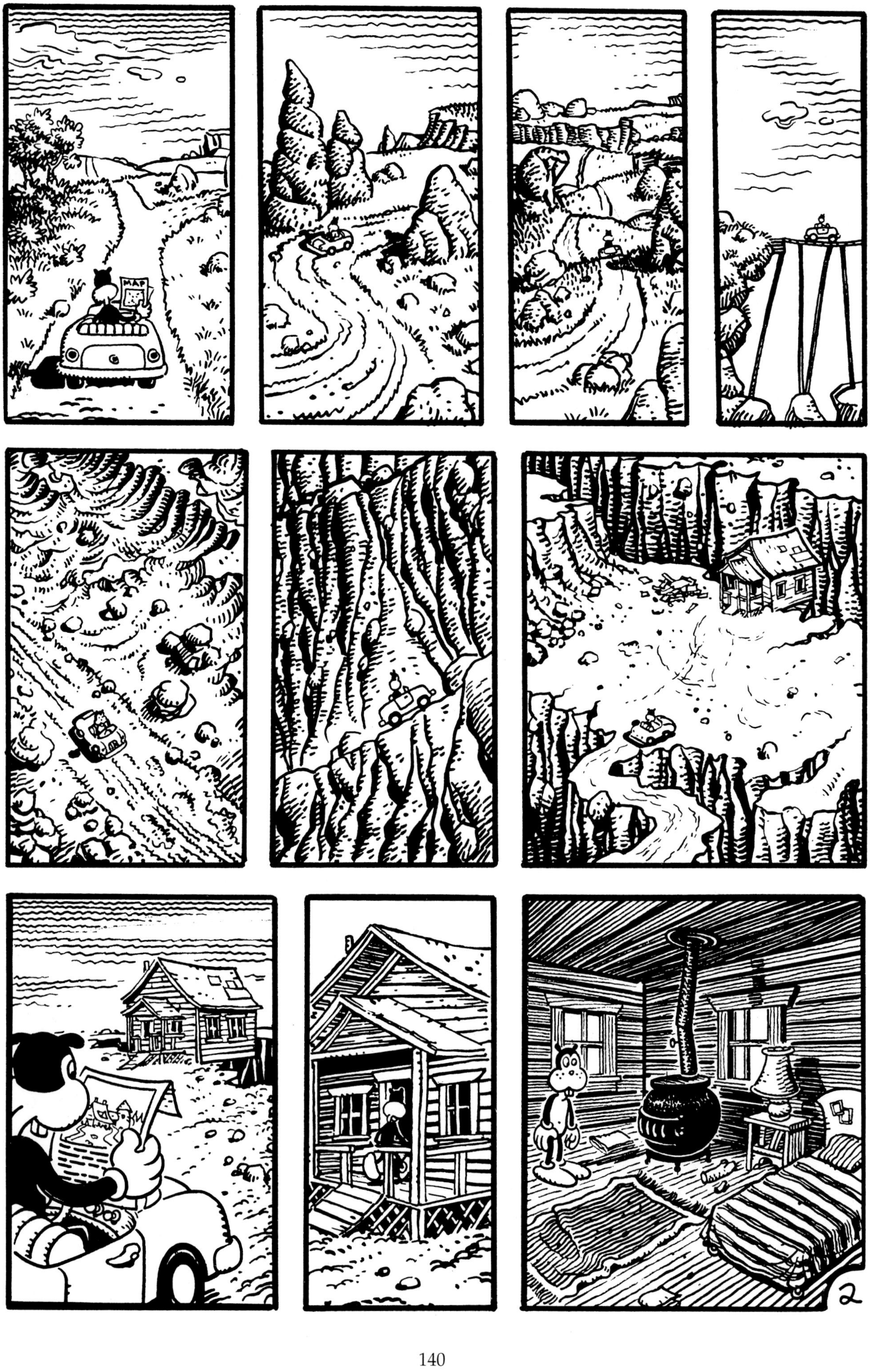
MAP
2

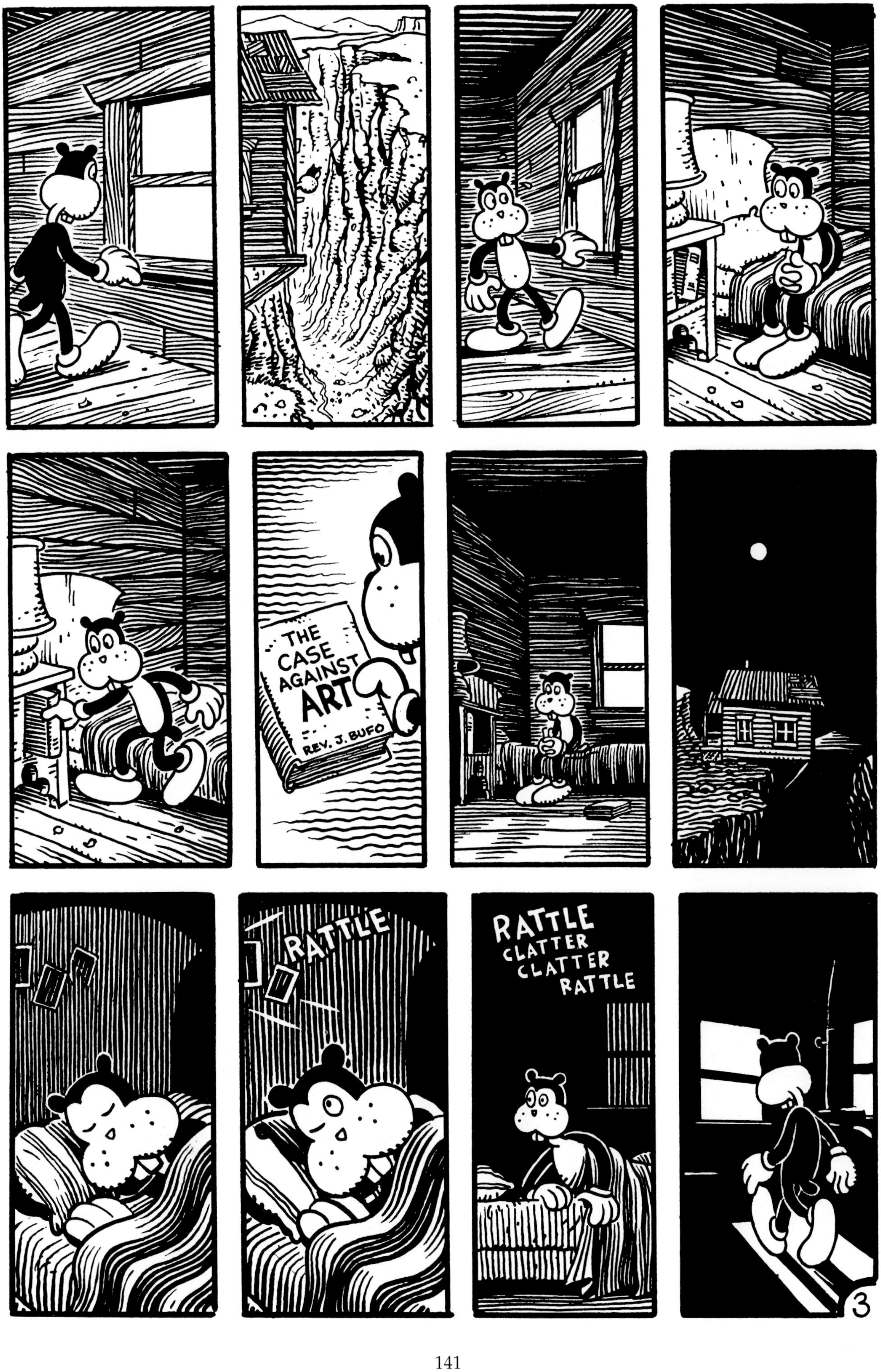
THE CASE AGAINST ART
REV. J. BUFO
RATTLE
RATTLE
CLATTER
CLATTER
RATTLE
3

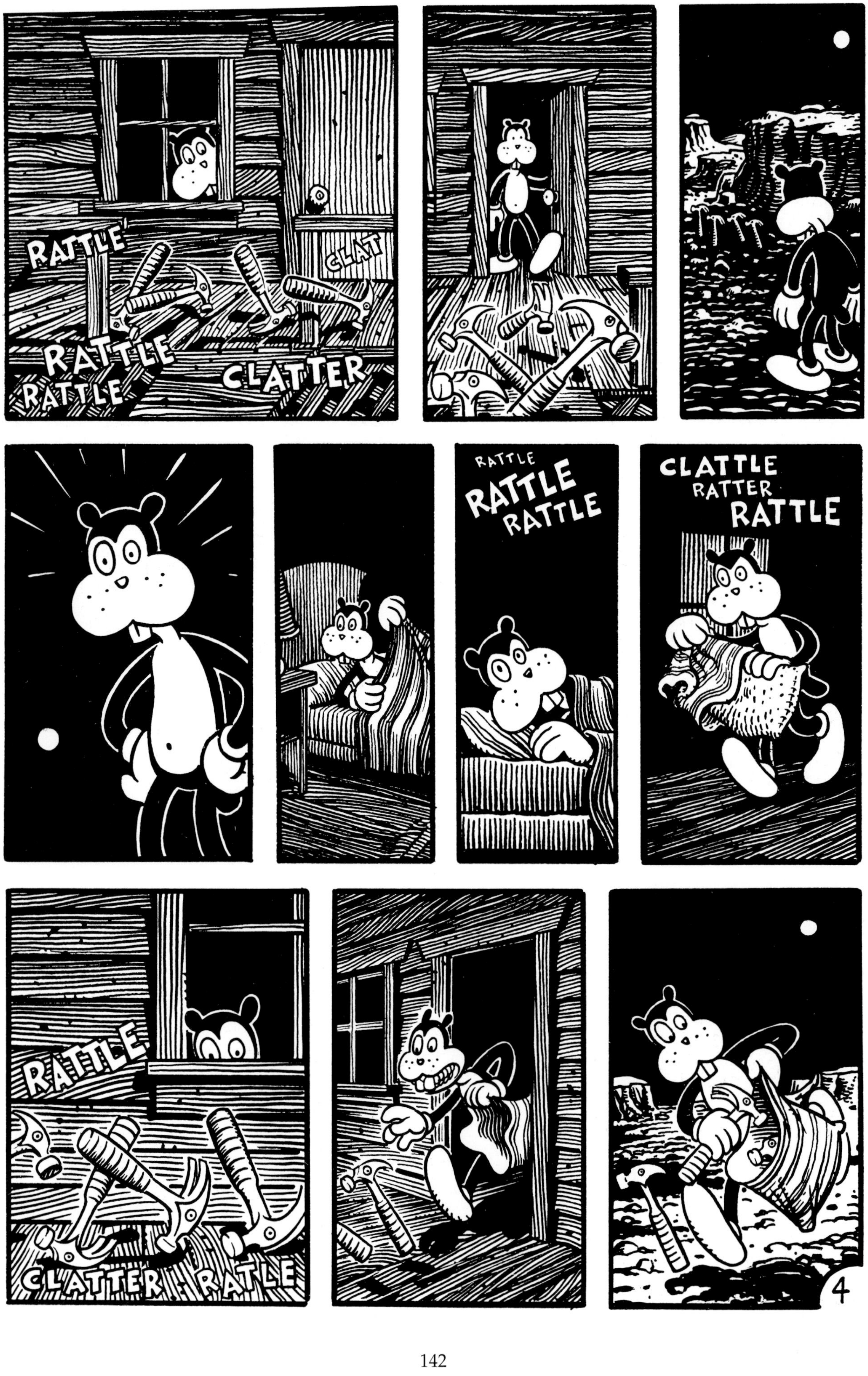
RATTLE
CLAT
RATTLE
RATTLE
CLATTER
RATTLE
RATTLE
RATTLE
CLATTLE
RATTER
RATTLE
RATTLE
CLATTER
RATTLE
4

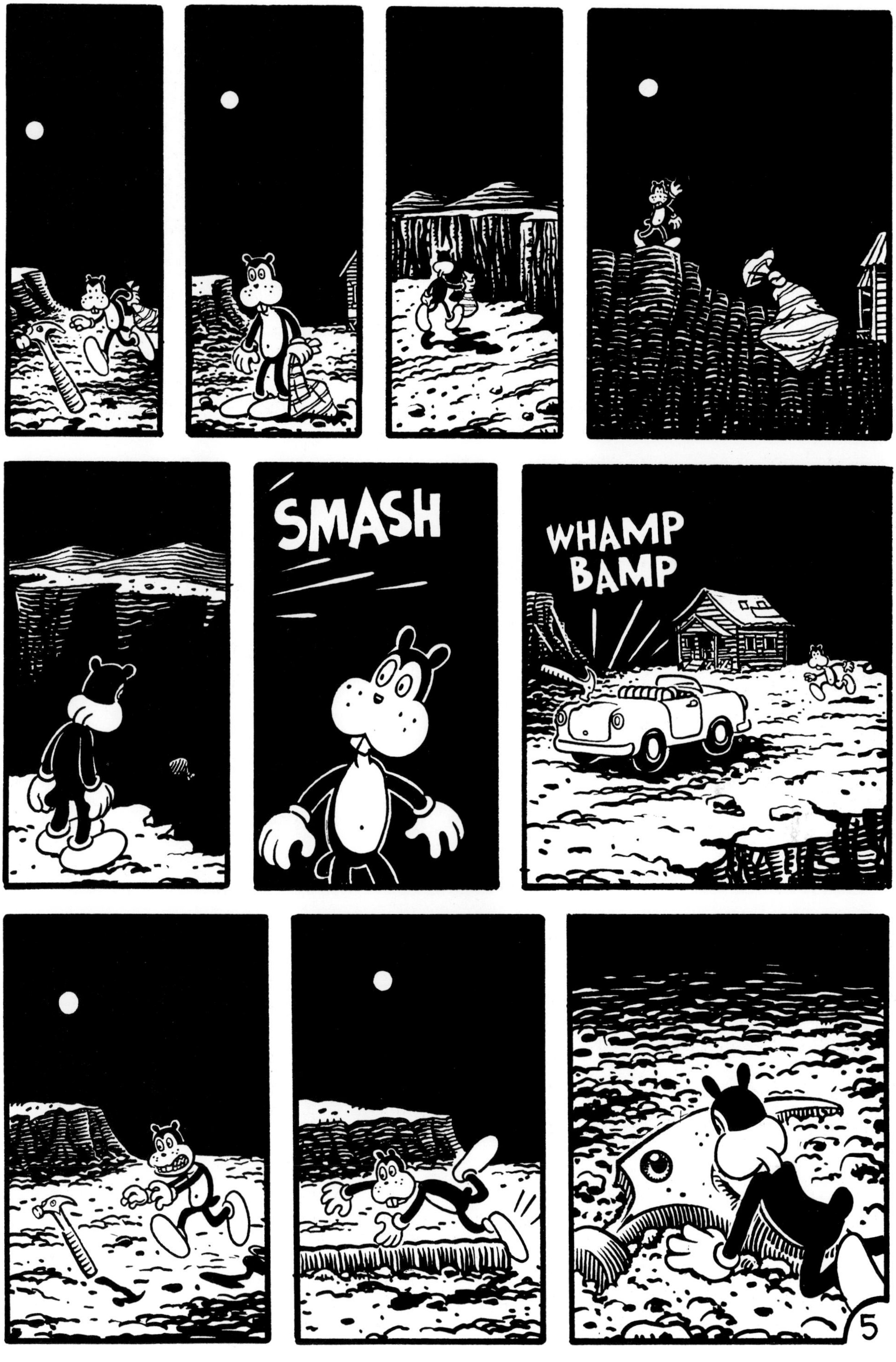
SMASH
WHAMP
BAMP
5

6

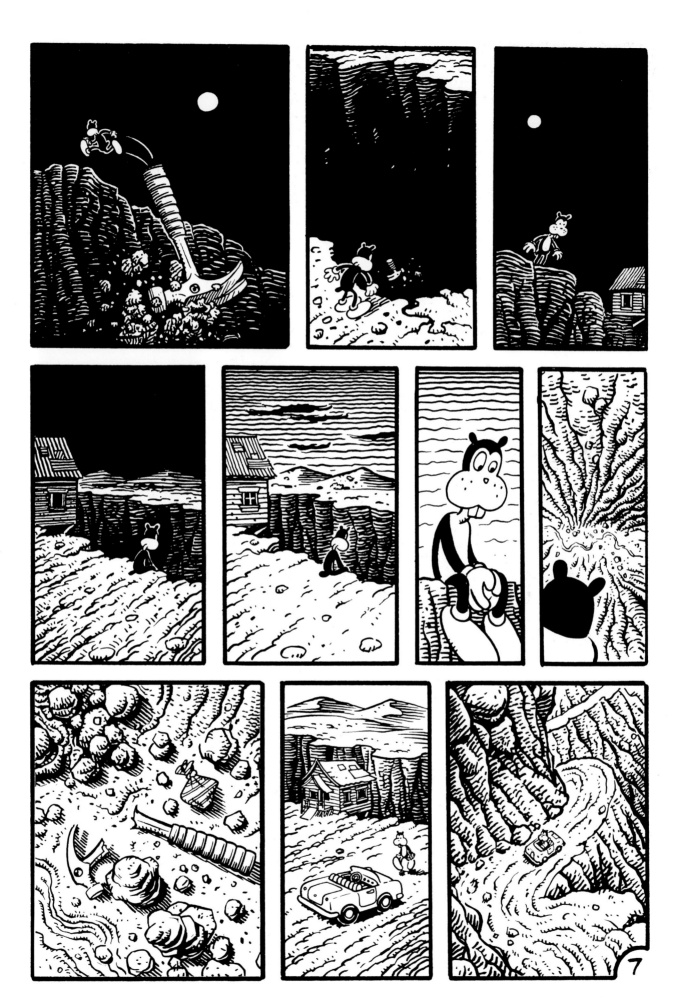

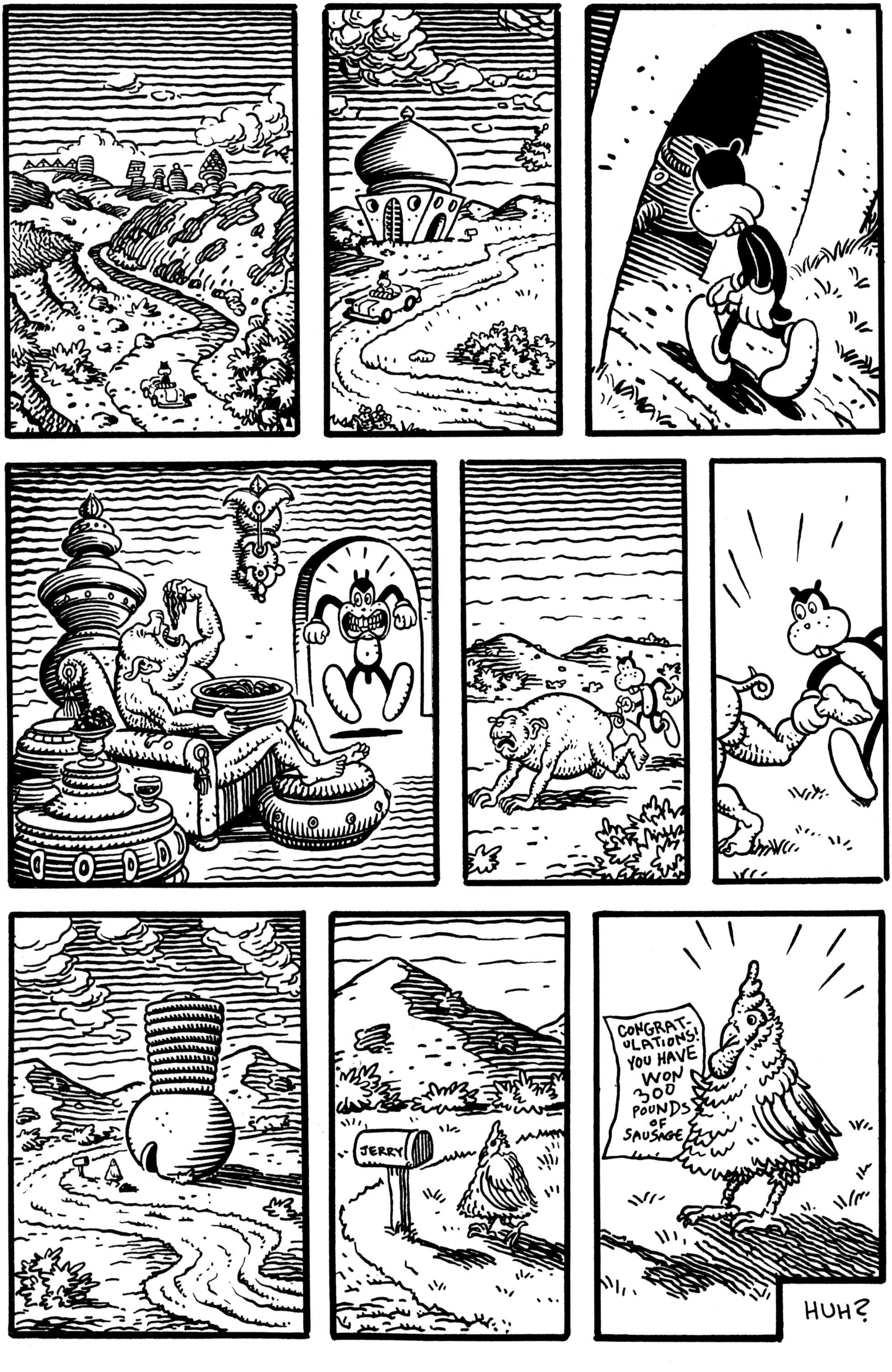
JERRY
CONGRAT-
ULATIONS!
YOU HAVE
WON
300
POUNDS
OF
SAUSAGE
HUH?

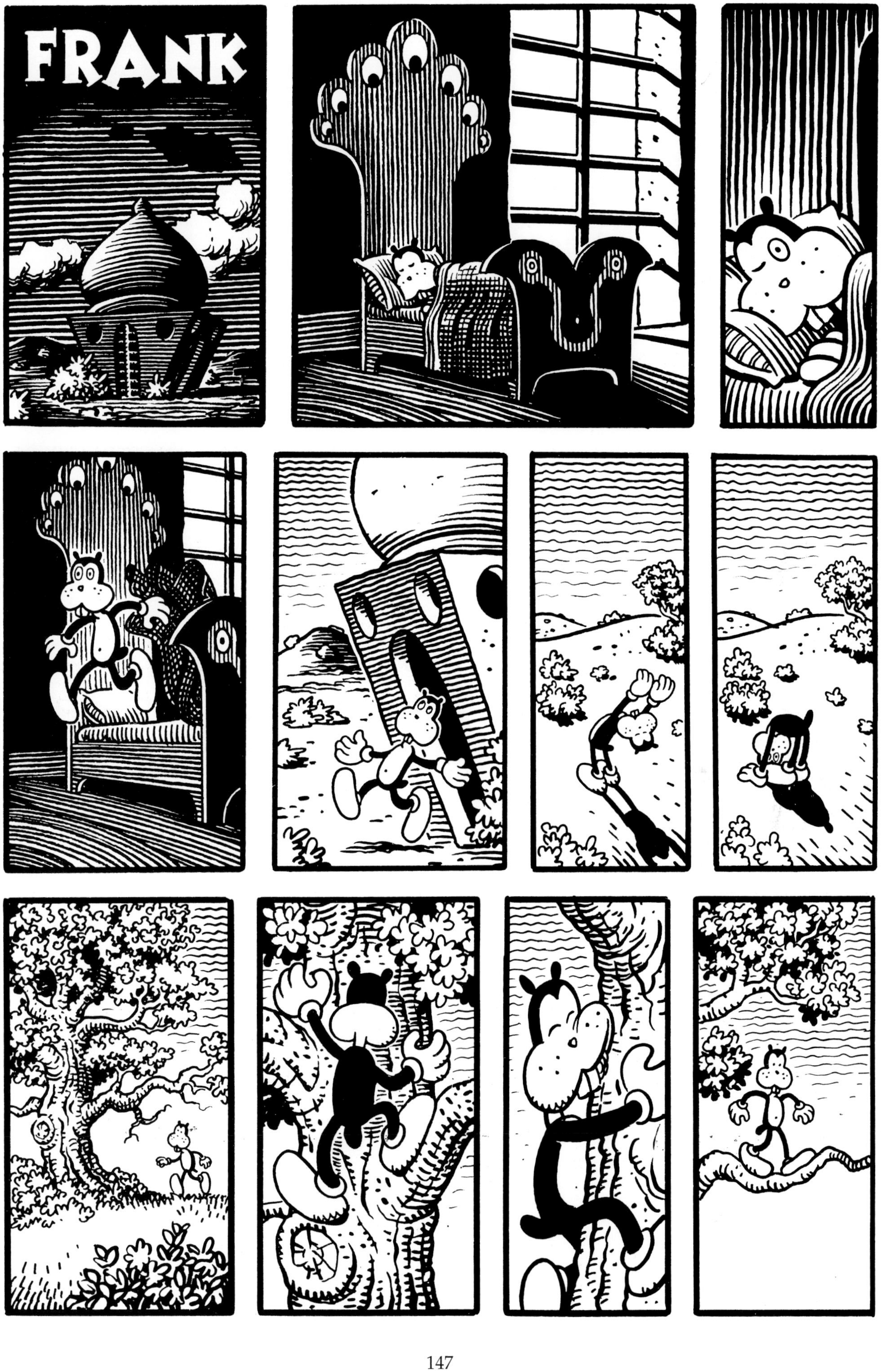
FRANK

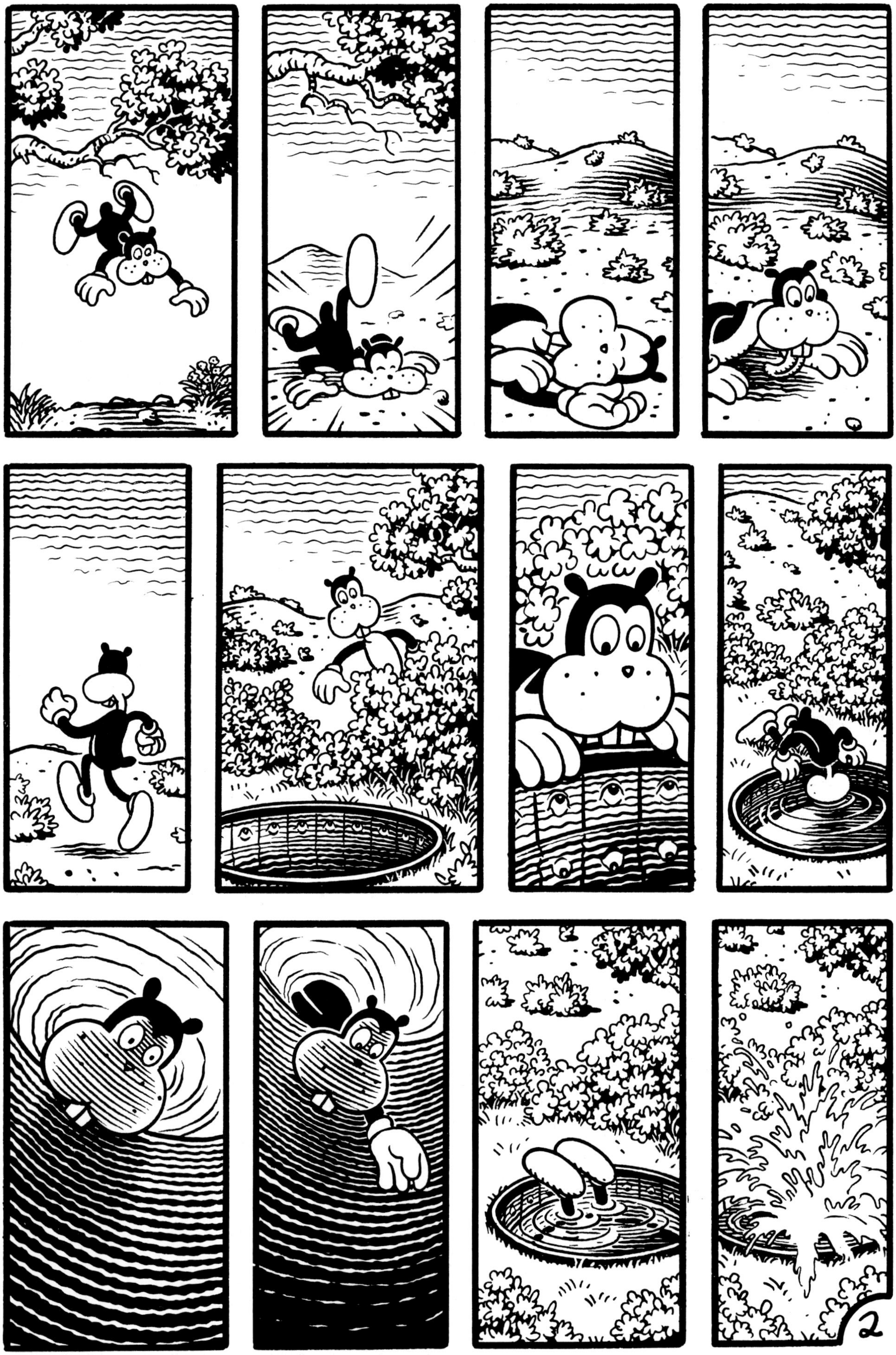
2

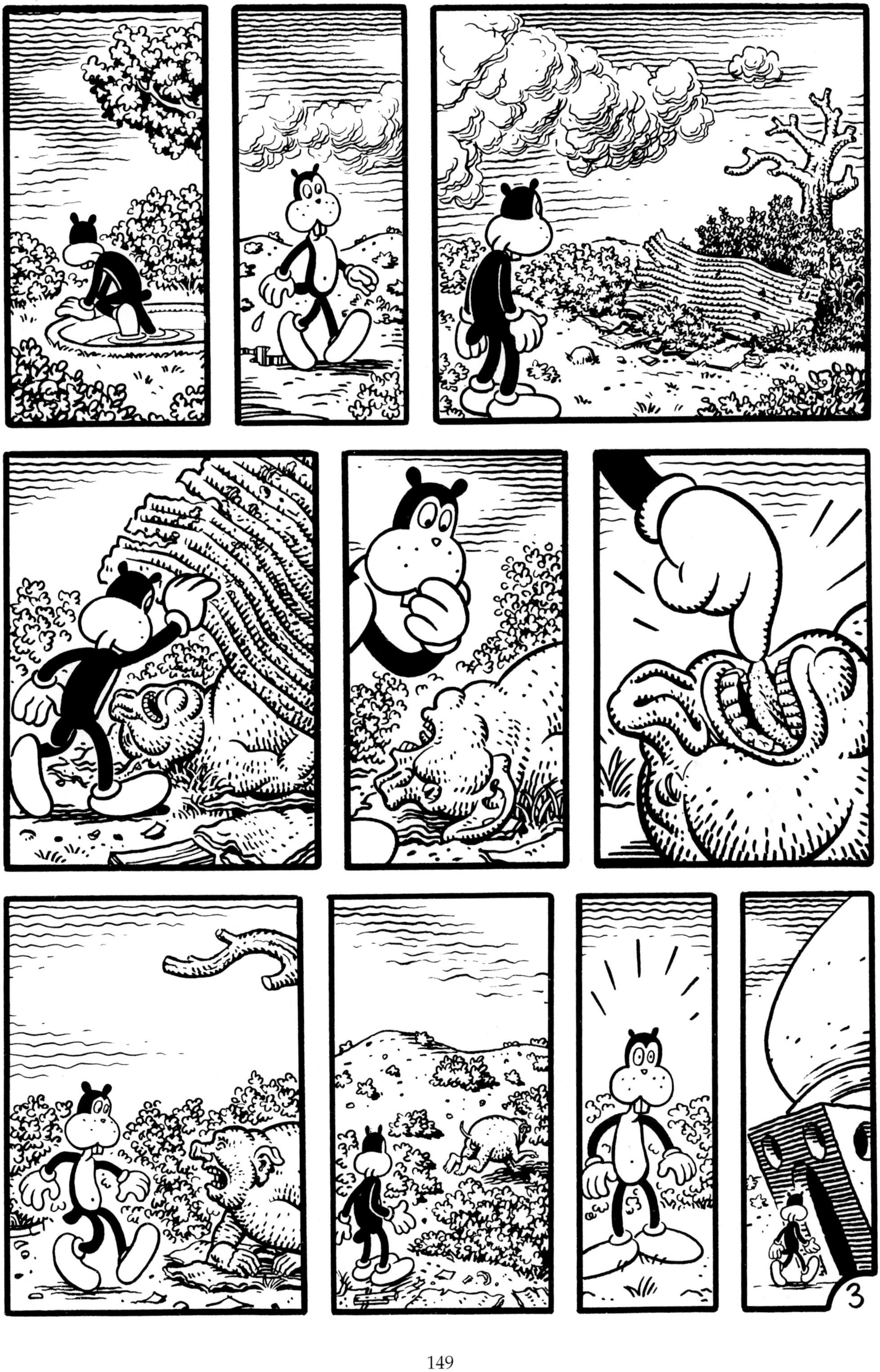
3

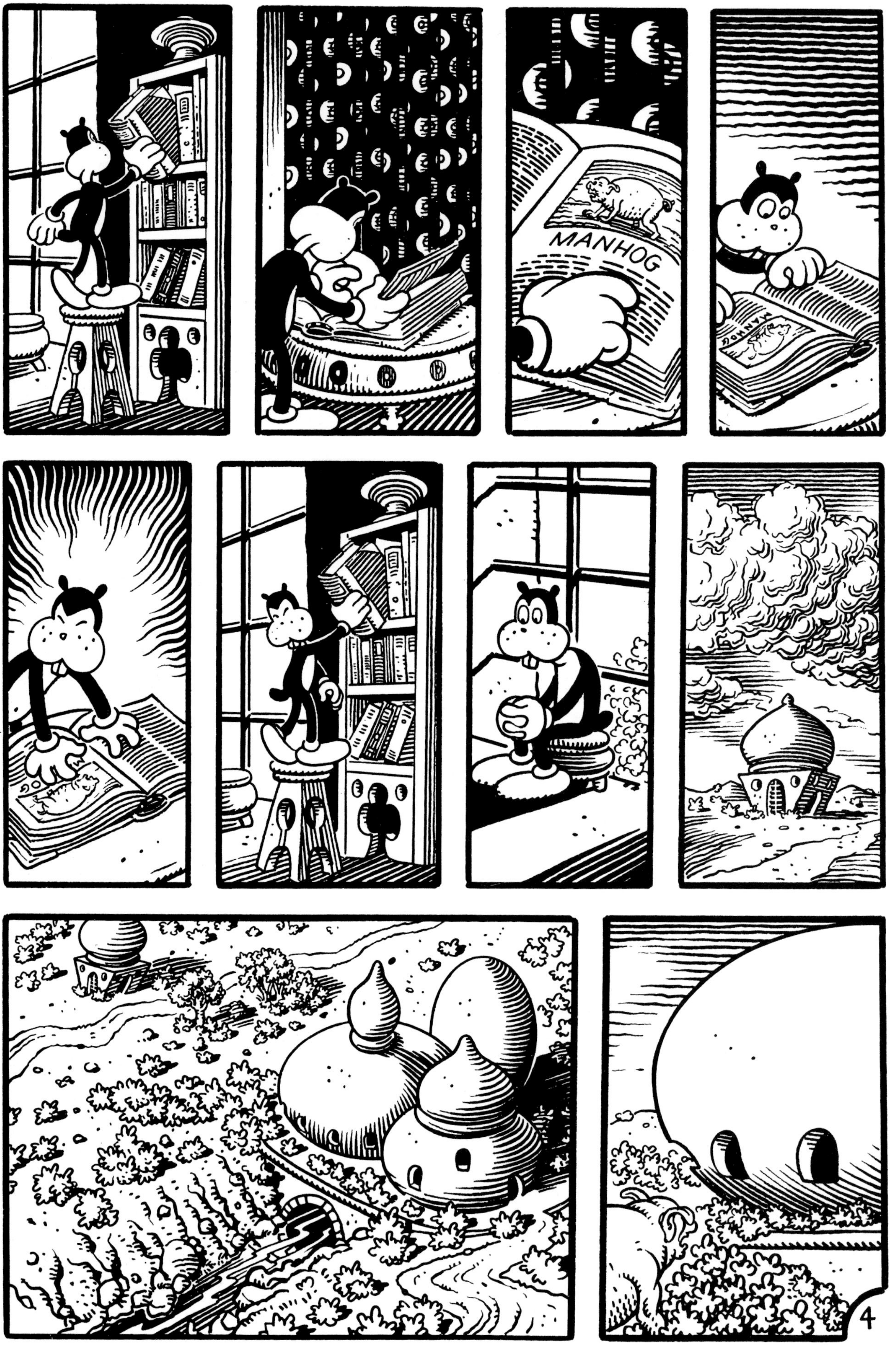
MANHOG
4

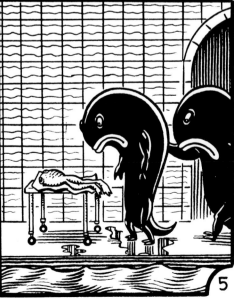

5

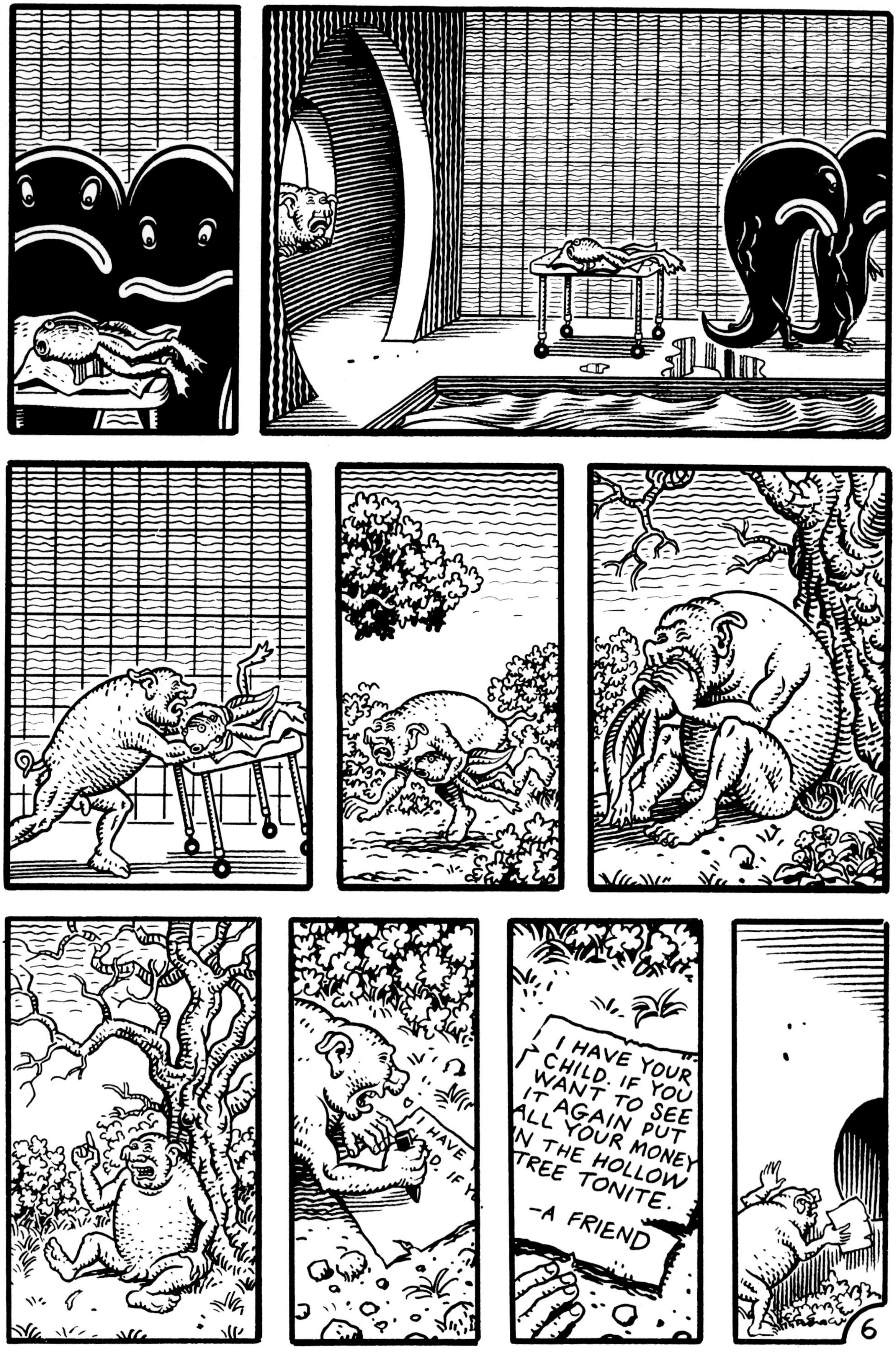
I HAVE YOUR CHILD. IF YOU WANT TO SEE IT AGAIN PUT ALL YOUR MONEY IN THE HOLLOW TREE TONITE.
-A FRIEND
6

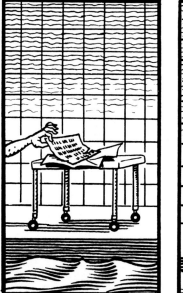

CLOBBERED
PLEASE
GIVE

7

153

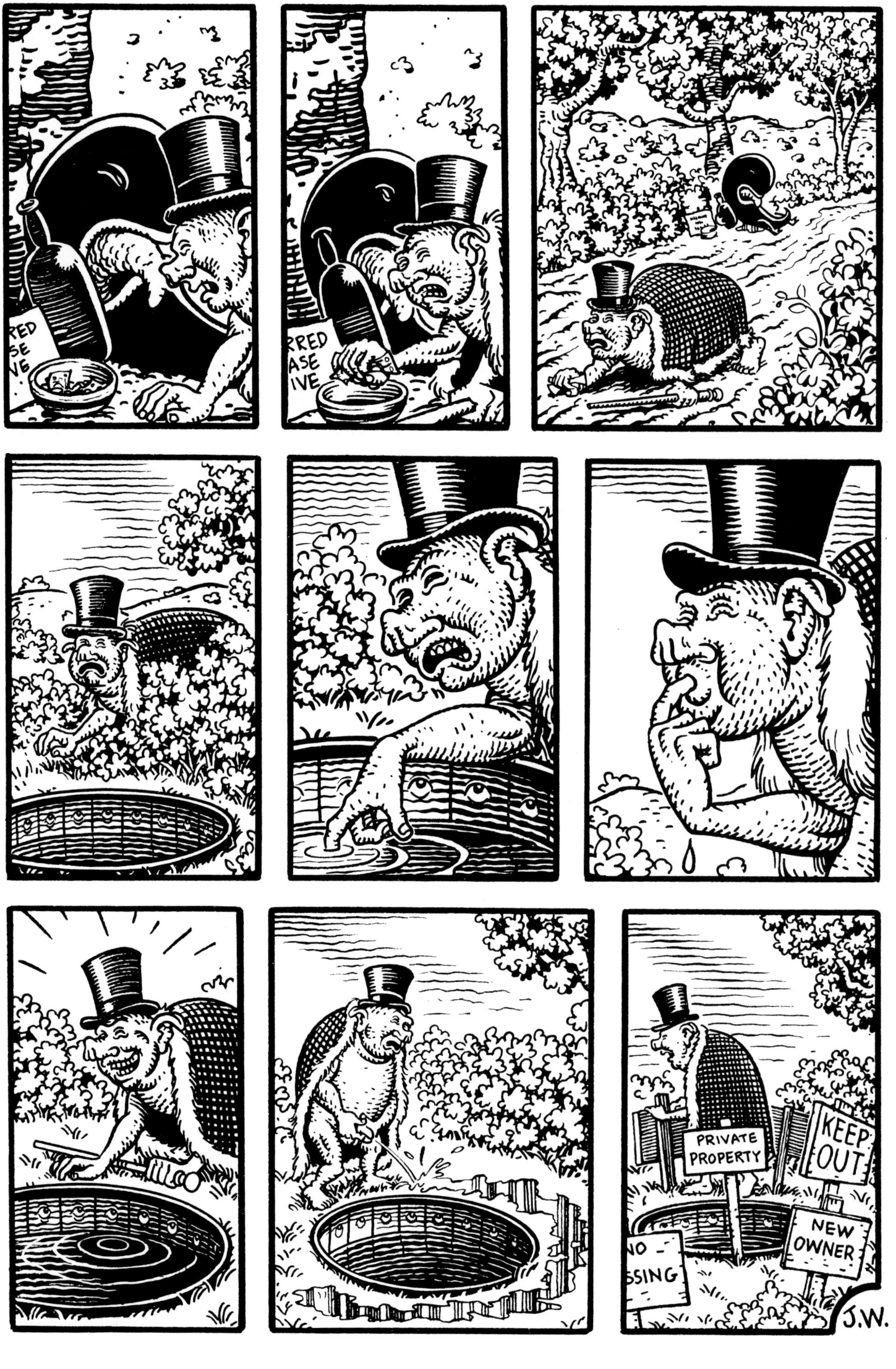
RED
SE
VE
RED
ASE
IVE
PRIVATE PROPERTY
KEEP OUT
NO -
SSING
NEW OWNER
J.W.

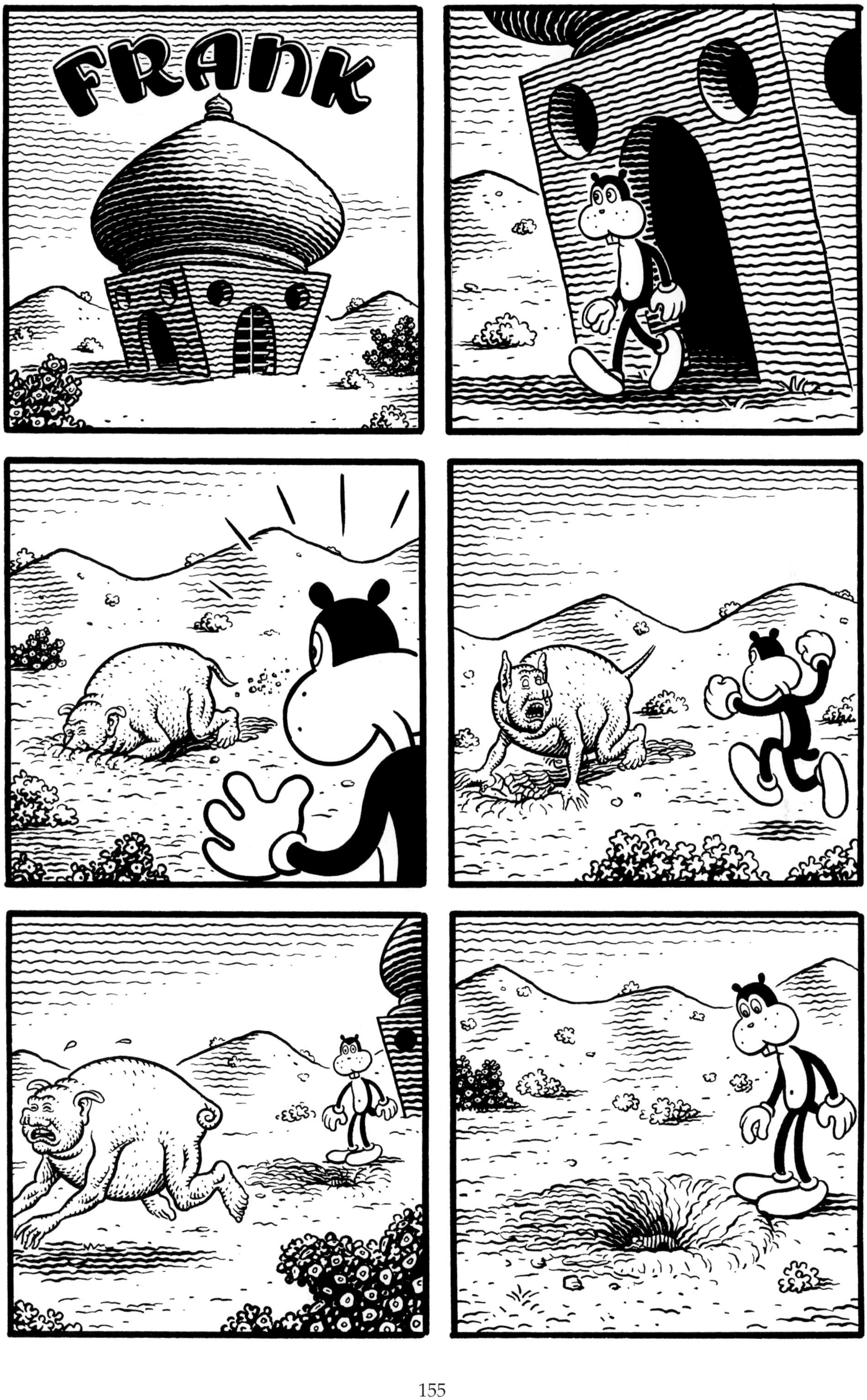
FRANK

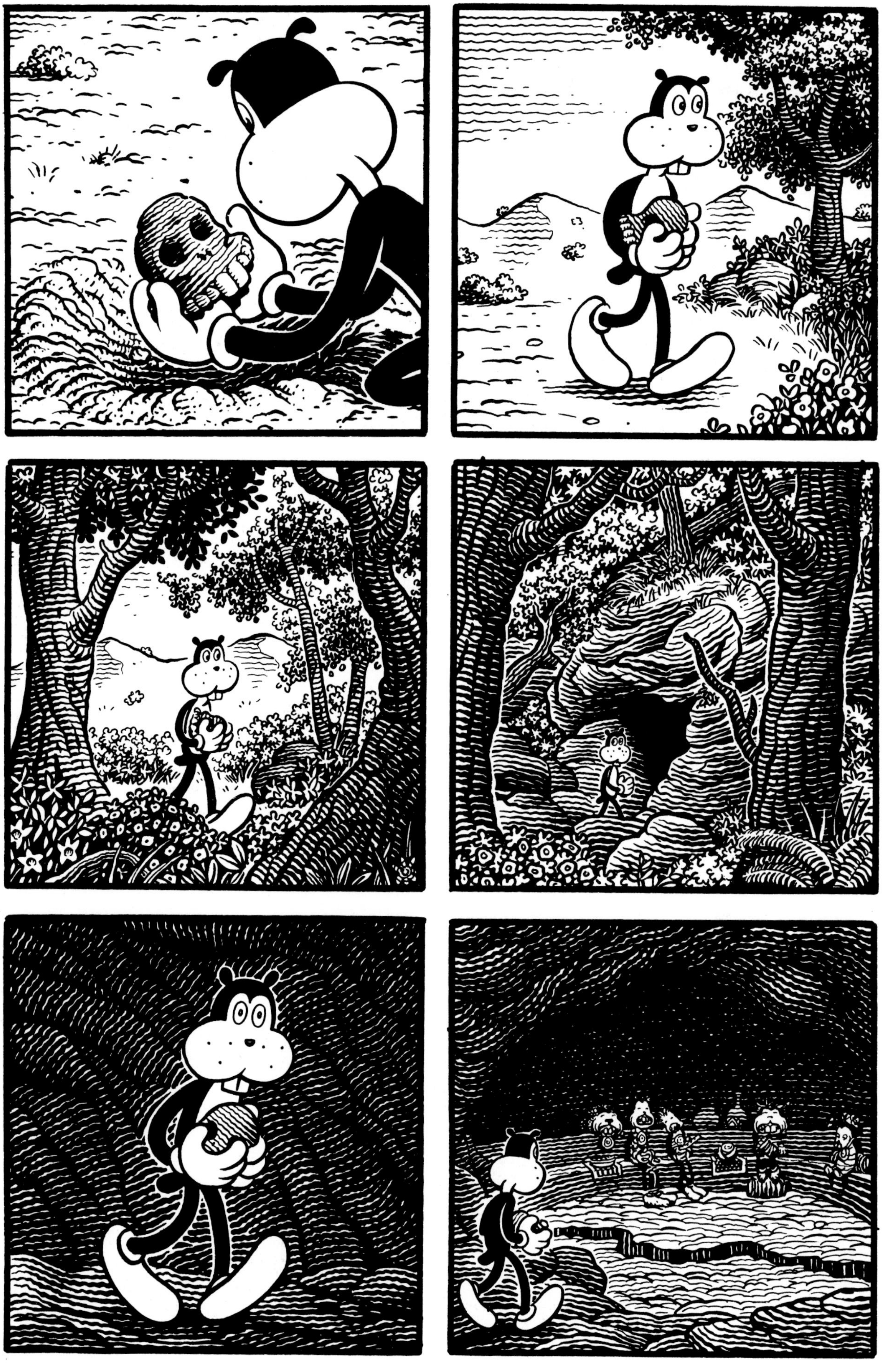

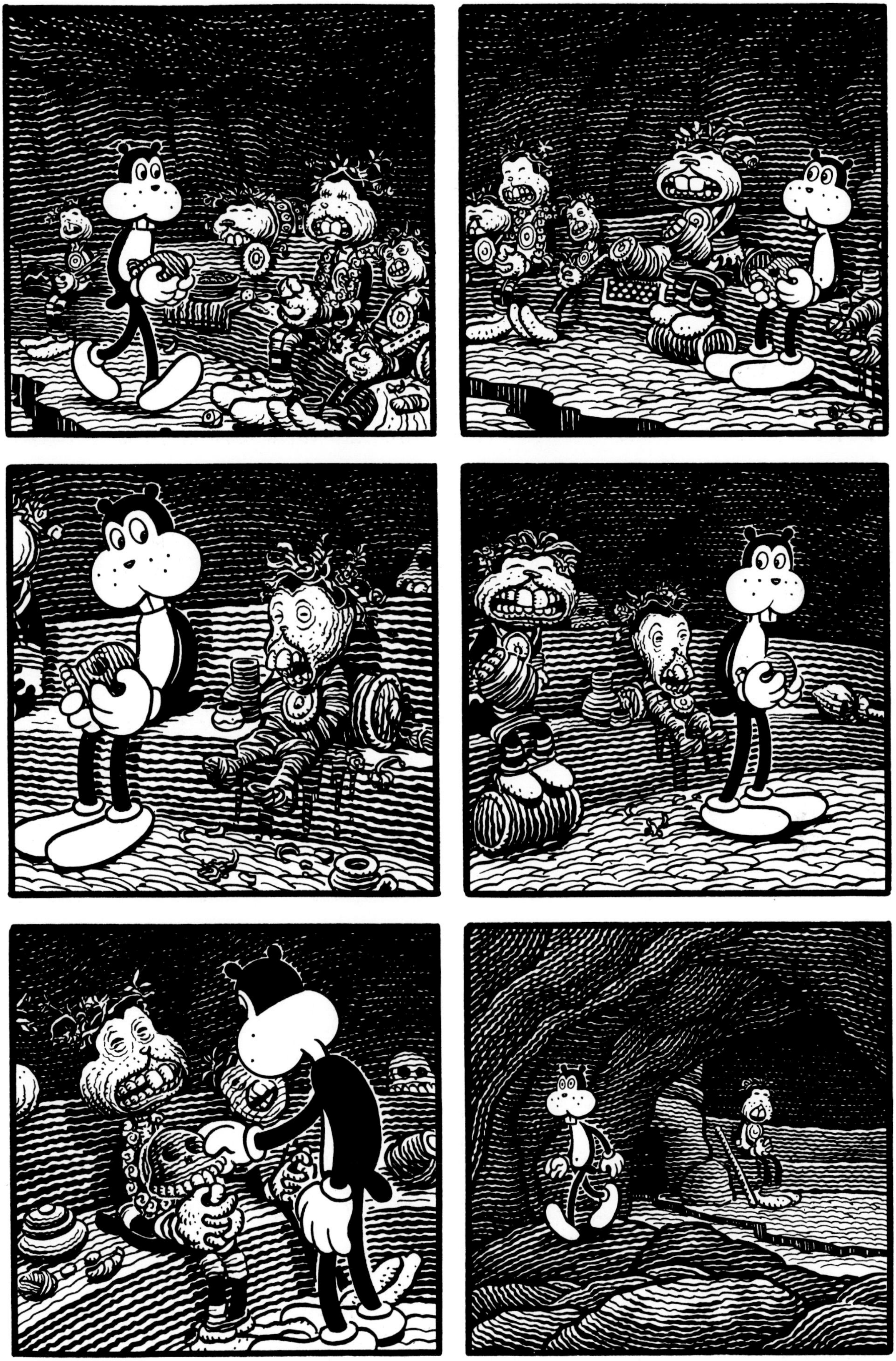

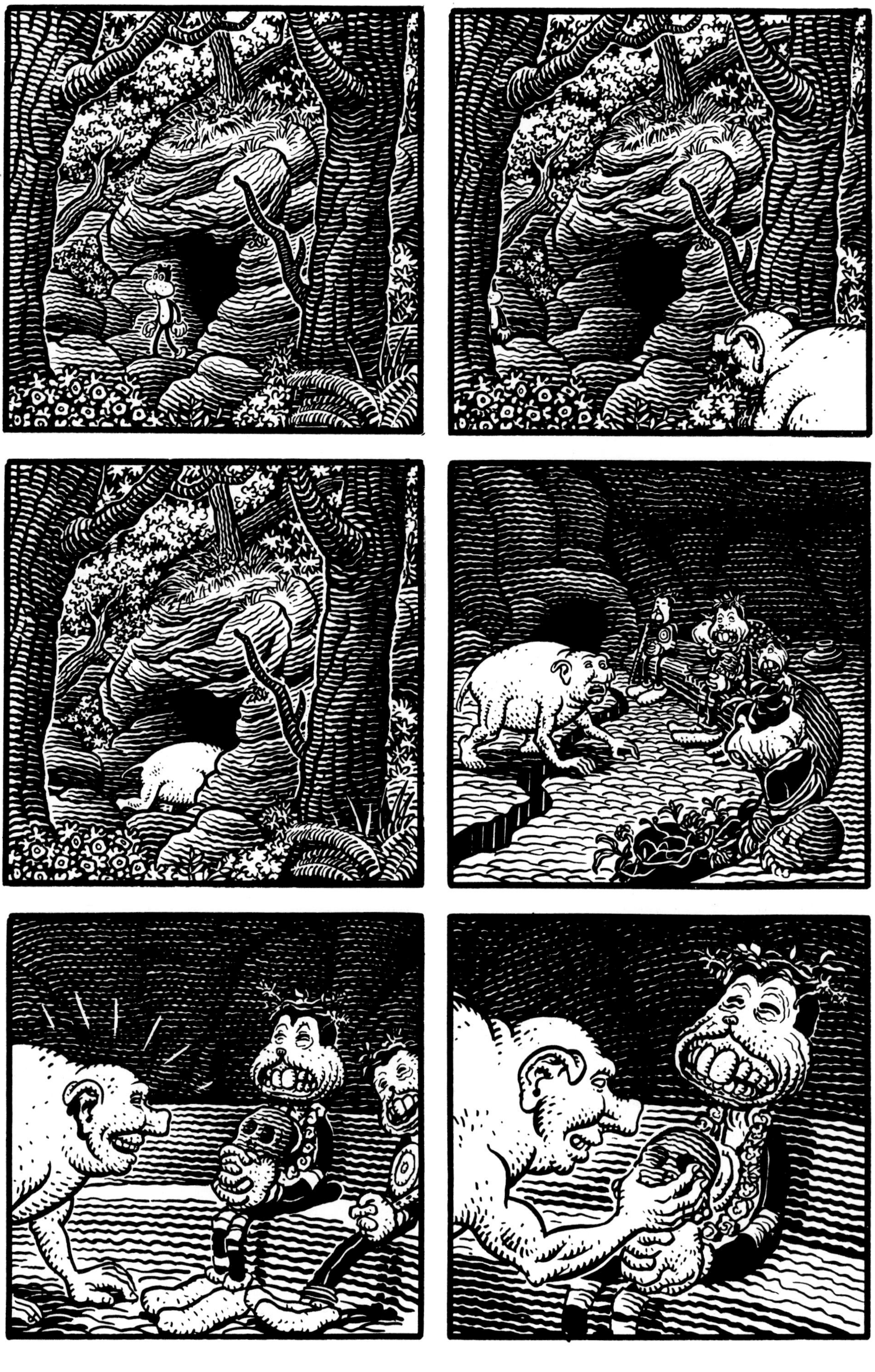

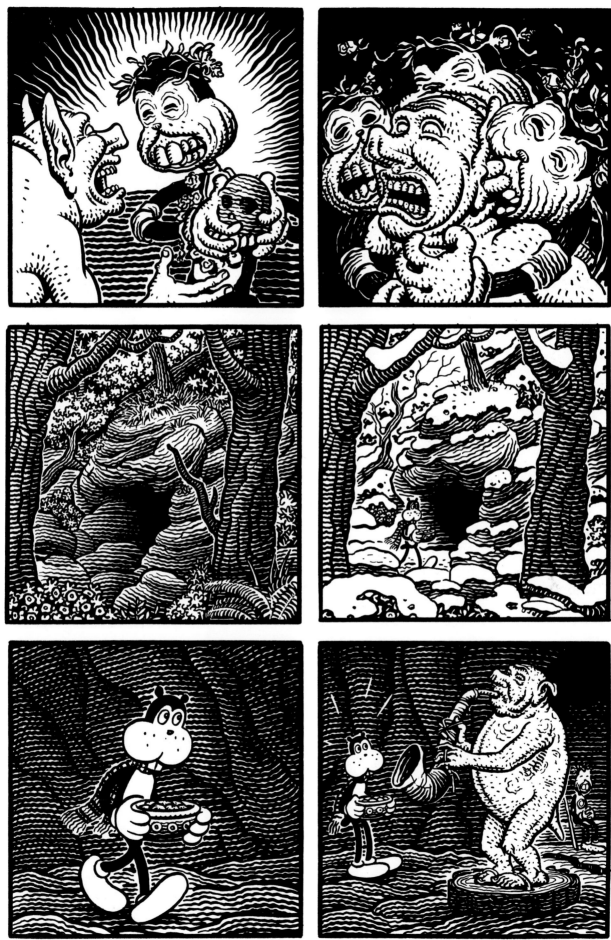

END

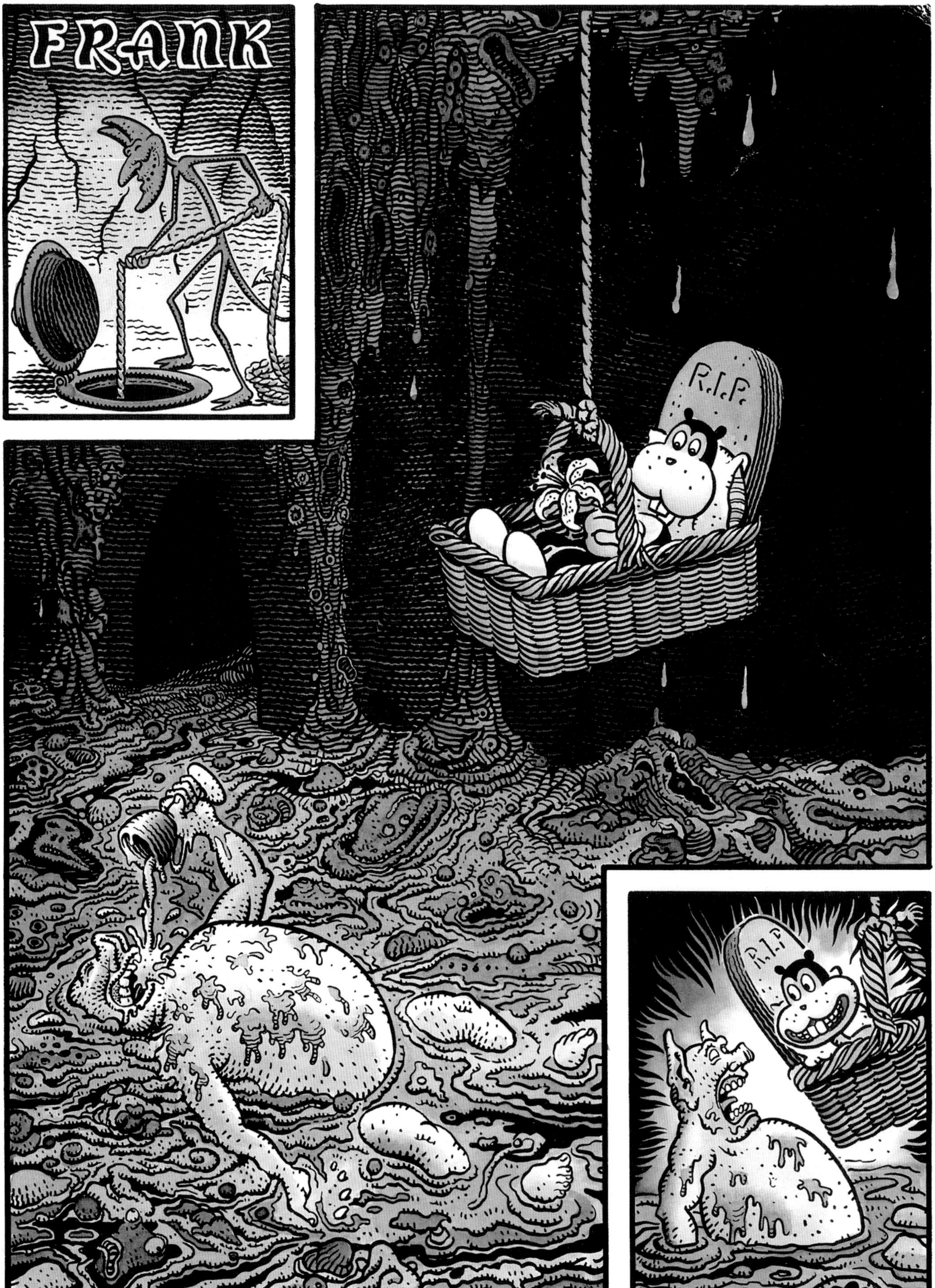
FRANK
R.I.P.
R.I.P.
END
© 1993 JIM WOODRING

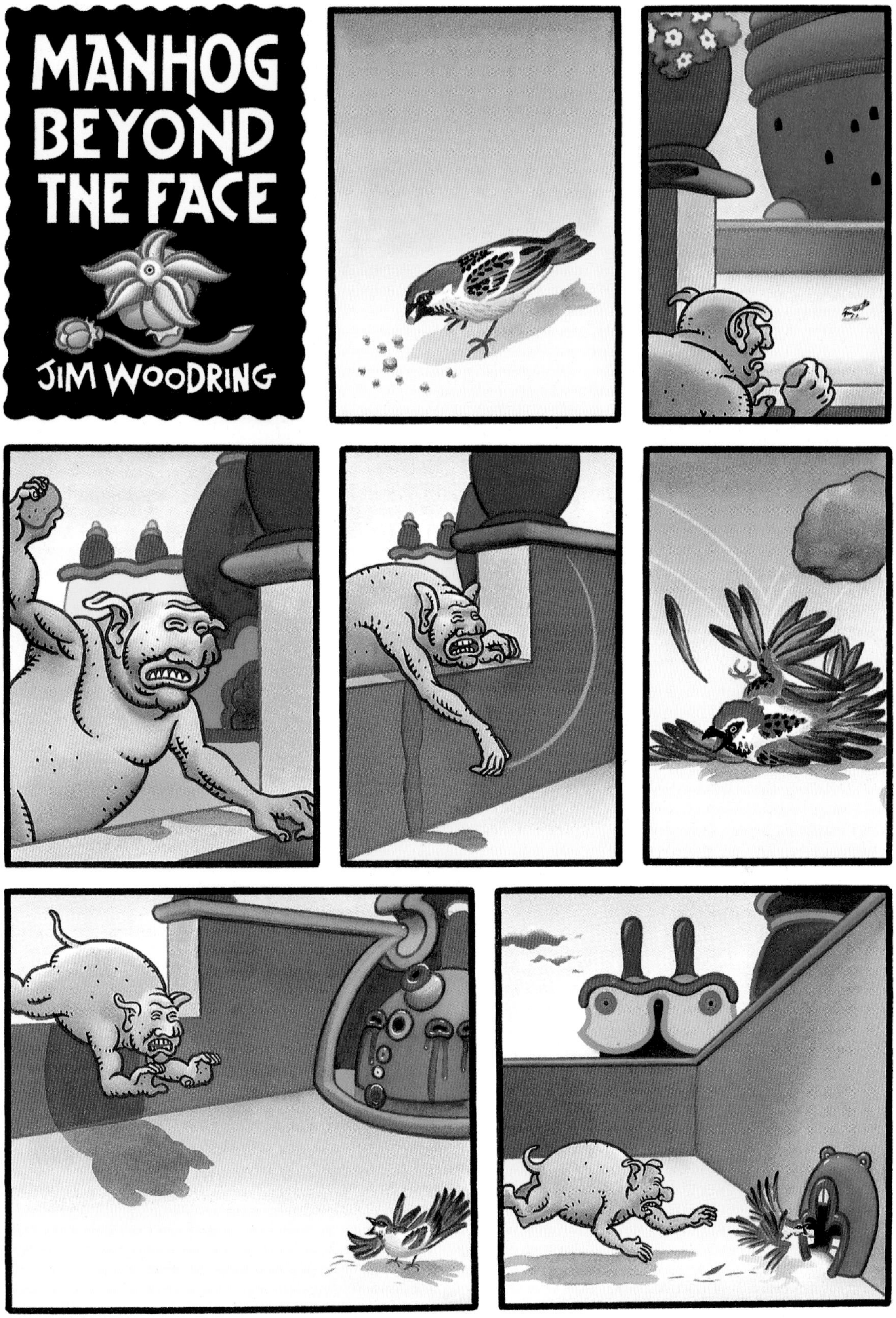
MANHOG
BEYOND
THE FACE
JIM WOODRING

Look at the sweet little bird! And there's Manhog, ready to cause some mischief as usual! Oh my God, he scored a direct hit! And here he comes. The bird will have to be quick if it expects to escape. There it goes, into that... er... drain. Hurry, Manhog!

Nuts! The bird got away. Poor Manhog! He was so eager to catch that tasty little wren that he forgot to stop in time. What a conk on the noggin he got! I bet he cracked his fat skull. Ouch! And look — Frank is passing by. Manhog is looking at him strangely.

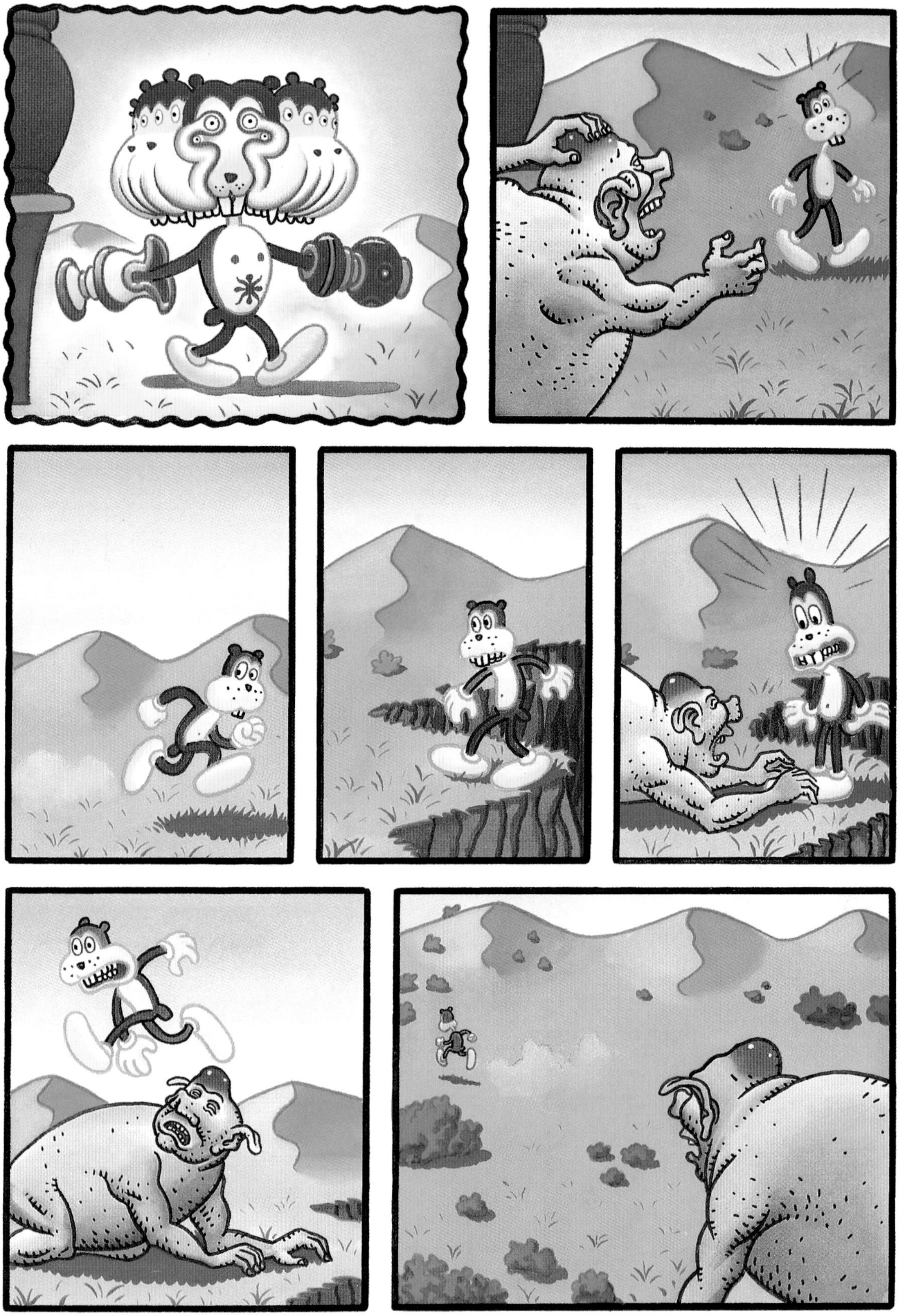

And no wonder! That bump on the head has affected Manhog's mind, and he sees Frank as no one has seen him before. In his pain and confusion he believes Frank is someone from heaven. He wishes to speak with Frank, and to worship him. Perhaps he thinks Frank can stop the pain in his head. But Frank wants nothing to do with Manhog and runs away.

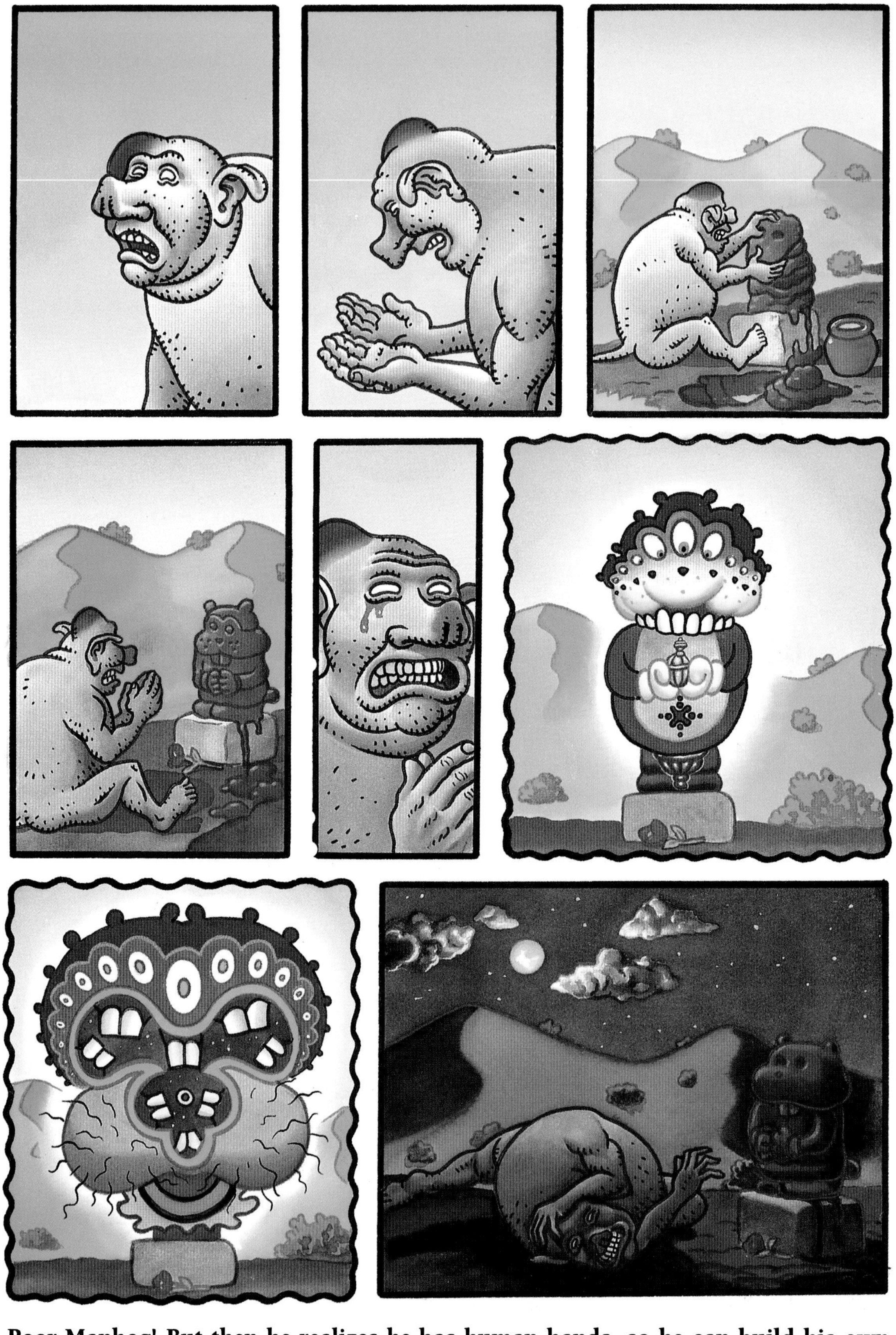

Poor Manhog! But then he realizes he has human hands, so he can build his own reality! In no time he makes a clay figure of Frank. He prays and prays to the clay idol. His injured mind plays tricks that scare him, and he passes an absolutely miserable night, rolling on the ground and praying in pain.

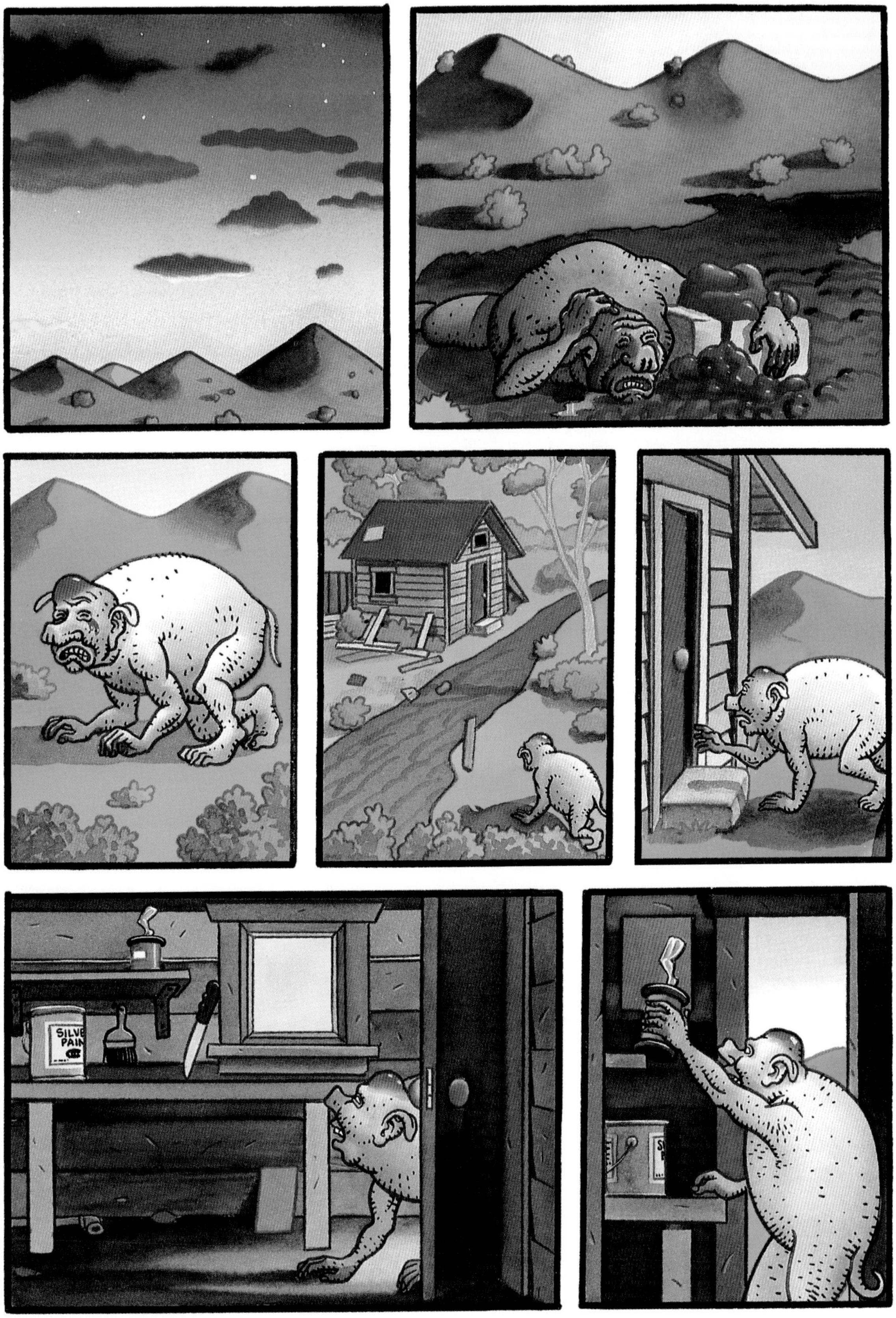

When morning finally comes Manhog feels as if he has spent eternity in Hell. He crawls aimlessly until he comes to a little shed. Perhaps Frank is in there! No, there's nothing but a few odds and ends. But what's that? It's what is left of a sports trophy. All that remains of the figure that was on it is a chromed leg.

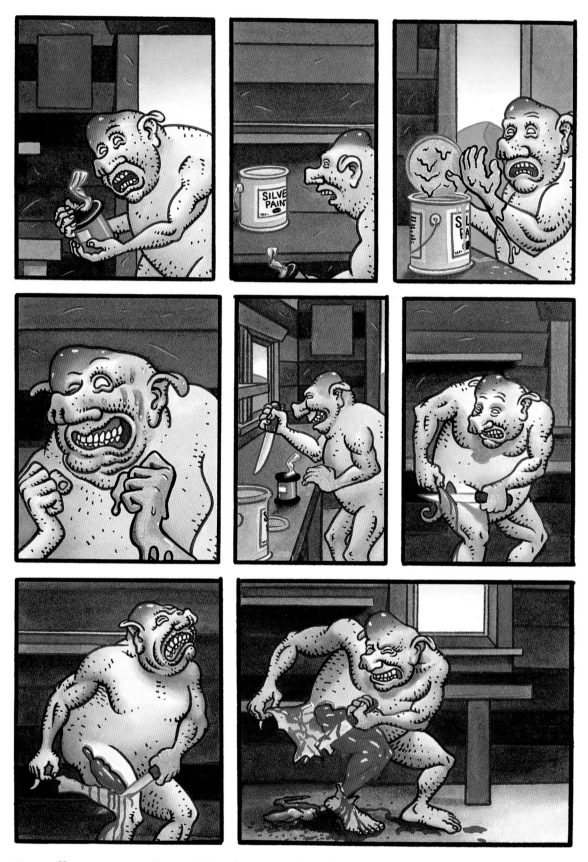

He really seems enchanted by that tiny leg, doesn't he. And there's a gallon of silver paint. Now what? He seems to be having a brainstorm. Now he's... I wonder what's going on outside the shed. I wish we could look out the window. I wonder how many grains of rice there are in a fifty pound sack.

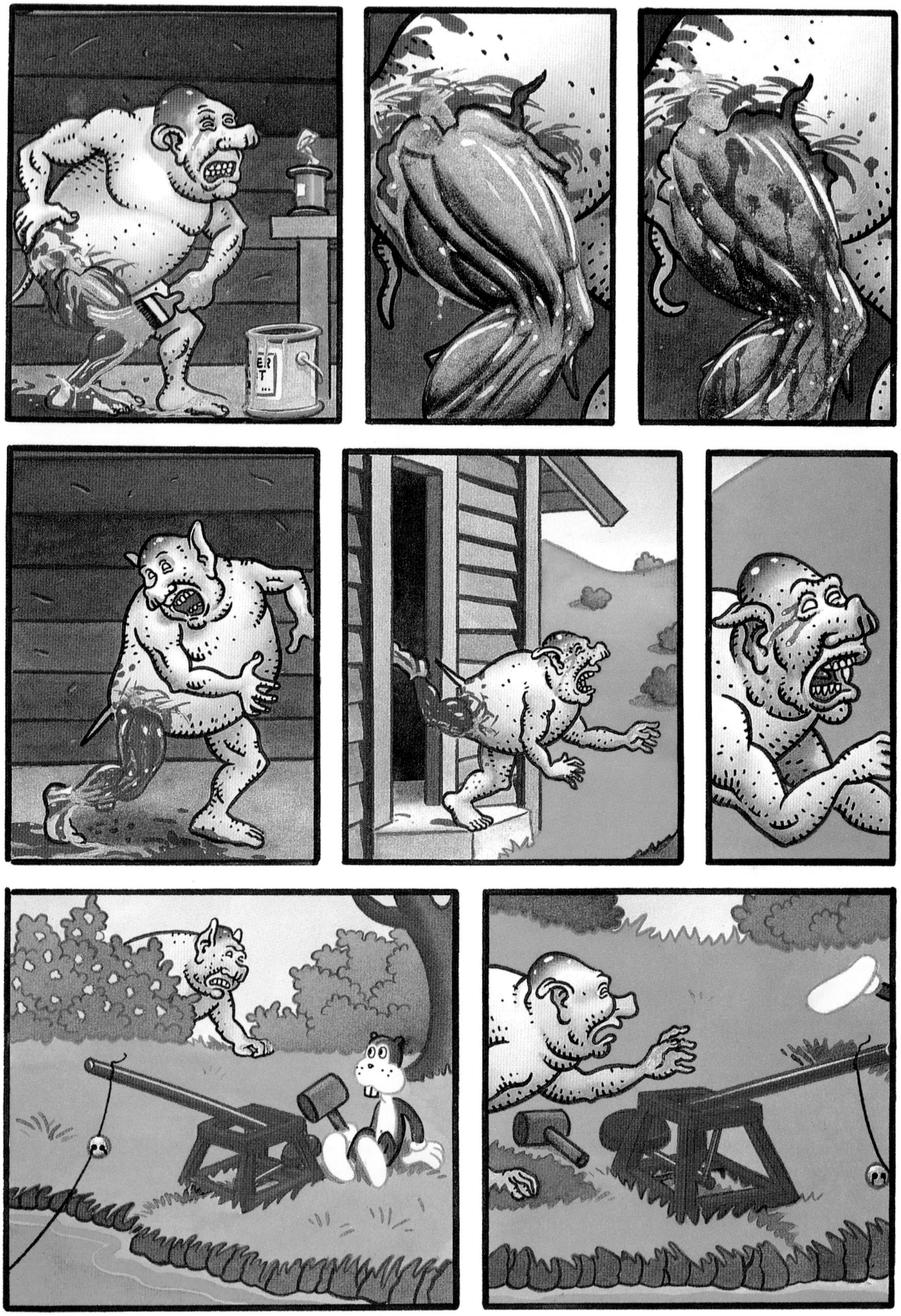

Now he's... Bobby wanted to move all his toys. He put them in a box so he could pull them, but it was very hard to move the box. The box seemed to have grown roots. Now Manhog is leaving the shed. His big idea didn't work out so well. But look! It's Frank! What is that contraption? Come back, Frank!

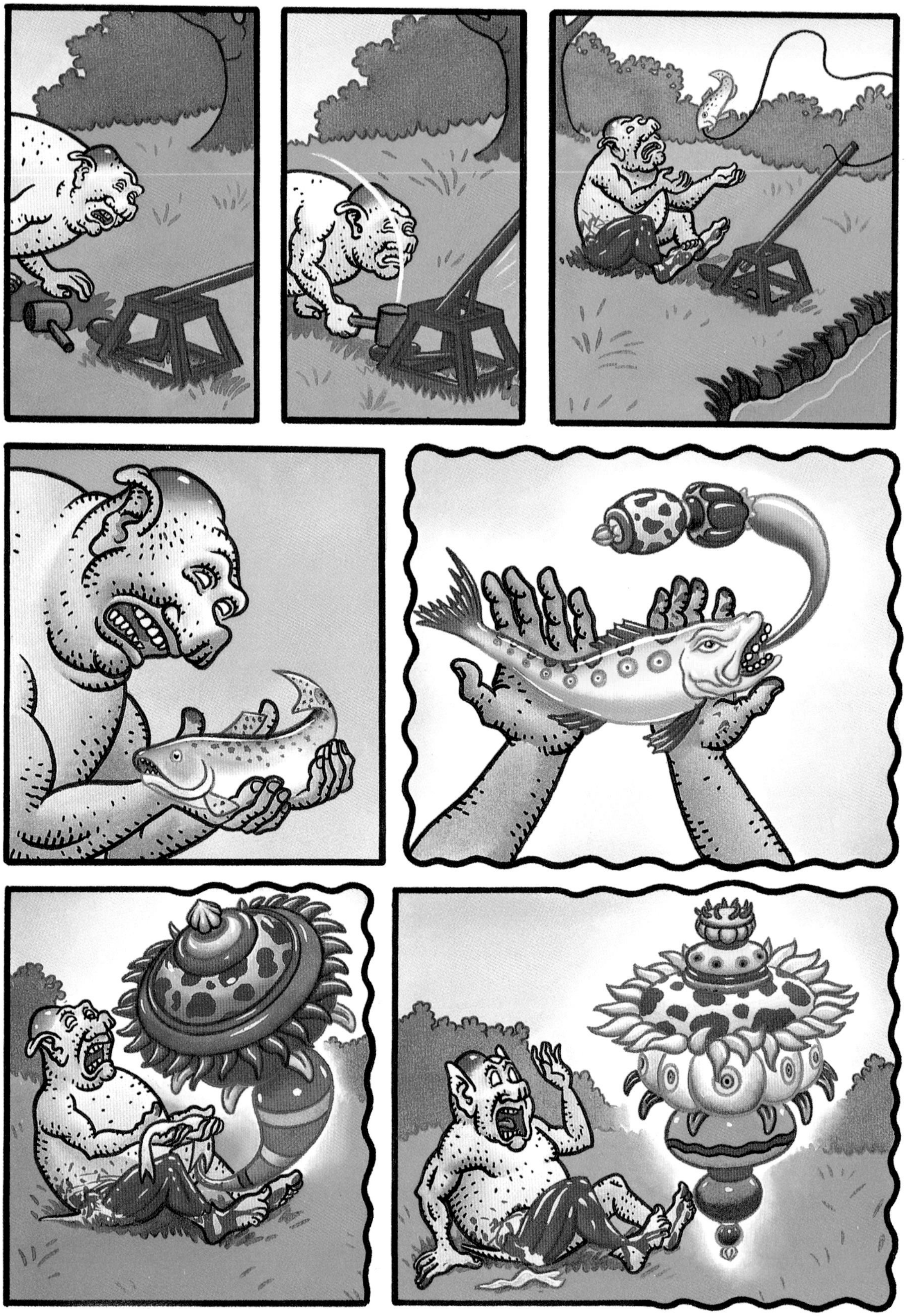

It looks to Manhog like the hammer is supposed to be applied to that disk. He tries it and catches a fish! What a surprise! And what a fish! Manhog's mind is playing tricks on him again. He really isn't ready for this kind of an experience.

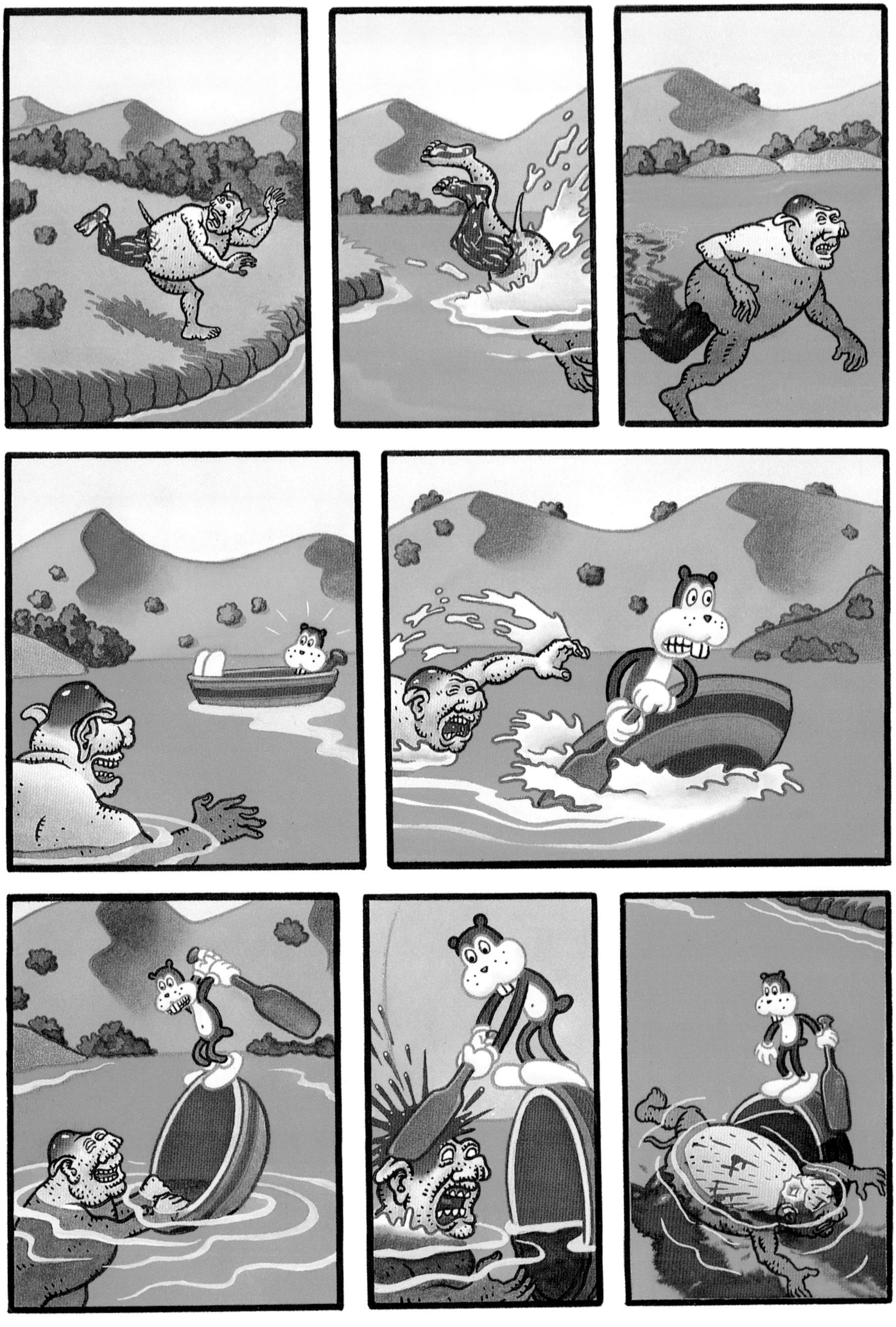

Ah! Into the cool, fresh water! Hello, Frank! It seems that Frank has nothing to say to Manhog. You better not pester him, Manhog; Frank has a real temper when he's feeling crowded. There, you see! Down comes the oar, right on Manhog's immense blood blister. Pow! What a noise! Like an exploding horse.

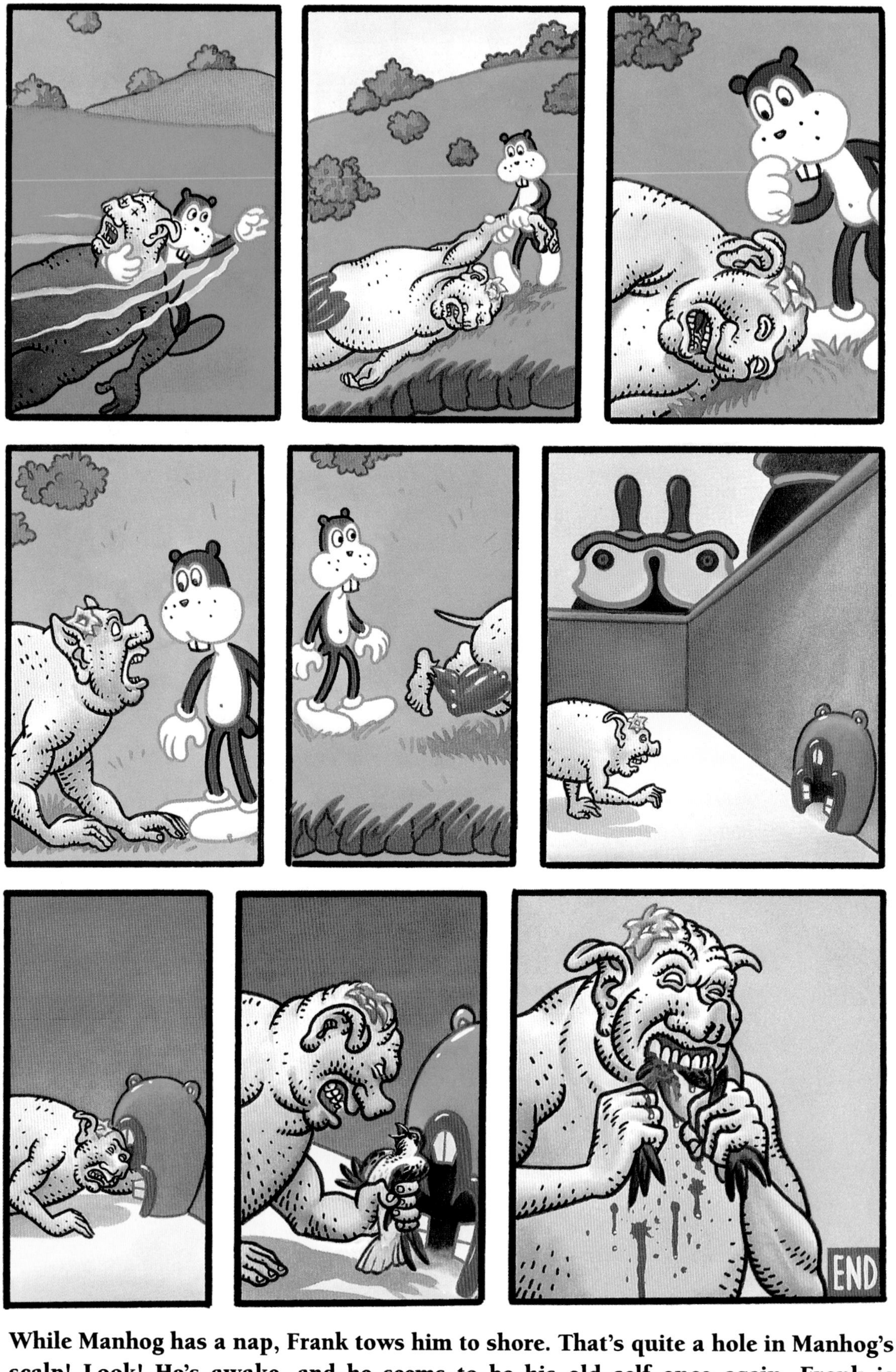
END

While Manhog has a nap, Frank tows him to shore. That's quite a hole in Manhog's scalp! Look! He's awake, and he seems to be his old self once again. Frank is relieved when Manhog screams like a woman and runs away. But is it just cowardice that causes him to rush off? No! He has unfinished business to attend. Good old Manhog!

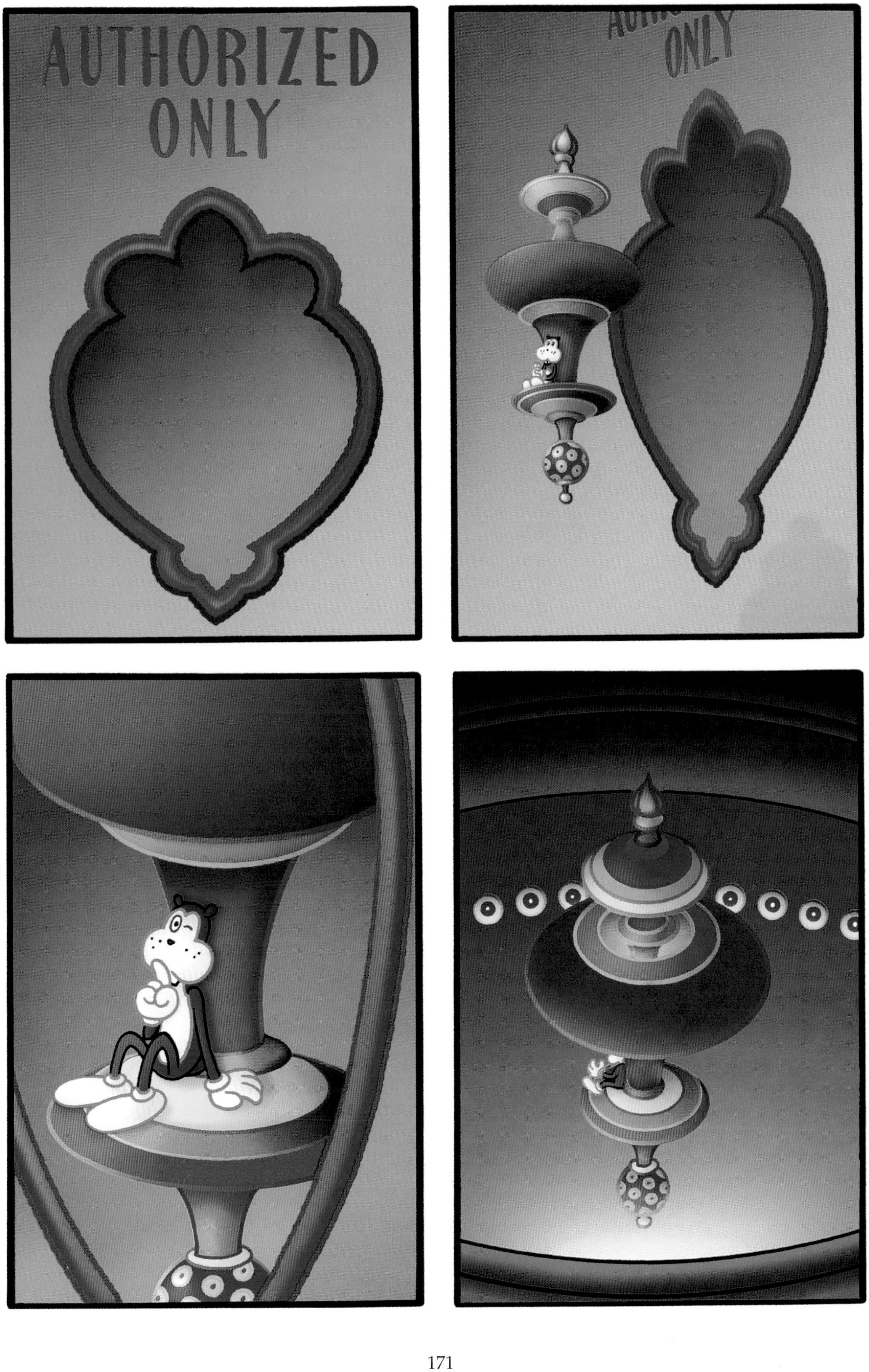
AUTHORIZED
ONLY

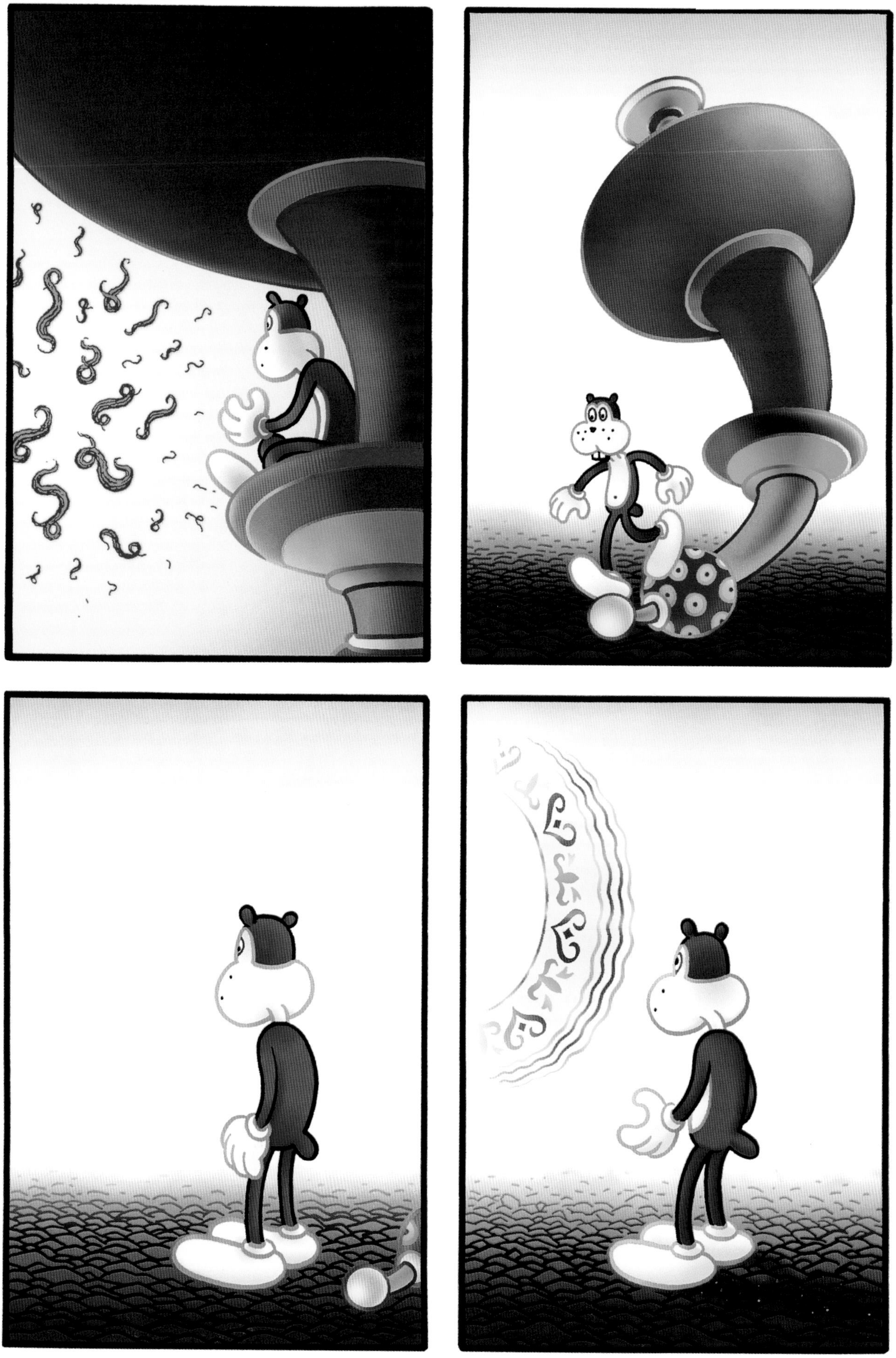

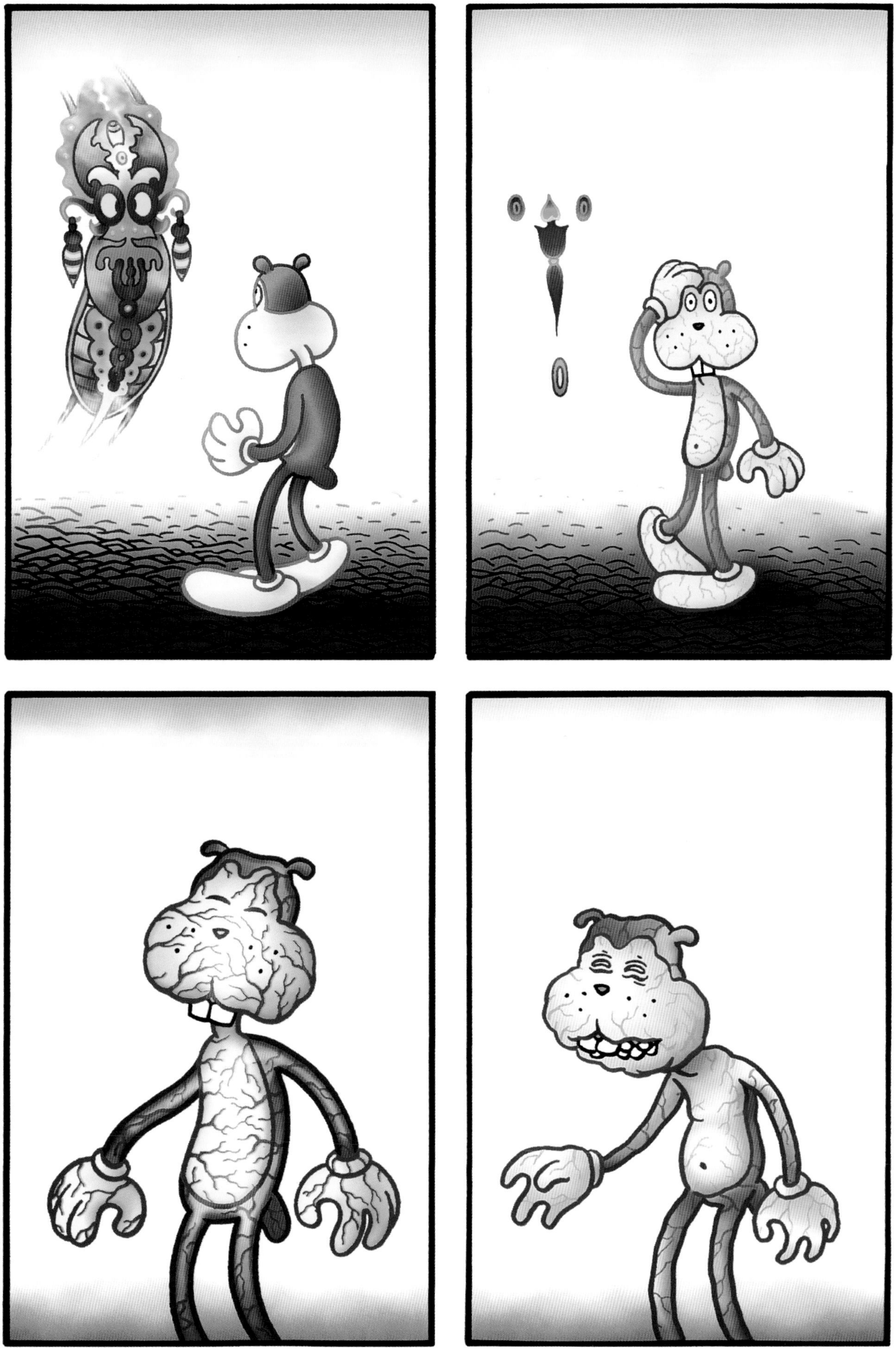

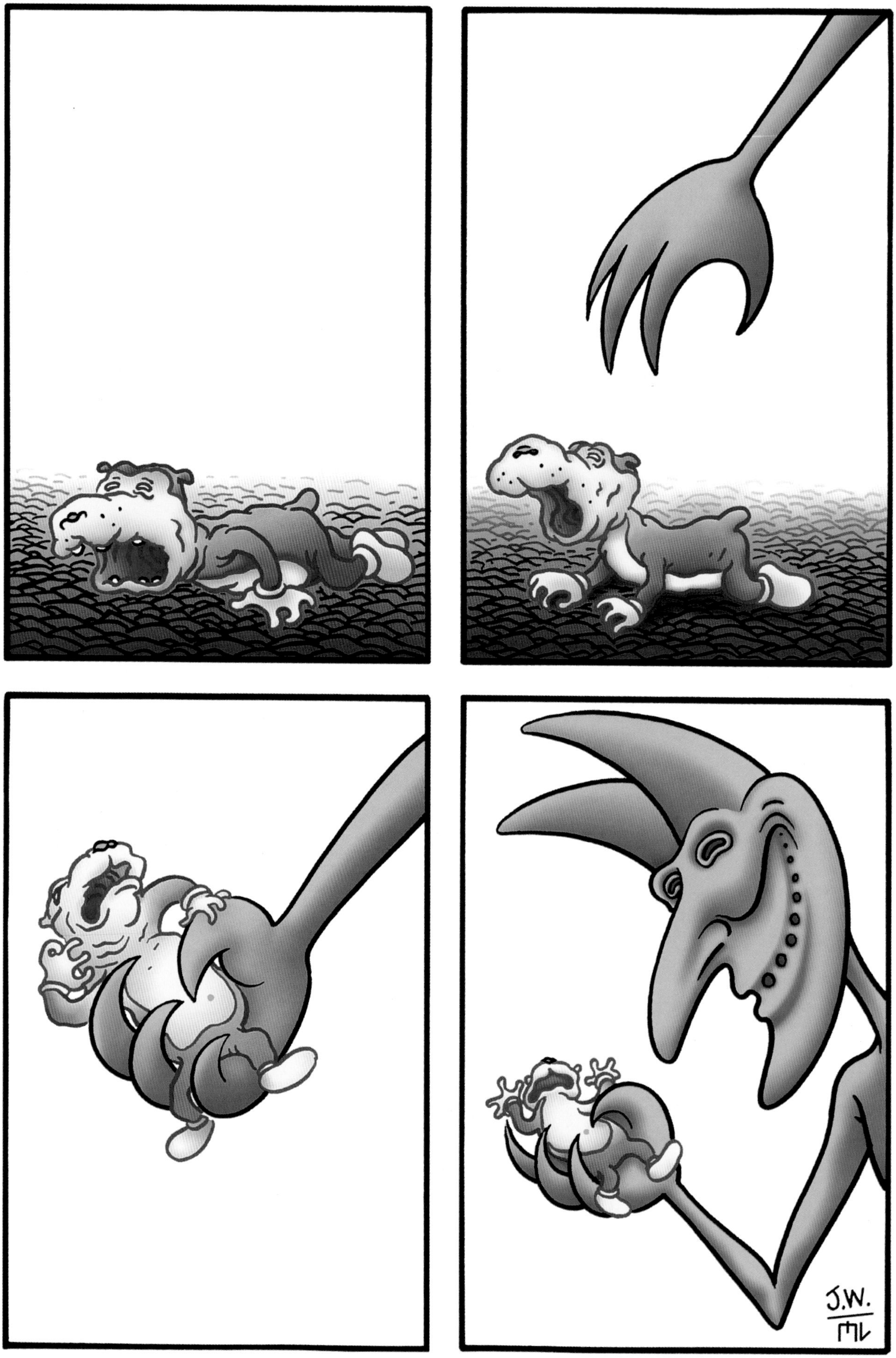

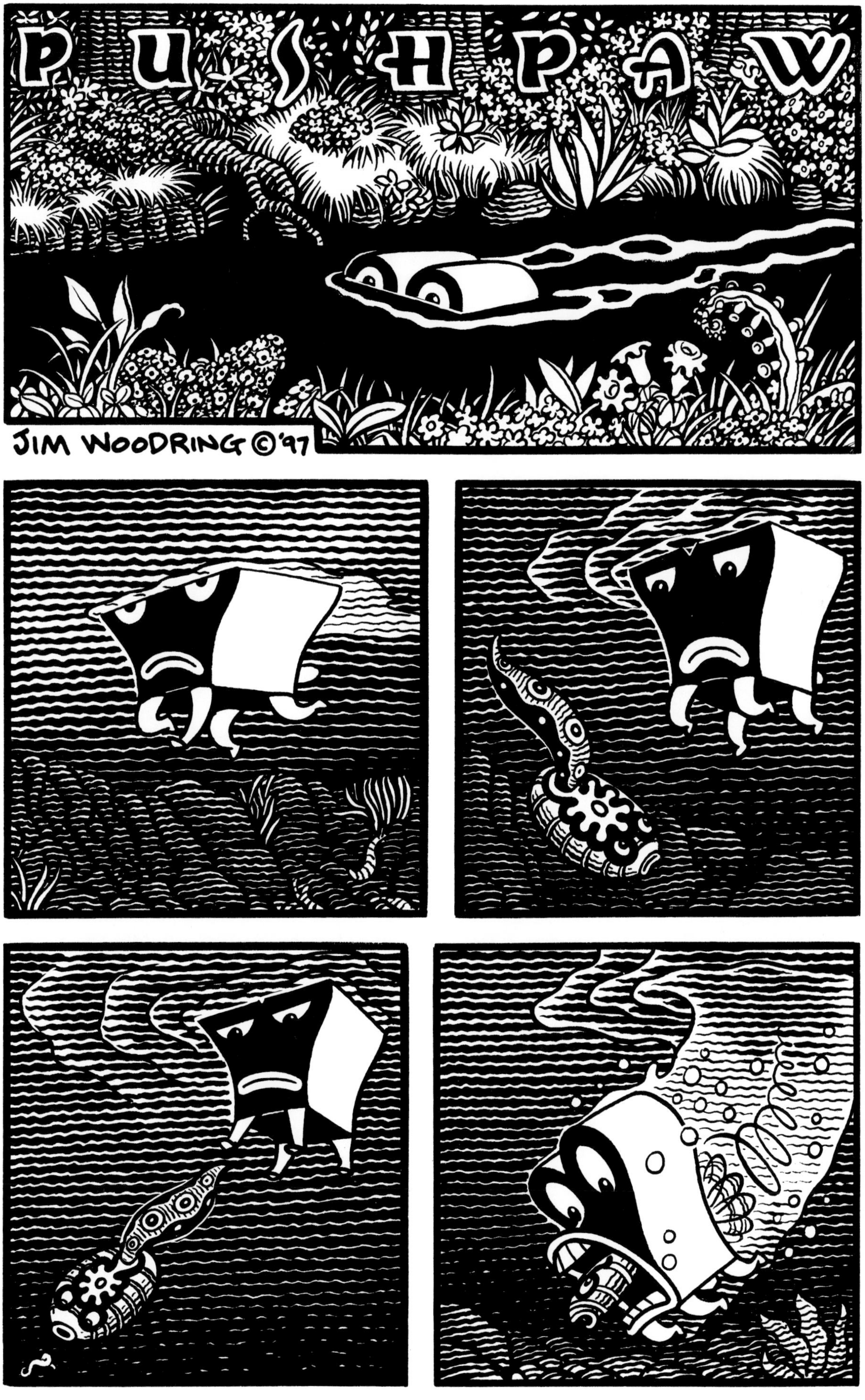
PUSHPAW
JIM WOODRING ©'97

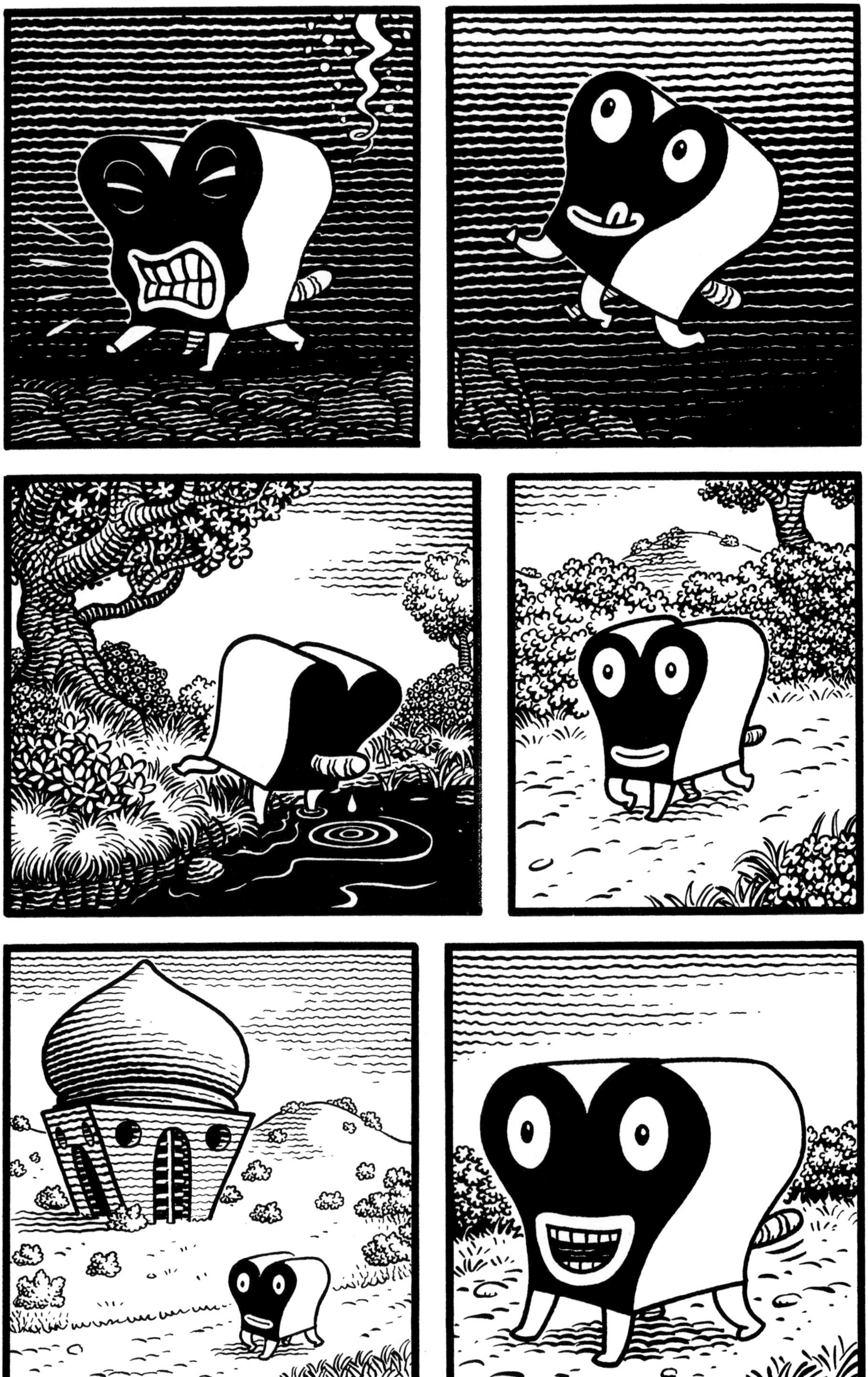

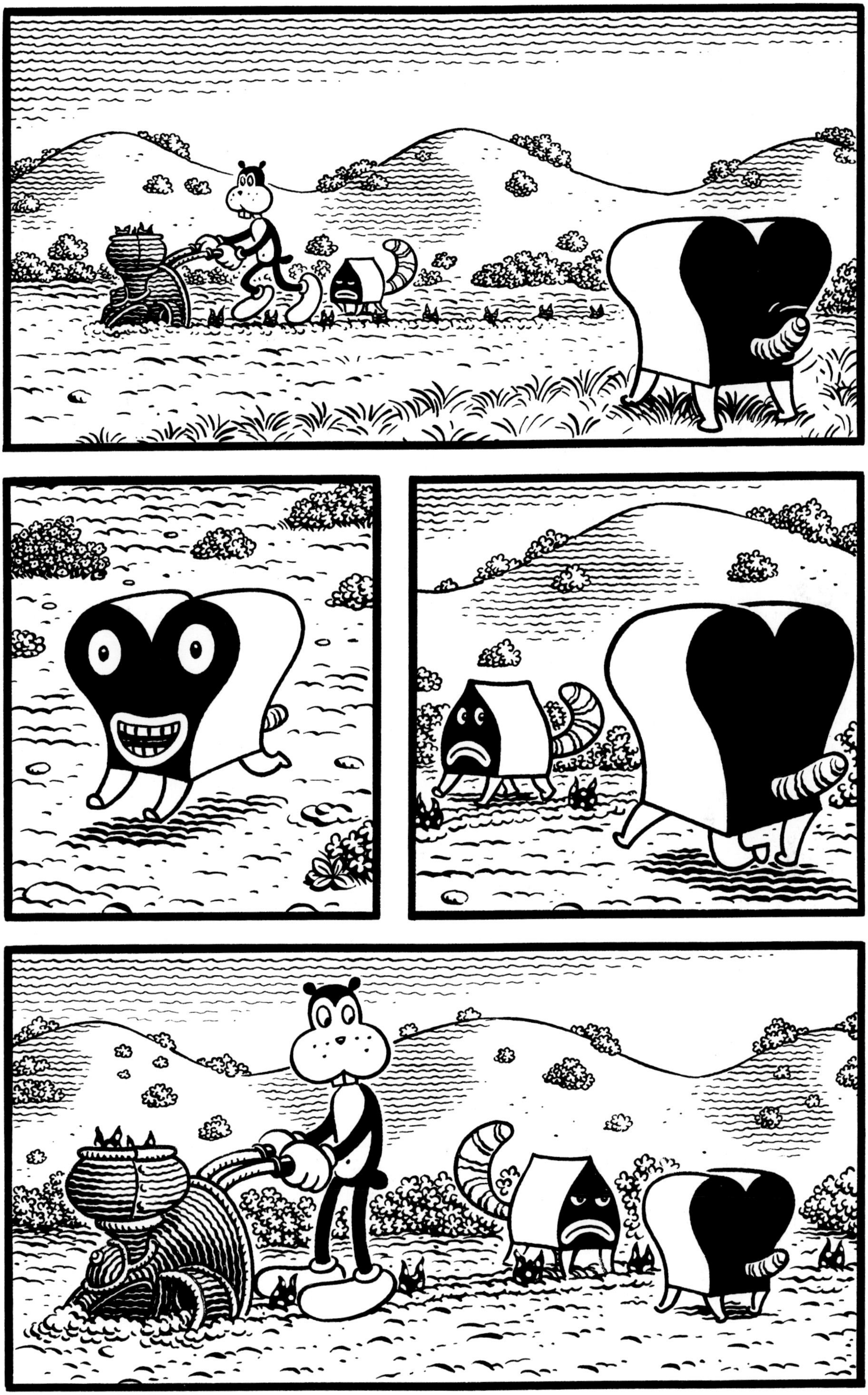

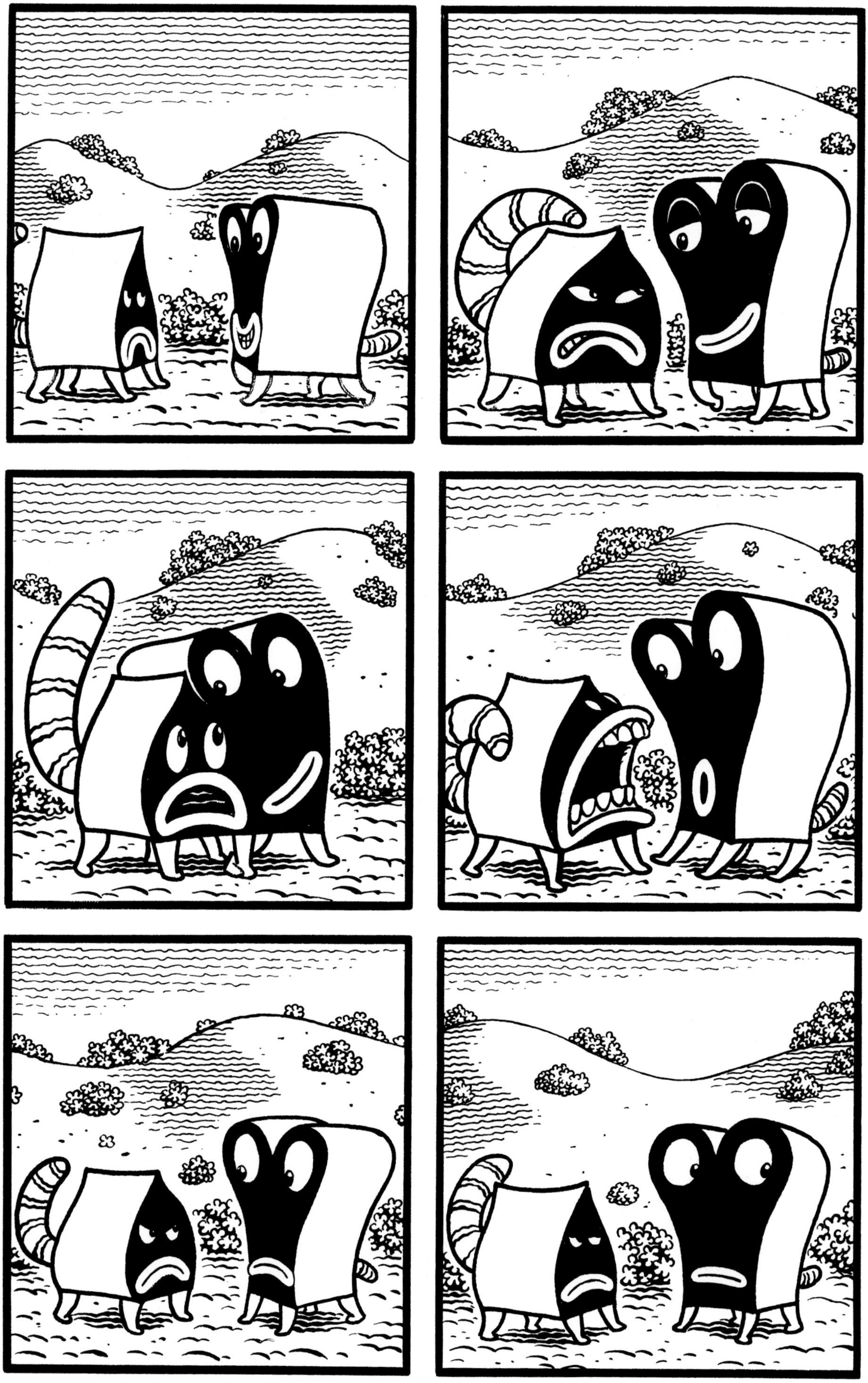

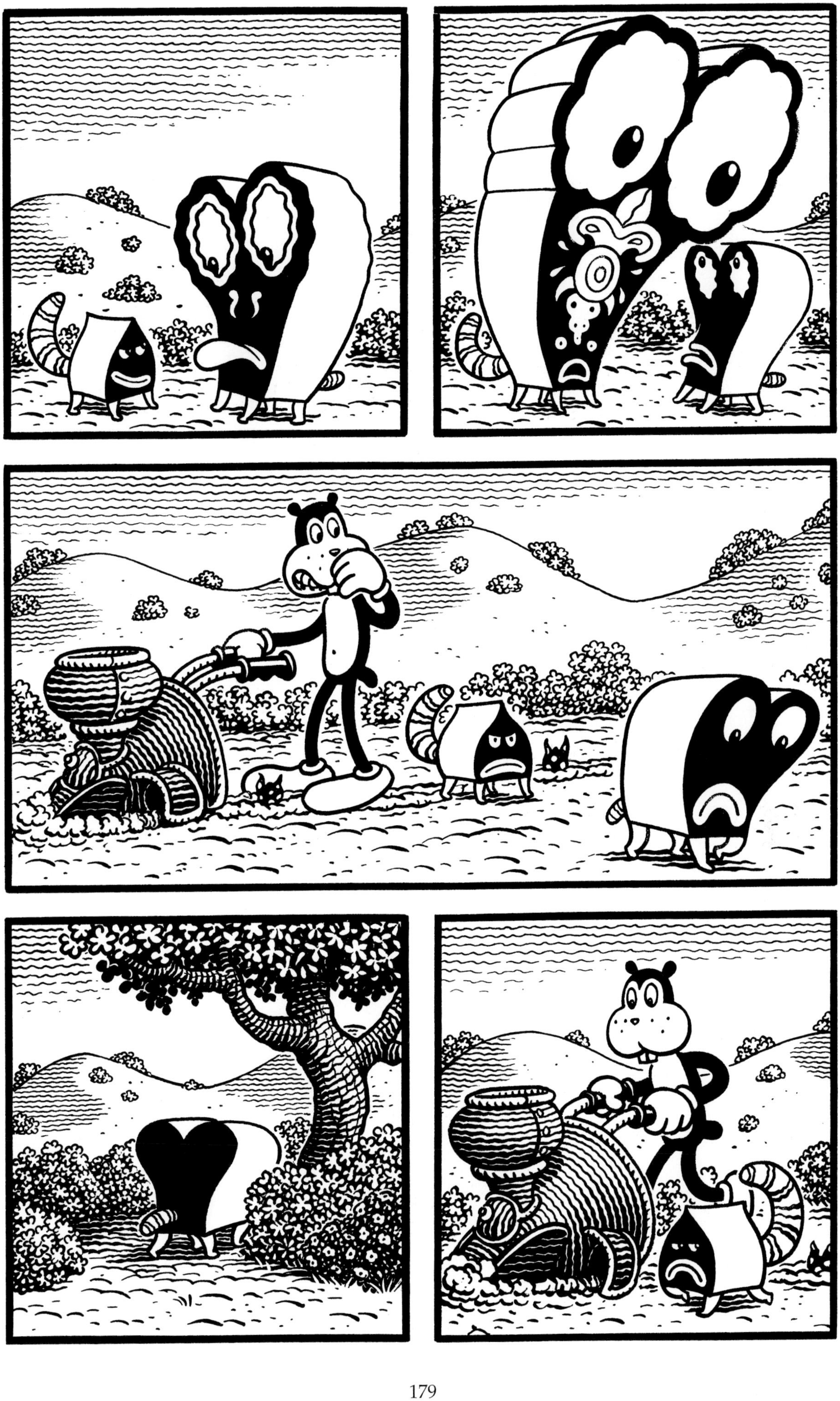

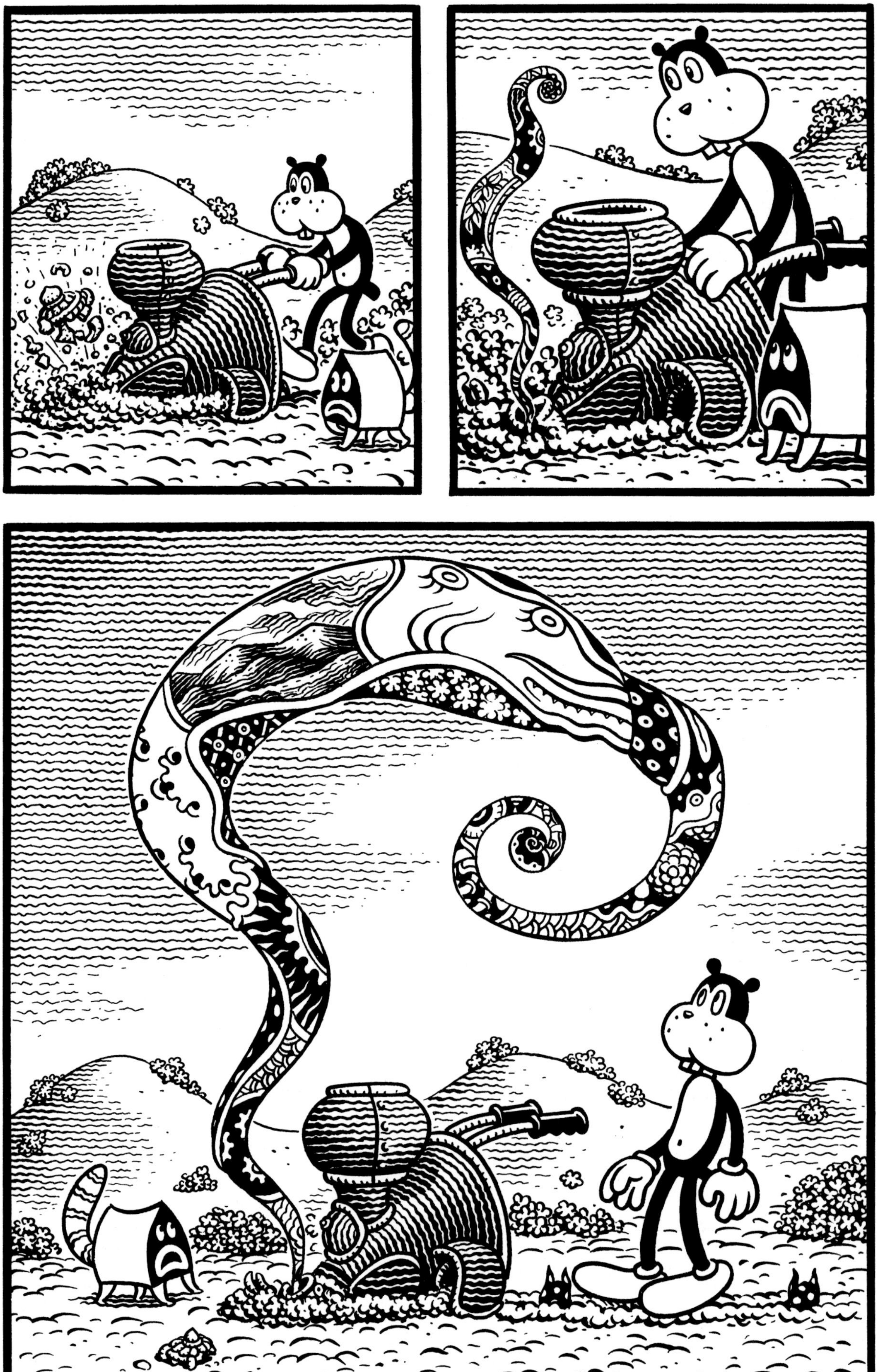

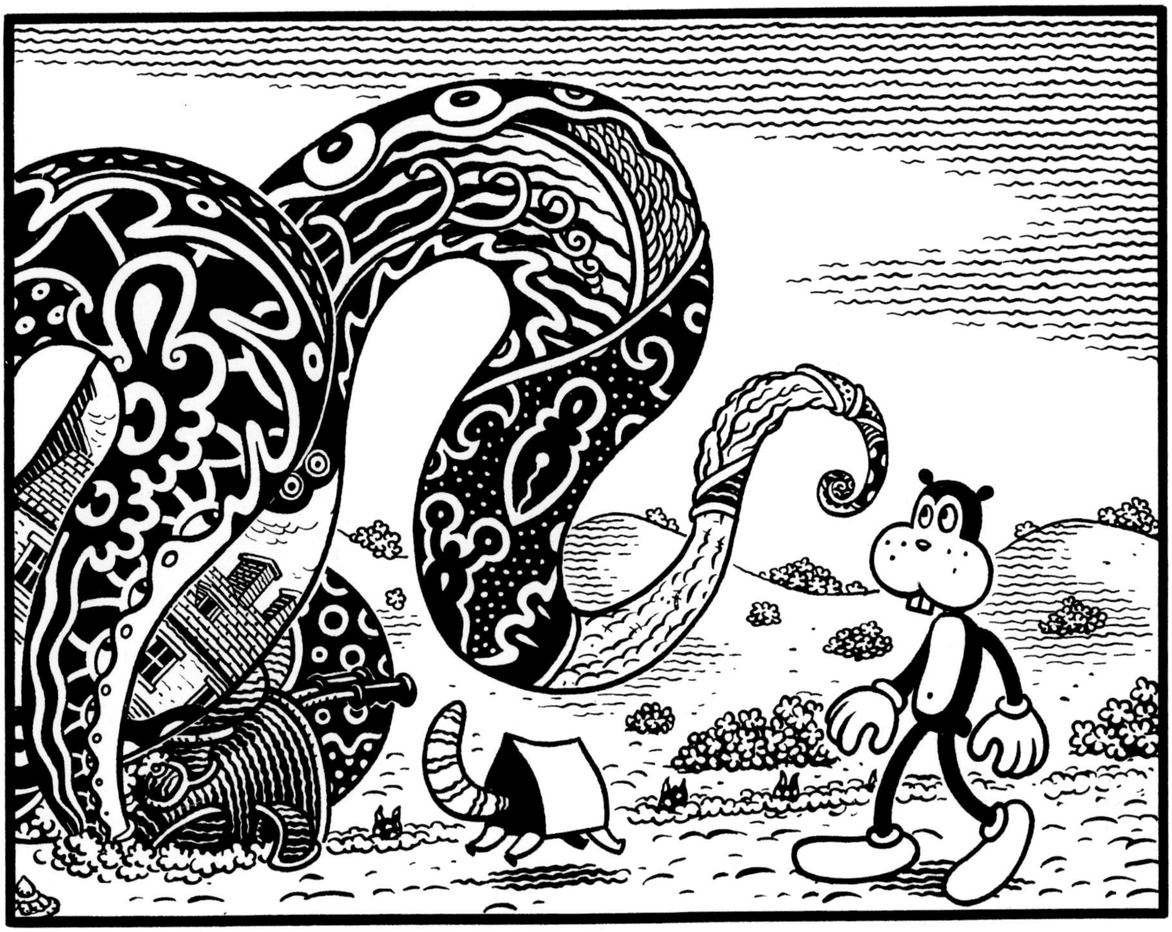

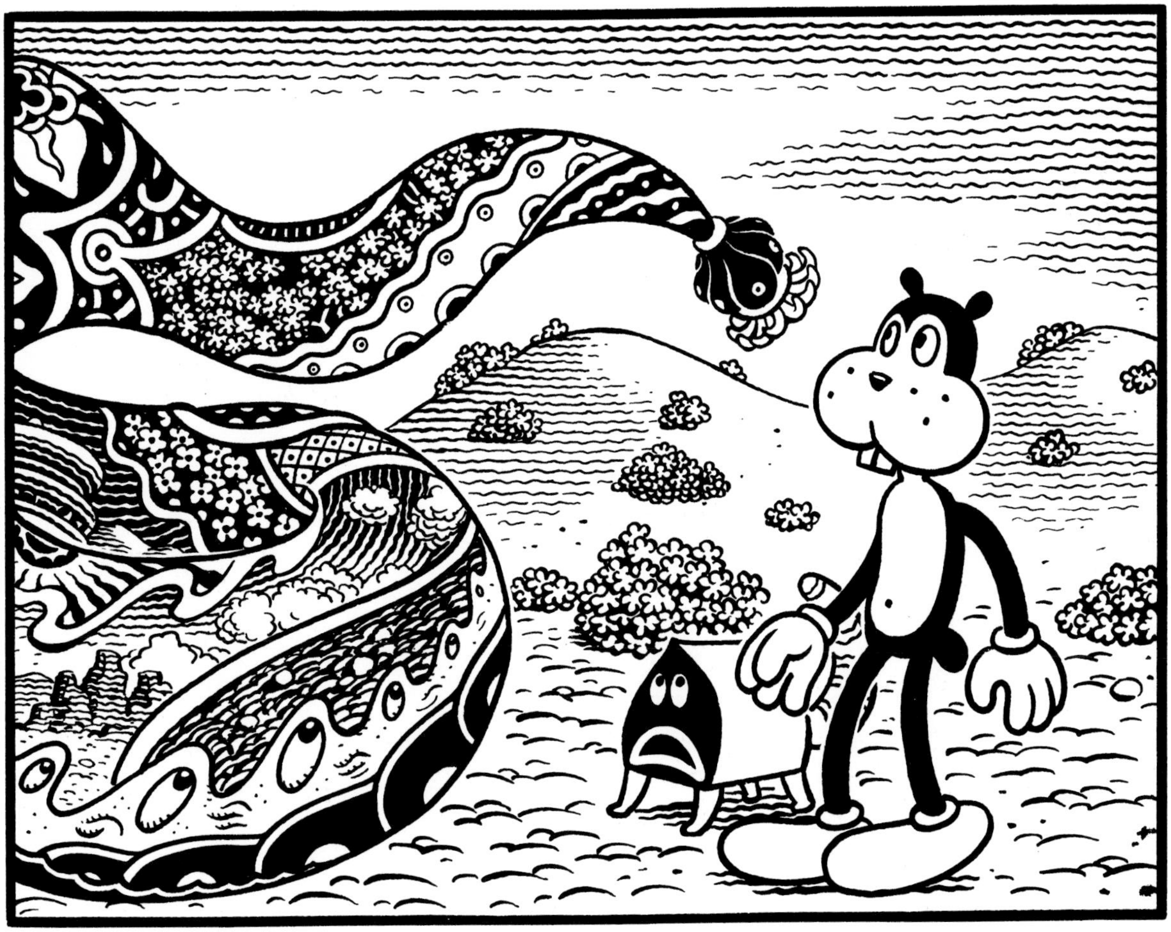

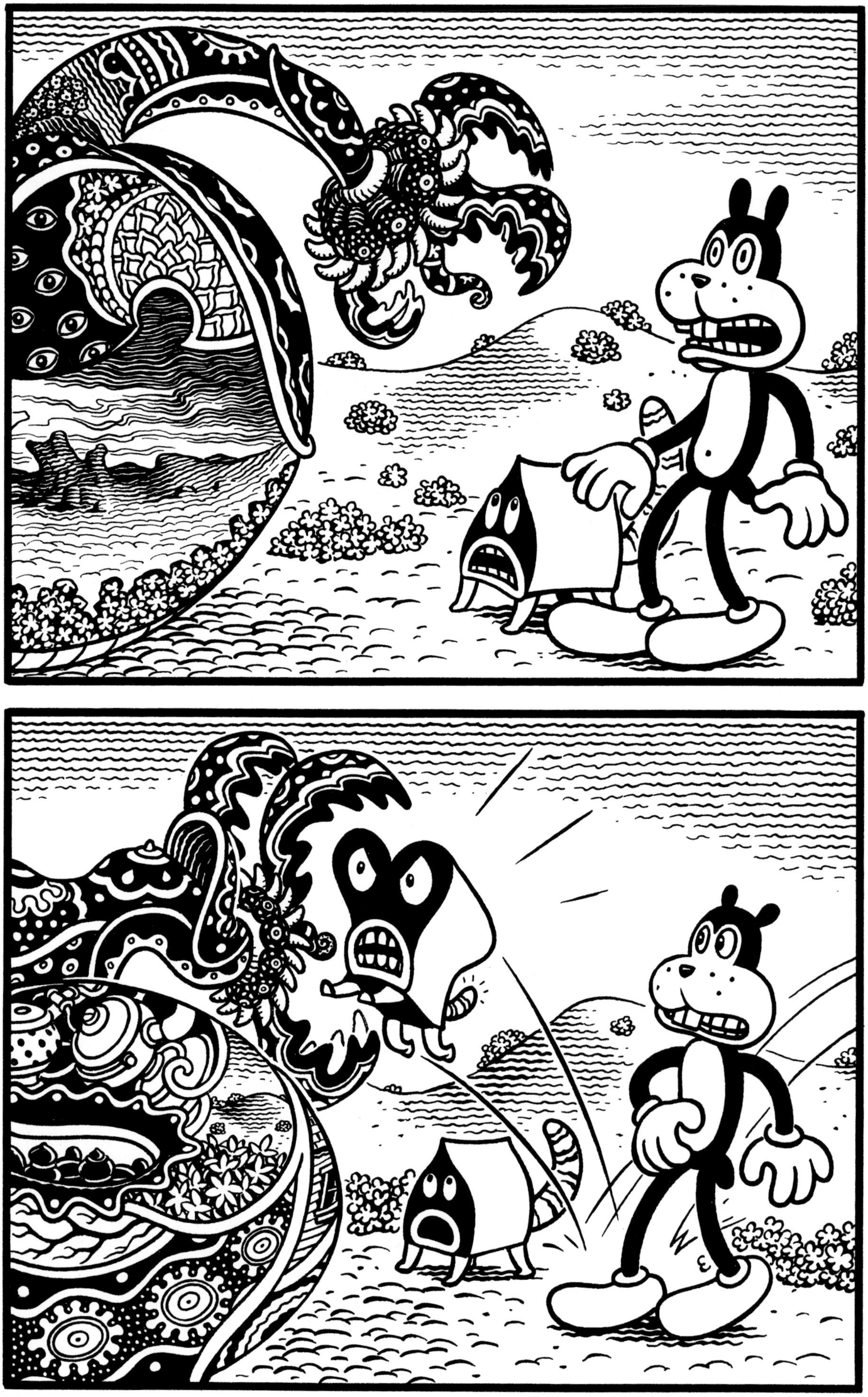

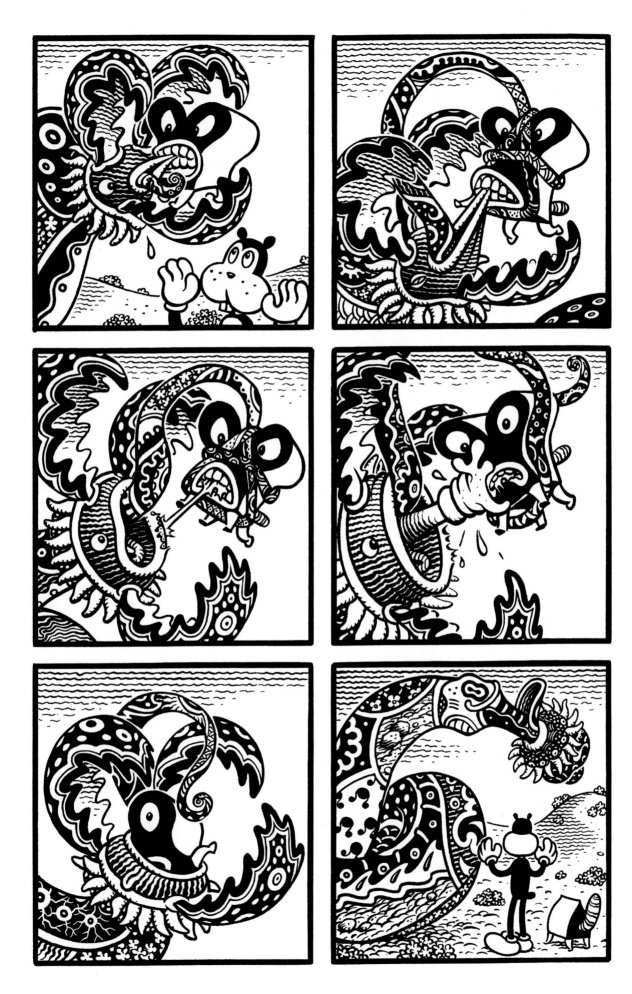

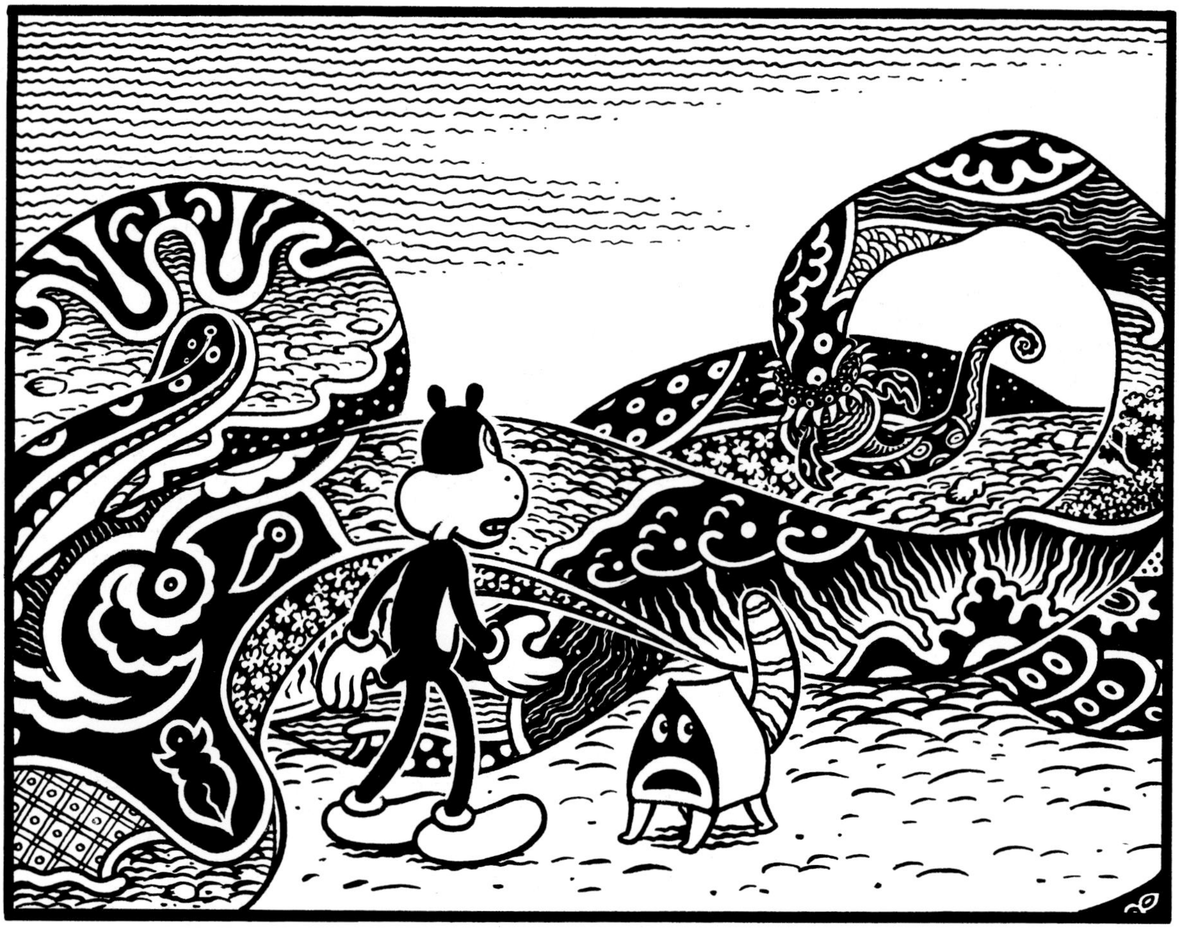

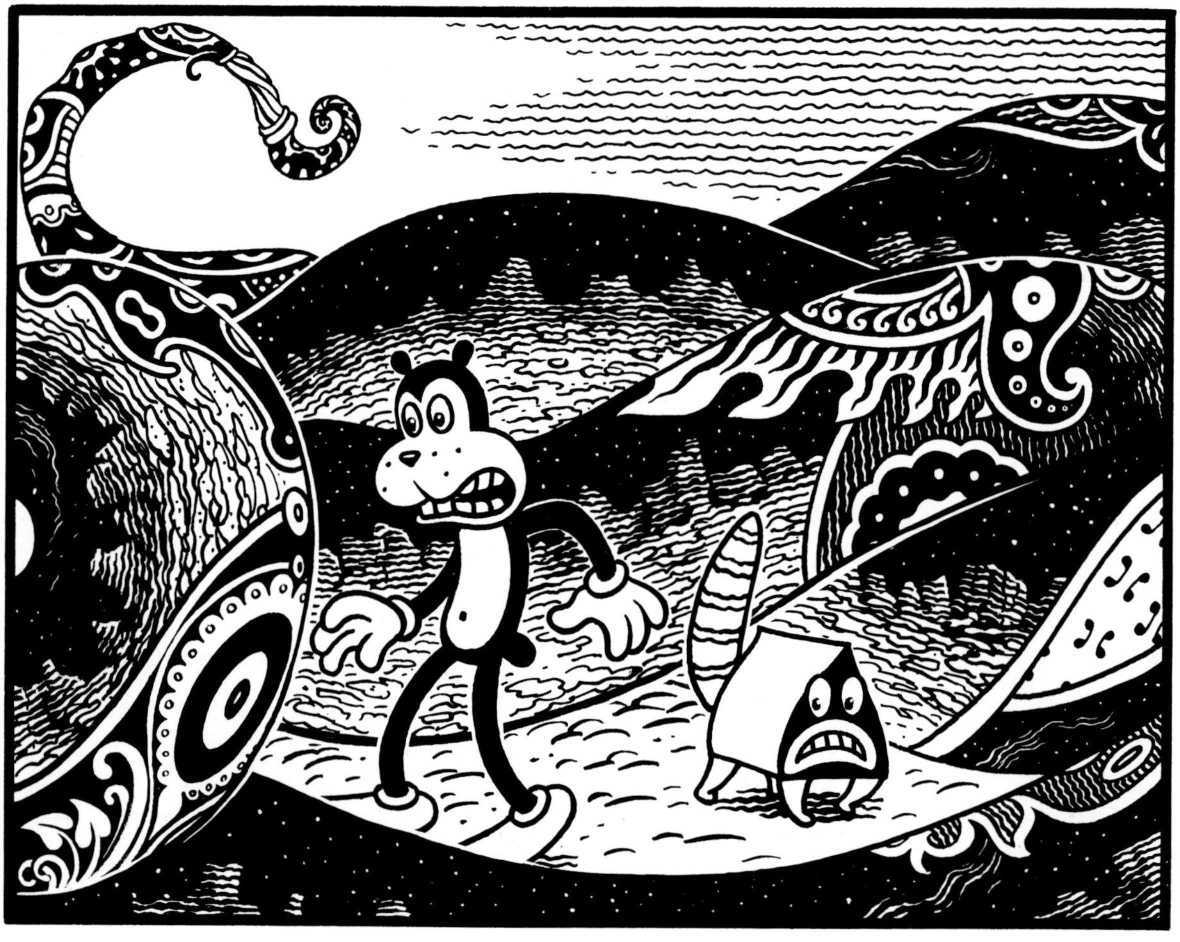

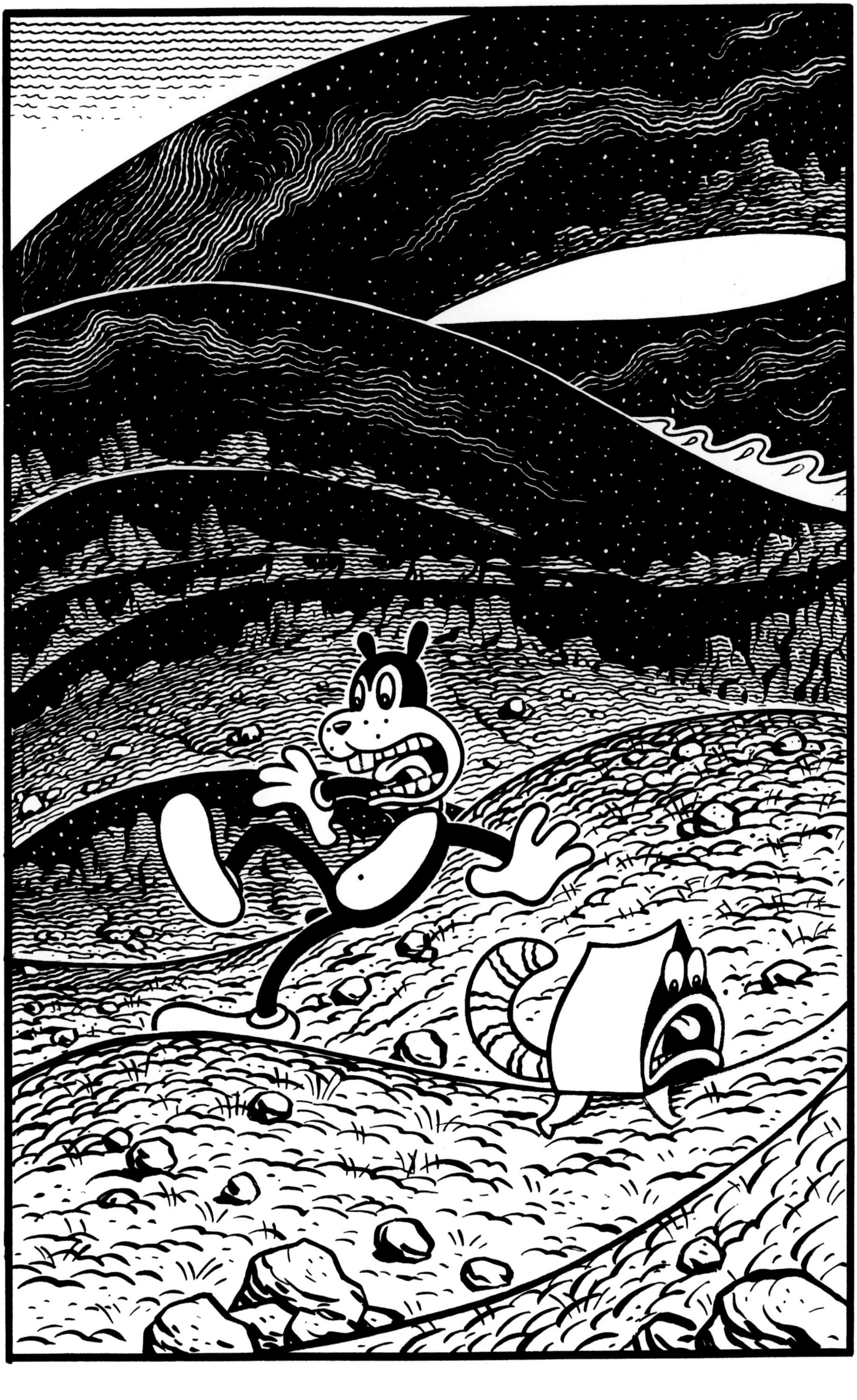

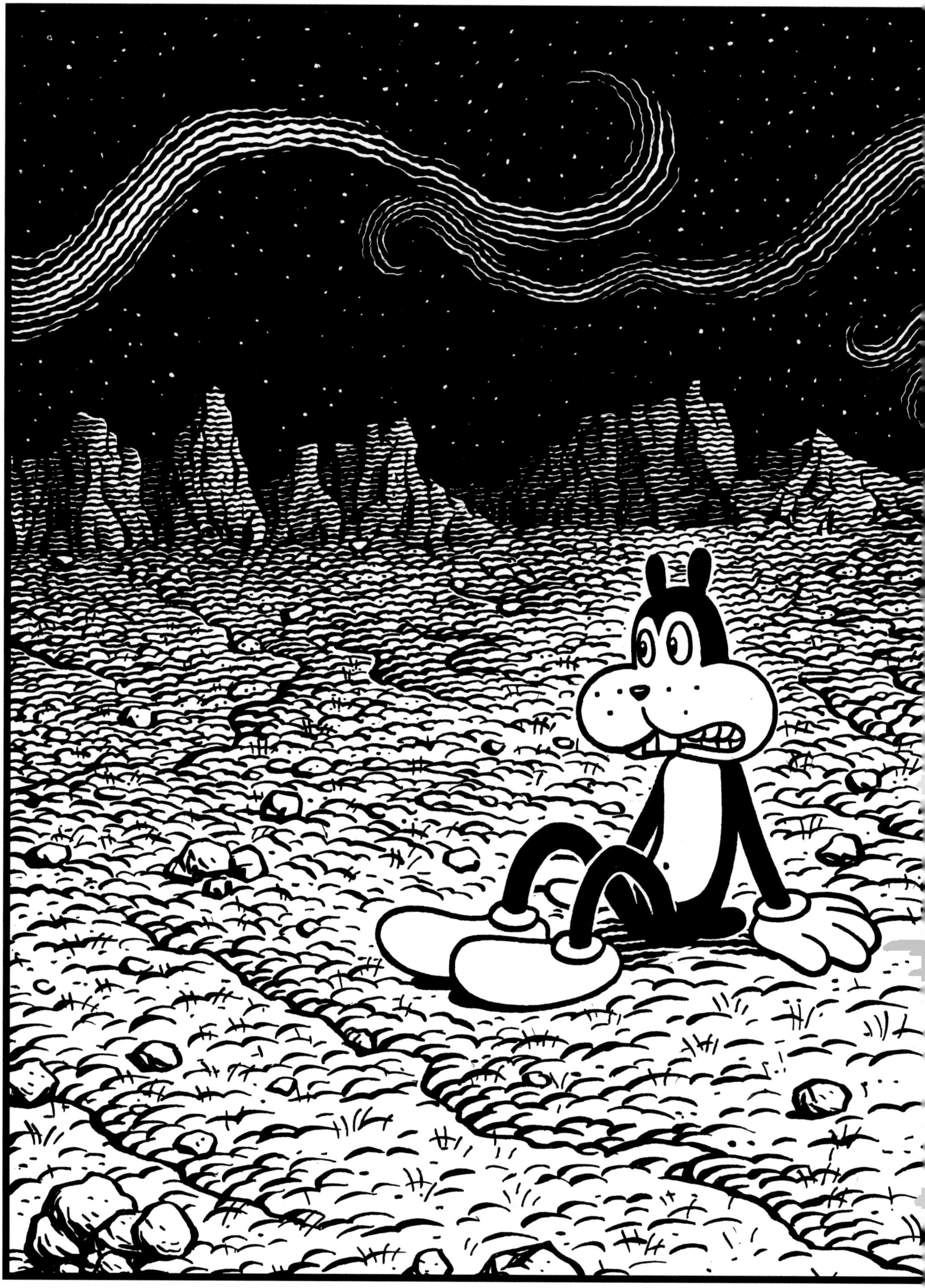

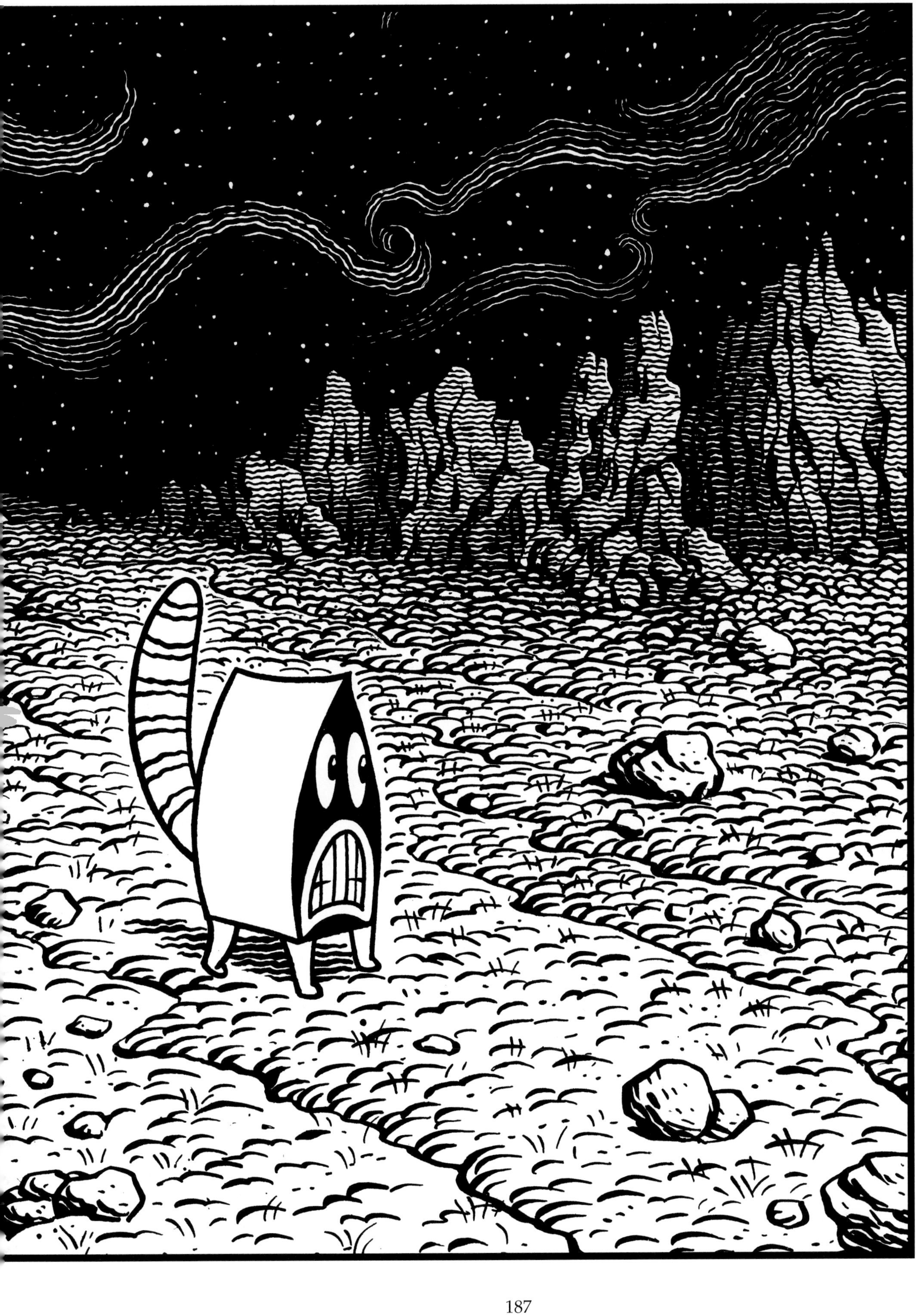

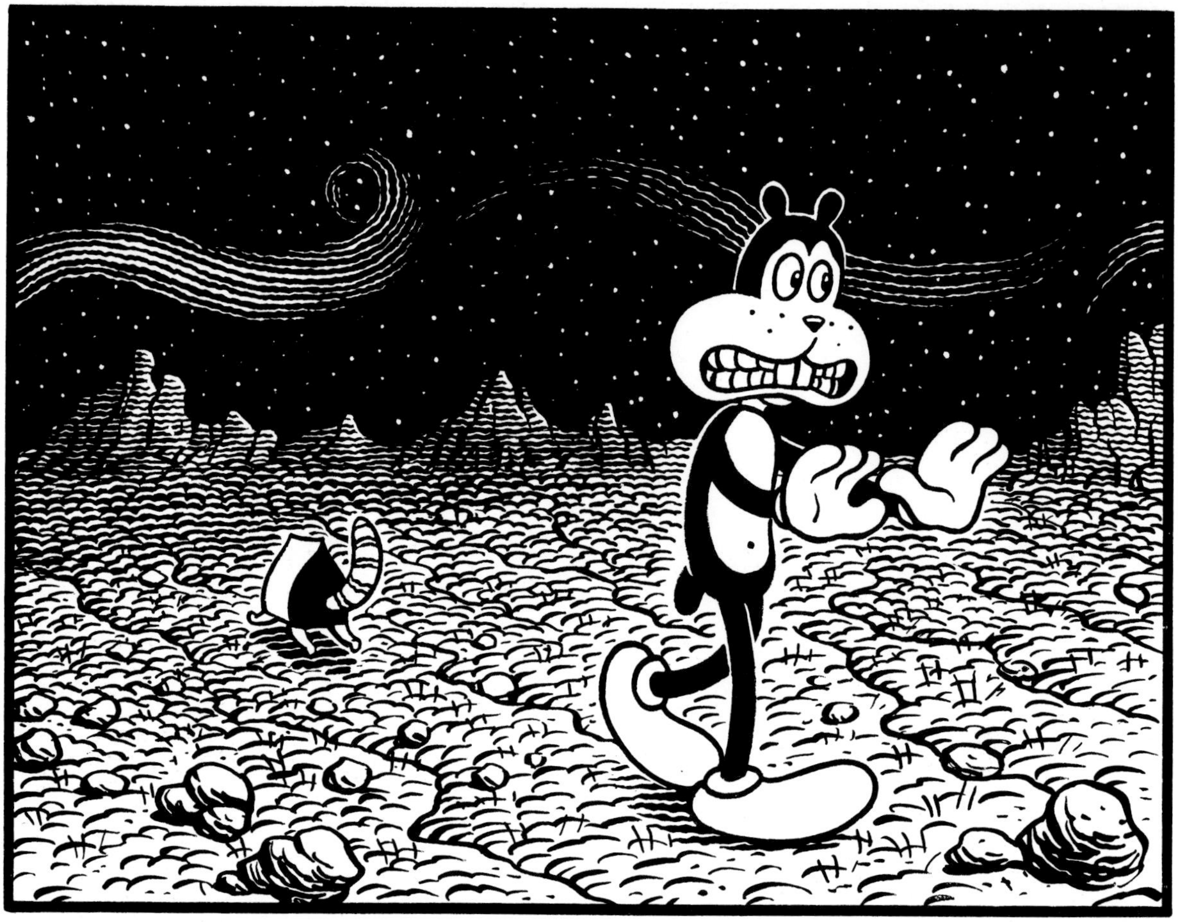

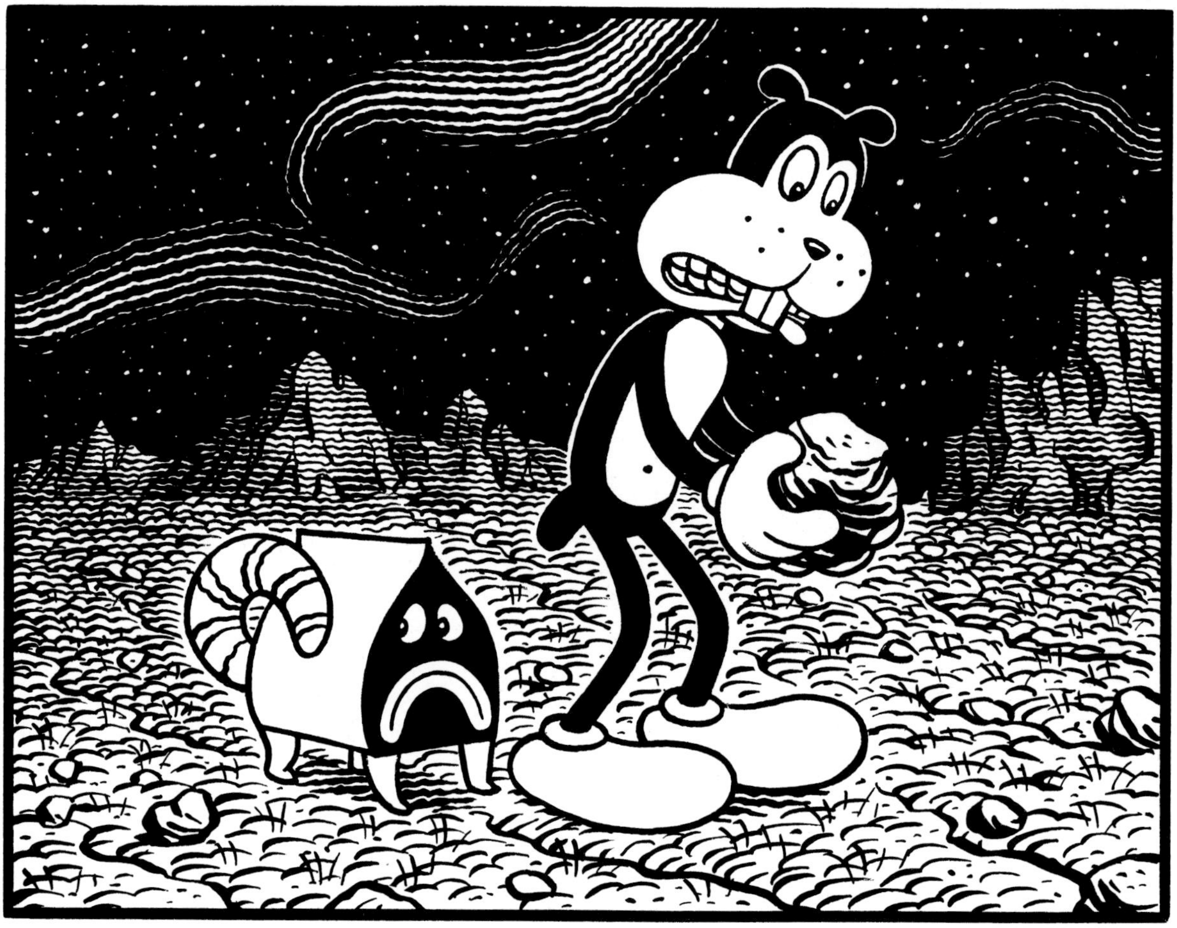

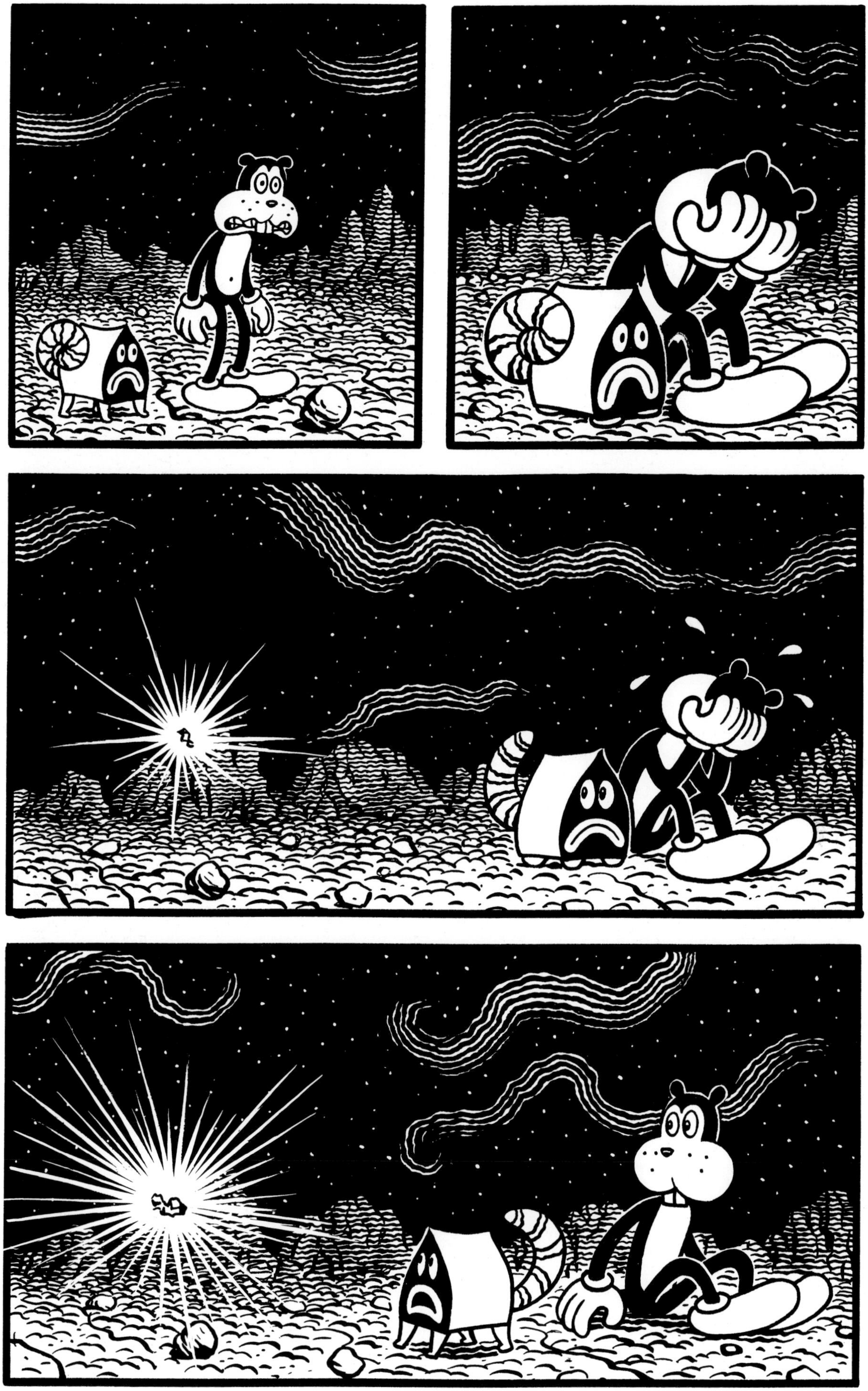

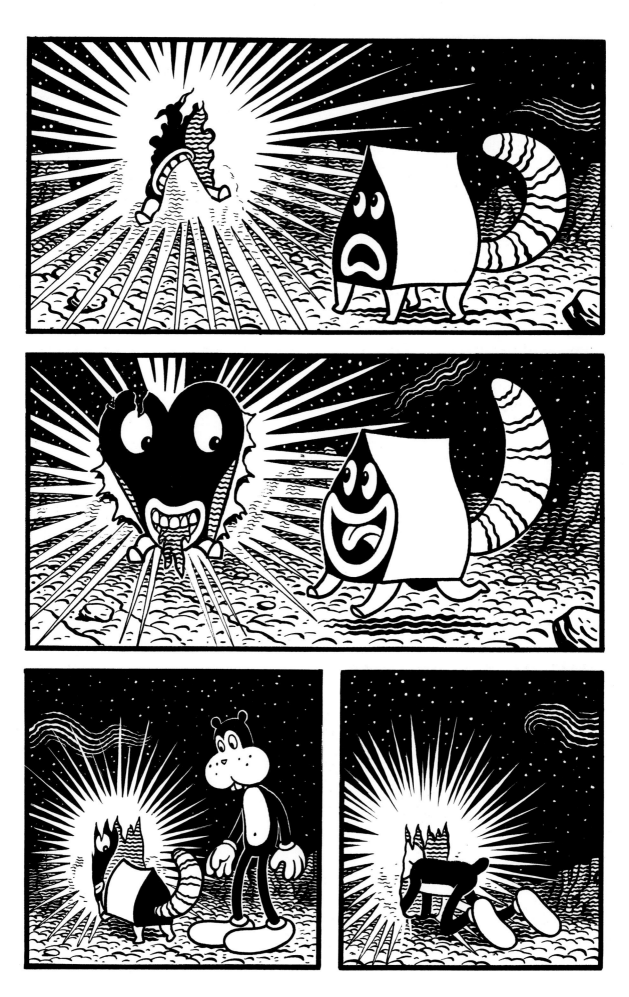

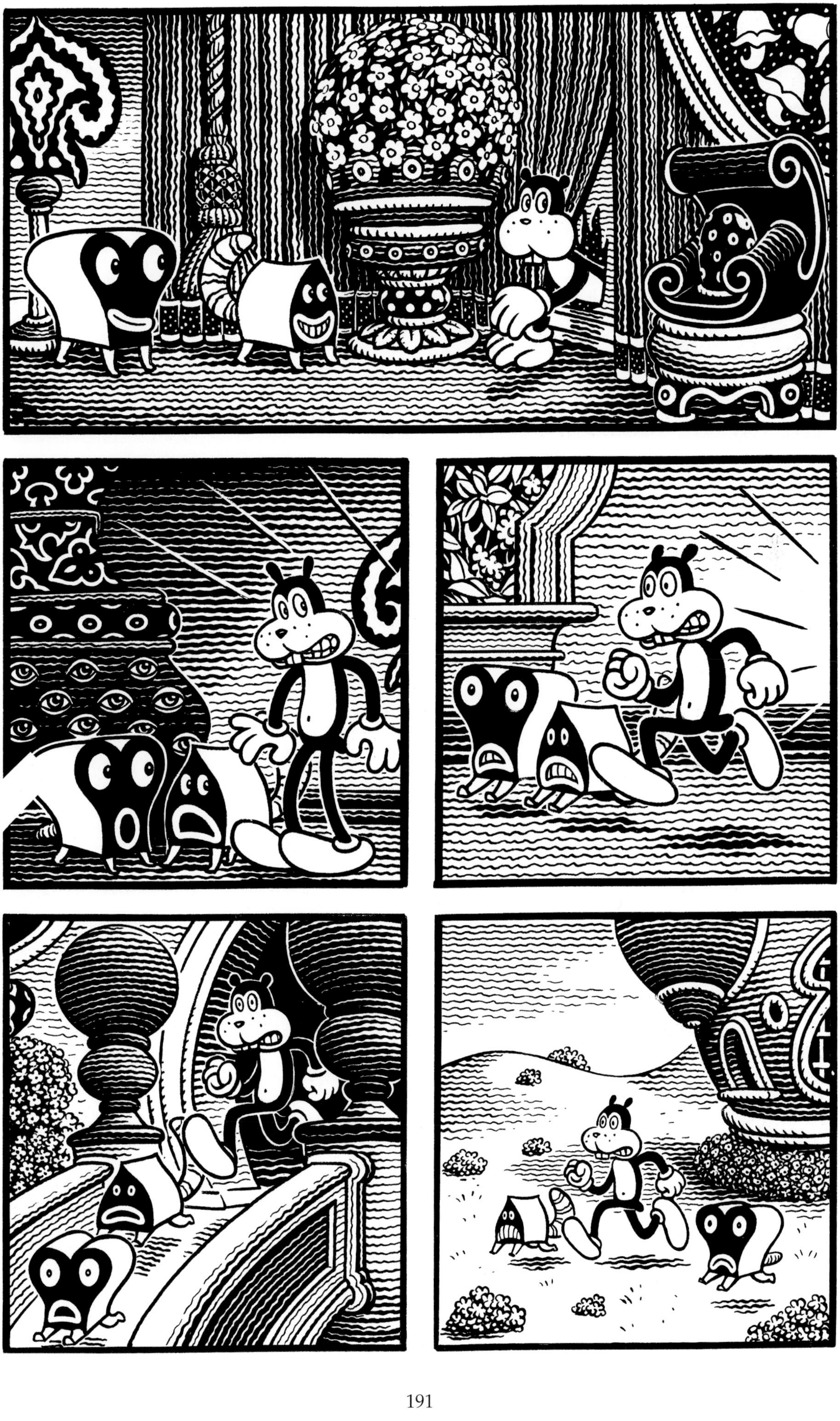

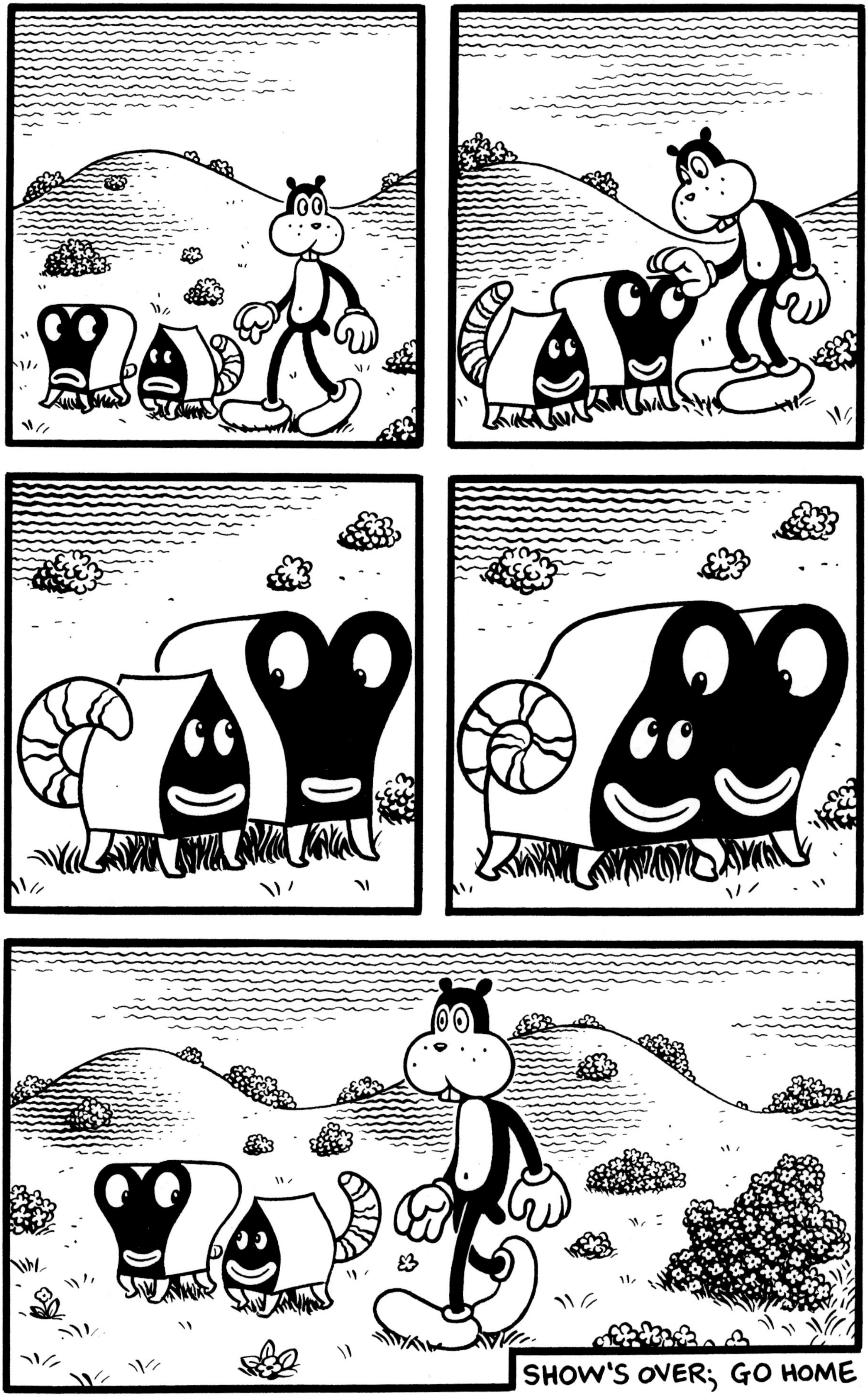
SHOW'S OVER; GO HOME

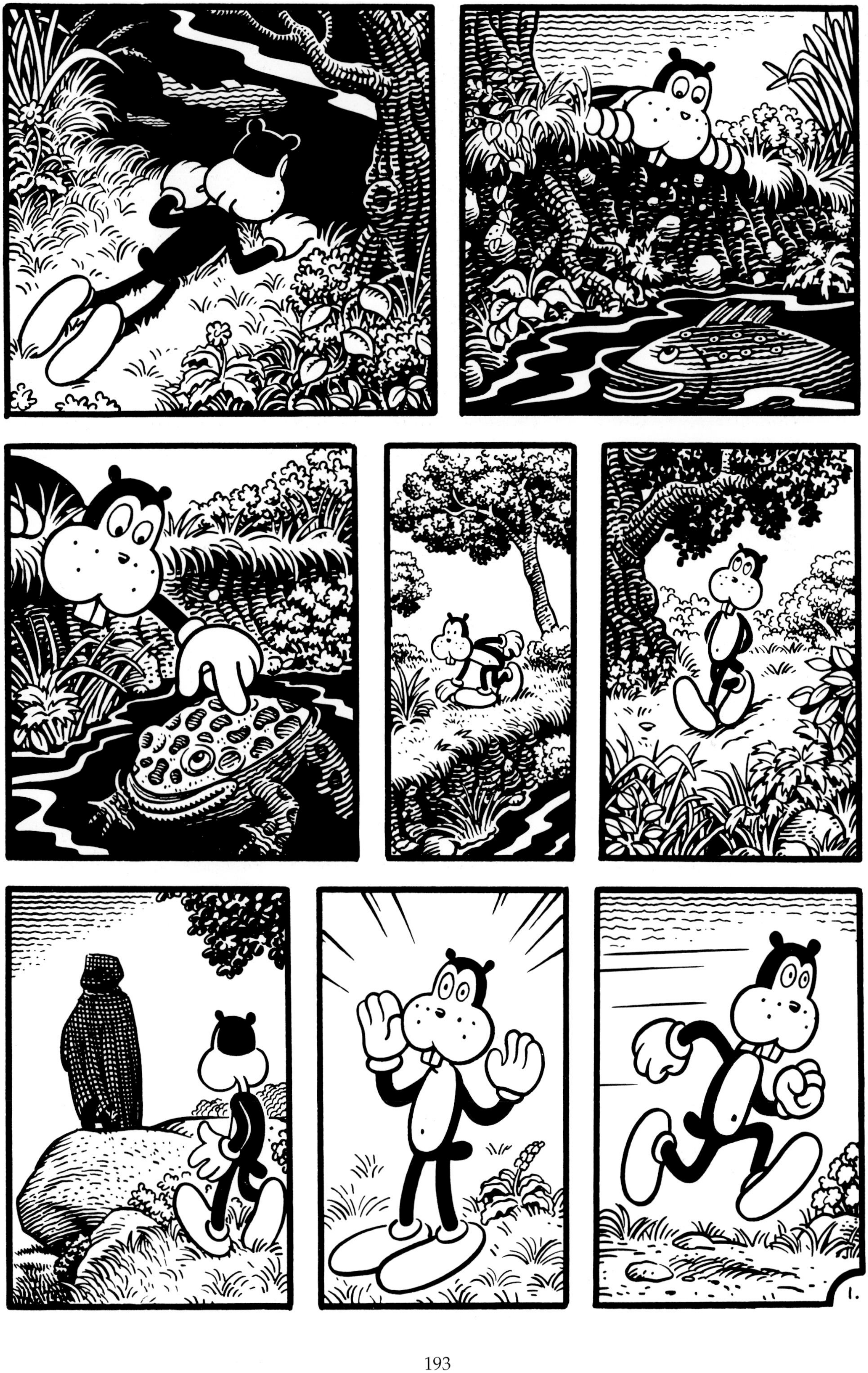
1.

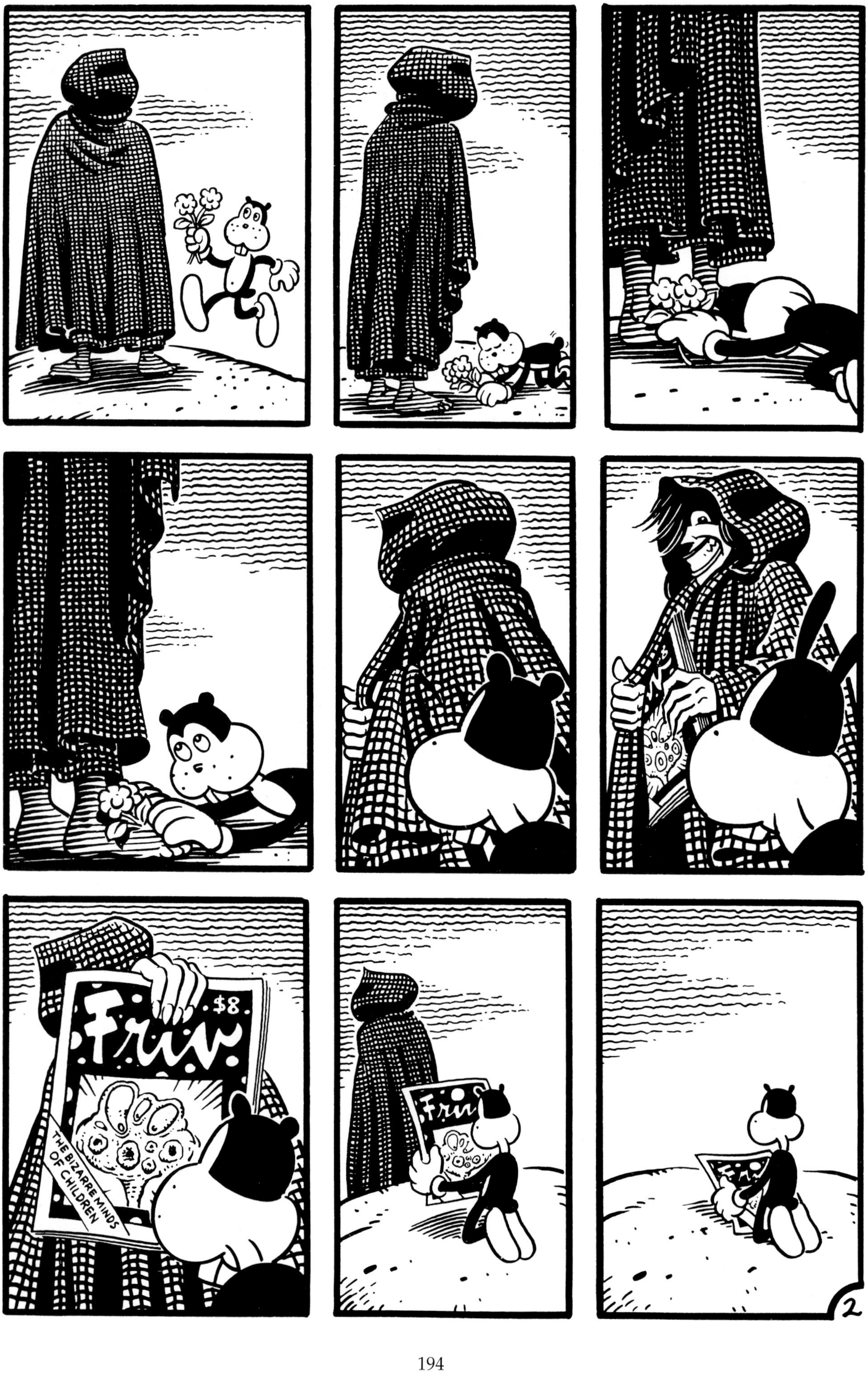
Friv
$8
THE BIZARRE MINDS OF CHILDREN
Friv
2

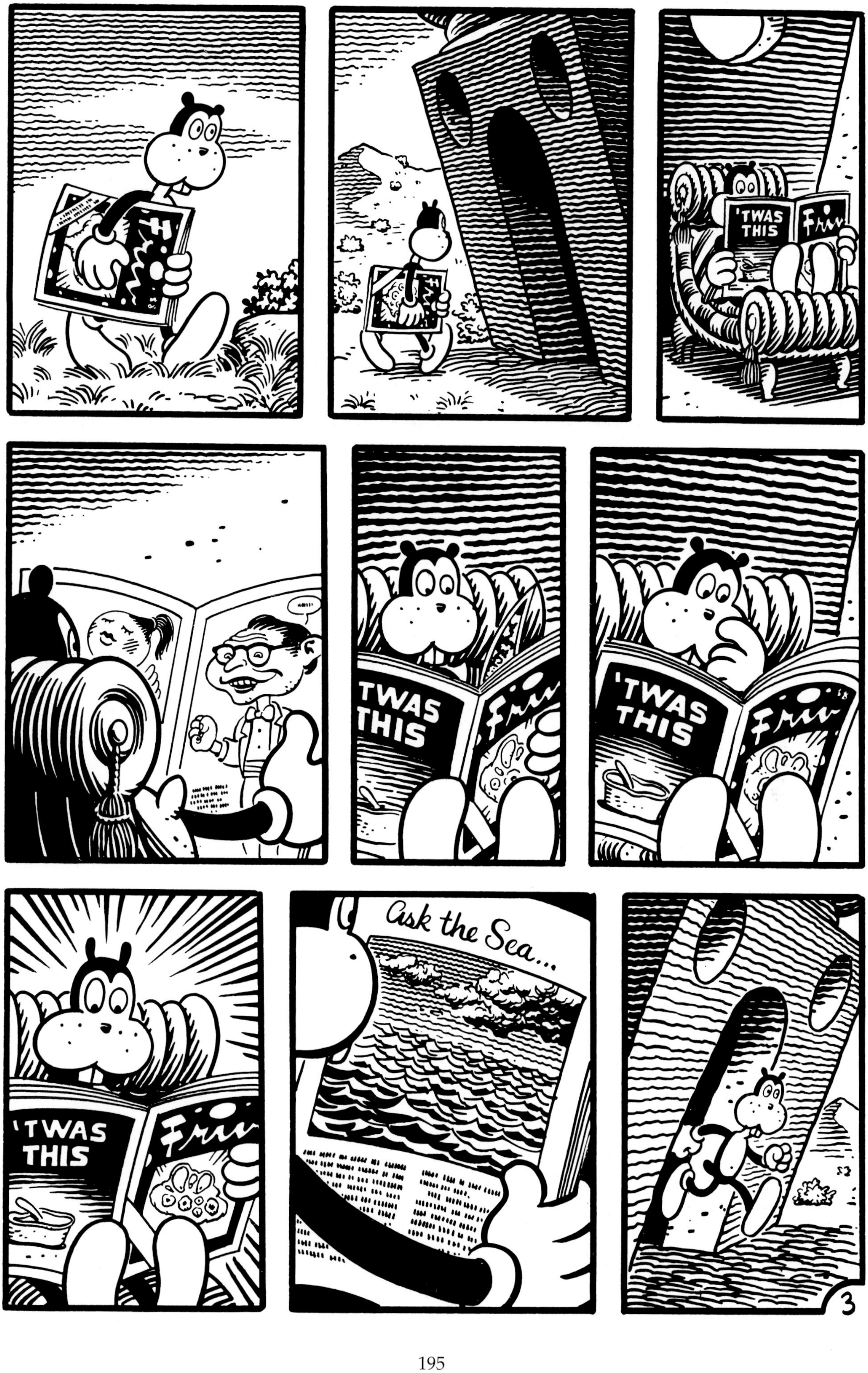
'TWAS THIS
Friv
'TWAS THIS
Friv
'TWAS THIS
Friv
'TWAS THIS
Friv
Ask the Sea...
3

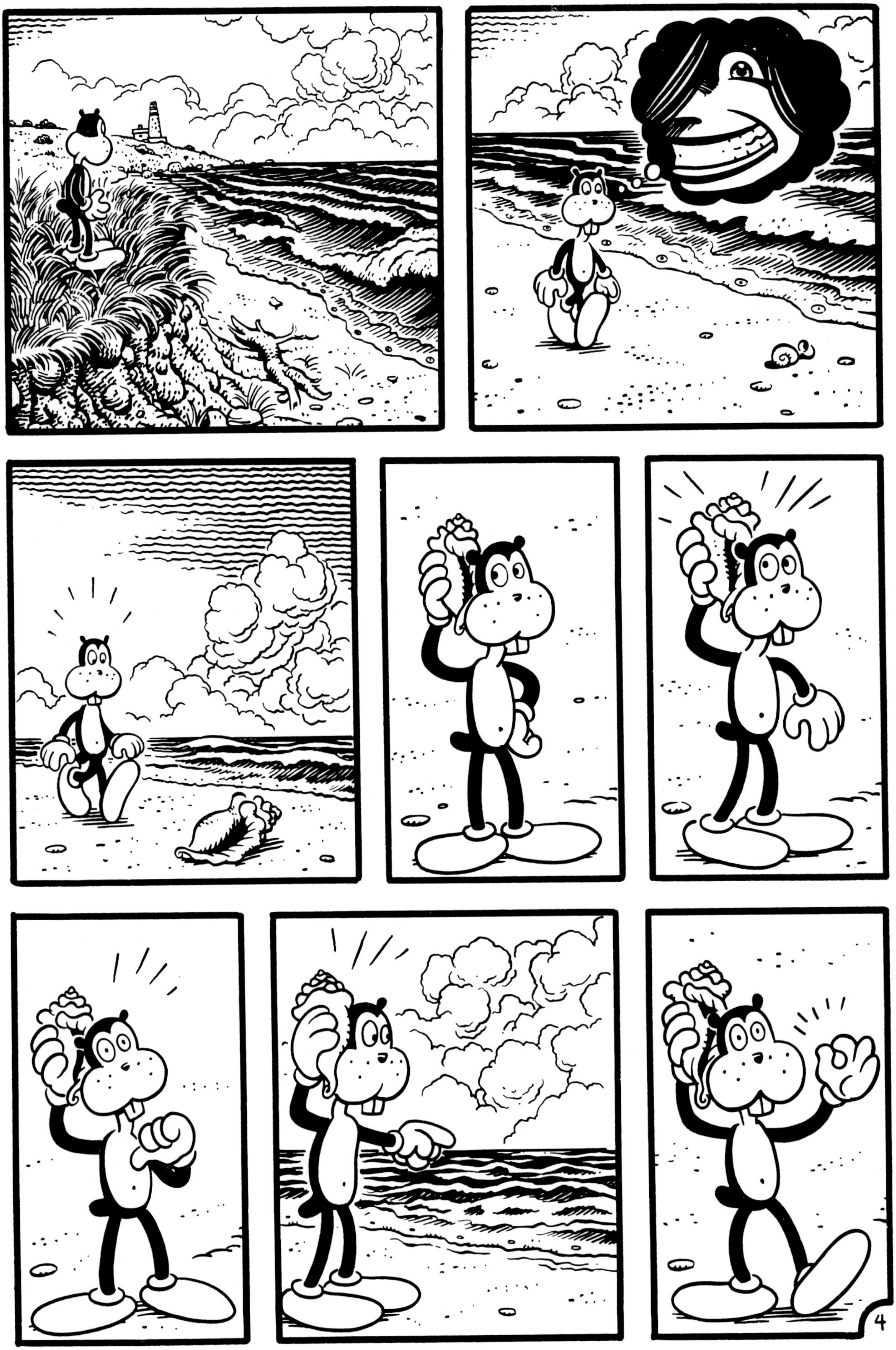
4

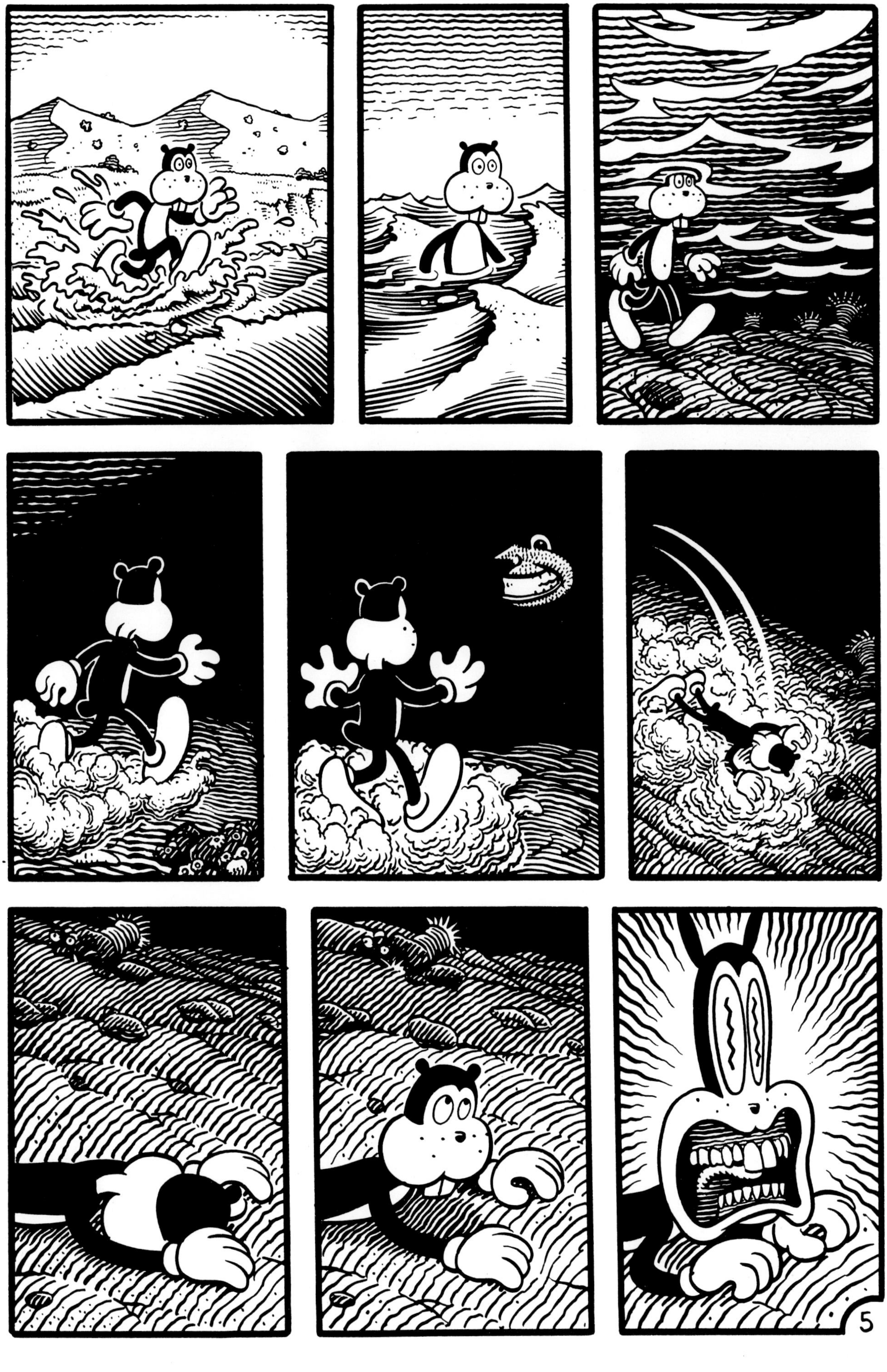
5

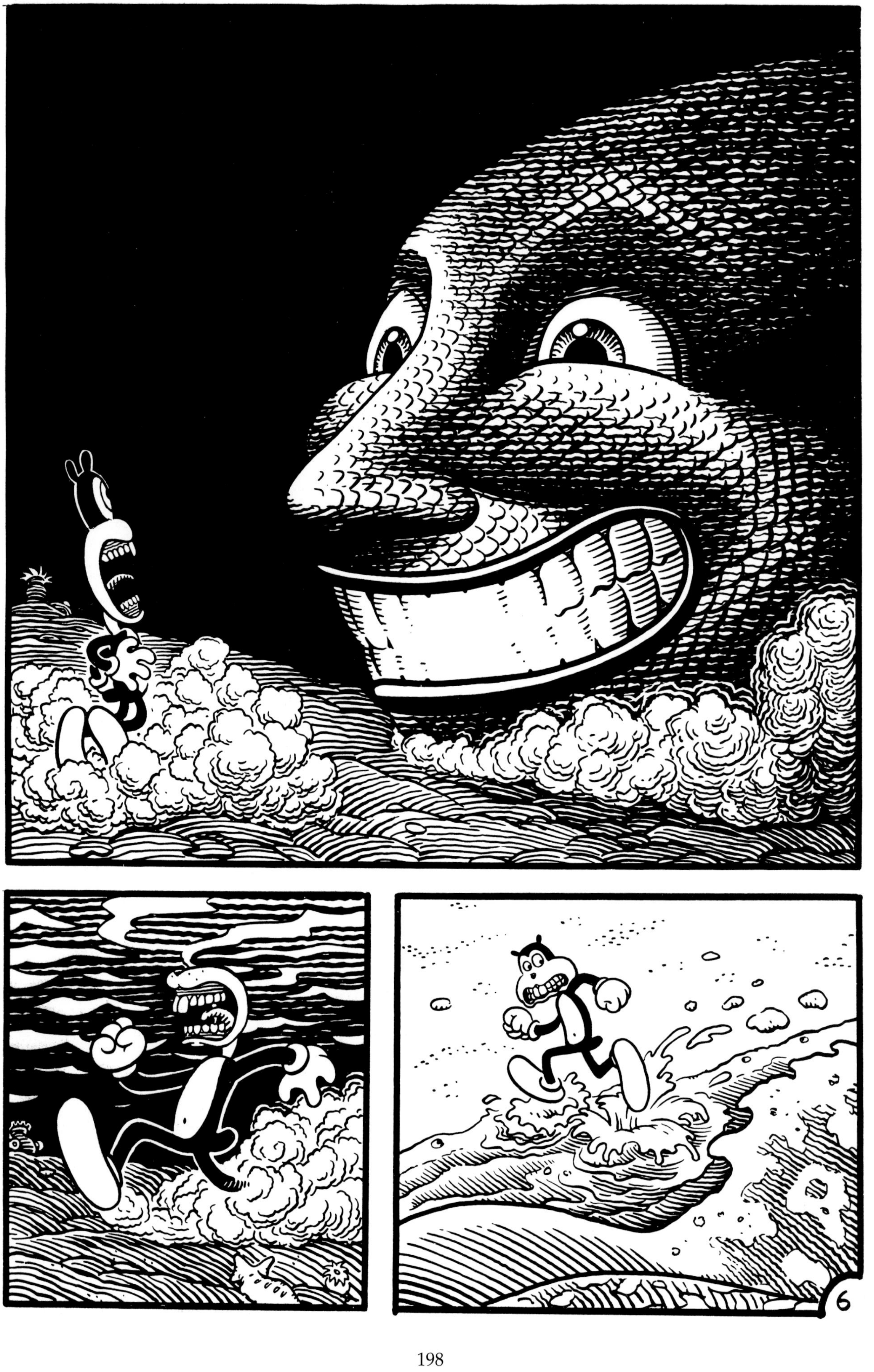
6

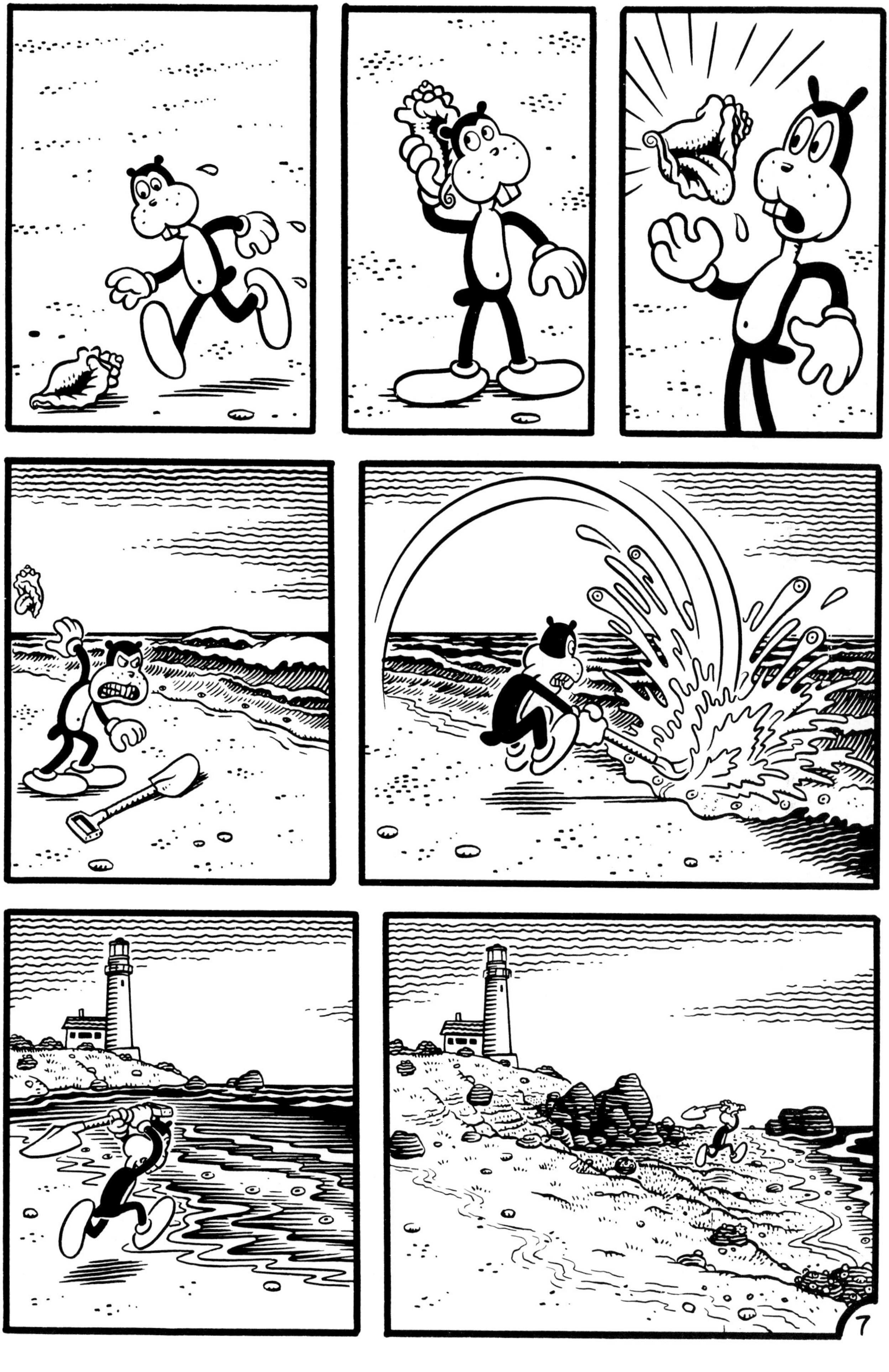
7

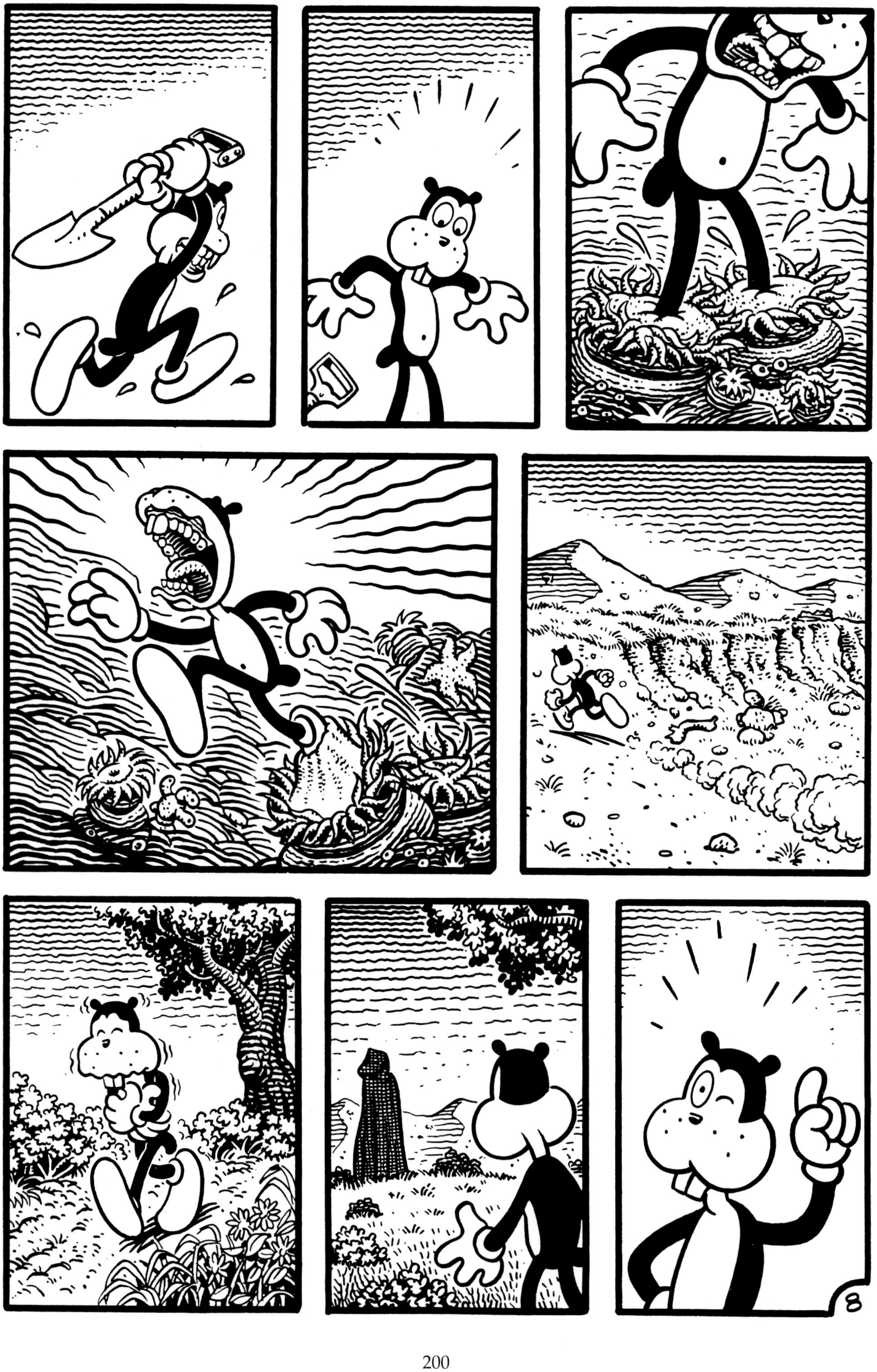
8

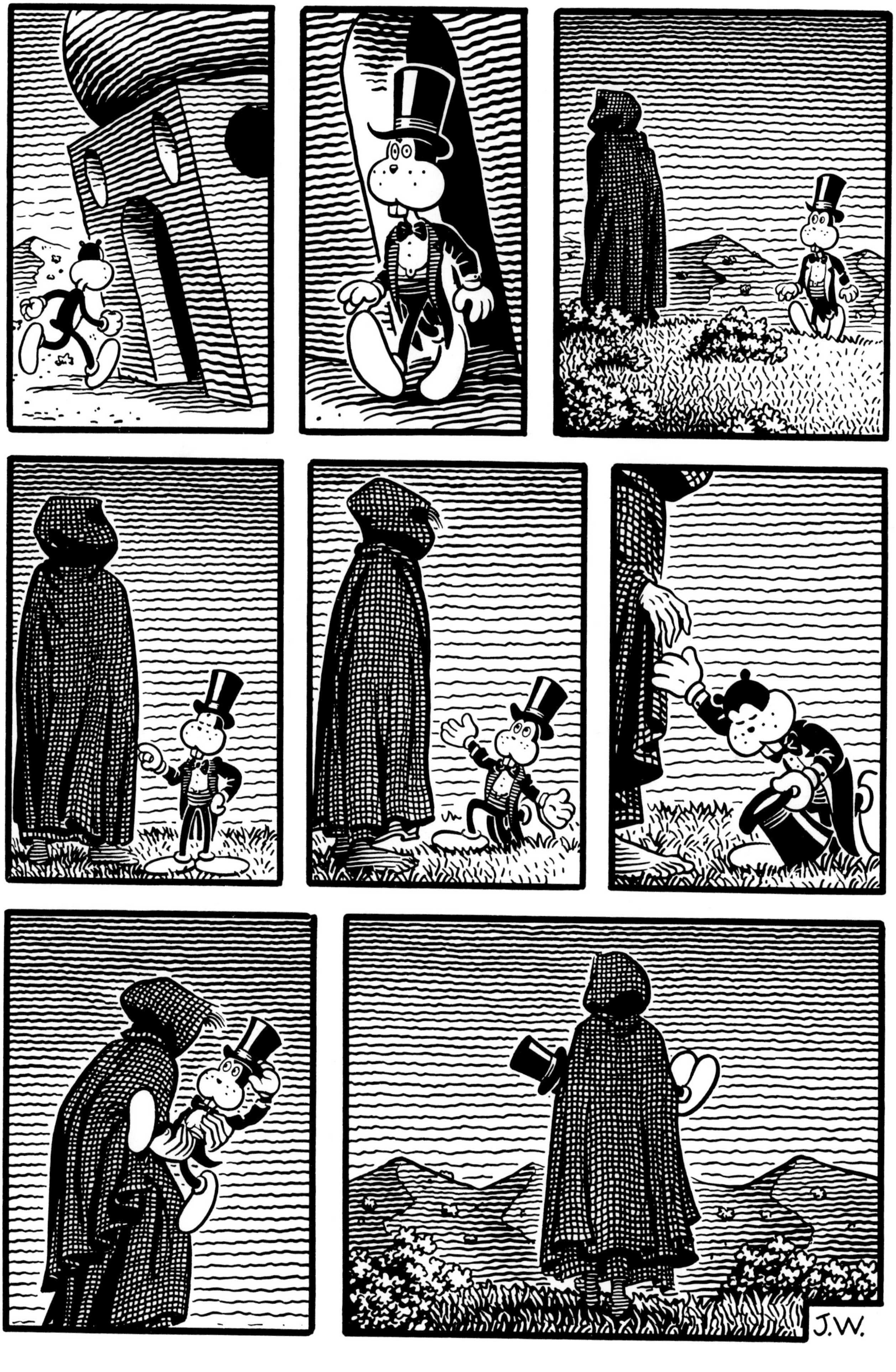
J.W.

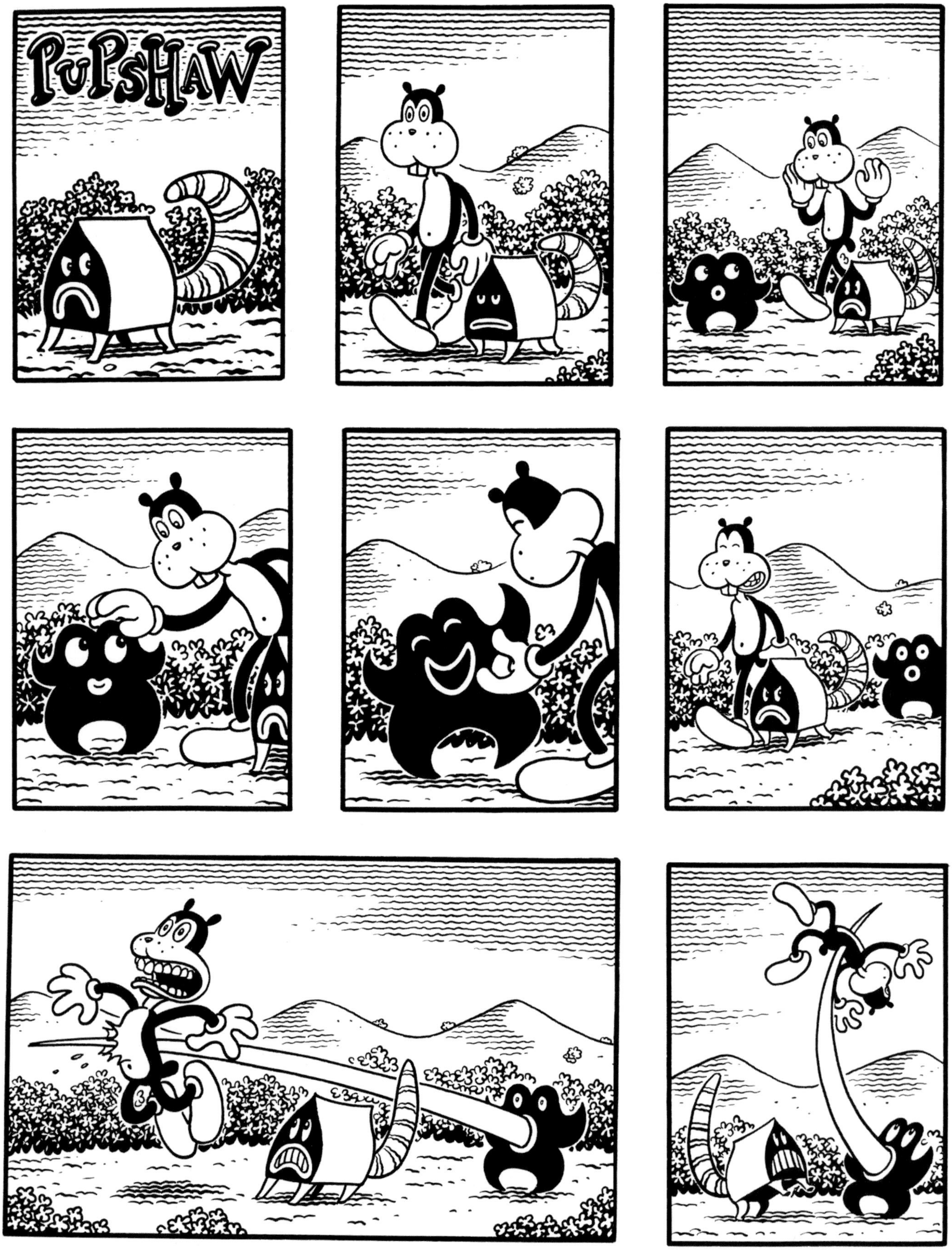
PUPSHAW

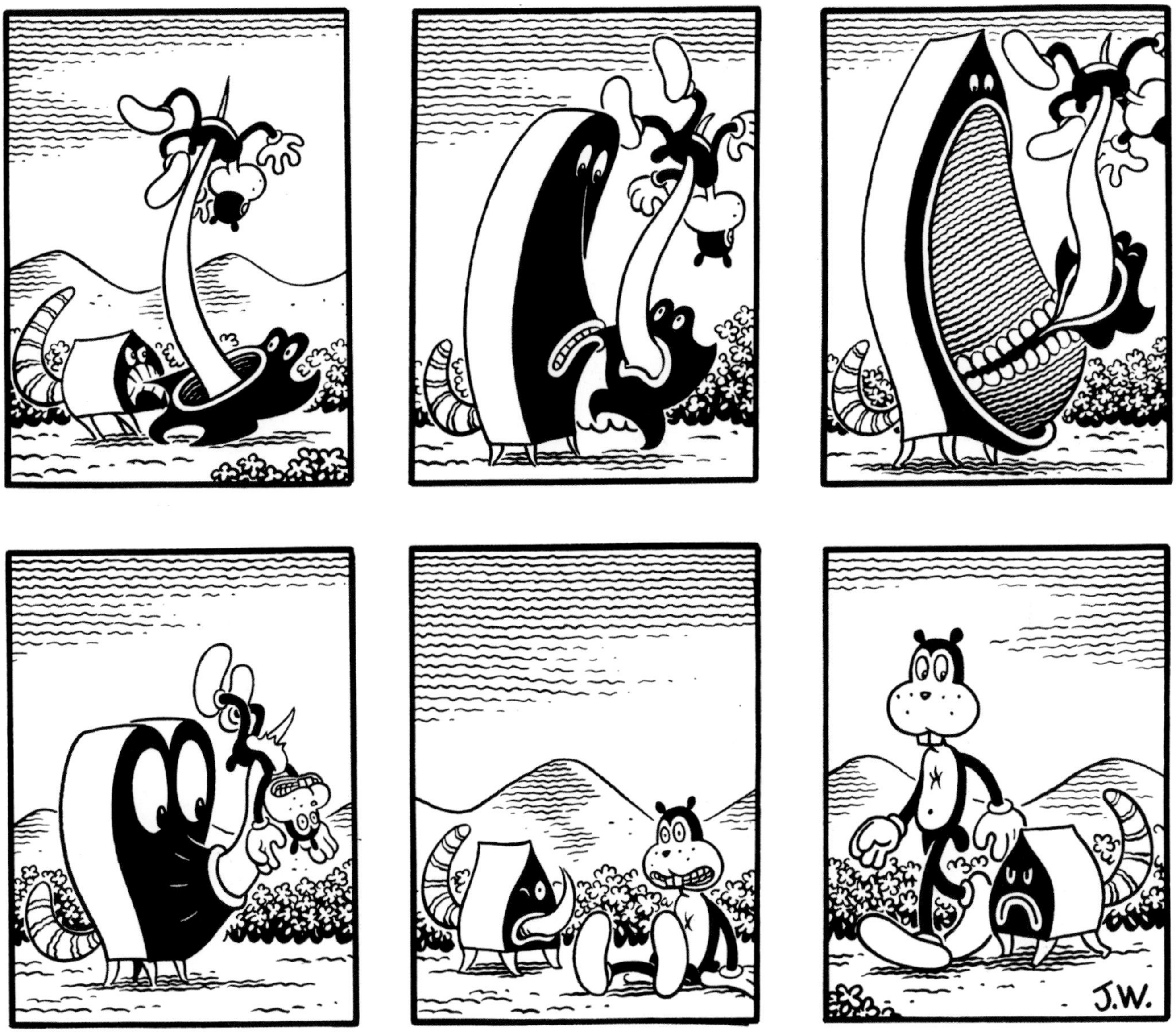
J.W.

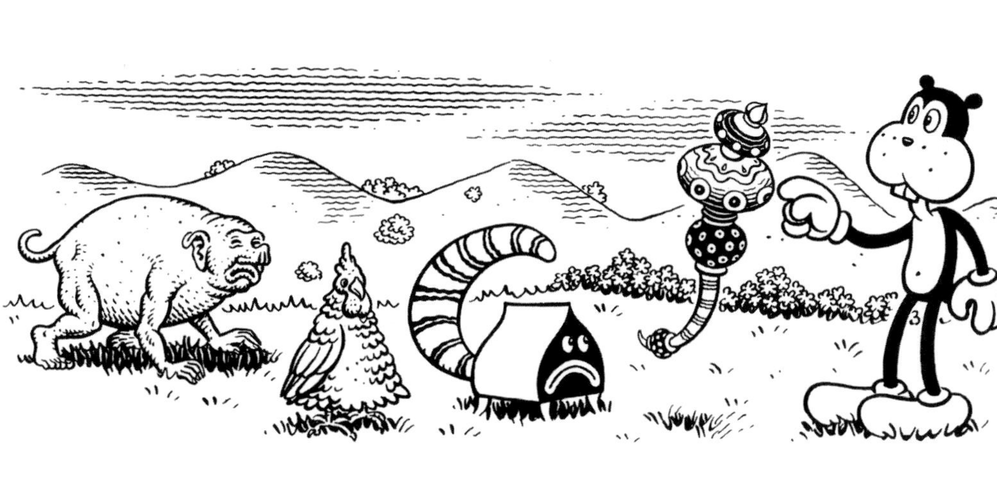

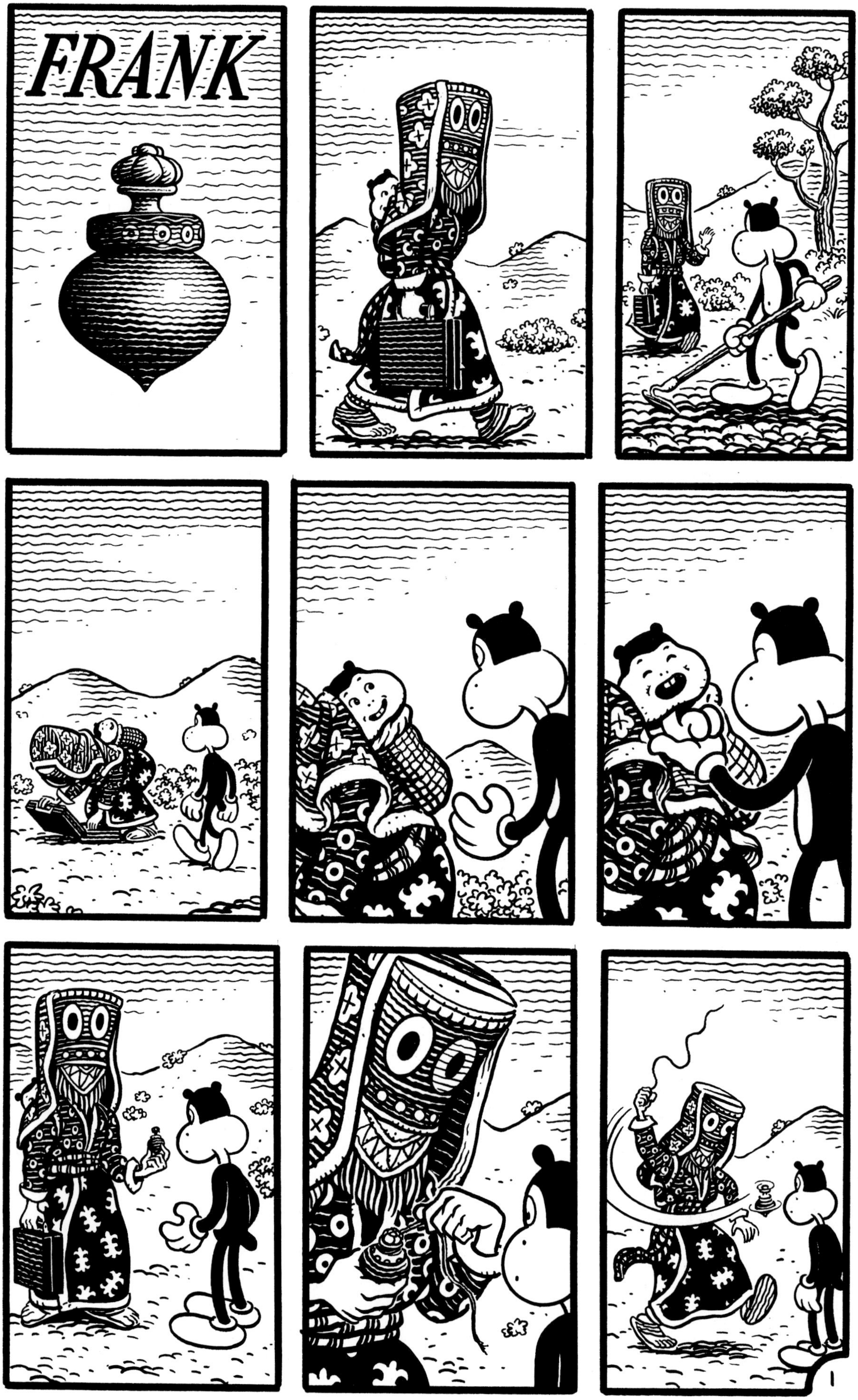
FRANK
1

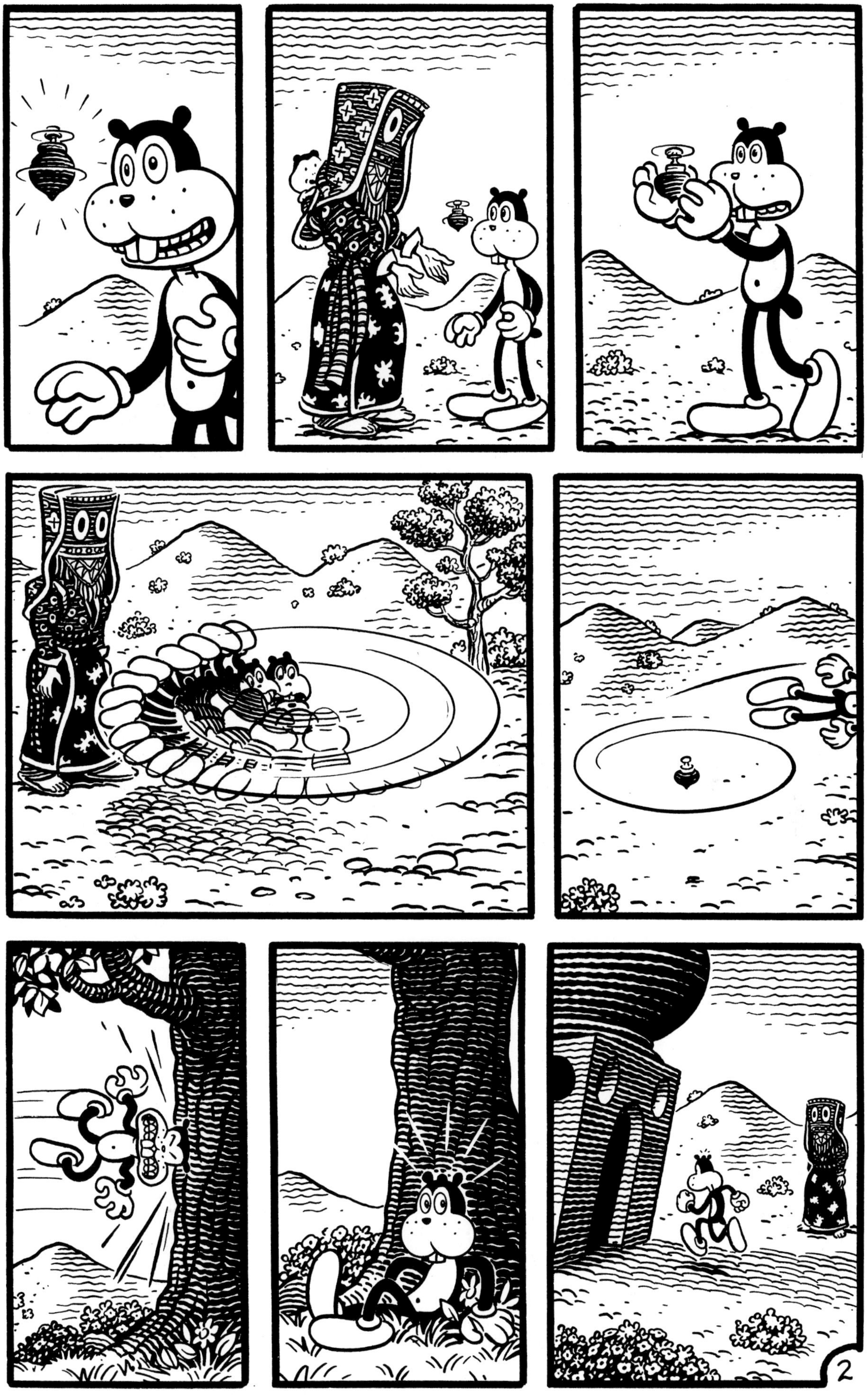
2

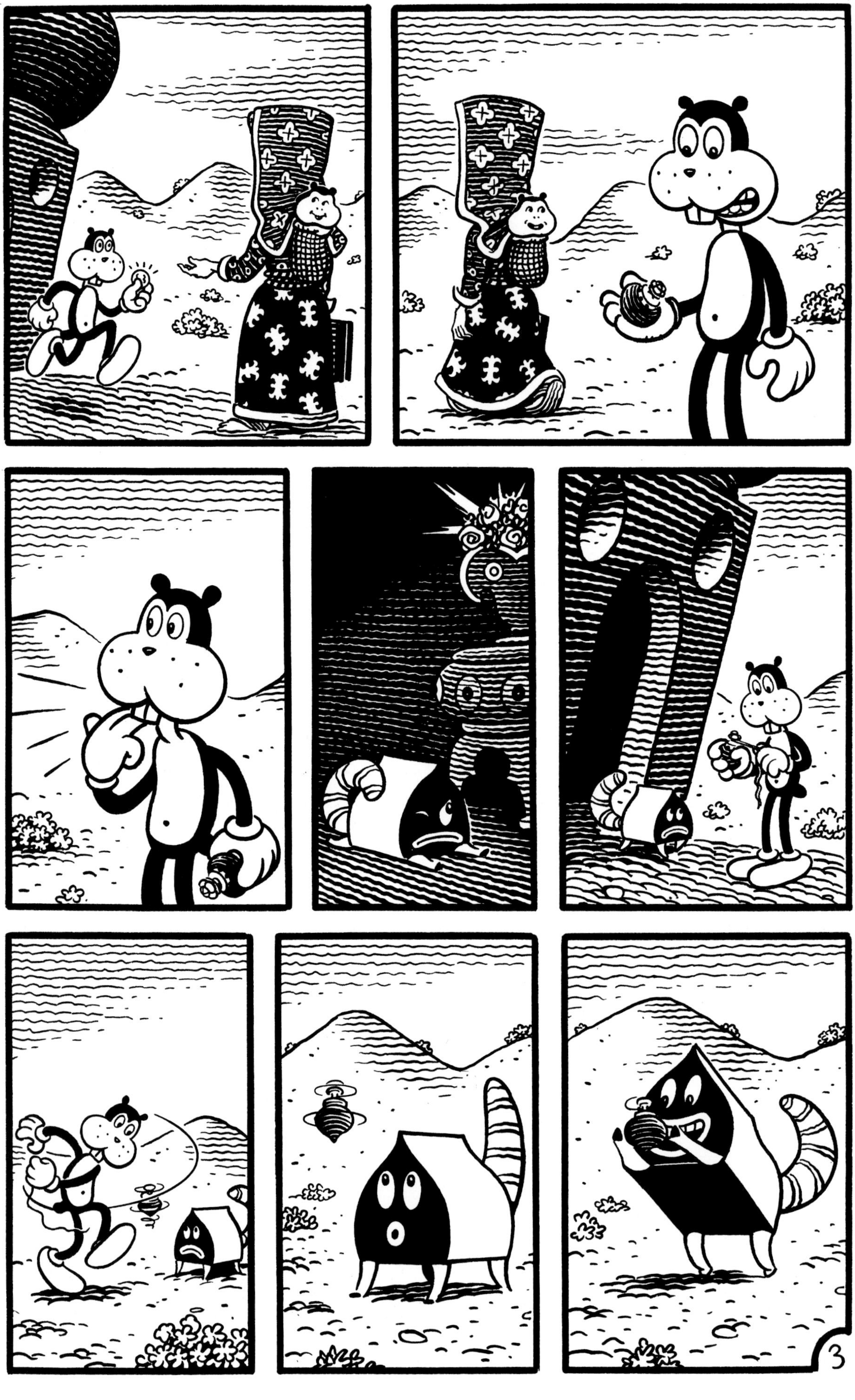
3

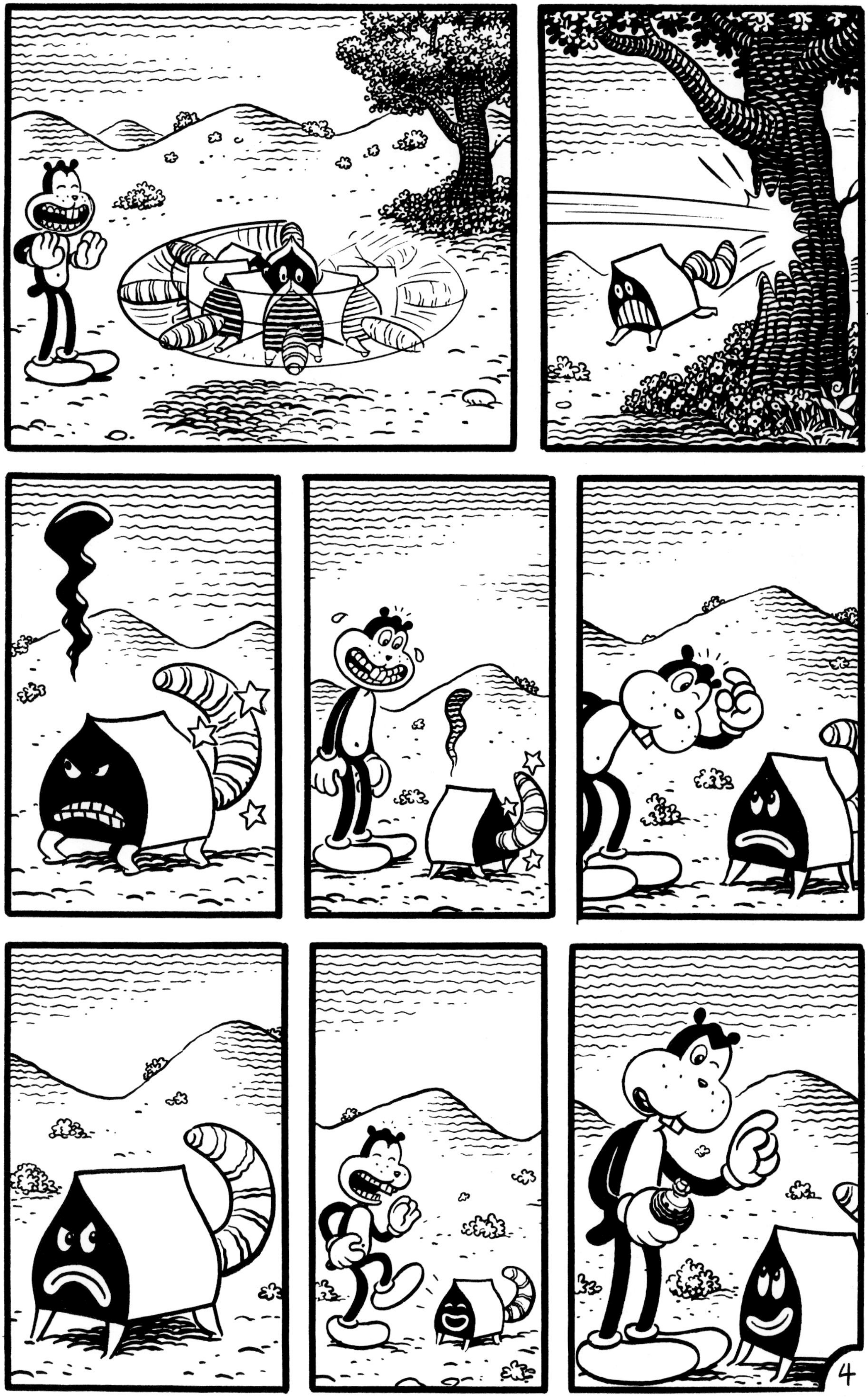

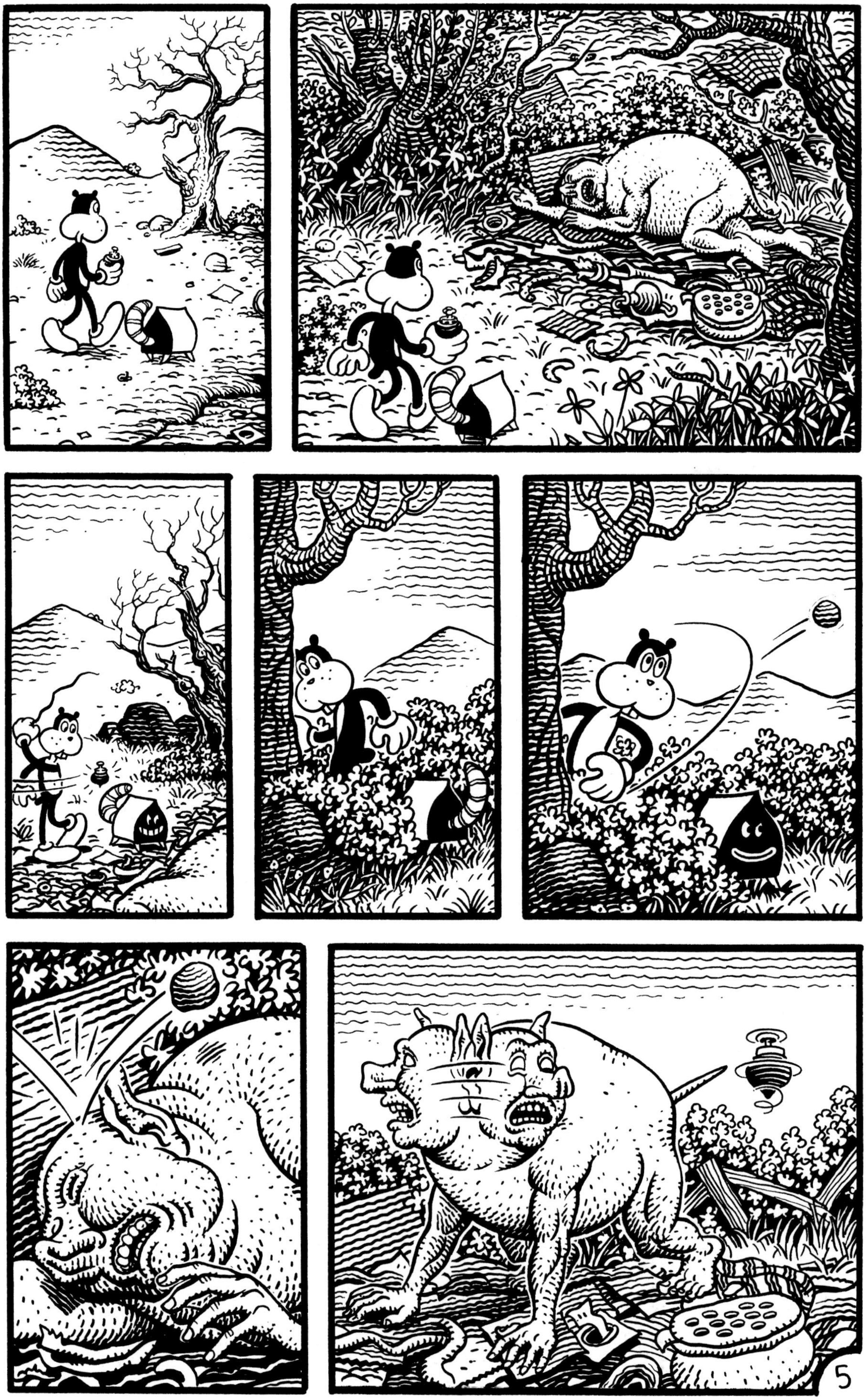
5

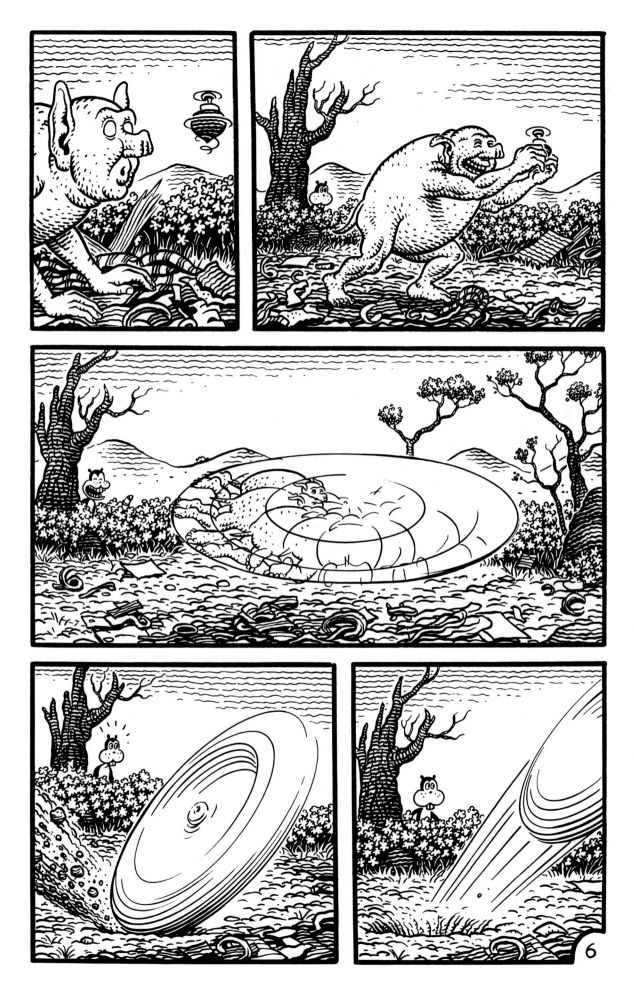

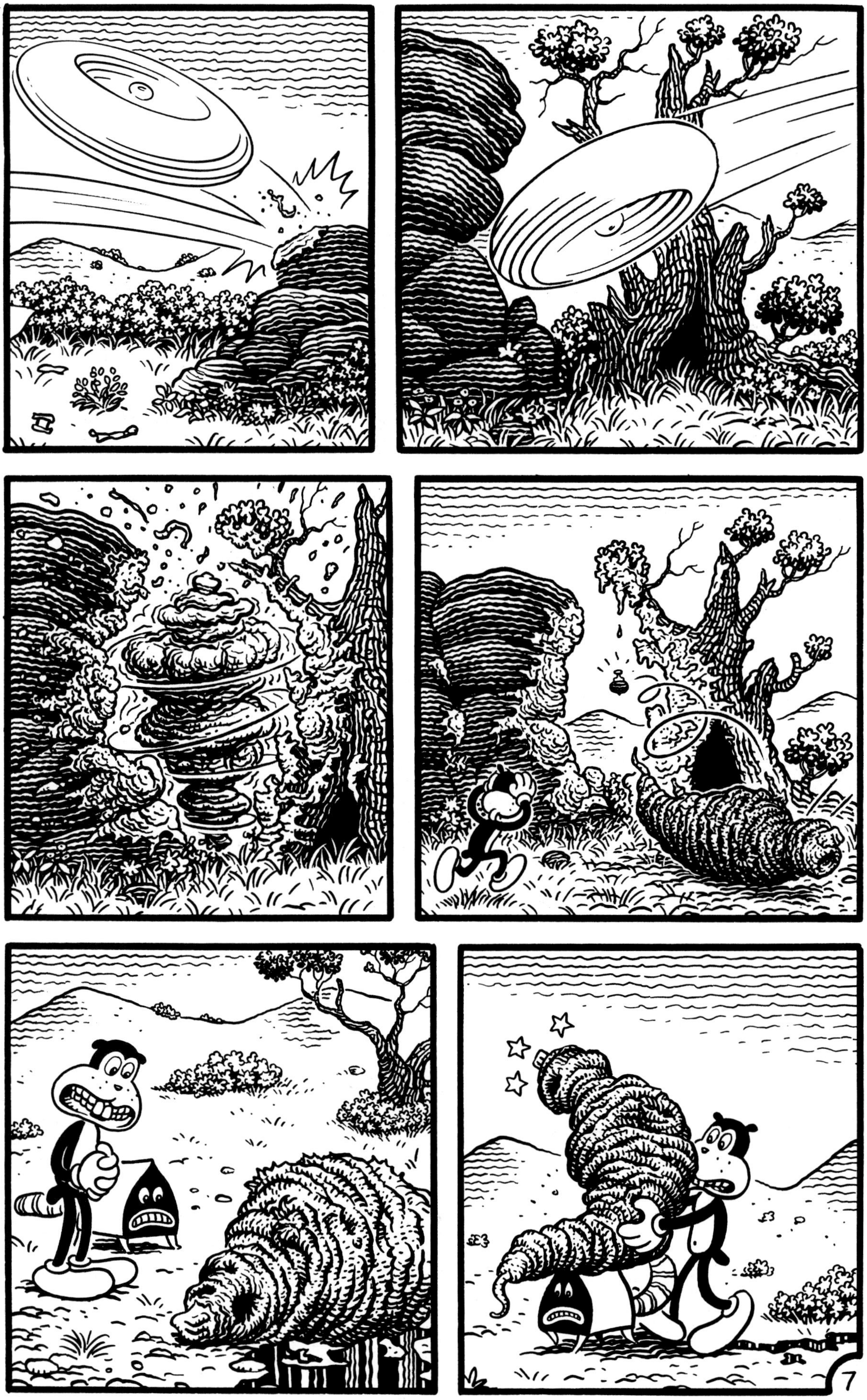
7

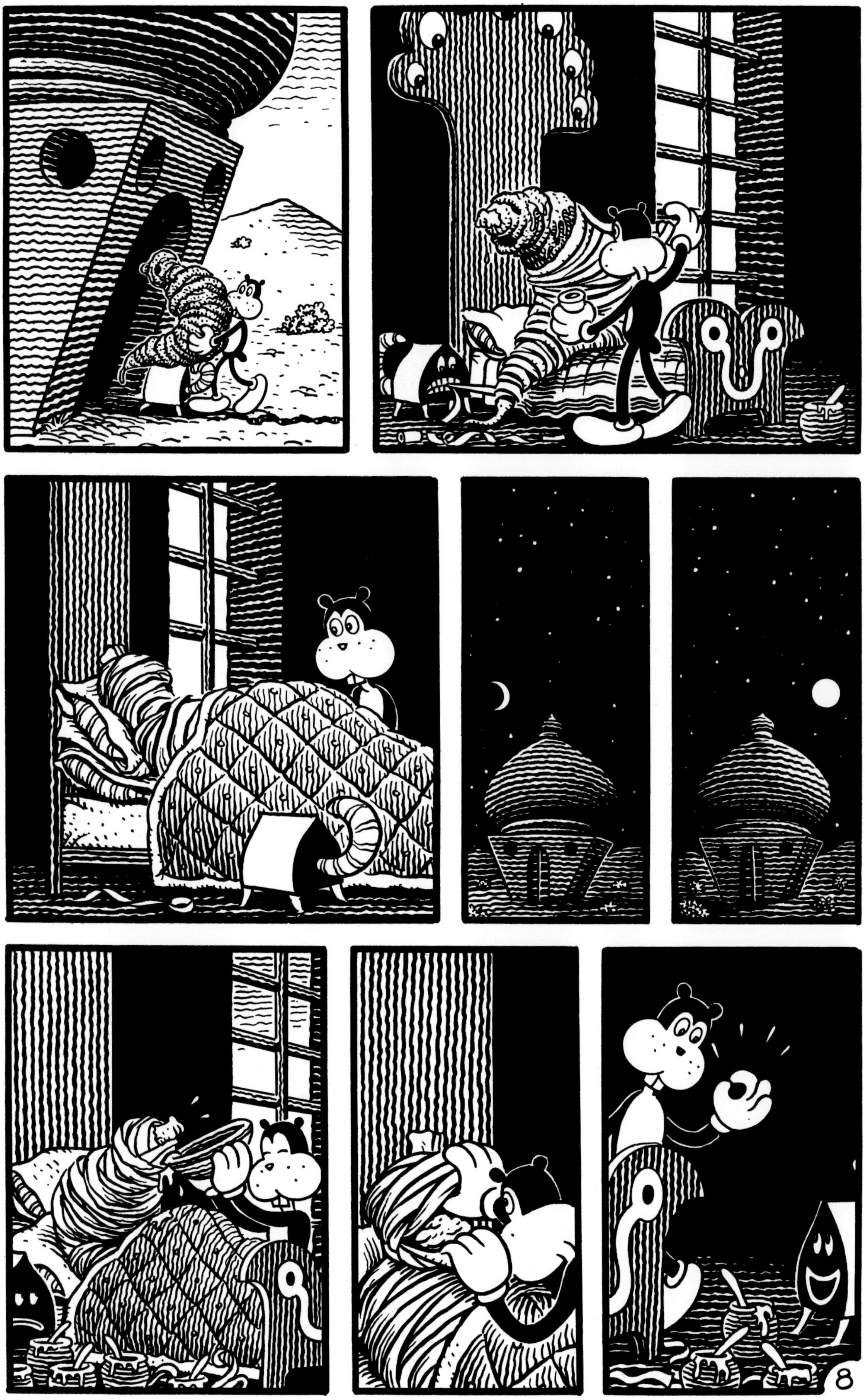
8

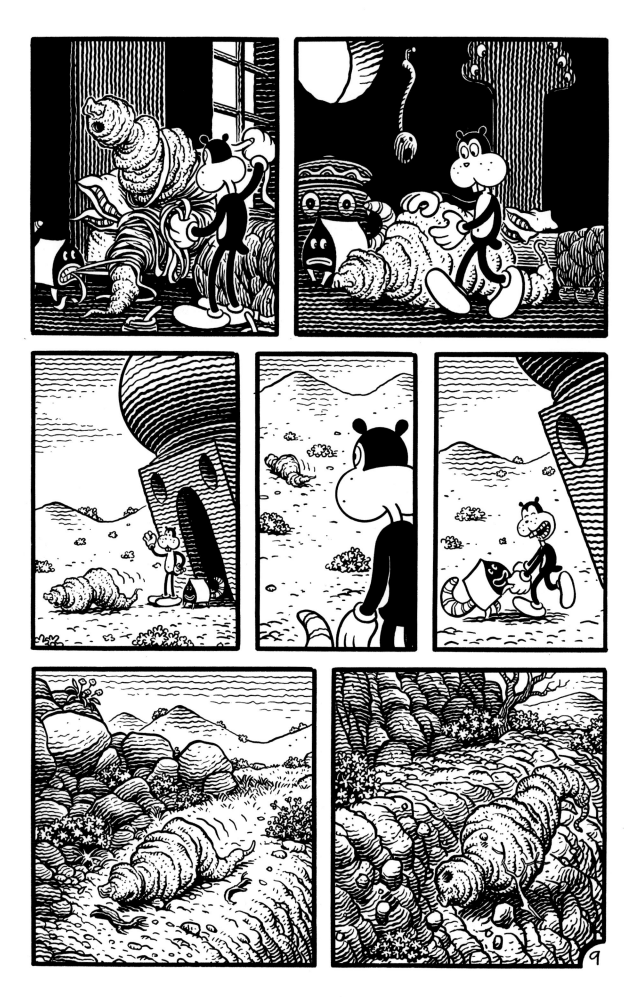

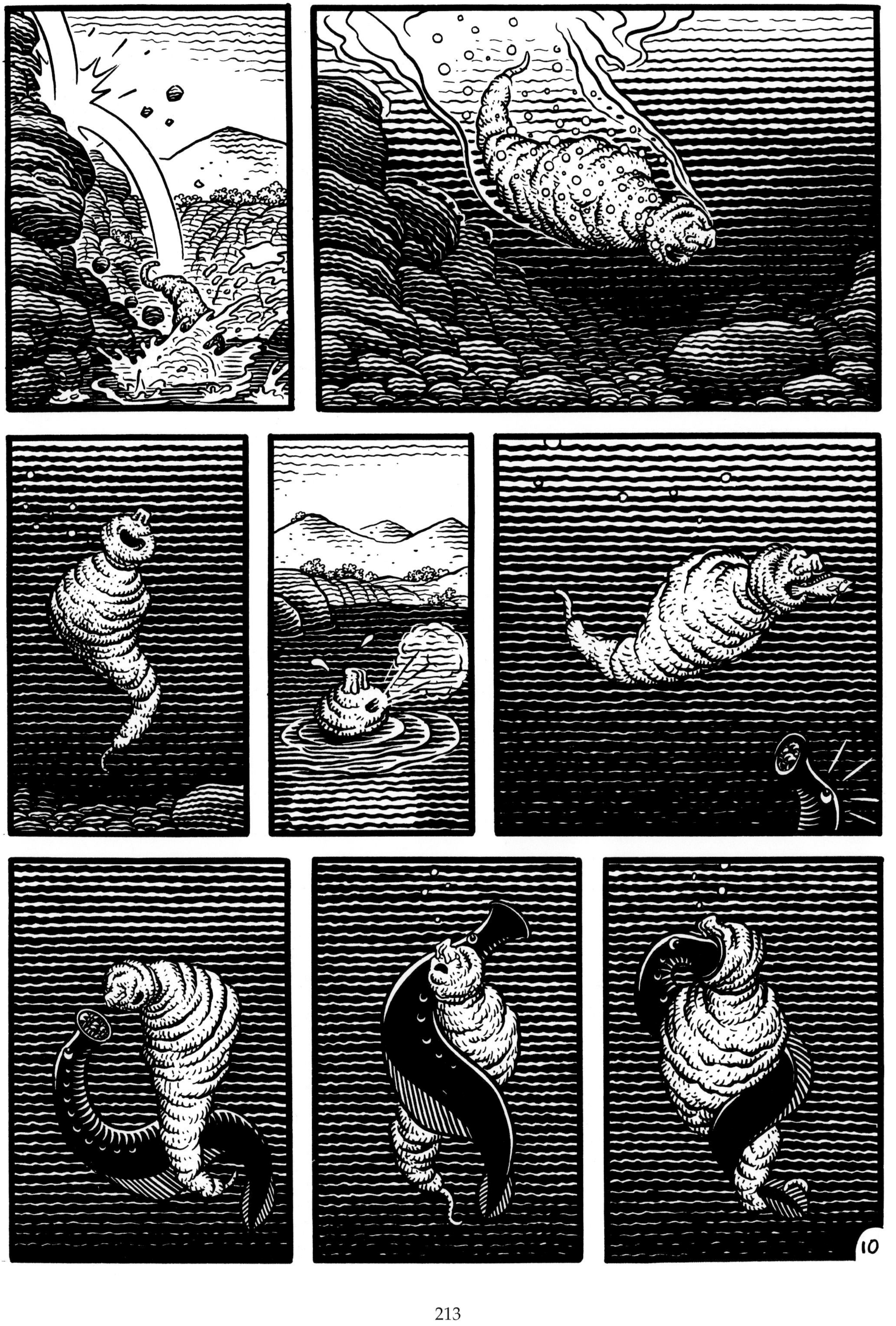
10

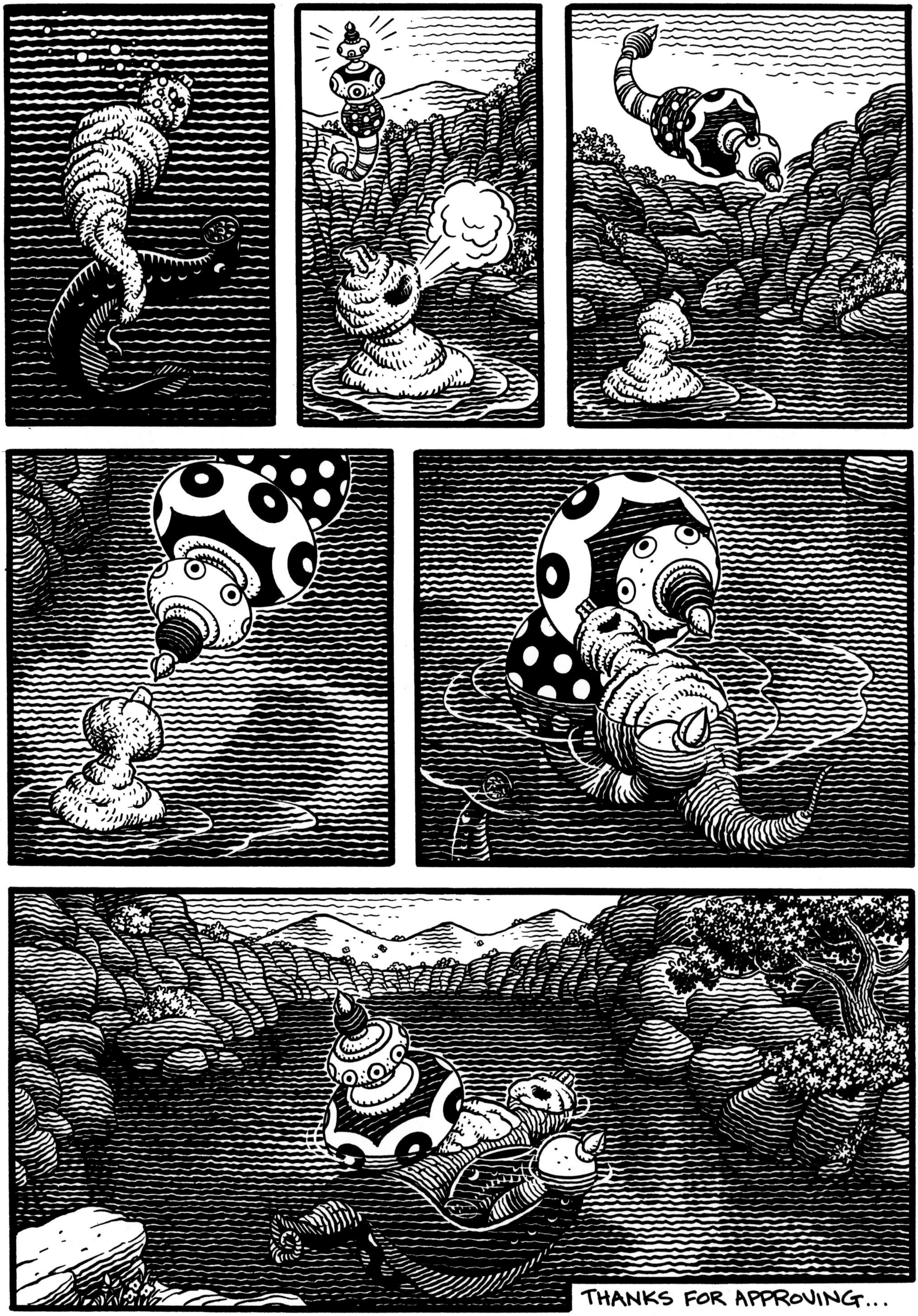
THANKS FOR APPROVING...

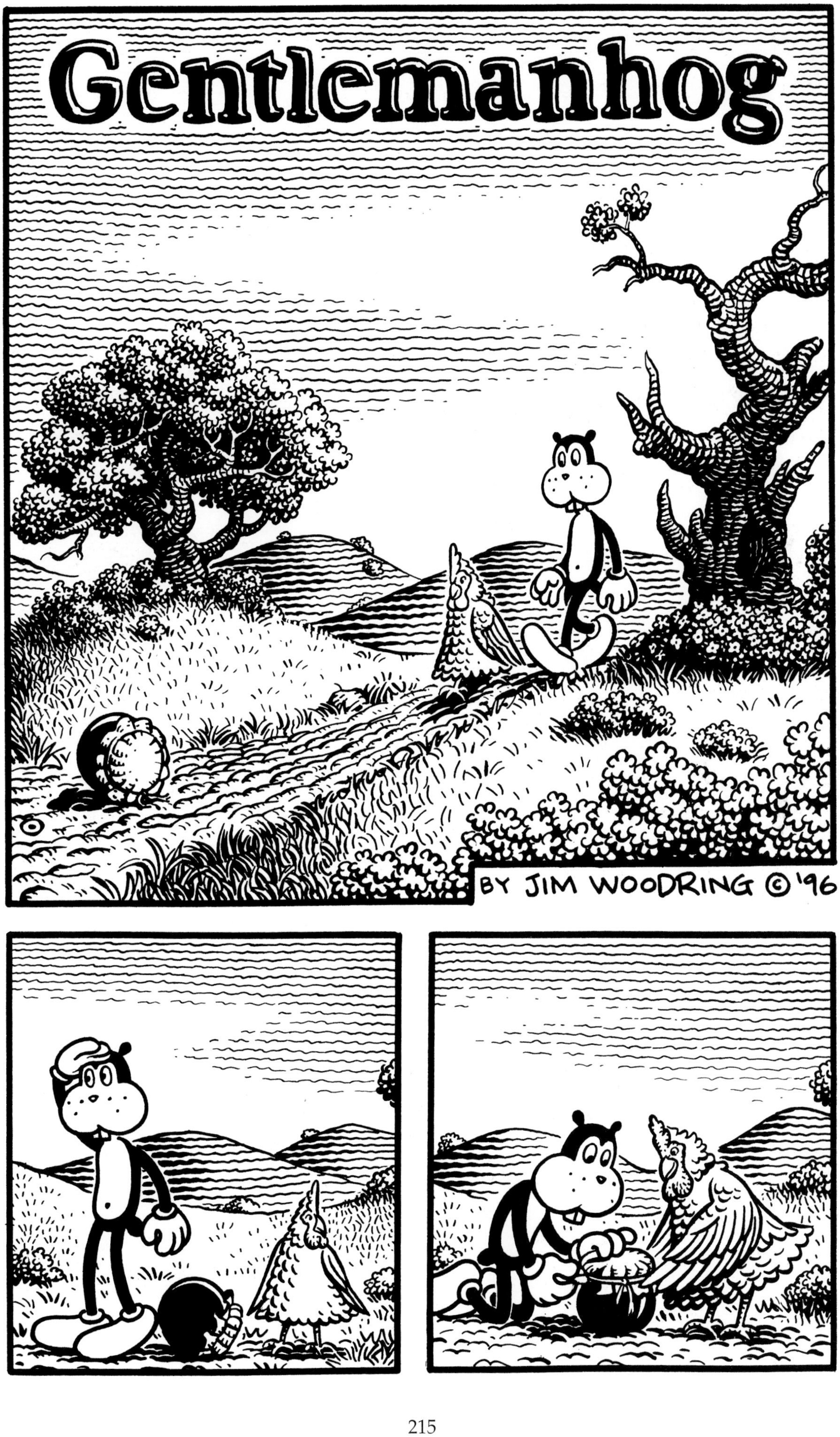
Gentlemanhog
BY JIM WOODRING © '96

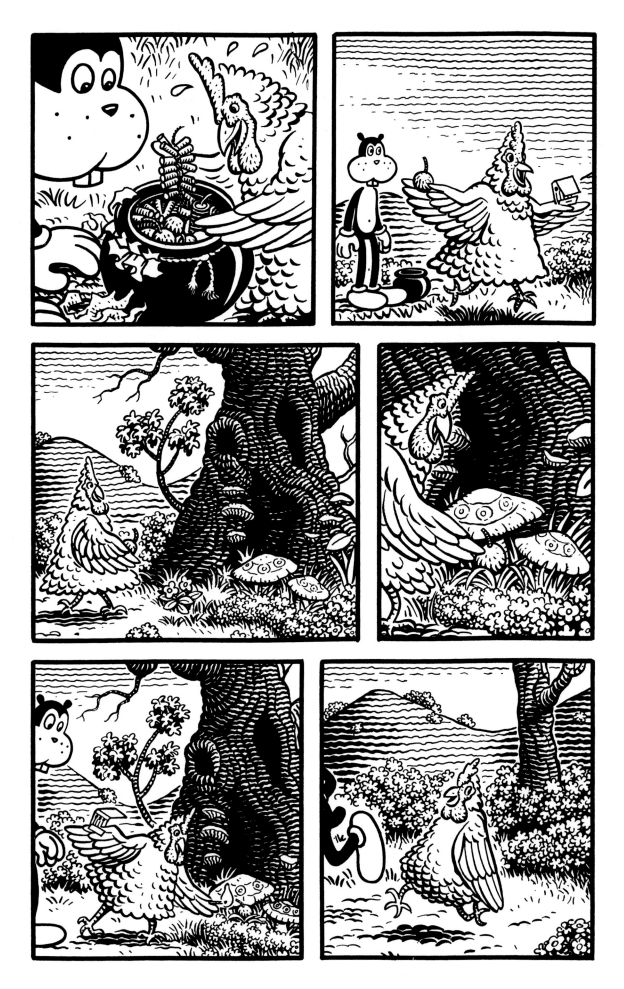

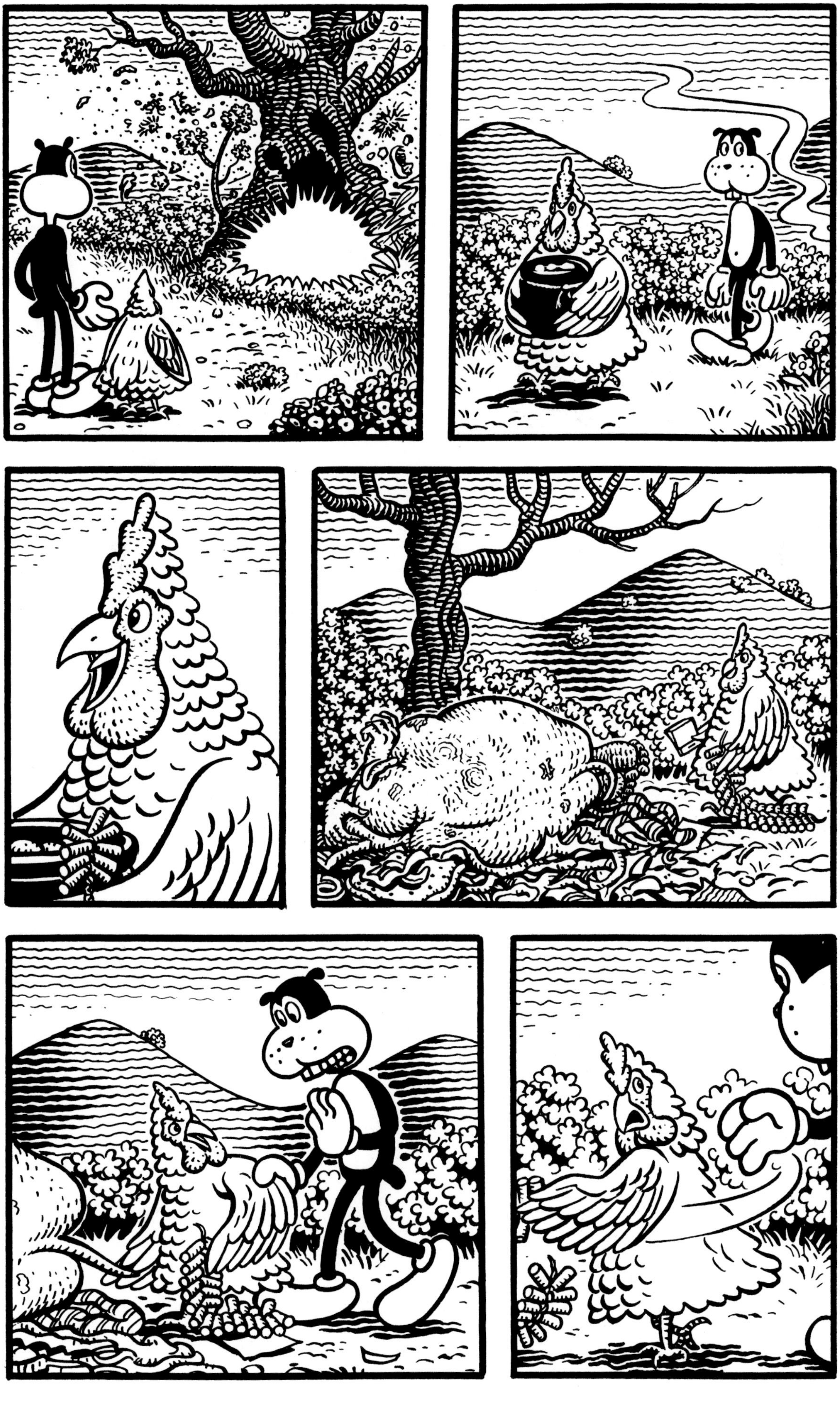

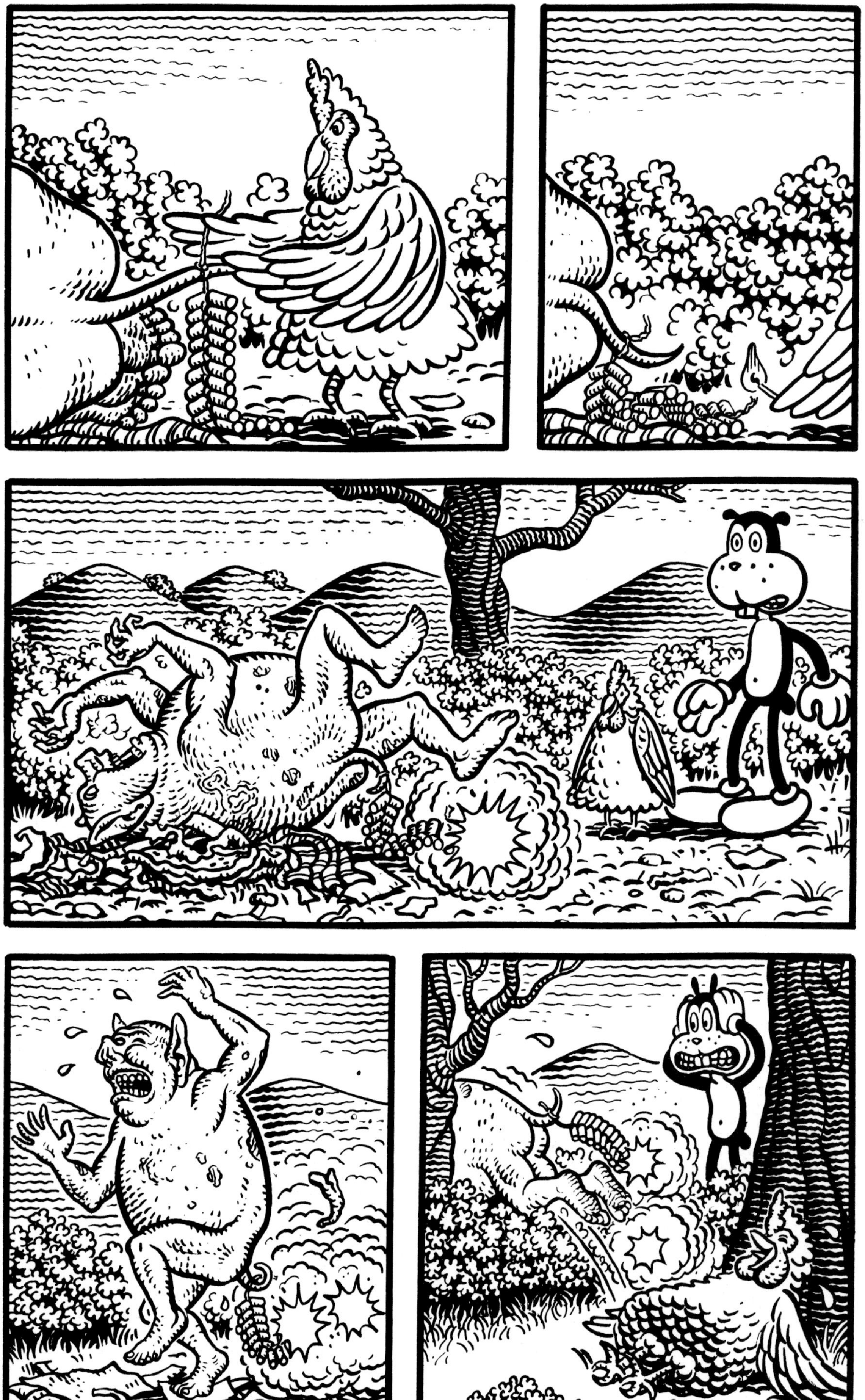

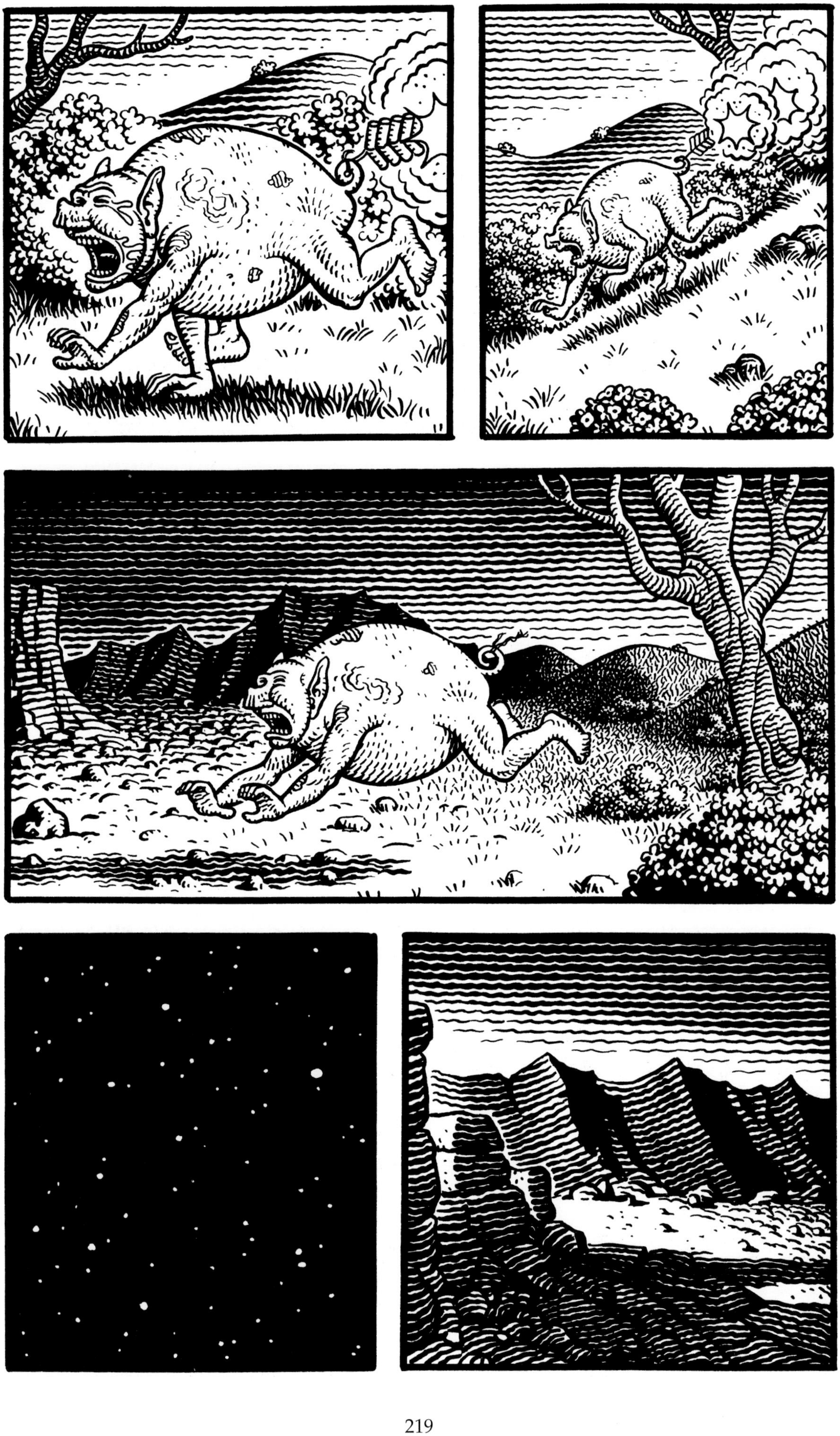

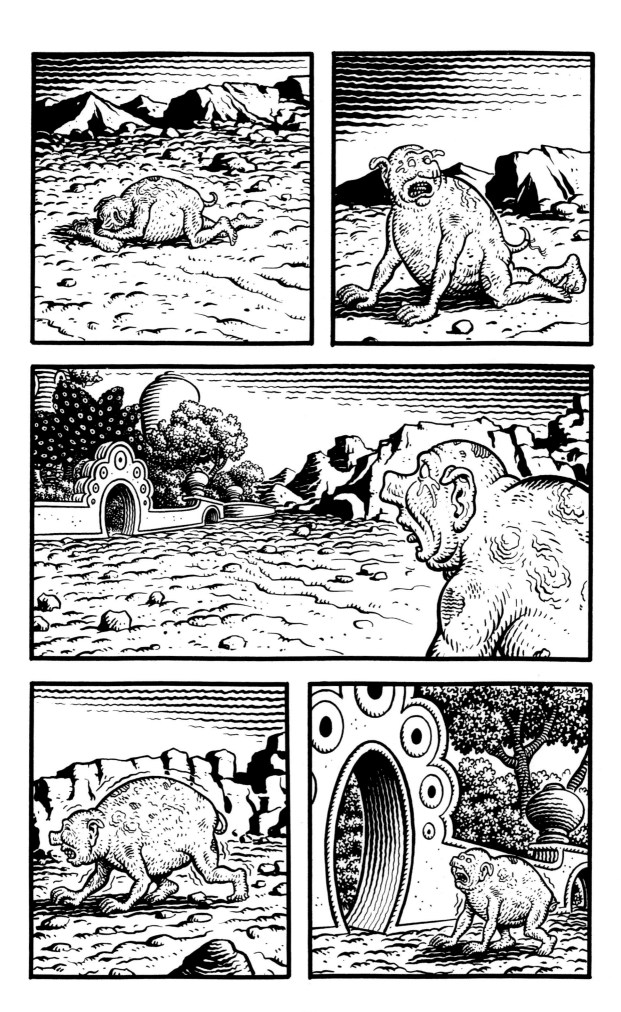

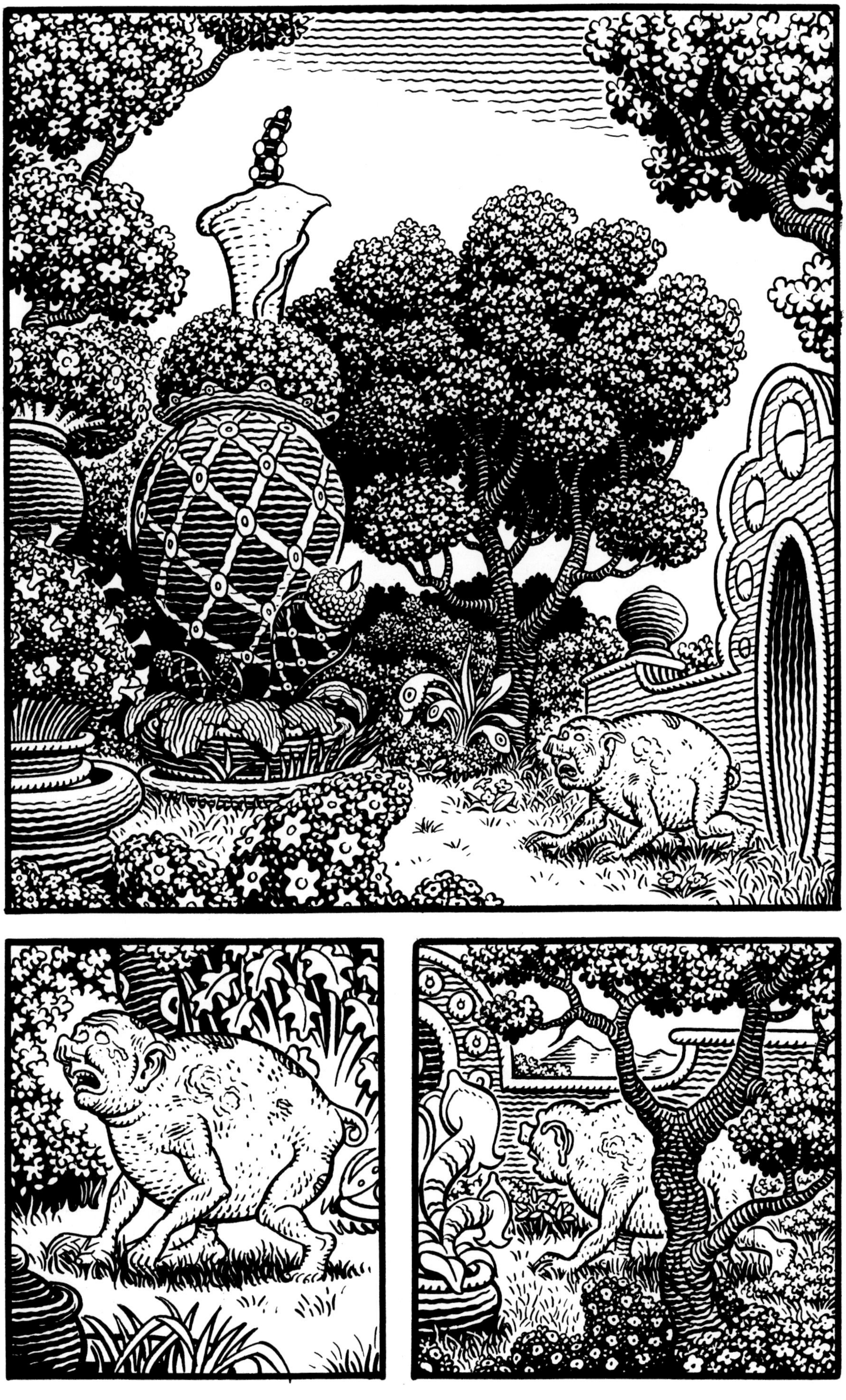

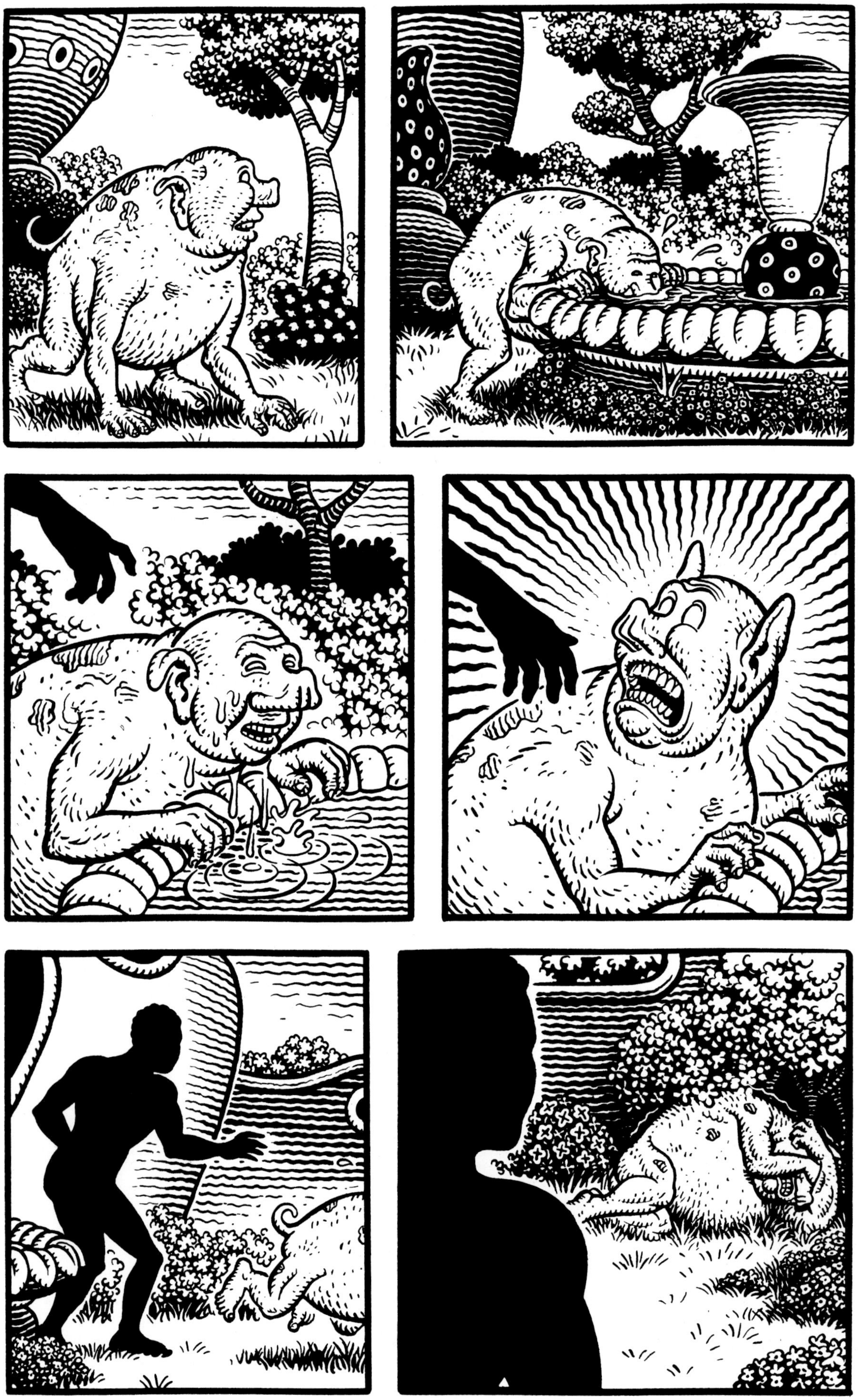

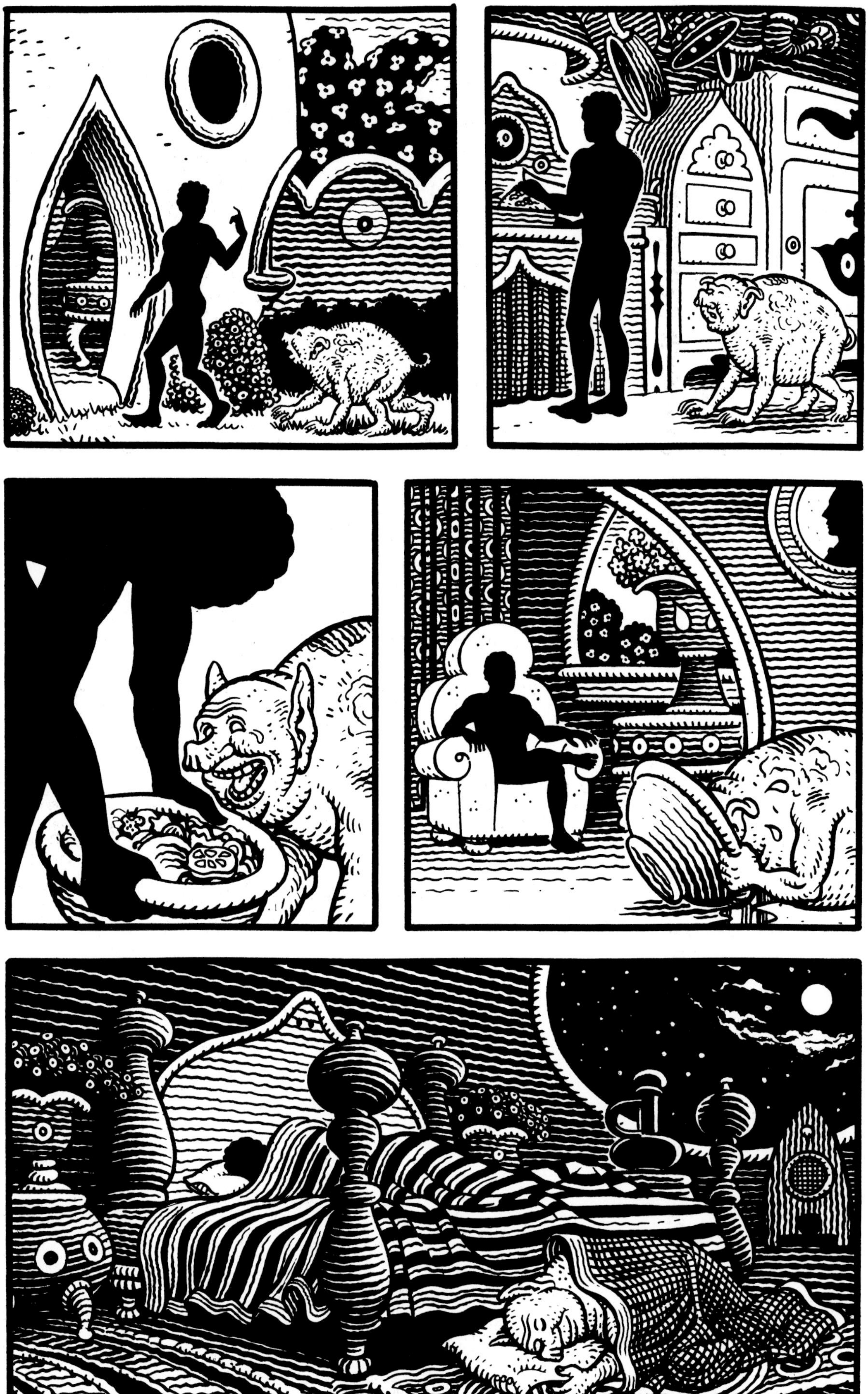

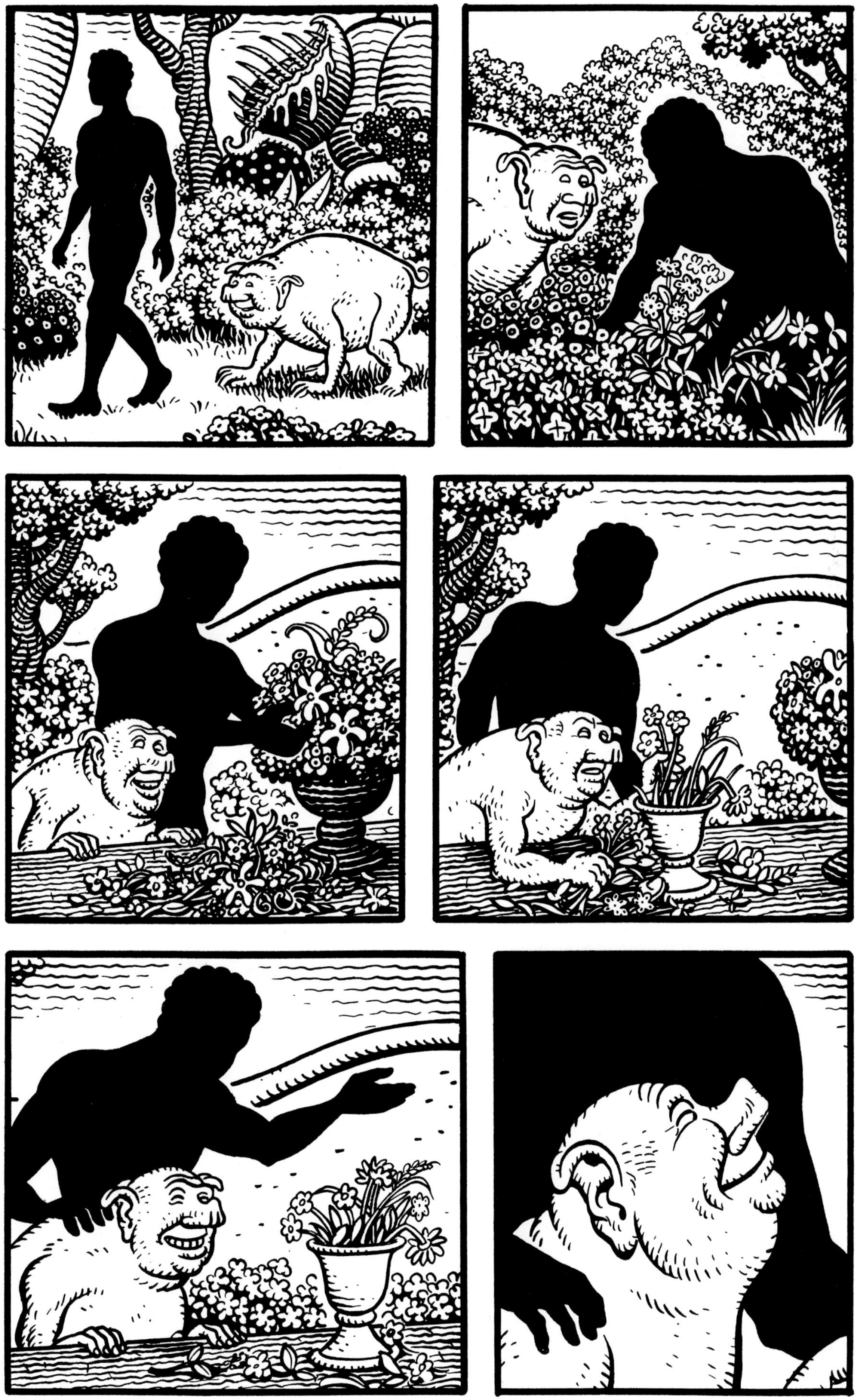

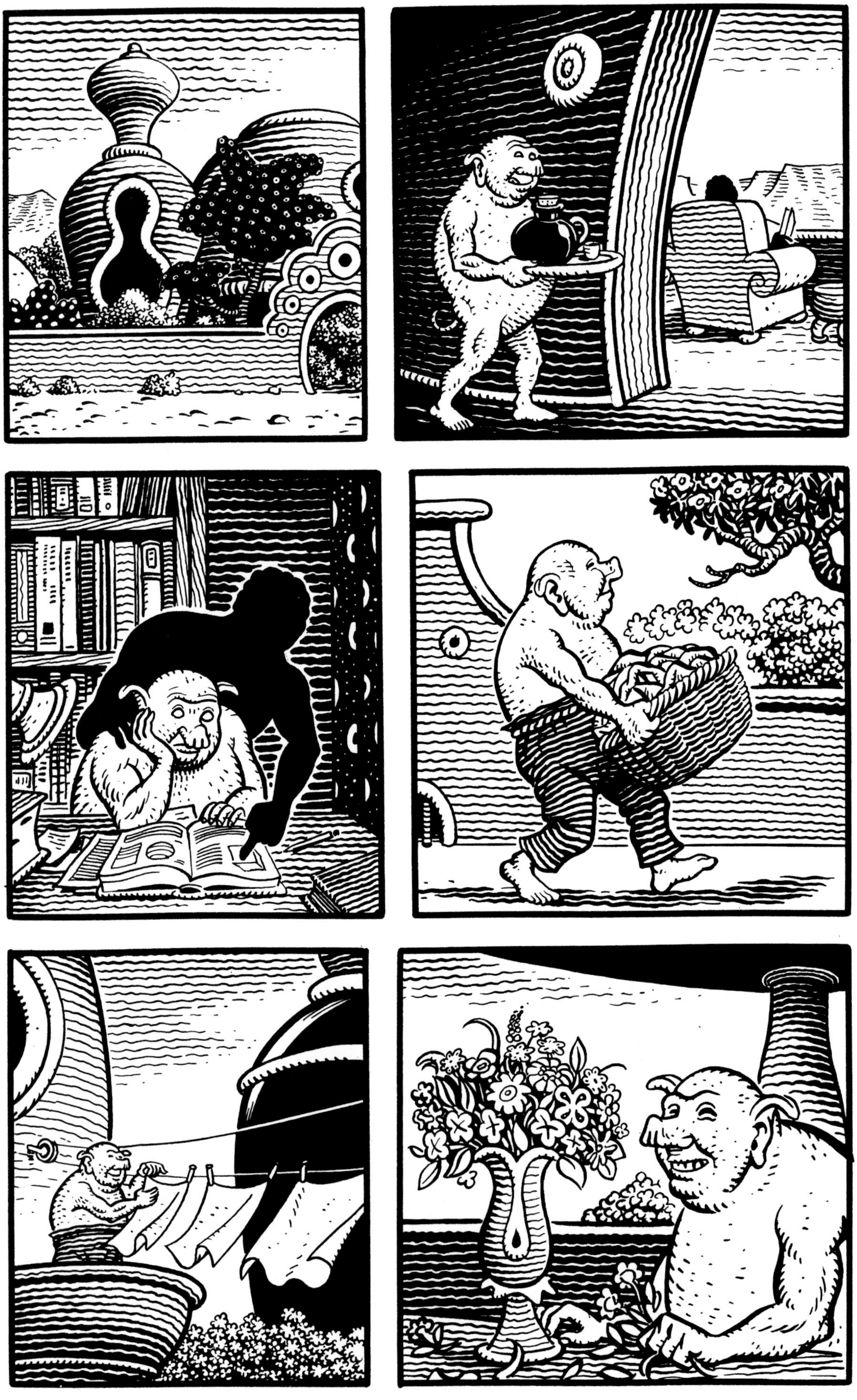

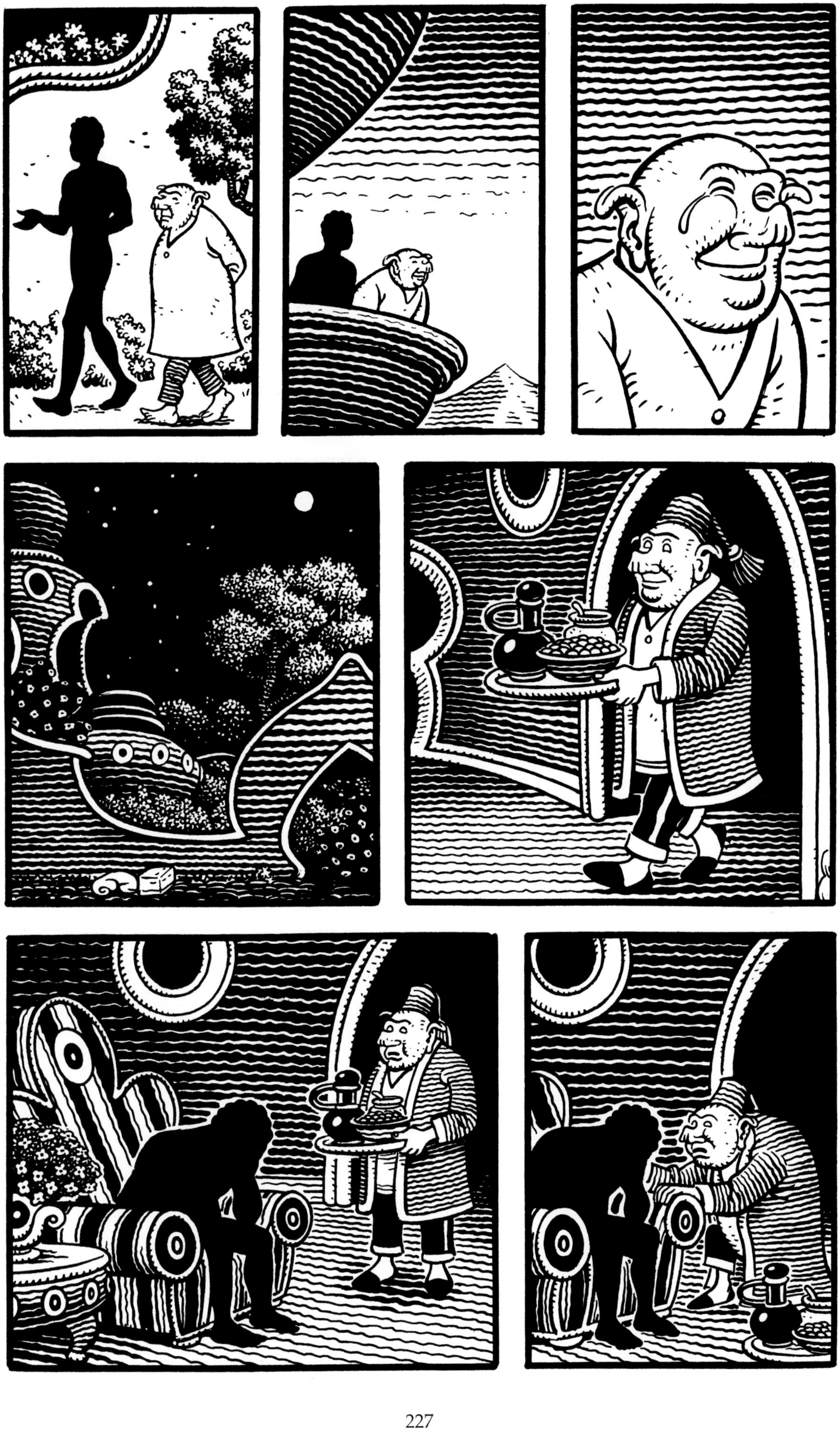

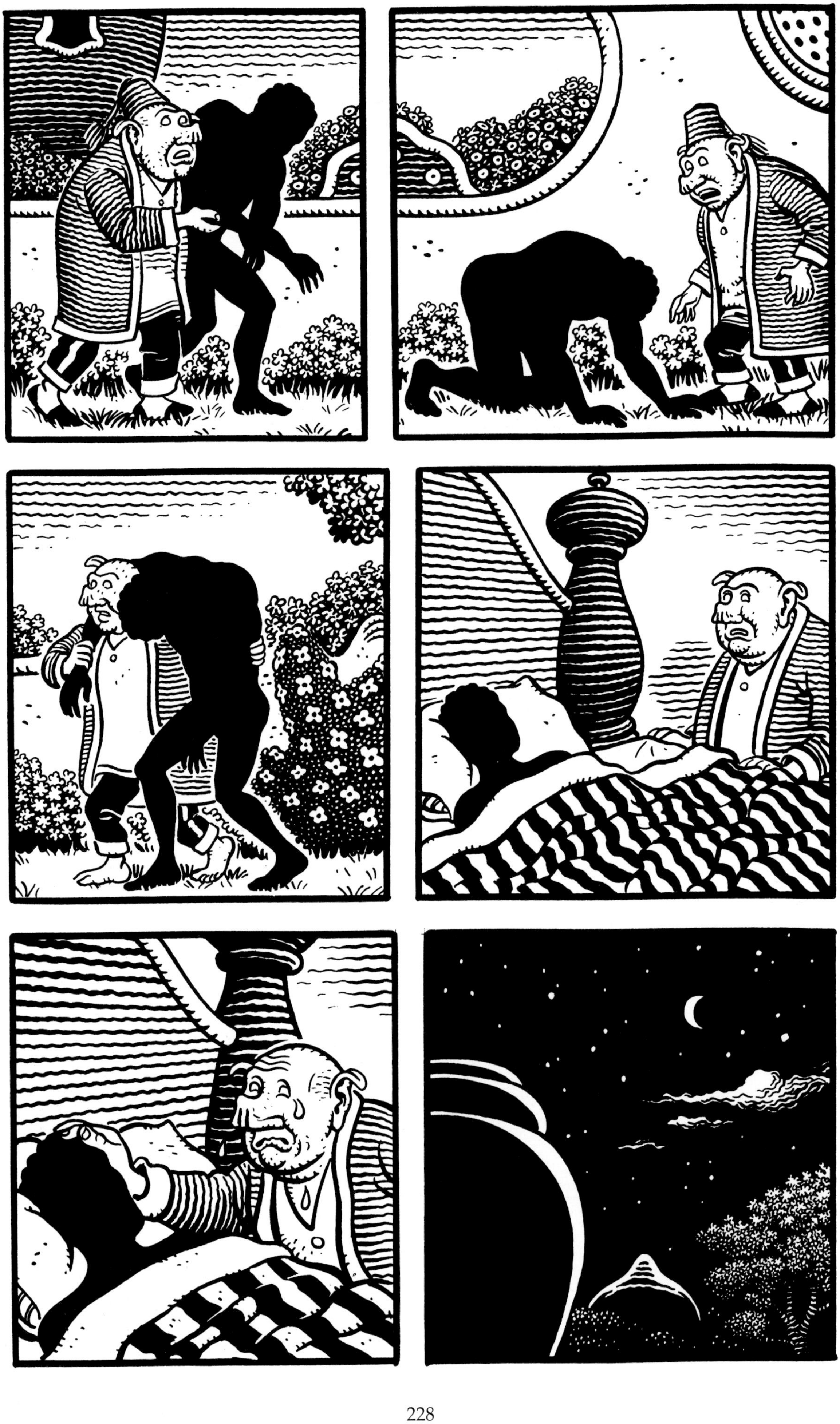

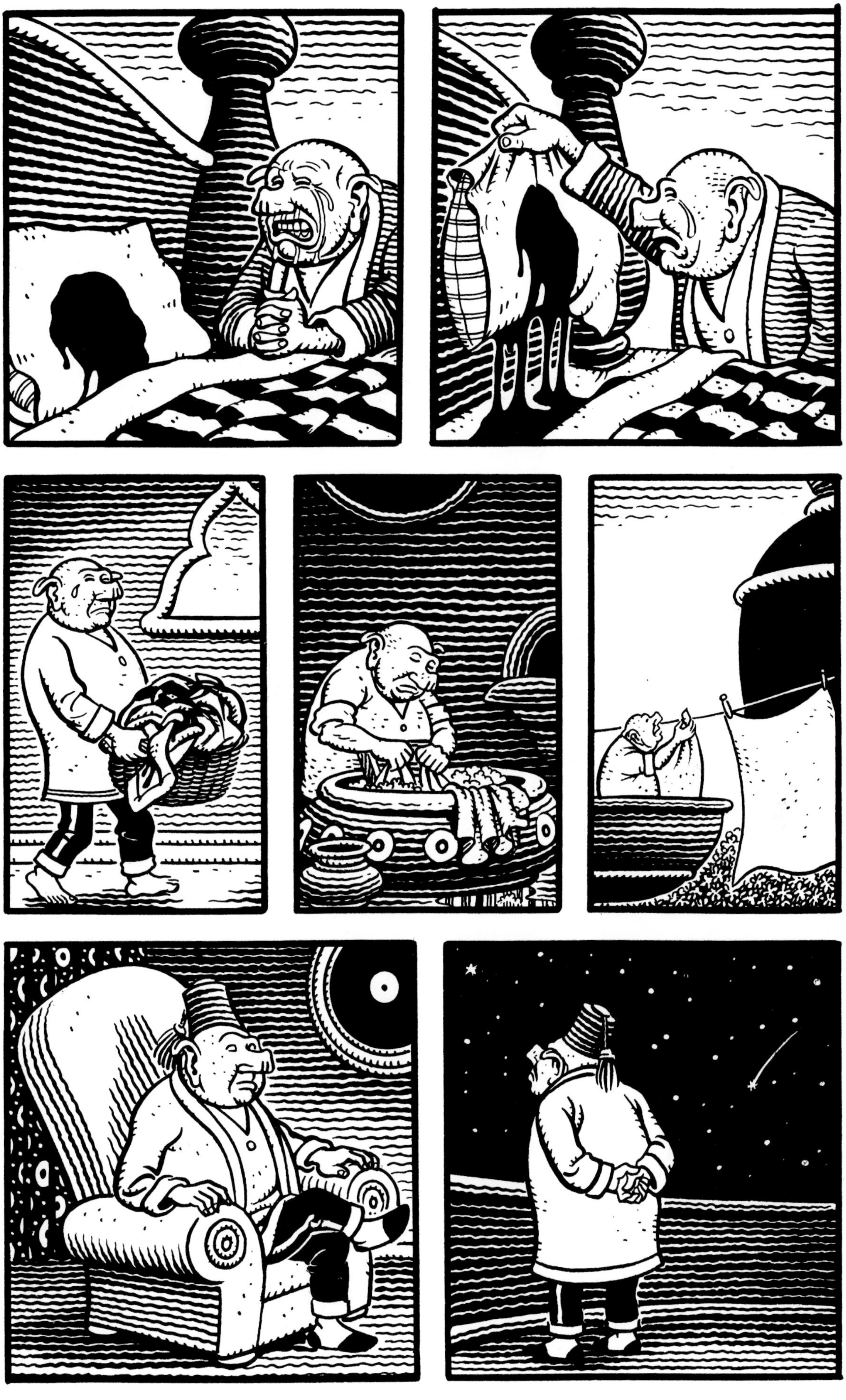

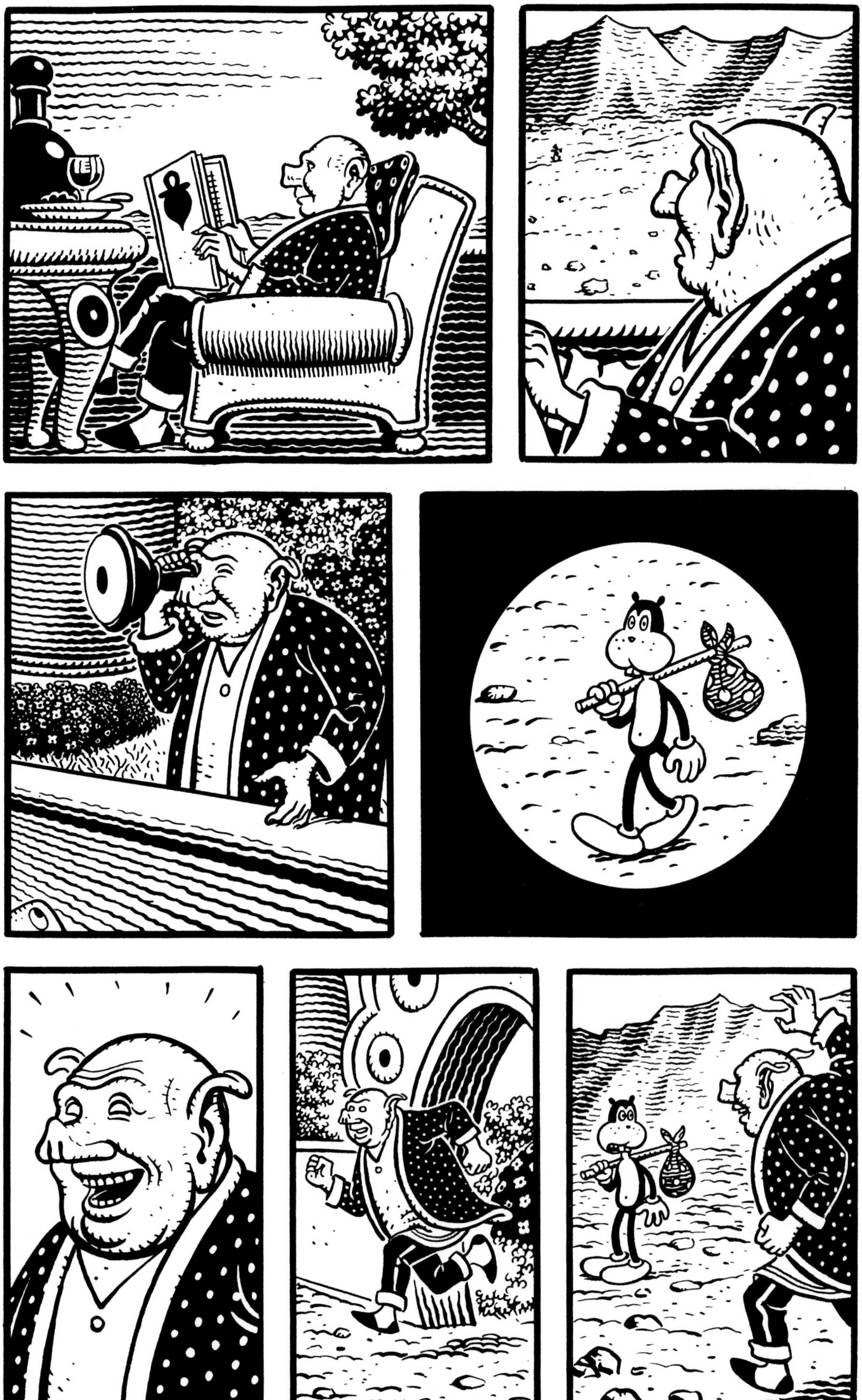

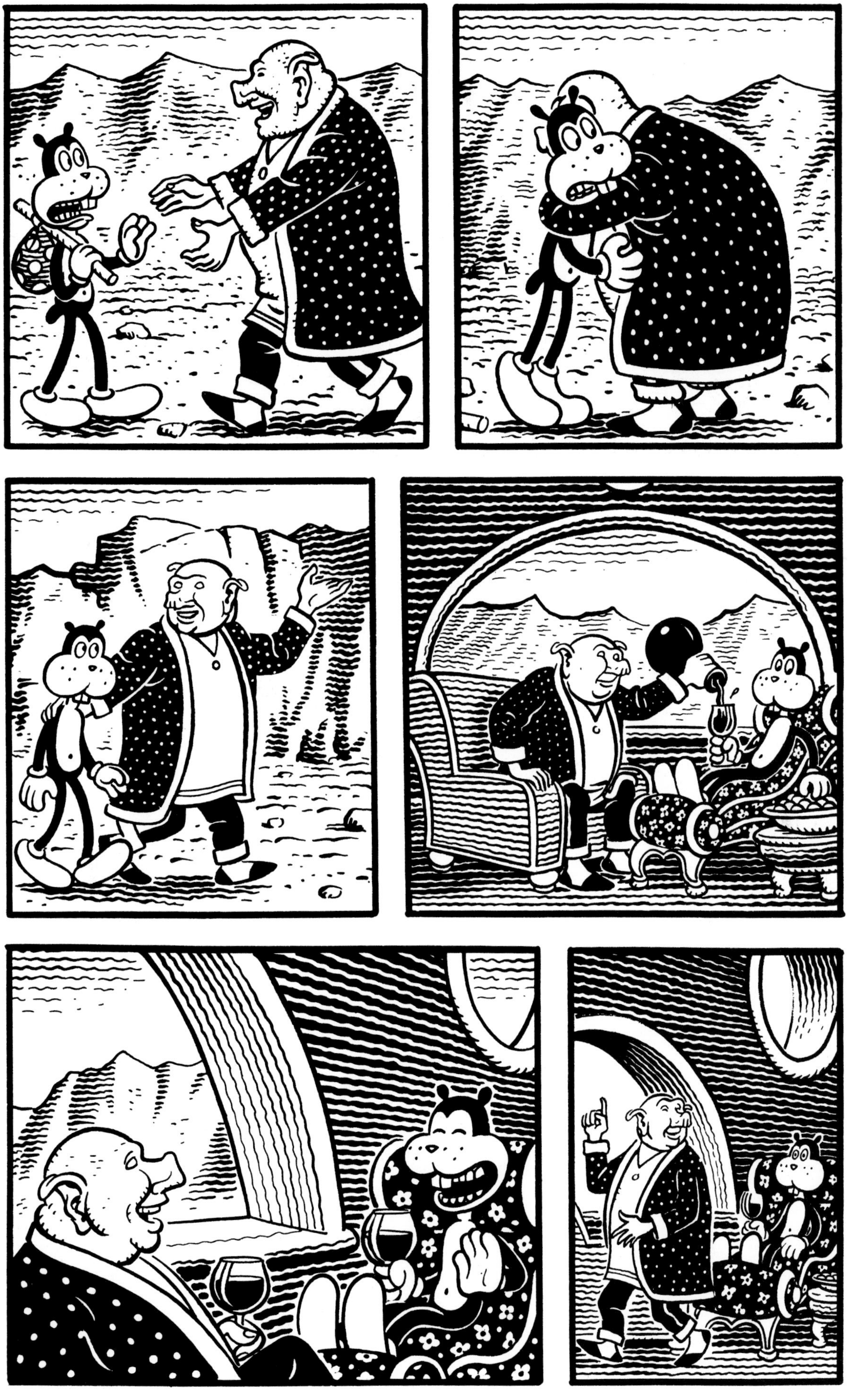

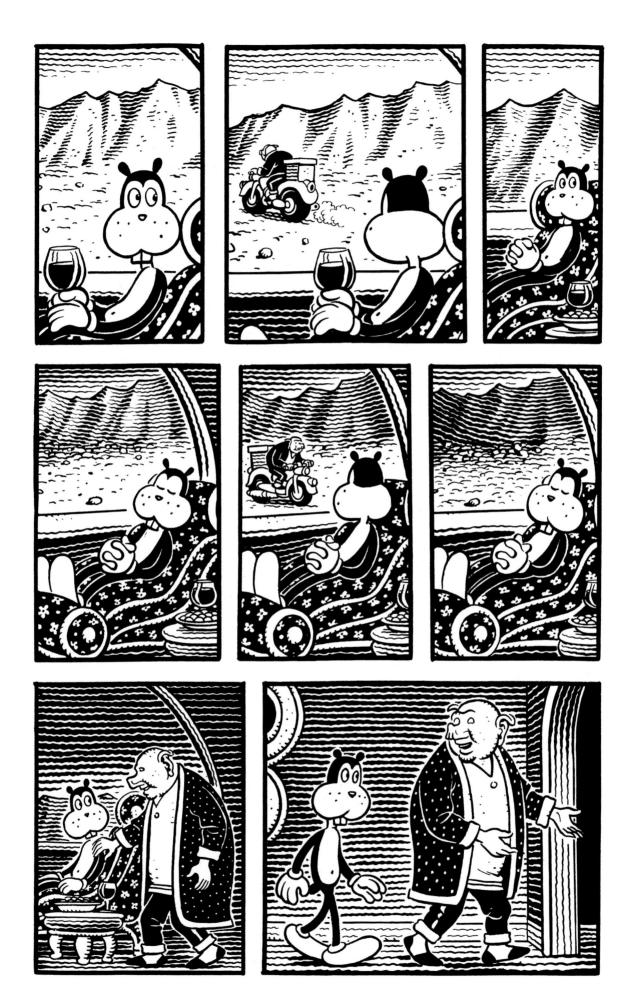

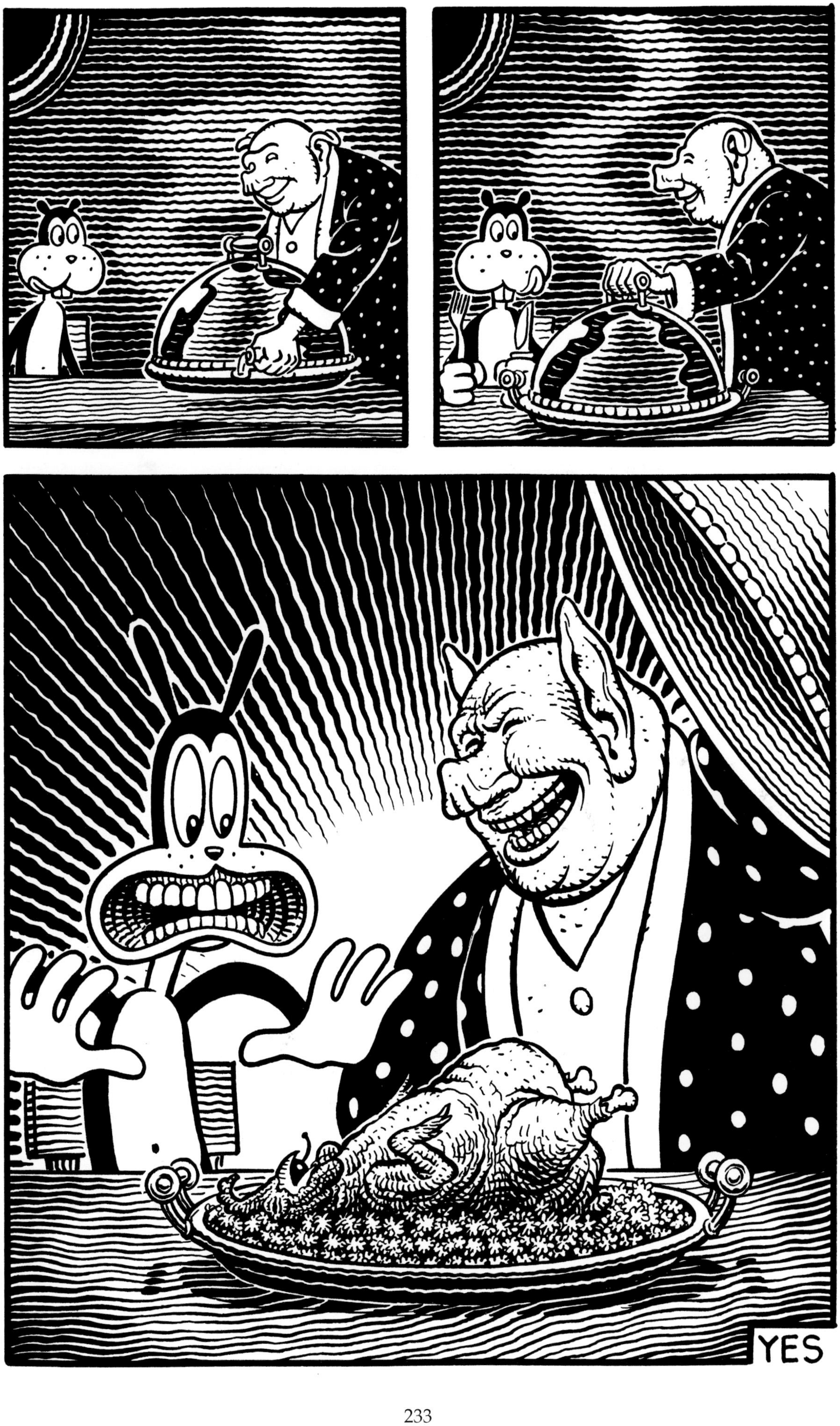
YES

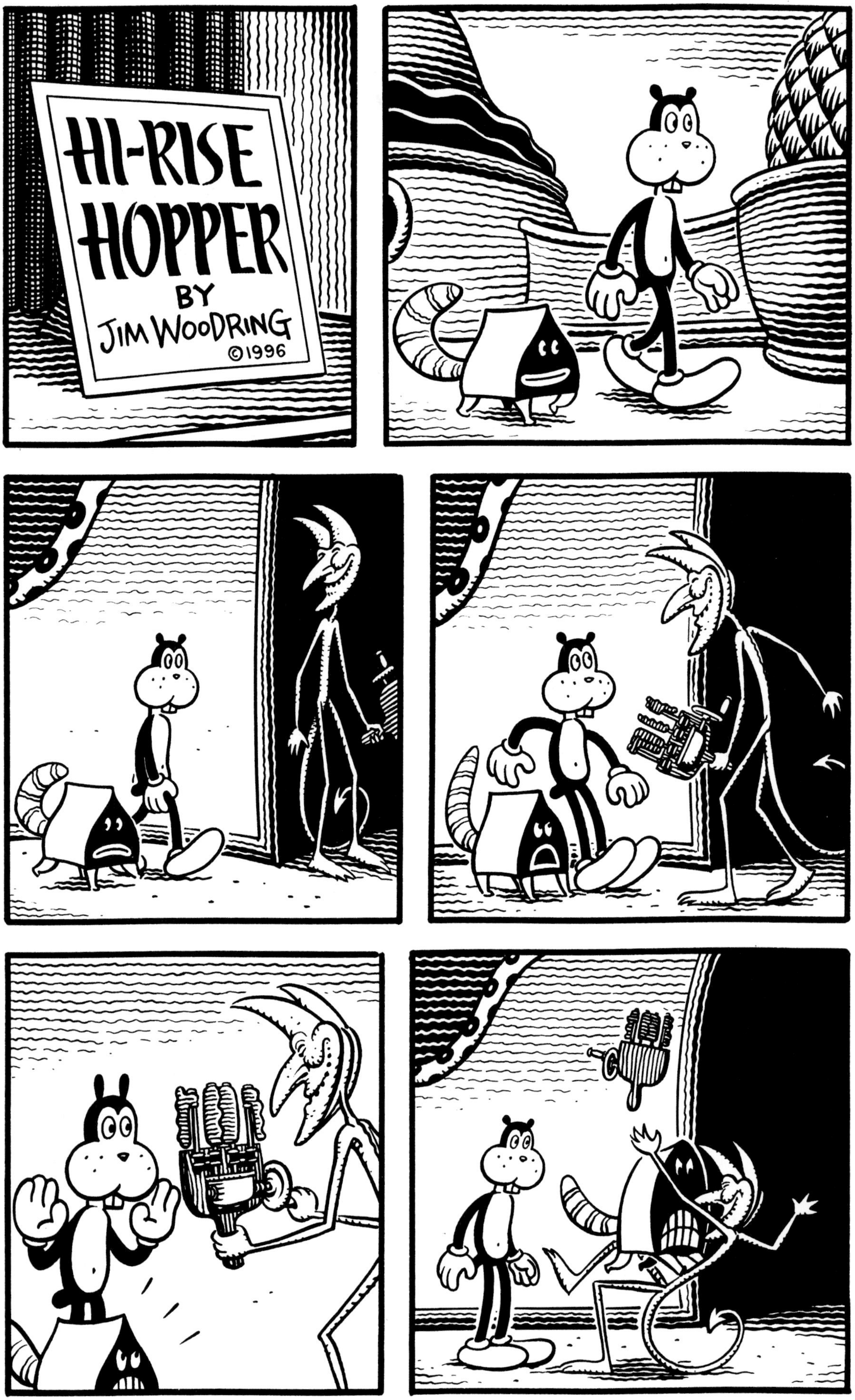
HI-RISE HOPPER
BY
JIM WOODRING
©1996

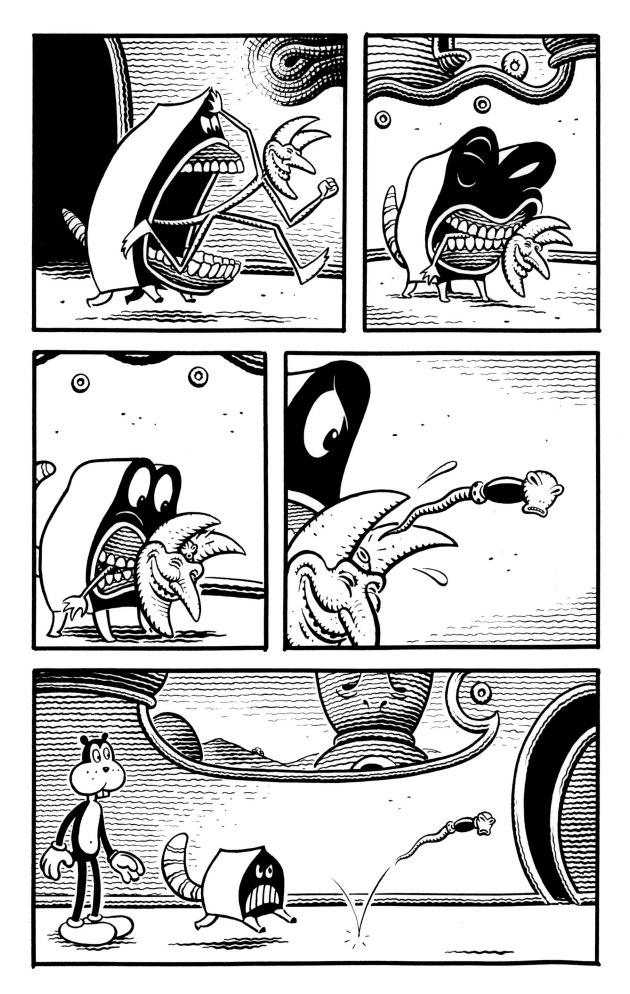

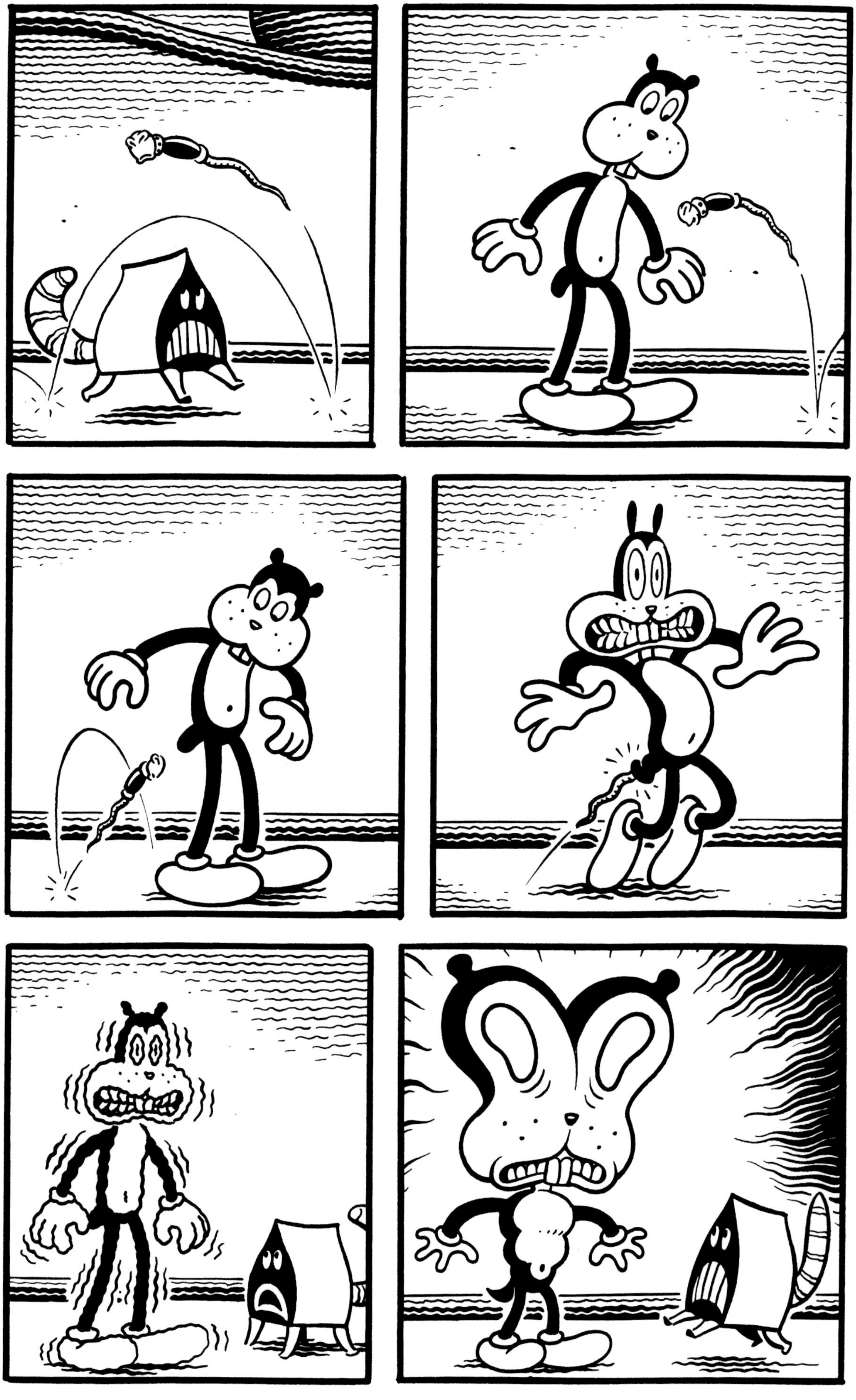

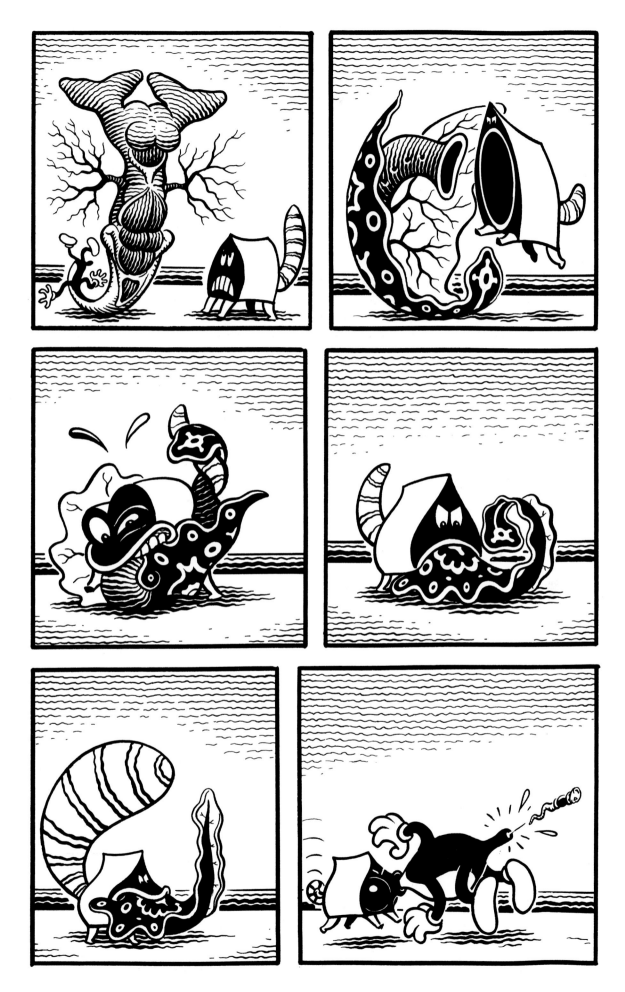

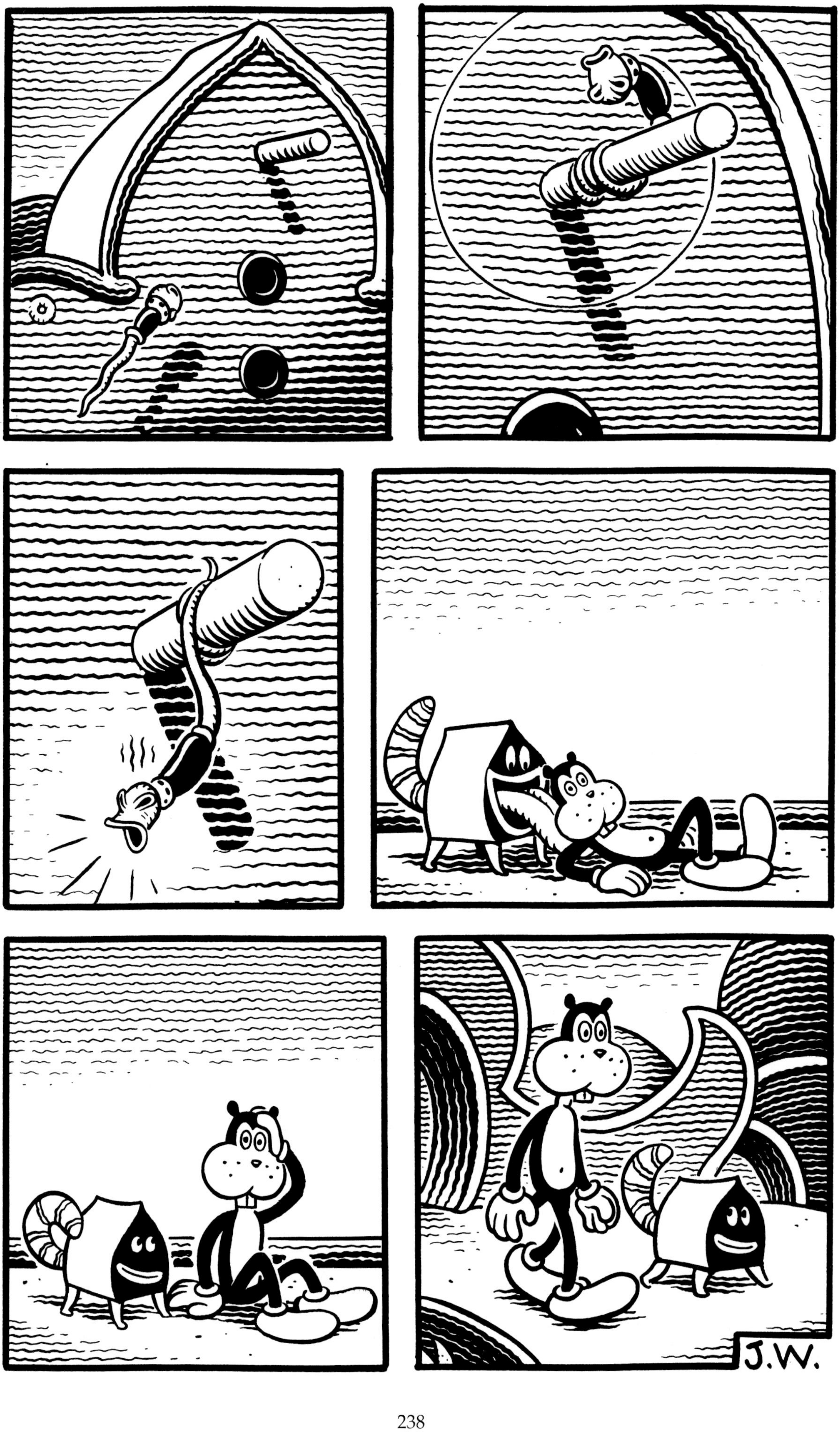
J.W.

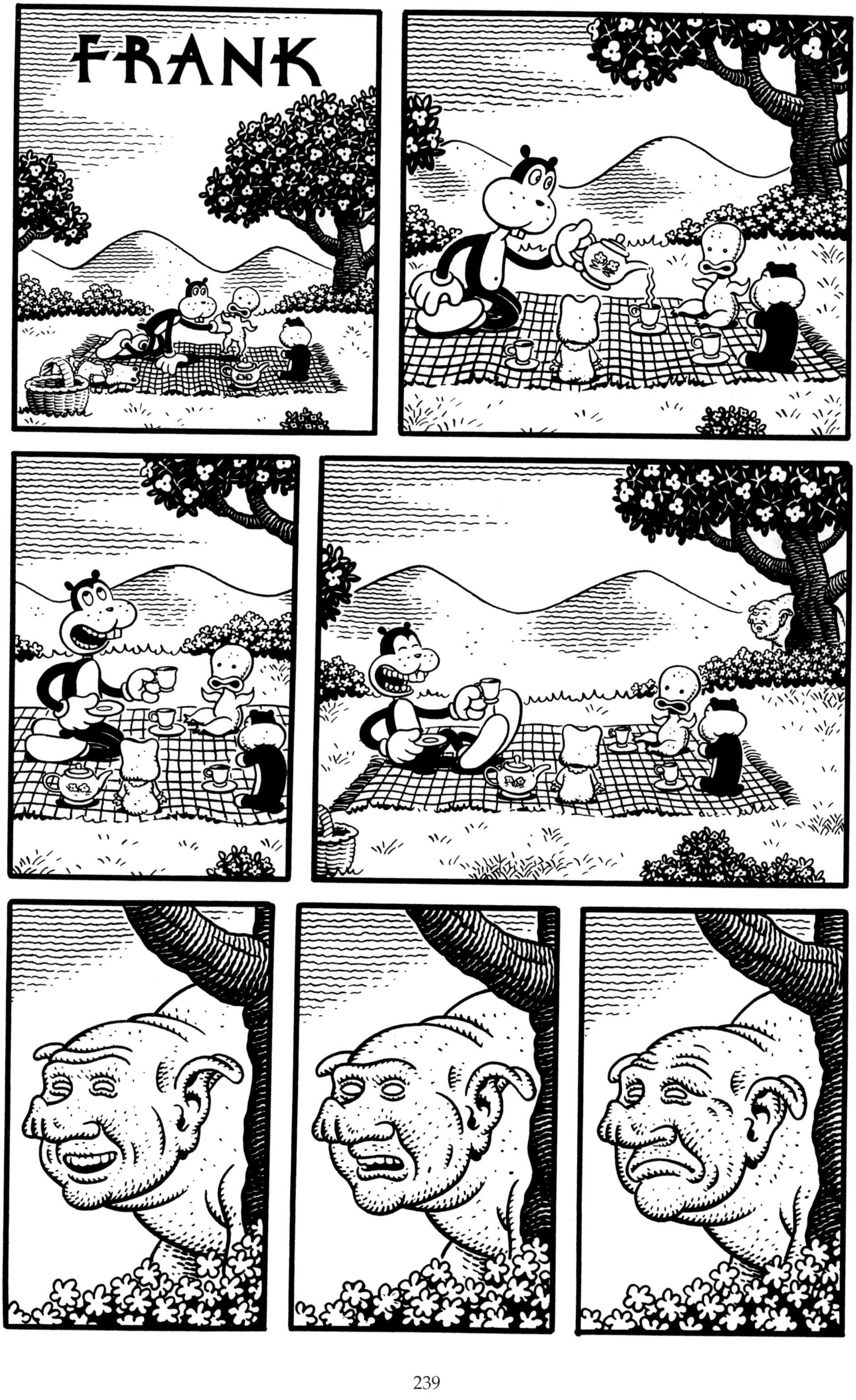
FRANK

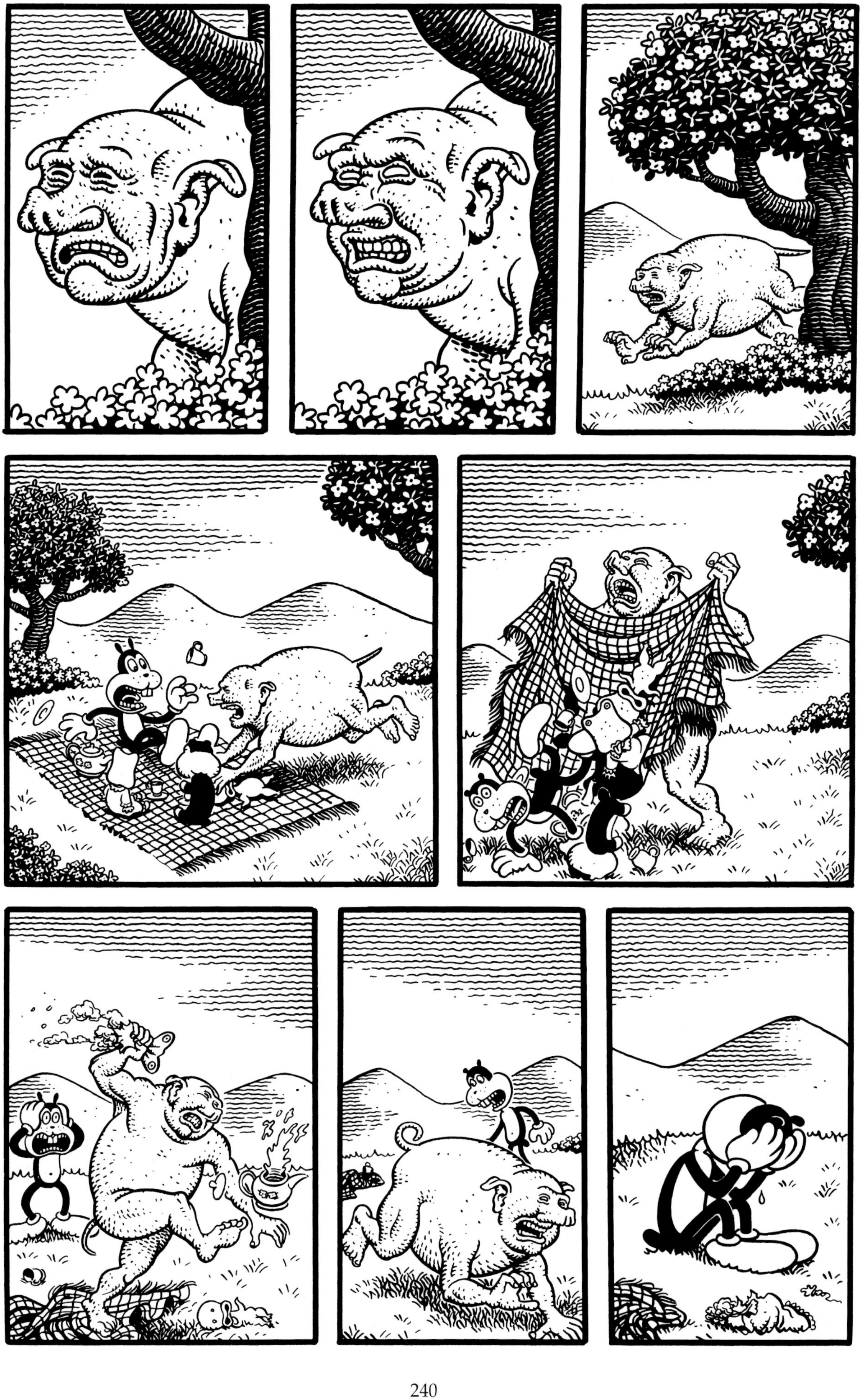

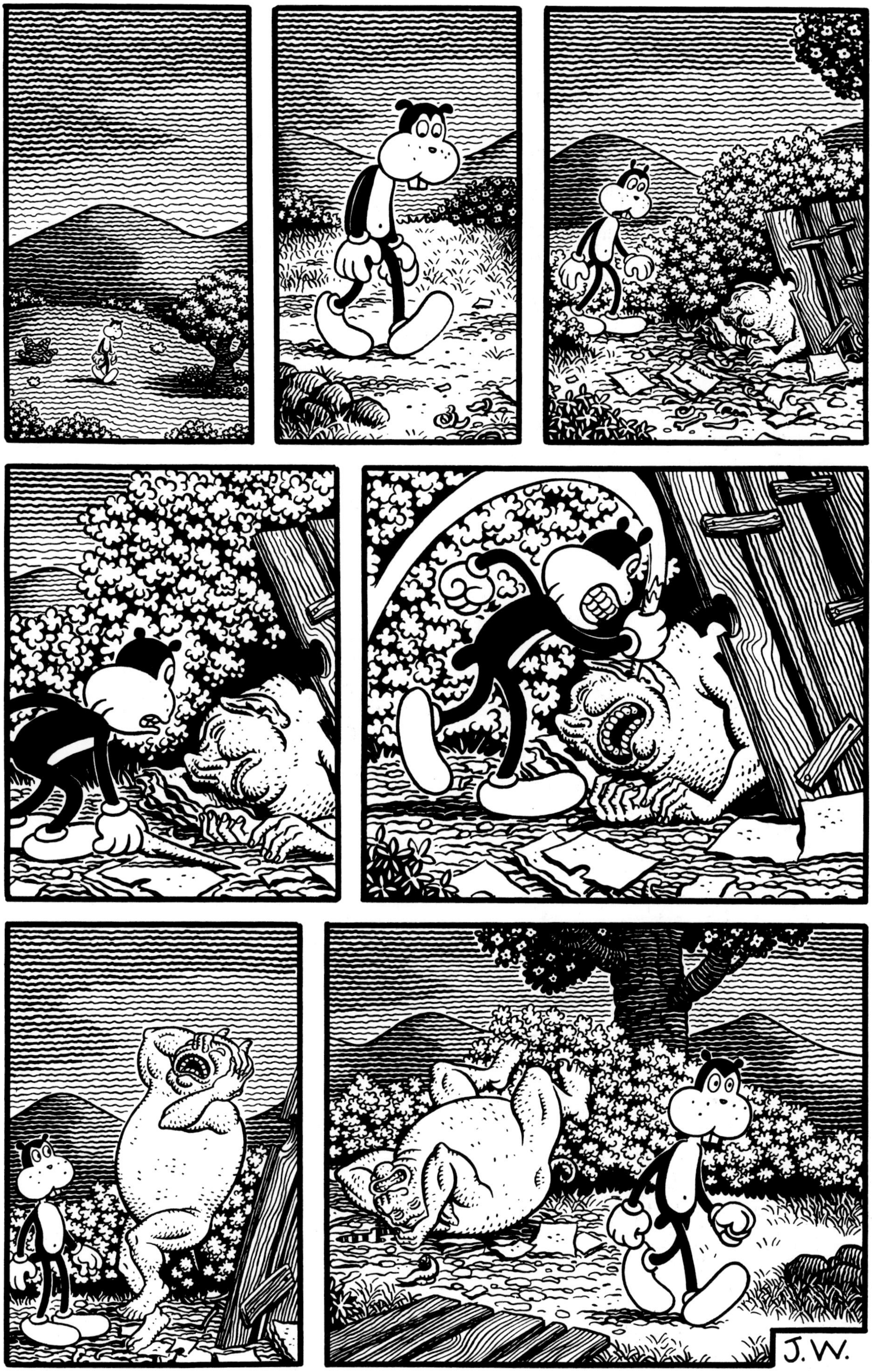
J.W.

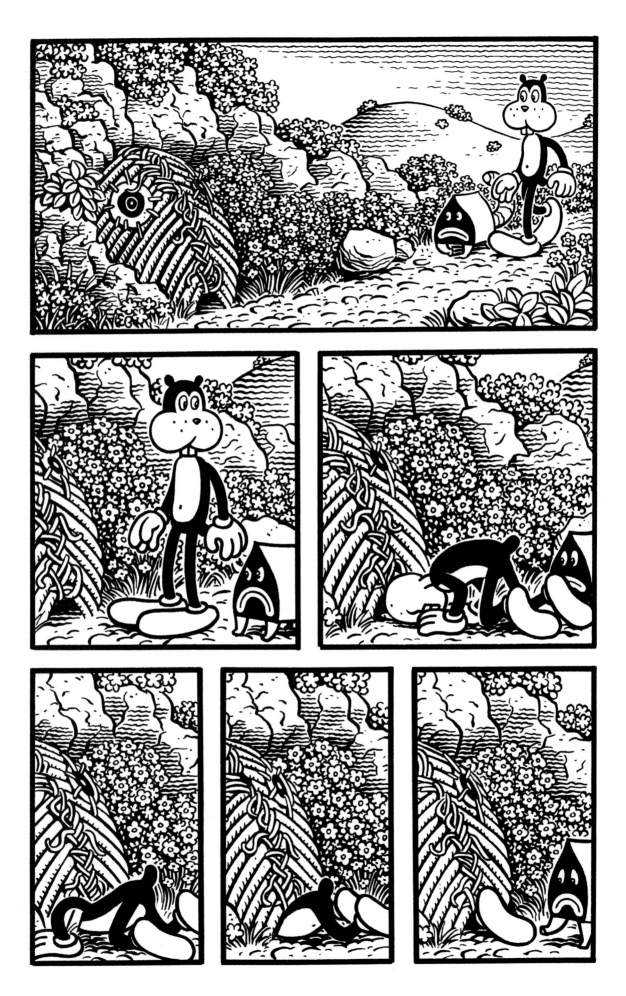

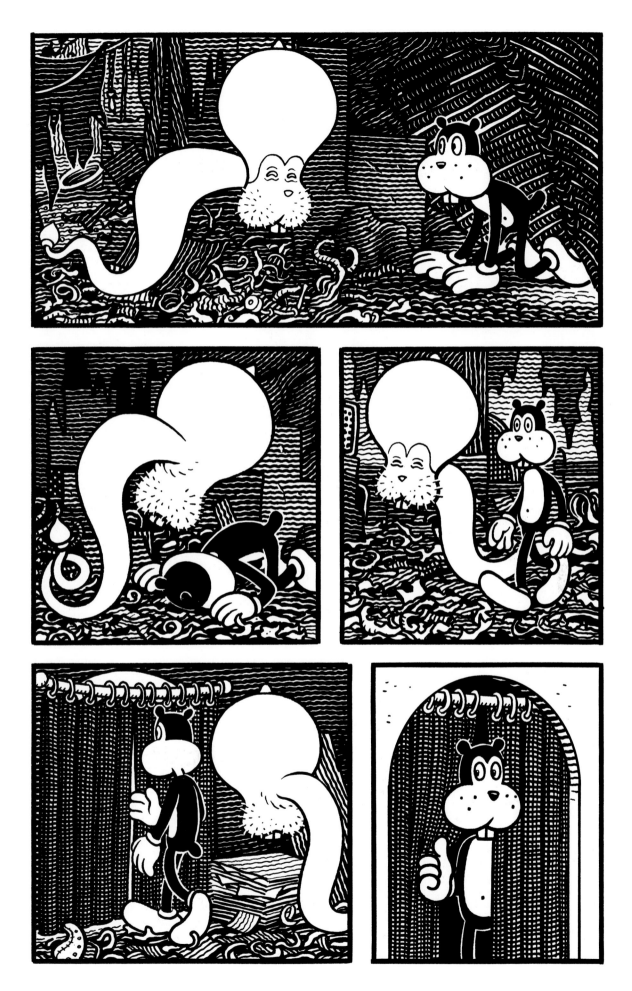

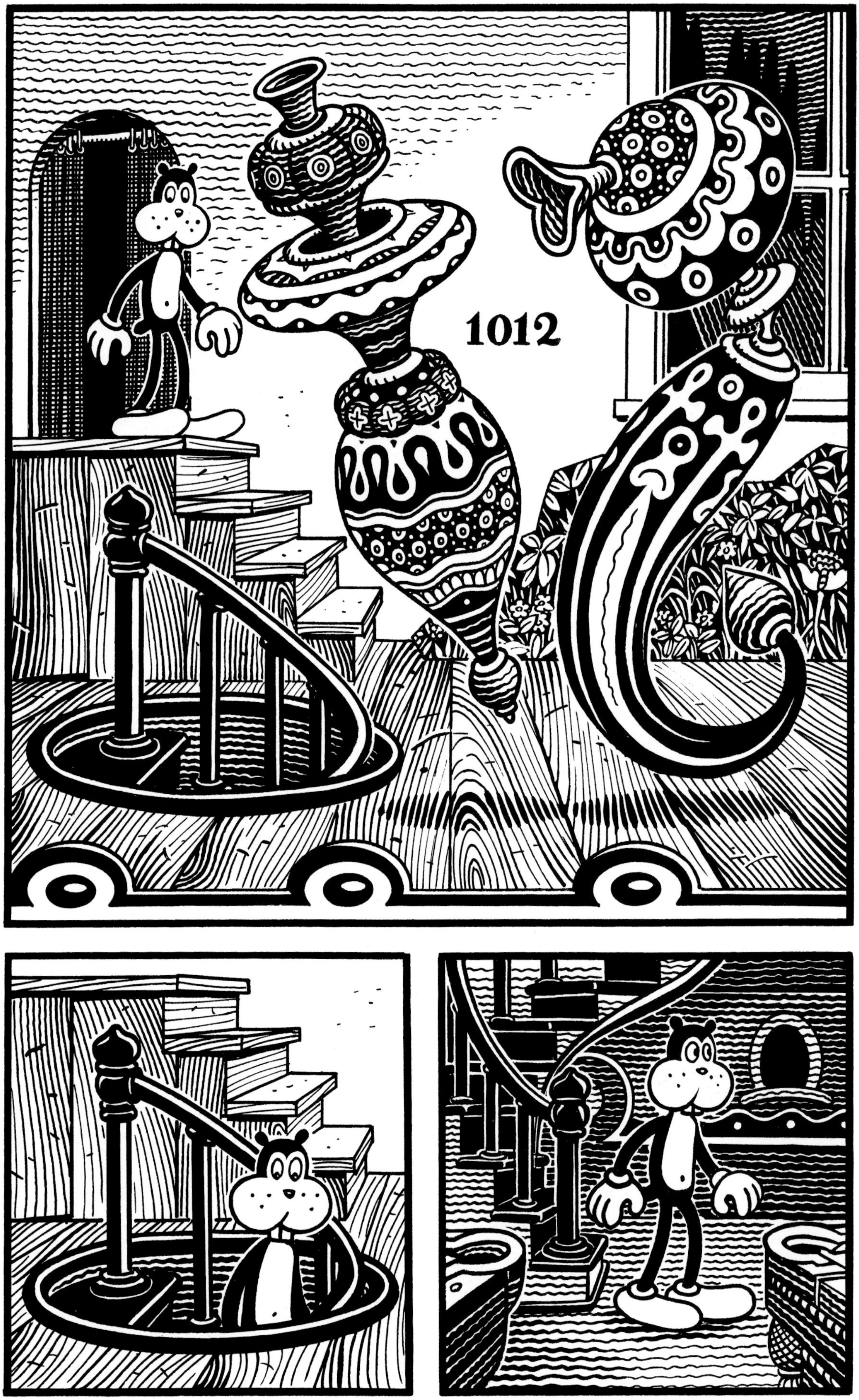
1012

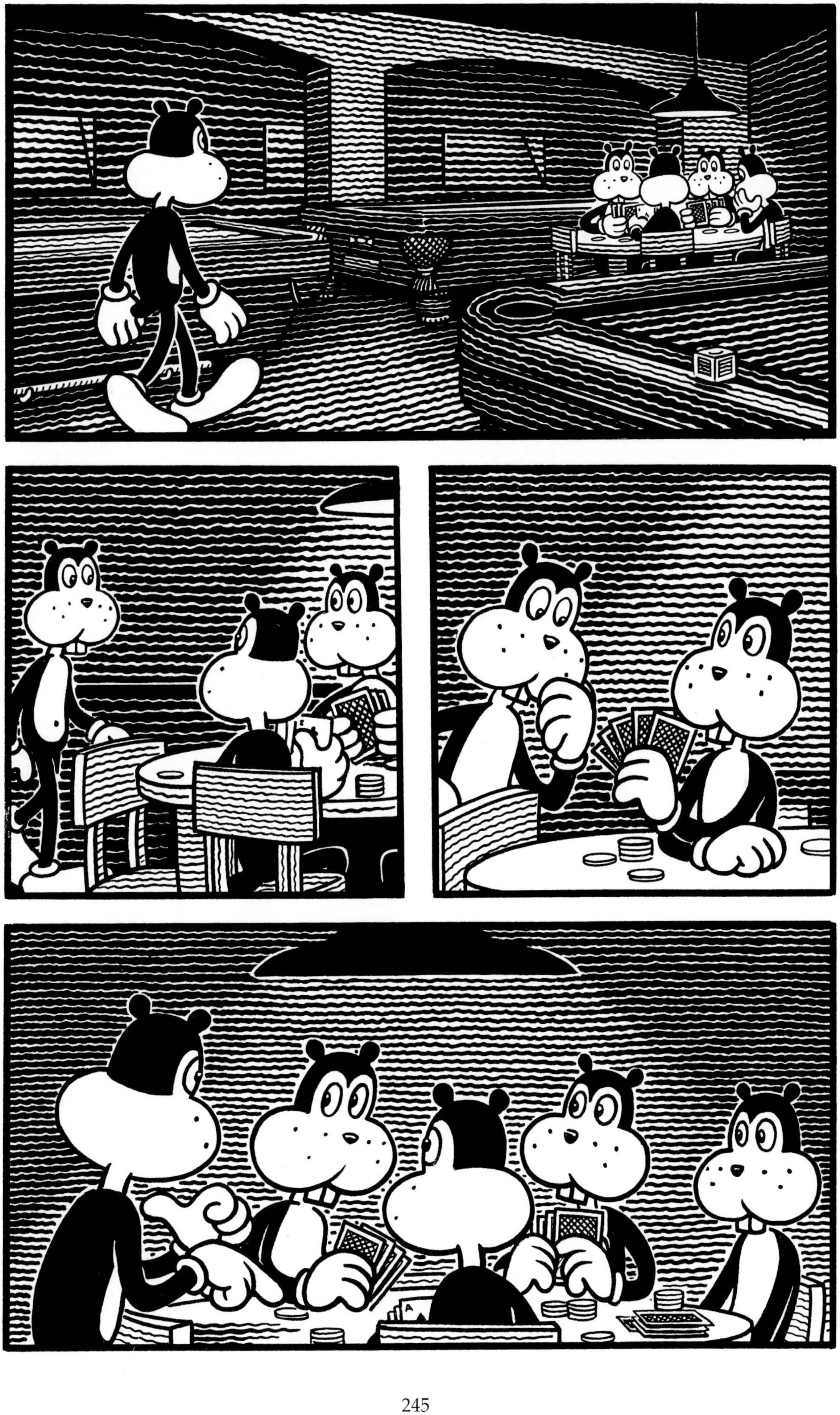

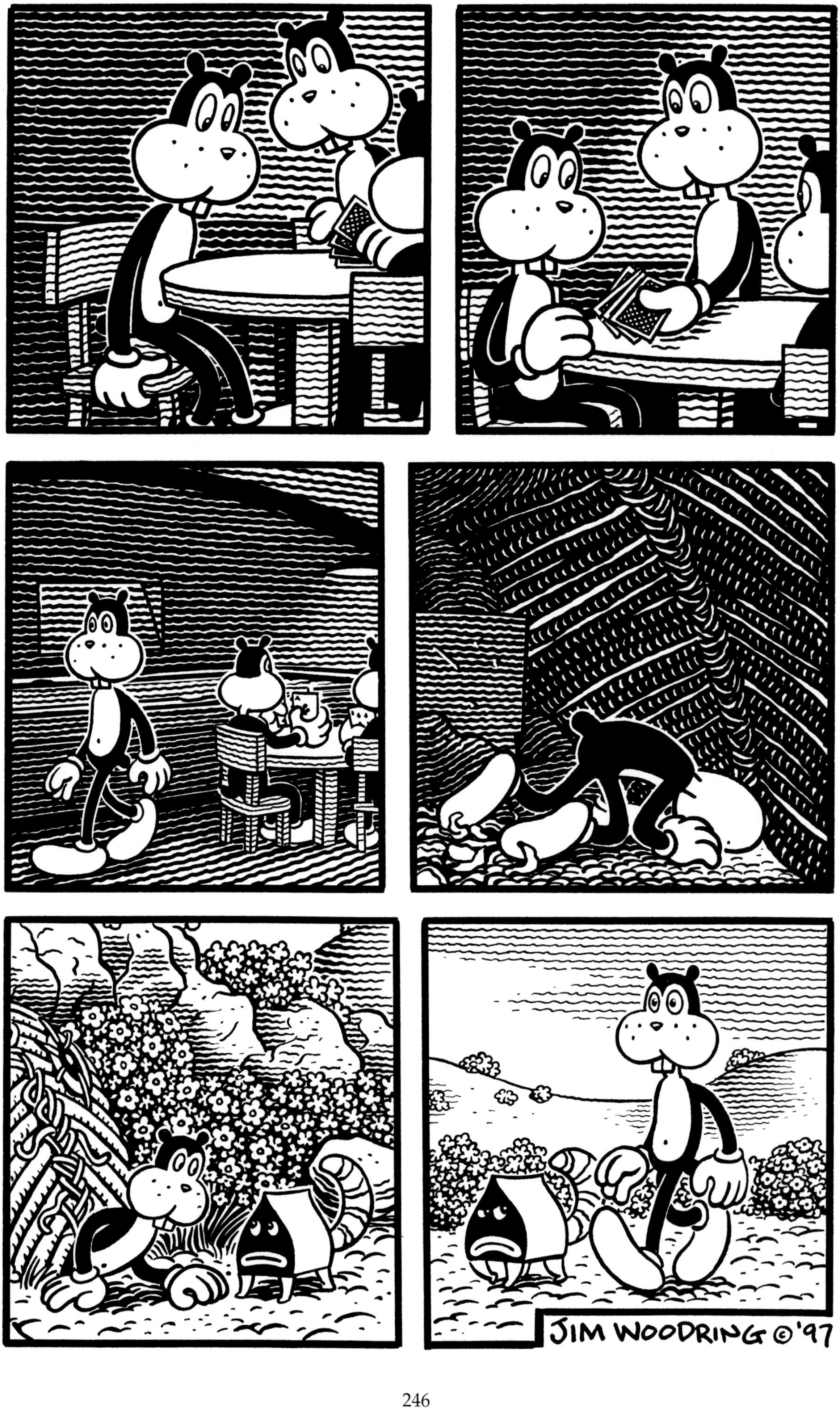
JIM WOODRING ©'97

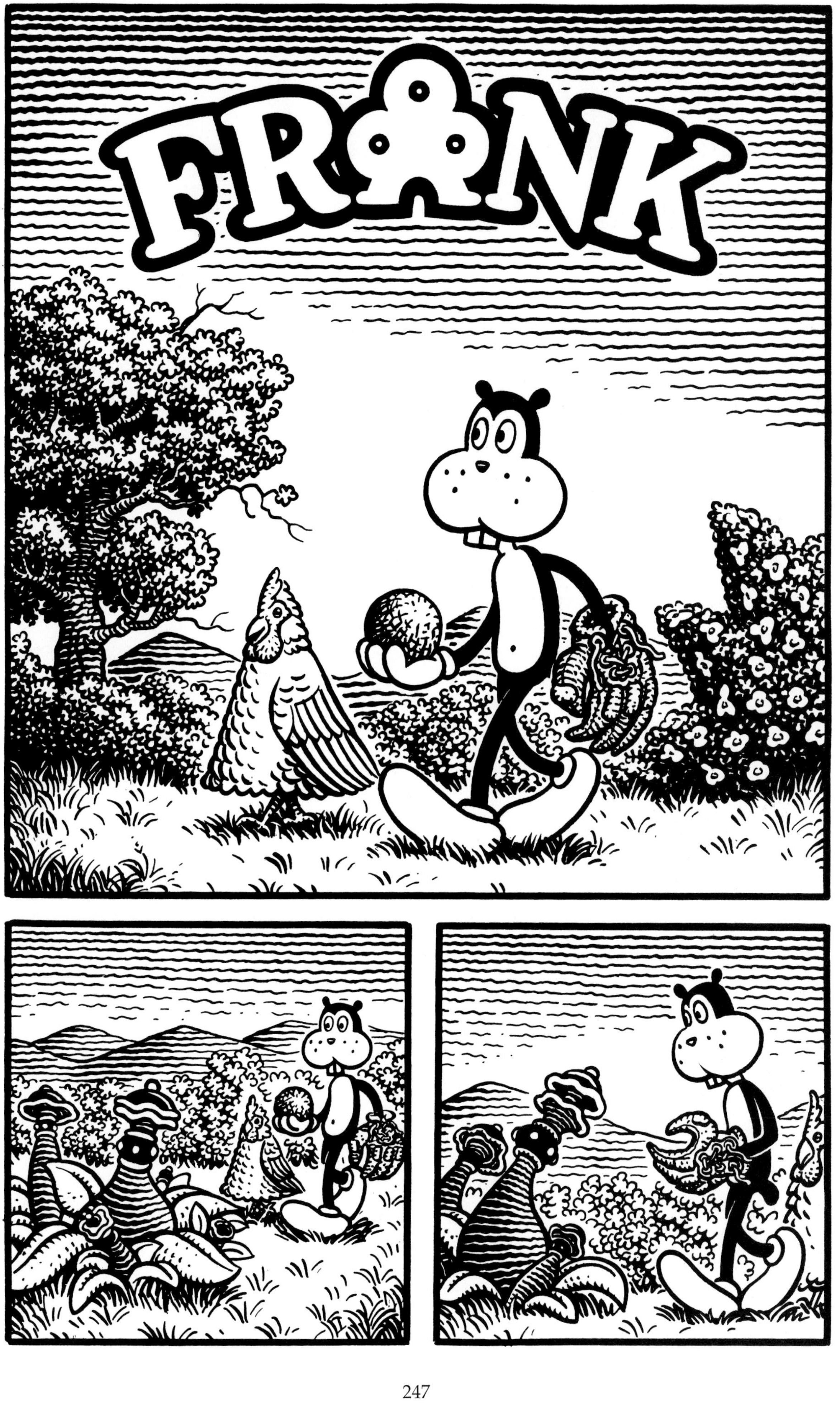
FRANK

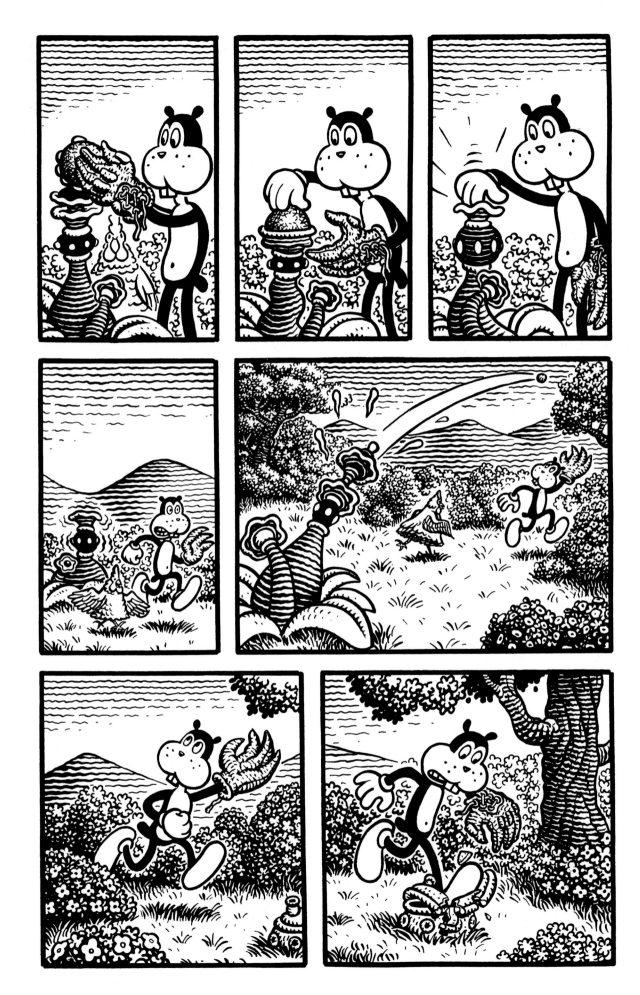

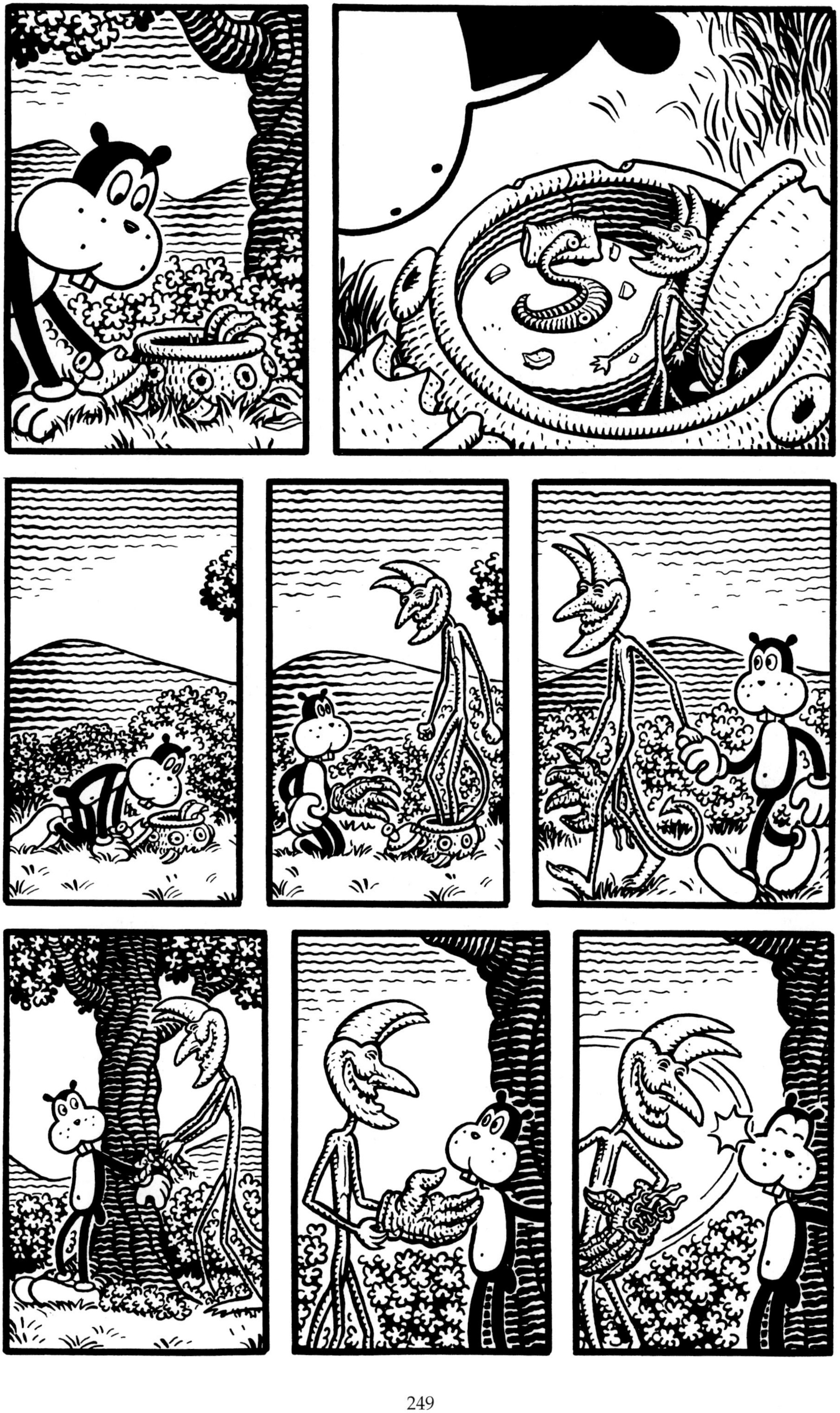

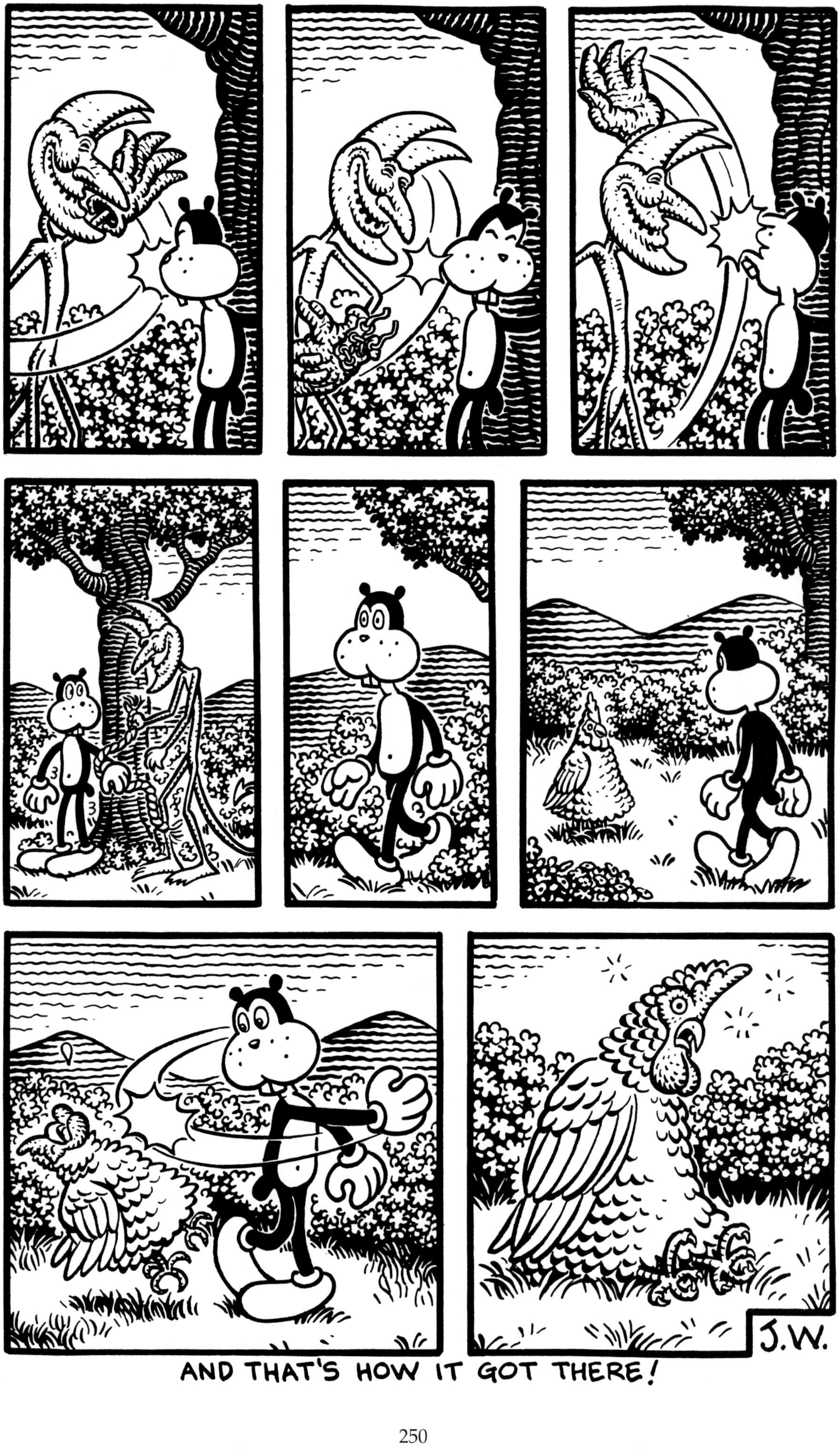
J.W.
AND THAT'S HOW IT GOT THERE!

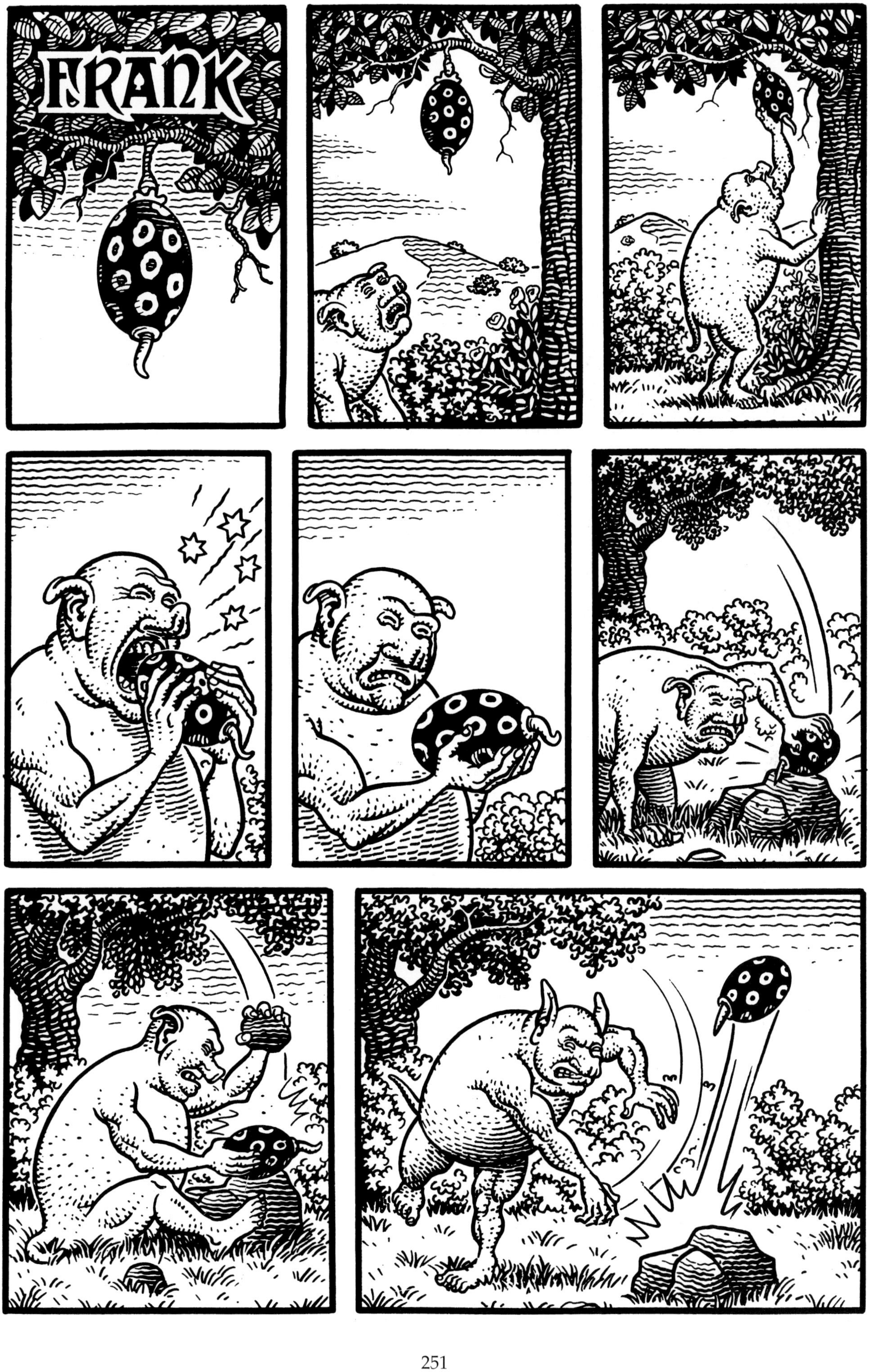
FRANK

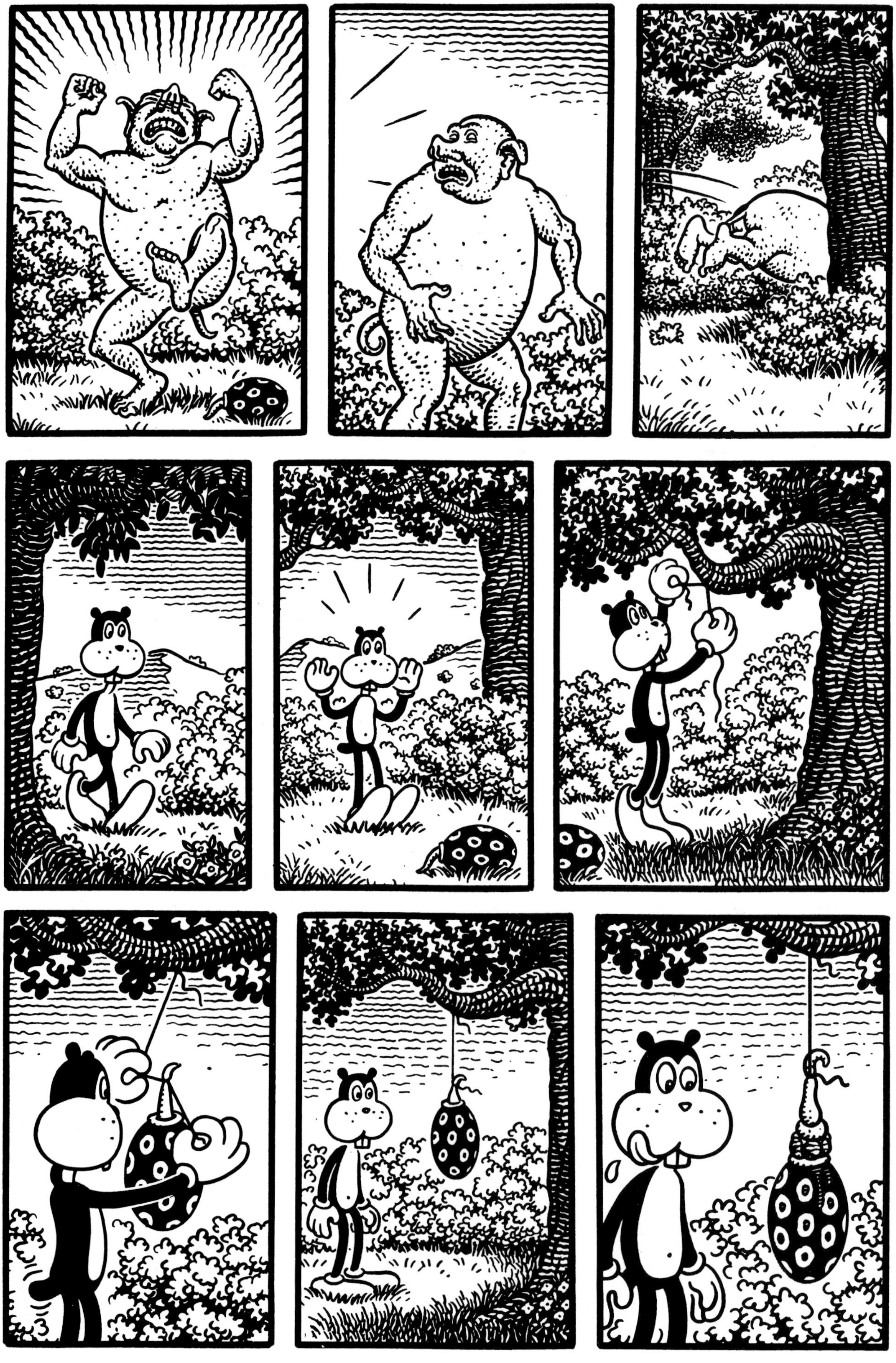

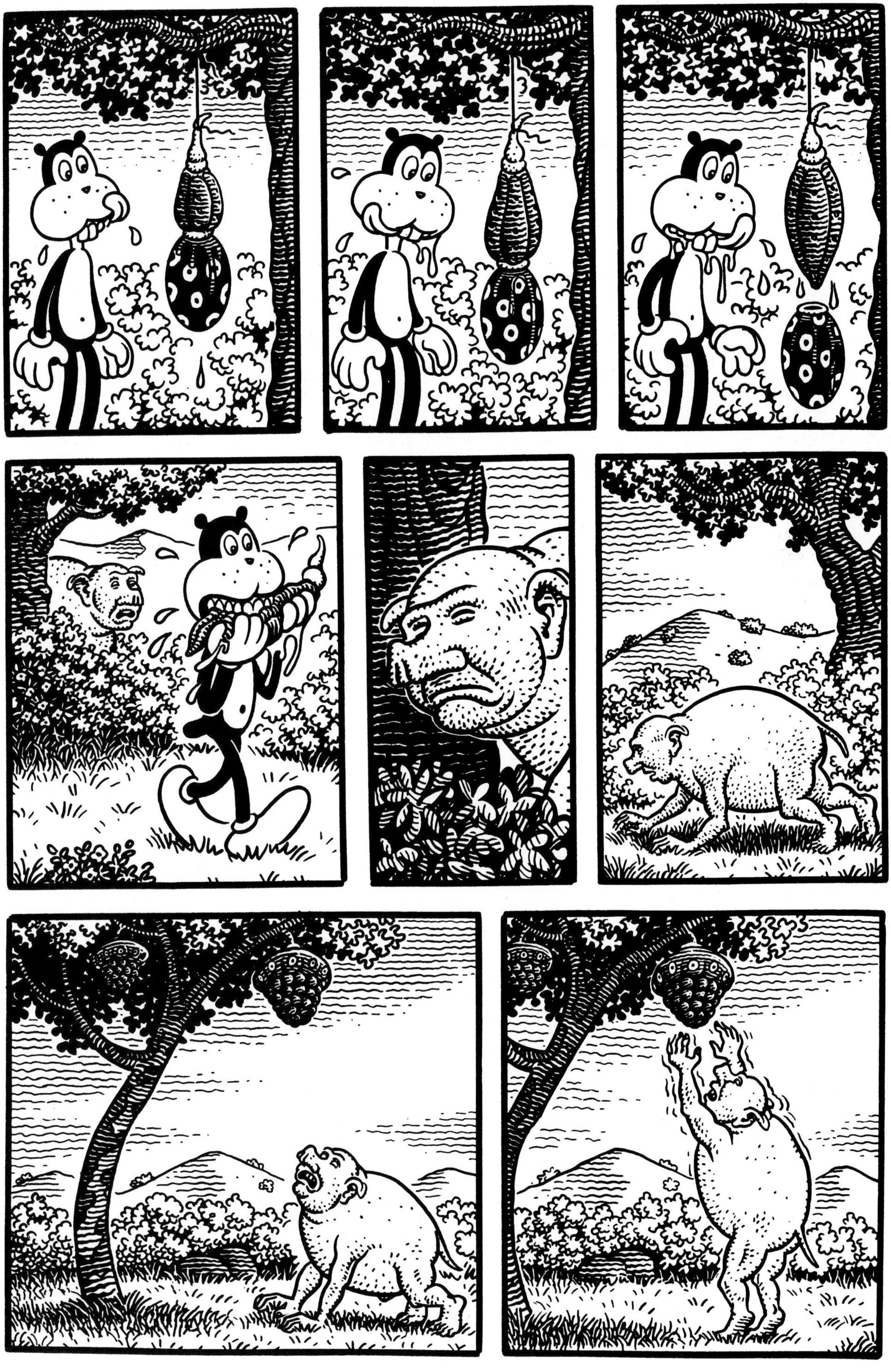

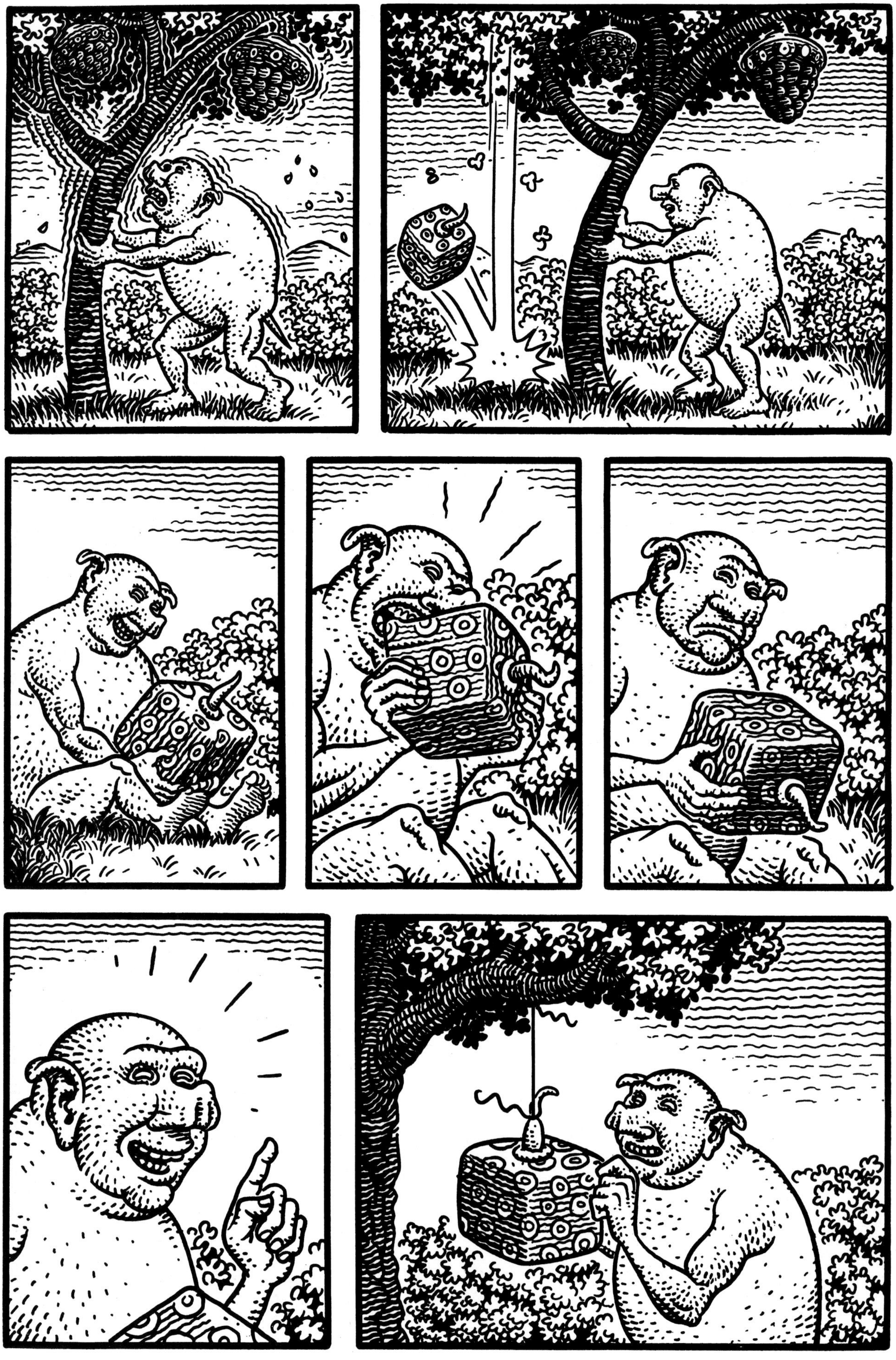

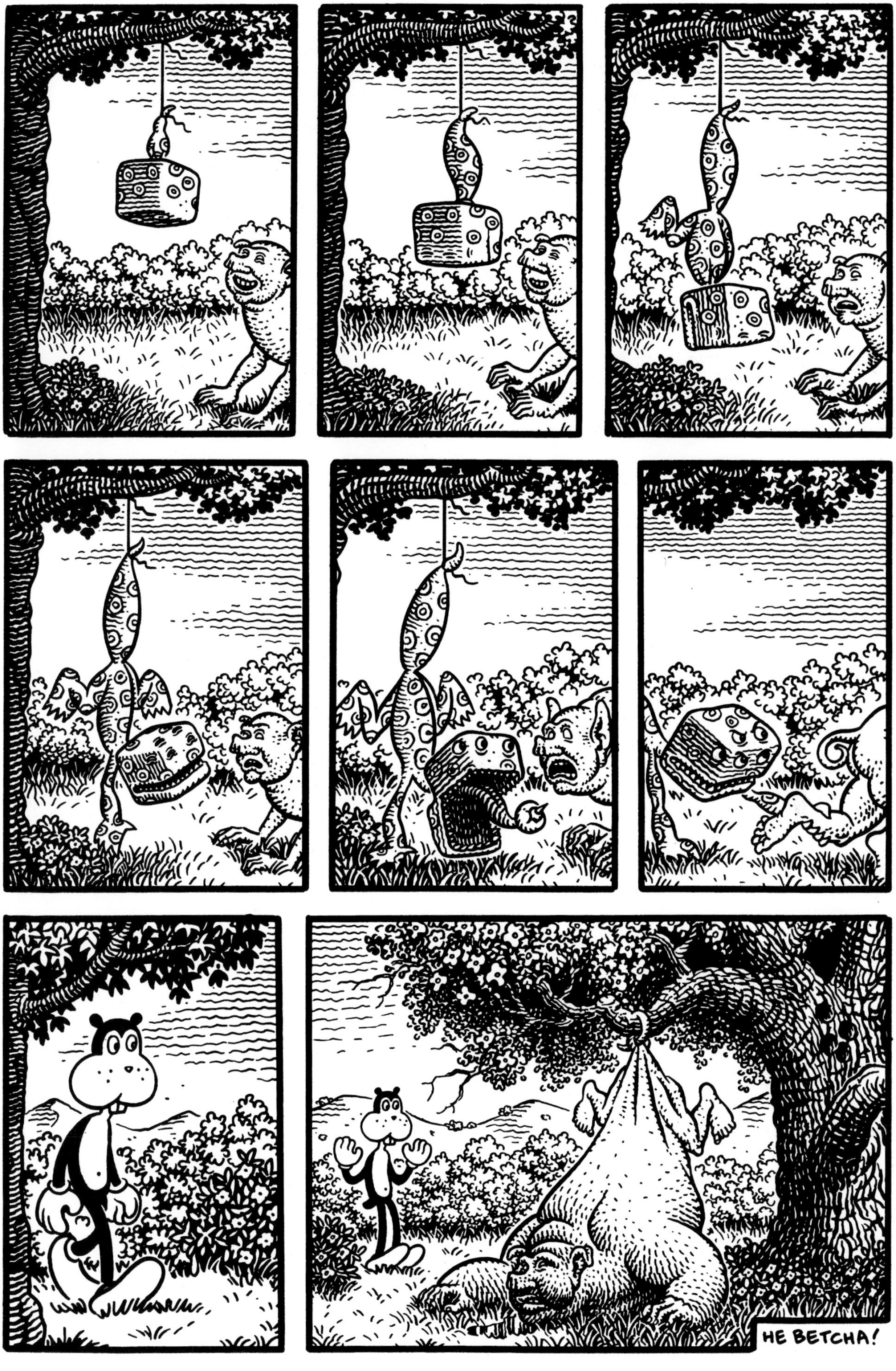
HE BETCHA!

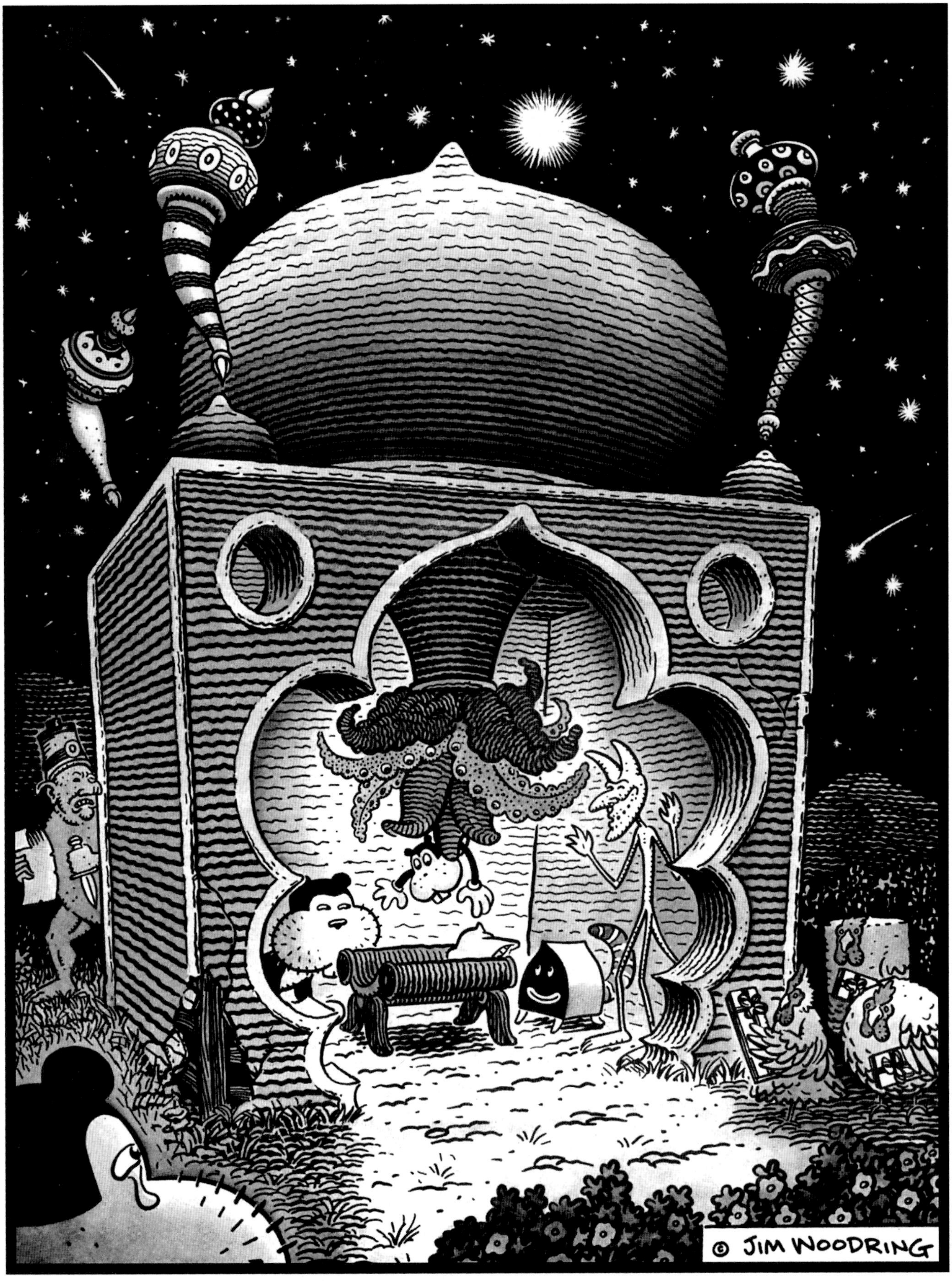
© JIM WOODRING

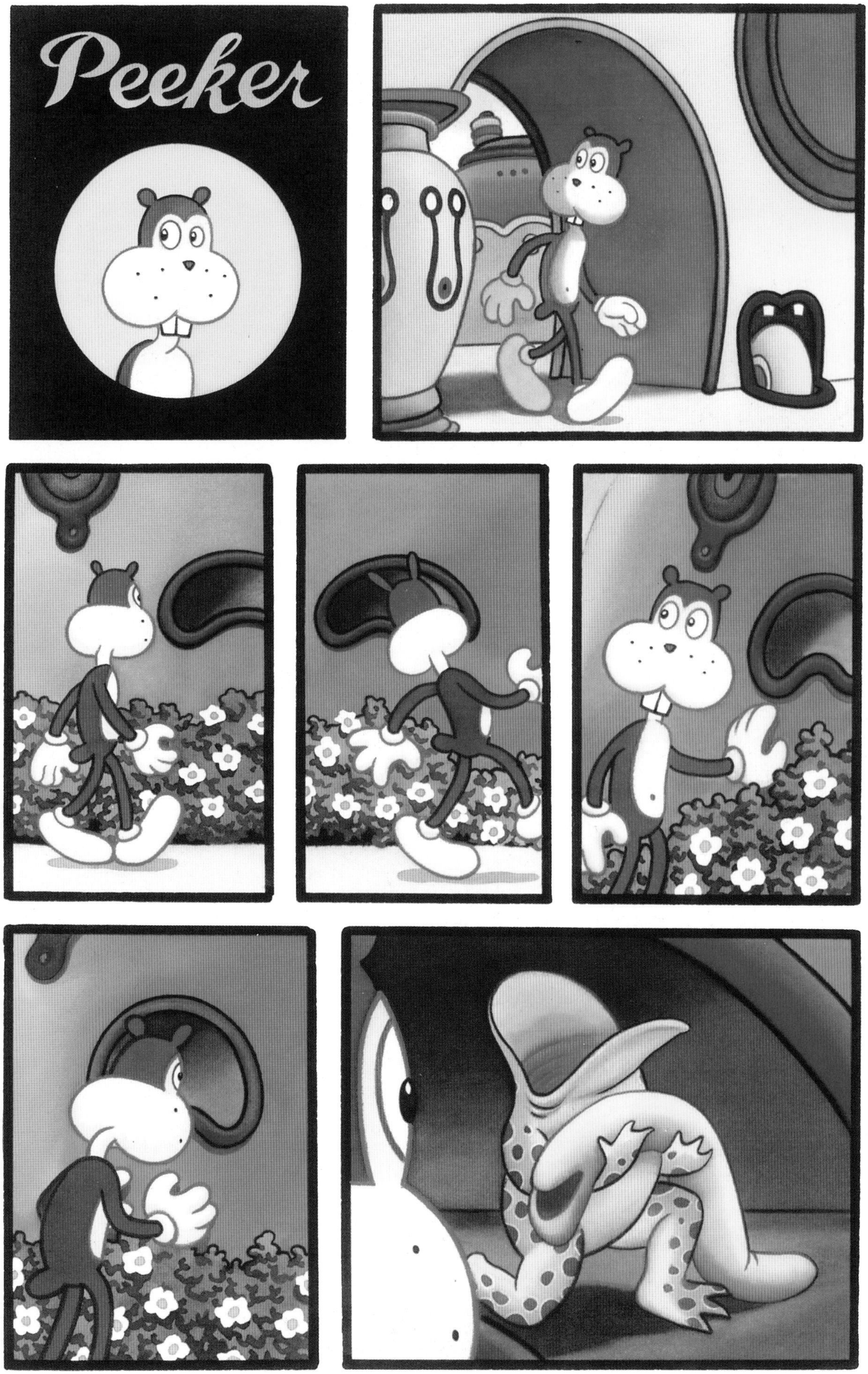
Peeker

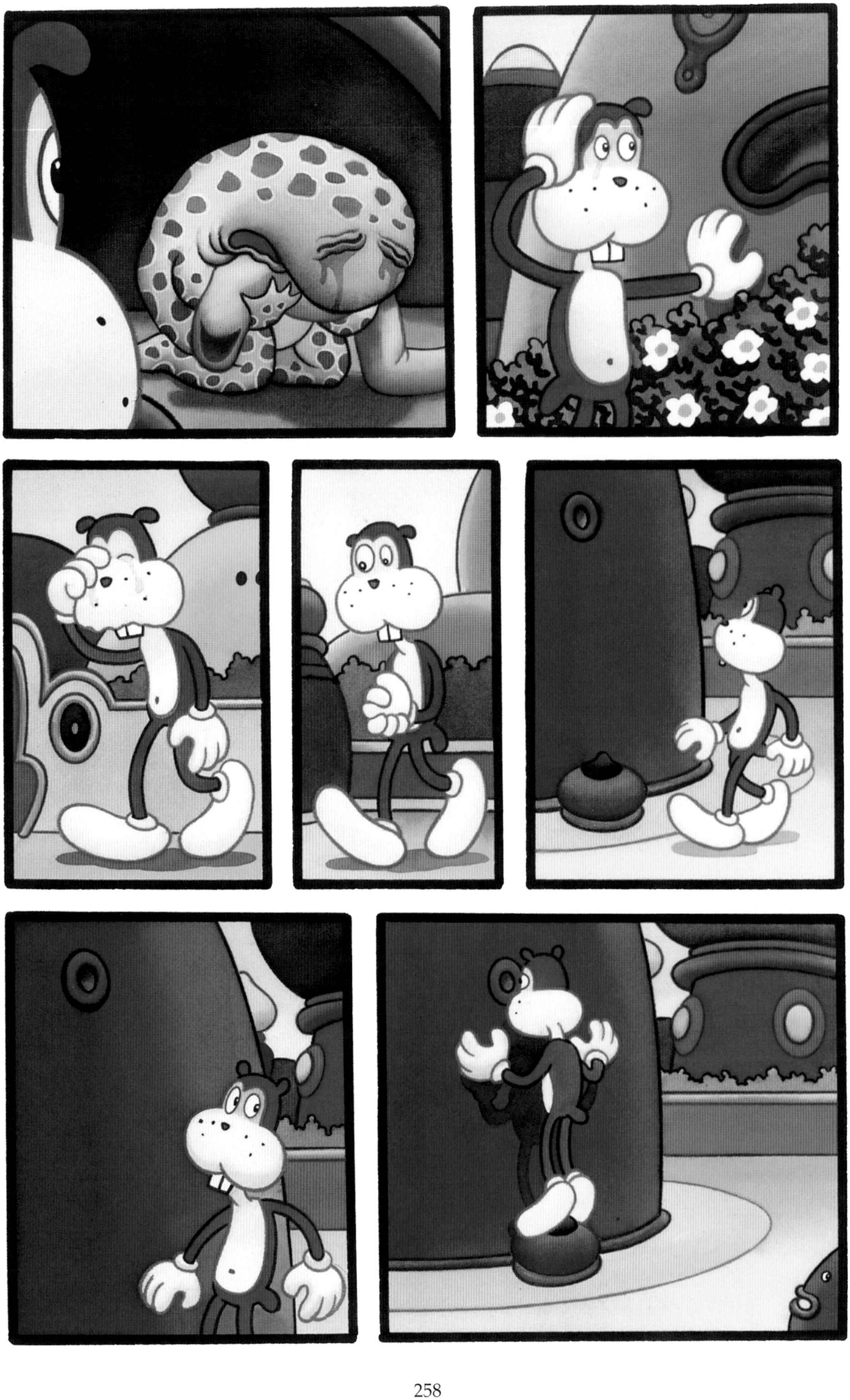

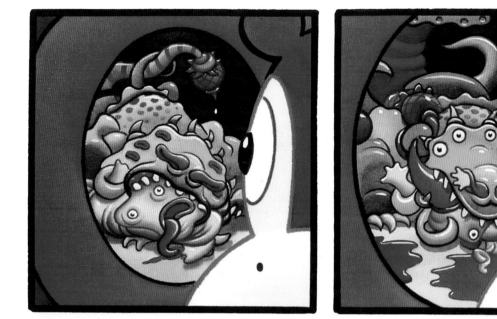

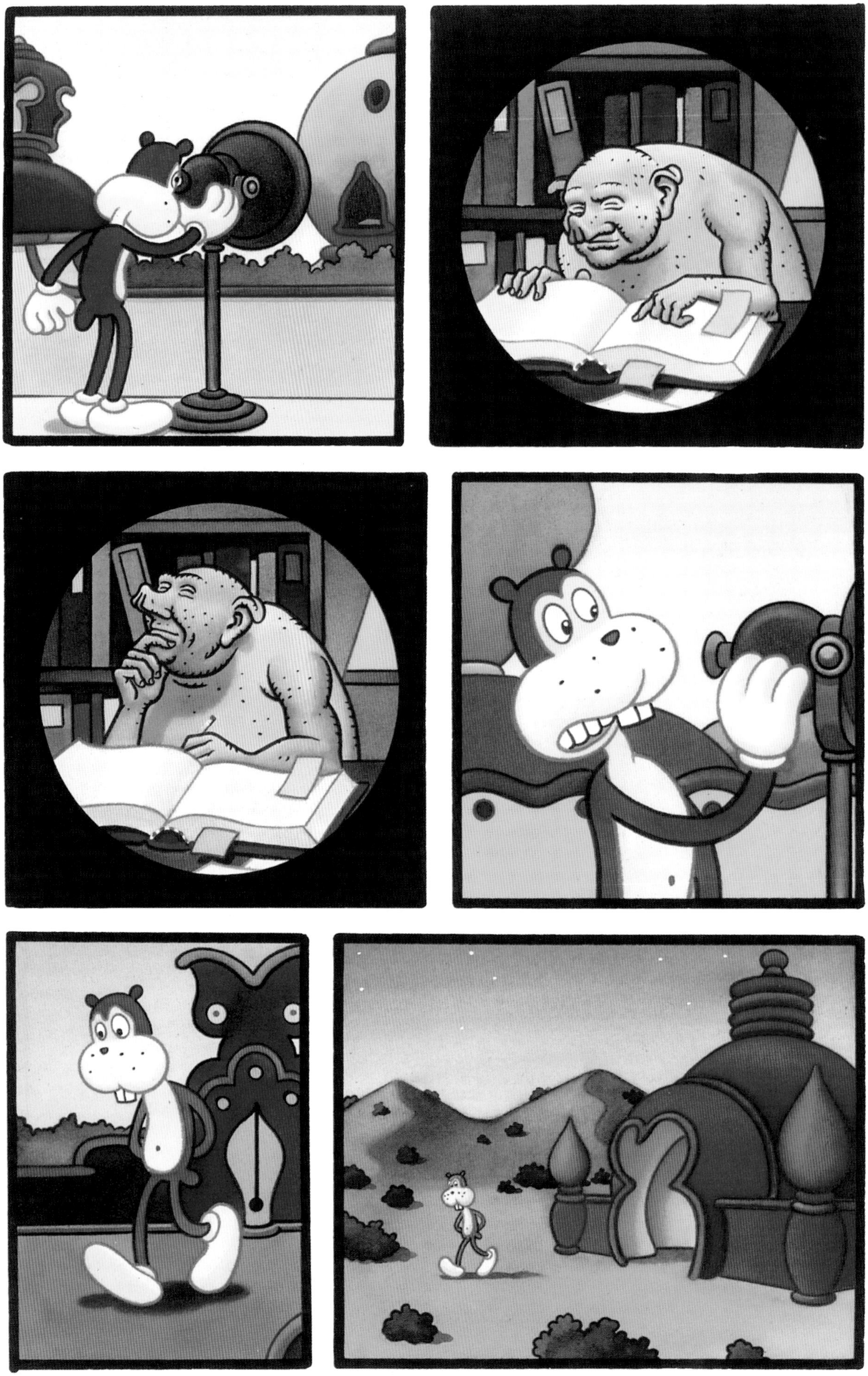

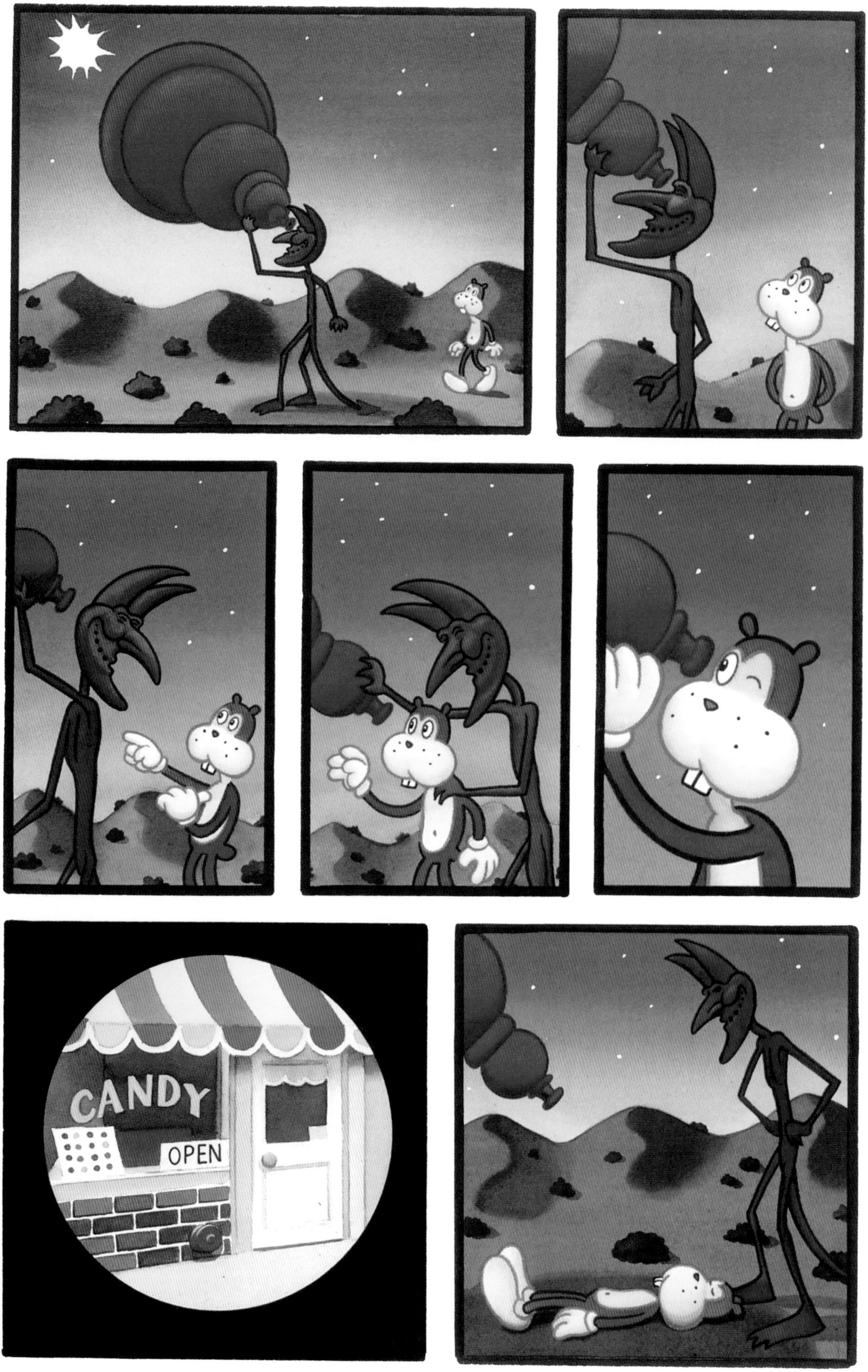
CANDY
OPEN

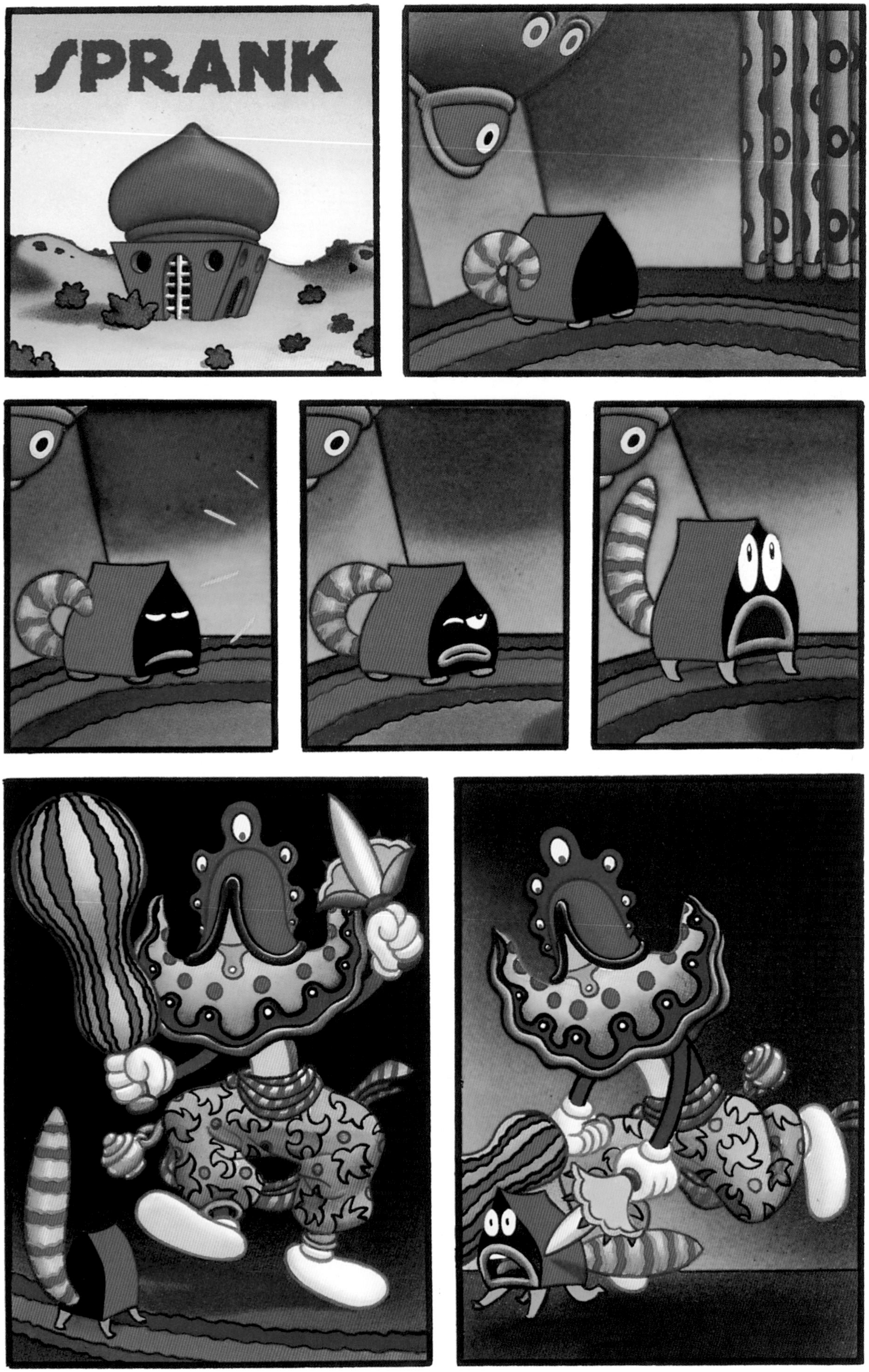
SPRANK

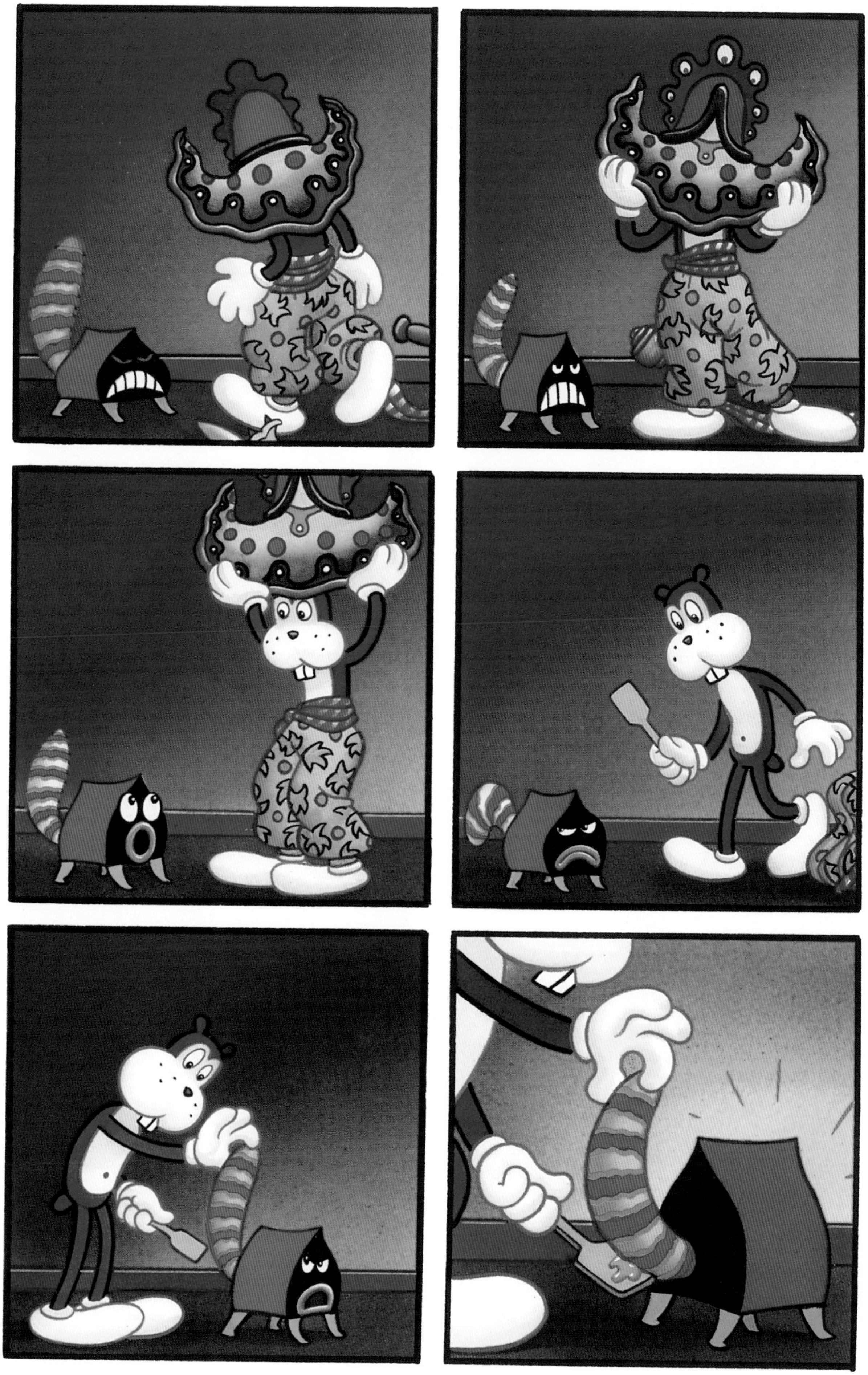

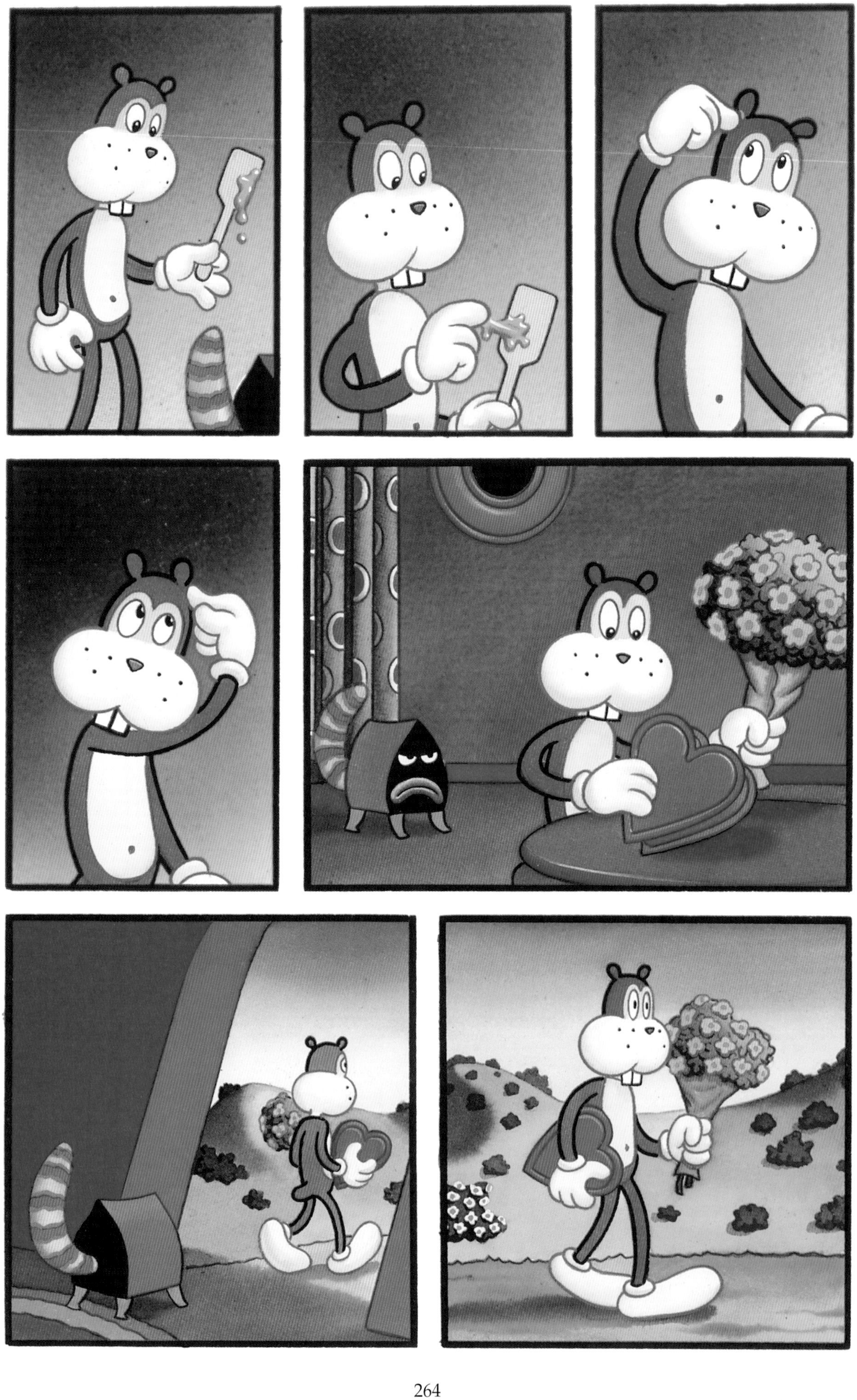

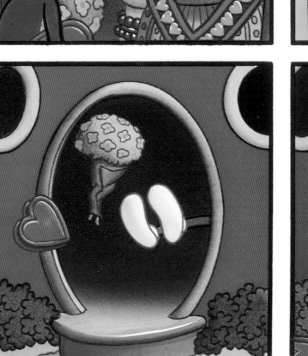

REMEMBER?

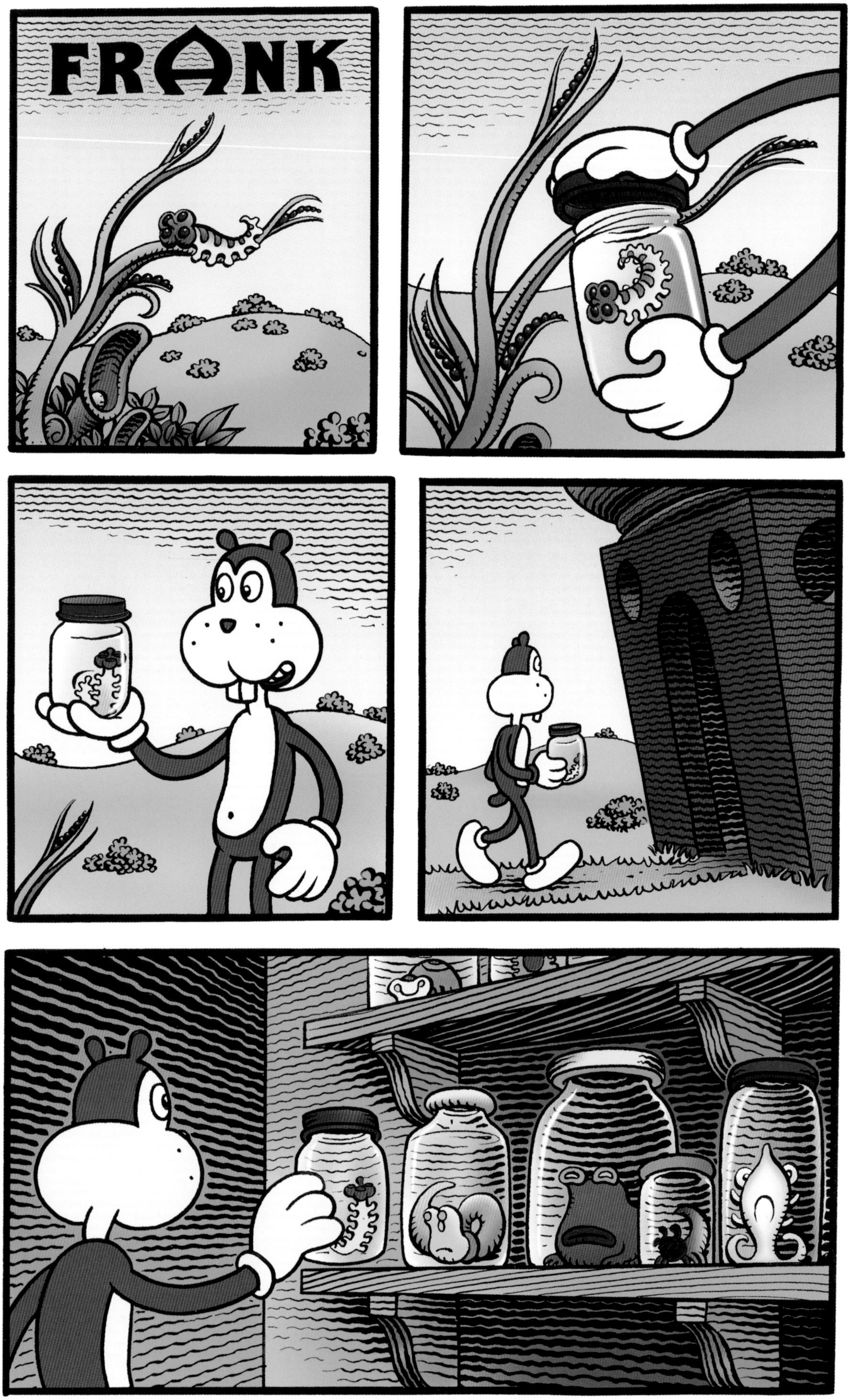
FRANK

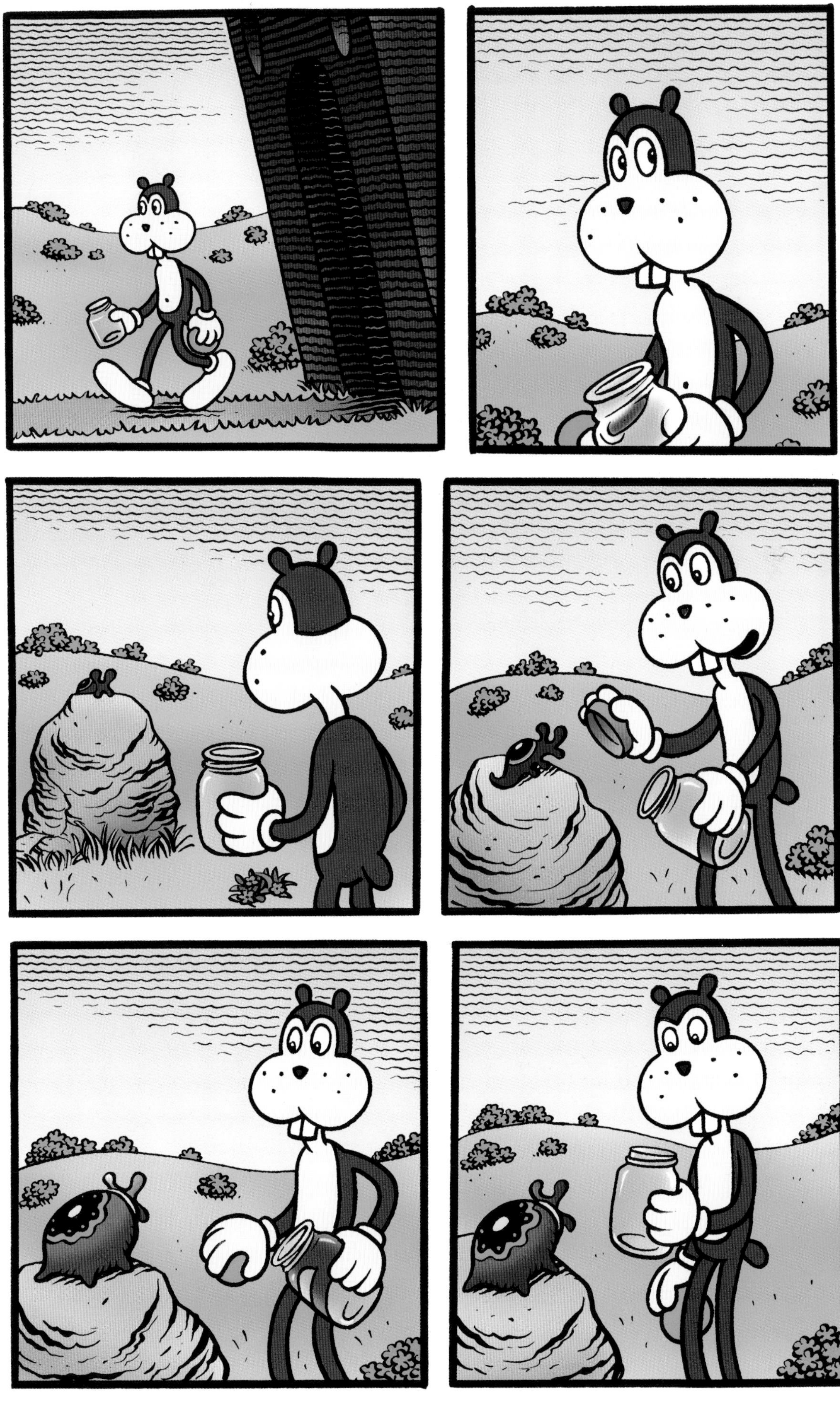

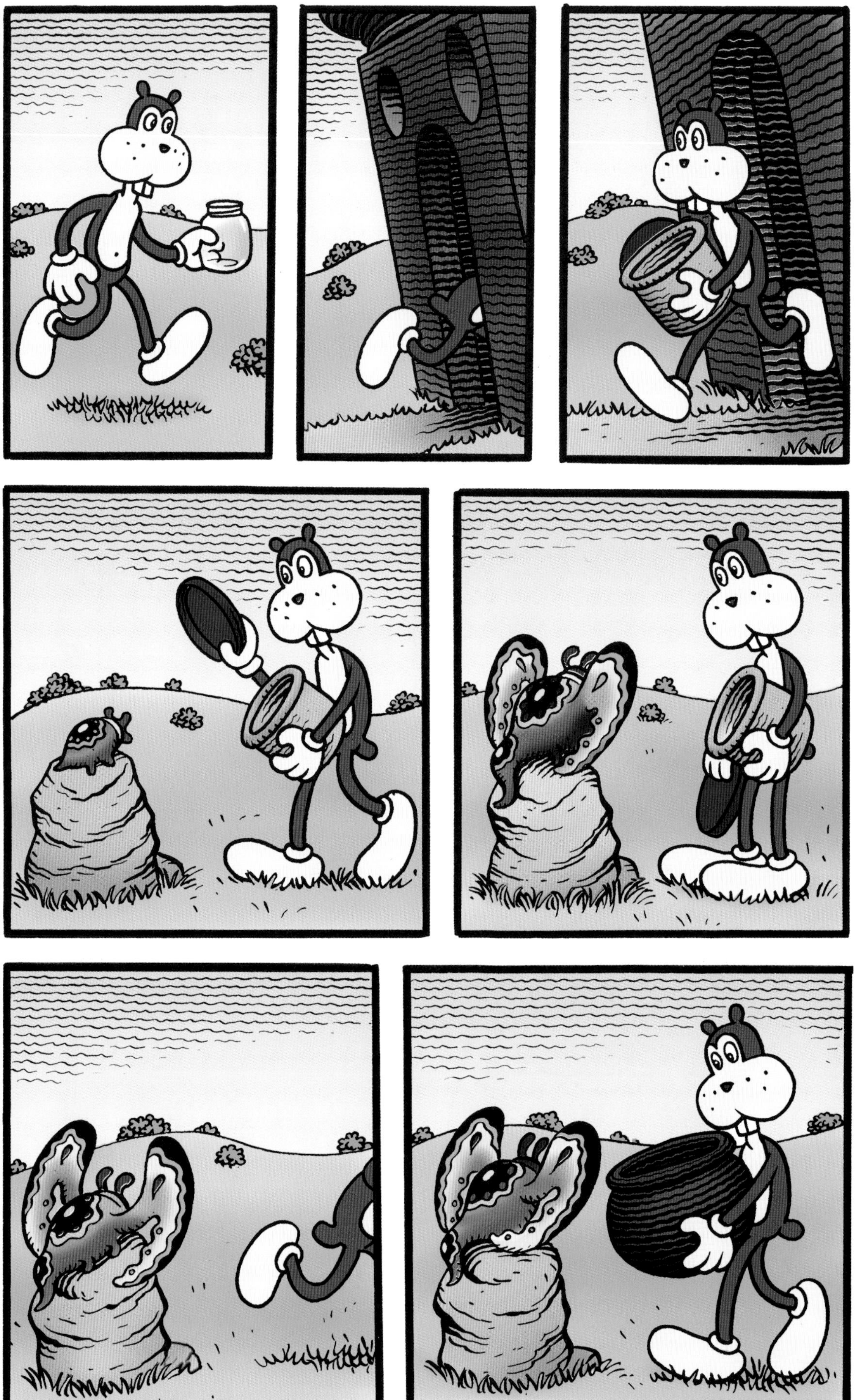

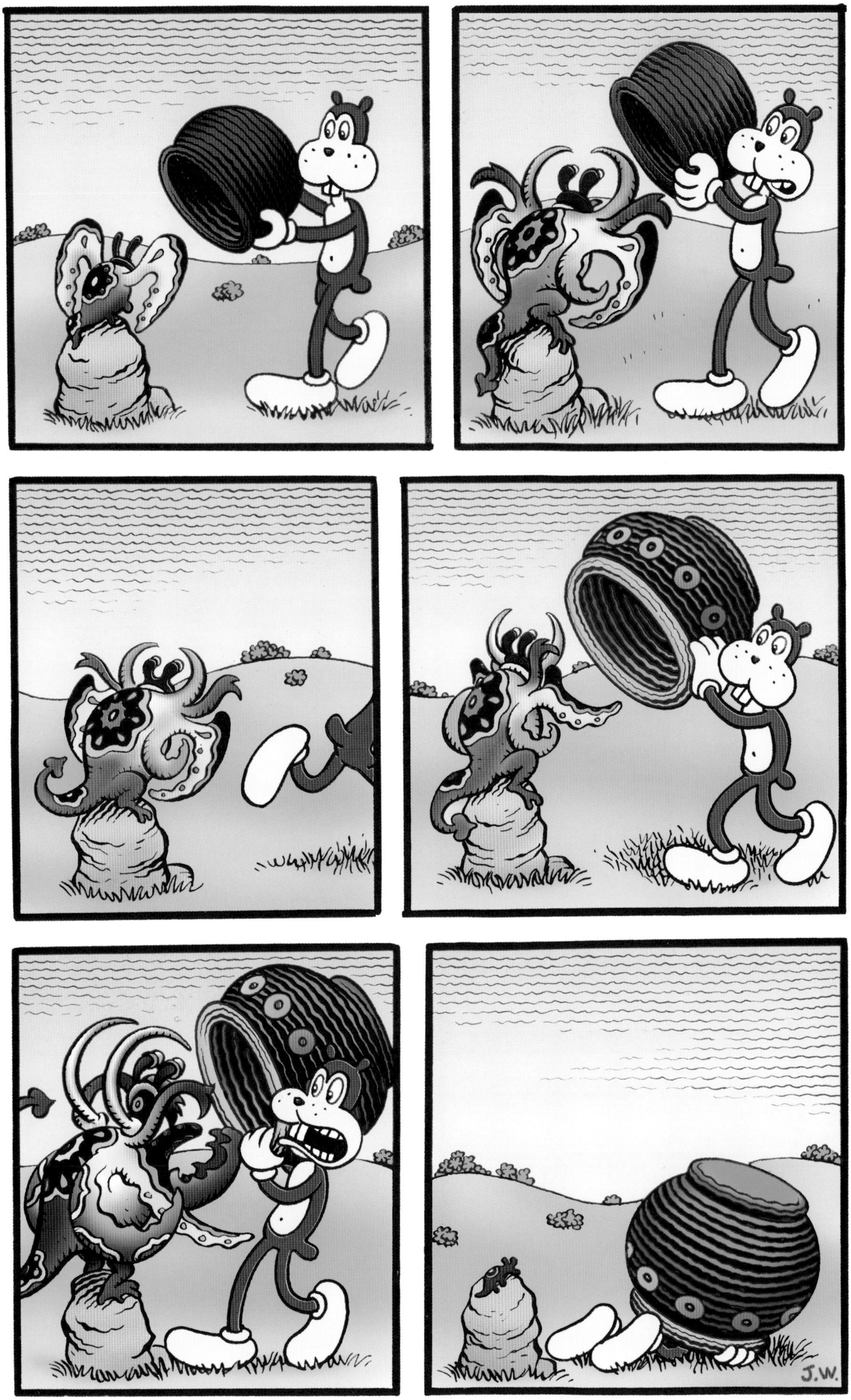
J.W.

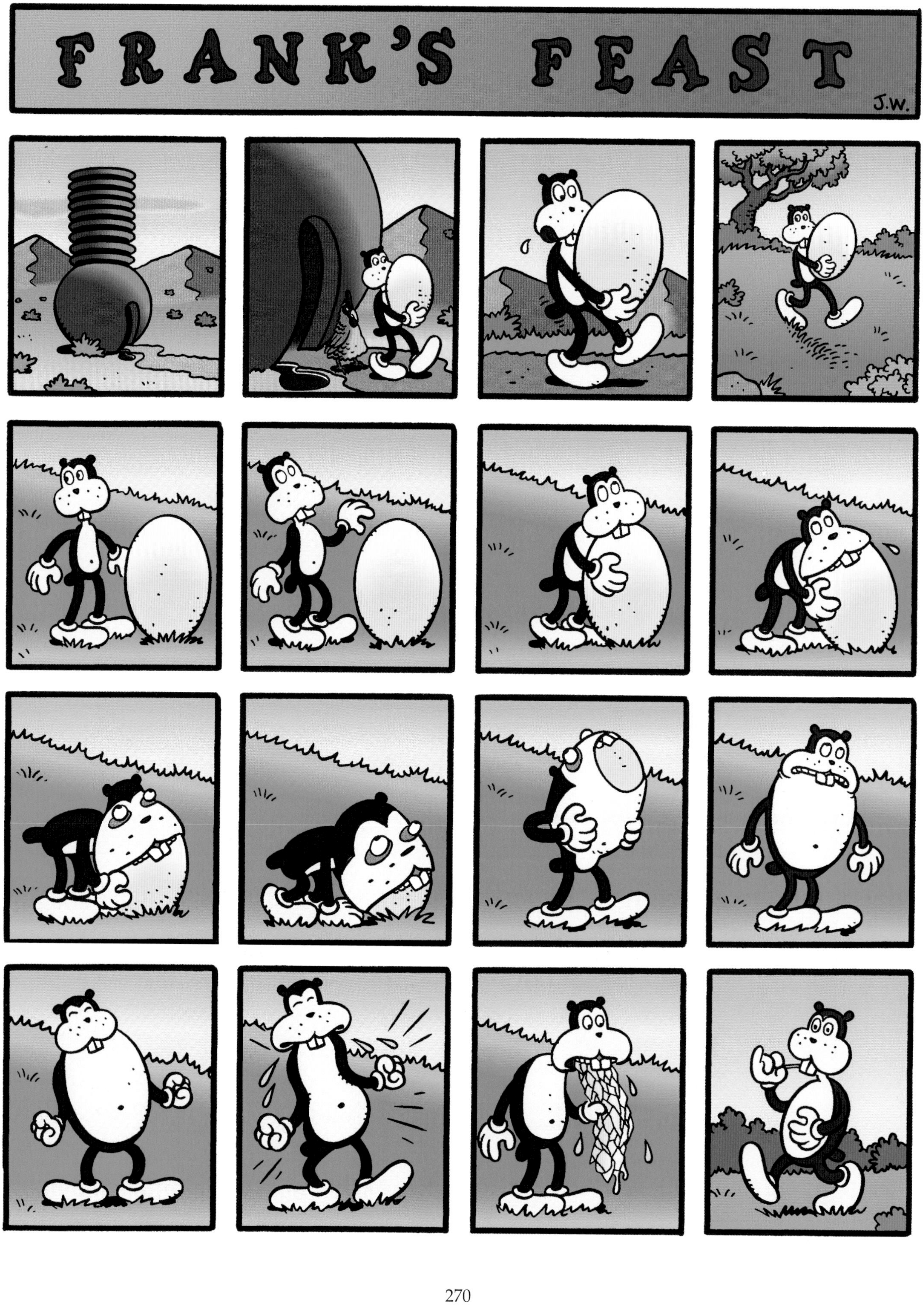
FRANK'S FEAST
J.W.

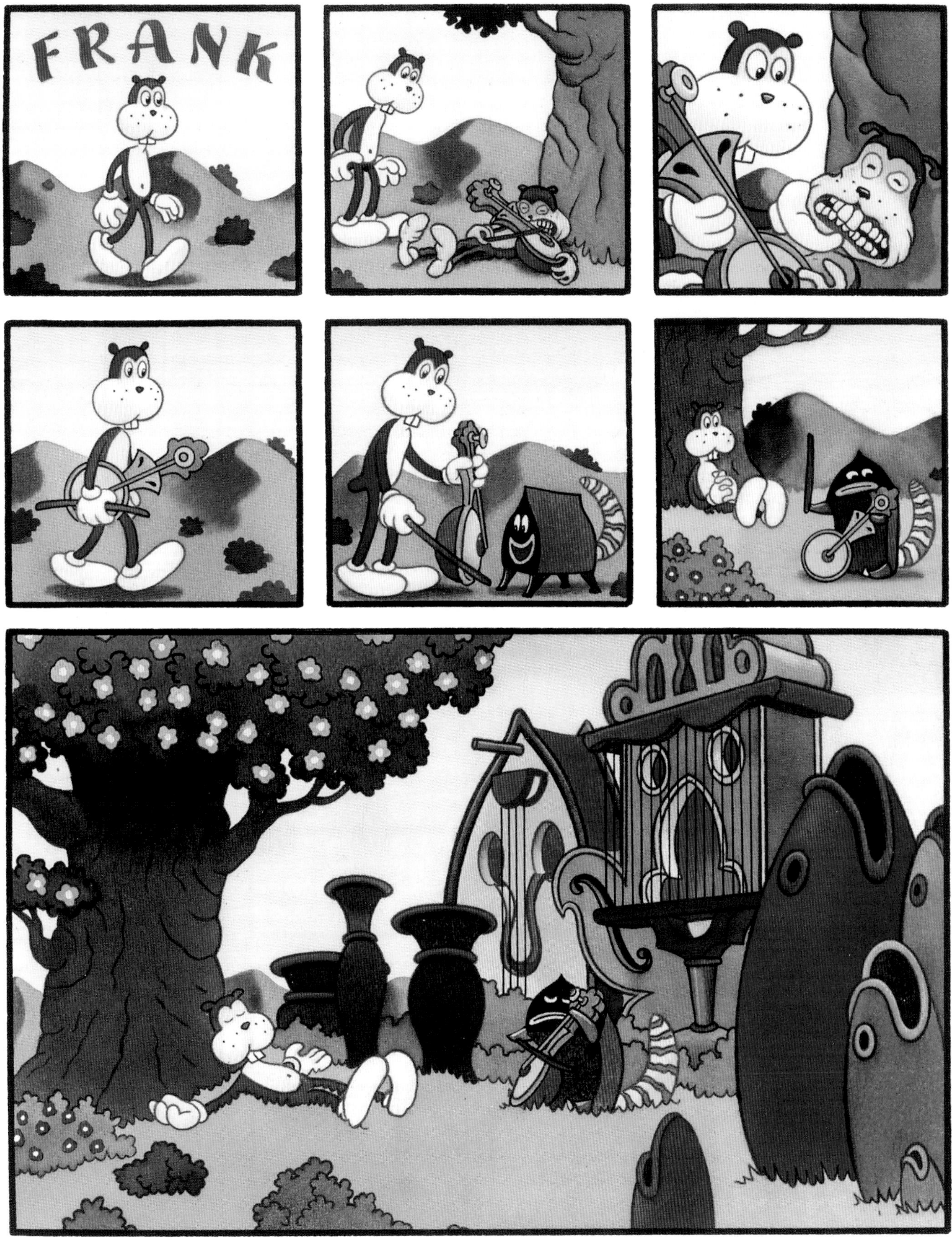
FRANK

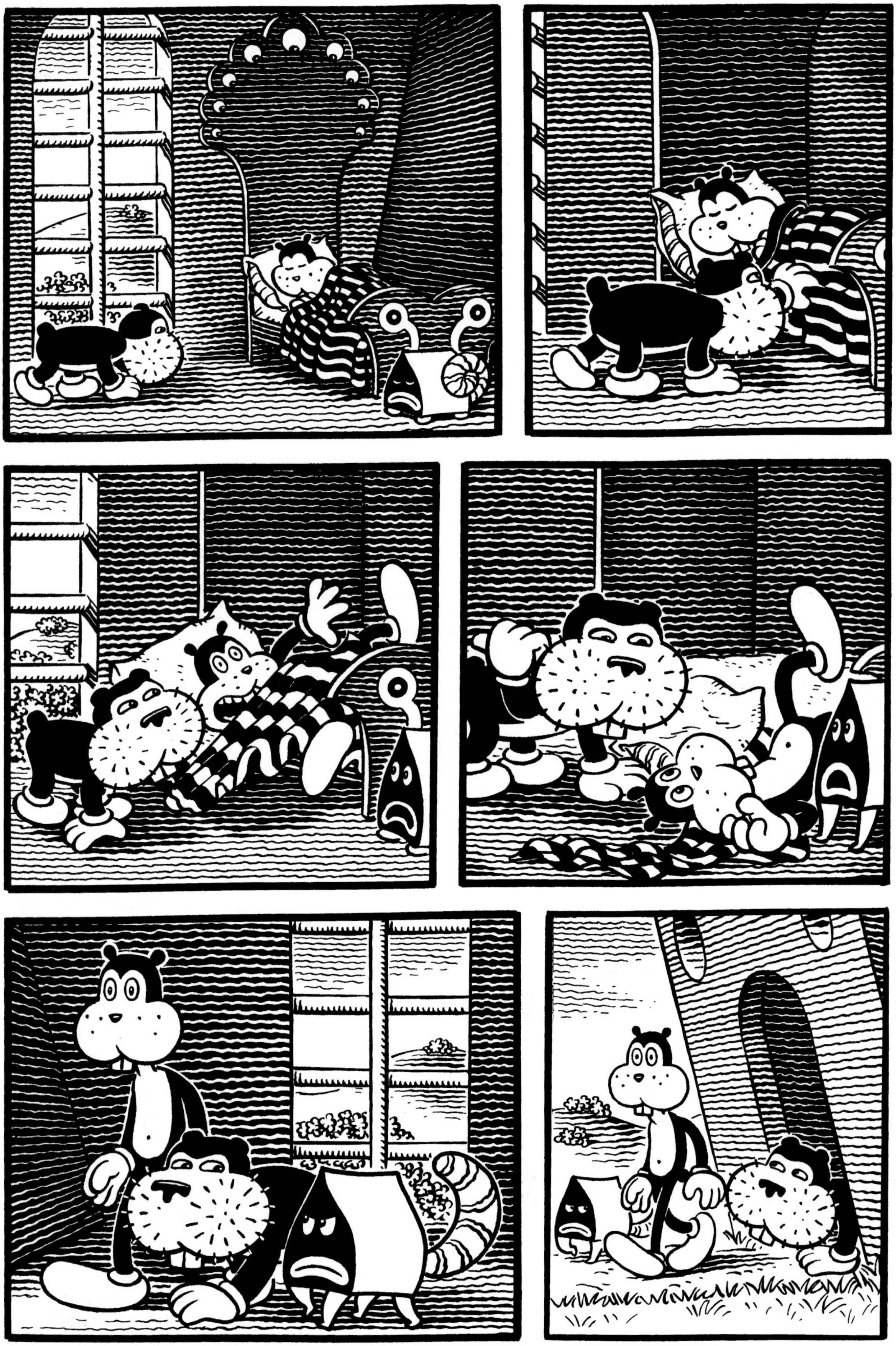

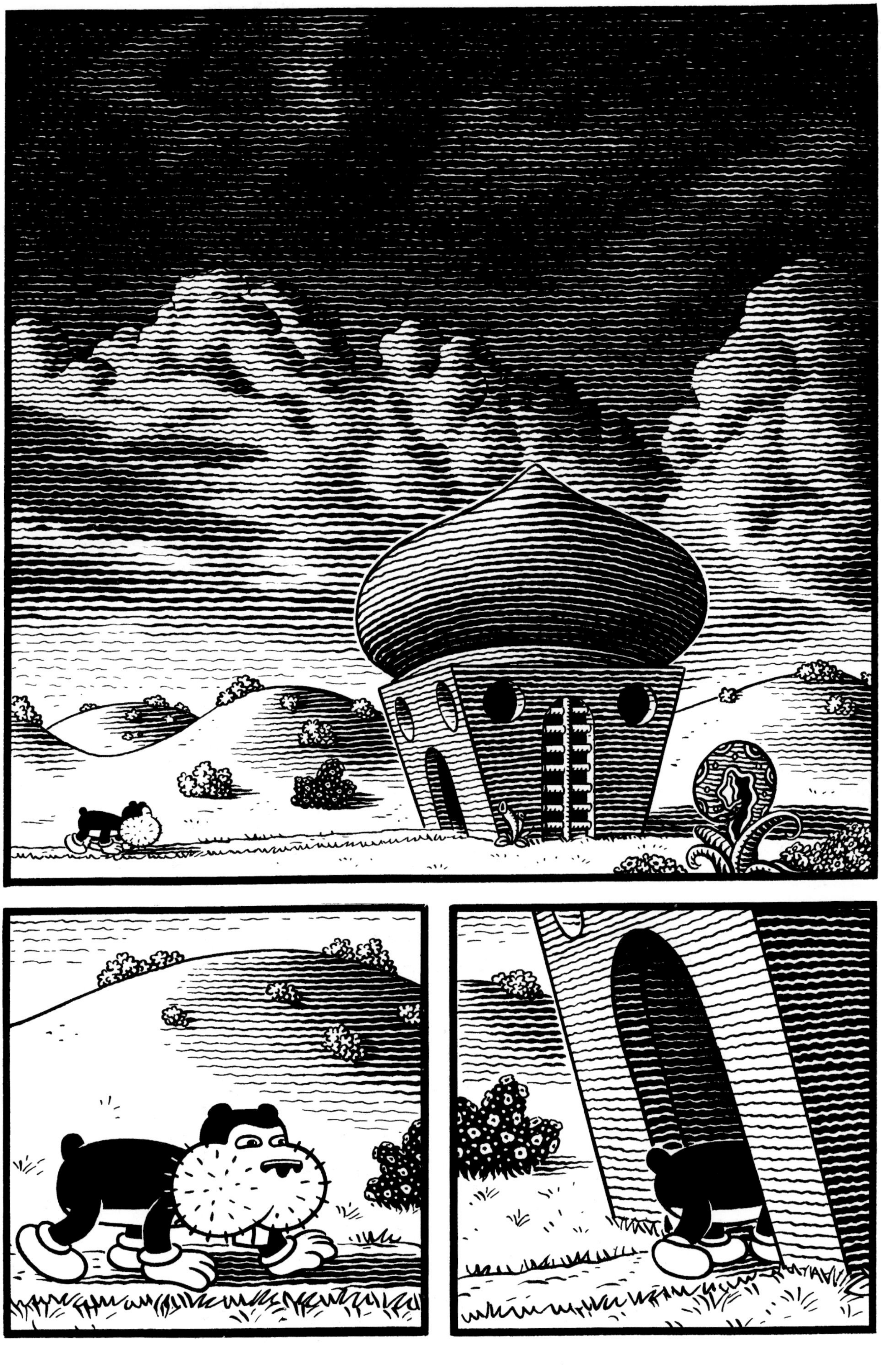

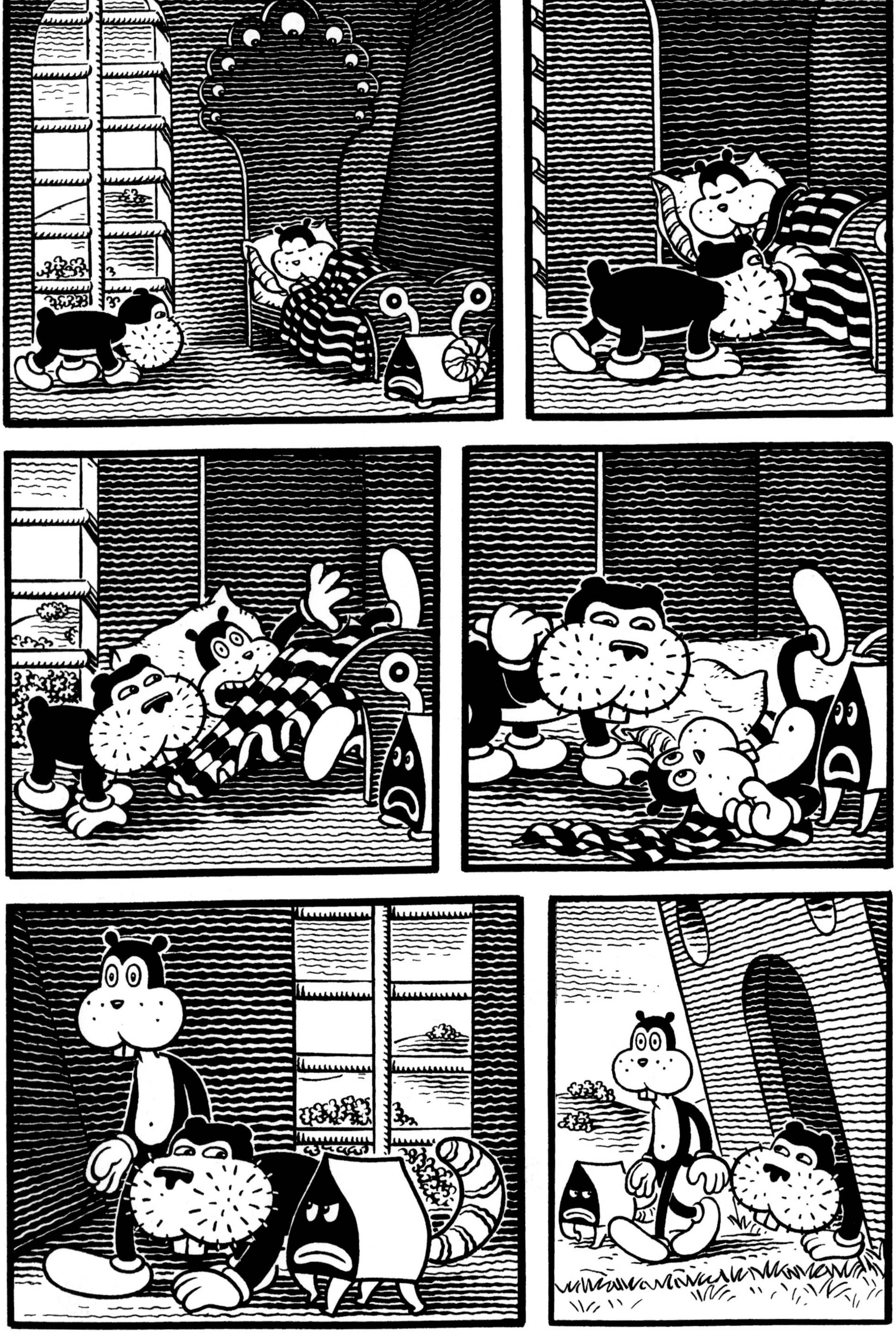

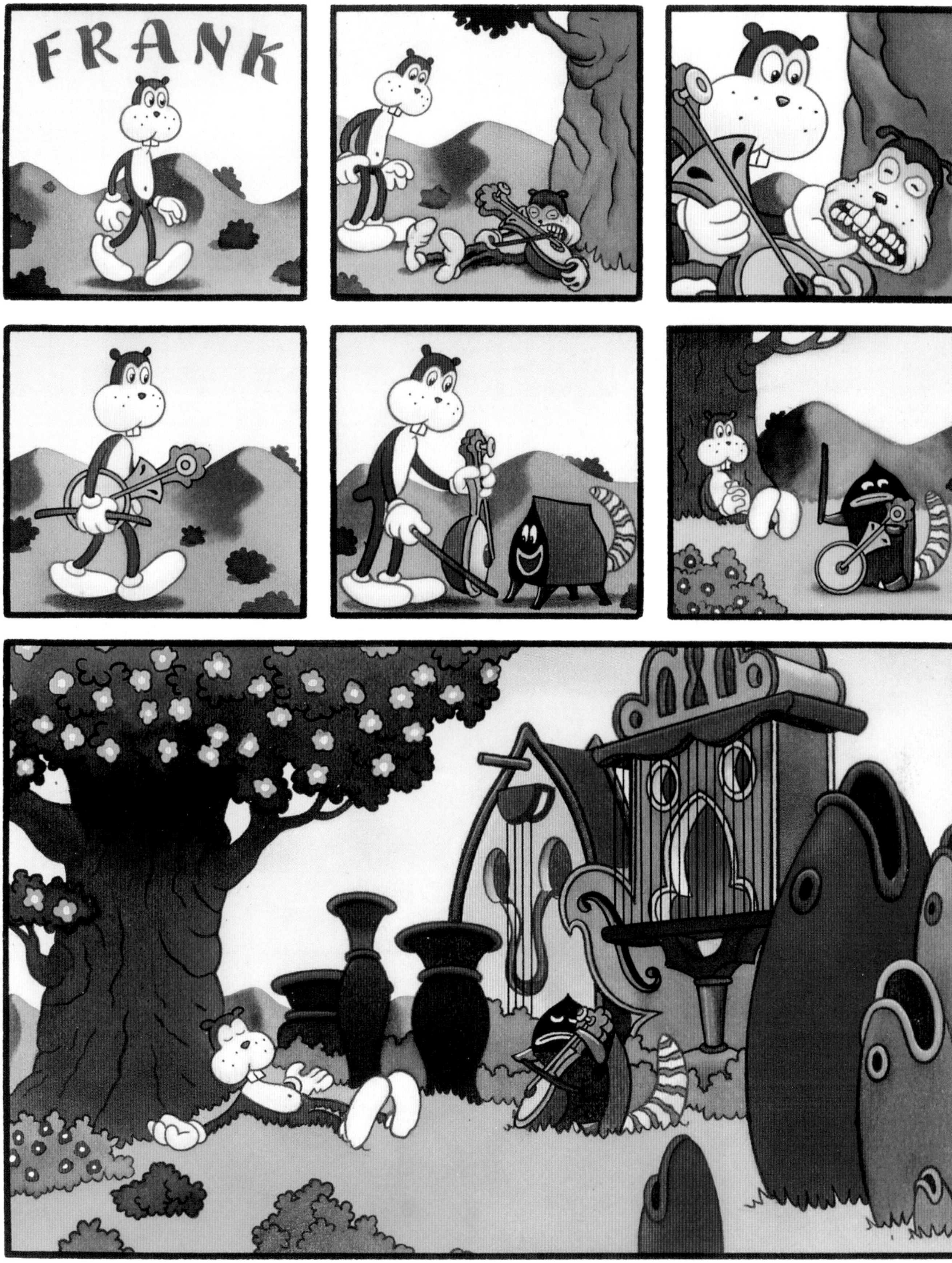
FRANK

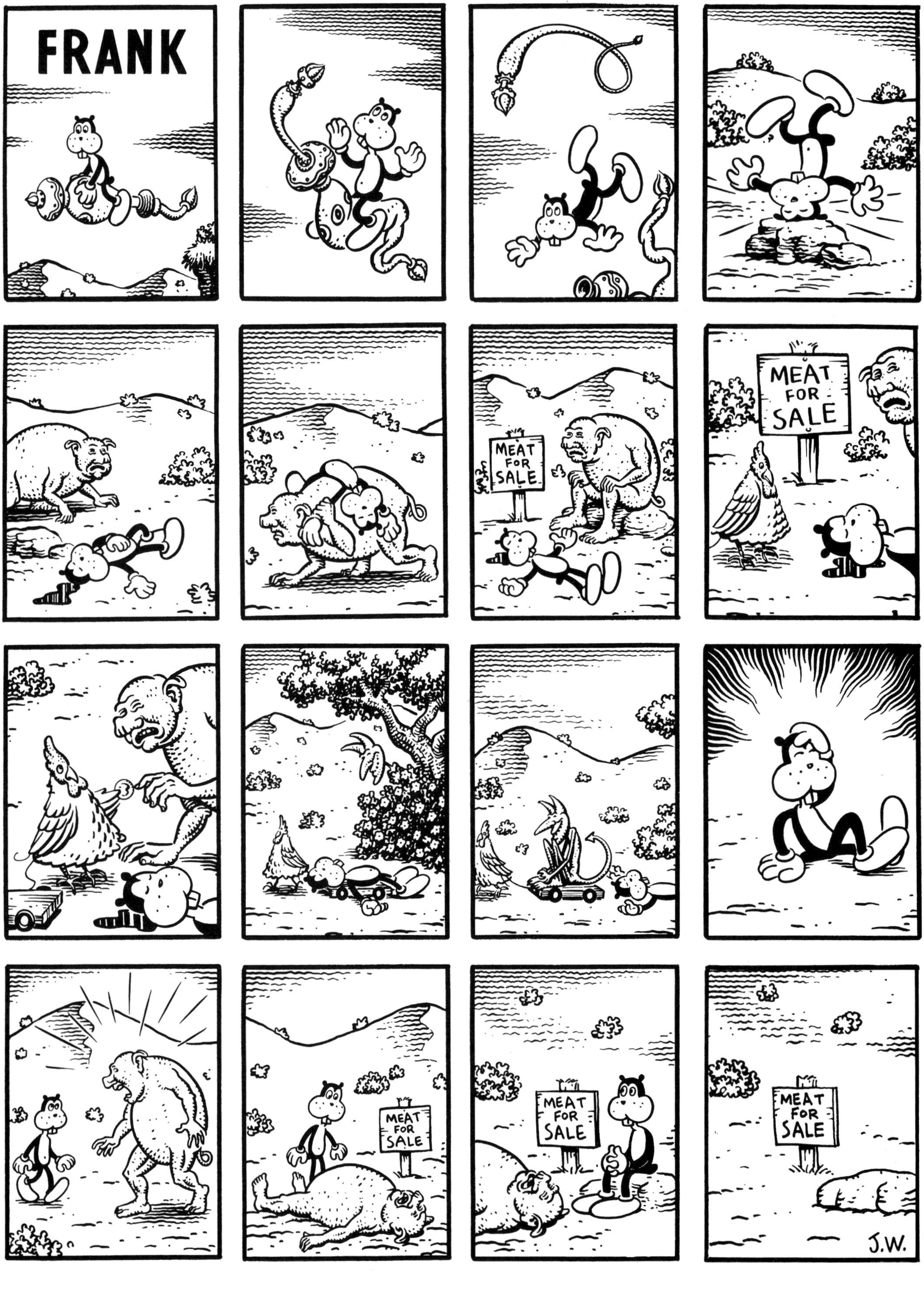
FRANK
MEAT FOR SALE
MEAT FOR SALE
MEAT FOR SALE
MEAT FOR SALE
MEAT FOR SALE
J.W.

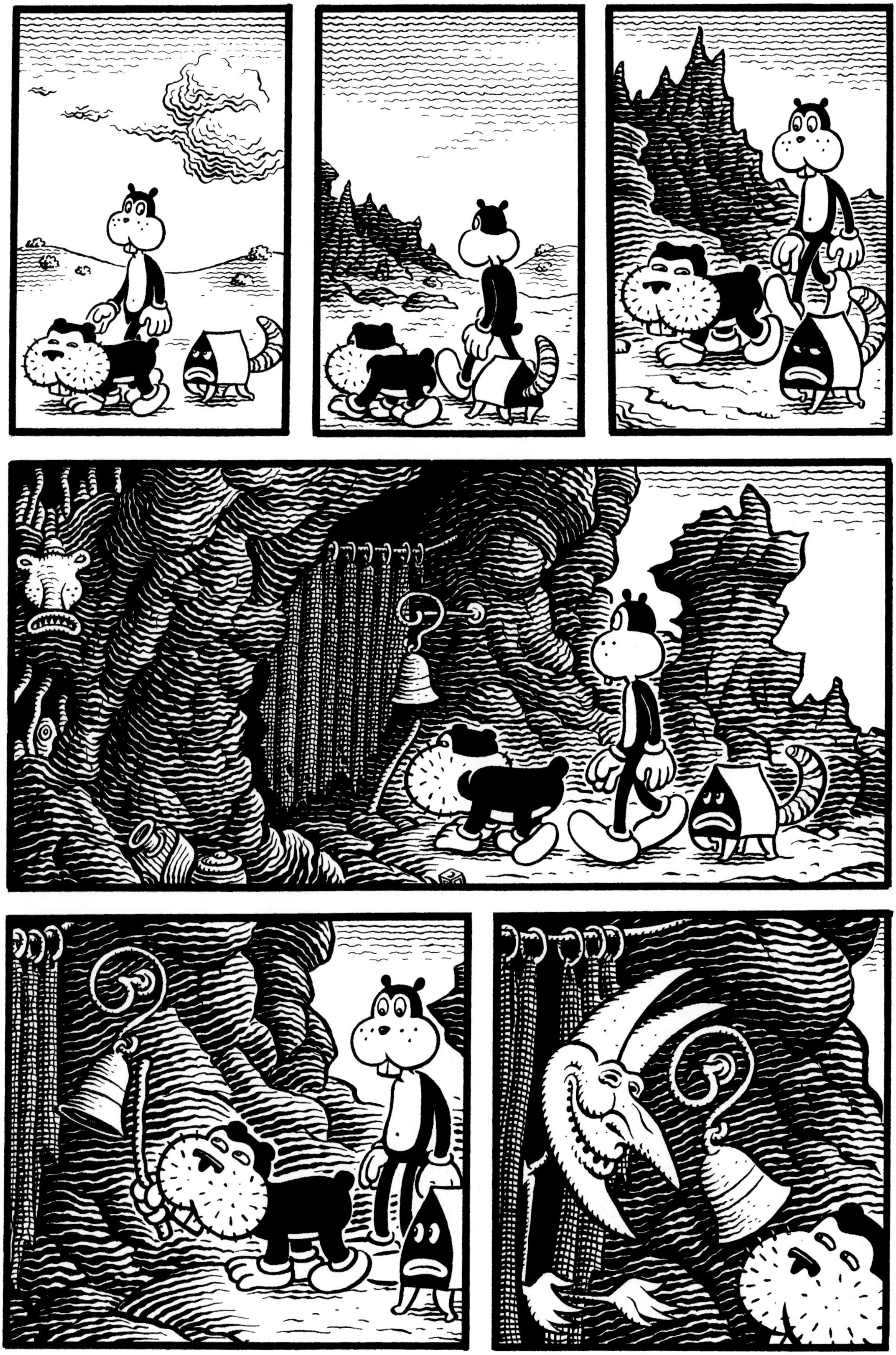

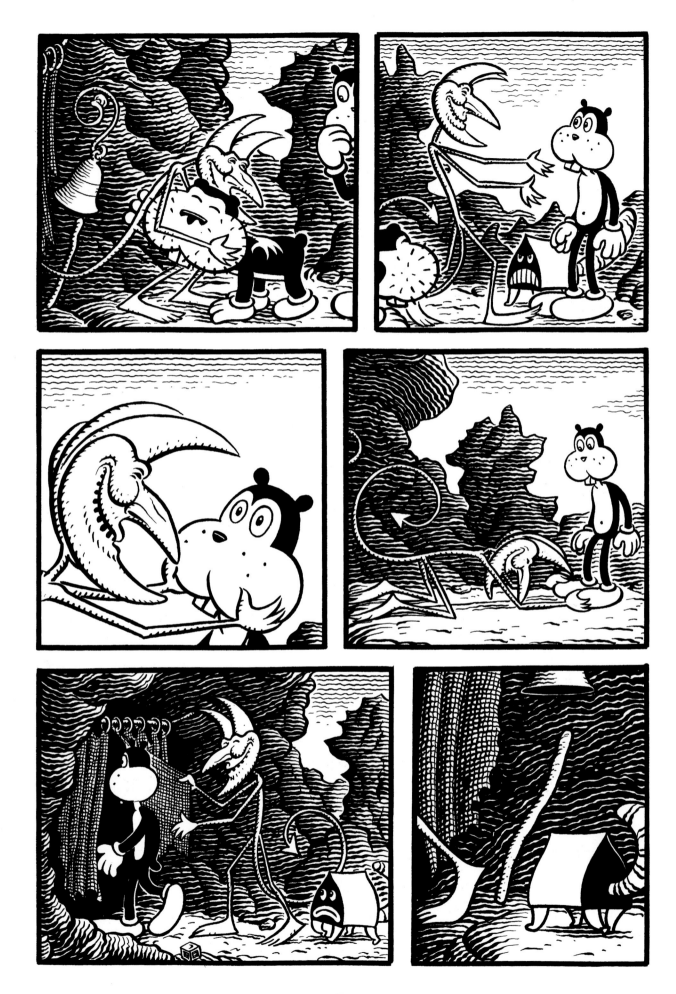

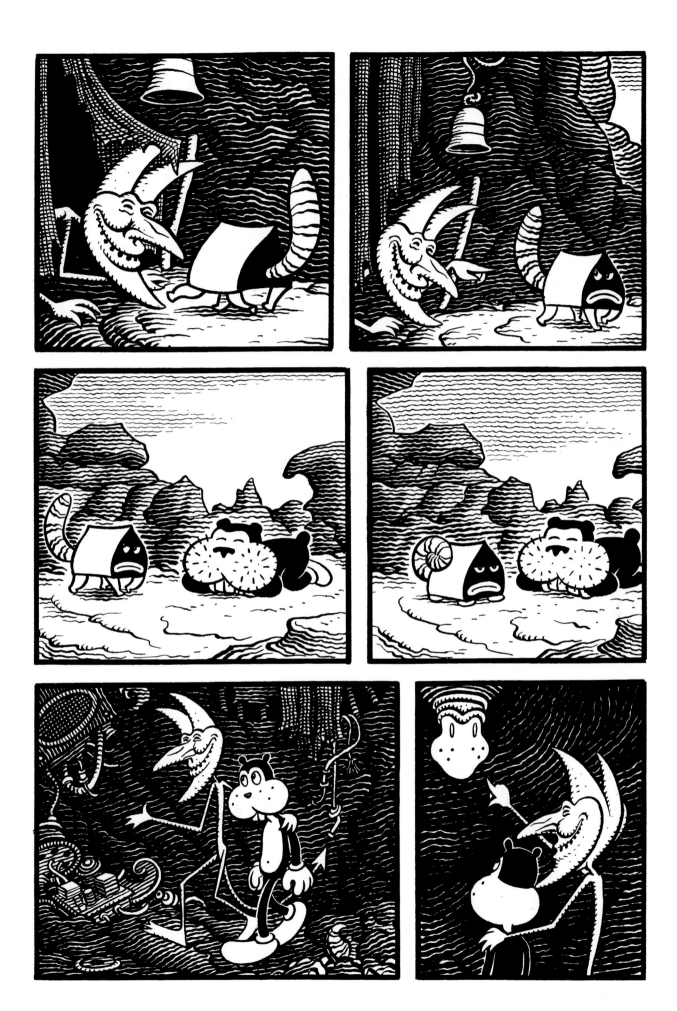

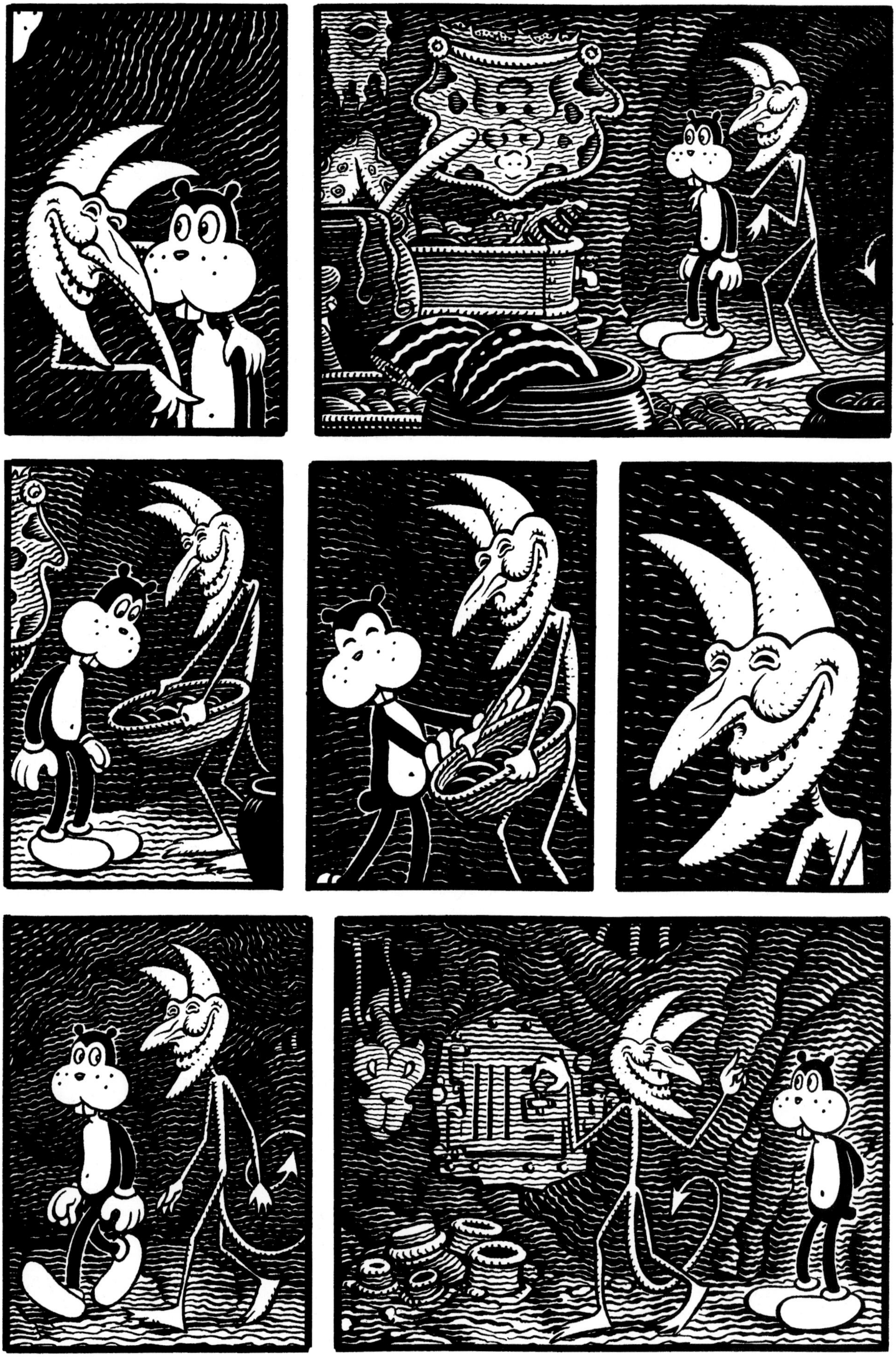

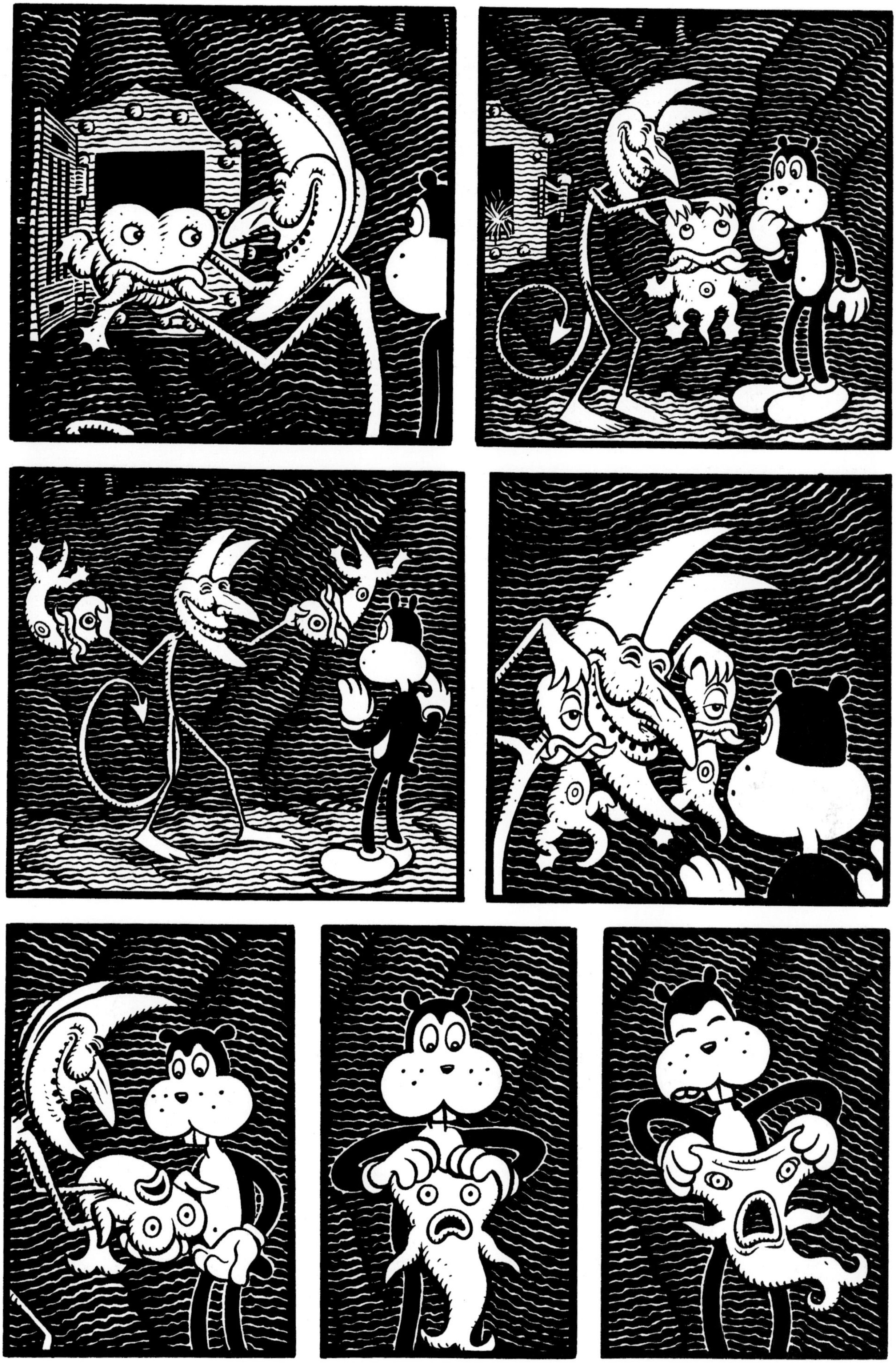

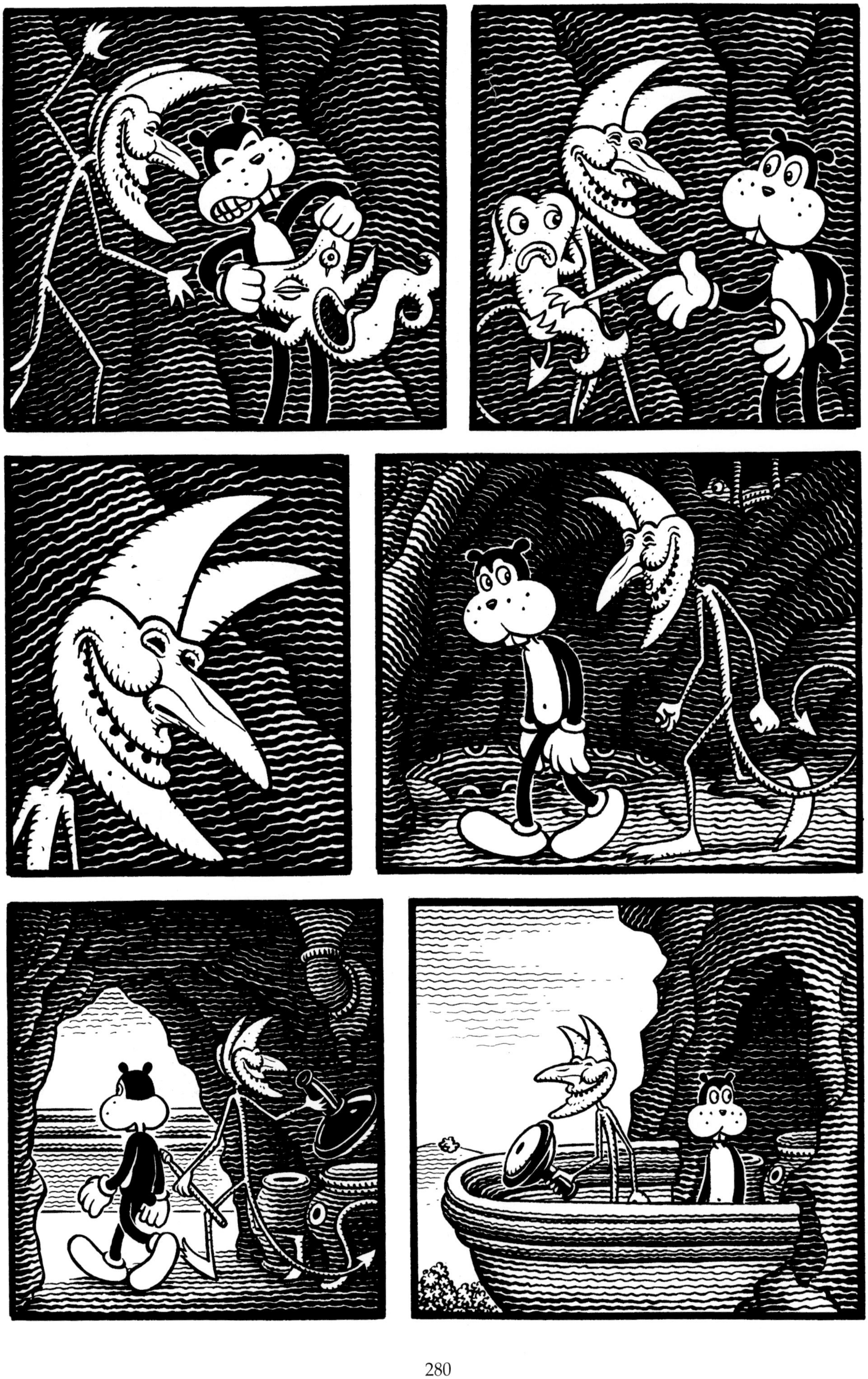

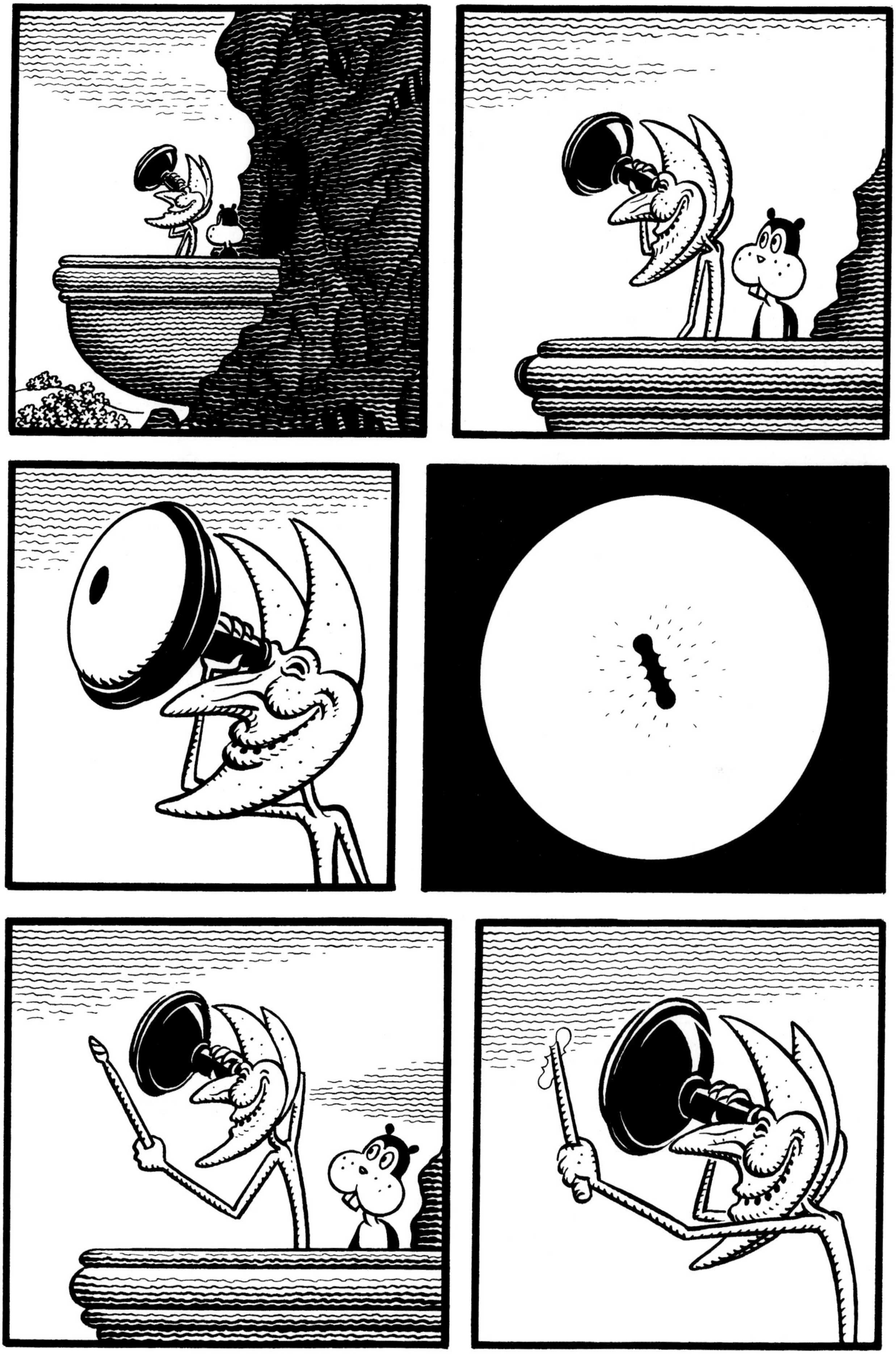

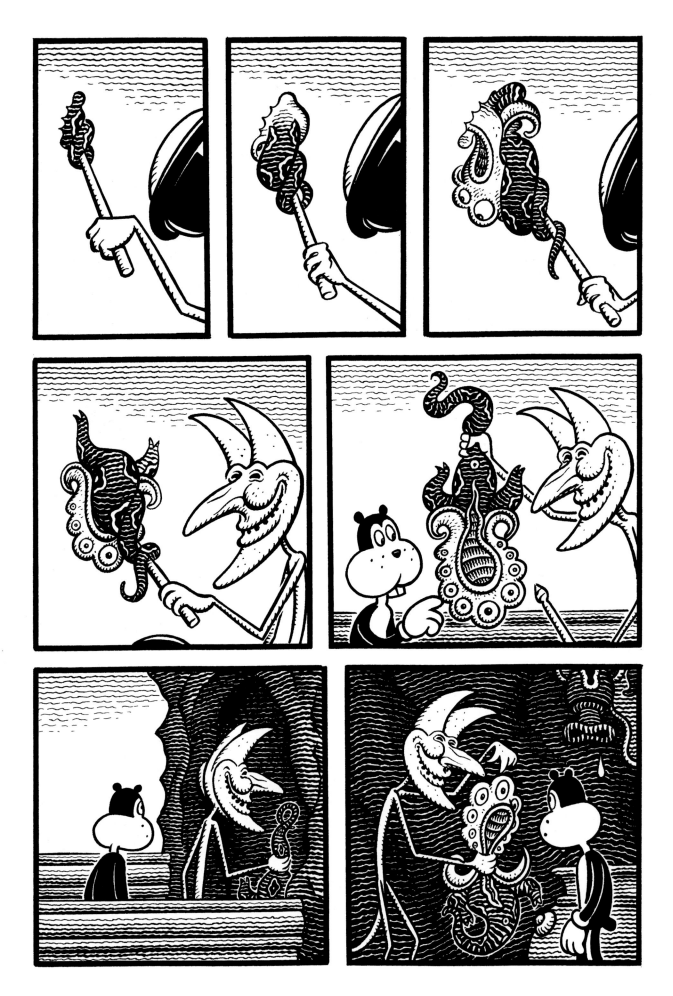

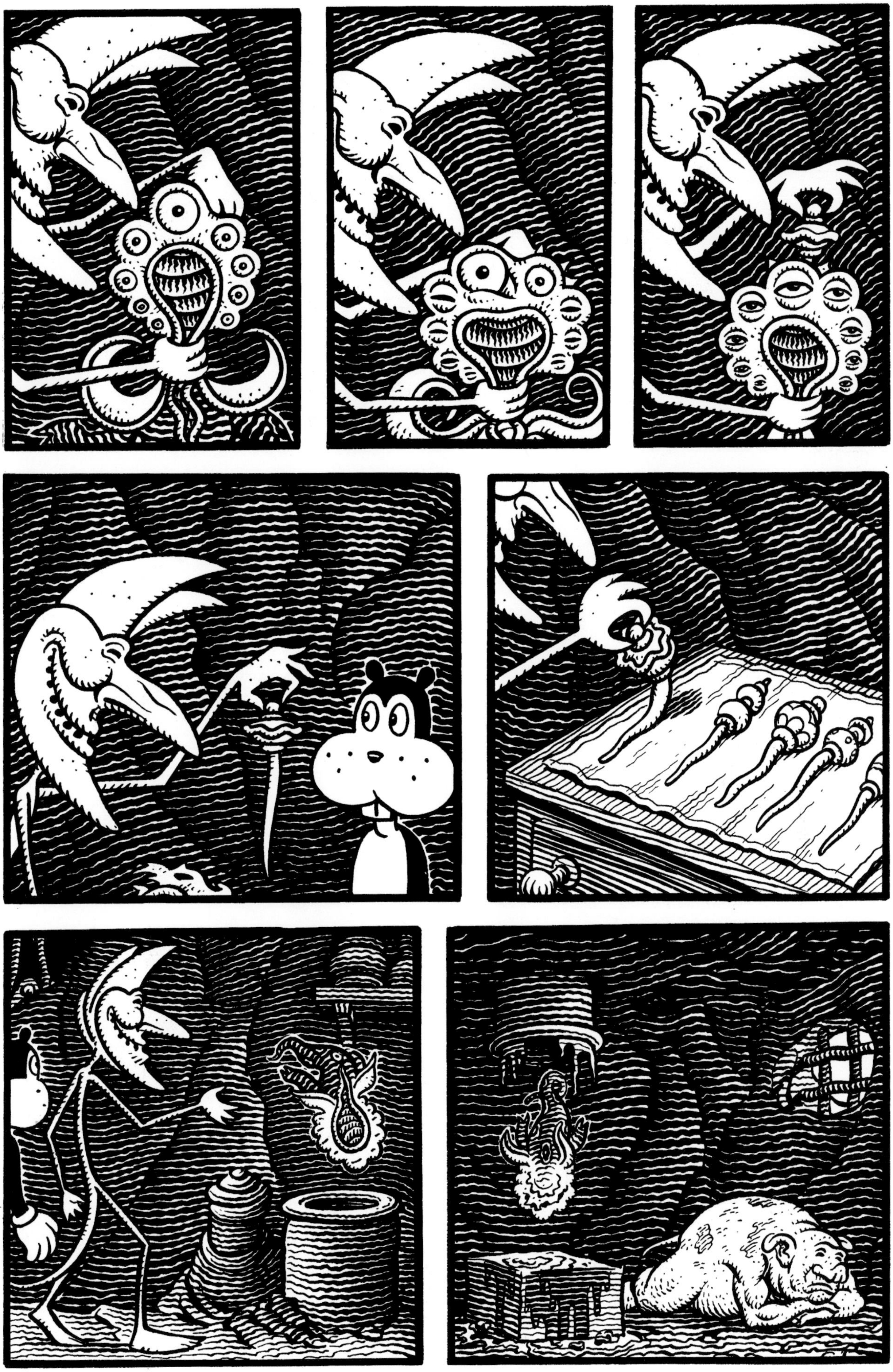

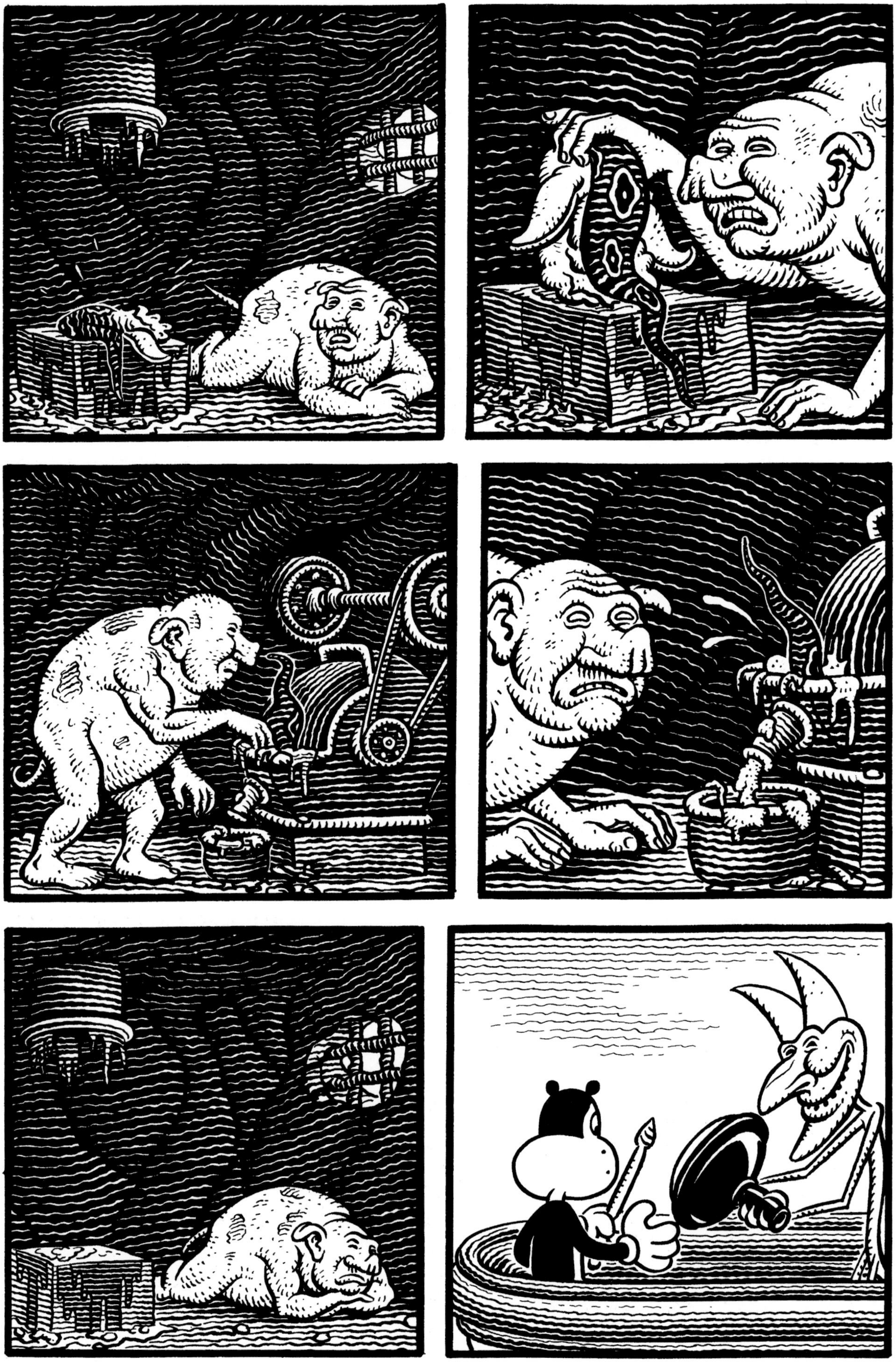

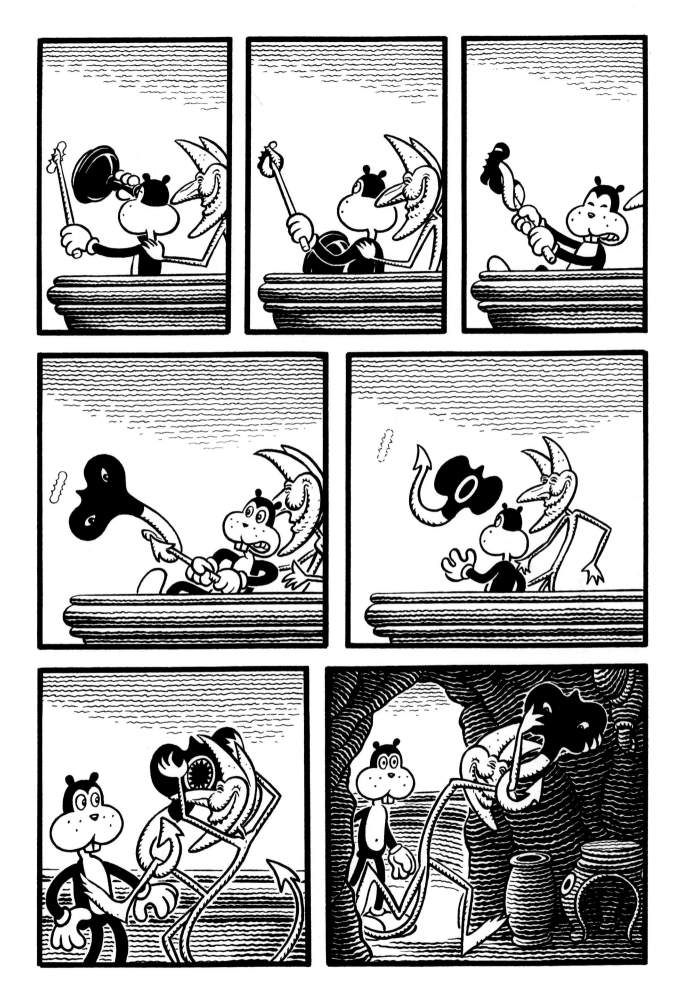

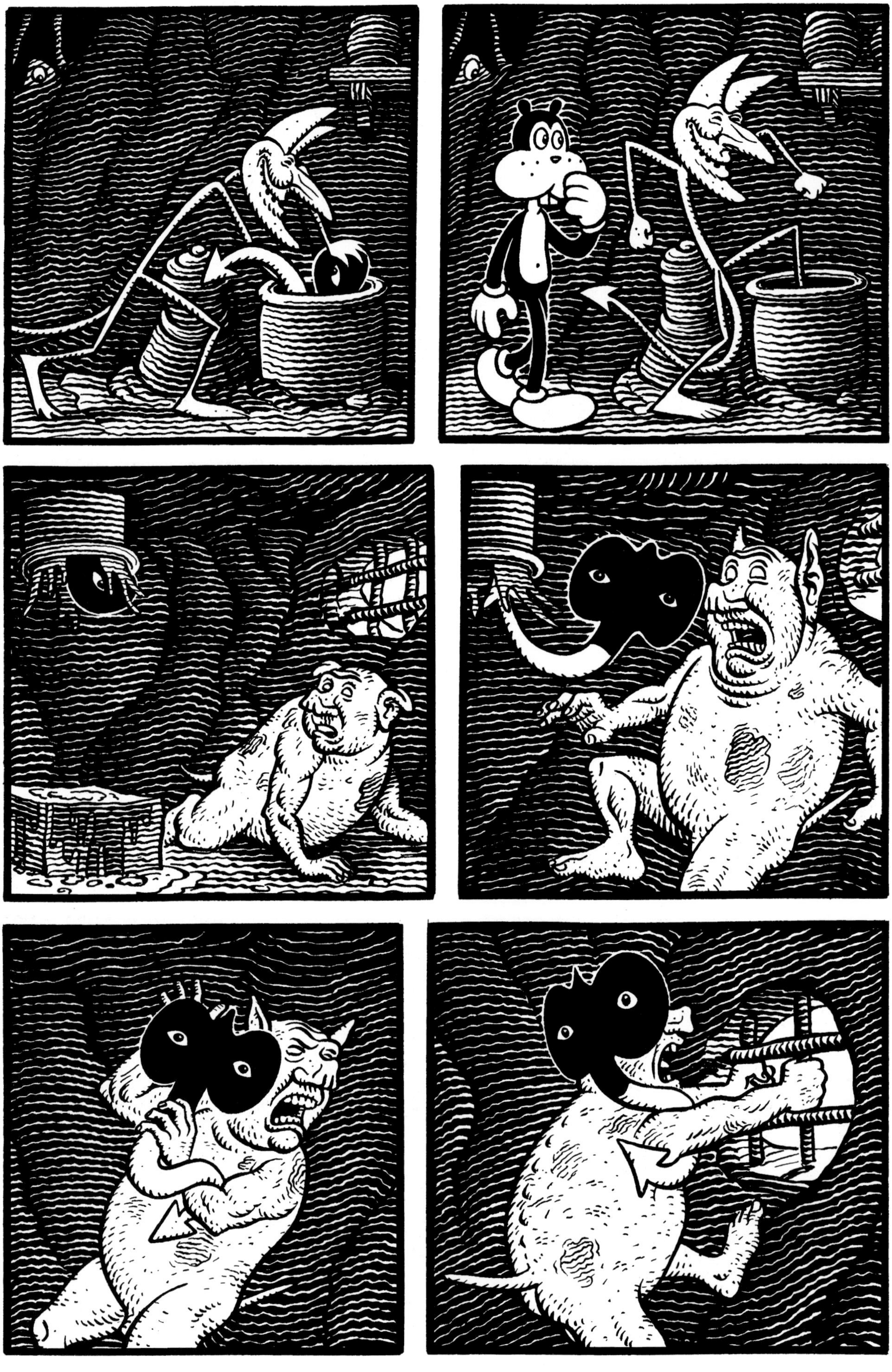

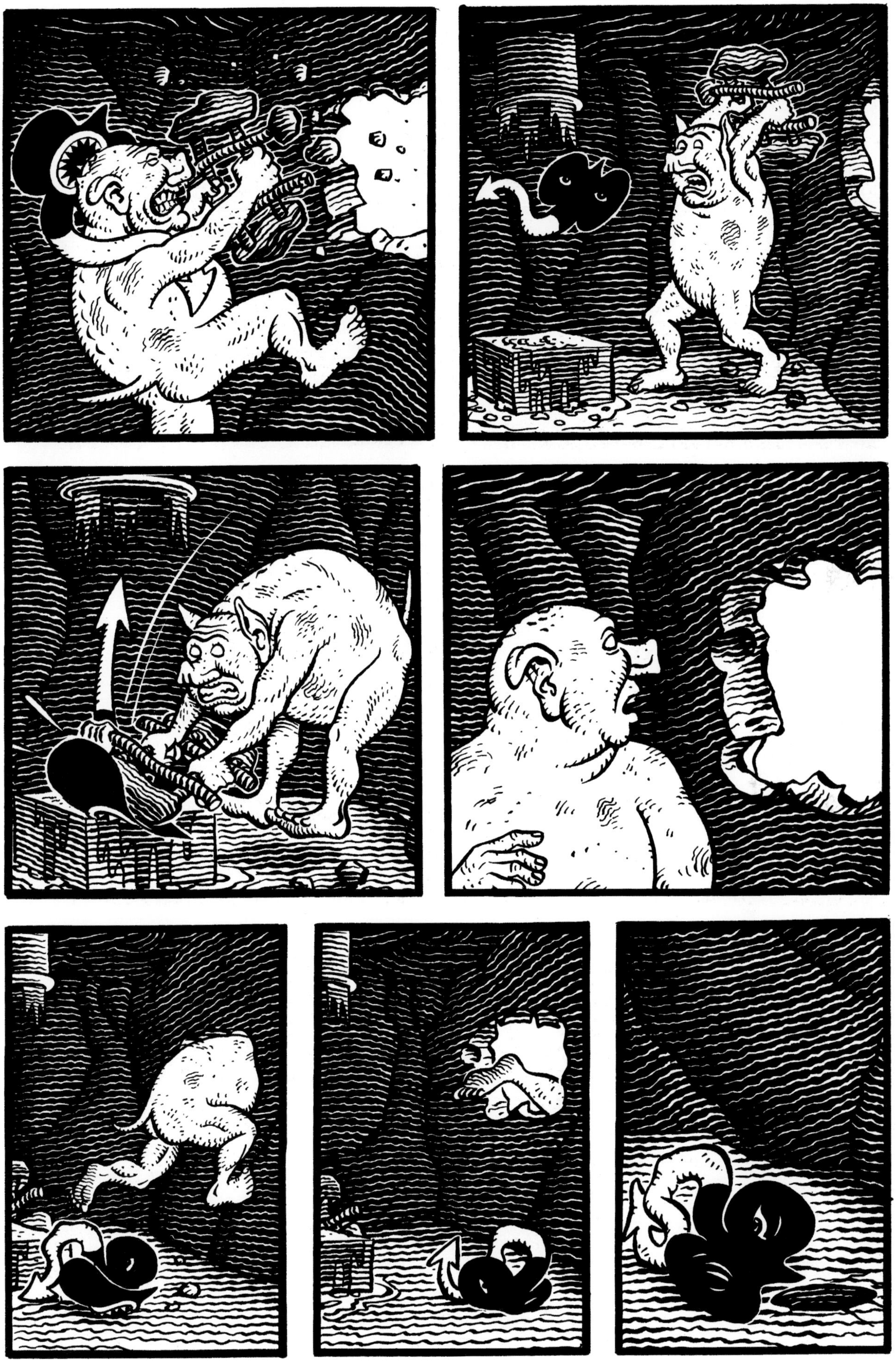

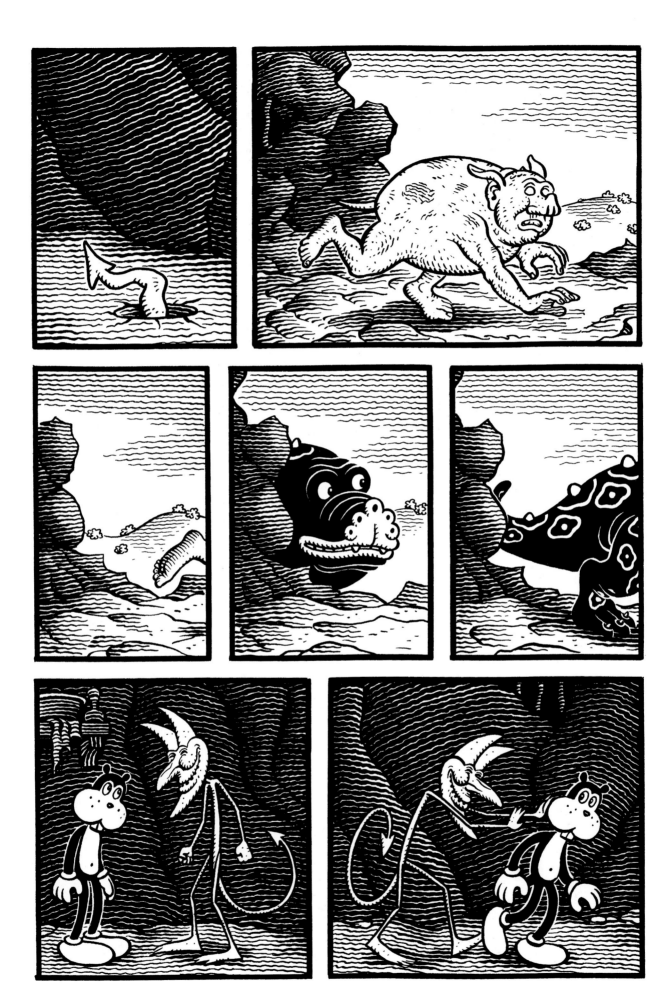

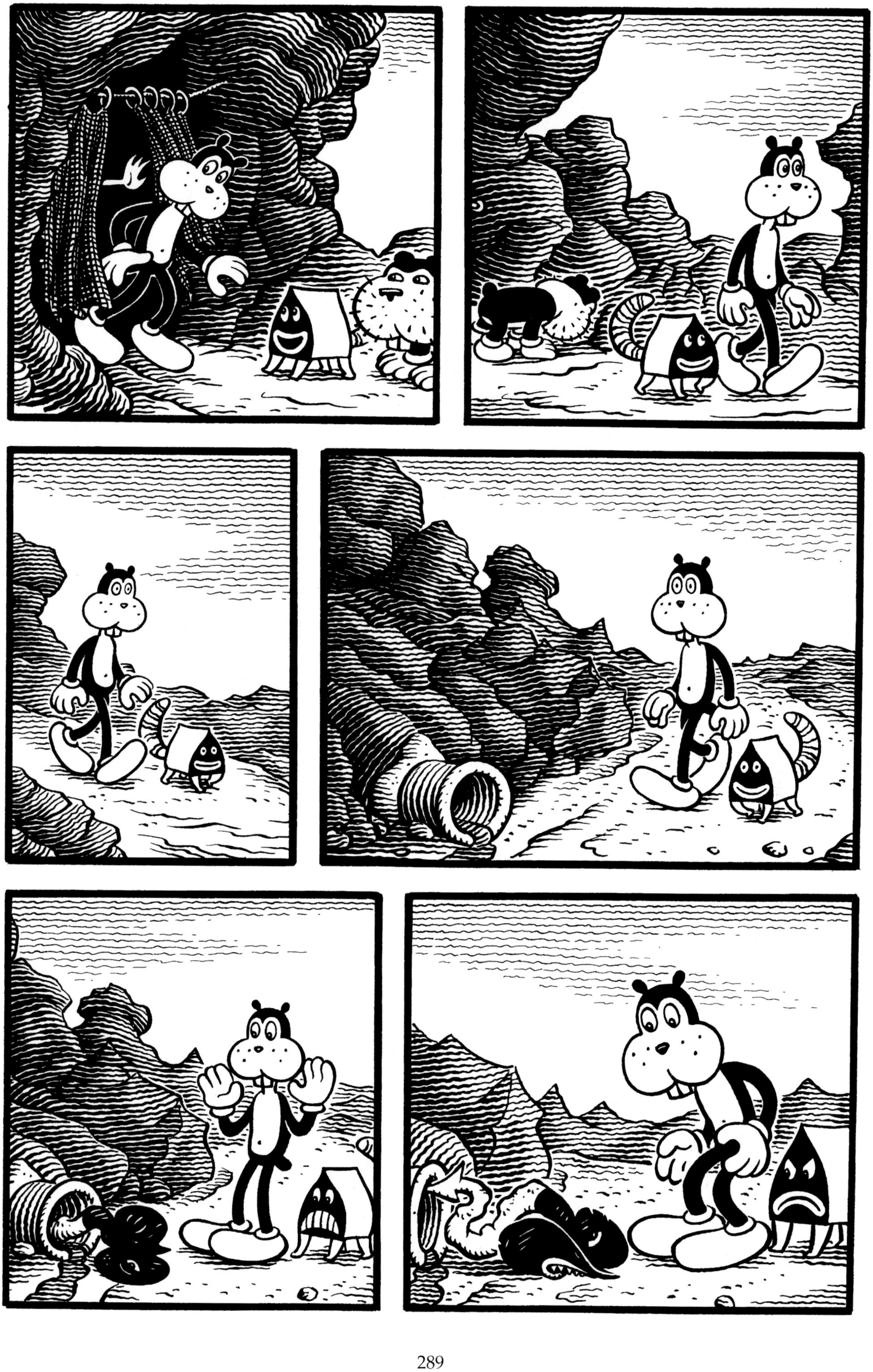

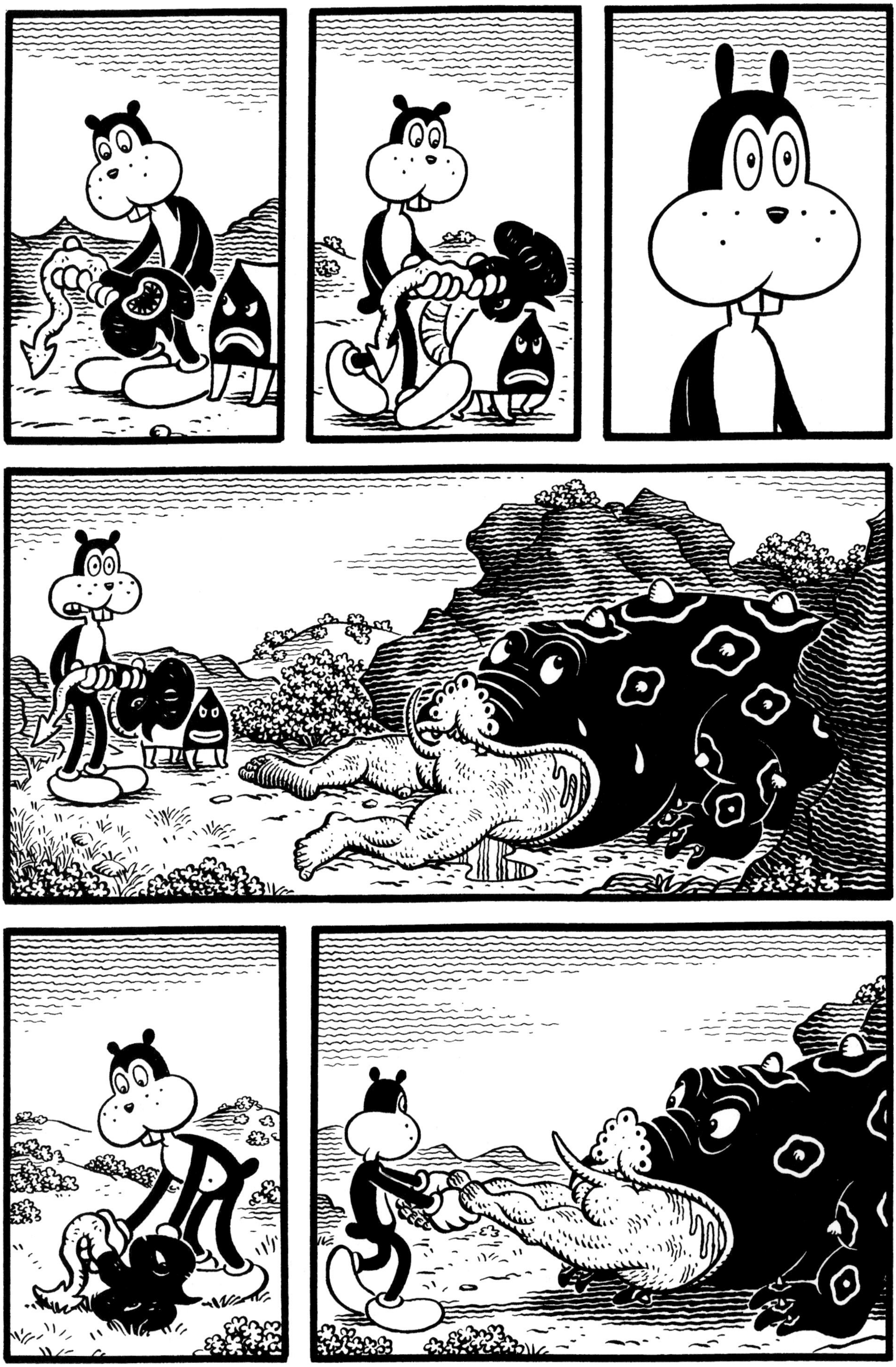

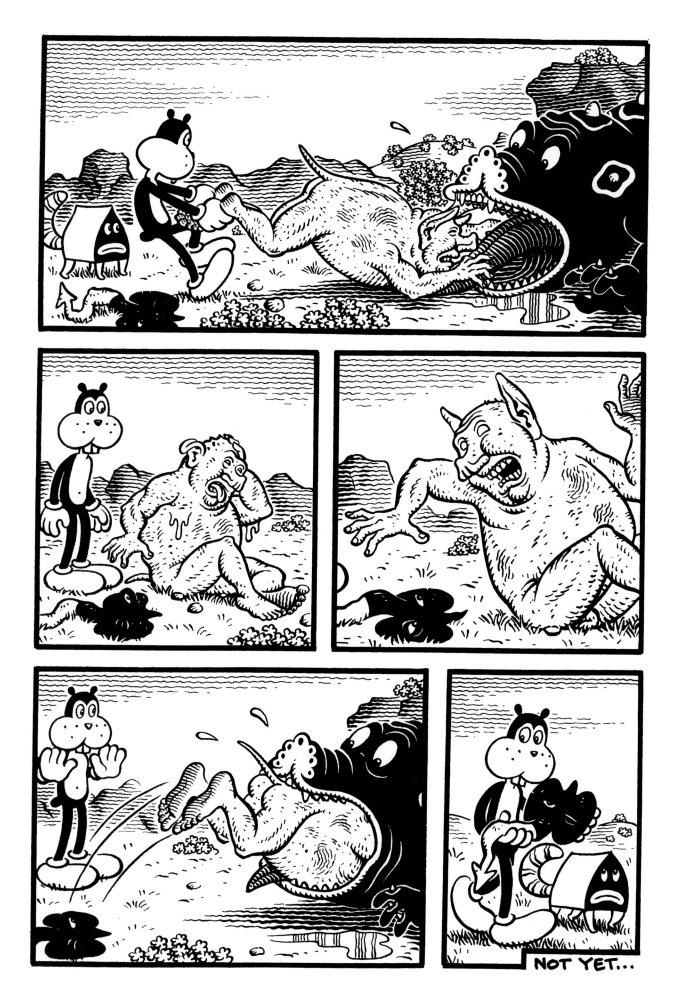

NOT YET...

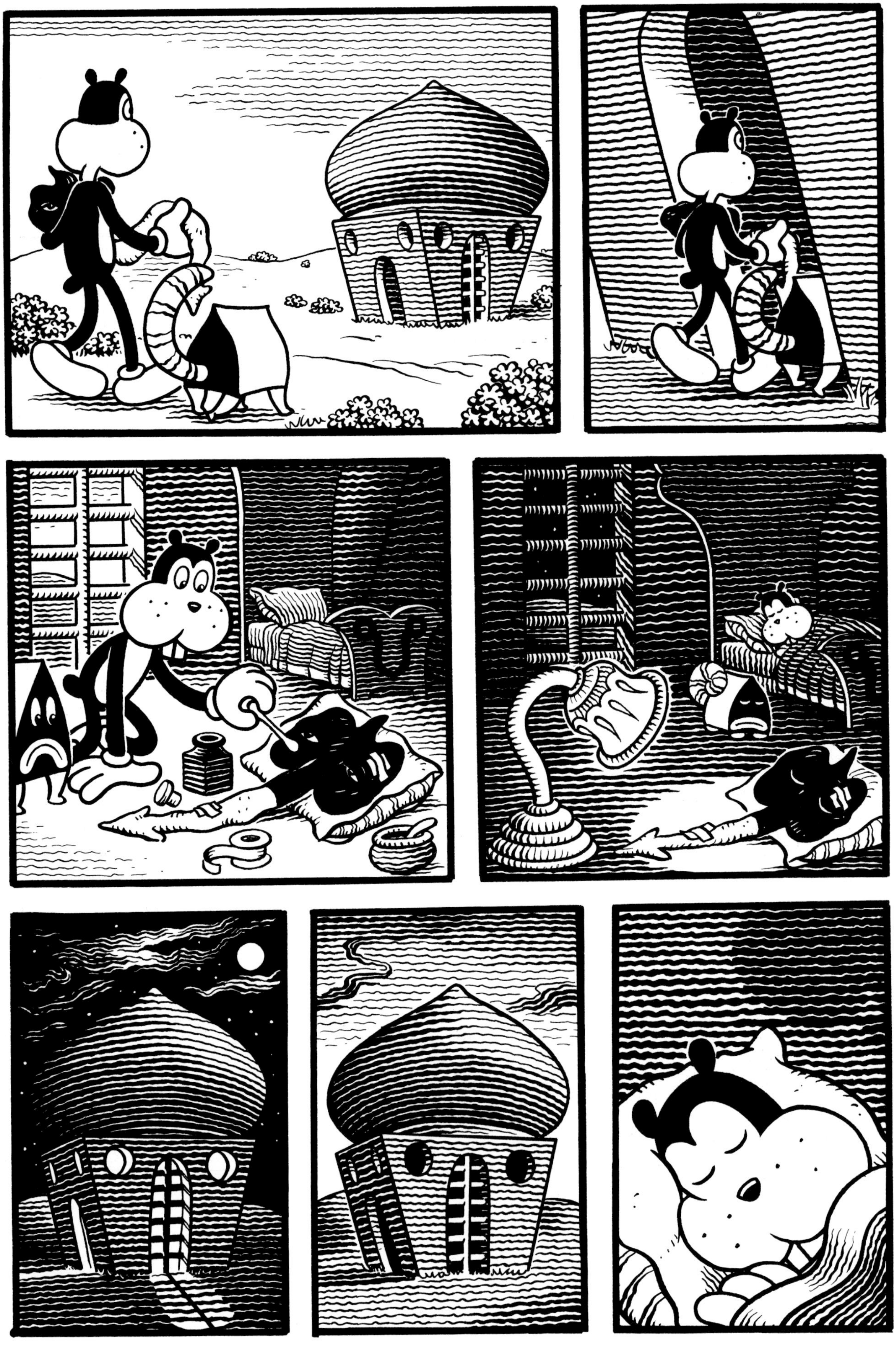

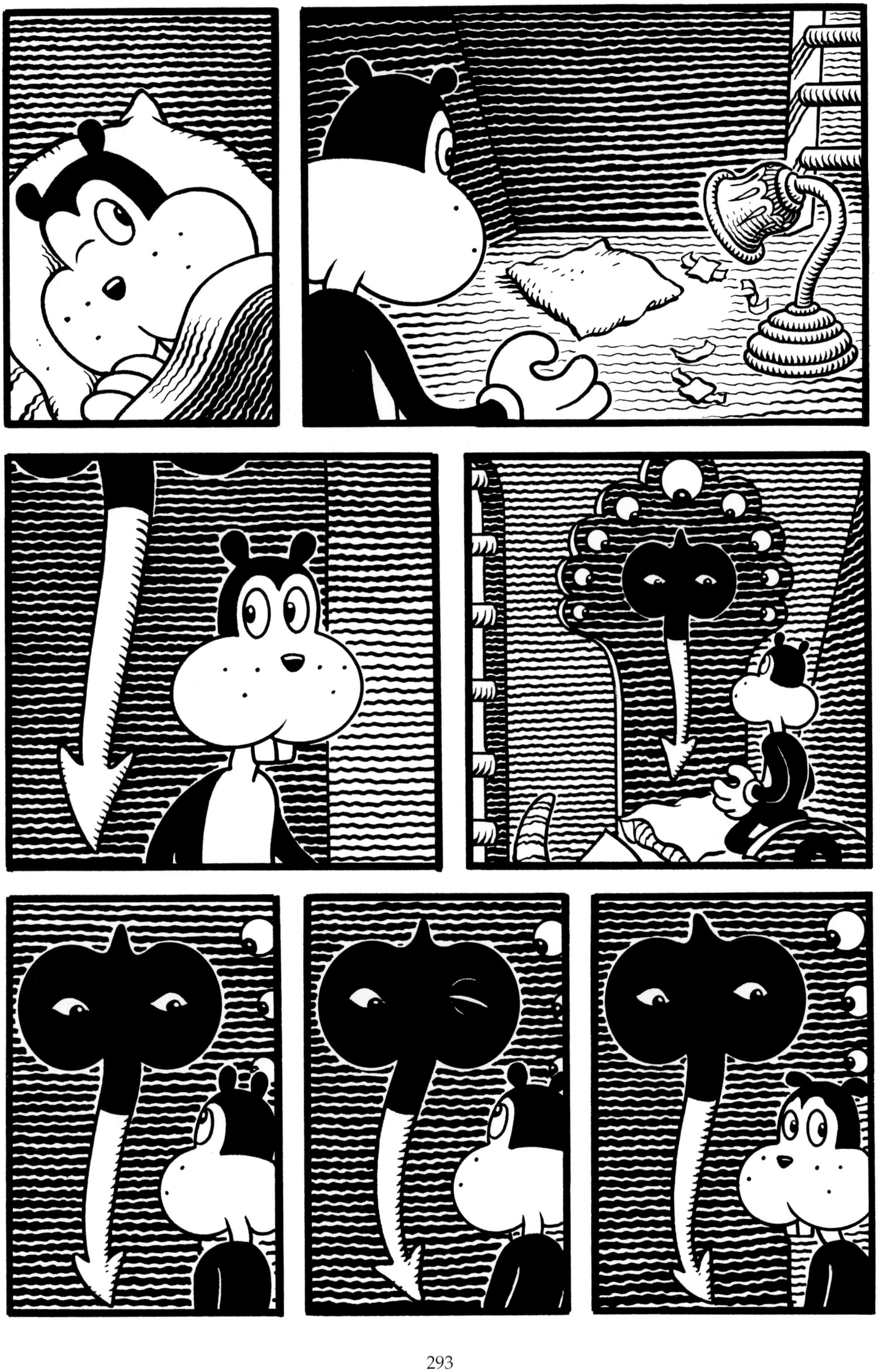

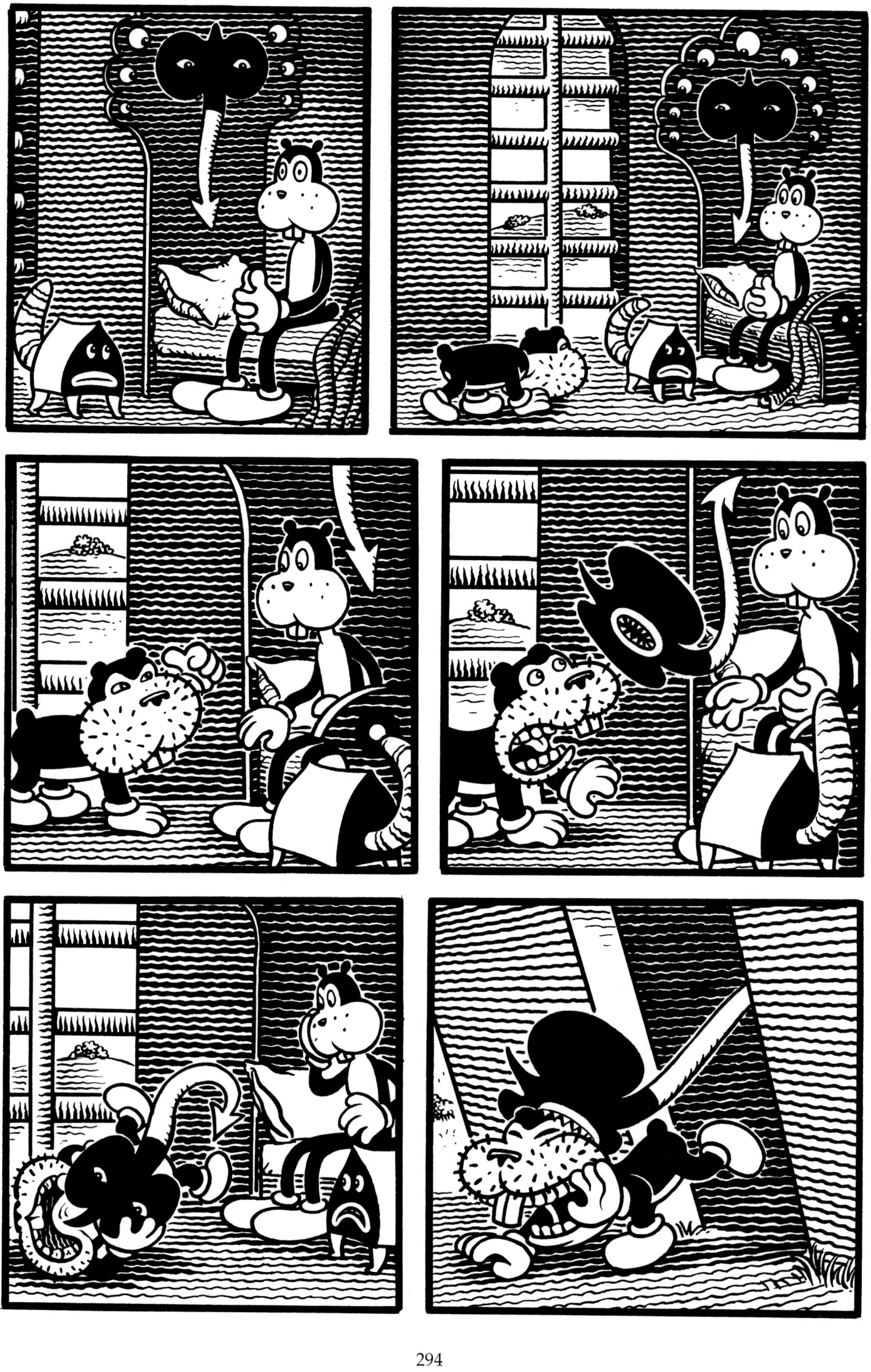

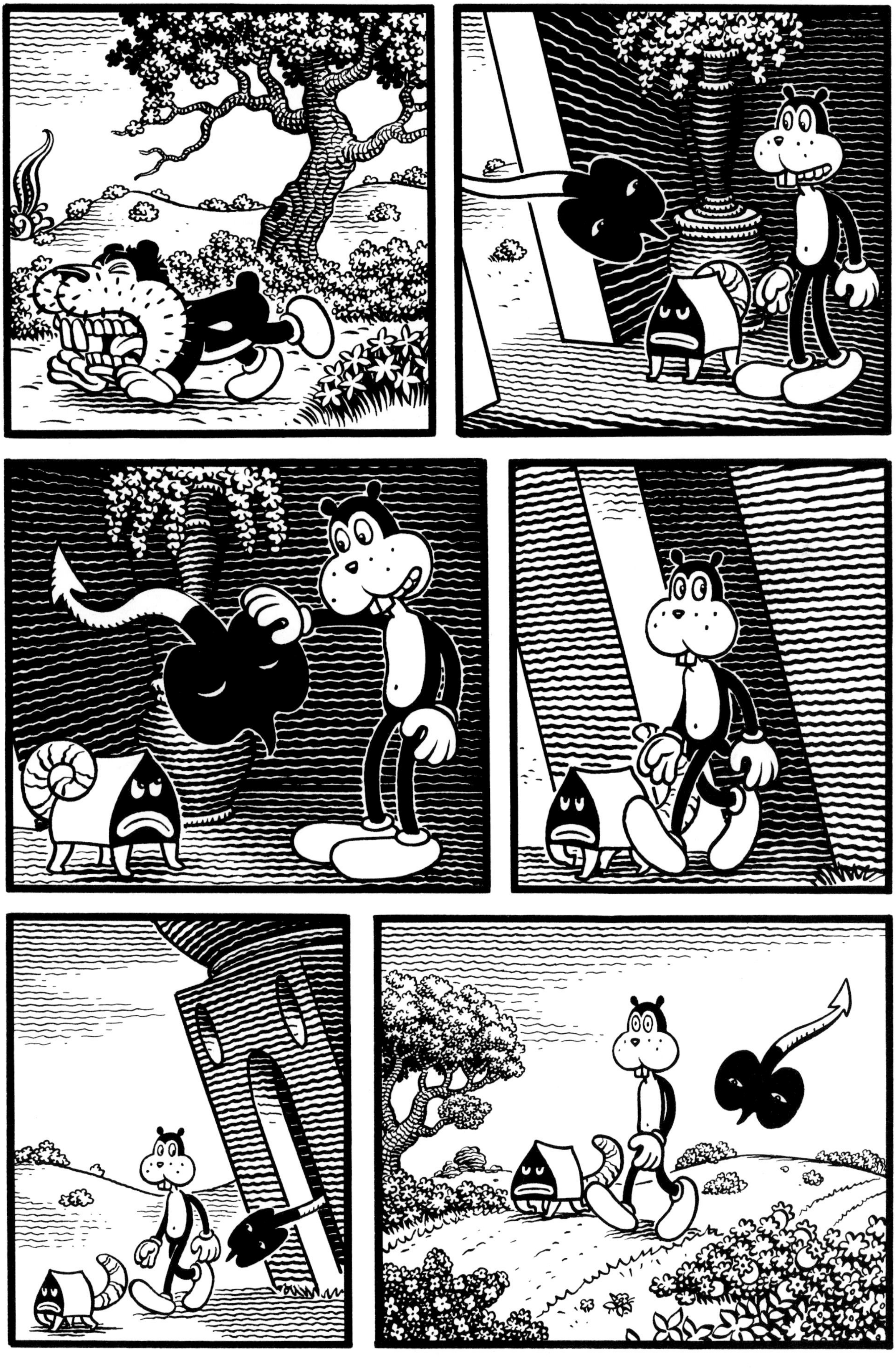

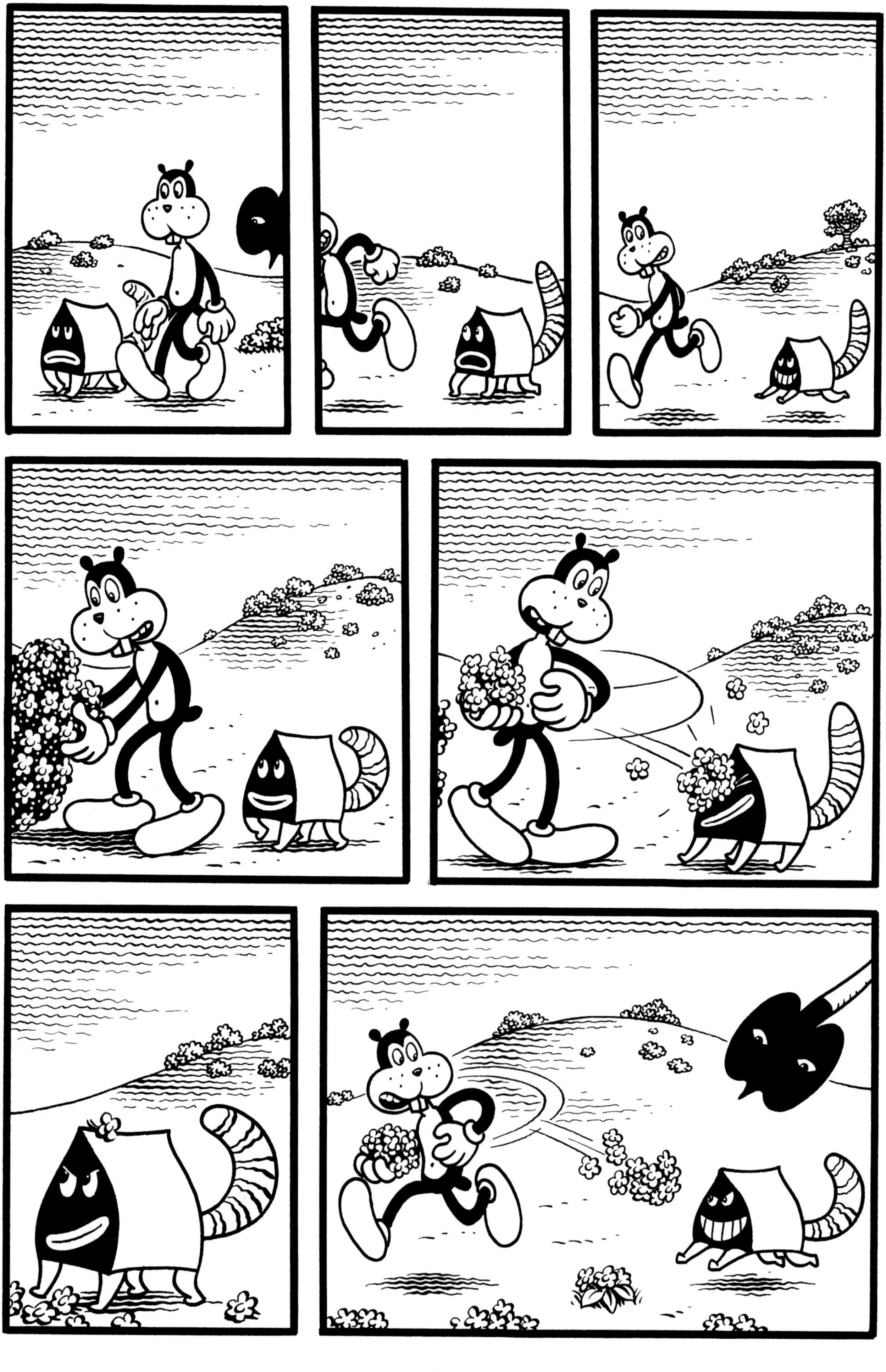

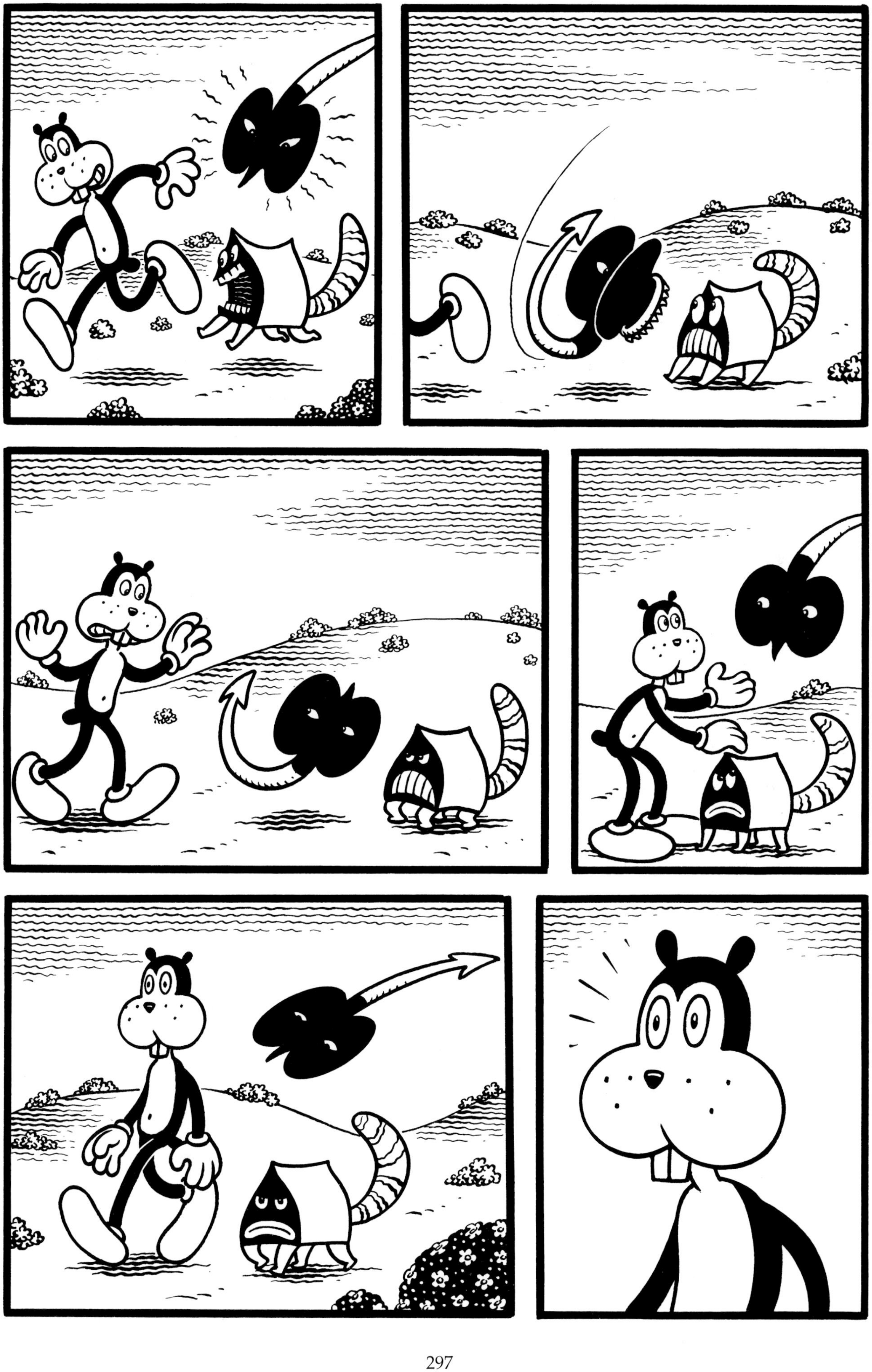

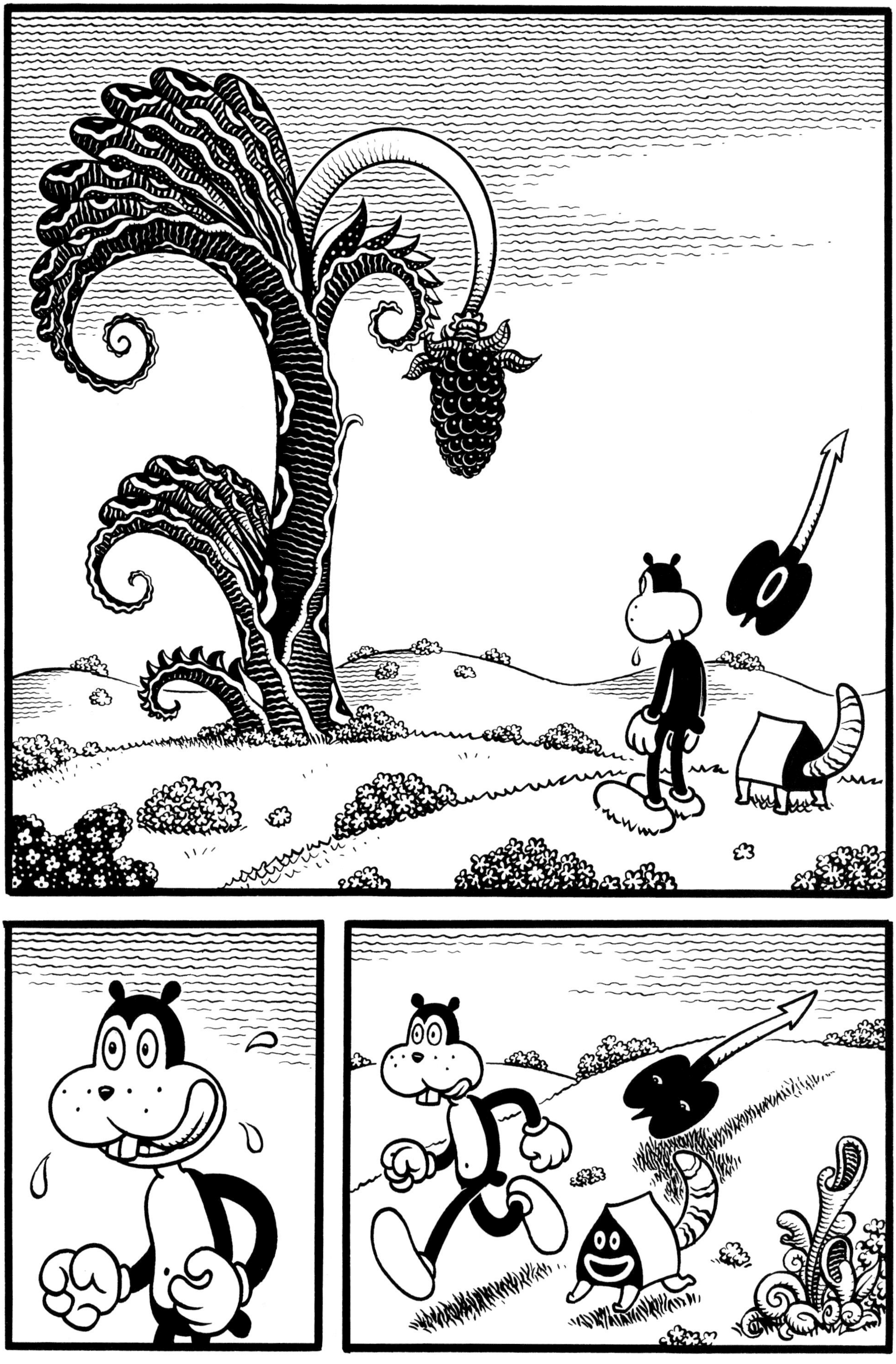

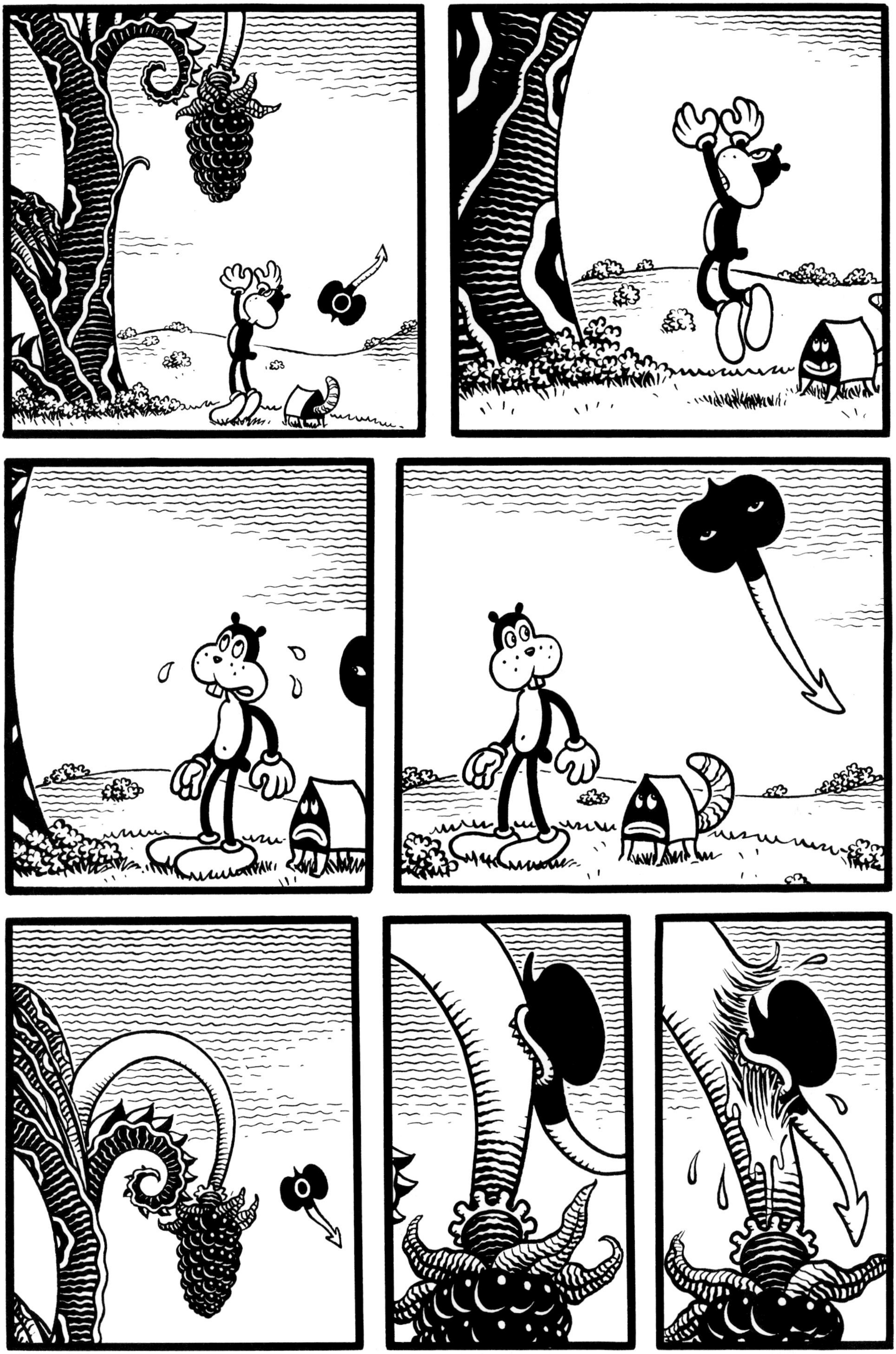

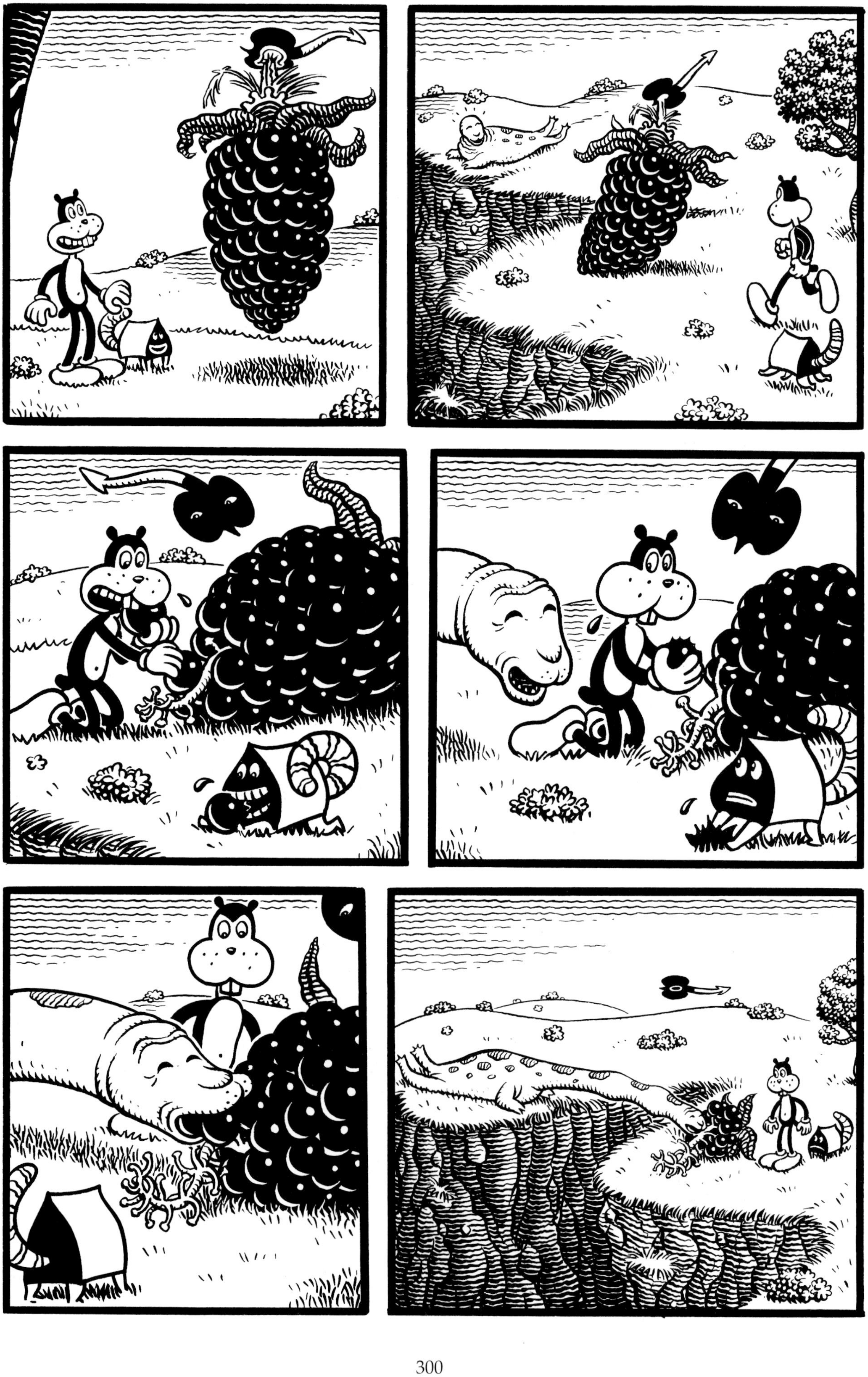

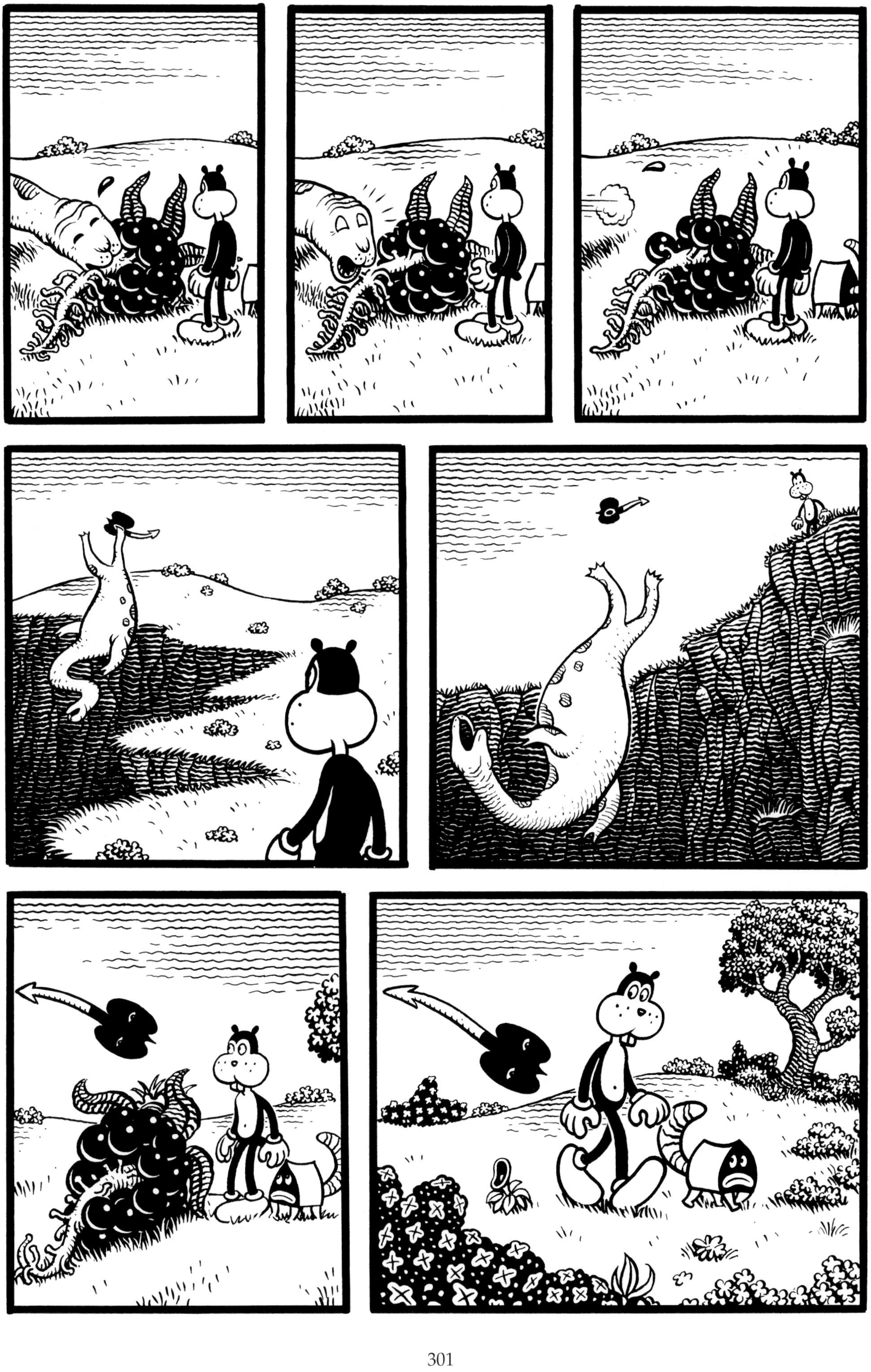

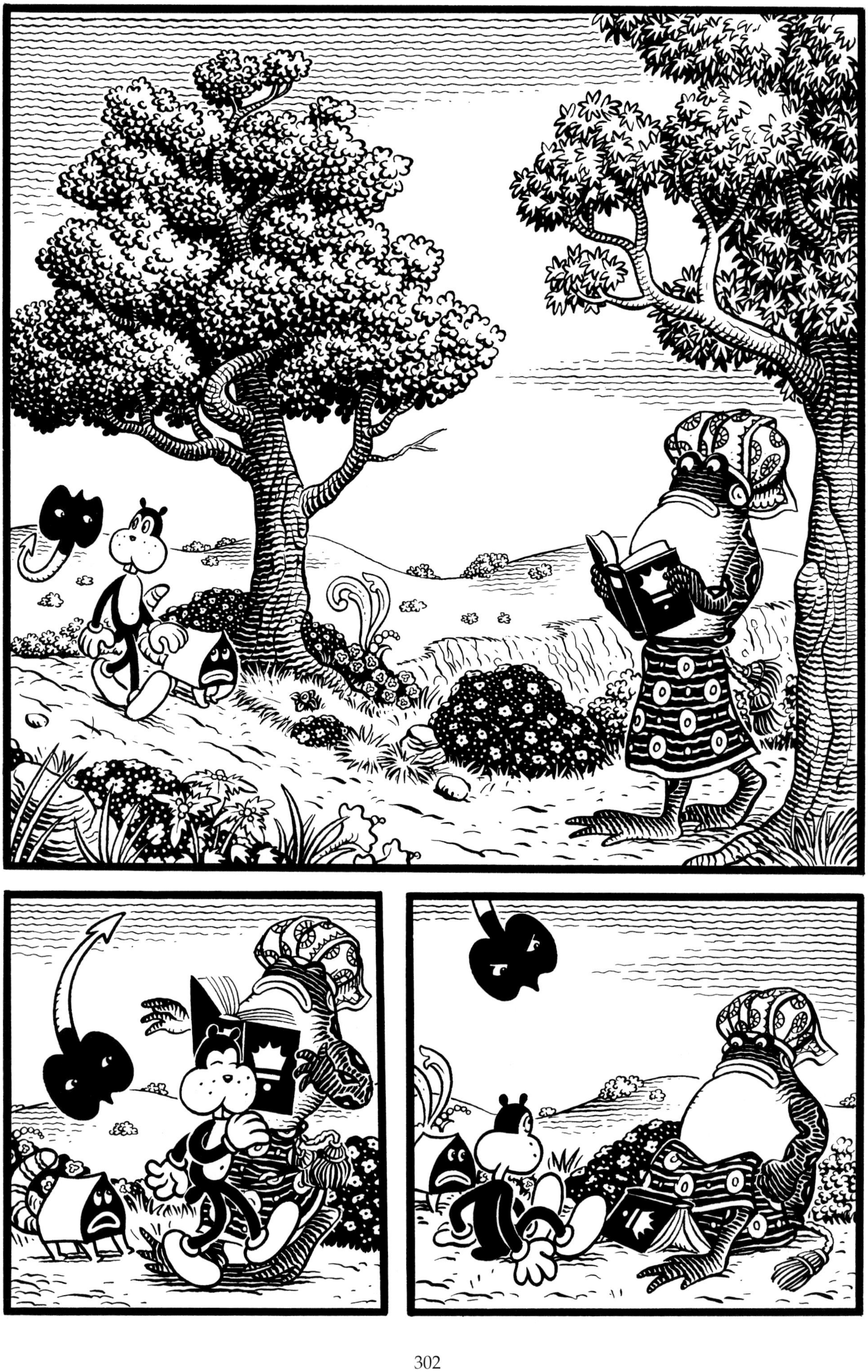

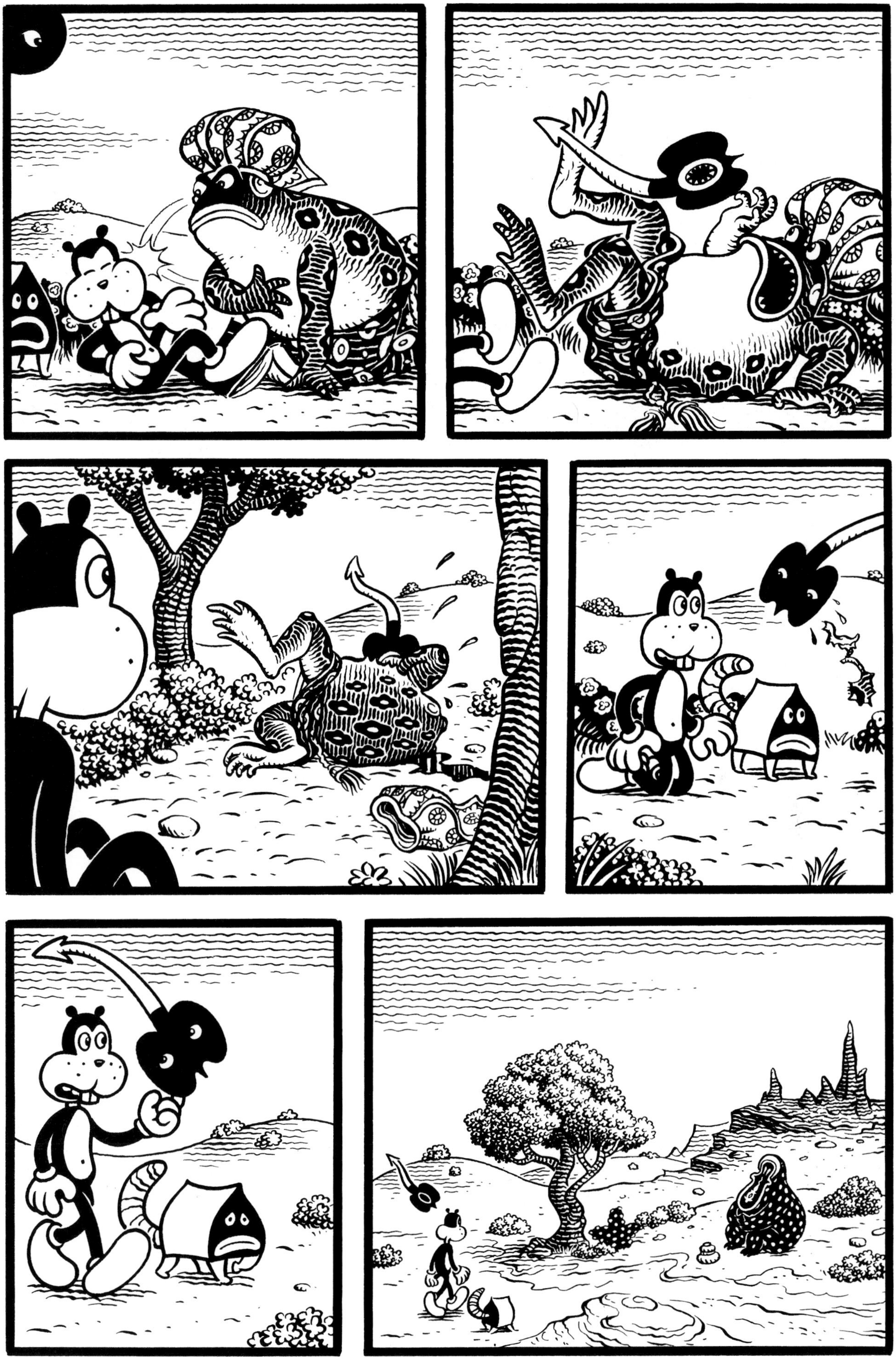

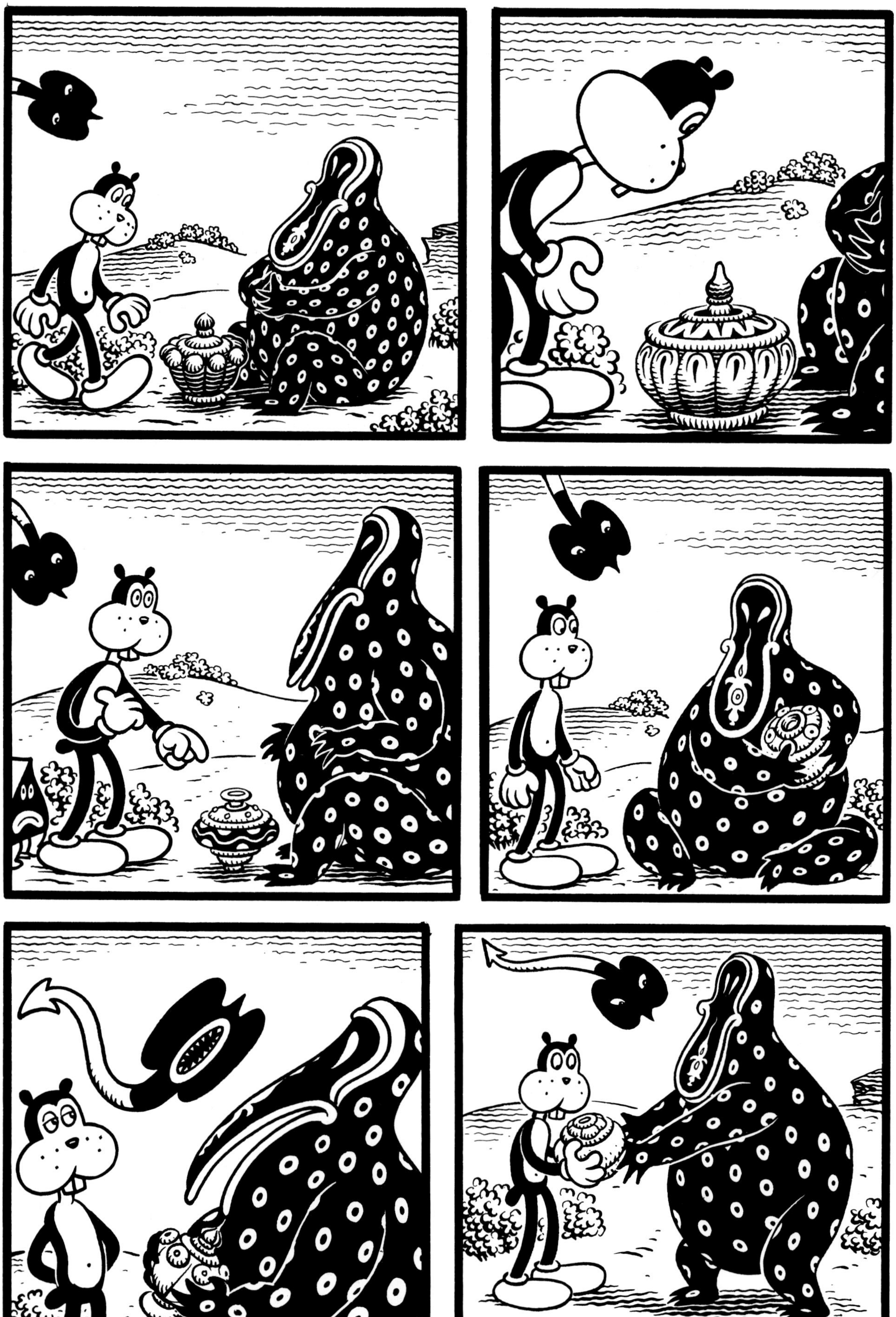

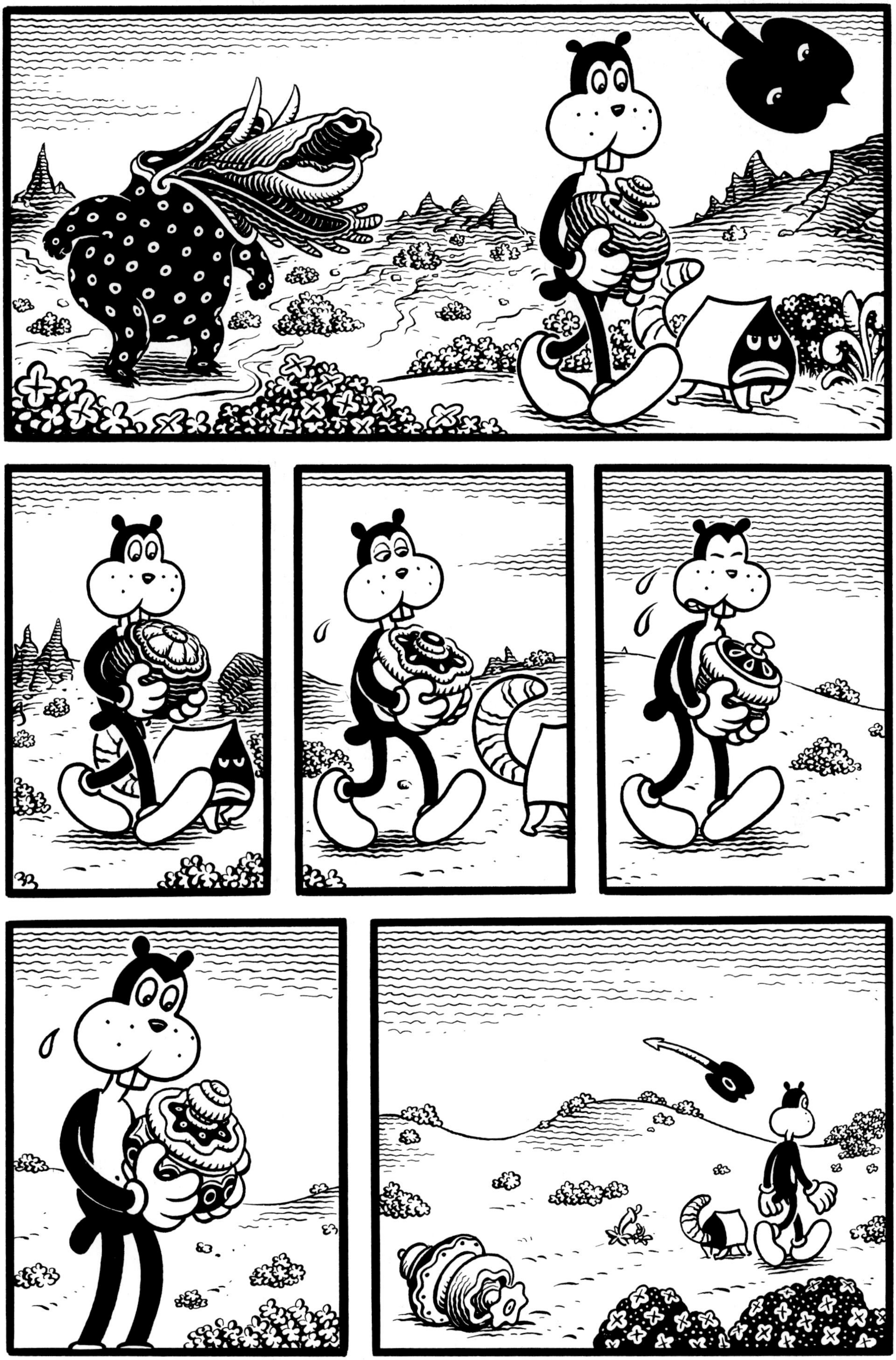

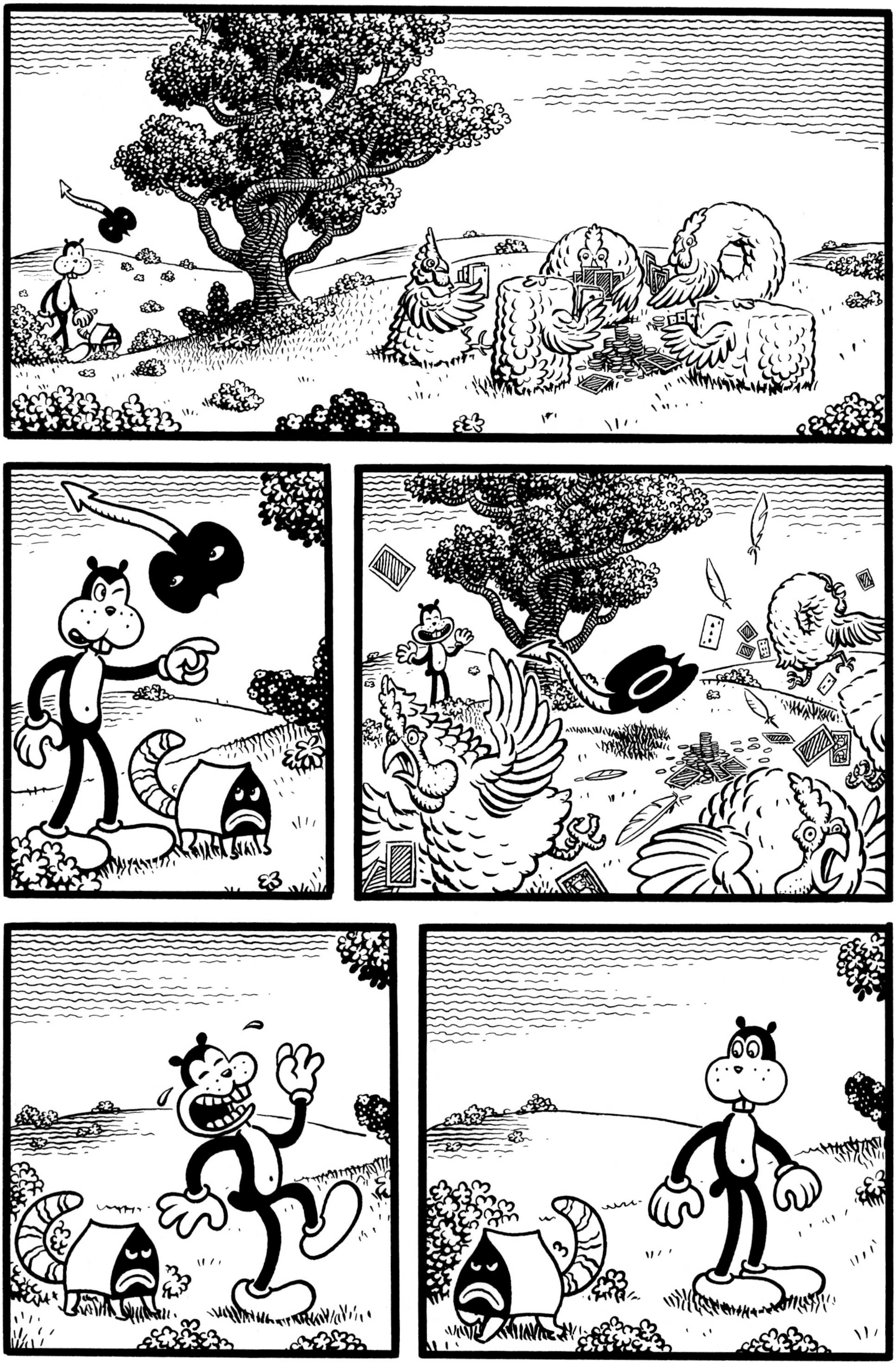

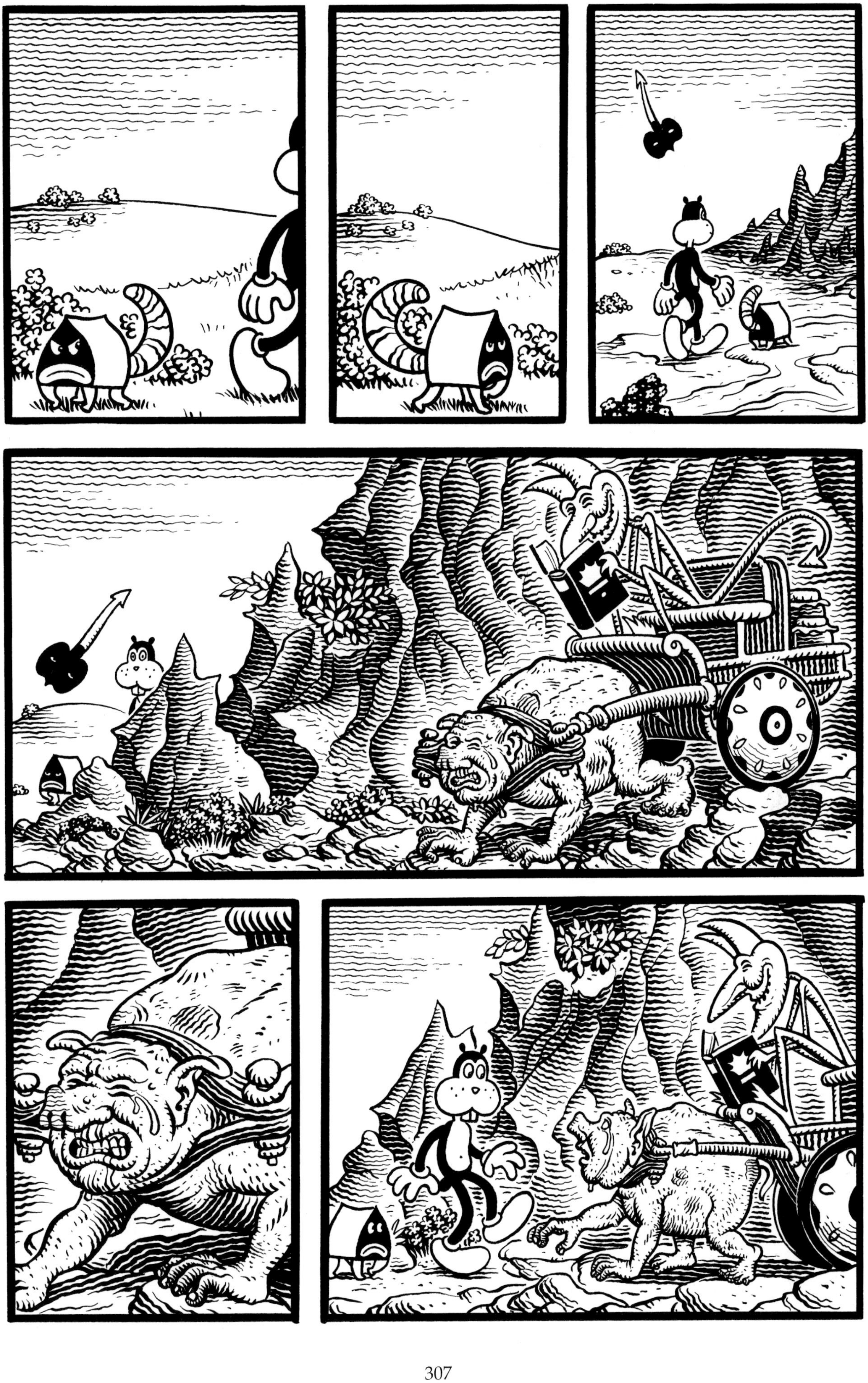

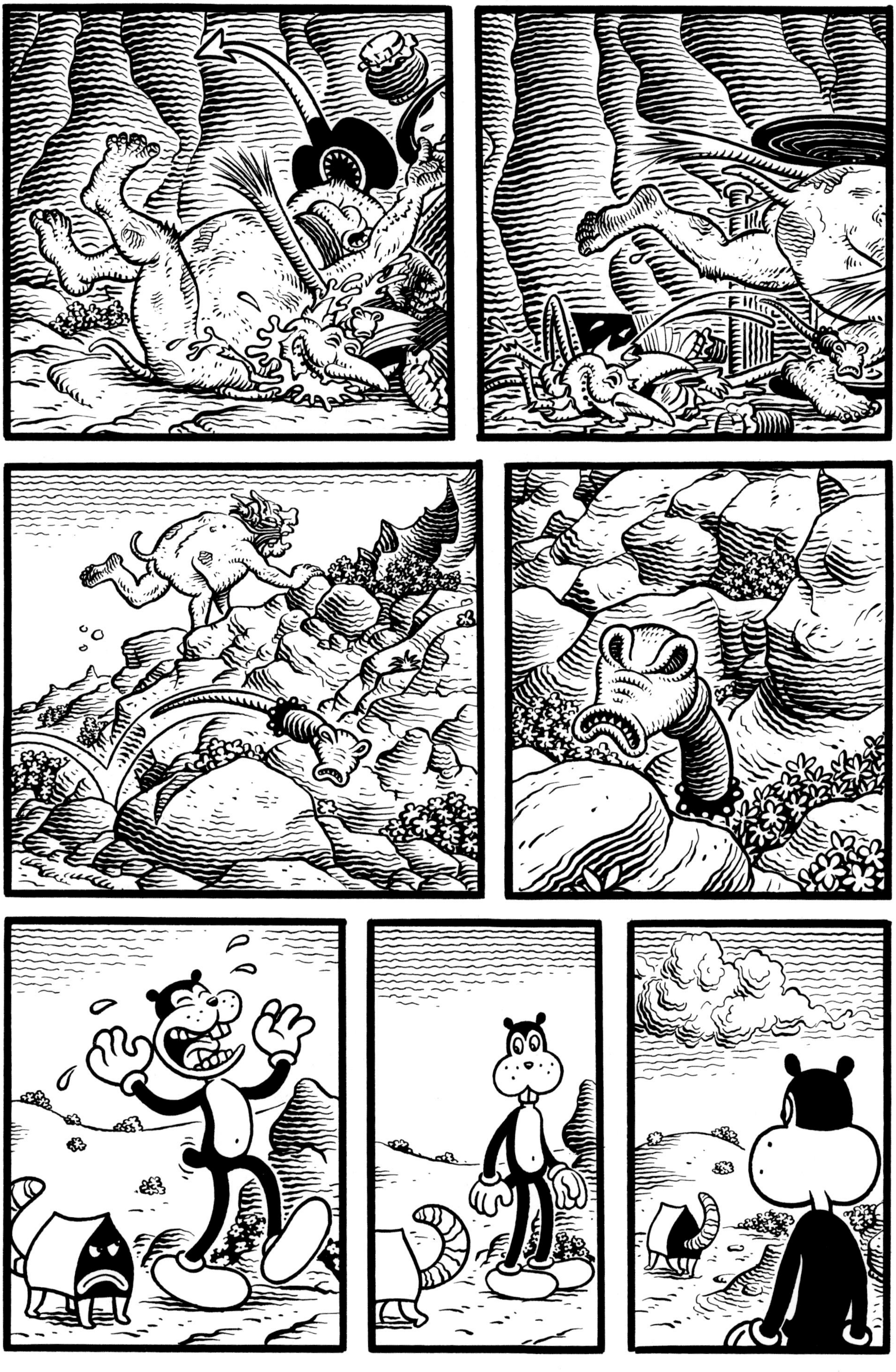

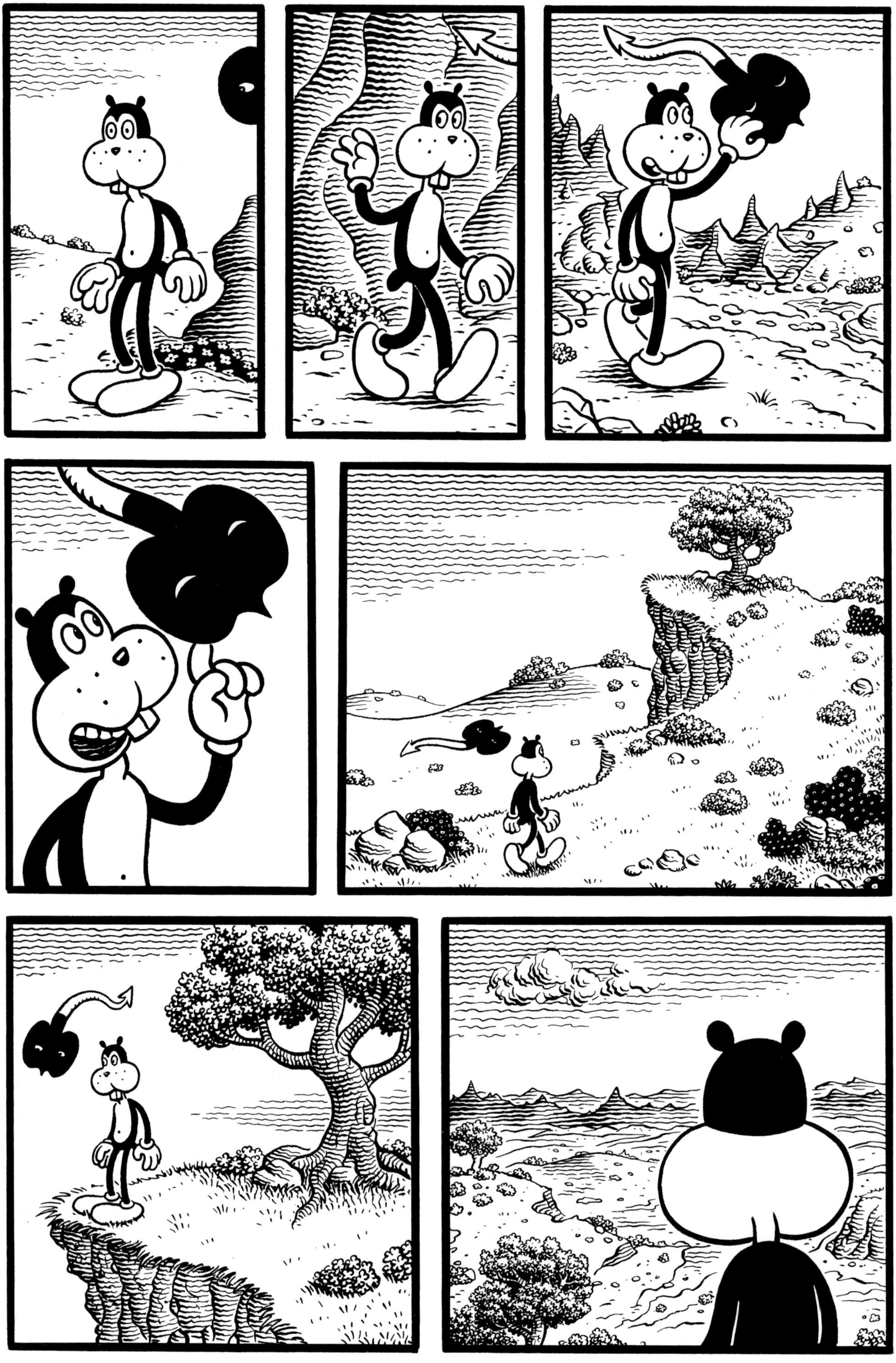

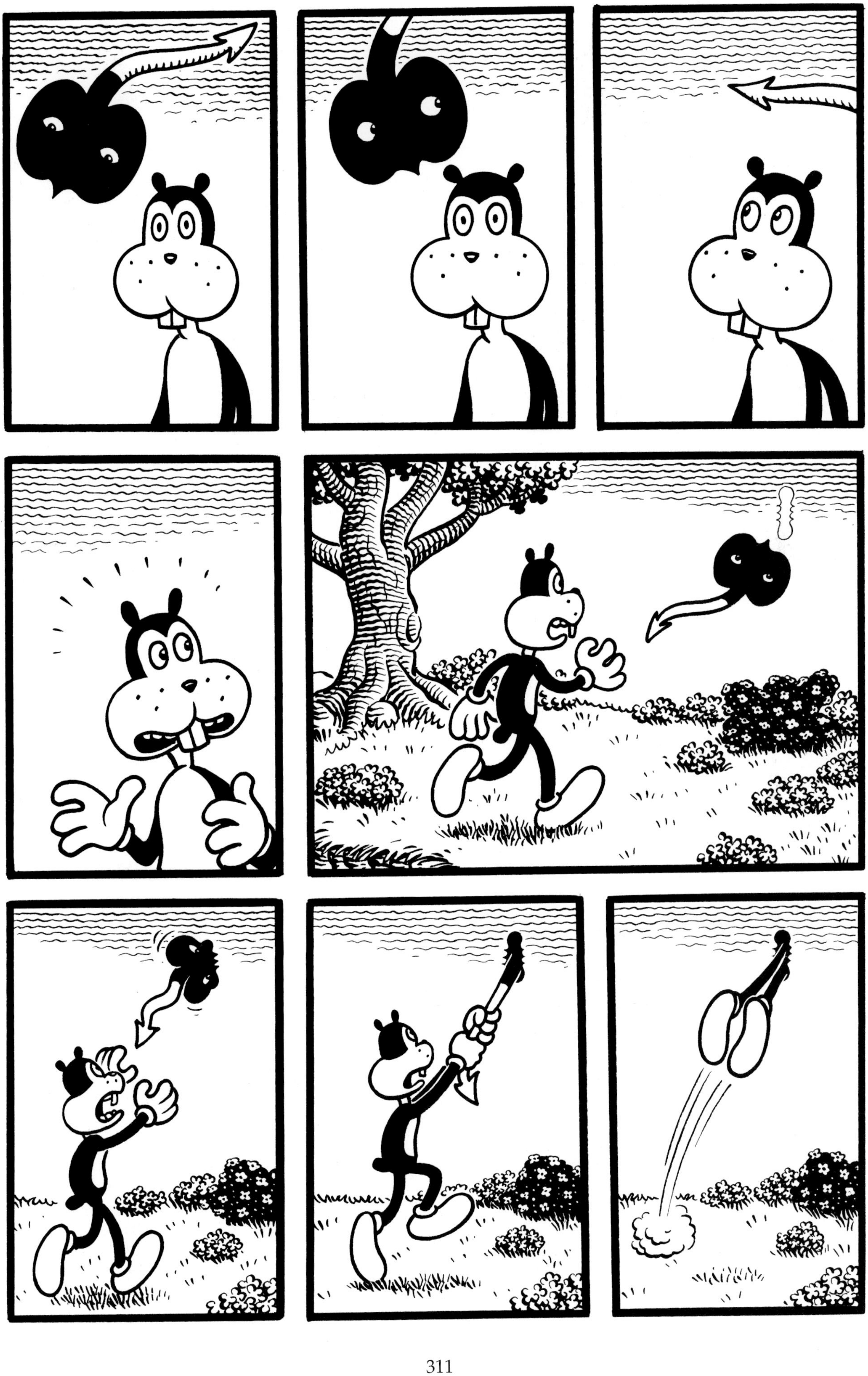

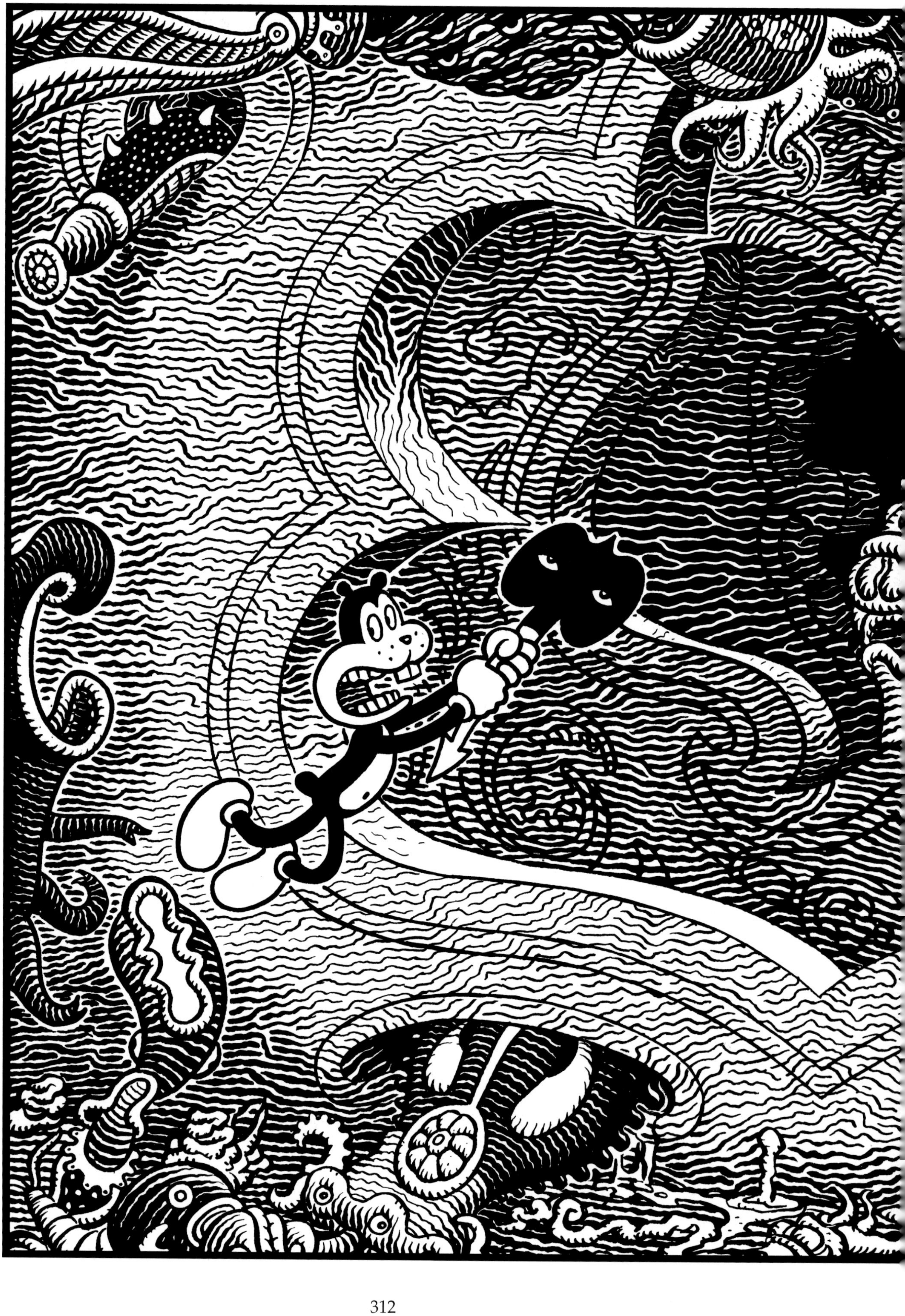

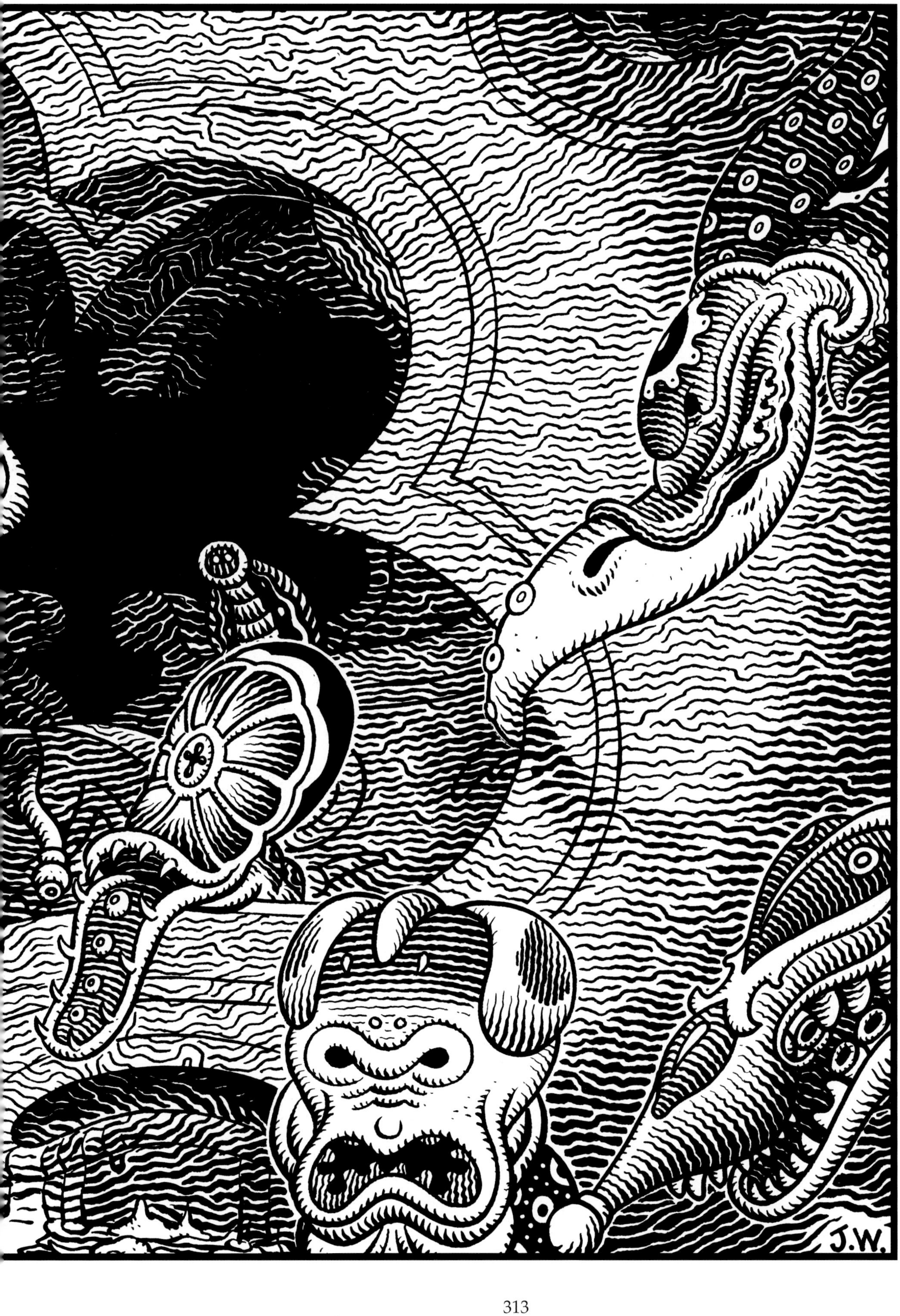
J.W.

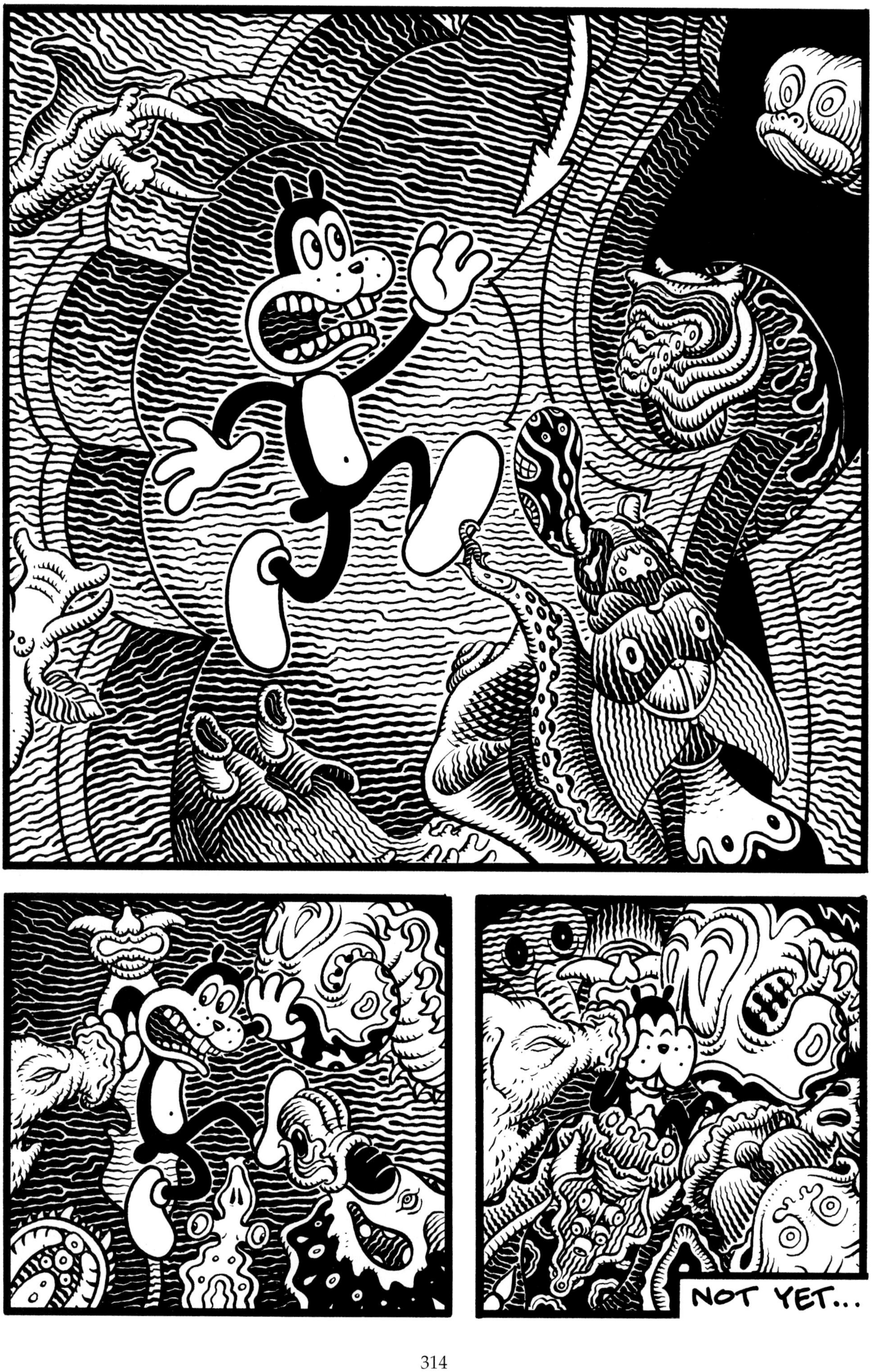
NOT YET...

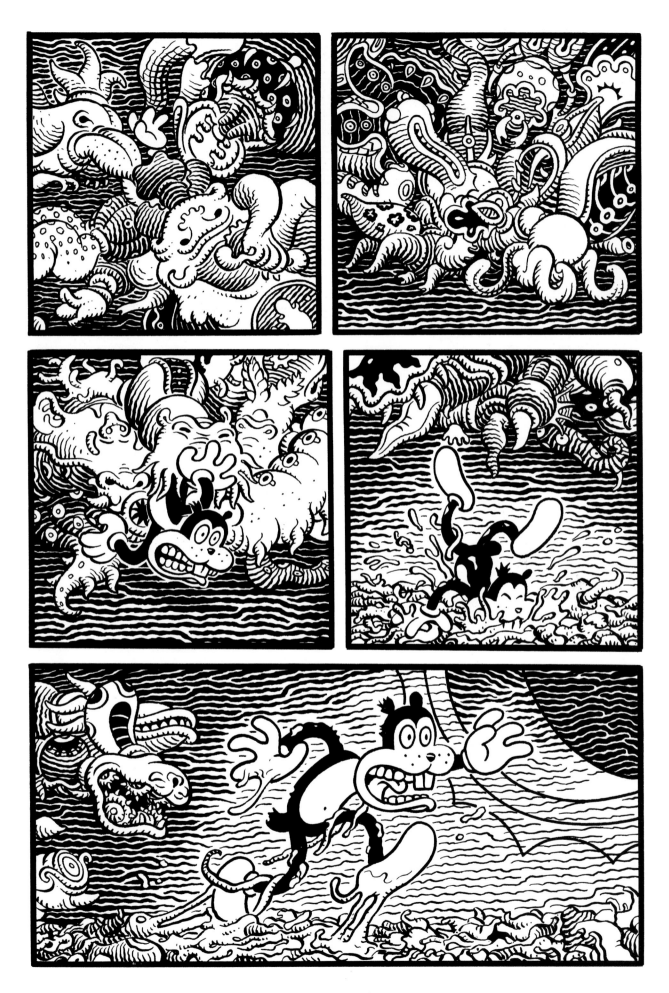

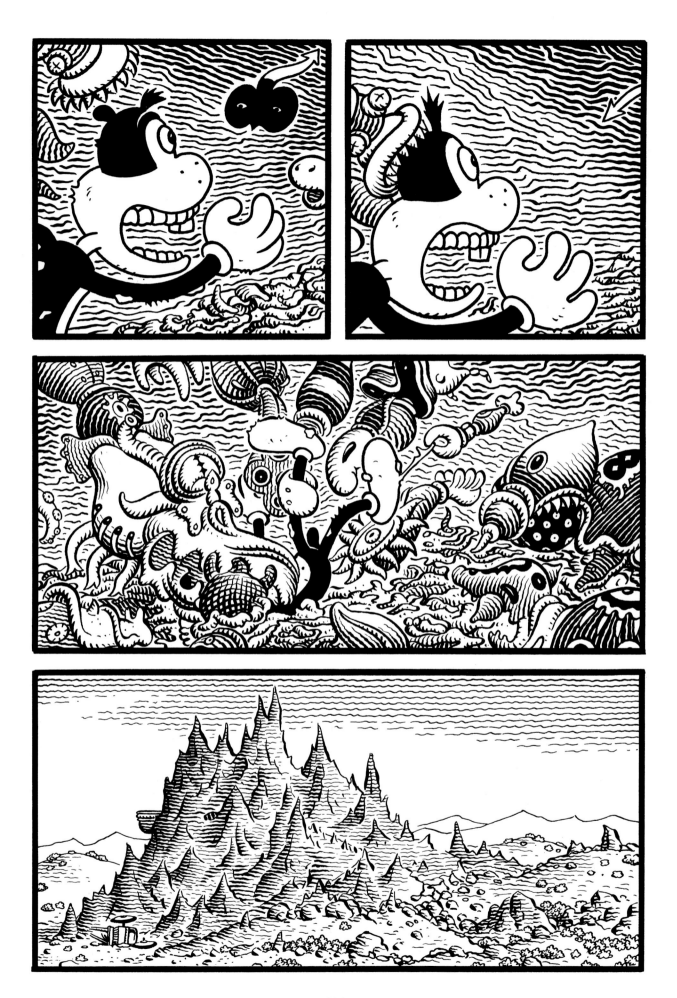

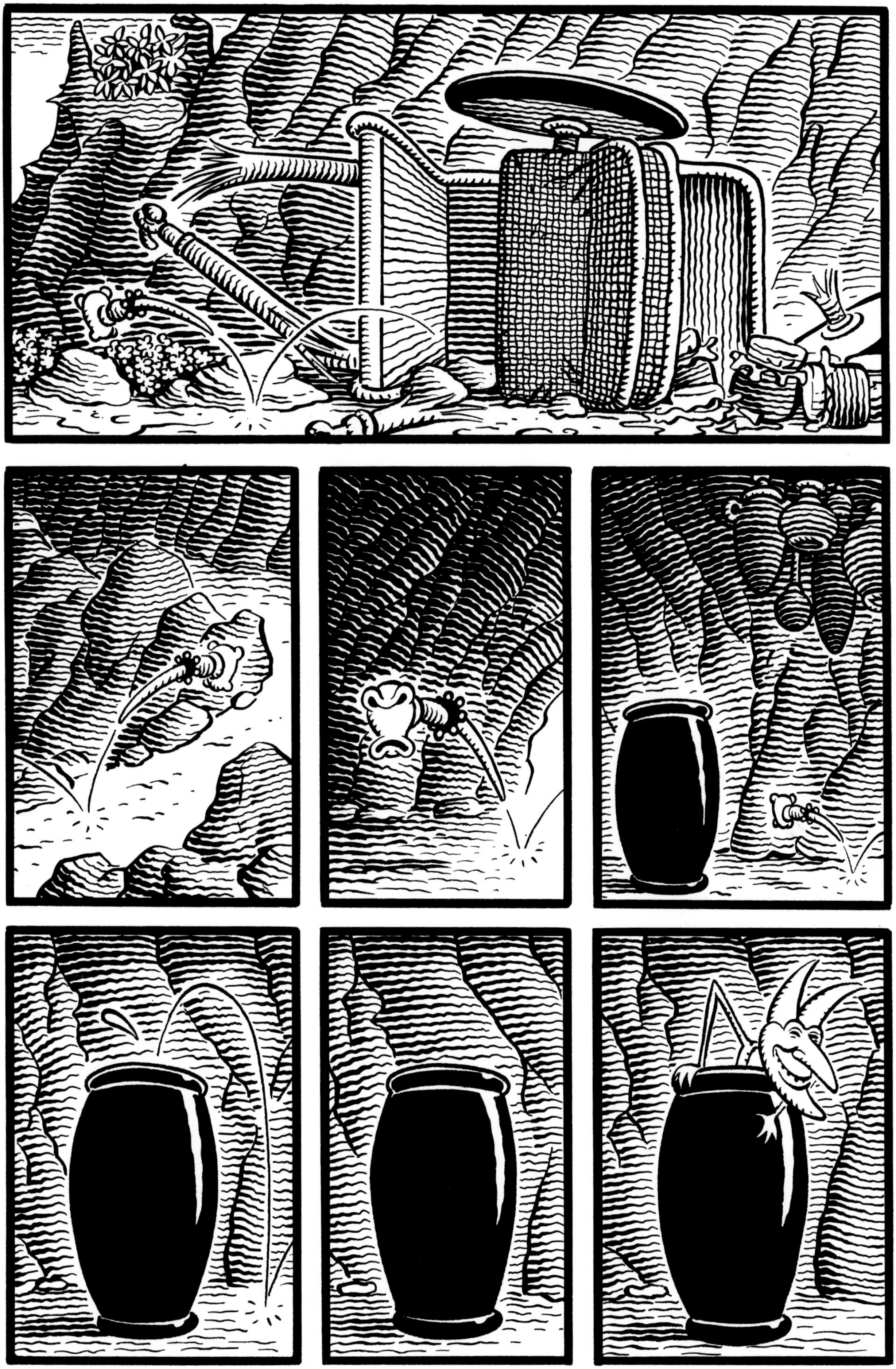

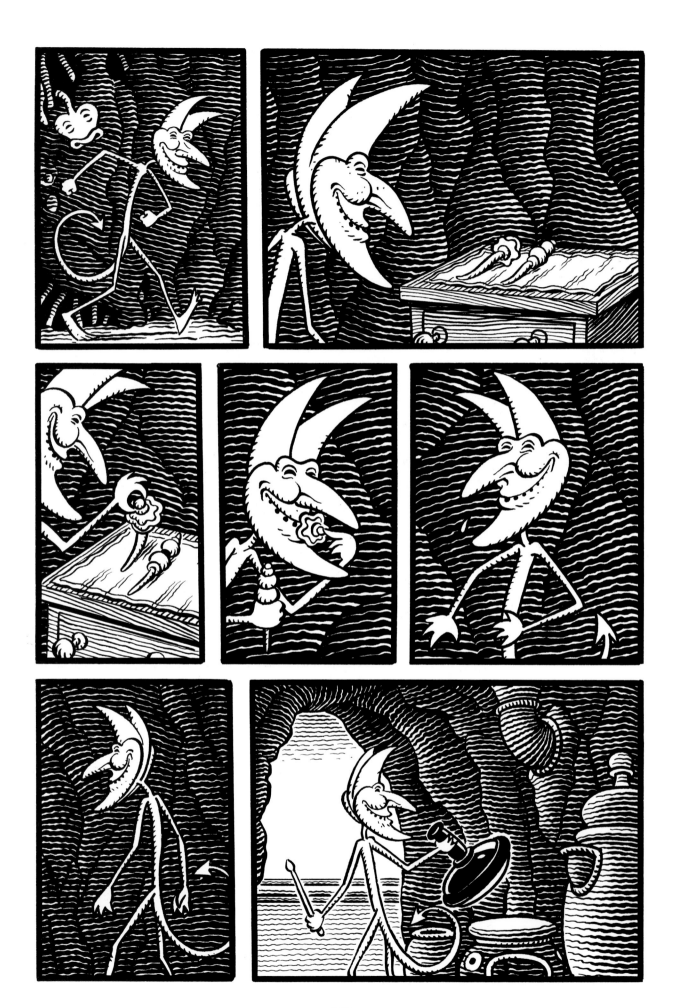

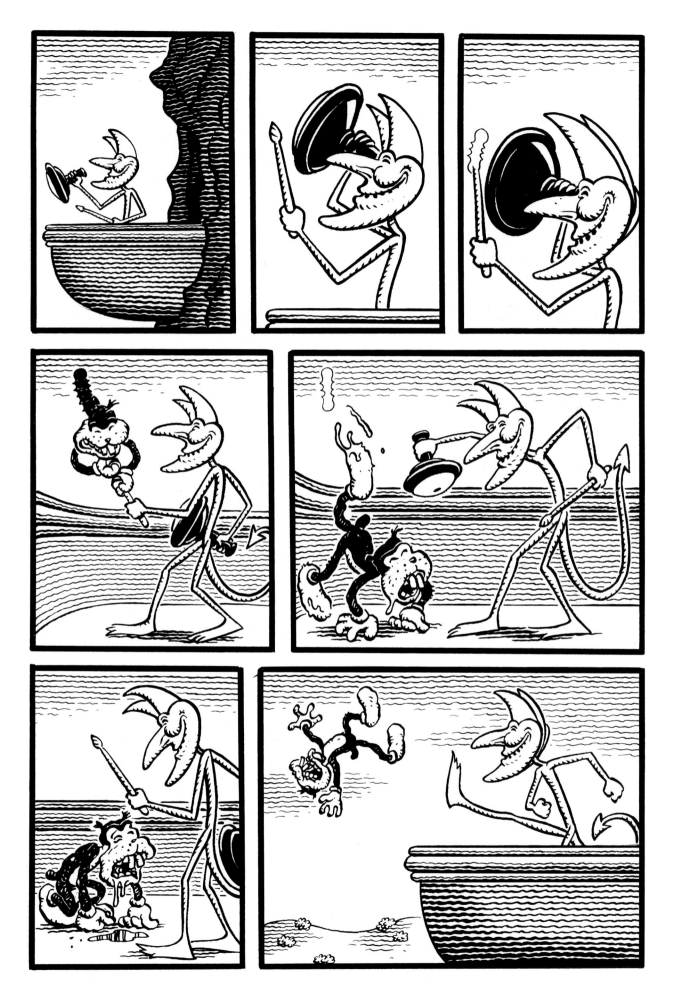

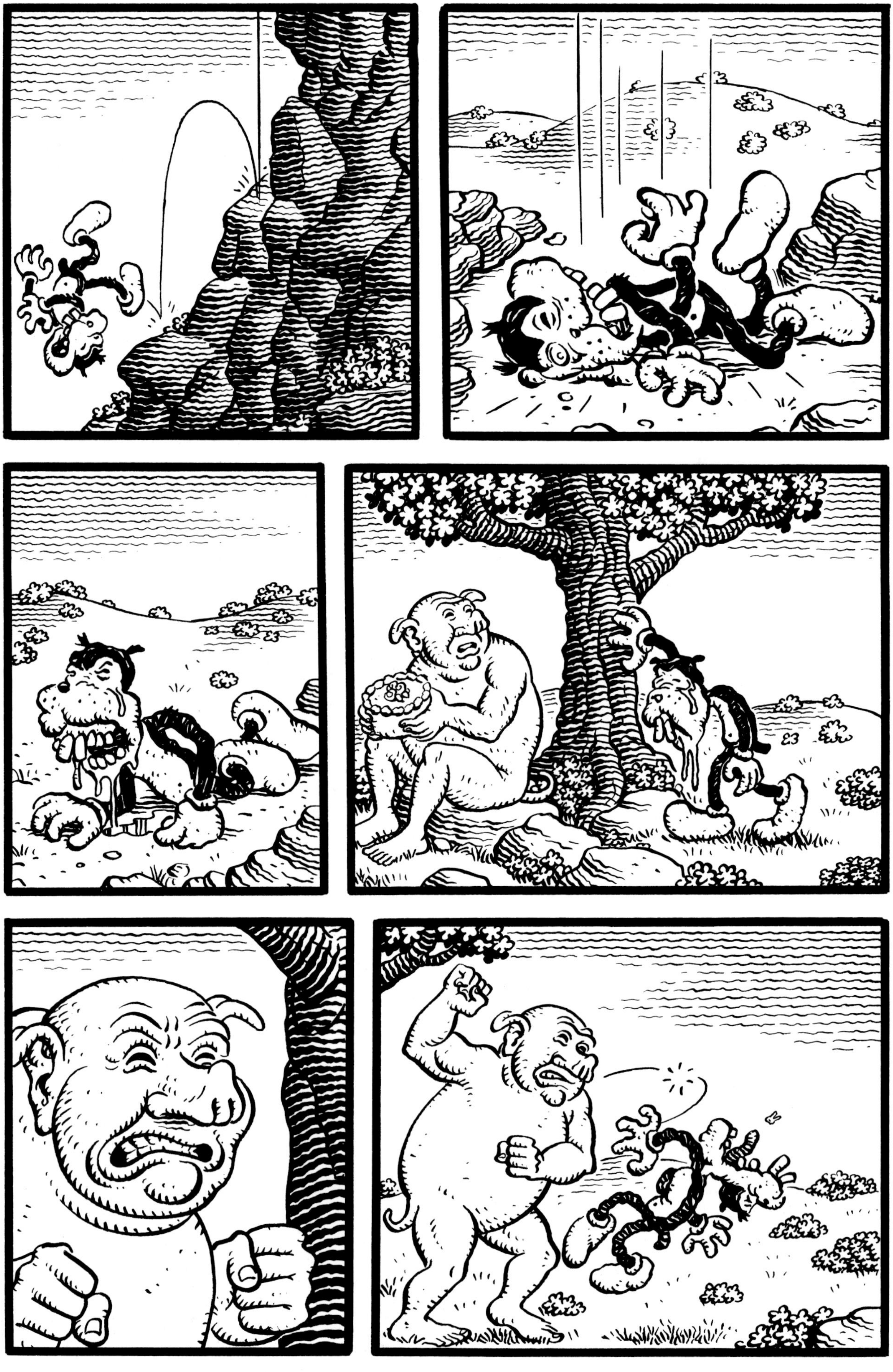

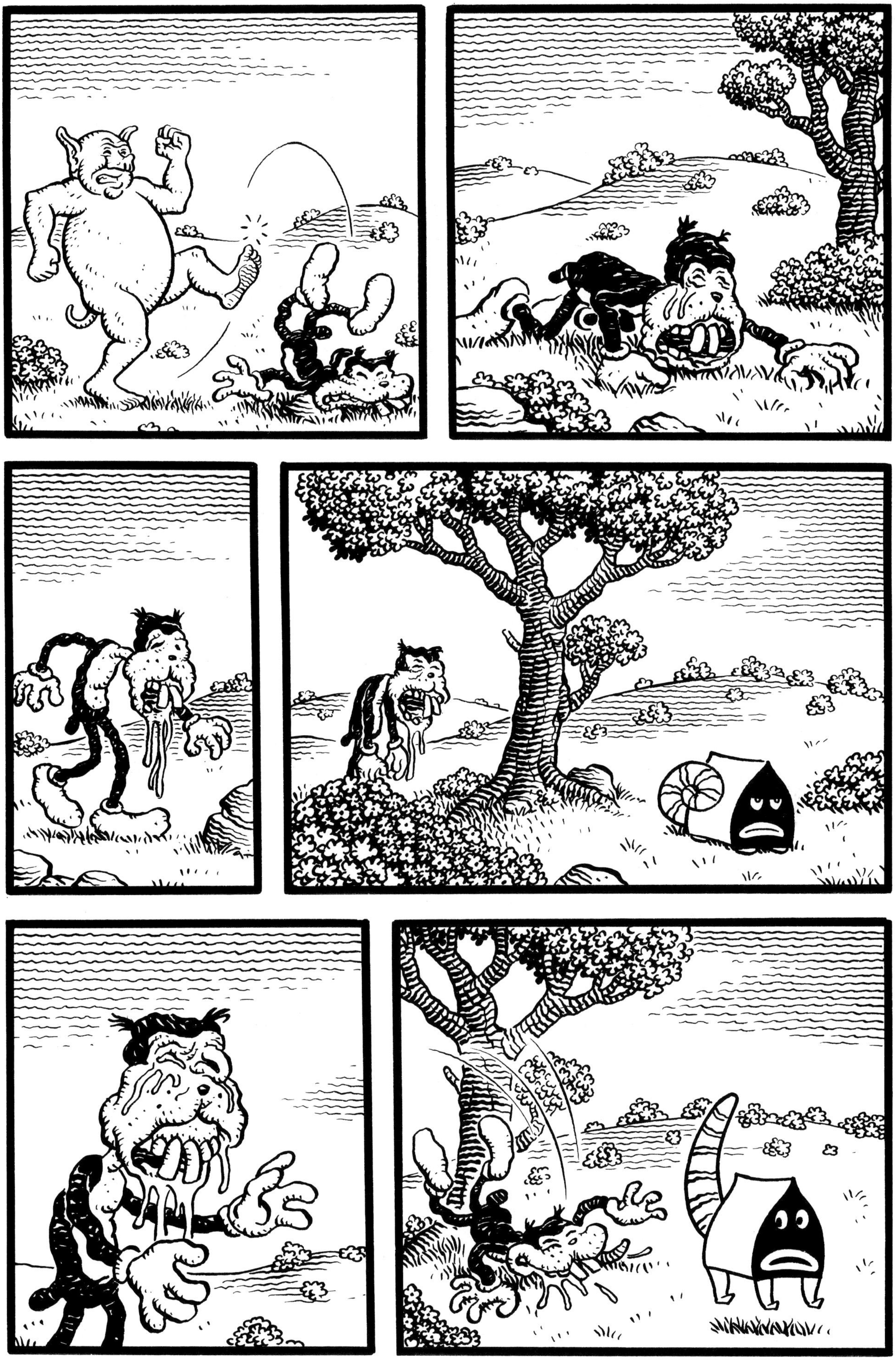

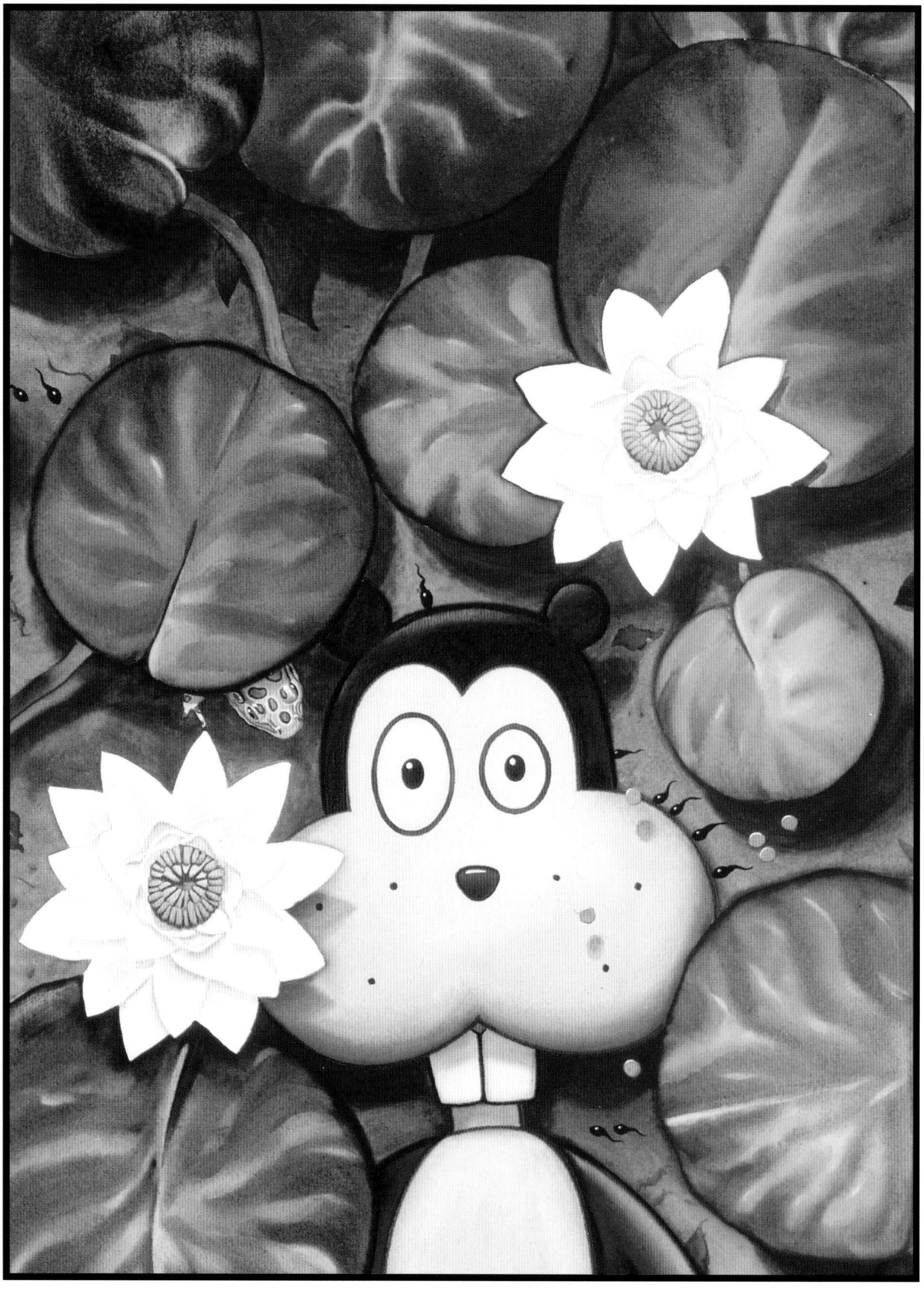

Cover, *JIM,* vol. 2, #1

Appendix

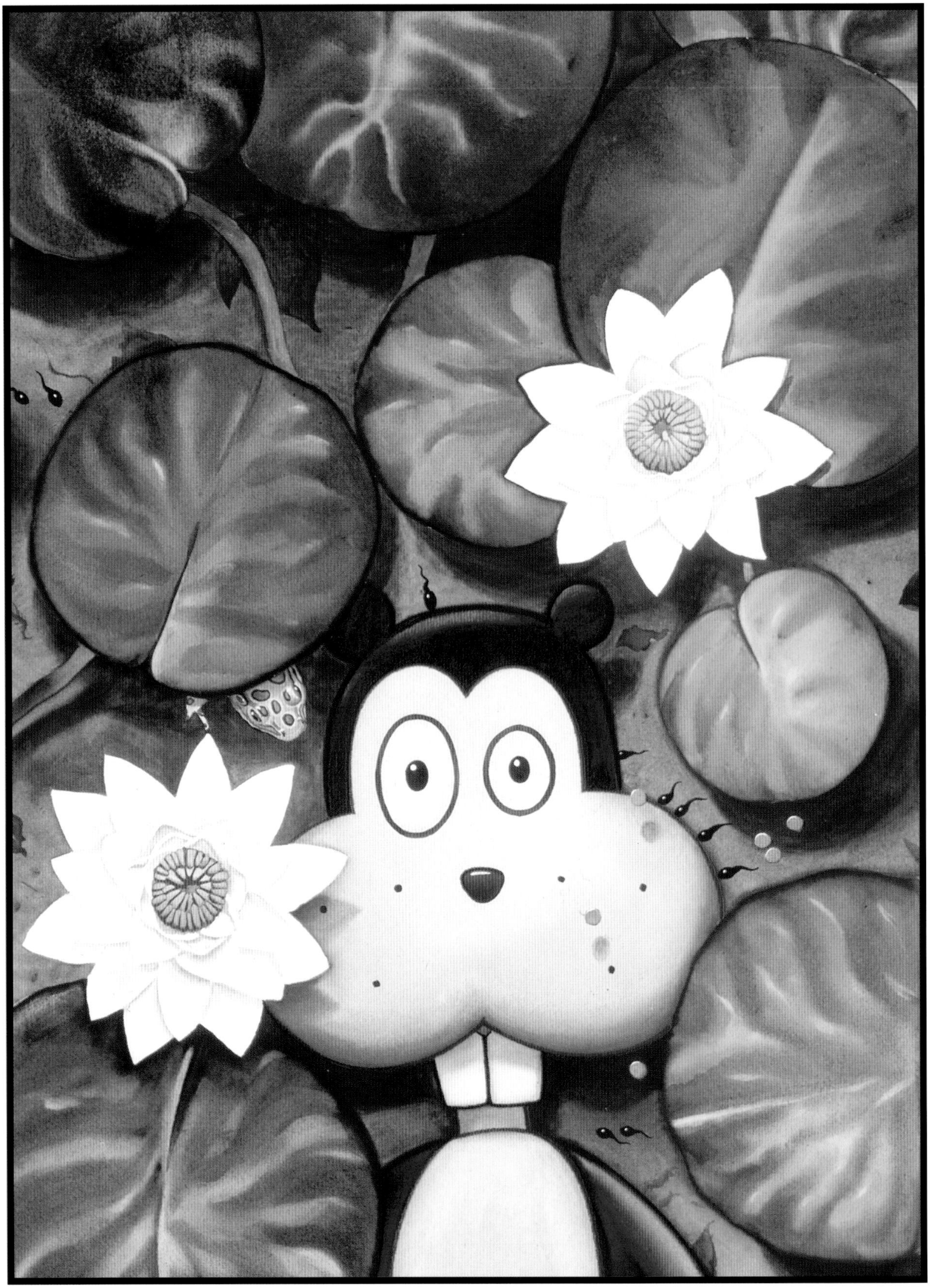

Cover, *JIM*, vol. 2, #1

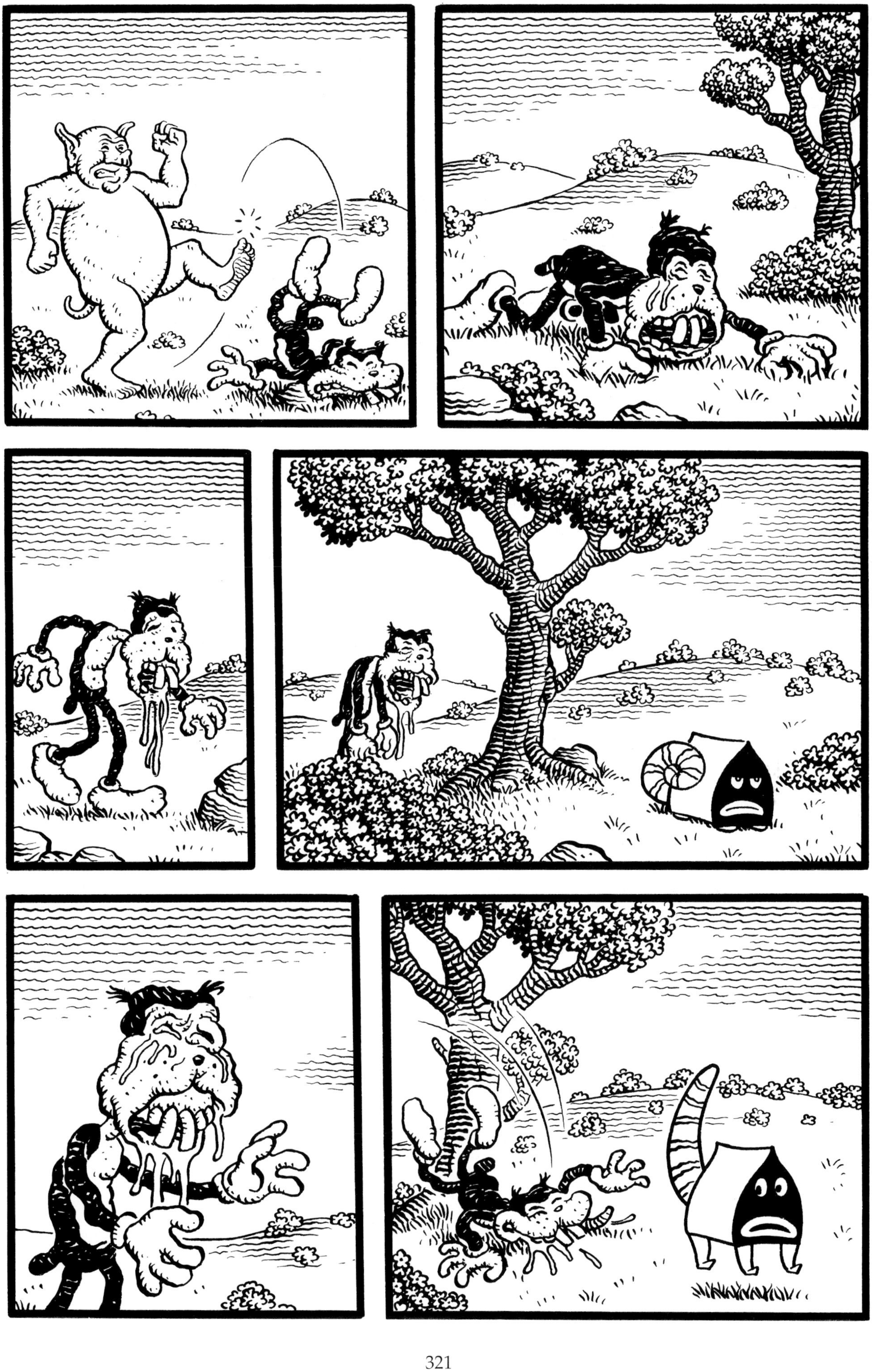

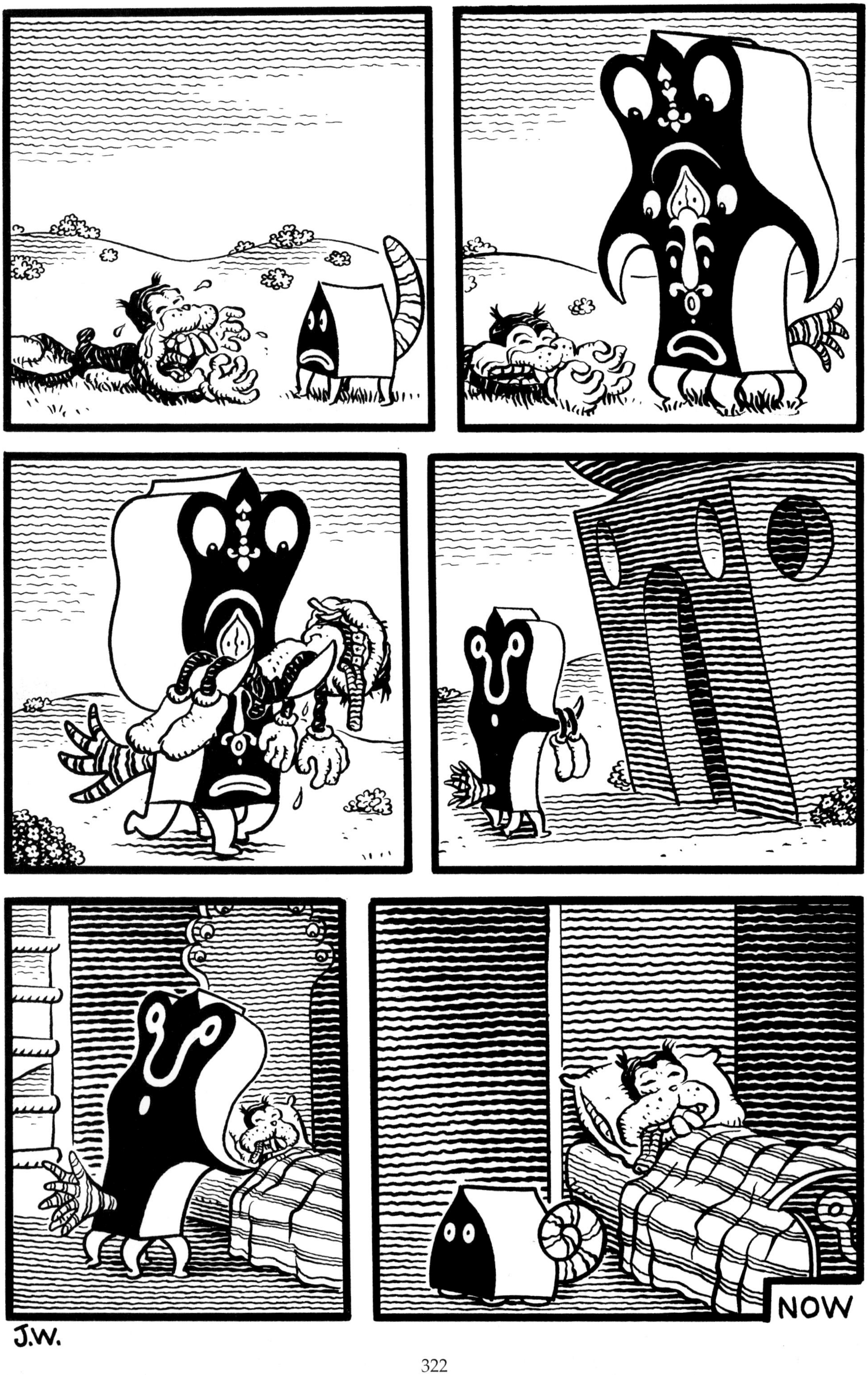
NOW
J.W.

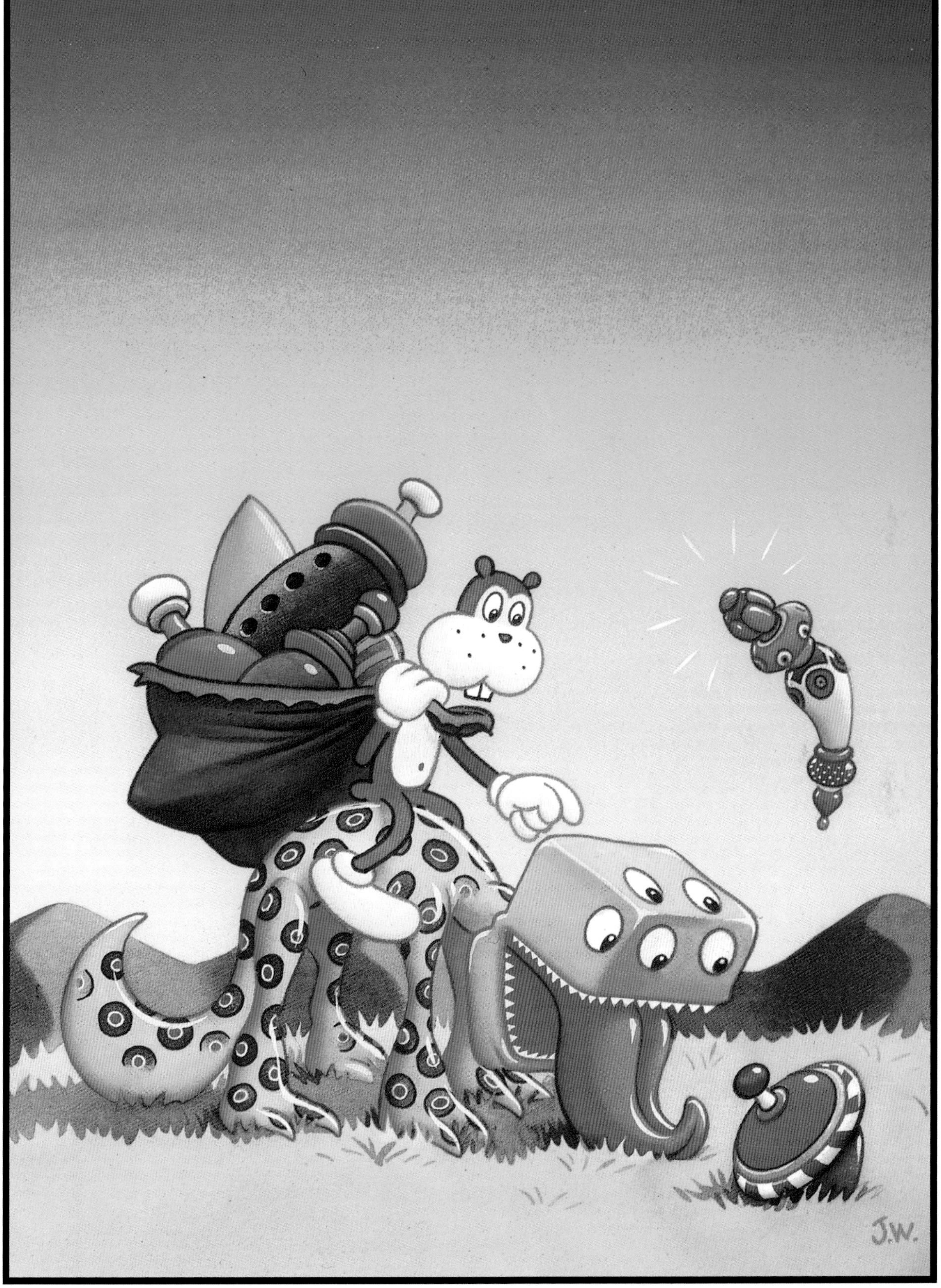
J.W.

Cover, *JIM,* vol. 2, #4

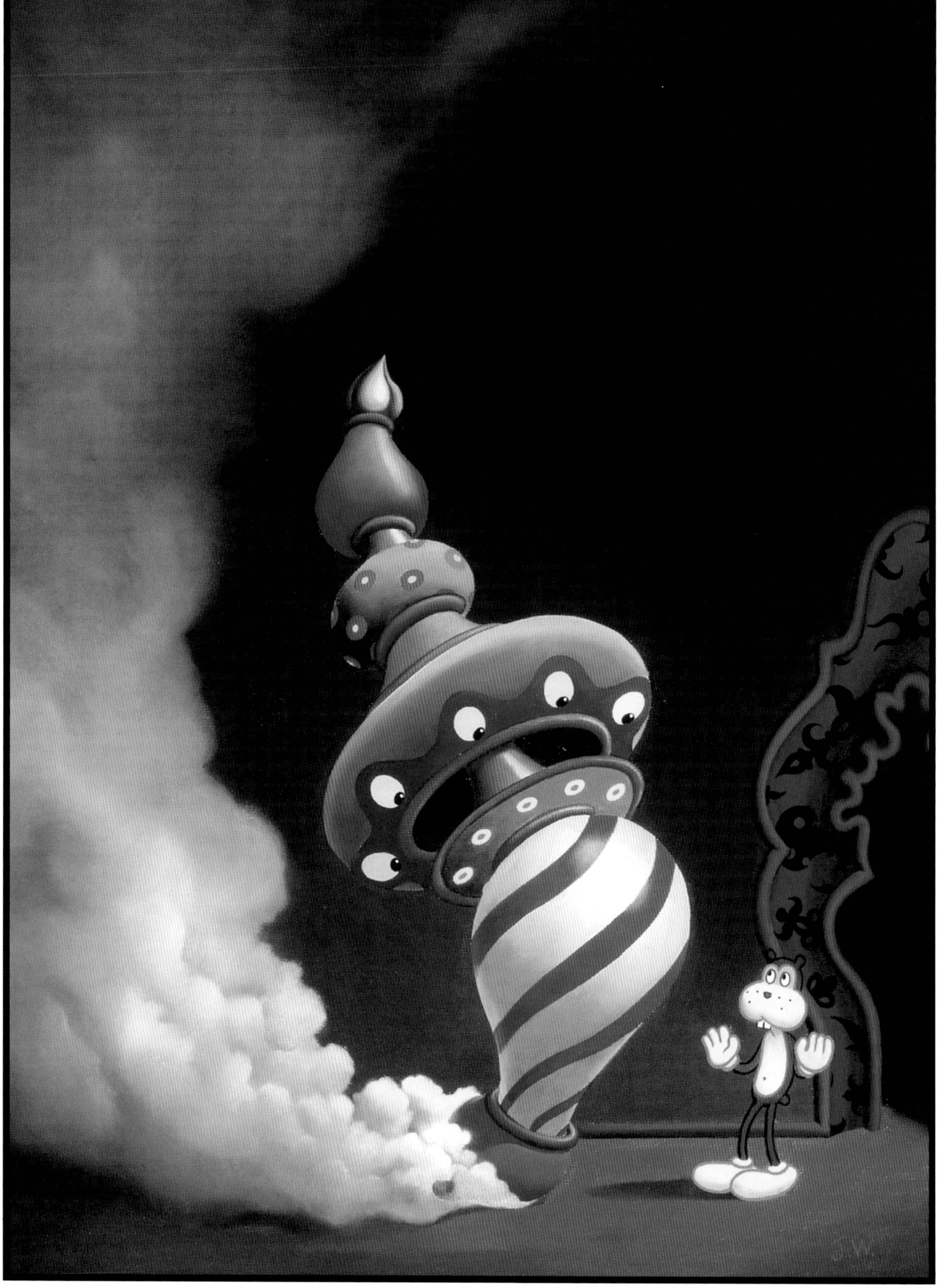

Cover, *FRANK*, #3

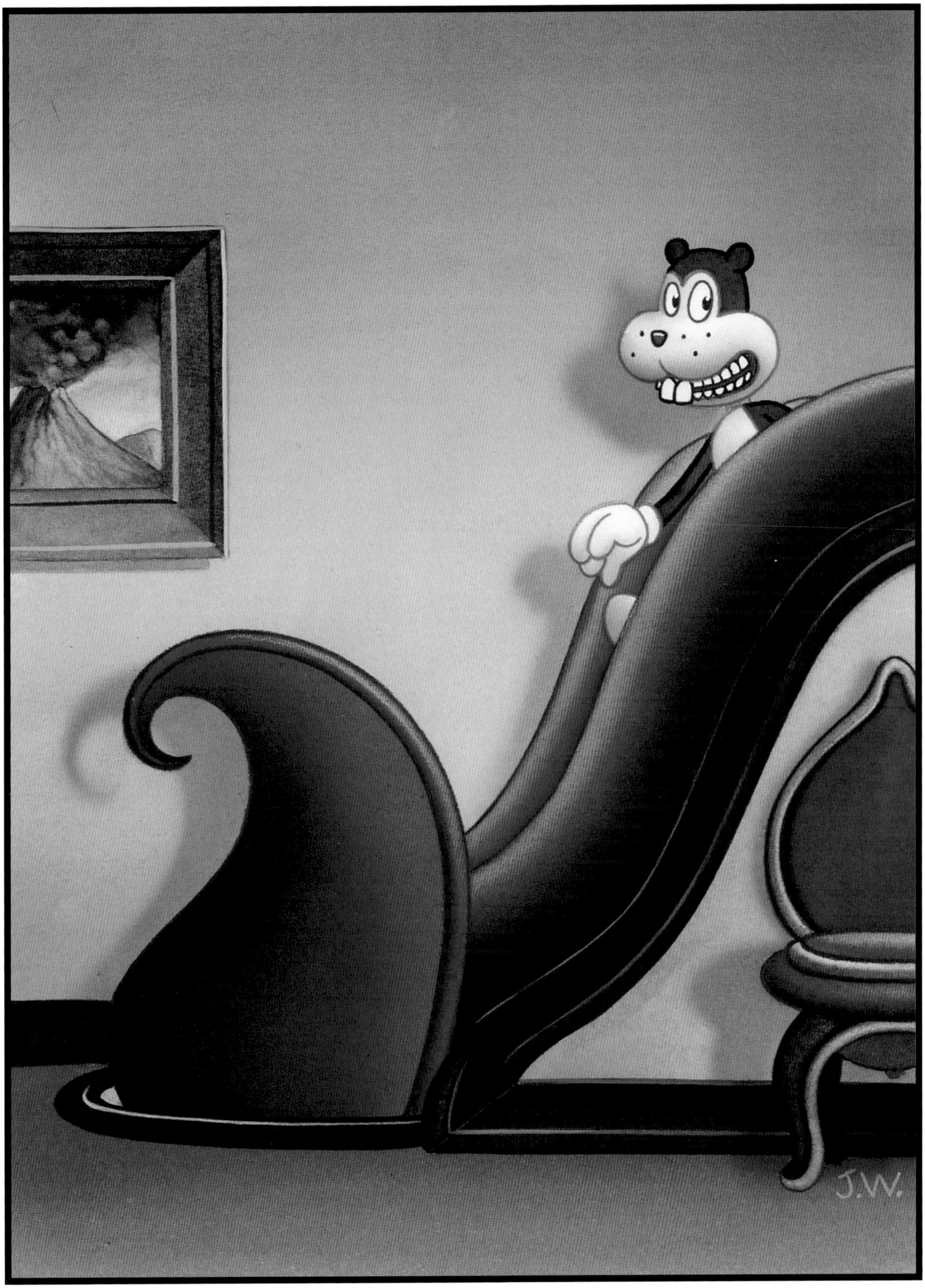
J.W.

Cover, *FRANK*, #2

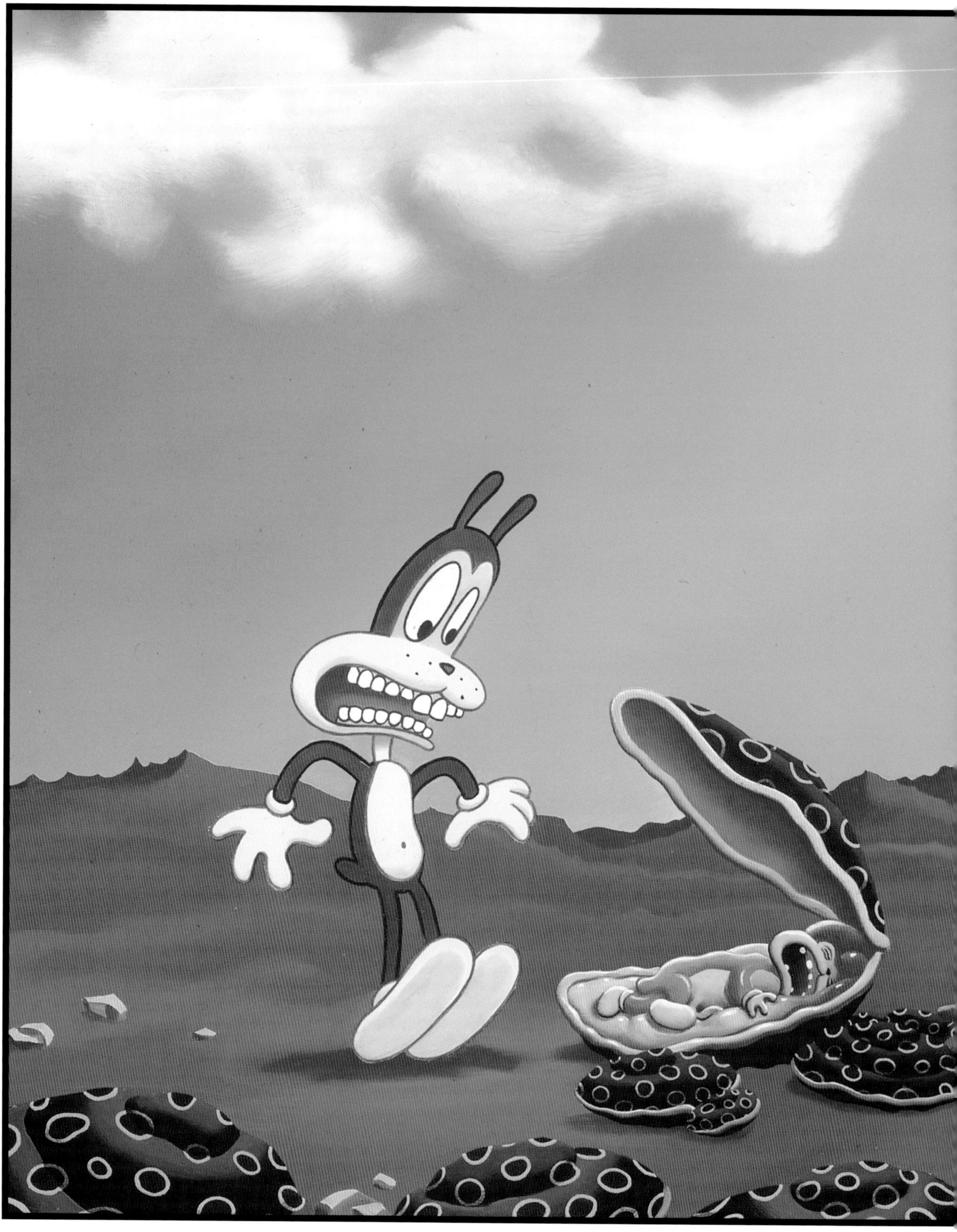

Cover, *JIM*, vol. 2, #5

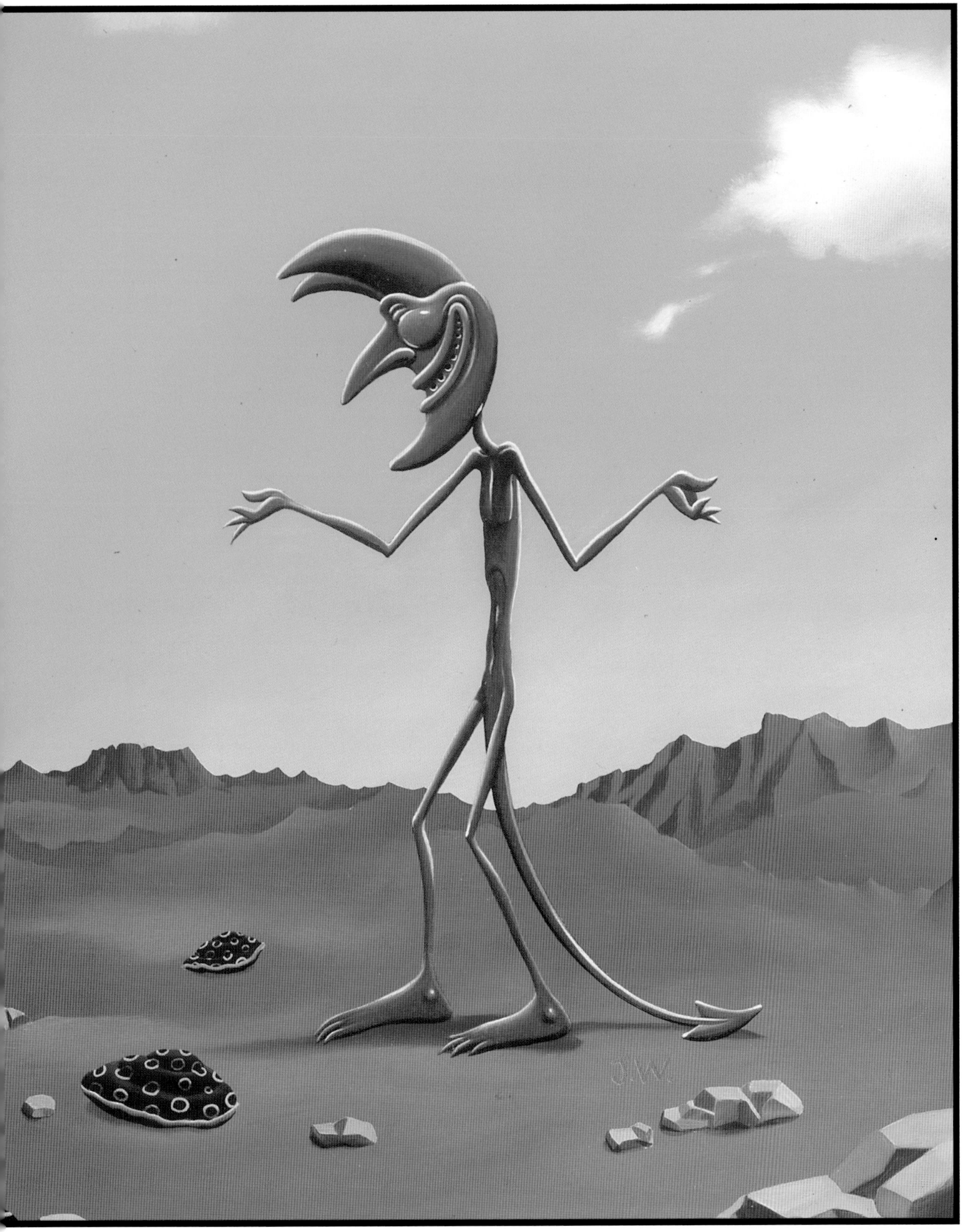

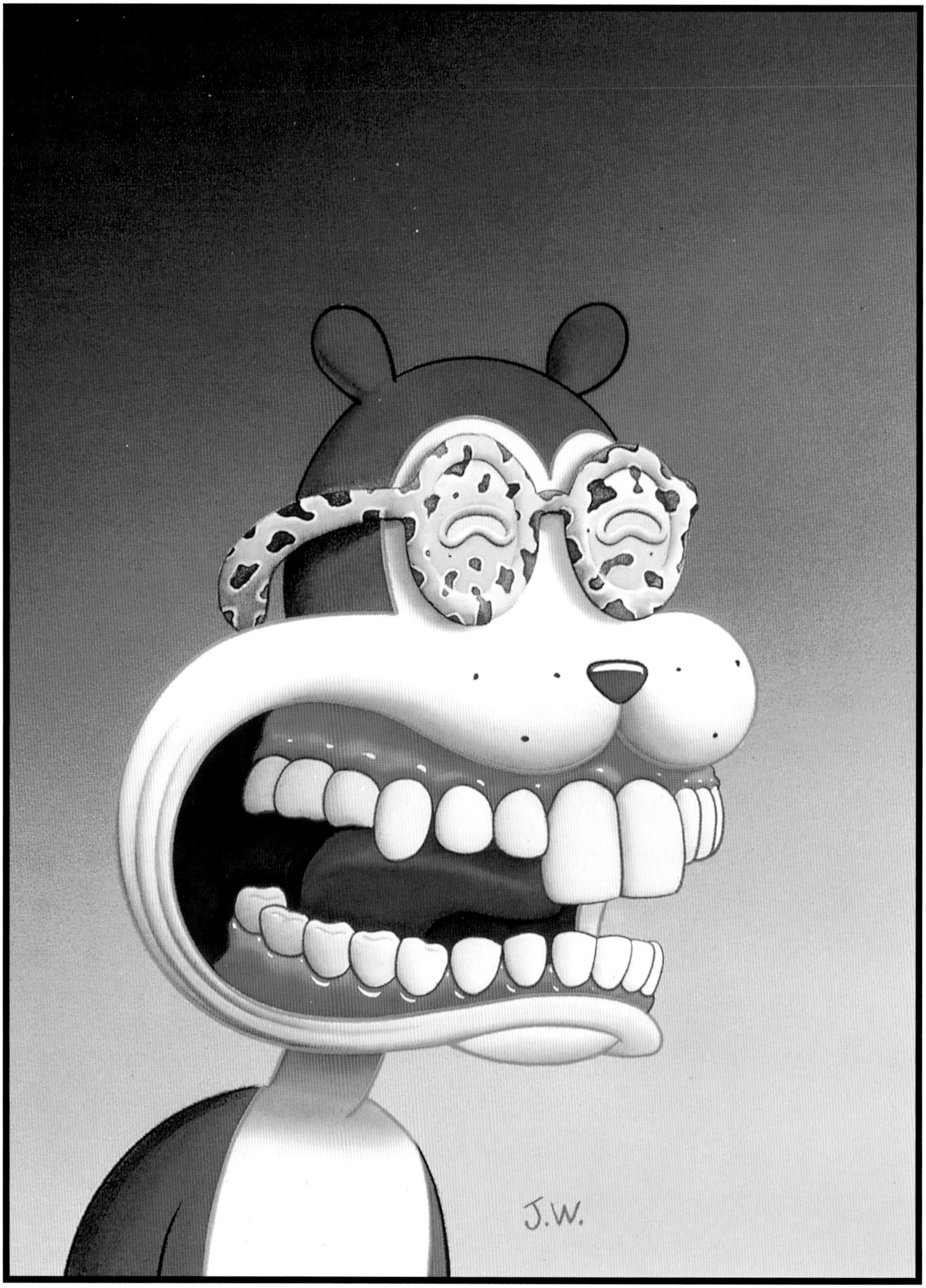
J.W.

Back cover, *JIM,* vol. 2, #4

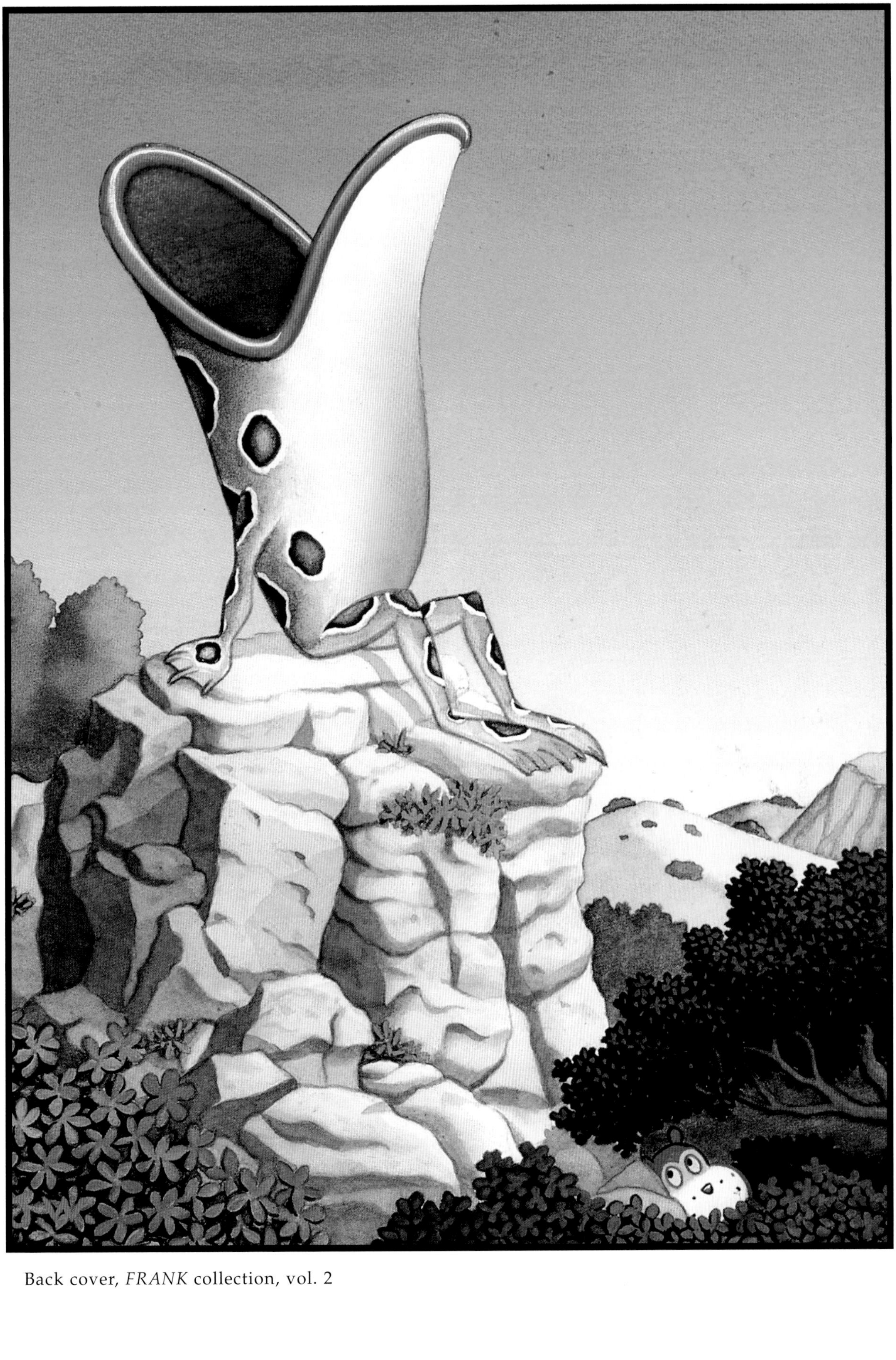

Back cover, *FRANK* collection, vol. 2

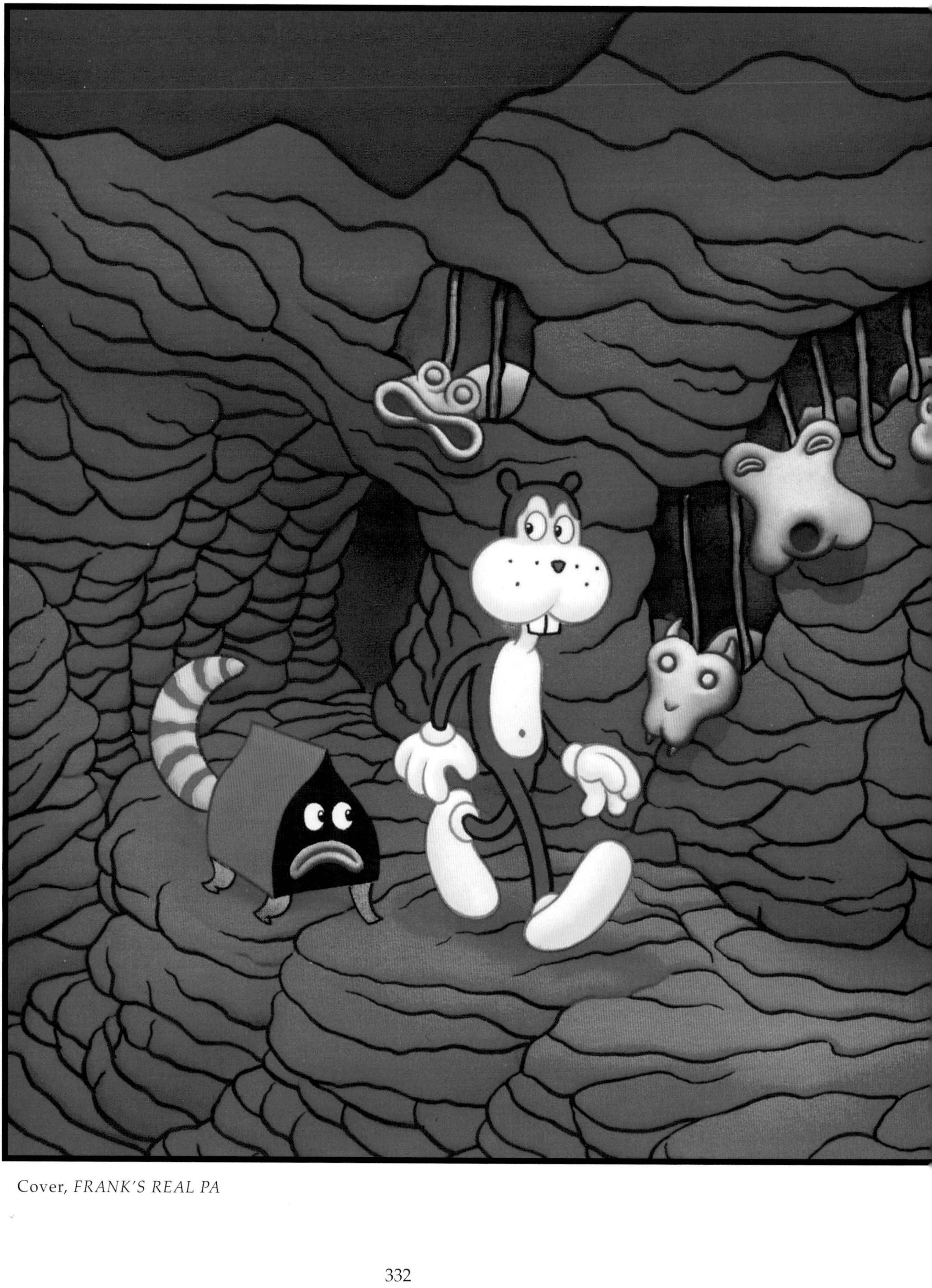

Cover, *FRANK'S REAL PA*

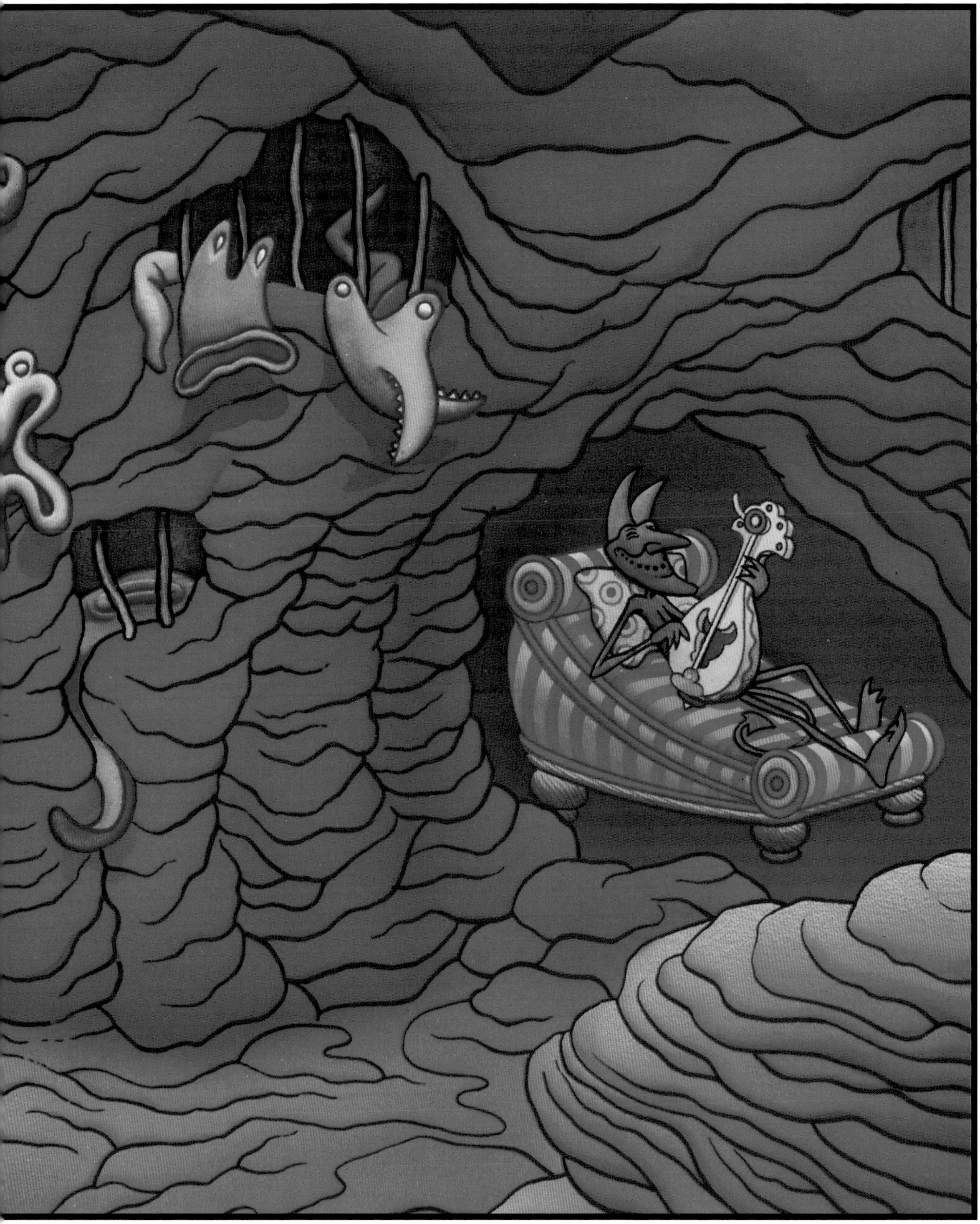

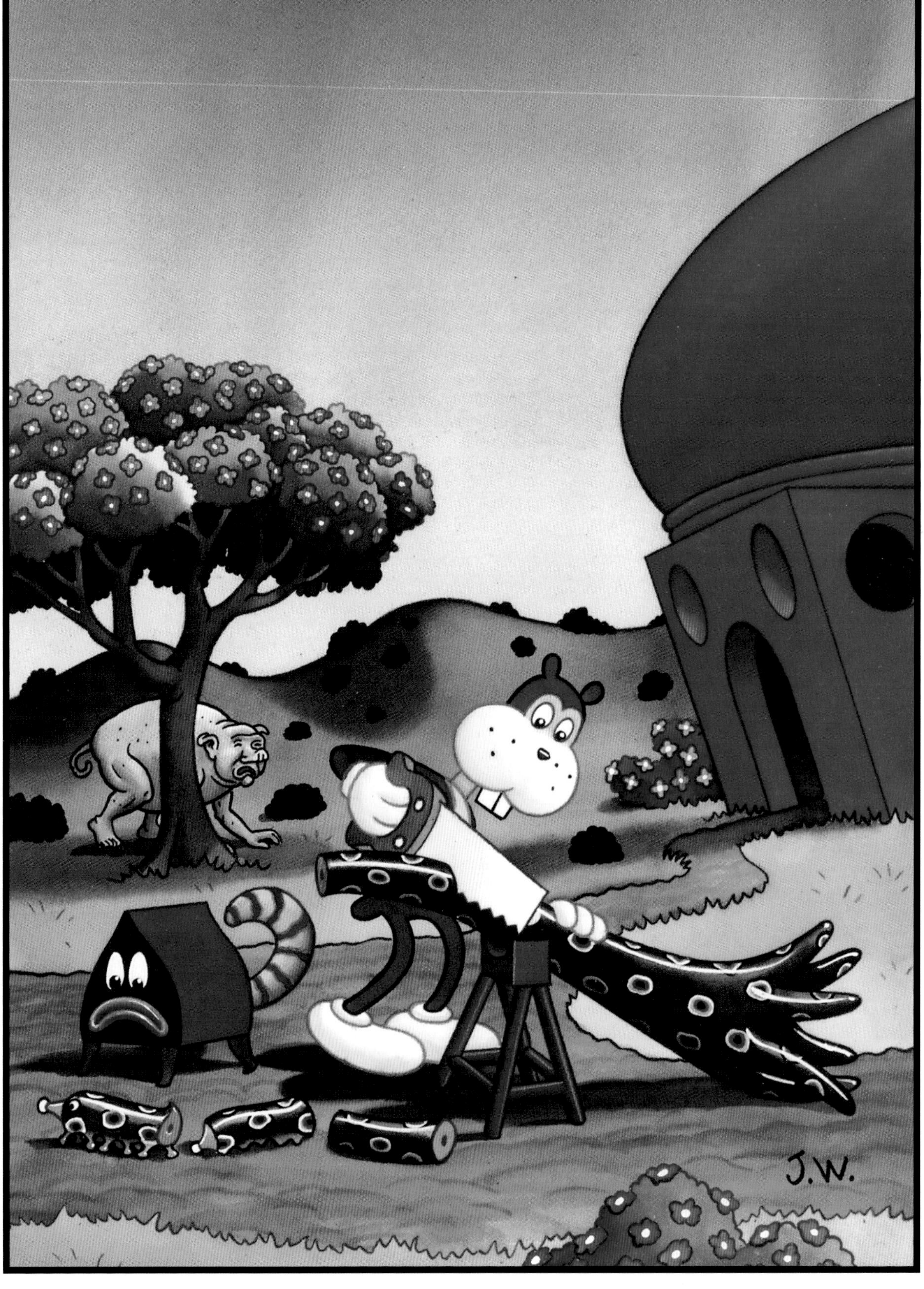
J.W.

Cover, *FRANK*, #1

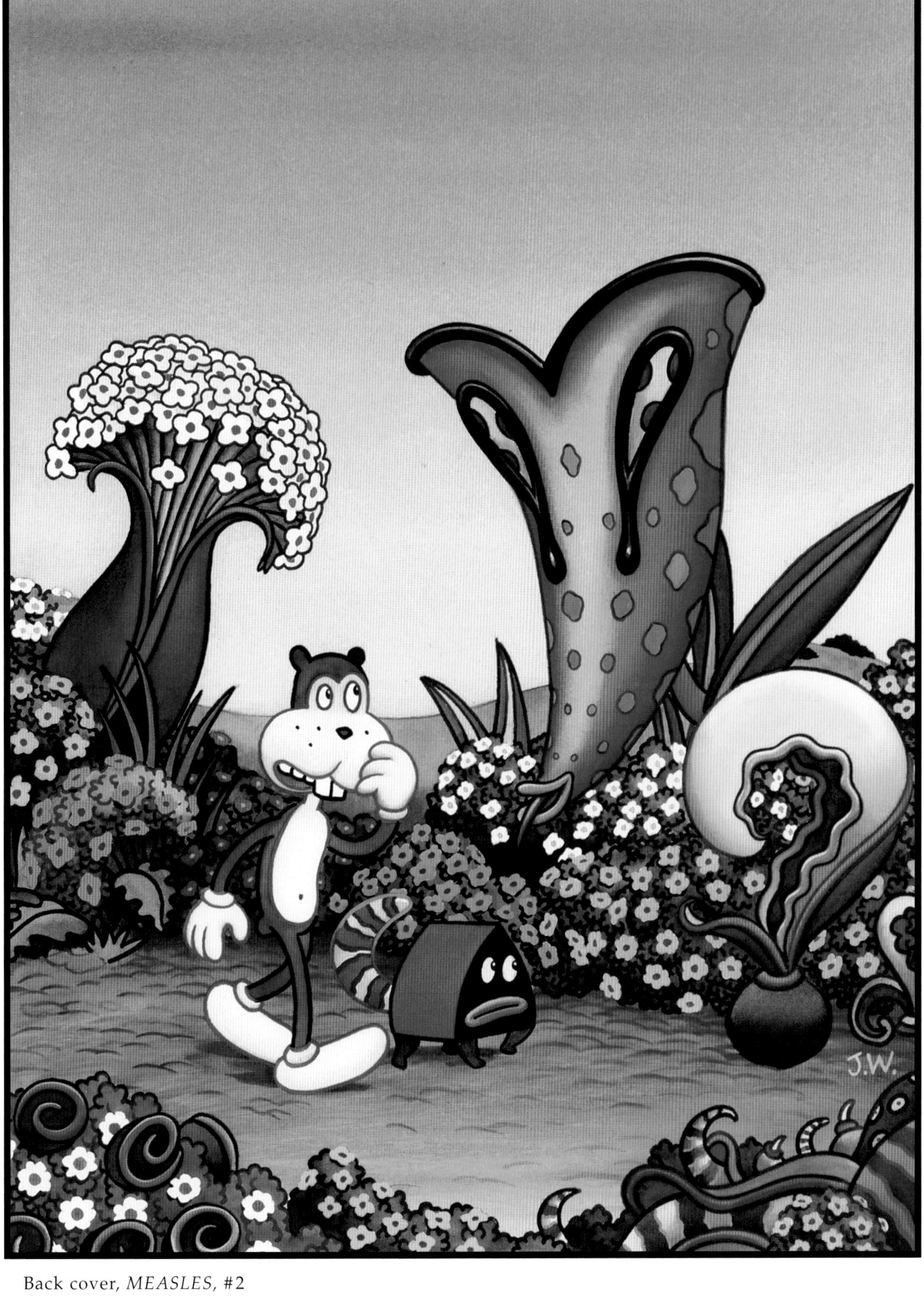
J.W.

Back cover, *MEASLES*, #2

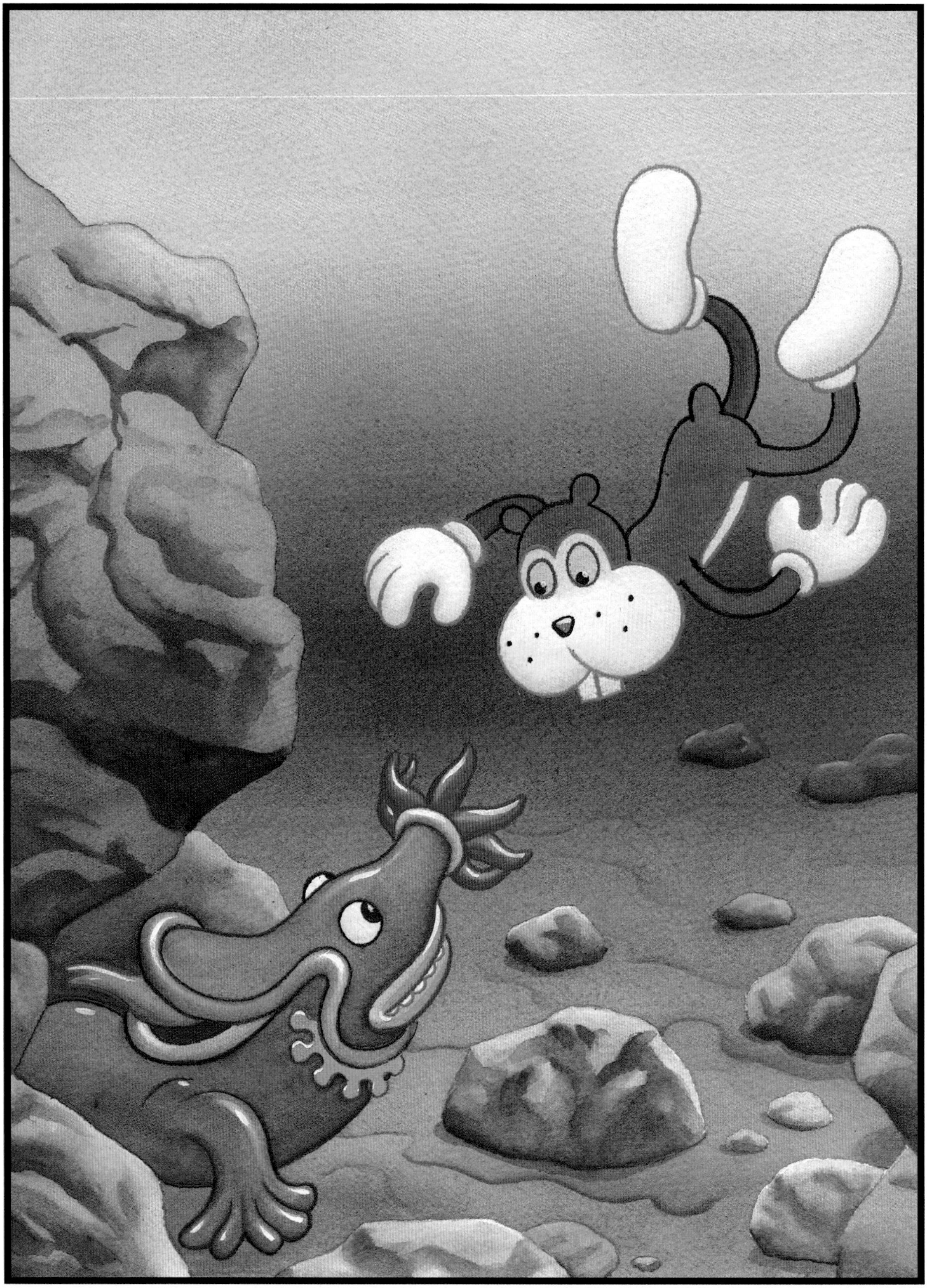

Aqueous Humor, an unused cover painting.

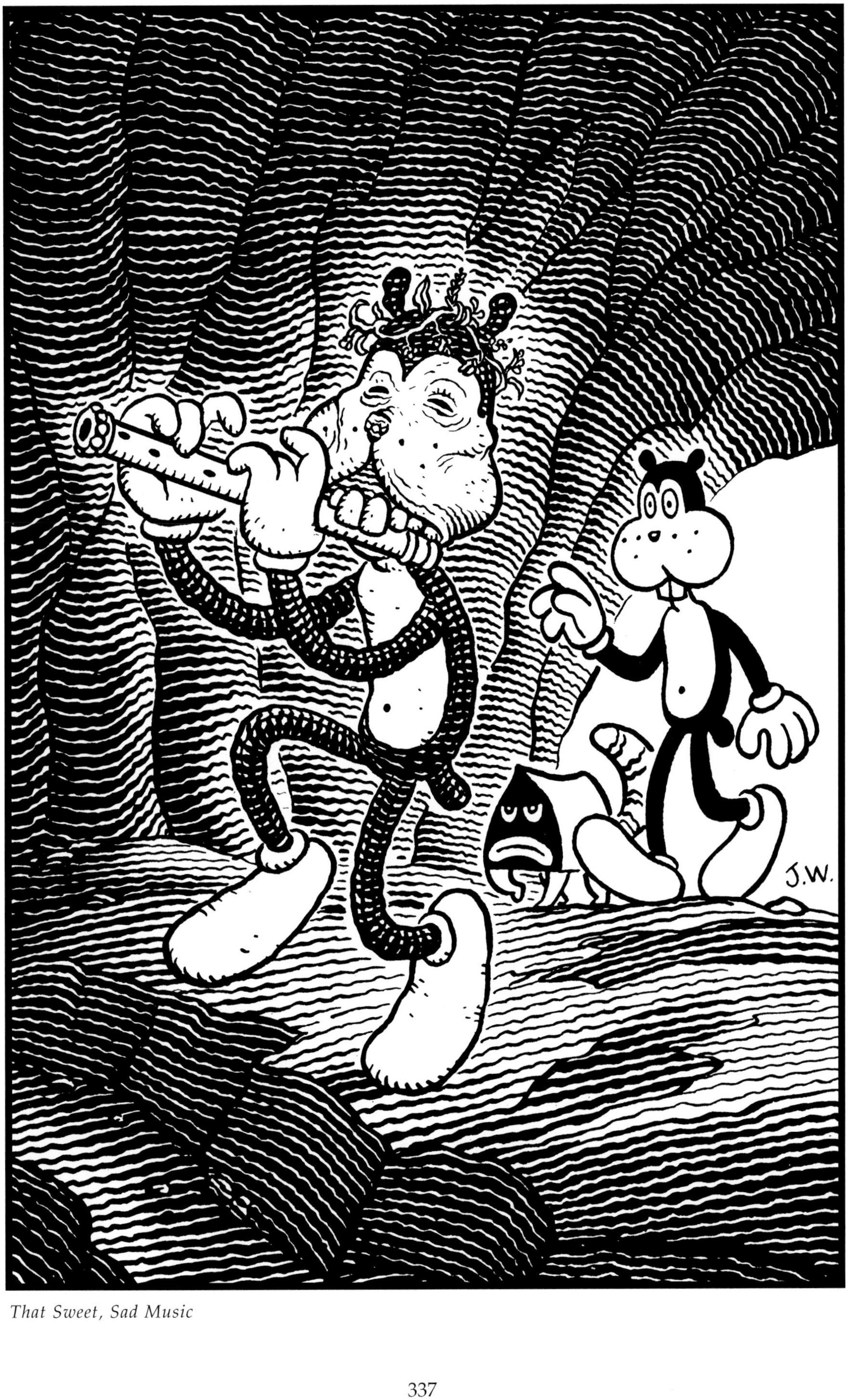
J.W.

That Sweet, Sad Music

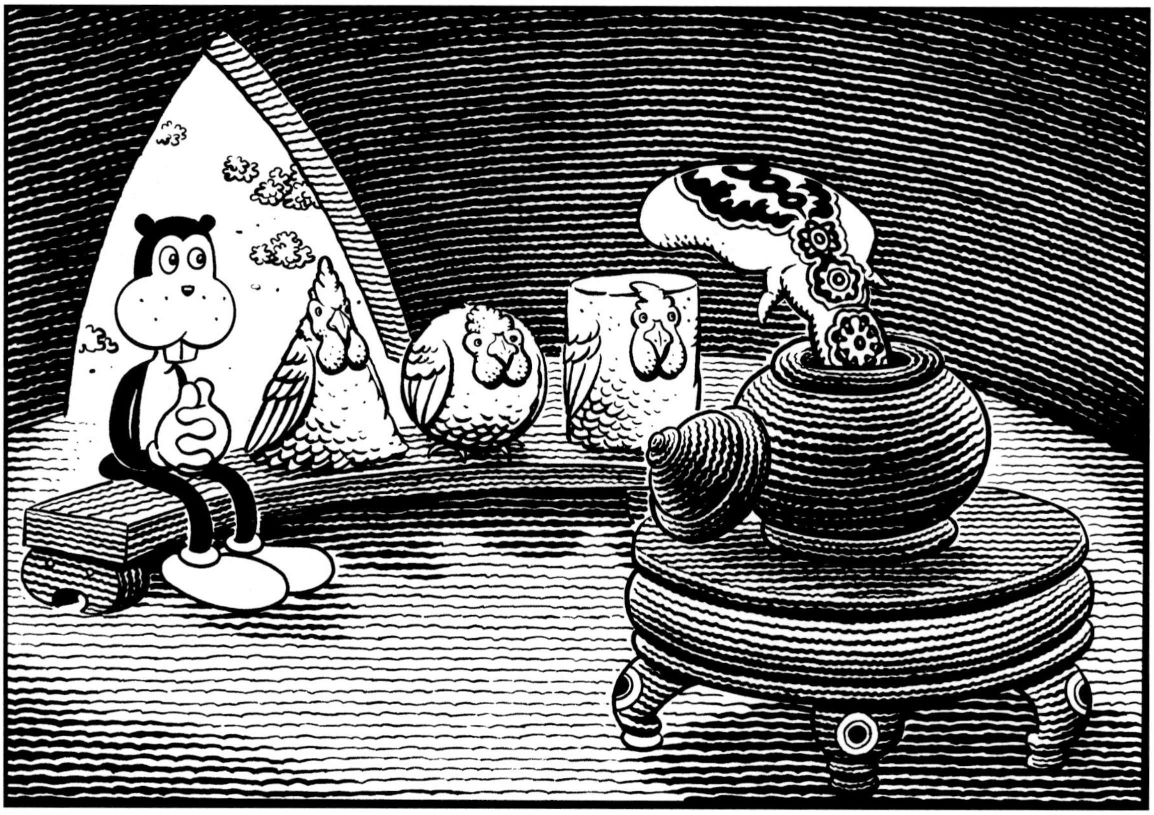

The Little Red Schoolhouse

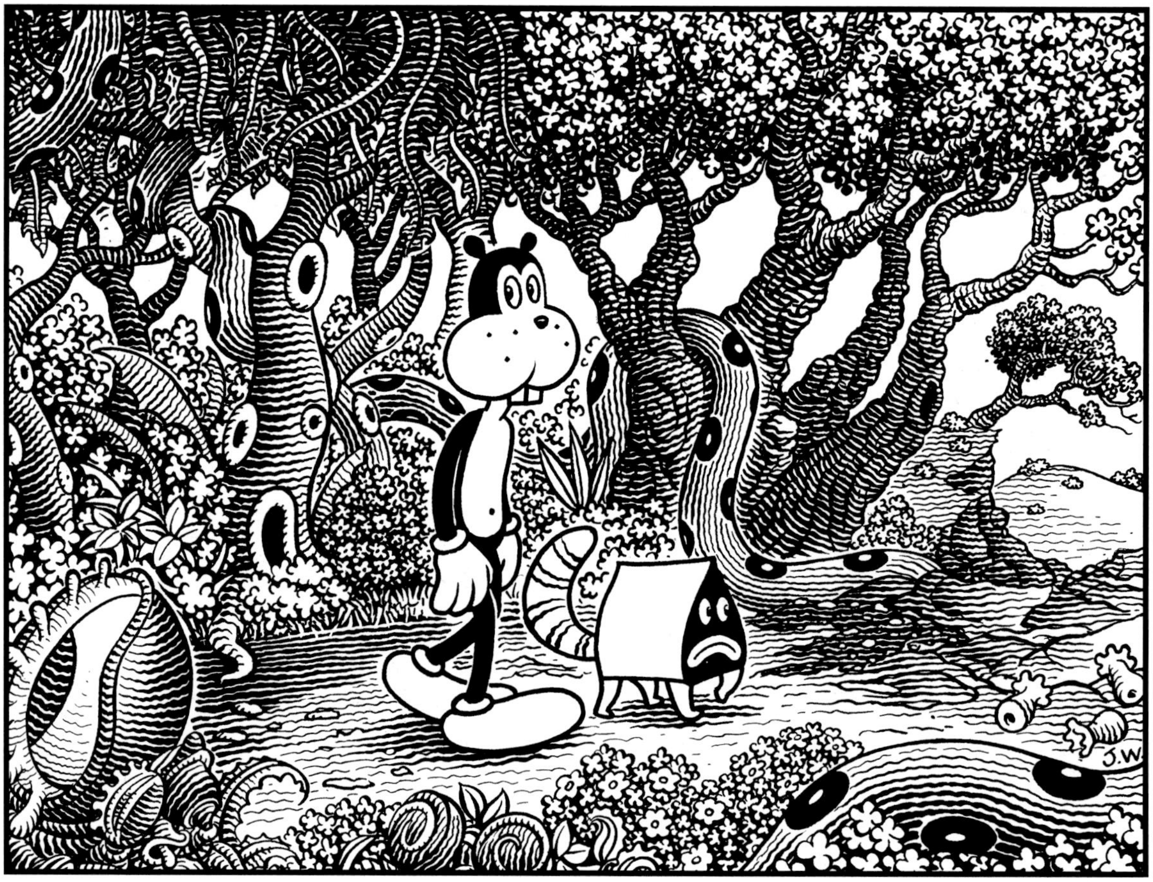

Squeaker in the Woods

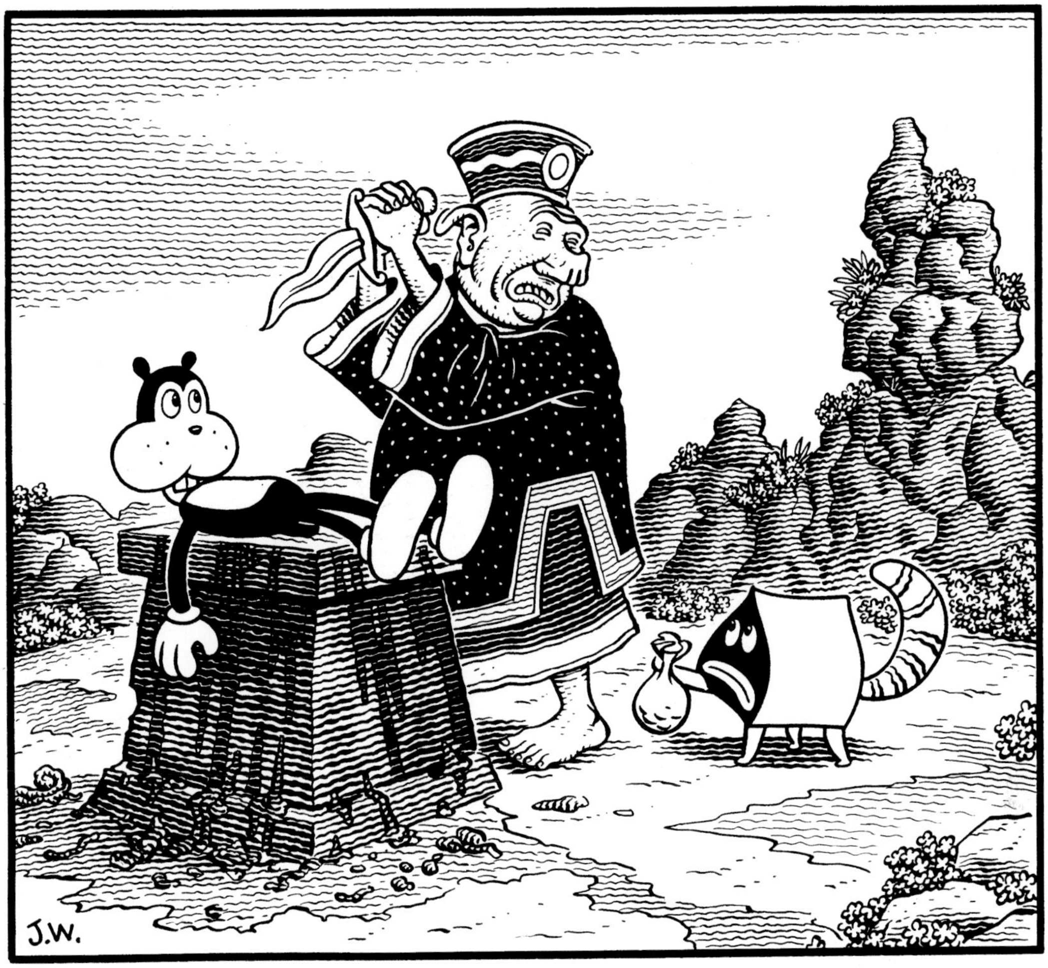
J.W.

The Counteroffering

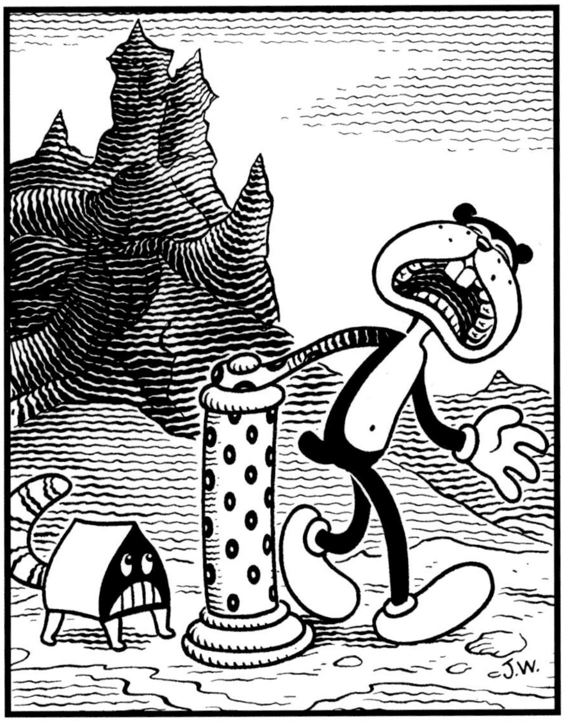
J.W.

Touch-Me-Not

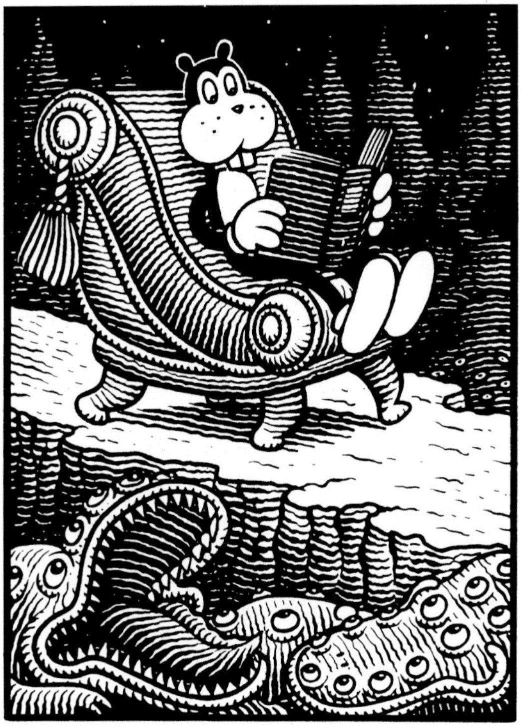

Bookplate

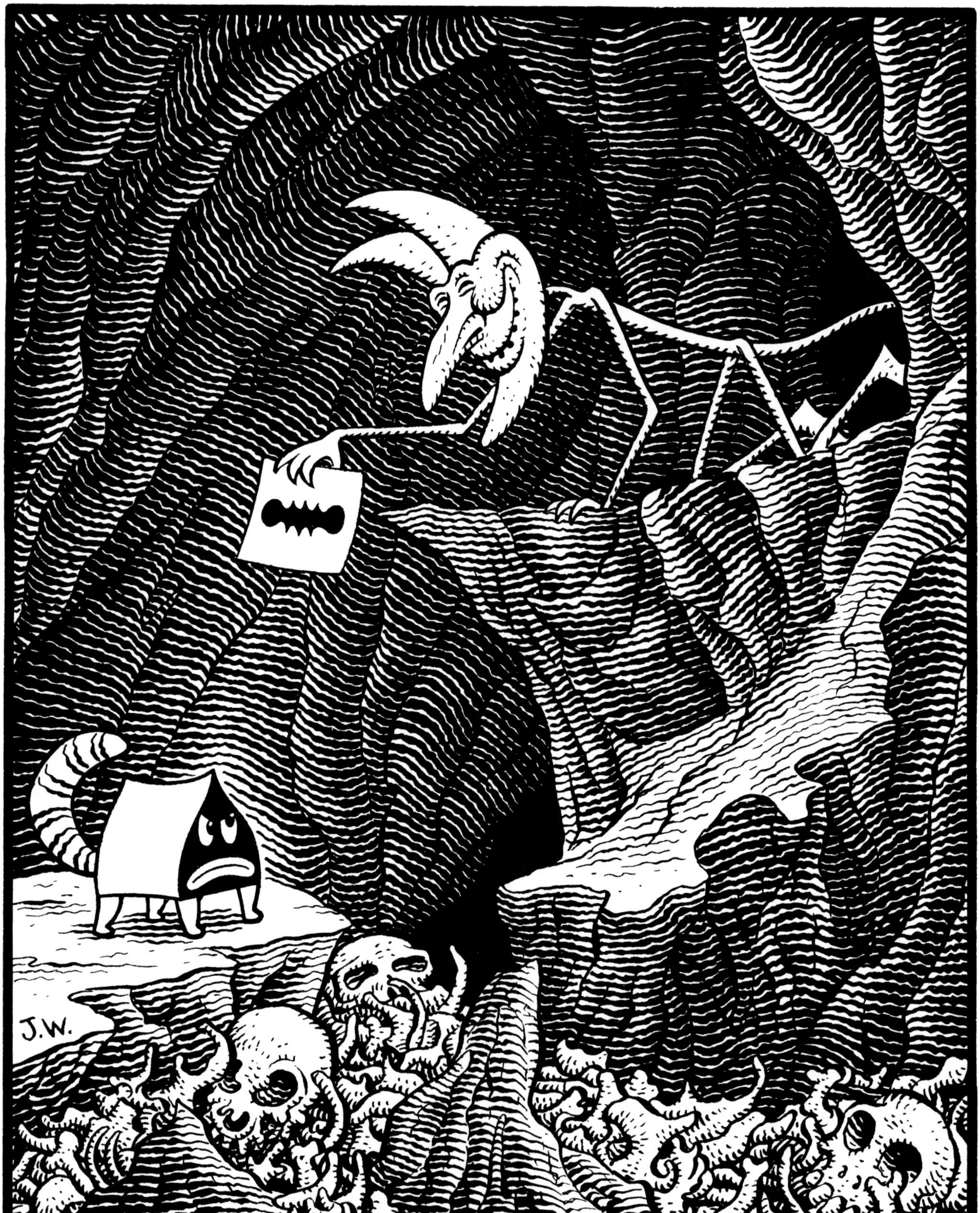
J.W.

Worse Than Useless

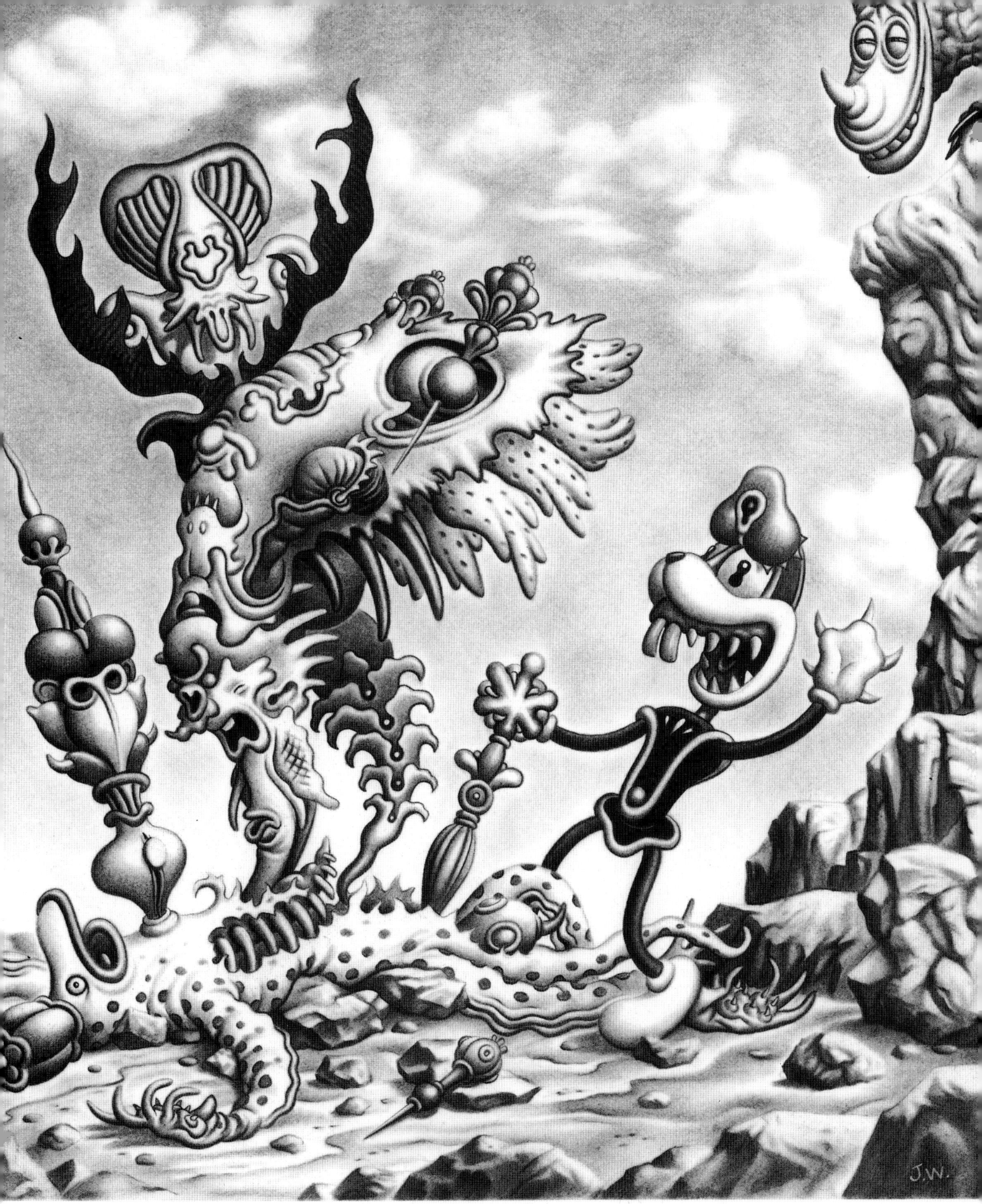
J.W.

Frank Amok This is the way the world looks to Whim, which goes a long way towards explaining his lousy behavior. You or I would see Frank weeping in empathy as he pulls a thorn from the side of an expiring demon. Overleaf: *Glendale*

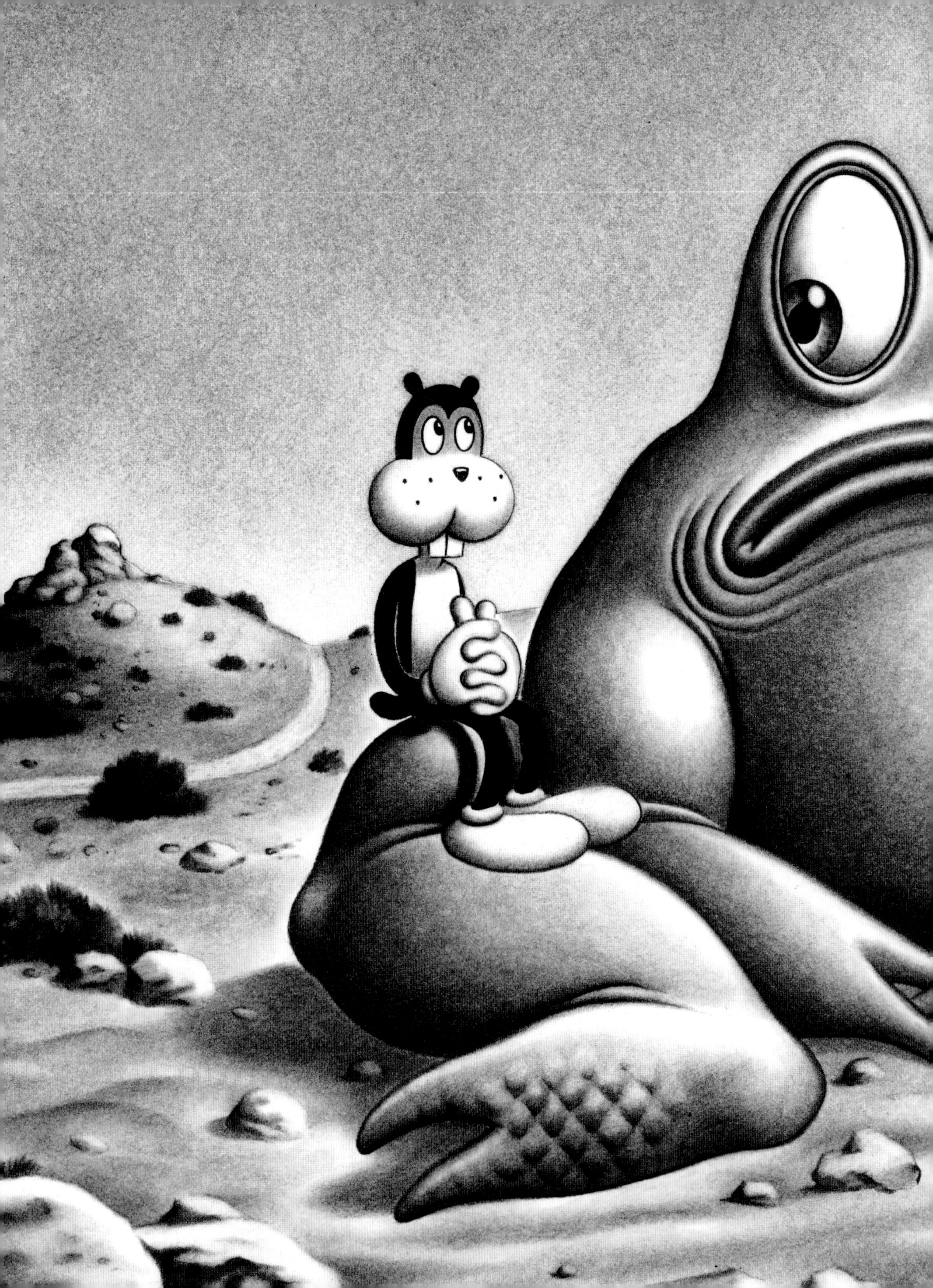

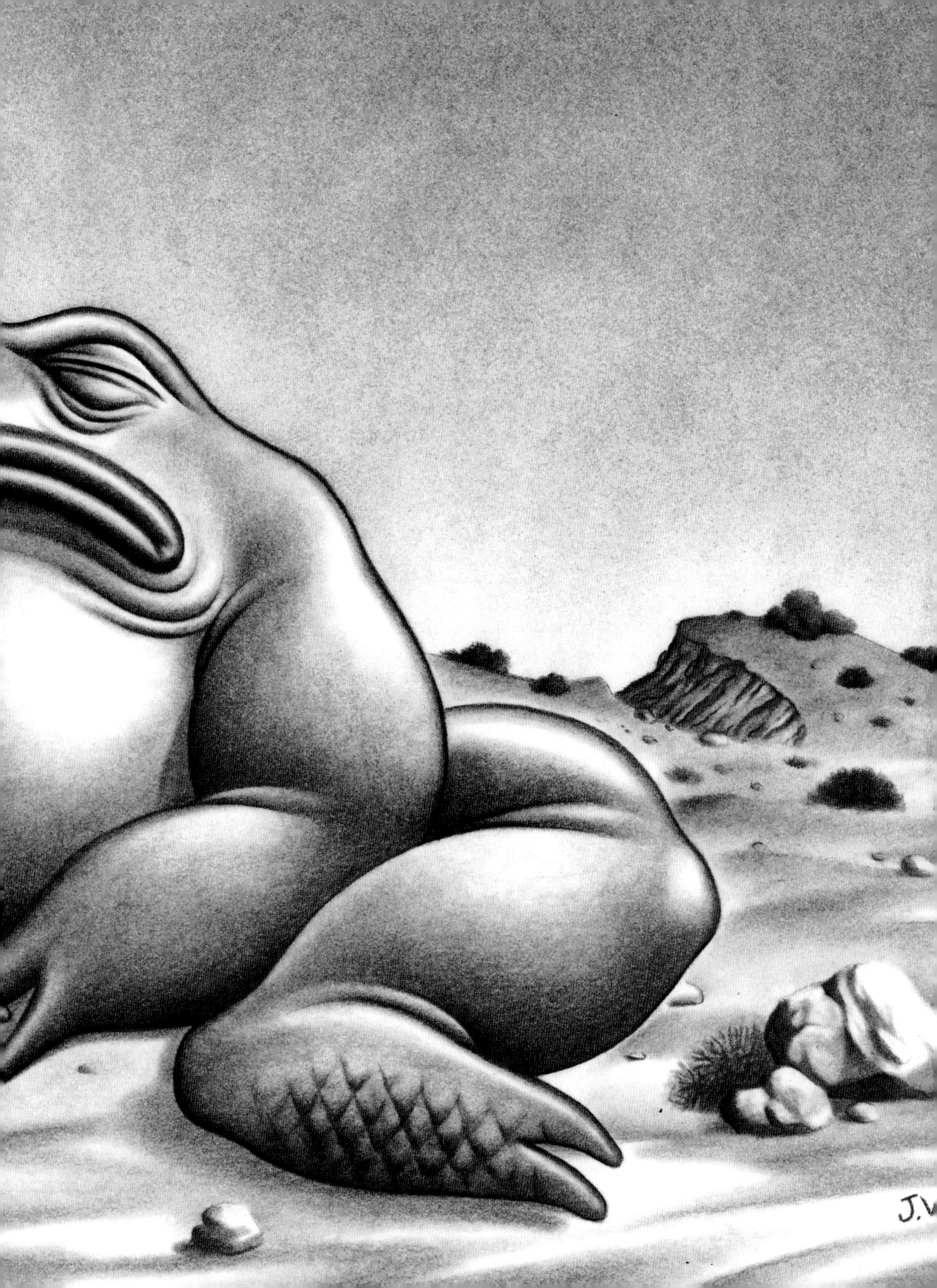

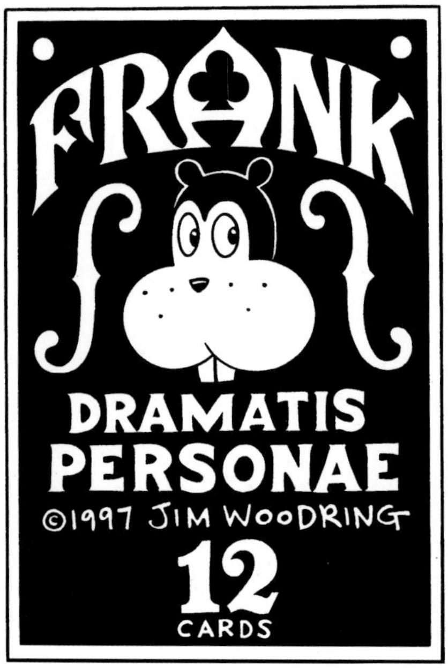
FRANK
DRAMATIS
PERSONAE
©1997 JIM WOODRING
12
CARDS

Originally published as a set of cards in 1997 by Michael Dowers and Brownfield Press. They have been edited for space here.

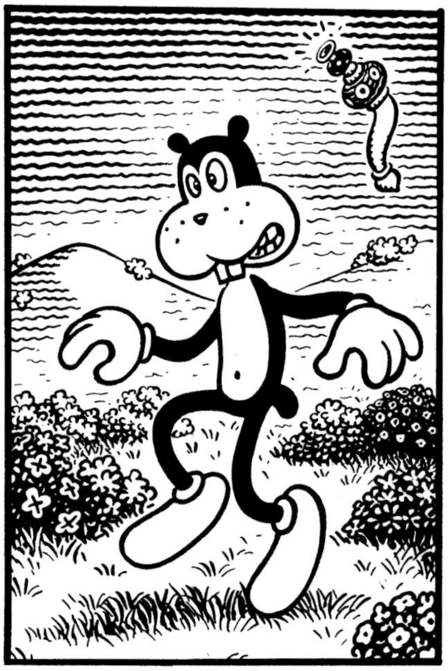

FRANK

Like Neptune, Frank enjoys the riches of the deep. His world works and rewards him vigorously, and Frank learns nothing, ever. Why should he? In his world there is no pattern, no law; only the incessant conversational cross-currents of nature and abstraction. Frank is innocent but not noble. What he is really looking for is a good scare. He knows that the blow never falls. Frank has many bodies, all identical.

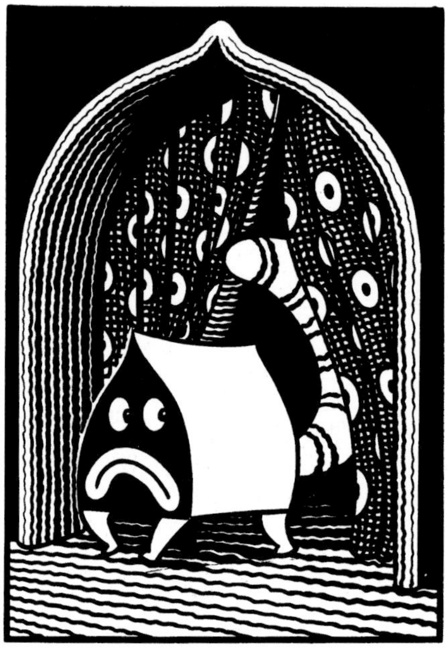

PUPSHAW

Frank's testy little bowser-box has the celestial stature of a demigod; yet she serves him muttishly. Her small squeaks are the collisions of stars, but when her bowl is empty and her stomach growls, the depth of her commitment to the trilobular chuck-buster is revealed; she never lifts a paw against her master. Pupshaw conceals in her brightness a dark concern; she knows that if Frank were to come to harm her life would be without purpose.

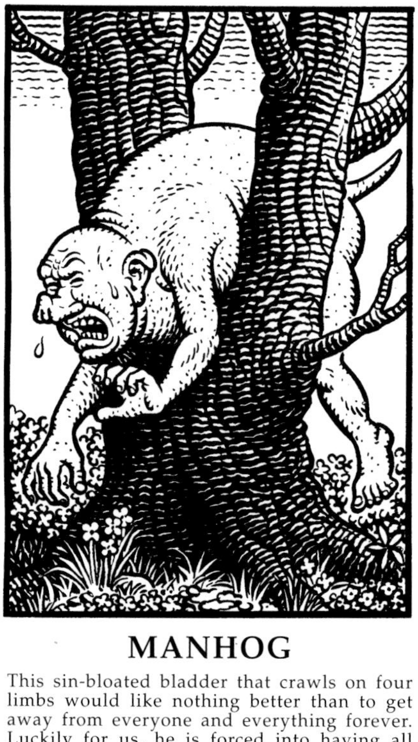

MANHOG

This sin-bloated bladder that crawls on four limbs would like nothing better than to get away from everyone and everything forever. Luckily for us, he is forced into having all sorts of exciting, horrible adventures. Manhog has been drowned, ground, filled with parasites, scraped to a nub, stabbed, stuffed, scared and driven away so many times that it's a miracle he sticks around. Perhaps he couldn't leave if he tried.

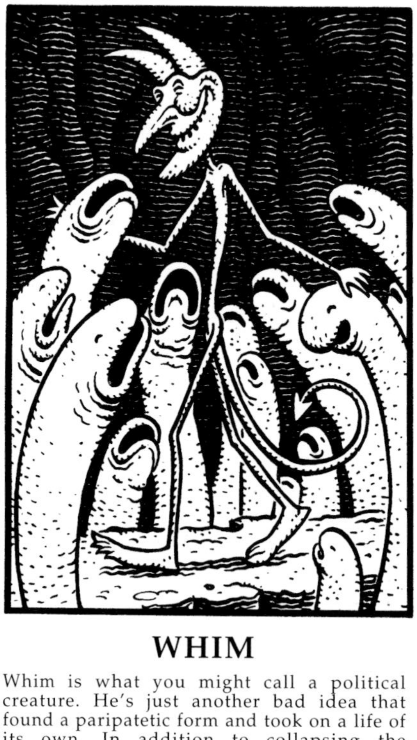

WHIM

Whim is what you might call a political creature. He's just another bad idea that found a paripatetic form and took on a life of its own. In addition to collapsing the material affairs of his neighbors, Whim is a practitioner of reciprocal brain-looting and is the inventor of the Whim-Grinder and the Looty. Naturally all his friends are brain-looted prisoners of his cavern home. Better to be his servant. Whim exists in three forms: biscuit, metal and liquid.

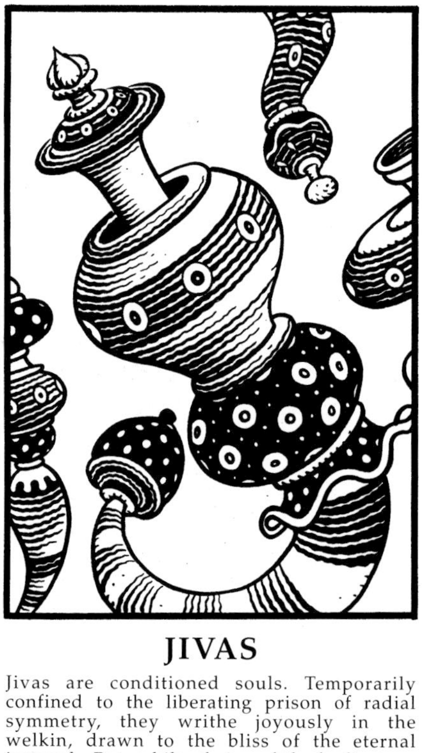

JIVAS

Jivas are conditioned souls. Temporarily confined to the liberating prison of radial symmetry, they writhe joyously in the welkin, drawn to the bliss of the eternal interval. But while their subtle bodies are nuzzling the absolute, the multicolored skins are available to Frank and his friends for riding or target practice. Jivas are independent; they are slow to notice and interact with Frank and his associates, but when they do the results can be appalling.

THE JERRY CHICKENS

The numerous Jerry Chickens demonstrate through their complex social maneuvers that anatomy is indeed destiny; the question is *whose?* Though they all carry within their misshapen skulls the capacity for sub-rational ministration, the conical Jerry has the greatest impact on Frank by virtue of the implications of his potentially infinite diminishment. Here we see them in their filthy coop, plotting a beakin' in the night.

A PA

This is either the Faux Pa or the Real Pa; they are physically indistinguishable from one another, except for one tiny difference. The Faux Pa assumes his role enthusiastically, giving Frank the worst possible advice. The Real Pa is another story altogether. When Frank is old he will look like this. Here is the real horse in the ointment: time will diminish them all, and their influences will no longer be felt.

PUSHPAW

He was just passin' through until he caught a glimpse of Pupshaw from afar; now he's her most ardent resident suitor. Pushpaw isn't the most exalted creature in the world, but what he lacks in subtle strength he more than makes up for in pluck and goodnaturedness. Pushpaw's inborn sense of fair play will never allow him to exploit an advantage gained falsely. When all is said and done he's just a lovable street scrapper with extra room in the bulkhead.

THE CART BLANCHE

Keeping to the little channels behind shrubs and along protected walls, the shy, silent, solitary, unresponsive, dead, white, slightly crunchy Cart Blanche travels slowly from place to place and from scene to scene. Its mood is that of a lost toy. Frequently present but hidden when fortune expands into disaster, the little trolley is well-respected as a catalytic presence whose bias is always inclined toward the chalky and austere.

LUCKY

One thing Lucky knows for sure is that even though there may be no jobs, there's always plenty of work. If ever there was a born drudge, it's Lucky. The nature of his curse overwhelms him, and he immerses himself in whatever toil is at hand in order to numb his uncomprehending sorrow. All he asks in return is a roof over his head and a panniken of chopmeat. Still, there's a light in his eye that bears watching.

THE UNIFACTOR

Did you know? Yes, you did. The golden mother of unknowing draws these bewildered creatures to her heaving bosom. This is the land of the phantom-smasher. The worst that can happen never happens. It already happened. Everything is terrible. The two-mouthed fear cow lives here.

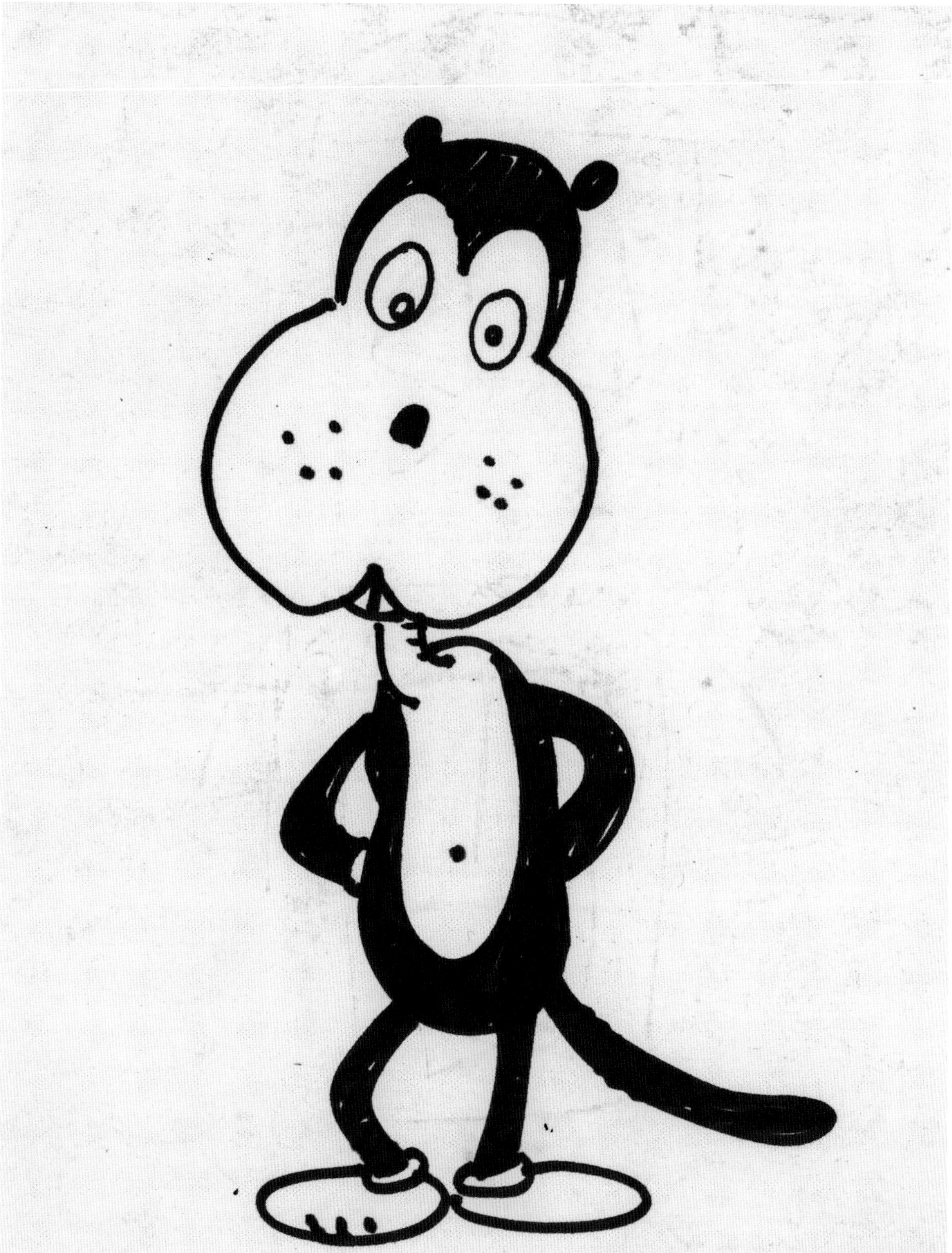

The first drawing of Frank

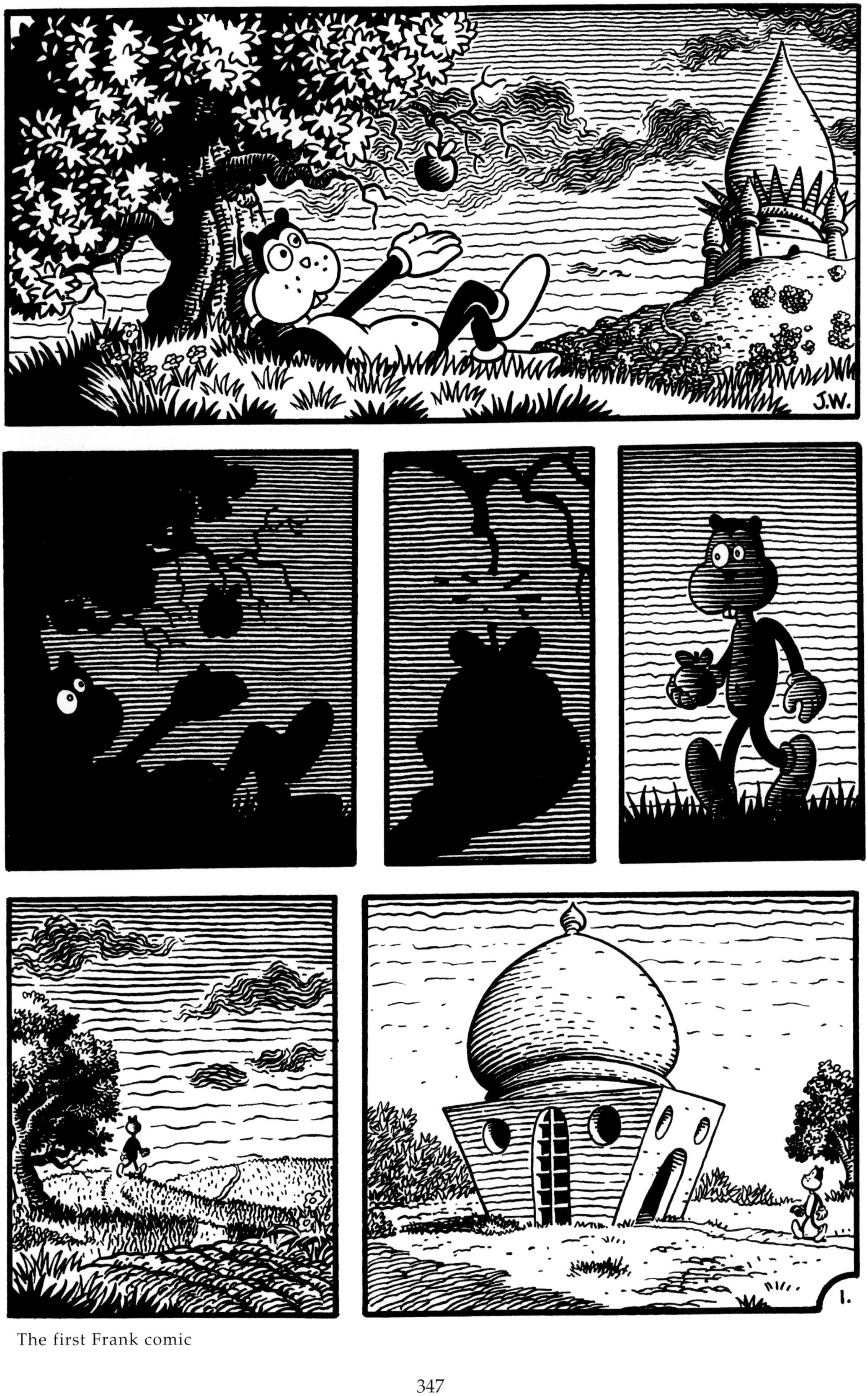
J.W.
1.

The first Frank comic

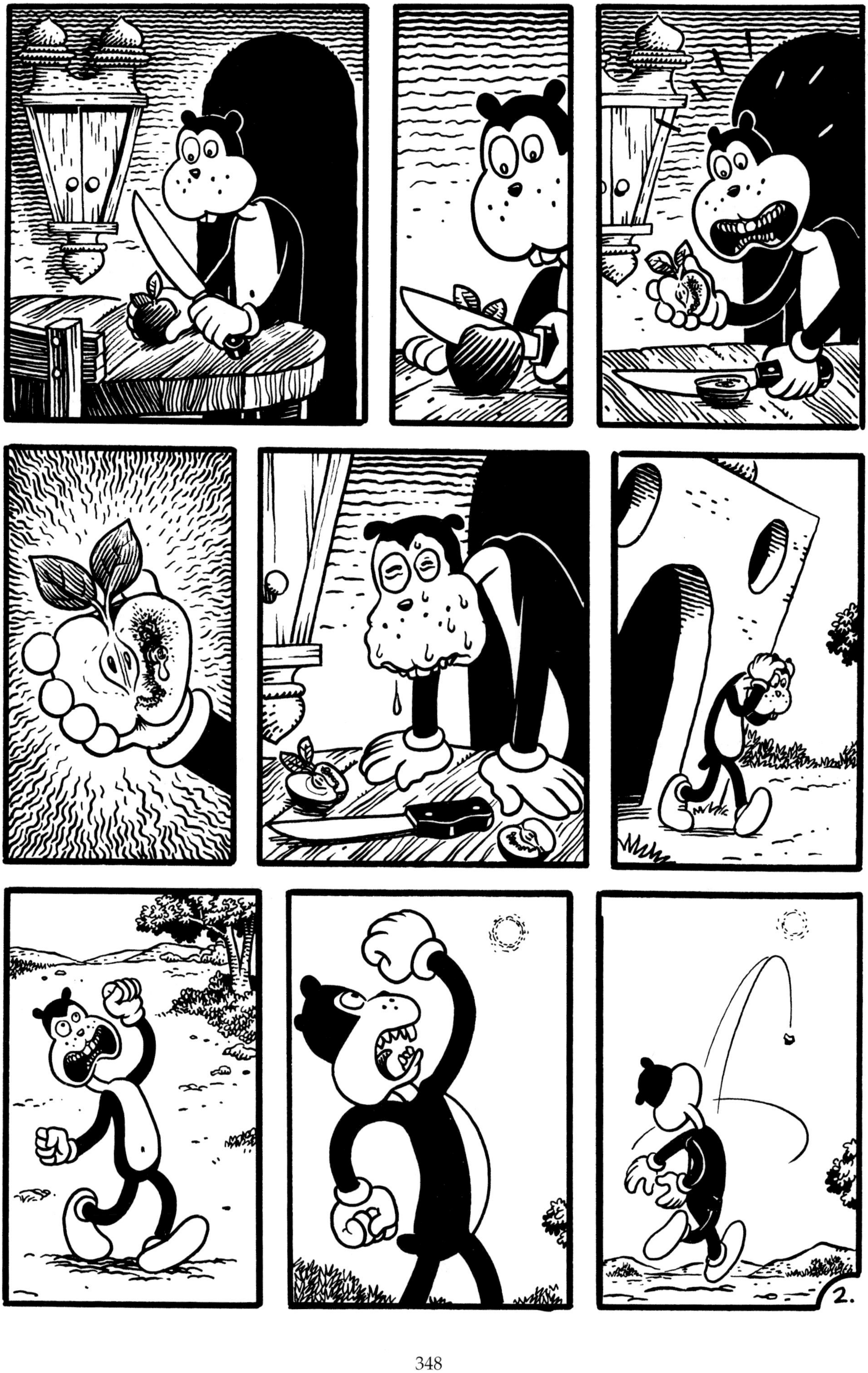
2.

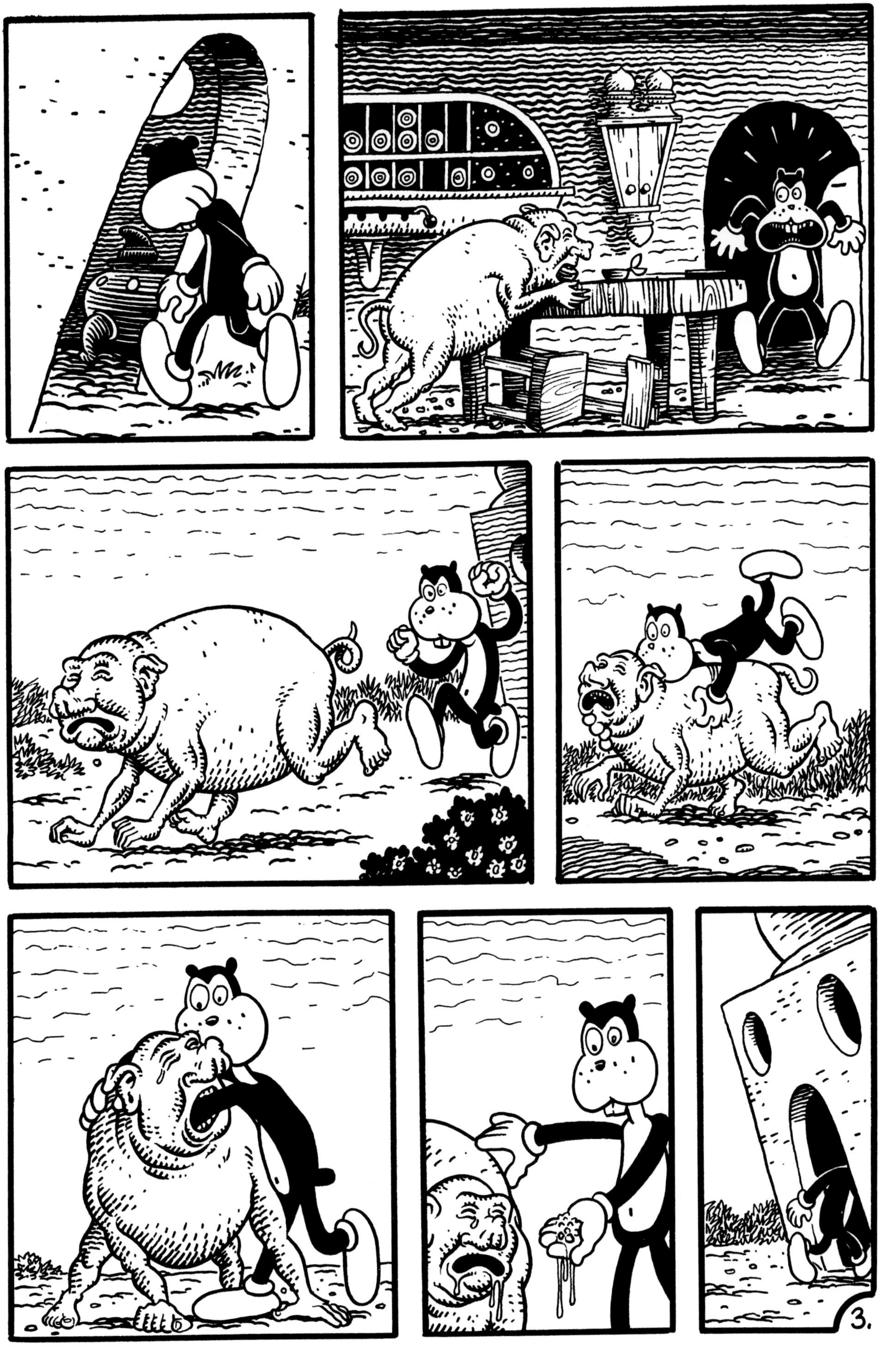
3.

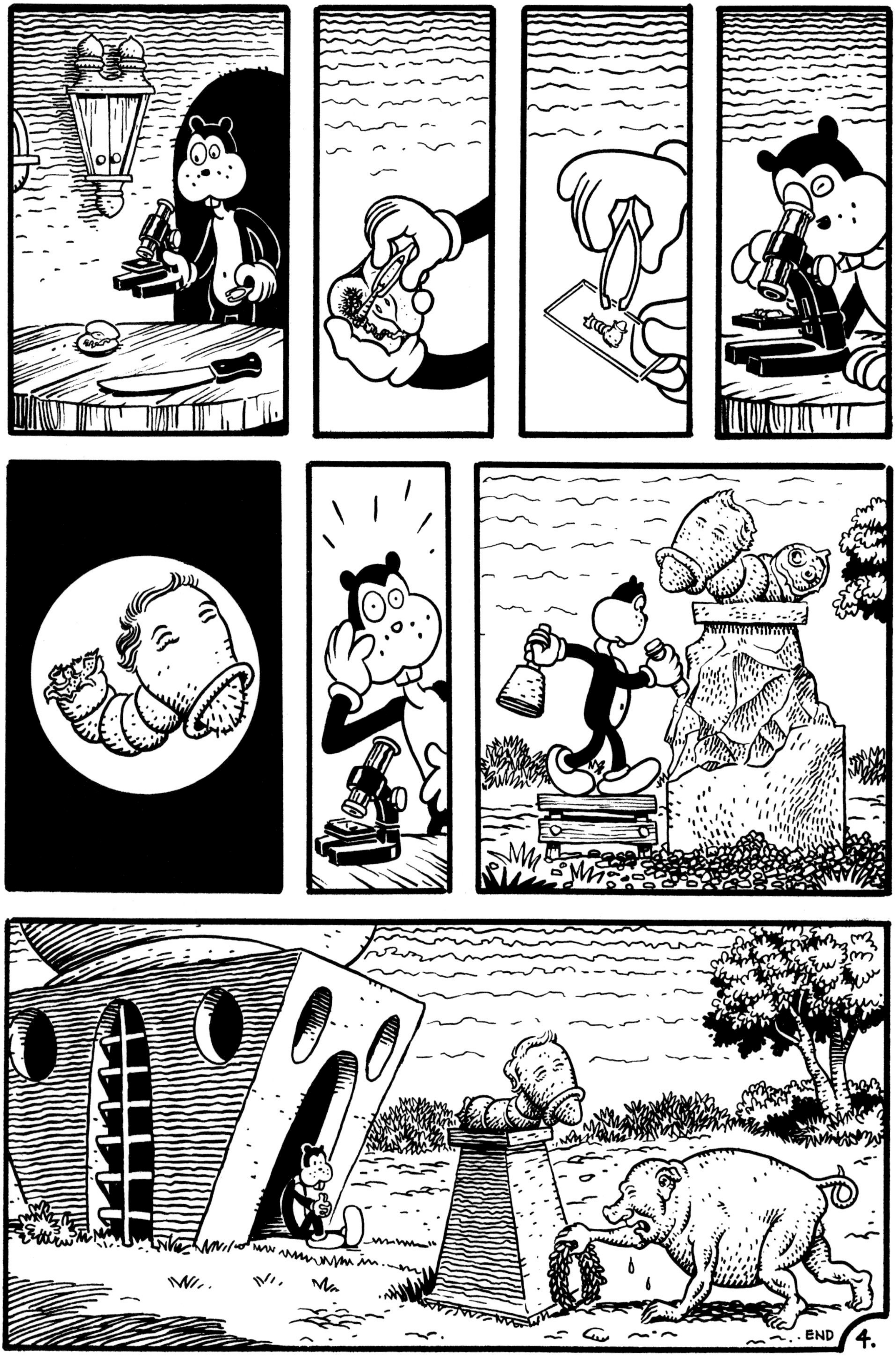
END
4.

Afterword

Frank was born in Los Angeles in 1989, out of the impulse to create a *sui generis* cartoon character; not a cat, or a mouse, or a beaver, or any other kind of creature, but a generic anthropomorph, beholden to nobody and with no expectations to fulfill. I showed the drawing (p. 346) to my former co-worker Ted Blackman, asking him what he thought of it, and saying that I myself thought it was quite interesting.

Ted got mad. "This is exactly what I hate about you," he said. "You play mind games. You make this nothing little scribble and ask me what I think of it. What *can* I think of it? It's *nothing!"* To spite him I decided to put a version of this drawing on the cover of the fourth issue of my autojournal *JIM*.

When I showed a copy of that magazine to the mother of my friend Meredith Lahr she pointed to the cover and said, "He looks like my cat Frank! You have to name him Frank!"

In 1990 Mark Landman asked me to do a story for his comic book *BUZZ*. When I asked him what sort of thing he wanted to see he said, "Why not do a comic that looks normal but isn't?" I decided that Frank filled the bill.

He needed a foil, so I put him to work with Manhog, a lamentable father figure. My own father had just died, and I was still angry at him. To further involve the family dynamic I based the story on the first joke I had ever heard, told to me by my mother: "What's worse than finding a worm in an apple? Finding half a worm!"

The first draft of that comic (p. 347) had the characters talking in a flowery, stylized dialect. The second draft had them using so much profanity that it made my eyes feel grimy to read it. Then it occurred to me that if I left dialogue out entirely it would reinforce the otherworldly mood of the story.

Readers have supplied many of Frank's attributes. Over time various individuals have determined that he is 11 years old, that he is covered with short, dense fur like a mole's, that he is innocent but not noble, and that he is mortal and must some day die.

All of the Frank stories have straightforward meanings which I usually recognize only after they are drawn and printed. I used to explain these meanings to anyone who asked, but I've stopped doing that because the stories are more powerful when their mysteries are undiscovered.

However, in the spirit of public service I will give a clue to the meaning of one story, Frank's Real Pa. There is a pun at the center of it that, once realized, snaps the whole story into sharp focus. This pun involves the eyepool into which Frank so desperately longs to jump, and the surrogate he finds at the Jerry Chicken's yard sale. The message is one that everyone can embrace with real profit to their lives. Don't go around saying I didn't warn you.

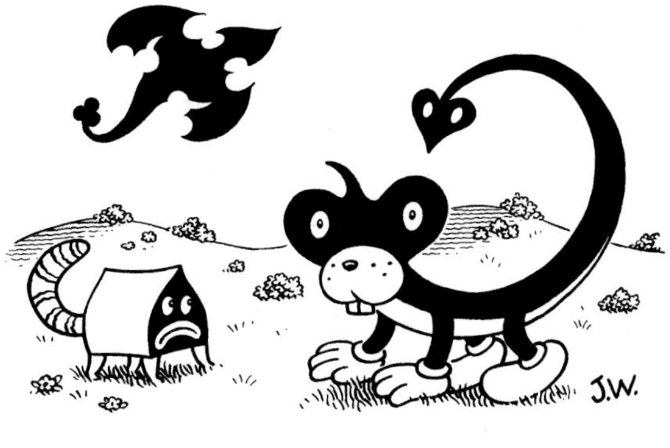
J.W.